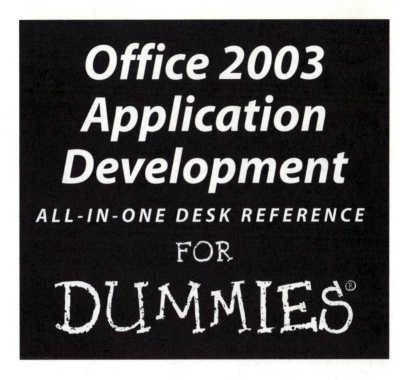

Office 2003 Application Development
ALL-IN-ONE DESK REFERENCE
FOR DUMMIES®

by Richard Mansfield

WILEY

Wiley Publishing, Inc.

Office 2003 Application Development All-in-One Desk Reference For Dummies®

Published by
Wiley Publishing, Inc.
111 River Street
Hoboken, NJ 07030-5774

Copyright © 2004 by Wiley Publishing, Inc., Indianapolis, Indiana

Published by Wiley Publishing, Inc., Indianapolis, Indiana

Published simultaneously in Canada

WILEY

Office 2003 Application Development All-in-One Desk Reference For Dummies®

Cheat Sheet

Frequently Used VBA Editor Shortcut Keys

Command Name	Shortcut Keys	Behavior
Edit.Copy	Ctrl+C Ctrl+Insert	Copies the currently selected item to the Clipboard.
Edit.Cut	Ctrl+X Shift+Delete	Removes the currently selected item but saves a copy in the Clipboard in case you want to paste it somewhere.
Edit.Undo	Ctrl+Z	Undoes previous deletion.
File.Save Normal.dot	Ctrl+S	Saves Normal.dot to disk, including any changes to its macros.
File.Import File	Ctrl+M	Load a .bas, .frm, or .cls file type.
File.Export File	Ctrl+E	Save a file as .bas file type.
File.Print	Ctrl+P	Print.
File.Quit	Ctrl+Q	Close VBA editor and return to Word.
Edit.Find	F3	Opens Find dialog box or finds next.
Edit.Replace	Ctrl+H	Opens the Find and Replace dialog box.
Display Members	Ctrl+J	Displays a list of an object's members.
Display Argument List	Ctrl+I	Displays the parameters you can pass to an object or method.
Display Procedure's Argument List	None	Displays the parameters you can pass to a procedure.
View Object Browser	F2	Opens the Object Browser.
Open Project Explorer	Ctrl+R	Displays the list of modules, documents, templates, UserForms, and other elements associated with the currently running instance of Word.
Open Properties Window	F4	Shows the properties of the currently selected object.
Toggle between Word and VBA editor	Alt+F11	If you're in a document, opens the VBA editor and vice versa.
Single Step	F8	Starts stepping through your code, line by line, for debugging.
Procedure Step	Shift+F8	Step through the code one procedure at a time.
Toggle Breakpoint	F9	Adds a breakpoint to current line of code (or removes an existing breakpoint) for debugging.
Run	F5	Executes current code (the procedure where the blinking cursor is).
Break	Ctrl+Break	Stops code execution (most of the time). If it doesn't work, press Ctrl+Alt+Del to go to the Task Manager.

Office 2003 Application Development All-in-One Desk Reference For Dummies®

Cheat Sheet

VBA Data Types

Name	Symbol	Range	Storage Required
Boolean	None	True or False.	2 bytes
Byte	None	0 to 255.	1 byte
Integer	%	−32,768 to 32,7672.	2 bytes
Long Integer (or Long)	&	−2,147,483,648 to 2,147,483,647.	4 bytes
Single (single-precision floating point)	!	−3.402823E38 to −1.401298E-45 (negative numbers); and 1.401298E-45 to 3.402823E38 (positive numbers).	4 bytes
Double (double-precision floating point)	#	−1.79769313486232E308 to −4.94065645841247E-324 (negative numbers); and 4.9406564584124E-324 to 1.79769313486232E308 (positive numbers).	8 bytes
Currency (scaled integer)	@	−922,337,203,685,477.5808 to 922,337,203,685,477.5807.	8 bytes
Decimal	None	+/−79,228,162,514,264,337,593,543, 950,335 if no decimal point; +/−7.9228162514264337593543950335 with 28 places to the right of the decimal. The Decimal type is not used in VB.NET.	14 bytes
Date	None	January 1, 100 to December 31, 9999.	8 bytes
Object	None	Any Object.	4 bytes
Text (string) (a string of variable length)	$	1 to roughly 2 billion.	The length plus 10 bytes
Text ("string") (a string of fixed length)	$	1 to roughly 2 billion (roughly 65,400 for Windows 3.1).	Length of string; the length of the text
Variant (when holding a number)	None	Any number.	16 bytes; can be as large as a Double
Variant (when holding text)	None	1 to roughly 2 billion (roughly 65,400 for Windows 3.1).	The length of the text plus 22 bytes
User-defined Variable (use the Type command)	None	The size of the defined contents. (You, the programmer, establish the range.)	Whatever is required by the contents

Copyright © 2004 Wiley Publishing, Inc.
All rights reserved.

Item 7067-6.

For more information about Wiley Publishing, call 1-800-762-2974.

For Dummies: Bestselling Book Series for Beginners

About the Author

Richard Mansfield's recent titles include *Visual Basic .NET All-in-One Desk Reference For Dummies, Visual Basic .NET Weekend Crash Course, Visual Basic .NET Database Programming For Dummies, Visual Basic 6 Database Programming For Dummies* (all from Wiley), *Hacker Attack* (Sybex), and *The Wi-Fi Experience: Everyone's Guide to 802.11b Wireless Networking* (Que).

From 1981 through 1987, he was editor of *COMPUTE!* magazine, during which time he wrote hundreds of magazine articles and two columns. From 1987 to 1991, he was editorial director and partner in Signal Research and began writing books full-time in 1991. He has written 34 computer books since 1982. Of those, four became bestsellers: *Machine Language for Beginners* (COMPUTE! Books), *The Second Book of Machine Language* (COMPUTE! Books), *The Visual Guide to Visual Basic* (Ventana), and *The Visual Basic Power Toolkit* (Ventana, with Evangelos Petroutsos). Overall, his books have sold more than 500,000 copies worldwide and have been translated into 11 languages.

Dedication

This book is dedicated to my mother, Florence Ethel Mansfield.

Author's Acknowledgments

I want to thank executive editor Greg Croy for his many kindnesses. I've always enjoyed working with Greg. He knows how to get the best out of authors (at least this author). Greg's one of the good guys.

I was also lucky to have two first-rate editors work with me on this book. Project editor Christopher Morris asked good questions when my writing needed some questions raised. He also made a number of very useful changes. He deserves credit for discernment and the high quality of his editing. Copy editor Teresa Artman kept a close eye on me and asked many good questions as well. In addition, she ensured consistency of punctuation, diction, and cross-reference. Thanks to her and Chris for the many improvements they made to this book.

Technical editor D. J. (Deepesh Jain) reviewed the entire manuscript for technical problems. For that, I thank him. I'm happy to report that he found few flaws but certainly glad that we fixed the flaws he did spot.

To these and all the other good people at Wiley who contributed to the book, my thanks for the time and care they took to ensure quality every step along the way to publication.

Finally, I want to give special thanks to my agent, Matt Wagner of Waterside Productions, who has been offering me good advice for over a decade.

Publisher's Acknowledgments

We're proud of this book; please send us your comments through our online registration form located at www.dummies.com/register/.

Some of the people who helped bring this book to market include the following:

Acquisitions, Editorial, and Media Development

Project Editor: Christopher Morris

Executive Editor: Gregory S. Croy

Senior Copy Editor: Teresa Artman

Technical Editor: Wiley-Dreamtech India Pvt Ltd

Editorial Manager: Kevin Kirschner

Permissions Editor: Laura Moss

Media Development Supervisor: Richard Graves

Editorial Assistant: Amanda Foxworth

Cartoons: Rich Tennant (www.the5thwave.com)

Production

Project Coordinator: Adrienne Martinez

Layout and Graphics: Andrea Dahl, Lauren Goddard, Denny Hager, Stephanie D. Jumper, Barry Offringa, Lynsey Osborn, Heather Ryan, Julie Trippetti

Proofreaders: Andy Hollandbeck, Carl Pierce, Evelyn Still

Indexer: Joan Griffitts

Publishing and Editorial for Technology Dummies

Richard Swadley, Vice President and Executive Group Publisher

Andy Cummings, Vice President and Publisher

Mary C. Corder, Editorial Director

Publishing for Consumer Dummies

Diane Graves Steele, Vice President and Publisher

Joyce Pepple, Acquisitions Director

Composition Services

Gerry Fahey, Vice President of Production Services

Debbie Stailey, Director of Composition Services

Contents at a Glance

Table of Contents

Introduction

Discover the world of Office 2003 programming and development. Microsoft has put many of its best cutting-edge tools into this power-house package. And you can also add .NET technology to Office 2003 quite easily, taking your programming to the next level. There's lots to explore.

This book shows you — the Office user, programmer, or developer — how best to exploit, expand, administer, and write code for Office 2003, the world's most popular application suite. And it certainly is popular: Experts estimate that Office has over 90 percent of the market share. I think I know why (and the answer isn't what Microsoft-haters claim).

I've Seen It All

I've seen all the software. Over two decades — first as editor of *COMPUTE!* magazine and since then as a full-time computer-book author — I've worked with review copies of most major software. I work daily with computers and have used most all the major applications.

Word processors? I've used SuperScript, XYWrite, WordStar, WordPerfect, Word, and more. I've also put in time with other products that are today little more than memories: dBase, early spreadsheet applications like VisiCalc, and so on.

In its day, WordPerfect was the word processor of choice, and I happily used it for years (the last half of the 80's), but when Microsoft Word appeared in 1989, I switched to it pretty fast. Right away, actually. I switched because I thought that Word was a better word processor than the competition. That's not because of any special ties I have to the Windows operating system or because I work for Microsoft. (They're not even giving me free software anymore when I write a book.) I'm mad at them because I have to buy all this software, truth be told. But truth should be told, and Microsoft does put out very good software. Microsoft-haters are wrong, in my opinion.

Today Word enjoys almost 100 percent market share in the word processing application market. Why? Because it's just plain the best word processor you can buy.

Whatever your politics, most of us living in the real world of practical computing use, manage, or program for Microsoft Office. And that's what this book is all about: how to take your current knowledge of Office to the next level. You'll find tips, solutions, code examples, clear explanations, migration paths, and lots of other useful information that you can apply to your everyday personal and business computing.

While writing this book, I've tried hard to give you information that is practical, makes sense, and helps you do the jobs you have to do.

Moving beyond VBA

This book has another, secondary goal: to help you migrate from VBA (the traditional Office programming language) to VB.NET, the next generation programming technology that offers you considerable additional muscle.

You'll find plenty of examples illustrating how to add .NET programming to your Office 2003 projects and how to tap into the various tools that the .NET editor (Visual Studio, the IDE) offers us programmers. Ignore .NET at your peril.

Connectivity, Internet programming, scalability, interoperability, stability, and more — VB.NET brings many qualities to the Office programmer's toolkit. VB.NET is the future of Office programming, and this book prepares you to make the move. You'll find code examples written in both VBA and VB.NET, showing you how to move to this important language and apply it to Office 2003 solutions. You need to know how to do things that VBA simply cannot handle by itself.

You can add .NET's power to your Office programming very easily — I show you how throughout this book.

But good old VBA isn't neglected. A mini-book is devoted to it (Book II, "Understanding Office Programming"), and much of this whole book's programming is written in it. VBA remains the "official" Office language in Office 2003. And we all have lots of VBA code that we've written over the years, either in VBA itself or its brother language, Visual Basic (versions 6, 5, 4, 3, 2, and 1).

Nonetheless, there are certain hints — suggestions of obsolescence — coming out of Redmond. For example: "There are no language enhancements to VBA 6.0 itself in the Microsoft Office System." In other words, VBA was not improved in Office 2003. (That's always a bad sign.) Further, Microsoft has announced that it will continue to support VBA in the future. Cue the "Jaws" movie music.

VBA code is legacy code!

Microsoft says that "if VBA is ever retired" (cellos: dunn-dit-dunn-dit-dunn-dit, as the shark approaches), it will provide utilities or other assistance to help us move our code from VBA to .NET. Here's a statement from a white paper on the MSDN site. Be afraid, VBA programmers, be *very* afraid:

> *VBA 6.0 is not going away in the next release of the Microsoft Office System, and Microsoft will provide a migration strategy if VBA is ever retired. There is quite a bit of legacy code that is written in VBA 6.0. In many cases, there may be no reason for existing code to be rewritten. However, the significant advantages and capabilities the .NET Framework offers may cause you to rethink whether to leave some solutions as they are. There are no language enhancements to VBA 6.0 itself in the Microsoft Office System.*

Here they're starting to refer to our beloved VBA programming as "legacy code." You know what legacy means: *done for.* So how should we react? Should we say:

"We, the programmer soldiers, salute you! Bring it on!"

or

"Do me baby one more time."

The choice is yours.

Recognizing VBA's excellence

VBA is to classical procedure-oriented programming as Bach's incomparable works are to Baroque music. They represent the finest example, the summation, of an epoch.

VBA is probably the most efficient and mature procedure-oriented language available today. And although VBA includes some object-oriented features, they seem a bit uncomfortable within the VBA structure — they feel more like workarounds and patches than integral elements.

By contrast, VB.NET was designed from the ground up to be object-oriented and to be an effective way to write *distributed* programs — programs that are divided into segments that execute on different machines.

Also, the .NET IDE offers a very powerful suite of programming tools. It's simply more capable and sophisticated than the VBA editor in Office 2003 applications. Given a choice, any serious Office 2003 developer — or indeed pretty much any programmer doing most kinds of Windows or Internet programming — likely prefers the Visual Studio programming environment.

Using the framework

Also, the .NET language itself, the .NET framework, is huge and contains effective, specialized, and generally powerful classes to accomplish whatever you might need to do. (Database, Internet, security, and nearly any other kind of programming are supported with advanced tools and versatile objects.) For example, NET lets you add classic Windows forms to Office solutions. These windows are superior to the UserForms available via VBA. And the VB.NET debugging facilities are among the most thoughtfully organized and robust available. .NET includes extensive XML and namespace support; ADO.NET — an advanced, highly scalable, database management technology — and ASP.NET (ditto for highly scalable Internet programming). The list goes on and on.

This book is not about .NET, but I do provide considerable information for Office programmers who want to find out how to add .NET to their Office solutions and in the process, see how to migrate from VBA to .NET.

The VB.NET language is not merely a revision of VBA or VB 6. Instead, it was rewritten from the ground up to be a brand-new, fully OOP language. Do realize, though, that if your programming projects are relatively small or you don't program as part of a programming team, OOP is often simply more trouble than it's worth. Fortunately, you can ignore OOP when writing code in .NET if you wish. You can just use familiar, tried-and-true, VBA-style procedure-oriented programming techniques if you wish. And you still get the double bonus of tapping into the powerful .NET framework of prewritten functions and also the use of the splendid .NET programming editor.

Understanding managed code

VB.NET — like the other VS.NET languages — runs under the supervision of the common language runtime (CLR), thereby earning Microsoft's new phrase: *managed code.* Such code is *validated* (checked to see that it doesn't violate memory restrictions and other illegal behaviors). It also offers code-based security features unavailable to unmanaged (non-.NET languages) code. However, compared with older languages — particularly the VBA built into Office applications — .NET requires that you deal with a bit of a learning curve, particularly when adapting to the .NET programming styles, language elements, and security settings. Also, after you come to grips with the essentials of OOP, communication between .NET and Office objects or VBA is generally quite smooth although there are a few data type discrepancies that now and then must be dealt with.

About This Book

My main job in this book is to show you the best way to create solutions for Office 2003 applications. You see how to master the various techniques that collectively put you on the path to true Office programming expertise.

If a task requires hands-on programming, I show you step-by-step how to write that programming. In other cases, I tell you when there's a simpler, better way to accomplish a job. Otherwise, you could spend days hand-programming something that's already been built — something you can create by clicking a simple menu option, adding a prebuilt component, firing up a wizard, using a template, or tapping into an object library.

This book is designed for Office programmers and developers or for people who want to become one. Most new computers ship with Office, and it is used in nearly every business today. What these businesses have in common is an ongoing effort to improve their efficiency. In many cases, developing or automating Office applications is one of the most effective ways to increase workplace productivity. Many workers know what they wish they could do, and this book shows you how to help them do it.

Office 2003 Application Development All-in-One Desk Reference For Dummies covers all the new features in Office 2003 and demonstrates how developers can best exploit them. Many of these features are designed to improve work-flow, boost productivity, and facilitate better communication between employees — just the sort of goals that Office developers themselves work to achieve. For example, InfoPath simplifies interaction with all kinds of data sources: everything from unformatted lists to legacy databases. SharePoint assists developers in building an automated collaborative environment.

Underlying many of the improvements in Office 2003 is XML and related technologies such as Web Services. This book explains precisely how to take advantage of XML's promise with simple, no-nonsense, real-world examples. Readers will understand exactly how to leverage their current work and communication patterns using the new and powerful data sharing techniques available in Office 2003.

Businesses understand the importance of remaining competitive. This book shows developers how to make the most of Office's tools and technologies. All the innovations in Office 2003 are fully explained, employing the famous *For Dummies* approach: clear explanations, step-by-step examples, and lots of practical advice.

No significant Office topic is ignored. I explain traditional but significant features such as Visual Basic for Applications (which are too often ignored in other books on Office). And I cover all the latest developments such as Smart Documents, Access 2003 Developer Extensions, programming task panes, managing Smart Tags, the new security features, and much more.

Anyone interested in building intelligent business applications will find the solutions they're looking for in this book. And the example code is practical: Not only do I show you how the code works, but as often as possible, I try to provide code that you can use in your own programs. You find out, for example, how to write a text search utility that searches across folders and directories for a specific word or phrase. What's the benefit? This search utility is far faster than the Windows search utility found on the Start menu.

Who Should Read This Book

This book is written for a broad audience: programmers, developers, office managers, IT staff, and even individual users of the Office 2003 suite of applications. In other words, the book has value for everyone who wants to be more efficient when using Office 2003.

The book shows how to exploit the Office applications by learning how to develop solutions to common business problems. The reader will understand how to solve those problems by using the many utilities, features, hidden shortcuts, wizards, add-ins, and other tools in the Office suite.

The book is also for would-be developers who want to get involved in customizing or automating the applications but just don't know how to get started. Whether you want to get Access to communicate with Outlook or are interested in building a sophisticated inter-office scheduling system, you'll find what you need in this book. The book is filled with useful macros and plenty of practical, real-world programming examples including

- ✦ Automating e-mail routing
- ✦ Administering the task pane from within an application
- ✦ Writing your own add-ins
- ✦ Building a distributed business system using Web Services

Making do in a shaky economy

No matter what they tell us from the bully pulpit, *we* know how shaky the economy is, don't we? The primary trend in nearly all industries today is toward making do with less: fewer workers, less time to complete tasks, and stretching resources as much as possible. This trend demands improved productivity.

Some offices respond by letting part of the staff go and heaping additional work on the remaining employees or by outsourcing or offshoring. In many cases, a more successful long-term tactic is to retain a high-quality, loyal staff but to improve the general efficiency of that staff. Microsoft Office 2003 is loaded with tools to improve productivity if you know how to exploit them. *Office 2003 Application Development All-in-One Desk Reference For Dummies* is the handbook that takes the reader from idea to finished business solution.

I hope that all my work these past years exploring programming and working with Office will benefit you, showing you the many useful shortcuts and guiding you over the rough spots. I won't pull any punches: I confess if it took me several hours wrestling with code to accomplish something. But after I've put in the time getting it to work, I can almost always show you how to do it in a few minutes. (I never got one new technology, Visual Studio Tools for Office, to work, but I confess that, too.)

Plain, clear English

Also, unlike some other books about Office 2003 programming (which must remain nameless), this book is written in plain, clear English. Novices will find many sophisticated tasks made easy: The book is filled with step-by-step examples that even beginners can follow even if they've never written a line of programming or designed a single computer application. And if you're an experienced programmer, better still. You'll find out how to accomplish sophisticated tasks quickly. You also discover how to harness the machinery built into Office 2003. And you also discover how to leverage your current skills to prepare for the future of Office programming: moving beyond VBA to VB.NET.

How to Use This Book

This book obviously can't cover every feature in Office 2003, VBA, and especially VB.NET. Instead, as you try the many step-by-step examples in this book, you'll become familiar with the most useful features of Office development and programming and discover many shortcuts and time-saving tricks (some that can take years to discover on your own). Believe me, some of them have taken me years to stumble upon.

Whether you want to turn a Word document into a Web site or create impressive Office 2003 solutions in Windows, this book tells you how to build what you want to build. Here are just a few of the goals that you can achieve with this book:

✦ Explore and program with new Office 2003 features such as Document Workspaces, shared attachments, OneNote, XML, and others. Some technologies explored in this book are not covered in other Office programming titles, including encryption programming and the new Visual Studio Tools for Office.

✦ Build professional-looking, effective programs.

✦ See how to connect the various Office 2003 applications and data stores into a seamless, distributed, and secure business solution (and how to be smart enough to know when to use wizards to help).

✦ Make the transition from Microsoft's traditional VBA Office language to the powerful new .NET technologies for database and other kinds of programming.

✦ Understand how to best use the many features built into VB.NET.

✦ Kill bugs using powerful debugging tools.

✦ Get the most out of the Office and .NET security features, including how to automate strong programmatic encryption.

Many people think that programming is impossibly difficult and that distributed (inter-application) programming is even more difficult. It doesn't have to be.

In fact, many common programming jobs have already been written for you in Office object libraries or the VB.NET framework, so you don't have to do the programming at all. If you're smart, you don't reinvent the wheel. Sometimes, all you need to know is where in VBA to find a particular component, wizard, template, or other prebuilt solution. Then drop it into your application. This book is your guide to building efficient Office 2003 applications, utilities, and large-scale solutions.

This book tells you whether a particular wheel has already been invented. It also shows you how to save time by using or modifying existing components or Help code to fit your needs instead of building new solutions from scratch. But if you're doing something totally original (congratulations!), this book also gives you step-by-step recipes for tackling many common tasks from the ground up.

Foolish Assumptions

In writing this book, I had to make a few assumptions about you, dear reader. I assume that you know how to use Office (except for the brand-new features in Office 2003) and understand the basics of programming in general.

I also assume that you don't know much, if anything, about VB.NET programming as it applies to Office. Perhaps most importantly, I assume that you don't want lots of theory or extraneous details. You just want to get programming jobs done, not sit around listening to airy-fairy theory about polymorphism and such. When a job can be done in VBA, I show you how. When you need to reach out to the more powerful .NET framework, I show you that, too. Whatever it takes, the job gets done.

How This Book Is Organized

The overall goal of *Office 2003 Application Development All-in-One Desk Reference For Dummies* is to provide an enjoyable and understandable guide for the Visual Basic programmer. This book will be accessible to developers and programmers with little or no .NET programming experience.

The book is divided into eight mini-books, with several chapters in each book. Just because the book is organized doesn't mean that you have to be. You don't have to read the book in sequential order from Chapter 1 to the end, just as you don't have to read a cookbook in sequential order.

For example, if you need to add today's most powerful encryption technology to your office solution programmatically, I suggest you read the last chapter first (Book VIII, Chapter 8).

If you want to brush up on VBA, Book II is for you. You're not expected to know what's in Book I to get results in Book II. Similarly, within each chapter, you can often scan the headings and jump right to the section covering the task that you want to accomplish. There is no need to read each chapter from start to finish. I've been careful to make all the examples as self-contained as possible. And each of them works, too. They've been thoroughly tested.

All of the source code for all the examples in this book is downloadable from this book's Web site at www.dummies.com/go/office2003dev.

The following sections give you a brief description of the book's eight main parts.

Book 1: Office 2003 Essentials

This first mini-book introduces Office 2003 — explaining its purposes, what's new in this edition, and Office's fundamental nature. You see how common tasks are accomplished, and you discover the elements of Office programming. You are introduced to the main new features in Office 2003 such as

OneNote, XML, task panes, the major overhaul of Outlook, and so on. Topics in this mini-book include managing menus and toolbars, how to find programming help online, understanding macro security, introduction to document workspaces, and joining the XML revolution.

Book II: Understanding Office Programming

Book II covers the primary elements of VBA. It's a refresher course for programmers to need to brush up on classic Visual Basic programming, and a full-on programming course for people new to programming VBA, the classic language built into Office applications. All the essentials are covered, from simple concepts such as data types to advanced subjects like various security measures that you can take to protect databases. This mini-book covers how to move Office documents and other elements to the Internet. You also see how to exploit the famous Visual Basic debugging tools.

Book III: Maximizing Word

Book III focuses on the world's greatest word processor. You see how to work with the Word object model to tap into the power of this huge dedicated language. You explore enums, ranges, selections, and the `dialog` object, among other topics. Then on to power editing — ways to maximize Word's editing features. Many (perhaps most) Office workers don't take advantage of Word's many powerful editing capabilities. You also see how to maneuver efficiently, use Smart Documents, import data, and manage mail merge.

You explore how XML and Word now work together synergistically to facilitate communication between any and all platforms, operating systems, data stores, applications, and whatever else might want to communicate with Word. You see how Word does a serviceable job for smaller Internet jobs, such as displaying your pictures or blogging your feelings for all to see. You find out how to transform DOC files into Web pages. This book concludes with power macro programming: how to contact and manipulate other Office applications from within Word, how to access and modify the behavior of Word's built-in features such as `FileSave`, and a set of what I consider the best Word macros available.

Book IV: Making the Most of Excel

This mini-book focuses on many aspects of programming Excel, beginning with an exploration of the Excel object hierarchy including all the expected classes, plus collection objects, ranges, charts, pivot tables, shapes, and so on. Concrete examples illustrate how you can get down deep into Excel and make it really glide across the ice like a champion skater. You also see how to respond programmatically to Excel events, automate data and XML importation, create datasets, and programmatically build pivot tables. You see how to manage goal seeking, scenarios, and summary reports and also explore problems with the Solver. You contact other Office applications from within Excel, employ UserForms, add macros to worksheet controls, automate formatting, add controls programmatically, trap keypresses, send workbooks via e-mail, and tell the differences between the activate and select methods. Whew! If I've left out anything you're interested in, send me an e-mail, and I'll include it in the next printing.

Book V: Advanced Access

There are dozens of books on Access 2003, but few I've found make a conscious attempt to integrate Access with the other Office applications. Access, poor darling, has always stood alone. It's always been the strange stepchild — the one that doesn't quite get into the act or the one off in the shadows in the family pictures. Access differs in many ways from the other Office 2003 applications, from its lack of direct keyboard modification to the peculiarities of its object model. Throughout this book, I've often found myself writing ". . . but of course, Access does this differently. Here's how to get Access to accomplish this task."

So I've done my best to always include Access in any important discussion all through the entire book. In this mini-book, though, I focus directly on Access. You see how to sort out the various database technologies and ODBC and how to move beyond VBA and DAO to ADO. You wrestle with the concurrency problem and benefit from various RAD efficiencies. Cutting-edge technologies are explored, including loading an Access database into .NET; data views; the XML Designer and XML dataset; loading XML into Access; using the new Access 2003 Developer Extensions; exploring the Package Wizard and Custom Startup Wizard; learning about the Property Scanner add-in; Smart Tags in Access; connecting to Access via automation; automating the Access runtime; using the new sandbox mode; and other topics that might interest you.

Book VI: Exploiting Outlook

No Office 2003 application has been as overhauled as Outlook. In this mini-book, you explore the new pane and other topics such as filters, spam blocking, encryption, special folders, and double calendars. As a programmer, you want to read the sections that show you how to exploit the Outlook object model, deal with namespaces, use MAPI objects, trap events, handle Contacts, send data between Outlook and Word or Access, create new folders, modify collections, search tasks, and manage the Outlook Calendar. Also covered are topics such as effective automatic routing (during your vacation), managing multiple accounts, using send/receive Groups, blocking virii, working with profiles, sharing schedules, planning meetings, searching e-mail, and ergonomics for your users.

Book VII: InterOffice: Working as a Team

This mini-book takes a closer look at ways to integrate workers and applications to improve overall workplace efficiency. I start with *OneNote,* the cool new utility and notes organizer that some people cannot live without. You also see how to work well with others. It's not always easy to avoid stepping on people's toes when several people try to edit the same document or plan the same project. You see how to best use Office 2003 to manage shared Contacts, handle document collaboration, set up a meeting workspace and permissions, use the new Information Rights Management, change workspace options, protect documents in Word, specify editing and formatting restrictions, create custom views, and deal with the version problem using Word's new versions feature. You also explore topics such as building Web pages, adjusting properties, viewing code, writing scripts, doing scripting in Excel, debugging script, using forms, and sharing information efficiently. InfoPath offers a variety of useful collaborative tools. You discover designing with InfoPath, viewing data hierarchies, generating InfoPath forms from XML, and building InfoPath forms from databases.

You also see how Smart Tags can be added to your Office 2003 projects to assist users in filling out forms, getting context-sensitive help, and other benefits. You see how to create, program, and test Smart Tags. You move on to the containers of Smart Tags — Smart Documents — and read about feeding data to Web sites, managing security issues, simplifying deployment, working with the elements of Smart Documents, using XML, attaching schemas, attaching the XML Expansion Pack, coding, and modifying a template.

Project 2003 isn't ignored. You explore creating and editing projects, dealing with dependencies, understanding Gantt charts, and employing Outlook features in your projects. Then you move on to SharePoint, beginning with the reasons why you might choose it over other collaboration technologies. You see how to install, specify permissions, use the Task Pane, manage SharePoint scalability, integrate SharePoint with office 2003 applications, and a bit about the ASP.NET connection.

Book VIII: Power Techniques: Advanced Office Automation, VBA, and .NET

If you're looking for real heavy-duty programmer info and industrial-strength development, many of those topics are gathered together in this mini-book. But don't be misled: Some seriously advanced topics are covered in other mini-books as well. It's just that I chose this last mini-book to focus on some of the more cutting-edge or sophisticated techniques.

This mini-book starts off with a discussion of the drawbacks of OOP programming and also a comparison of the qualities of VBA versus VB.NET (when you should choose one over the other). You also see code that introduces a cool .NET feature called *streaming*. You then create your own add-in — one of several techniques whereby you add the power of .NET to your Office 2003 programming.

Chapter 2 is all about XML and associated technologies such as XSD, XML data types, schemas, and XML programming. You wallow in objects in Chapter 3: discovering techniques for using objects in VBA, understanding .NET data types, making declarations and using events in VBA, and managing collections and arrays of objects. Then you move on in the next chapter to some advanced Internet programming topics, including working with Web Services and how XML and Office work with this interesting Internet technology.

Chapter 5 is a dive into .NET — something every serious programmer must master sooner or later. Sure, it's a learning curve at first; Visual Basic will never be the same again, after VB.NET. But believe me, what you spend in time mastering .NET, you gain in considerable additional programming capability. You see how to use software services, Internet initiatives, .NET database technologies, and general programming practices. This chapter is for those readers who understand that the migration from VBA to .NET is essential (unless they're near retirement and don't have to worry about the future of their career).

Chapter 6 continues this migration topic by focusing on Visual Studio Tools for Office. It sounds like just the ticket. (*Visual Studio* is the set of utilities, editors, and languages that collectively contain .NET.) It might sound like the ticket, but at this point, it's maybe a little too unfinished to be of much real use to programmers. It has a little two-page wizard that merely sets up a template that you can use to build an Excel or Word document, using some *code-behind* features: that is, programming in .NET that can be used when a user opens these documents (thereby also running Excel or Word).

Read Chapter 6 to see the struggles I faced trying to get VSTO to work. Maybe it has been improved by the time you read this book, or maybe the days I spent trying and failing to get it working correctly were a result of temporary confusion on my part. Whatever. I got it *mostly* working — right up to the final step. So perhaps you'll succeed where I failed. (Some on the VSTO newsgroup seem to have it working.) One other point, though: Even if it works, there are other ways to do what VSTO does. Thus, unless I'm missing something, I actually don't understand VSTO's *raison d'être*. I might not have conquered VSTO, but I do know French.

Chapters 7 and 8 move you into an area of computing that is of increasing interest to all of us who program or simply use computers — security. Chapter 7 walks you through the various ways you can tighten Office 2003 security. You read about IRM, virus protection, file- and folder-based systems, macro security, signing, and hashing.

Chapter 8 is my personal favorite because to me, encryption is one of the most compelling aspects of programming. There's something intriguing about the contest of intellects on either side — those cooking up new attacks versus those thinking up new defenses. And the computer brings an entirely new dimension to this ancient spy-versus-spy game.

For example, computers can try millions of passwords in less than an hour. This speed wasn't possible before computerization. It's called a *brute force attack*. This attack is countered by brute force encryption systems, as you'll see in Chapter 8. When you finish this chapter, you'll be able to employ today's strongest encryption systems in your own programming. It's quite a bit of power for just a little extra work.

You also discover how to harness the DES system, used today by most banks and other commercial institutions to secure their data and the messages that they send over the Internet. But you also see how to add public key encryption (RSA) to your programming. RSA is today's most powerful encryption system, used by the military and others to transmit shorter pieces of data, such as passwords and keys. RSA isn't generally used for actual messages (because they're too lengthy), and although it's fantastically secure, it's really too slow to practically encrypt large amounts of data. But combine the two technologies, and you'll have today's most powerful encryption system at your disposal. Use RSA to exchange passwords or keys and then use fast DES to exchange messages.

This chapter also shows you how to avoid storing your messages on a hard drive (where, even if "deleted," they can be recovered by widely available utilities). Instead, you see how to employ .NET streaming technologies to keep your information floating in the air like smoke — then disappearing without a trace into the encryption. These memorystreams and cryptostreams have lovely, poetic names, but they embody important, potent technology . . . technology that you'll want to understand.

Conventions Used in This Book

This book is filled with step-by-step lists that serve as recipes to help you cook up finished Office 2003 solutions. Each step starts off with a boldface sentence or two telling you what you should do. Directly after the bold step, you might see a sentence or two, not in boldface, telling you what happens as a result of the bold action — a menu opens, a dialog box pops up, a wizard appears, you win the lottery, whatever.

A primary convention used in this book is that I've tried to make the step-by-step examples as general as possible but at the same time make them specific, too. Sounds impossible, and it wasn't easy. The idea is to give you a specific example that you can follow while also giving you a series of steps that you can apply directly to your own projects. In other words, I want to illustrate a technique but in a way that employs real-world, useful code.

In some of the examples, particularly when exploring Access 2003, I use the Northwind sample database that comes with Office 2003. With Access running, choose Help⇨Sample Databases and then select Northwind Sample Database. If it's not there in the Help menu, go to the Windows Control Panel, choose Add/Remove Programs, find and click Microsoft Office, click the Change button, and follow the instructions to install the Northwind sample database. You'll need it, even for some programming involving other Office 2003 applications as well.

Also, note that a special symbol shows you how to navigate menus. For example, when you see "Choose File⇨New⇨Project," you should click the File menu, click the New submenu, and finally click the Project option.

When I display programming code, you see it in a typeface that looks like this:

```
Dim pfont As Font
pfont = New Font("Times New Roman", 12)
```

If I mention some programming code within a regular paragraph of text, I use a special typeface, like this: `Dim pfont As Font`.

If I ask you to type something in, **it shows up in bold, like this.**

Find All the Code Online

Every line of code that you see in this book is available for downloading from this book's companion Web site at `dummies.com/go/office2003dev`. Take advantage of this handy electronic version of the code by downloading it from the Web site so that you can then just copy and paste source code instead of typing it by hand. This will save you lots of time and help you avoid those pesky typos.

The Searchable VBA/VB.NET Dictionary

Also, over the years I've compiled a book-length Rosetta stone dictionary of traditional VBA programming commands alongside their VB.NET equivalents. VBA programmers can look in this *Dictionary of VB.NET* online for a VBA function that they already know (such as InStr) to see how that same job is done the VB.NET way. Even readers who are not familiar with traditional VBA will also find this searchable Appendix of use. If you want to quickly find out, for example, how to change a property of Form1 from within Form2, search the dictionary and you get your answer. Find this dictionary at the following Web site:

http://www.dummies.com/extras/vb_net_all_in_one_fd/

What You Need to Get Started

To use this book to the fullest, you need only one thing: a copy of Office 2003 — preferably the Professional or Enterprise versions — to take full advantage of all the topics covered in this book. However, this book does not require the high-end Enterprise version or even the Professional version. The book covers what I consider the most significant topics in whatever version you use.

Although throughout this book (and particularly Book VIII), I cover OOP in depth, it does help to understand a few basic terms upfront. VBA programmers have not traditionally written classes. They use procedure-based programming techniques, which is usually quite sufficient for many Office programming jobs. But time marches on, and fashions arrive and fade. The current fashion in programming is OOP, and you have to come to grips with it. Here are some essential OOP concepts:

✦ A *class module* is a container for OOP source code that you write in the VBA editor. And after you define a class in your source code, when you execute that source code (by pressing F5 or otherwise running the code), an *object* comes into being. (The object is *instantiated;* an *instance* of the object comes alive.) So class is to object as recipe is to cookie: The class is the blueprint, the latter is the resulting thing.

✦ An *object* is an entity that comes into existence when you run your project by pressing F5 or otherwise triggering the code to execute. The object's characteristics and behaviors are based on the description of that object you provided in the class. For example, a UserForm becomes an object when you press F5 and thereby execute your program.

✦ Classes (and the objects that result from them) are primarily composed of two types of code: *properties* (the object's characteristics, like its BackColor) and *methods* (the object's behaviors, like its Show method that makes it visible to the user). Properties are similar to traditional variables, and methods are similar to traditional functions (or Sub procedures). Collectively, an object's methods and properties are called *members.* There's another member, *events,* but let's not go too far, too fast.

Icons Used in This Book

Notice the eye-catching little icons in the margins of this book. They're next to certain paragraphs to emphasize that special information appears. Here are the icons and their meanings:

The Tip icon points you to shortcuts and insights that save you time and trouble.

A Warning icon aims to steer you away from dangerous situations.

A Technical Stuff icon highlights nerdy technical discussions that you can skip if you want to. I'm not too fond of unnecessary technical stuff, so this icon is used rarely.

Book I

Office 2003 Essentials

The 5th Wave
By Rich Tennant

"The new technology has really helped me get organized. I keep my project reports under the PC, budgets under my laptop and memos under my pager."

Contents at a Glance

Chapter 1: Getting with the Program

In This Chapter

✔ **Exploring what you'll find in this book**

✔ **Managing menus and toolbars**

✔ **Creating your first Office program (it's easier than you think)**

✔ **Customizing the keyboard**

✔ **Getting programming help online**

*O*ver the years, Office has evolved. As the result of hundreds of focus groups, ergonomic studies, user feedback, and hard-won experience, the Office design teams have come up with a highly effective suite of applications.

One of Office's strong points over the years has been its considerable depth. You can find literally thousands of features within the Office applications, yet the surface that you interact with can be as smooth and simple as you wish. You can even hide the toolbars and menu bars.

Put another way, Office applications are highly customizable. Throughout this book, you discover ways to manage and exploit Office 2003 to take it to a new level of efficiency. You see how to write programs that make your work easier as well as how to build utilities that facilitate communication between Office applications and automate other common business tasks. I also show you hundreds of other useful techniques and tools.

Most new computers ship with Office, which is also used in nearly every business today. What these businesses have in common is an ongoing effort to improve their efficiency. And in many cases, developing or automating Office applications is one of the most effective ways to increase workplace productivity. Many workers know what they wish they could do — and this book shows them how to do it.

Office 2003 Application Development All-in-One Desk Reference For Dummies covers all the new features in Office 2003 and demonstrates how developers can best exploit them. Many of these features are designed to improve work-flow and facilitate better communication between workers — just the sort of goals that Office developers want to achieve. You'll find everything you need to know to make Office 2003 an effective, valuable, and customized workplace engine.

For example, InfoPath simplifies interaction with all kinds of data sources: everything from unformatted lists to legacy databases. SharePoint assists developers in building an automated collaborative environment. And eXtensible Markup Language (XML) as well as related technologies, such as Web Services, underlies many of the improvements in Office 2003. Among many other topics, this book explains precisely how to take advantage of XML's promise with simple, no-nonsense examples. You'll understand exactly how to leverage your current work and communication patterns by using the new and powerful data sharing techniques available in Office 2003.

No significant Office topic is ignored here. Read on to discover how to use classic but important features such as Visual Basic for Applications (VBA). And I cover all the latest developments such as Smart Documents, Access 2003 Developer Extensions, and the new security features. Anyone interested in building intelligent business applications will find the solutions they're looking for here.

Modifying the User Interface

This chapter starts things off with an introduction to some relatively easy modifications that you can make to Office 2003 applications. (No point jumping immediately into the deep end of heavy-duty programming; there's time enough for all that in subsequent chapters.) And although these modifications are on the simpler side, some of the techniques that I describe in this chapter are powerful, new, or both.

I show you various ways of manipulating the user interface, the surface that you work on when using Office applications. If you're already an Office guru, you might want to skim this chapter to search for techniques you don't yet know. Less-experienced readers are likely to find many ideas in this chapter that are of immediate practical use, such as hiding a new Help feature or modifying and editing menus.

You will find a bit of programming in this chapter, too, but it's not very advanced, and you're not even expected to understand it at this point. You can just benefit from the exercise, and you might find the results (such as quickly turning toolbars on and off) a valuable addition to your bag of tricks.

Turning off mini help

Begin by seeing how to get rid of that new little Office 2003 Help field. It seems as if Microsoft introduced a new, cute Help feature. Remember the little paper clip fellow (Clippit) that started annoying many people a few

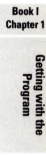

years back? Most people find the animated Office Assistant rather bother-some, not to mention unprofessional looking. At least it's easy enough to turn off that annoying paper clip by just deselecting Office Assistant on the Help menu.

Now to get rid of that new Help field, located by default at the upper-right corner of Office applications such as Word and Access, as you can see in Figure 1-1.

The Help field

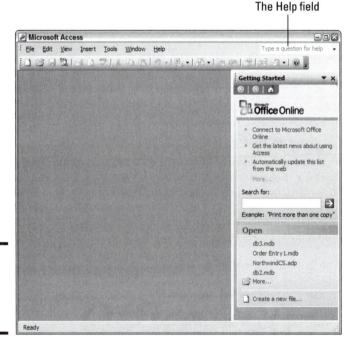

Figure 1-1:
Type Help questions here or hide Help.

What I don't like about this feature is that anyone can see your last Help request, which could be embarrassing. Personally, I don't want people seeing the kind of help that I last requested. It lets them know what I didn't know. Your last question stays up there for all to see, even after you've closed the Help pane. And even though there's no obvious way to make this little feature go away, I know the easy secret.

Before I lead you through this example, note something important about the Customize dialog box. When it's open, Office 2003 applications freeze and wait to see whether you're modifying something. All the menus and toolbars are loosened, so you can drag and drop items from the dialog box onto tool-bars or remove items by dragging them off toolbars and dropping them into the document workspace.

Here are the steps for removing the Help field:

1. **Choose Tools⇨Customize.**

2. **Click the Toolbars tab of the Customize dialog box.**

3. **Right-click the little Help field.**

You see a check box with a check mark in it.

4. **Remove the check and then close the Customize dialog box.**

The discomforting little critter won't ever advertise your personal short-comings again.

If you want this feature back, just repeat these steps, but mark the check box to select it.

Making this change in Word won't get rid of the Help field in other Office 2003 applications; you have to turn it off in each application.

Modifying menus

Menus can be adjusted to suit your needs. You can move the menu bar itself the same way that you move toolbars: Just drag the dotted line on the left or top of the menu bar and drop the menu elsewhere on the screen. To switch between long and short menus (short menus display only the most frequently used options), choose Tools⇨Customize⇨Options, and then select the Always Show Full Menus check box.

To modify a menu's location on the menu bar, follow these steps:

1. **Choose Tools⇨Customize.**

2. **While the Customize dialog box is open, you're free to drag around the menu headings on the menu bar, reorganizing them any way you wish.**

If you want to remove a menu heading entirely, drag it away from the menu bar and drop it somewhere in the document.

Editing menus

The contents of menus can be modified, too. To modify the order of items within a menu, follow these steps:

1. **Choose Tools⇨Customize.**

2. **In the Customize dialog box, click the Commands tab.**

3. **Click the Rearrange Commands button.**

The Rearrange Commands dialog box opens, as shown in Figure 1-2.

Figure 1-2:
Add, delete,
or adjust the
order of
commands
here.

4. **Select a command you want to rearrange; then click the Move Up or Move Down buttons.**

Click the Modify Selection button in Figure 1-2 to rename menu items, change their icon, and otherwise manipulate them to suit yourself, as shown in Figure 1-3.

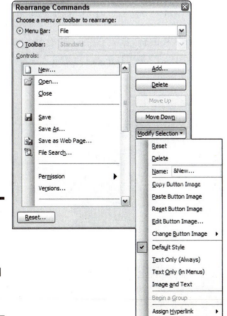

Figure 1-3:
Here's
where you
can really
take control
of your
menus.

Creating your own menus

You can even create a new menu of your personal favorite features. Just follow these steps:

1. **Choose Tools⇨Customize and then click the Commands tab.**

2. **Click New Menu in the Categories list.**

3. **Drag the new menu icon from the Customize dialog box and drop it on the menu bar.**

4. **Right-click the new menu to name it whatever you want.**

    To add commands to your new menu, click the Rearrange Commands button. Then locate the name of your new menu in the Choose a Menu or Toolbar to Rearrange list.

5. **Click the Add button and select which features you want to include on your new custom menu.**

Customizing shortcut menus

Shortcut menus, also called *context menus,* are those little menus that appear when you right-click something. In Office 2003, you can customize these menus in Access, Word, or PowerPoint.

Although thousands of shortcut menus exist, never fear. Here's how to add a new command to a shortcut menu in Access. Follow these steps to add the Help command to the default database background shortcut menu:

1. **Open a database window in Access; then right-click the window to open the default context menu, as shown in Figure 1-4.**

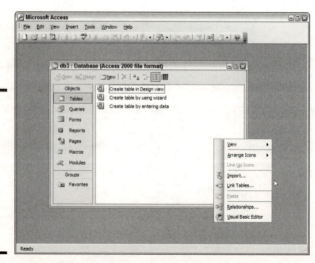

Figure 1-4:
BEFORE:
Many
objects in
Office 2003
come with
a context
menu that
you can
modify.

2. **Choose Tools⇨Customize.**

3. **Click the Toolbars tab.**

4. **Select the Shortcut Menus check box.**

   A special shortcut toolbar appears, as you can see in Figure 1-5.

A special shortcut menu toolbar appears.

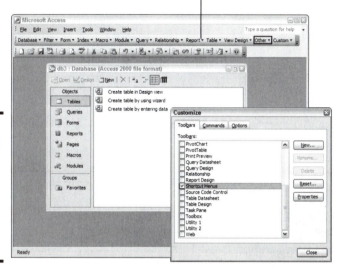

Figure 1-5:
This special
toolbar
allows you
to choose
which
shortcut
menu to
modify.

5. **From this special toolbar, choose Database⇨Background, as shown in Figure 1-6.**

6. **Click the Commands tab of the Customize dialog box.**

7. **Choose the category that contains the command you want to add to the shortcut menu.**

8. **Drag the command from the Commands list to the shortcut menu (position it where you want it to appear).**

9. **Drop the command (release the mouse button) into the shortcut menu, as shown in Figure 1-7.**

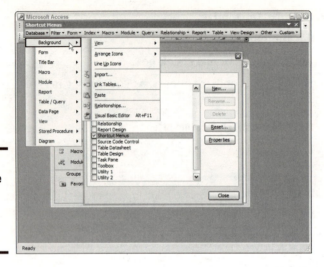

Figure 1-6:
Choose the shortcut menu you want to modify.

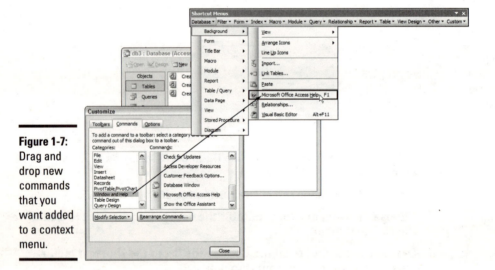

Figure 1-7:
Drag and drop new commands that you want added to a context menu.

In this example, I add the Help feature to the shortcut menu that pops out when I right-click the background of a database, as shown in Figure 1-8.

Figure 1-8:
AFTER:
Success!
This context
menu now
has a Help
command.
Compare
this menu
with Figure
1-4.

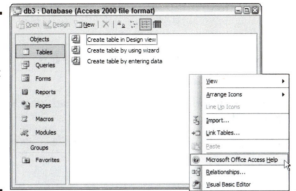

You can edit context menus in many of the same ways you edit ordinary menus — rename, rearrange, add icons, and so on. However, you can't add or delete an entire context menu.

Personalizing Toolbars

You can manipulate toolbars, tailoring them to suit yourself, much the same way you customize menus. In fact, a toolbar is simply another kind of menu. Although toolbars are more graphic and they are always open, they're just another way for you to trigger behaviors in Office 2003 applications. Some people prefer menus; others consider toolbars more convenient. (You say *toe-may-toe,* and I say *toe-mah-toe.*) As usual in Office, how you work is largely up to you, as long as you know how to modify the applications. After all, it's your work surface, so you should be able to decide where things go and how best to manage it, just as you arrange your desk to suit yourself.

In addition to adding built-in commands (such as File➪Open), to menus and toolbars, you can also add macros. A *macro* is simply a short program, designed to work within and improve the efficiency of the application that hosts it. (See Book I, Chapter 2.) Writing macros allows you to really take control of the elements of an Office application and do with it what you will. You can also add special hyperlinks, such as a link to a worksheet or workbook in Excel or to a Web page.

Adding hyperlinks

As with menus, you modify toolbars via the Customize dialog box. Just add a custom button, change its image (if you like), and name it. You can even turn the button into a hyperlink. Follow these steps to see how to add a hyperlink to CNN News to the standard Excel toolbar.

First add the custom button:

1. **Choose Tools➪Customize.**

2. **Click the Commands tab in the Customize dialog box.**

3. **Click Macros in the Categories list.**

4. **Drag a custom button from the Commands list and drop it on the Standard Excel toolbar.**

   You don't have to detach the Standard toolbar as it's shown in Figure 1-9.

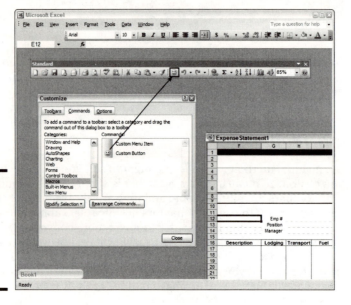

Figure 1-9: Add a new button to a toolbar by dragging and dropping.

Don't worry about the smiley face default icon; you can always change this icon by right-clicking it and choosing another graphic. In fact, try that now (with the Custom dialog box still open from the preceding step list).

1. **Right-click the smiley face and choose Change Button Image.**

   You get a palette of images to choose from.

2. **Select the microphone image to remind you that this is CNN, which is broadcast.**

   Smiley is gone, replaced with the microphone image.

Now rename the custom buttom:

1. **Right-click the new button and click the Rename option from the context menu.**

2. **Rename it from Custom Button to CNN.**

Finally, make the button *hot* (into a link):

1. **Right-click the button once again and this time choose Assign Hyperlink, and then Open, from the context menu.**

   The Assign Hyperlink: Open dialog box opens, as shown in Figure 1-10.

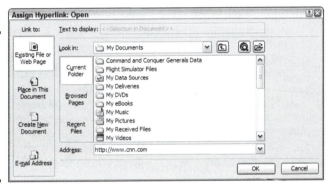

Figure 1-10: Use this dialog box to create hyperlinks to workbooks, Web sites, and so on.

Note in Figure 1-10 that you can link to various destinations: specific cells or ranges in an Excel workbook; files; e-mail addresses; or new documents, workbooks, Word files, or Notepad TXT files.

2. **Type** http://www.cnn.com **into the Address field (refer to Figure 1-10).**

3. **Click OK.**

   The dialog box closes.

4. **Click the Close button on the Customize dialog box.**

Now try your new hyperlink. Click the microphone icon on the Standard toolbar, and you should see CNN appear, with all the latest shocks, scandals, and scary celebrity agony.

Follow essentially the same steps to add links to menus instead of toolbars. Hyperlinks can also be inserted into Excel workbooks (just right-click a cell and choose Hyperlink from the context menu), Word documents (right-click the document), and so on.

Access, however, is, as usual, the odd stepchild and does things its own, different way. You add hyperlinks to reports, forms, and so on in Access. (It just creates a `Label` control containing the link.) However, the links don't work in Access itself. You must output the report to Excel, HTML, Word, or some other host before the links can actually do their job. As you'll see throughout this book, Access often trods a different path than other Office applications. It appears to exist in a parallel, although similar, universe.

Vaporizing interface elements programmatically

Throughout this book, you'll find all kinds of programming techniques that you can use to exploit and unify Office 2003 applications. Although you've not yet explored the vast VBA language built into most Office applications, create a useful little macro right now while I'm talking about toolbars. You don't have to understand what's happening in the programming at this point: Monkey-see, monkey-do is just fine at this stage.

Many games and programs have a key you can press that removes all the extraneous, distracting menus, help windows, gauges, and other things from the screen. This frees you up to simply see the essentials. It's similar to choosing View⇨Full Screen in Word: All the rulers, scroll bars, menus, and toolbars vanish, and you see the immortal words of the document's writer (you) unadulterated by debris. However, note a couple of problems with Full Screen mode in Word: You lose the scroll bars, and an annoying little bar appears right in the document, which allows you to restore the view to Normal mode.

Here I show you how to write a macro to improve on Word's clean-screen mode. In this macro, I preserve the scroll bar, and you won't need that annoying back-to-Normal-mode bar. Instead, you just use the shortcut key combination Alt+V to toggle Full Screen mode on and off. Simple, clean, and — for those of us who like to type on a blank piece of "paper" without distracting icons all over the edges — a real pleasure to use.

Programming a macro to hide a toolbar

Here's how to write a macro to hide one or more menus and toolbars so that you can selectively clear the screen any way you choose or toggle between sets of toolbars/menus for different purposes.

Many people have the primary menu (File, Edit, View, and so on), and the Standard and Formatting toolbars visible at all times while using Word. But you use them only now and then. Most of the time, you're just typing. Wouldn't it be nice to have a clean screen in which to type? Figures 1-11 and 1-12 show before and after examples.

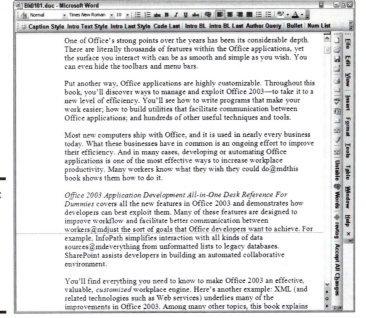

Figure 1-11:
BEFORE:
Toolbars
and menus
can clutter
up a word
processor
screen.

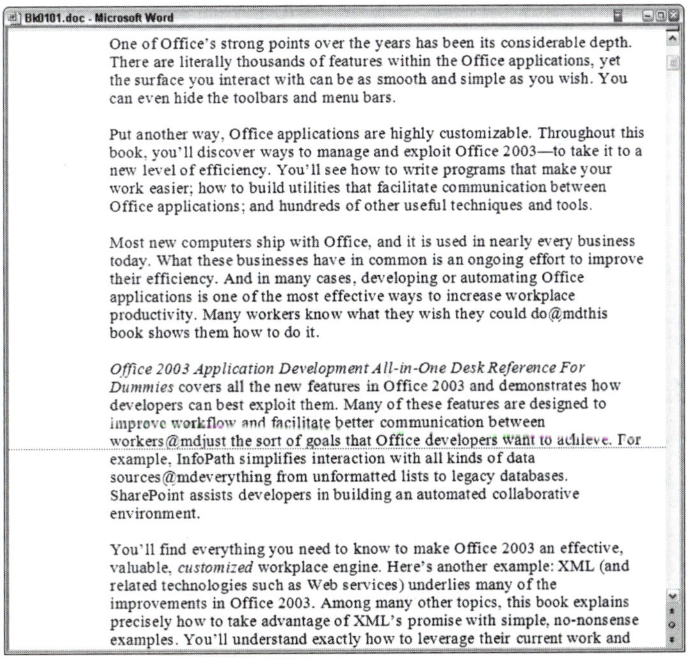

Figure 1-12:
AFTER:
Some
people
prefer a
clean
screen to
write on.

Here's how to make distracting menus and toolbars disappear, or reappear, every time you press the Alt+V key combination (V for *vanish*).

1. **In Word, choose Tools⇨Macro⇨Macros.**

2. **Type** Alt+V **in the Name field in the Macros dialog box.**

   You're later going to assign this macro to the Alt+V key combination, so it's useful to name the macro after these keys. It helps you remember.

3. **Click the Create button in the Macros dialog box.**

   A powerful editor opens, about which you can find more in Book II and other places in this book.

   Your insertion cursor (the blinking, vertical line) is now located within your AltV macro.

4. **Type in the following VBA commands so that the** AltV **macro (a** Sub, **technically) looks like Listing 1-1.**

Listing 1-1: AltV Macro

```
Sub AltV()
'
' AltV Macro
' Macro created 11/25/2003 by Richard
'

If CommandBars("Standard").Visible = True Then

    CommandBars("Standard").Visible = False
    CommandBars("Formatting").Visible = False

Else

    CommandBars("Standard").Visible = True
    CommandBars("Formatting").Visible = True

End If

End Sub
```

5. **Close the Visual Basic editor by clicking the small X icon in the upper-right corner.**

When reviewing the code, you can ignore the lines that begin with single quote marks. They're simply *comments* that the programmer (or in this case, VBA itself) inserted as hints or notes to the programmer. VBA ignores such lines when executing a macro.

You can also ignore these programming commands, but for the curious, the above code translates into English like this: If the Standard toolbar is showing, make it and the Formatting toolbar invisible or else make them both visible. And that's just what you want. Pressing Alt+V toggles their visibility, just the way you toggle a light switch on and off.

Using macros to remove menus

If you want to hide the main menu, too, you have to do things a bit differently. Menus are not part of a `Menus` collection but are in the `CommandBars` collection. (*Collections* are, simply put, arrays of objects. Like arrays, collections can be manipulated programmatically in loops.) What's more, you can't specify the primary menu (the one with File, Edit, View, and so on) by name but instead must refer to it as the `ActiveMenuBar`. Finally, you can't use the `Visible = False` approach that works with toolbars. Instead, you must use `Enabled = False`. There's no rhyme or reason for these differences: It's just one of the challenges faced by programmers every day. Consistency is attempted in computer languages like VBA but is never fully achieved. Anyway, here's the code that you should add to the above macro to toggle the visibility of the main menu. Insert the bold lines in the places indicated.

```
If CommandBars("Standard").Visible = True Then

    CommandBars("Standard").Visible = False
    CommandBars("Formatting").Visible = False
    CommandBars.ActiveMenuBar.Enabled = False

Else

    CommandBars("Standard").Visible = True
    CommandBars("Formatting").Visible = True
    CommandBars.ActiveMenuBar.Enabled = True

End If
```

Modify this code to add any additional command bars — beyond Standard and Formatting — that you use in Word.

Assigning the macro to hide menus and toolbars

After you program the macro to hide toolbars and menus (see the preceding sections), all that remains is to assign this macro to the Alt+V key combination. Follow these steps:

1. **Choose Tools⇨Customize.**

2. **Click the Keyboard button at the bottom of the Customize dialog box.**

3. **Choose Macros in the Categories list.**

   A new list named Macros appears, with all your macros displayed, including the new one you just wrote, AltV.

4. **Choose AltV in the Macros list.**

5. **Click in the Press New Shortcut key field in the Customize Keyboard dialog box.**

   The insertion cursor begins blinking in this field, ready for you to press the key combination that will launch the AltV macro.

6. **Press Alt+V.**

   You are informed that Alt+V is unassigned unless you've already assigned it to something previously, in which case you must decide whether to override the previous assignment or choose a new key combination.

7. **Click the Assign button of the Customize Keyboard dialog box.**

8. **Click the Close button of the Customize dialog box.**

Let Office do the programming

If you're unsure what commands to use when programming in VBA, you can always try a shortcut: Let Office do the programming for you. Here's how. Choose Tools⇨Macro⇨Record New Macro. The Record New Macro dialog box opens. Click the OK button to begin the recording process. Then do something — type, click the mouse, choose menu options, whatever — while the recorder runs and writes programming for everything you're doing. When you've finished, click the blue square in the Macro Recorder toolbar to stop the recording. Now press Alt+F11 (in Word) to display the VB editor and the programming that was generated for you by the recorder. You can now edit this code, copy and paste it into other macros, or just learn from it. For example, if you choose File⇨Save while the recorder is running, you'll find the following code in the VB editor later:

```
Sub Macro6()
'
'  Macro6 Macro
'  Macro recorded 11/25/2003 by
    Richard
'
        ActiveDocument.Save
End Sub
```

The currently visible Word document is the `ActiveDocument` object. You can append a period after this object's name to perform various tasks that can be accomplished with the `ActiveDocument`.

Now for the fun. Press Alt+V in Word's Normal document view. The toolbars disappear. Press Alt+V again, and they reappear, just as you'd hoped. You can take this technique as far as you want, showing or hiding pretty much whatever you want, whenever, however . . .well, you get the idea. More about VBA in chapters to come.

If you want to go the whole way and create a macro to toggle Full Screen mode, use the following code. (Use this *instead* of the code in the previous sections, not *in addition to*.)

```
ActiveWindow.View.FullScreen = Not ActiveWindow.View.FullScreen
```

Customizing the Keyboard

Just as you have essentially total freedom to manipulate Office 2003 menus and toolbars, you can also reassign keys to suit your needs. Key combinations can be assigned to trigger all the features in the applications as well as macros and other targets. These combinations are *hot keys* or *shortcut* keys. However, when you open menus via built-in keyboard shortcuts featuring the Alt key (such as Alt+F to open the File menu), this behavior is also called *shortcut keys* or *keyboard shortcuts*. Never mind. Whenever you want, you can change the classic key assignments to whatever you want.

To see the shortcut keys assigned to toolbar buttons when you pause your mouse cursor over a button, choose Tools⇨Customize and then click the Options tab. Mark the Show ScreenTips on Toolbars and the Show Shortcut Keys in ScreenTips check boxes to select them. Making these changes affects the behavior of all the other Office 2003 applications. (*Note:* Excel displays only the Show ScreenTips on Toolbars check box, so you can't make this change from Excel.)

Restoring Classic Key Behaviors

When you first start using Office 2003 Word, you might notice that several traditional keyboard behaviors have been rather strangely altered. For example, the Delete key has for decades been used to delete a selected block of text. Now, when you select (drag) some text (so it reverses color, to white on black), pressing the Delete key merely displays a little (and for most of us who are capable typists, highly annoying) question: Delete block? No (Yes). Repeatedly pressing the Delete key has no effect. You must also press Y to actually perform the job that pressing the Delete key used to accomplish.

Similarly, keys that maneuvered you through a document have been reassigned. You used to get to the start of a line of text by pressing the Home key. Now you must press Home+←. You used to be able to press Ctrl+Home to get to the beginning of the document; now this displays the Find and Replace dialog box, with the Go To tab selected.

If you're finding these strange behaviors, you won't be able to remap these keys by using the usual approach (choosing Tools⇨Customize and then clicking the Keyboard button). The Delete key is set to Edit⇨Clear, which is what it's supposed to say. It just behaves oddly.

Here is the solution: For reasons unknown, when Word is installed, it sometimes switches on the Navigation Keys for WordPerfect Users option. To fix this and restore your familiar Word behaviors, choose Tools⇨Options and then click the General tab. Deselect the Navigation Keys for WordPerfect Users option.

Getting Online Help

Microsoft provides extensive online help for developers and programmers, and its Office information is no exception.

Your portal to Office 2003 help online is `http://office.microsoft.com`. (You'll find a link to this site in the Office applications' Help menu.) At this location. you find a list of the individual Office applications and utilities. (See the left side of Figure 1-13.)

Click the <u>Access</u> link, for example, and you'll be told that in Office 2003, you need to upgrade to Jet 4.0 if you want Access to be able to offer all its features yet at the same time block unsafe expressions that could cause virus-like damage.

Another useful online resource is MSDN, the Microsoft Developer Network. Here at `http://msdn.microsoft.com`, you can find advanced tutorials, a search engine, white papers, downloads, free software trials, and other often useful items. MSDN is also a subscription service that sends out early versions of Microsoft products, CDs full of various kinds of programmer-oriented tools, and so on. However, you don't have to be a subscriber to take advantage of the wealth of information online.

If you're looking for answers to specific questions, try joining one of the newsgroups dedicated to the various Office applications. Try this address: `http://support.microsoft.com/newsgroups/default.aspx`. Then drill down until you find the application, topic, and messages of interest to you.

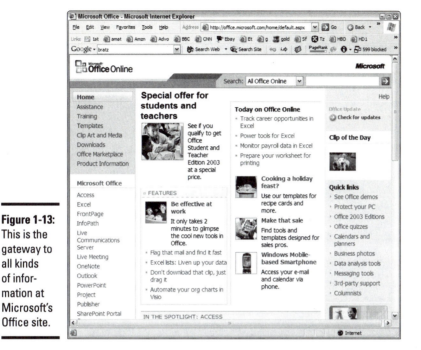

Figure 1-13:
This is the
gateway to
all kinds
of infor-
mation at
Microsoft's
Office site.

Chapter 2: Programming Lite: Making the Most of Macros

In This Chapter

✓ **Knowing what you can and can't record**

✓ **Assigning macros to toolbars and keyboard shortcuts**

✓ **Viewing standard macros**

✓ **Using the** `Auto` **macros**

✓ **Understanding macro security**

*P*erhaps you've created *macros* (little programs) in an application such as Word. (Nobody knows how macros got their name: *Macro* means large, but macros are small. Whatever.)

Macros can be real timesavers, automating tasks that you perform frequently. Macros are available for every other major Microsoft application. Even Visual Basic .NET and the Visual Studio .NET editors now have macro capabilities.

Discovering the Pluses of Macros

You can automate and customize your applications in many ways: assigning layout configurations to function keys, adding new shortcut keys, building custom add-ins, creating your own wizards, modifying toolbars, and even extending the existing menus with your own utilities.

However, for those of us who love to program, macros (also known as *VBA subs* or *procedures*) are among the most enjoyable ways to modify how applications behave — easy, little utilities that can be quite simple to create but are also sometimes surprisingly useful.

The most obvious reason to use a macro is to accomplish instantly what might take you a fair amount of time to do. For example, if you find yourself doing something repeatedly, such as having to fill out your address, create a macro to do the job for you.

The ABCs of BASIC and C

BASIC (Beginner's All-Purpose Symbolic Instruction Code) has been around for a long time (think mid-1960s). An early programming language, it's the most popular, straightforward, and efficient computer language ever invented. Prior to 1995, most Office applications had their own, unique version of BASIC: WordBasic, AccessBasic, and so on. That was unfortunate, but now these special languages have all been replaced by VBA.

It's a great relief that Microsoft had the wisdom to use BASIC as the macro language rather than the alternative (the crypto-mathematical, pseudo-scientific C language and its many derivatives). Had C been chosen — and doubtless there were some programmers advocating it — few people would bother to write macros.

Nonetheless, over the years, some aspects of C have leaked into BASIC, most notably the academic theory of object-oriented programming (OOP). VBA is somewhat less straightforward, intuitive, and plain-English than previous versions of BASIC such as WordBasic, which VBA replaced. That's because OOP has moved into VBA in various ways, adding some complexities while offering some benefits as well. But VBA will never be fully object-oriented. For that, you must move to Visual Basic .NET.

Macros can be composed of a simple series of application commands, such as creating a new Access database with certain parameters. Or macros can be quite complex, involving .NET libraries and other low-level (sophisticated programming) activities. You can read how to create complex macros in Books II and VIII.

In essence, a macro is a computer program. No, it's not as large or complex as a typical utility (such as a spell checker), but it's a program nonetheless. You tell the macro how to do something for you. Then, forever after, it carries out your instructions flawlessly.

Although macros are just one way to write a computer program, they're widely used because they're efficient — both easy to create and useful. Most commercial applications contain an embedded programming language: the macro language. In Microsoft applications, that language is Visual Basic for Applications (VBA).

Macros run within their applications; they can't run if the host application isn't also running. However, you can build small programs by using Visual Basic 6, VB .NET, or other languages outside of Office applications while you're working in any application or even just on the desktop or in Explorer. And with a third-part utility that I use all the time, you can even imitate the way macros are usually launched. These outside programs can be launched with shortcut key combinations, such as W+Tab to launch Word.

In other words, regardless of whether any applications are running, you can launch a program, substitute text, open a document, send e-mail, go to an Internet site, open a folder or Windows peripheral (such as printers, disk drives, and so on), and even launch scripts that you write to do such things as switching screen resolutions with a single keypress. (*Script languages* are similar to regular computer languages such as BASIC, but they usually lack the ability to directly modify or delete files on the hard drives, or other potentially malicious, virus-like actions.) This Windows-wide, keyboard shortcut-capable macro utility is available from ActiveWords (`www.activewords.com`), which offers a free 60-day trial and two versions. (The more expensive one includes the scripting feature among other enhancements.) I find this utility indispensable.

Recording Macros

Whenever you find yourself doing some small task repeatedly, that task is a candidate for a macro. For example, I often need to see how many words are in a document I'm writing in Word. I could take the long route through the menu system: File⇨Properties⇨Statistics. Or I could record this activity into a macro and then simply add that macro to a toolbar, so I could see the word count with a single click. Or I could assign that macro to a keyboard shortcut such as Alt+W. Either way, macros make frequent tasks a snap.

Try an example. You can read in Chapter 1 how to write a macro directly — to program it — in the Visual Basic editor. You can also record macros, which is the simplest (but most limited) way of creating a new macro. (However, you can't record a macro in Access. You can write them, but you can't record them.)

Recording a simple Word macro

Assume that you're running a little eBay business, selling Samoan straw dolls. Every time you write a letter to a customer, you have to type *We're hoping you enjoy your new MuNaa Doll! Remember, though,* never *put it in the microwave.*

This tedious, repetitive task is a perfect candidate for a macro. What's the point of typing those sentences over and over, day after day? The following steps show you how to create a macro to automate the process.

1. **In Word, choose Tools⇨Macro⇨Record New Macro.**

The Record Macro dialog box appears, as shown in Figure 2-1.

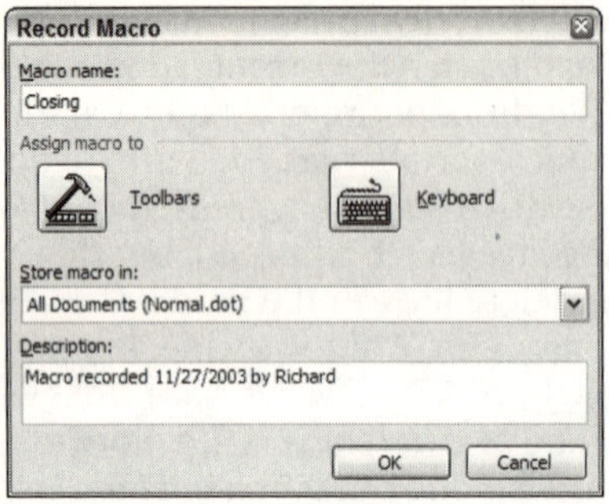

Figure 2-1:
Begin
recording a
Word macro
from this
dialog box.

2. **In the Macro Name text box, type** Closing **as the name for your new macro.**

3. **Decide how you want the user to activate the macro: mouse or keyboard.**

   You can also opt to assign your new macro to a toolbar, but that requires that you move your hands from the keyboard and reach for the mouse. (Bad.) It also requires that the toolbar be visible at the time. (Double bad.) In my view, creating a keyboard shortcut is often preferable. So, click the Keyboard icon of the Record Macro dialog box.

   The Customize Keyboard dialog box opens, as shown in Figure 2-2.

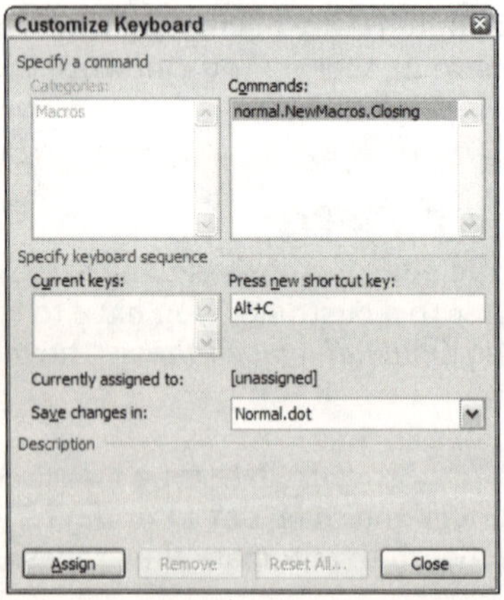

Figure 2-2:
Assign your
new macro
to a key
combination
here.

4. **Click the Press New Shortcut Key field to put the blinking insertion cursor there; then press Alt+C (or whatever other combination you want to use).**

5. **Click the Assign button and then click the Close button.**

   The Record Macro toolbar appears on the upper left of your document, with a blue square (End Recording) and a red circle (Pause).

6. **Type in the following text, which is what you want to automatically insert whenever this macro is run.**

   We're hoping you enjoy your new MuNaa Doll! Remember, though, *never* put it in the microwave.

7. **Click the blue square on the Record Macro toolbar.**

   The toolbar disappears, and your macro is finalized.

Now whenever you press Alt+C, the text is typed in for you.

Although the macro recorder can detect mouse clicks on such things as menu items (it sees this as simply the same as a keyboard menu selection via Alt+keypress), some mouse behaviors can't be correctly interpreted (such as dragging to draw a line). So, if possible, use the keyboard when recording a macro, especially in Excel and PowerPoint.

If a dialog box appears while you're recording a macro, note the settings displayed in the dialog box. Every setting will be recorded by the macro, even if you're merely trying to adjust one of the settings. For example, if you decide to switch to boldface, you can open the Font dialog box by choosing Format⇨ Font during recording. However, all the following information (everything this dialog box is capable of modifying) is inserted into your macro:

```
With Selection.Font
        .Name = "Times New Roman"
        .Size = 10
        .Bold = True
        .Italic = True
        .Underline = wdUnderlineNone
        .UnderlineColor = wdColorAutomatic
        .StrikeThrough = False
        .DoubleStrikeThrough = False
        .Outline = False
        .Emboss = False
        .Shadow = False
        .Hidden = False
        .SmallCaps = False
        .AllCaps = False
        .Color = wdColorAutomatic
        .Engrave = False
        .Superscript = False
        .Subscript = False
        .Spacing = 0.3
```

```
                    .Scaling = 100
                    .Position = 0
                    .Kerning = 0
                    .Animation = wdAnimationNone
            End With
```

This is fine if forcing all these parameters is your intention. However, if you just meant to make the text you've selected boldface, you'd be better off avoiding the dialog box altogether when recording the macro. Try using Ctrl+B instead.

Understanding the VBA behind recorded macros

If you want to view or modify the macro you just recorded, press Alt+F11 to open the VB editor and scroll until you find the macro named `Sub Closing`. It should look like this:

```
Sub Closing()
'
' Closing Macro
' Macro recorded 11/27/2003 by Richard
'
Selection.TypeText Text:="We're hoping you enjoy your new
    MuNaa Doll! Remember, though, never put it in the
    microwave."

End Sub
```

A short overview of objects

To understand .NET, Office applications' object models, the XML object model, and other contemporary programming, you need to know about a few key qualities of objects.

You can divide computing into two broad categories: information and processing (manipulating the information). Similarly, objects are made up of two broad categories: properties and methods. *Properties* are similar to information; properties describe an object's characteristics, like the format of an XML attribute (format= ounces, for example). *Methods* are similar to processing. A method is a behavior or job that an object knows how to perform, like make a copy of yourself. Another way to look at this

distinction is that properties are similar to what a programmer thinks of as traditional variables, but methods are similar to traditional functions. Collectively, an object's methods and properties are known as its *members*.

These distinctions between object, properties, and methods are hardly new to computer programming, much less an invention of OOP or XML. Instead, they are built into reality and can be found in the simplest childhood grammar: "Black storm go boom!" is more than a two-year-old's poetic description of thunder. It reveals the fundamental nature of object/member relationships: Black (property), storm (object), go boom (method).

The Selection object

The `Selection` object is not well-named. *Selection,* in computer terms, typically means that you've dragged your mouse across text or held down the Shift key while using the arrow keys to highlight some text. The selected text reverses to white letters on a black background to indicate that it's a selection. Unfortunately, this is not what is commonly meant by *selection* in VBA. A `Selection` object is merely a fancy way of saying *the current insertion cursor position* (although it can also confusingly mean a true, classic selection of text).

The lines `Sub` and `End Sub` surround all macros, and mean *start here* and *end here,* respectively. The commands and information between those two lines tell VBA what to do when the macro is executed. Lines that start with apostrophes are comments and are ignored during execution.

You can delete this macro `Sub` if you wish, but be sure to delete everything, including the `End Sub`. Or you can modify the message by typing something else as the text. In other words, you can directly modify the macro programming in the VB editor.

What does the programming mean? It's written in BASIC (see the sidebar, "The ABCs of BASIC and C"). But because of the influence of OOP, instead of simply writing `Insert "This Text"`, as would be the case in WordBasic, you must refer to a selection object and its `TypeText` method: `Selection.TypeText`. Then you have to provide a `Text` object. (Some would call it a *property.*)

Today's programmers face the job of transitioning from classical computer programming (typified by VBA) to the current trend of object-oriented programming, as exemplified by VB.NET. Throughout this book, I illustrate migration paths that you take to ease this transition if you're used to traditional Office programming techniques but now need to move beyond them to VB.NET. If you aren't yet familiar with the fundamental concepts of OOP (objects and their properties, methods, and events), don't be concerned. You'll pick up the jargon as you go along.

 Briefly, and somewhat simplified, an *object* can be practically anything (a visible button, single word of text, range of words, calendar utility, and so on). An object's *properties* are its qualities (such as its color, size or length, position on the screen, and so on). An object's *methods* are things that it can do, such as a calendar object's ability to calculate the number of days between two dates. *Events* are things that can happen to an object, such as the user clicking the object to trigger it or select it, and so on.

The point is that with OOP-inflected BASIC, your programming becomes more verbose than traditional BASIC programming as well as less clear, less descriptive, and less easy to read and modify. The punctuation also becomes awkward and strange (such as the : = used instead of the more sensible =). And, c'mon: You're simply inserting text here. Why not just use the obvious programming (WordBasic's version), like this?

```
Insert "We're hoping you enjoy your new MuNaa Doll! Remember,
    though, never put it in the microwave."
```

The answer is that a generation of programmers has graduated from schools that teach only the OOP way, so that's what they tend to prefer.

Using Special Macros in Access

Although Access includes VBA, it has a separate (albeit rather awkward) macro facility as well. However, for reasons of backward-compatibility (surely it's not nostalgia for ungainliness), Access retains its old macro programming system as well as VBA. Also, Access contains a utility that can translate legacy Access macros into VBA macros.

I don't spend much time exploring Access macros, but you should know that you can't *record* a macro in Access. In fact, if you open the Tools⇨Macro menu in Access, all you see are three options: the VB editor, Run Macro, and Convert Form's Macros to Visual Basic. *Form's Macros* are Access's old-style macros: You select various actions from a list box; when translated into VBA, these actions become methods of the DoCmd object. In all the other Office 2003 applications, macros are what I've been describing in this chapter, namely VBA Subs (also called *procedures*). However, Access (always the maverick) requires you to explicitly request (via Tools⇨Macro) that a particular Access-style "macro" be translated into VBA.

Creating an Access macro

To create a legacy Access macro, go to the primary database window, click the Macros option in the left pane, and then click the New button. The special Macro window appears, as shown in Figure 2-3, from which you choose actions from a drop-down list:

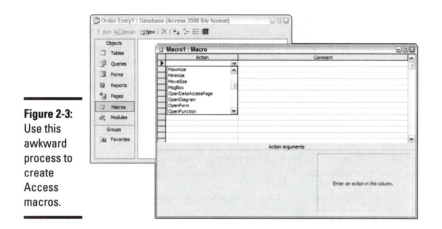

Figure 2-3:
Use this
awkward
process to
create
Access
macros.

Never fear, however. As you'll see in Book II and elsewhere, you can create whatever you need via VBA in Access perfectly well, just without the freedom to use a recorder to assist you.

Converting Access-style macros to VBA

If you do have legacy Access macros that you want to convert to VBA — so you can edit them along with your other, newer Access macros — follow these steps:

1. **Click the Macros option in the Objects pane of the database window.**

   Your macros are listed.

2. **Click the name of the macro you want to convert.**

3. **Choose File⇨Save As.**

   The Save As dialog box opens.

4. **Choose Module in the lower text box.**

5. **Click OK.**

6. **Choose Convert in the Convert Macro dialog box.**

Working with Auto Macros

Word, Excel, PowerPoint, and Outlook each permit you to use a special type of macro. If you use special names when naming a macro, the macro is handled in a special way by VBA. These special macro names begin with Auto and other special, reserved names. Office applications recognize that such macros must be executed in response to events that happen while the application is executing. In fact, in OOP, these macros would actually be called *events*.

The most useful Auto macros are

+ AutoExec: This executes when you first start the application running (or also if you load a global template in Word).

+ AutoNew: This executes each time you create a new document, workbook, or presentation.

+ AutoOpen: This executes any time you open an existing document, workbook, or presentation.

+ AutoClose: This executes every time you close a document, workbook, or presentation.

+ AutoExit: This executes when you shut down the application (or also if you unload a global template in Word).

Auto macros are useful if you need to do some housekeeping before an application runs or a document loads (such as loading in the last two documents you worked on, or calculating the latest sales tax). Other housekeeping — such as saving a special backup file — might need to be done during document or application shutdown.

Word includes several specialized Auto events, but you will probably need to use only AutoOpen and AutoClose (put these in a Normal module), Document_Open, Document_Close, and Document_New.

Excel also offers a variety of Auto macros — New Sheet, Sheet Activate, and so on — but the spelling is a bit different. (AutoOpen becomes Auto_Open, for example). Press Alt+F11 to get to the Excel VBA editor and then look in the Project Explorer for Name.Personal.xls. Double-click this entry and choose Modules, Module1. You're now in Module1 of your Personal Macro Workbook. Choose Insert⇨Procedure. You see the Add Procedure dialog box. Type **Auto_Open** in the Name field. Click OK.

Access does permit a limited Auto event facility, but you cannot use VBA. You must use that early macro legacy technology that Access (alone among Office applications) includes. Search Access help for *AutoExec* to find instructions.

Outlook uses this format:

```
Private Sub Application_Startup()

End Sub
```

PowerPoint wants you to put any `Auto` macros in a class module. Beyond that, you must trigger the macros from a code in a different location. I don't have time or space or patience to outline the unnecessarily convoluted process to execute PowerPoint events, but if you must do it, search PowerPoint Help for *Application Events.*

If the user holds down the Shift key, `Auto` macros are blocked and will not execute. Also, you might have a macro that creates new documents, which would, therefore, trigger the `Document_New` macro. If you want to block the `Document_New` event from triggering in your programming, use this code:

```
WordBasic.DisableAutoMacros
```

Dealing with Macro Security Issues: What You Need to Know

The struggle to achieve computer security is doomed. It's impossible to completely secure a computer, just like it's impossible to build a car that can't crash, you cannot completely secure a computer. (You could secure a computer or car by encasing them in cement and then burying them in a salt mine, but then they'd no longer do their jobs.)

Of course, you know that your computer can delete files: Just right-click a filename in Window Explorer, and then choose Delete from the shortcut menu. However, if a file can be deleted, a virus can potentially delete it, too. Or reformat an entire hard drive, or use your computer to launch blizzards of span, and so on.

All you can do is minimize the risks; you can't eliminate them. Similarly, macros are executable programs, albeit small programs. And therefore, they can be used for good, or ill.

Administrators (and if you work on a personal computer at home, you should be the administrator) are people who are permitted to do everything to modify how Windows behaves. They can hide files from other users, change passwords, adjust security settings, and make many other modifications.

Administrators can specify how macros behave, as well as any other executable code located in documents, presentations, templates, workbooks, and most objects attached to these various elements via linking or other techniques. (Remember that objects are famous for including not merely data, but also executable code — known as *methods* — that can act upon that data.)

Windows has various kinds of built-in security. In XP, an administrator can assign levels of "trust" to various different users. (For example, some are not allowed to delete files, for example). In addition, the .NET languages have built-in security features. Office 2003 applications contain their own kinds of security. As you see, there are layers upon layers of security measures.

By far, the most effective security that you can personally achieve is to take these relatively simple steps:

+ **Make frequent backups.** This prevents a file-deleting virus attack from doing much harm.

+ **Install a firewall like Zone Alarm.** This blocks (so invaders from the Internet will be blocked, and spyware can't send secret messages out from your machine).

+ **Set your macro security level to High.**

+ **Simply refuse to install software from unknown sources.** This includes opening e-mail attachments.

Microsoft recommends the following additional safety measures: "run up-to-date antivirus software on your computer; clear the Trust All Installed Add-ins and Templates check box (described below); use digital signatures; maintain a list of trusted publishers." To me, these are fine precautions if you want to take them, but personally I've never found much use for anti-virus software because it interferes with some software installation processes (even though you trust the source); it exacts a speed penalty; it's a hassle to continually update it with the latest versions; and if you take the steps I suggest at the start of this tip, it's not necessary.

When your macro security settings are set to High, macros created by you are trusted, as are other sources of *executables* (runnable programs) that you can specify. However, nothing prevents a virus author from posing as you. Somewhere in the computer, a macro's author is identified — and identity theft is not impossible; indeed it's rather common.

VeriSign (www.verisign.com) — and other sources such as Microsoft's own Authenticode technology — attempts to ensure security by verifying the origin of software via digital signatures. A digital signature usually does two things

+ **Certification:** They certify that the sender of a message or the author of a piece of code (like a macro) is who he says he is.

In this sense, digital signatures are like a driver's license.

✦ **Verification:** The other job they perform is to verify that the message or code has not been modified after the author signed it.

In other words, you can rely on the message to be accurate, or the code to be benign.

Technically, an electronic signature is usually generated by hashing a public key, which is, itself, encrypted using an associated private key. The terms *hash* and *public/private* key pairs are explained in detail in Book VIII, Chapter 8, if this topic is of interest to you and you want to try programming using these technologies.

Digital signatures are better than nothing, but viruses can imitate signatures, just as people can put on police uniforms as a disguise. Likewise, they might get caught relatively quickly but not before they've done some damage.

You can also self-certify your own macros. Choose Start⇨All Programs from the Windows toolbar, and then choose Microsoft Office⇨Microsoft Office Tools⇨Digital Certificate for VBA Projects. In the dialog box that opens, type in whatever name you want to use for your personal certification. Note that this is a pretty weak certification process. (Not that any of them are completely secure.) This self-certification is kind of like issuing yourself a homemade driver's license — it's not likely to impress the sheriff. It works on your computer, but if your programming is run on a different machine, a warning message appears. Commercial certificate issuing companies can revoke their certificates, if necessary, and can trace signatures back to their origin. Neither of these capabilities are available when you self-certify.

If you want to digitally sign your own macros for use on other computers, choose Tools⇨Digital Signature in the VBA editor. (You have to sign up with VeriSign or another vendor before this will work. Prices vary depending on the size of your business and other factors. Contact VeriSign sales for details at 866-893-6565.)

Adjusting macro settings

To see your current Office 2003 macro security settings, choose Tools⇨Macro⇨Security. You see the Security dialog box, where you can adjust the levels of macro security. By default, security is set to High, as shown in Figure 2-4.

The macro security settings (Tools⇨Macro⇨Security) work as follows:

Low

Anything goes! Live dangerously, hellzapoppin'! Every macro or eXtensible Stylesheet Language (XSL) script file can do whatever it will. This is crazy and dangerous. Nobody should use this setting.

Figure 2-4:
Set macro
security
here.

Medium

For unsigned macros, the user is shown a dialog box requesting permission to run this macro. Signed macros are first examined to see the quality of the digital signature.

✦ A signature from a trusted source and by a trusted digital signature company (such as VeriSign) executes automatically.

✦ A valid source but by an unrecognized author displays the permission dialog box.

✦ An invalid signature causes the macro to be disabled and the user to be warned.

✦ A signature that can't be verified or certificate (validation method) that has expired displays a dialog box and requests user permission to execute.

High

This setting is similar to Medium except that

✦ No dialog box is shown for unsigned macros.

✦ Network administrators can lock the list of trusted sources so that users can't accidentally add new (but nasty) trusted sources.

✦ In all additional situations, macros are summarily disabled, along with dialog boxes displaying warnings.

Although I'm the administrator on my personal machine, this is the setting I use.

Very High

New in Office 2003, this most conservative setting disables all Smart Tag DLLs, COM add-ins, and any macros not from trusted locations. *DLLs* are dynamic link libraries (collections of executable code, loaded as needed by applications: hence, the term *dynamic*). COM add-ins are similar to macros, but they are sometimes larger, utility-size programs and are written and execute outside of documents or worksheets. Add-ins can also be used to globally change the behavior — or add functionality — to several Office 2003 applications simultaneously and automatically. What's more, add-ins execute more quickly than the typical macro.

You build an add-in for yourself using .NET (see Book VIII, Chapter 1). To prevent any macros from running on a particular computer, choose Tools⇨ Macro⇨Security, click the Trusted Sources tab, and deselect the Trust All Installed Add-ins and Templates check box, as shown in Figure 2-5:

Figure 2-5:
Here's how to disable all macros entirely.

Different Office 2003 applications display different options in the Security settings. And, always the odd stepsister of the Office system, Access 2003 doesn't offer the Very High option, although all other Office 2003 applications do.

Triggering trouble

No matter what settings you choose for the macro security feature in Office 2003, other sources of potential damage lurk. In early versions, VBA was *VBScript,* which was a language without such potentially dangerous capabilities as file deletion. However, VBA does have `FileSystemObject.` `DeleteFile` and `FileSystemObject.DeleteFolder` commands. What's more, Word documents and Excel workbooks can execute code from within

.NET assemblies. This execution ignores any security settings within the dialog box shown in Figure 2-4: .NET security is managed by the .NET framework itself.

You can avoid .NET assembly code execution from within Office 2003 applications by removing any `_AssemblyLocation0` or `_AssemblyName0` properties from a document (or template) or workbook's list of custom document properties. To do so, choose File⇨Properties⇨Custom.

Alternatively, you can handle the problem from within .NET itself by deleting a .NET assembly's associated code group from the computer or by modifying code group properties by using the Code Access Security Policy Tool or the Microsoft .NET Framework Configuration tool. For information on this tactic, see the Microsoft .NET Framework Developer's Guide that comes with Visual Studio .NET. These are rather drastic steps, however.

Office 2003 includes a new capability to scan XML files to see whether any references to XSL exist, which can contain executable scripts. If the macro security level is set to High or Very High, all scripts are disabled. With the security at Medium, the user is prompted to decide whether to permit the script to execute. Set macro security to Low, of course, and Office allows any scripts to execute and also invites angry ex-cons to your house for Thanksgiving dinner.

Setting security for your needs

Here's how to achieve whatever level of security you want:

✦ **To prevent all executables from running:** Disable the Trust All Installed Add-ins and Templates option and set the macro security level to Very High.

✦ **To prevent all executables from running, other than those from a trusted location:** Enable the Trust All Installed Add-ins and Templates option and set the macro security level to Very High.

✦ **To allow trusted signed executables to run automatically:** Set the macro security level to Medium or High.

✦ **To prevent unsigned executables from running:** Set the macro security level to High.

✦ **To display a prompt to users to see whether they want to allow an untrusted executable to run:** Set the macro security level to High.

✦ **To display a prompt to users to see whether they want to allow any executable to run:** Set the macro security level to Medium.

✦ **To allow all executables to run with no prompt:** Set the macro security level to Low.

Administrators can set these levels for an entire office by using these various approaches:

Book I
Chapter 2

Programming Lite:
Making the Most
of Macros

✦ **Custom Maintenance Wizard**

✦ **Office Profile Wizard**

✦ **Custom Installation Wizard**

✦ **Group Policy snap-in**

A *snap-in* is a utility that can be added to a Microsoft Management Console (MMC).

The Office 2003 Editions Resource Kit Tools can be downloaded from

```
http://www.microsoft.com/downloads/details.aspx?familyid=
    4bb7cb10-a6e5-4334-8925-3bcf308cfbaf&displaylang=en
```

This resource kit is a set of utilities and information. It includes the Custom Maintenance Wizard (and the CMW File Viewer), Office Profile Wizard, Custom Installation Wizard, Policy Template files, customizable alerts, HTML Help Workshop, international information, Office Converter Pack, Office information, Outlook Administrator Pack, Package Definition Files, MST File Viewer, and OPS File Viewer.

The Group Policy allows administrators to specify and govern how network resources, applications, and the operating system itself will behave. The administrator can configure security settings for domains, computers, and individual users by manipulating the MMC. To open the MMC, choose Start⇨ Run. In the Open field, type **mmc**. Click OK to launch the console. To get further information on using snap-ins, choose Action⇨Help in the MMC.

Chapter 3: What's New in 2003?

In This Chapter

- Seeing an overview of task panes
- Introducing Document Workspaces
- Discovering OneNote
- Joining the XML revolution
- Discovering the redesigned Outlook

Many users and developers are upgrading from previous versions of Office to Office 2003. Perhaps you've been using Office XP or even Office 2000, and you're wondering what the primary new features are in Office 2003 and how they can be used to your advantage. If so, this chapter's for you.

On the user interface level, Smart Tags and task panes are more in evidence in Office 2003, and Outlook has undergone quite major changes. However, many Office applications should seem pretty much as you remember them. A quick look at the surface of Office 2003 will seem rather familiar, but you'll soon discover significant changes under the hood, where we programmers spend most of our time.

For example, Office 2003 emphasizes interoffice communications in two major ways: communication between office workers, and communication between Office applications.

In fact, Microsoft is no longer calling the Office applications a *suite*. Instead, it's now the Microsoft Office *System*. This new terminology suggests that you should consider Office a kind of special network, with lots of improvements designed to assist the flow of data among workers. No longer are Office applications merely isolated, individual applications running on separate, self-contained computers. Instead, there is a great push to integrate the system into a client-server network. After all, how many company documents are generated by one person working alone?

Throughout this book, you'll find lots of examples showing how to exploit Office's new collaborative features. In this chapter, I take you on a brief introductory tour of some of the major new tools and utilities in Office 2003.

Opening Task Panes

In various Office 2003 applications, you see a *pane* (a zone within a window) open up, usually on the right side, as shown in Figure 3-1. These panes have never been used as extensively as they now are in Office 2003, although they've been around for several years. For example, in many XP applications, the Help system opens a pane on the right side of the application.

In Office 2003, task panes are frequently used to provide context-sensitive links, templates, help, and various other kinds of information. These panes pop up in various ways: if the user clicks certain words, loads an XML-based document, works on a shared document, opens a new document, chooses View⇨Task Pane, and several other actions.

For example, if you need to do research, be sure to check out the new Research task pane. Just hold down the Alt key while clicking a word in a document, and the Encarta encyclopedia pops open in the Research pane, as shown in Figure 3-1.

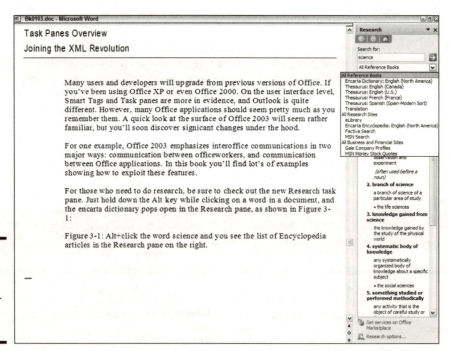

Figure 3-1:
Alt+click a word for a list of ency-clopedia articles.

In addition, you can open the All Reference Books list box to see various the-sauri, translation services, and other research sites.

To see research for an entire phrase, highlight it before Alt+clicking it.

Security: Adjusting Permissions and Protections

All the new collaborative features of Office 2003 are welcome, but sometimes too much collaboration isn't a good thing. For example, the accounting department gets to look at everyone's salary, but fights would undoubtedly break out around the water cooler if the whole office could see just who's being slighted and who's rolling in cash.

Each Office application now has a Permission item on its File menu, as shown in Figure 3-2. And you'll also find various other options, such as the Protection option on the Excel Tools menu or the Protect Document option on the Word Tools menu.

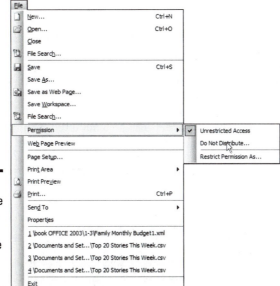

Figure 3-2:
Specify here how widely this document can be distributed or viewed.

One new security aspect is Information Rights Management (IRM). With this, you can decide to mark documents so they can't be forwarded, copied, or printed. Of course, forbidding copying or printing can be a rather weak security feature, given that (although the PrintScreen key is disabled) third-party utilities can still copy a document as a graphic that can then be merrily forwarded, copied, or printed.

You can also specify an expiration date on a document as well as lock documents (or parts of documents) from modification. If an organization prefers not to use IRM, it can use the *Passport system* (Microsoft's authentication system, permitting quick and easy log on/password entry and verification).

SharePoint Everywhere

To streamline and improve workflow, Office 2003 is designed to work successfully with SharePoint. With SharePoint, anyone in an office, or indeed an entire distributed company, can easily collaborate with others to produce documents, diagrams, presentations, or whatever other computer-based task is required.

To this end, a core *SharePoint portal* hosts newsgroup-like discussions, links, database features such as disconnected recordsets drawn from the corporate database, files of all types, annotated multimedia content, and so on. Making all this more effective is that you're not called upon to use special utilities to communicate, with all the inconvenience and copying and pasting that implies. You don't need to open an Internet browser to e-mail a paragraph from a Word document to a colleague. You can hold a chat discussion or show someone part of a Word document right from within Word itself, via the Shared Workspace task pane. You can invite others into a Shared Workspace session by using the instant messaging feature of Microsoft Office Live Communications Server 2003.

To use Office 2003's collaboration features, you need to install on your server either Windows Server 2003 (which includes SharePoint and costs around $1,000 for five clients) or the SharePoint Portal Server 2003, which costs $3,999 and $71 per user. Client computers can simply install Office 2003 itself.

Sharing with Document Workspaces

A *Document Workspace site* is a SharePoint Services site devoted to allowing colleagues to collaborate efficiently on a document (or set of related documents). It's similar to the idea behind other project management utilities that permit people to check out documents and then update the common copy of those documents in the shared library.

You can use the Shared Workspace task pane to launch a Document Workspace in Office 2003 Word, Excel, PowerPoint, or Visio. After you choose Tools⇨Shared Workspace in one of these applications, the Shared Workspace Task pane appears, as shown in Figure 3-3.

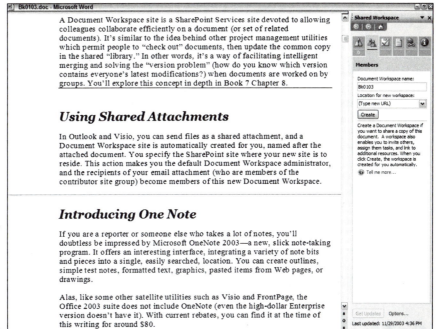

Figure 3-3:
Here's a
way to
create a
new Shared
Workspace.

In other words, use Document Workspace to facilitate intelligent merging and solve version-control problems when documents are worked on by groups. You know, how do you know which version contains everyone's latest modifications? Use SharePoint to handle this version problem for you by permitting designated users read-only access to a document that you (feel the power) can freely edit. Or you could choose to let everyone in your group see the changes that you're making in real-time if you wish.

Cool factor: Perhaps the most interesting aspect of this feature is that it mimics a group of workers standing around a table, simultaneously modifying a document. To prevent version collisions when two people try to edit the same word, when anyone makes a change, everyone else's mouse pointer disappears. The final version of the document is then saved to the SharePoint server after the collaborators have agreed on the changes. Explore these concepts in more depth in Book VII, Chapter 8.

Introducing OneNote

If you're a reporter, office worker, or anyone who takes a lot of notes, you'll doubtless be impressed by the new, slick note-taking program, Microsoft OneNote 2003. Featuring an interesting interface, it can integrate a variety of note bits and pieces into a single, easily searched, location. You can create outlines, simple test notes, formatted text, graphics, pasted items from Web pages, or drawings. OneNote can even include handwritten notes, diagrams, and audio snippets (synchronized to your other notes), providing you with very convenient ways to organize and retrieve disparate kinds of information.

OneNote offers many of the other formatting features of Word, but it's specifically designed for quick organization and easy retrieval, including sections, tabs, running heads, specifying which notes are particularly important (by using note flags: icons such as stars, question marks, and check boxes), and other visual aids to help put notes in order systematically. You don't even have to remember to explicitly save a note: After you create a note, it's automatically saved for you. Also, cutting and pasting can be avoided because you can e-mail and otherwise access the Internet directly from within OneNote itself.

 Think of OneNote as an electronic briefcase full of miscellaneous items: diagrams, handwritten notes, audiotape snippets, and so on. You want to accomplish two primary objectives with this collection of items. First, you want to be able to organize them efficiently. Second, at some point, you're likely to want to combine some of them into an actual document to show others. Both of these needs are thoughtfully and effectively met as a result of all Microsoft's efforts to make the product anticipate your researching, searching, and document-generating needs and behaviors.

Alas, like some other satellite utilities such as Visio and FrontPage, the Office 2003 suite does not include OneNote. (Even the high-dollar Enterprise version doesn't have it.) With current rebates, you can buy OneNote at the time of this writing for around $80.

XML under Everything

As with most Microsoft products — such as Visual Studio — Office 2003 rests on eXtensible Markup Language (XML). XML is a daughter language of HyperText Markup Language (HTML), which is a communication scheme becoming increasingly popular as a way to send messages over the Internet (among other uses).

Markup languages

XML shares HTML's inability to compute. They are fundamentally *markup languages:* that is, they're used to describe how things look or how information should be arranged but are not themselves capable of processing information. Information processing is the definition of computing; however, by themselves, languages such as HTML and XML can't even add 2 + 2. (A derivative language, XSL or XML transforms, however, can include executable script. Other derivative languages can perform various document editing functions. XML itself, though, is by definition merely structured data with no processing capability.)

XML's primary benefit for Office 2003 users is that it offers yet one more way to avoid having to use the Clipboard for copying and pasting information — or worse, copying data by hand. XML permits you to automate the process of transferring data between applications or between a *data store* (a database, or perhaps another place where data is stored, like a list) and an application.

Using InfoPath with Word

New in Office 2003, InfoPath offers you a way to create templates that take data from a database and change it into forms that can be added to your corporate database. InfoPath — unlike the rest of Office — stores data directly as XML. InfoPath can be used by itself, but it's especially valuable as a tool to connect front-end users to back-end data stores. You can build forms where users enter, view, or modify data, and the data store — and perhaps a set of proprietary, legacy user-input interfaces — remain invisible to the user. InfoPath can be a significant part of any Office 2003 data-related system. And, of course, XML is now also available to all Office 2003 applications, if not as directly as it is to InfoPath.

For example, after translating a table in a Word document into an XML file, it's then relatively easy to automatically flow that data into an Access database (or indeed, any other kind of database). XML deconstructs data into the famous self-describing format and then reconstructs it according to the rules of the target.

To put it another way: When you choose File⇨Save As and then select Save As Type XML document, the process of translating a spreadsheet, database table, or Word document separates the formatting from the raw data. The formatting is preserved. An italicized word, for example, gets a tag pair like these — `<italic>`*identifying*`</italic>` — that is indeed italic. However, if the data is sent to a target application where italics are not available as part of the presentation, the italic tags are ignored. In other words, formatting is not lost, but it can be recast if the recipient application prefers to display it — or otherwise manipulate it — a different way.

Here's how it all looks. Suppose you enter a recipe into a Word table and then send that table to a co-worker or store it in a database. The Word table is translated first into XML format, with each element *delimited* (surrounded) by tags describing the raw data inside those tags:

```
<?xml version="1.0"?>
  <recipes>
    <recipe>
    <name>Paste</name>
    <cook>Mrs. Sprud</cook>
    <date>2/12/03</date>
    <size format="ounces">14</size>
    <recipe>
    <ingredients>
    <dry>flour</dry>
    <wet>water</wet>
    </ingredients>
  </recipes>
```

Using InfoPath with Excel

Here's an example showing how InfoPath can be used with Excel. Data that you type into an Excel spreadsheet doesn't always remain in the classic Excel format. Instead, like everywhere else in Office 2003, the data can become XML. The advantage here is that the time-honored and terribly inefficient process of printing out a hardcopy of an Excel spreadsheet and then having someone type that data into a database or report is no longer necessary. The connection between Excel and the database becomes possible via XML's universal data format.

Another time factor, too, is improved by XML. Because Excel data can now appear immediately in various structures, formats, applications, and reports, people all over the organization can see various views of data right away. They don't have to wait until it's retyped or otherwise massaged into a different format via some cumbersome process. XML offers instant communication.

Figure 3-4 shows a sample Excel spreadsheet that I saved in an XML spreadsheet format:

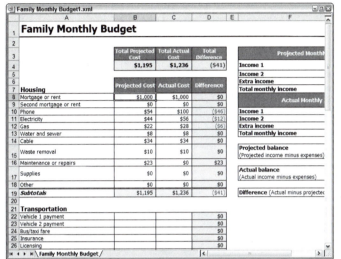

Figure 3-4:
This classic spreadsheet can be saved in XML format.

To save data in XML in Excel, choose File⇨Save As and then change the Save As Type selection at the bottom of the Save As dialog box to XML Spreadsheet (*.xml). When you look at this file (it's in plain, unformatted text, as XML usually is), it describes the data in the classic <tag></end tag> format and includes considerable redundancy (for clarity when this data is translated into the target format). In Listing 3-1 is part of the XML file generated from the spreadsheet in Figure 3-4:

Listing 3-1: XML Generated by the Spreadsheet Data Shown in Figure 3-4

```
 </Row>
<Row ss:StyleID="s41">
 <Cell ss:StyleID="s42"><Data ss:Type="String">Mortgage or rent</Data></Cell>
 <Cell ss:StyleID="s43"><Data ss:Type="Number">1000</Data></Cell>
 <Cell ss:StyleID="s43"><Data ss:Type="Number">1000</Data></Cell>
 <Cell ss:StyleID="s44" ss:Formula="=RC[-2]-RC[-1]"><Data
          ss:Type="Number">0</Data></Cell>
 <Cell ss:StyleID="s39"/>
 <Cell ss:MergeAcross="1" ss:MergeDown="1" ss:StyleID="m18355140"><Data
   ss:Type="String">Actual Monthly Income</Data></Cell>
</Row>
```

```
<Row ss:StyleID="s41">
 <Cell ss:StyleID="s42"><Data ss:Type="String">Second mortgage or
          rent</Data></Cell>
 <Cell ss:StyleID="s43"><Data ss:Type="Number">0</Data></Cell>
 <Cell ss:StyleID="s43"><Data ss:Type="Number">0</Data></Cell>
 <Cell ss:StyleID="s44" ss:Formula="=RC[-2]-RC[-1]"><Data
          ss:Type="Number">0</Data></Cell>
 <Cell ss:StyleID="s39"/>
</Row>
<Row ss:StyleID="s41">
 <Cell ss:StyleID="s42"><Data ss:Type="String">Phone</Data></Cell>
 <Cell ss:StyleID="s43"><Data ss:Type="Number">54</Data></Cell>
 <Cell ss:StyleID="s43"><Data ss:Type="Number">100</Data></Cell>
 <Cell ss:StyleID="s44" ss:Formula="=RC[-2]-RC[-1]"><Data ss:Type="Number">-
          46</Data></Cell>
 <Cell ss:StyleID="s39"/>
 <Cell ss:StyleID="s45"><Data ss:Type="String">Income 1</Data></Cell>
 <Cell ss:StyleID="s43"><Data ss:Type="Number">4000</Data></Cell>
</Row>
```

Excel also has a feature that translates and saves spreadsheets in an XML
data format that's more like a traditional database table than the XML
spreadsheet format above with its cell identifiers and other spreadsheet-
specific tags.

Checking Out Outlook's New Features

Outlook has been considerably improved. It's a hotbed of collaborative features, as you would expect. For one thing, you can now look at two calendars
at the same time. This is the sort of thing that people do in their offices all
the time, reconciling their personal day planner or PDA with their wall calendar, for example, or comparing their schedule with a co-worker's.

Several years ago the Microsoft Office team must have sat down and said:
"What do people do in offices a lot that we're not offering in Office?" The
result is the many collaboration features supported by the SharePoint engine
as well as many individual touches like Outlook's dual calendars.

In Outlook and Visio, you can send files as shared attachments, and a
Document Workspace site can be automatically created for you, named after
the attached document. You specify the SharePoint site where your new site
is to reside. This action makes you the default Document Workspace administrator, and the recipients of your e-mail attachment (who are members
of the contributor site group) become members of this new Document
Workspace.

Among the many other new team-centric features in Outlook, when you attach a document to an e-mail, you see a pane open with many options, as shown in Figure 3-5. One notable new option is the suggestion that you might not want to e-mail the attachment in the traditional way but instead use the Shared Attachment feature. If you choose this option, the document is placed into a shared workspace rather than sent to individual client computers.

Figure 3-5:
Outlook offers to create a shared document when you add an attachment to e-mail.

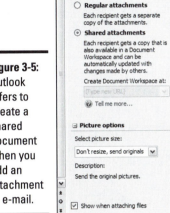

Book II

Understanding Office Programming

The 5th Wave   By Rich Tennant

Re·al Pro·gram·mers

Real Programmers code in pen.

Contents at a Glance

Chapter 1: The Basics of Office Development with VBA

In This Chapter

✔ **Using the IDE**

✔ **Introducing the Object Browser**

✔ **Understanding objects and collections**

✔ **Employing events**

*I*n this chapter, you orient yourself to the Visual Basic for Applications (VBA) editor, also known as the *Visual Basic editor* or *IDE (Integrated Design Environment* or *Integrated Development Environment)*.

Although the VBA editor isn't the powerhouse development environment available in the Visual Studio IDE, the VBA editor is nonetheless full of useful tools, a mature and effective Help system, and other features that help move your programs from idea to finished product. This chapter also explores the Object Browser utility and examines objects themselves (their uses, collections, and events).

Discovering the IDE

To get started with the grand tour of the editor, press Alt+F11 and behold the Visual Basic editor, as shown in Figure 1-1.

For now, you can close the Properties window, the Project Explorer pane, and any other windows that are visible, except the normal (Normal.dot) macros window, as shown in Figure 1-1.

Here you get to do some real programming. You can use VBA to create macros, but it's also a very powerful language in its own right. The common use of the term *macro* suggests a limited series of commands, similar to those of the old AccessBasic language, but don't be misled: VBA is full of commands and capabilities. Indeed, its capabilities exceed those needed for many macro tasks, but Microsoft figured why not just go whole hog and give us everything we could possibly ever want?

Figure 1-1:
This editor sits on top of the VBA engine, providing you with high-level tools.

In fact, both VBA and VB.NET (VBA's likely successor as the Office application development language) give you access to many thousands of programming commands, and most of them have multiple variations: You can use each command in various ways. Remembering all the commands and their variations would be impossible for most of us, so in this chapter, I show you how to find help quickly when programming in BASIC.

Navigating the Complex VBA Vocabulary

Over the years, BASIC source code has grown far more complex. Visual Basic (VB) Version 1 in 1991 had a vocabulary of approximately 350 words. When VB made its first, tentative moves toward object-oriented programming (OOP) in version 4, the vocabulary began to balloon. Now, in VBA and VB.NET, the lid has blown off: You can program with thousands of objects, and each of them can have dozens of *members* (methods, properties, and events). Each of these members can include yet more *diction* (various arguments). The total vocabulary now available to the VBA programmer is many thousands of words. For example, when you use VBA in Word, you're not only accessing all the VBA commands but also the thousands of Word objects and all their properties and methods.

How are you going to remember all these commands and their grammar?

Using AutoListMembers and parameter info

Fortunately, you don't have to remember all the properties and methods (known as the object's *members*). Always at your service is the Help feature, which continues to improve with each new version of Visual Basic.

Also, Microsoft has IntelliSense features — AutoListMembers and parameter info — that pop up while you're writing your source code, listing all the members. And then after you choose a member, all that member's parameters are listed, too. This list displays the number, names, and data types of both required and optional parameters used by a function, template, or attribute.

**Book II
Chapter 1**

**The Basics of Office
Development
with VBA**

Displaying a reminder

Whenever possible in this book, the examples will kill two birds with one stone. They illustrate a technique, but they're also useful in their own right. (You discover how to do something actually worth doing rather than its underlying theory.) In this example, I show you how to use the AutoListMembers feature and also see how to display reminder or comment messages to users in the title bar of Office applications. This is less obtrusive than a message box as a way of communicating with users: They don't have to close the message box before continuing with their work.

For some of the code examples in this book, you need to make sure that the Office Object Library is available (is *referenced*) by the VBA editor. Press Alt+F11 to open the Word VBA editor and choose Tools⇨References. Ensure that the check box next to *Microsoft Office 11.0 Object Library* is marked.

Now follow these steps:

1. **Run Word and press Alt+F11.**

   The Visual Basic editor opens.

2. **In the editor, choose Insert⇨Procedure.**

   The Add Procedure dialog box opens.

3. **Type ChangeTitle as the name for your new procedure.**

4. **Click OK.**

   The dialog box closes, and a new, empty Sub procedure appears, waiting for you to insert some programming.

   ```
   Public Sub ChangeTitle()

   End Sub
   ```

You want to add *Remember to Save!* to the title bar at the top of the current Word document(s). Most Office applications have an object that represents them. Not surprisingly, it's the `Application` object. Like most objects, it has lots of properties and methods, including a `Caption` property that affects what you see on the title bar. To see one kind of `AutoListMembers` feature, type this line just below the `Public Sub` line:

```
Dim App As
```

As soon as you finish typing the word `As`, a list of objects appears, as shown in Figure 1-2.

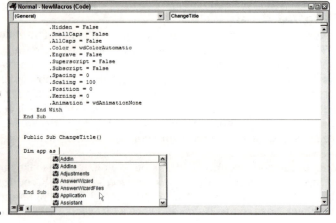

Figure 1-2: Here's one kind of automatic Help list that VBA displays.

5. **Type the following lines, ending with a period after the word** `app.`, **like this:**

```
Public Sub ChangeTitle()

Dim app As Application
Set app = Application

app.
```

Don't worry about the strange `Dim` and `Set` redundancy. I explain those commands shortly in the upcoming section, "Instantiation woes." As soon as you type the period following `app`, the AutoListMembers window opens, showing you all the properties and methods available to the Word `Application` object, as shown in Figure 1-3.

Figure 1-3:
An object's
members
are all listed
here for you
to choose
from.

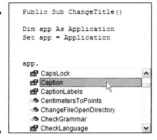

```
Public Sub ChangeTitle()

Dim app As Application
Set app = Application


app.
    CapsLock
    Caption
    CaptionLabels
    CentimetersToPoints
    ChangeFileOpenDirectory
    CheckGrammar
    CheckLanguage
```

6. **Scroll down in the list with the down-arrow key until you highlight the** `Caption` **property; then press Enter.**

   The `Caption` property is inserted into your source code, and the list disappears.

7. **Finish the line by assigning your text message to the** `Caption` **property, as in the following:**

   ```
   app.Caption = "Remember to Save!"
   ```

8. **Just below the line you entered in Step 7, type** MsgBox **and press the spacebar.**

   As soon as you press the spacebar, a list of the arguments available to the `MsgBox` (message box) command is displayed. This handy AutoQuickInfo feature, as shown in Figure 1-4, reminds you of the required arguments, the optional arguments shown in brackets, and the order of the arguments.

Figure 1-4:
This small
argument
list Help
feature is
AutoQuick
Info.

```
MsgBox |
    MsgBox(Prompt, [Buttons As VbMsgBoxStyle = vbOKOnly], [Title], [HelpFile], [Context]) As VbMsgBoxResult
End Sub
```

9. **Complete your little macro procedure by assigning text to the message box prompt.**

Your entire macro should look like this:

```
Public Sub ChangeTitle()

Dim app As Application
Set app = Application

app.Caption = "Remember to Save!"

MsgBox ("Done.")

End Sub
```

10. With your blinking insertion cursor somewhere inside the new `ChangeTitle` **procedure in the VBA editor, press F5 to execute and test the macro.**

When you look at Word's title bar now, you should see the name of the currently opened document, followed by the message `Remember to Save!`

Using the Object Browser

Some people like to use the VBA Object Browser utility instead of (or in addition to) the IntelliSense features. Press F2 to see the Object Browser, as shown in Figure 1-5.

Figure 1-5:
Find the class names and hierarchies of objects in this browser.

Click the various classes in the left pane to see the members of the objects that interest you. Figure 1-5 illustrates the `Document Close` event that I discuss at the end of this chapter. Of course, you do run into the old paradox from time to time: How do you look up a word in the dictionary if you don't know how to spell it? You might have a tough time finding what you're looking for in Help, the Object Browser, or the IntelliSense features. I don't know of any solution to this problem other than memorizing the necessary names for important, but strangely named, classes.

Understanding Objects

What, you might well ask, is an object? Simply, *objects* are items like message boxes, but lots of other things are called objects, too, as you'll soon see. Truth be told, *everything* in today's programming languages is an object — even a lowly integer is an object in VB.NET.

If everything is an object, is there any meaning to the concept *object?* Does the term *object* have any value in categorizing things? Good questions, friend. But you're getting ahead of yourself.

To try to get a sense of what an object is, first ask this question: How does an object differ from a traditional variable? An object is more powerful and sophisticated; some objects are like self-contained mini-programs (quite mini). A *variable* contains a value: a single piece of data. An object, on the other hand, usually contains several pieces of data, sometimes arranged in a hierarchy. Some of an object's data are known as its *properties,* such as a document's typeface style, called its `FontName` property. Another piece of data, its `FontColor` property, specifies a graphic that is displayed within the button.

In addition to its data, an object also usually includes programming: that is, things it knows how to do with its data (or data passed to it), such as a Word document object's `Add` method, which adds a new Word document to the current collection of open documents. An object's programming is known as its *methods.*

All the currently open documents in a Word application are, collectively, considered an object (technically a *collection,* but with all the features of an object, such as methods and properties). And, each document within the documents collection is itself an object. So you can have objects nested within other objects. (For more on collections, see the sidebar, "Objects versus collections.")

Objects versus collections

Take a look at this little Word macro to understand the relationship between objects and collections:

```
Sub ShowFonts()
Documents.Add

s = "You have these " &
    FontNames.Count & " fonts
    you can use:"

ActiveDocument.Range.
    InsertAfter s & vbCr & vbCr

For Each afont In FontNames
    ActiveDocument.Range.
    InsertAfter afont & ", "
Next afont

End Sub
```

Here you use the `Add` method of the `Documents` collection to create a new blank document. It's the same behavior as if the user had chosen File⇨New⇨Blank Document, but here, you're accomplishing that job programmatically.

Then you compose a text string (`s`) incorporating the `Count` property of the `FontNames` collection. It tells you how many typefaces are available to you. They're in an array. A *collection* is often just a simple array, with index numbers so you can access each member of the collection, such as `FontNames(2)`. Then you use the `InsertAfter` method of the `Range` object to type the variable `s` into the newly created blank document, followed by two carriage returns. (`vbCr` imitates what happens when the user presses Enter.) Finally, you use the `For Each` command to step through the entire `FontNames` collection, typing in the name of each font name. Try typing this macro into the VBA editor, and then pressing F5 with your blinking insertion cursor inside the macro text to run it.

Most applications have collections that can provide you with useful information that might be important during program execution. Here's an example that tells you how many tables are in an Access database:

```
Sub infoAccess()

With Application.CurrentData
    s = "This database has " &
    .AllTables.Count & "
        tables."
    MsgBox s
End With

End Sub
```

Finally, objects can (but don't necessarily) have *events,* which are places for a programmer to define how the object behaves in the event that some outside action happens to that object, such as an Excel workbook object's `BeforeClose` event. In this case, when a user attempts to close a workbook, your macro can respond to that event by putting up a message box that reads `Would you like to back up your work?` **The workbook's** `BeforeClose` event can contain optional programming that you insert into the event to display the message box.

To summarize: An object can have properties (qualities), methods (abilities), and events (responses). Together, this entire group of features is known as the object's *members*.

Also note that an object can (but doesn't necessarily) include a visible user interface. For example, a `Button` object has a visible user interface, but a `Timer` component does not. Some objects just do math calculations or search for a particular name in a database, but other objects display the results of that calculation or that search to the user or invite the user to modify the object's data.

However, don't get the idea that objects are limited to components like buttons or text boxes. True, all components are objects, but not all objects are components. Some objects that you program with are located inside applications — like the `workbook` object in Excel and other objects that you create within your programs for your own purposes.

Objects can be used in two main ways when programming in VBA. First, you can take advantage of the many objects available in the Office 2003 applications. This is useful. Second, you can create your own objects for programming purposes in VBA. Generally speaking, this is not useful. It's overkill unless you're creating a large, complex project or programming in a group (where such features as OOP's encapsulation assist in helping people avoid stepping on each other's code).

Should You Go Fully OOP?

Some programmers believe that all Visual Basic programs — indeed all computer programs — should be written with OOP. I'm not one of them. I feel that objects are most useful with large, complex programs, or when you're writing a program with other programmers as a group effort. Some people also advocate OOP for all programs because they claim that you can easily reuse objects in future programs.

It is true that programming with objects forces you to follow some strict rules that can help avoid problems commonly encountered when group-programming, working with complex applications, or reusing code. However, smaller, simpler applications generally don't benefit from most OOP techniques, and macros (of course) individually need not be made into classes to be useful — that would be dreadful overkill.

For macros and small utilities — the primary use of VBA — OOP imposes a superstructure more sophisticated and heavy-handed than is called for. What's more, VBA still employs outdated programming techniques for instantiation, property procedures, and so on. Unless you have a compelling reason to employ OOP, you're better off with classic structured (procedure-oriented) programming in VBA.

If you've never been exposed to OOP, you might find the following paragraphs helpful. I show you some of what OOP can do for you, should you need to use it.

Encapsulation

Perhaps the primary benefit of OOP is *encapsulation,* which means that an object doesn't permit outside programming to directly manipulate its data. (In programming terms, this means that none of the encapsulated object's variables should be declared `Public`. They're all `Private` or declared with some other self-application-only scope.)

Any properties that you want to permit outsiders (source code that uses the object) to read (query) or set (change) can be exposed to those outsiders in a special way: by using property procedures. The outside code must contact these procedures, and then the procedures in turn deal directly with the object's data. It's rather like having someone answer the phone for you — to run interference in case you don't want to accept the call. The outside code doesn't get to manipulate an object's actual data directly. This allows you (the programmer) to validate that incoming behaviors, properties, or other data are proper and won't cause problems for your encapsulated objects.

To illustrate the idea of encapsulation, first create an object (a class). It has a `Private` (encapsulated) string variable. It can't, therefore, be changed, or even accessed for viewing by outsiders (any code outside the class itself, such as a macro that activates the class). For comparison, the object also includes a `Public` variable that outsiders can modify. Follow these steps to create the object:

1. In the Word VBA editor, choose Insert⇨Class Module.

A new window appears, with a default initialize method (Sub).

You can view this `Sub` by opening the drop-down list in the upper-left corner of the Class code window and choosing Class. This `Sub Class_ Initialization` method is carried out every time the class is *instantiated* (brought into being) by being accessed from code inside a macro. *Initialization* is similar to the traditional Visual Basic `Form_Load` event: the place a programmer usually writes any code that has to execute before the user interacts with the form (such as loading in some data).

You can ignore this Sub by writing no programming inside it if you don't need to do any housekeeping during initialization. (There's also a terminate method for handling any necessary tasks when the object is about to be destroyed.)

I illustrate how a class in VBA works, though, by displaying some messages.

2. **By default, your new class is named** Class1. **Move your insertion cursor up to the top of the Class1 editor window and type in the following private variable:**

```
Private m_OutsideMessage As String
```

This Private property can't be accessed directly from code outside the class itself.

Book II
Chapter 1

The Basics of Office Development with VBA

3. **Now just below that, type in the** Property **procedure:**

```
Public Property Let TheMessage(ByVal s As String)
  If Len(s) > 10 Then 'validate
    MsgBox ("ERROR. LIMIT 10 characters.")
  Else
    Let m_OutsideMessage = s
  End If
End Property
```

This property is Public, so it can be accessed from outside the class, but the string passed from the outside is validated. In this case, if it's greater than ten characters, the outside code is warned. If it passes the test, you assign the outsider's string to the private property m_OutsideMessage. It's traditional to prepend an m or m_ to private property names, as I did here.

4. **Inside the** Initialize **method, type this:**

```
Private Sub Class_Initialize()
  s = "Initializing..."
  MsgBox (s)
End Sub
```

The purpose of this method is just to indicate when the initialization takes place by displaying a message.

5. **Finally, type this to create a method that the outside code can access.**

```
Public Sub OurClass()

MsgBox (m_OutsideMessage)

End Sub
```

Just as a `Public Property` is a property of an object, a `Public Sub` is a method of an object. This method displays the `Private` property `m_OutsideMessage`, showing that the user's string was correctly assigned. The entire class should look like Figure 1-6.

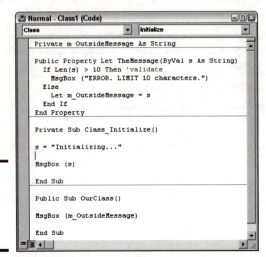

Figure 1-6: This is the VBA class editor window.

To test your new macro, go to the Normal New Macros window (where most of your ordinary Word macros are). If it's not visible, press Ctrl+R to see the Project Explorer (see Figure 1-6), choose Normal⇨Modules, and then double-click New Macros. Now type in this new macro to test your class, as follows:

```
Sub TestClass()

Dim o As Class1  'create object variable
Set o = New Class1 'assign object variable

o.TheMessage = "Hi, Bobbi!"
o.OurClass

End Sub
```

The first two lines of code within this `Sub` instantiate the object (that you just created as `Class1`). Then, using the object variable `Office`, you send a message to the object's `TheMessage` property. Finally, you request that the object's `OurClass` method be exectued.

Instantiation woes

You must first instantiate the object before you can access its public members. The approach shown in the previous section — using `Dim` and then `Set` and then `New` commands — is not only cumbersome, but it's technically indefensible. It simply makes little sense and is highly redundant. Fortunately, VB.NET has simplified the process of instantiating objects, and presumably VBA will eventually adopt the superior approach. But for now. . . .

The code works like this: After you create your object variable `o`, you then assign the object variable to point to your `Class1`. Then you set the message property with `o.TheMessage` and display the message with the `o.OurClass` method.

Press F5 to run the `TestClass` macro to see how it instantiates, and then employs, the class.

Class modules in VBA never have a user interface. (You choose Insert↝ UserForm to add user interfaces to your VBA programming.) When you want a class to do some computing that doesn't require a user interface, choose a class module.

Using Events

The Word `Document` object includes a variety of events, as do the primary objects in Excel, Access, and other applications. *Events* are behaviors, like methods, but they're not hard-wired into an object. Instead, outside programmers can write code that goes inside an event that executes when the event itself is triggered. For example, many objects have a `Click` event that triggers whenever a user clicks the mouse on the object.

In this example, you display a reminder to anyone who closes the current document that a copy of the document needs to be sent to a co-worker. Follow these steps:

1. **Run Word.**

2. **Open a document file.**

3. **Press Alt+F11.**

   The VBA editor opens.

4. **Press Ctrl+R.**

   The Project Explorer opens, showing all macros, references and other items associated with the currently running application.

5. **Locate the name of your currently open document in the Project Explorer window.**

6. **Locate and then double-click** ThisDocument **under the currently open document title (in boldface, Project (*Document name*)), as shown in Figure 1-7.**

Figure 1-7:
Click This Document under the currently open Project (document), not under Normal.

As soon as you double-click, you see a code window for the ThisDocument object, as shown in Figure 1-8.

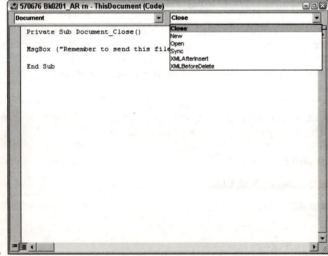

Figure 1-8:
Use the two drop-down lists at the top of this code window to choose Document from the left list, and Close from the right list.

The list box on the right in Figure 1-8 contains the available events that are built into the document object. You chose the Close event.

7. **Type the following into the** `Close` **event:**

    ```
    MsgBox ("Remember to send this file to Suzanne when it's finished.")
    ```

8. **Now return to Word and close the current document.**

    Your message is displayed before the Word document closes.

Book II
Chapter 1

The Basics of Office
Development
with VBA

Chapter 2: Managing Data

In This Chapter

✔ **Using variables and arrays**

✔ **Handling operators and expressions**

✔ **Understanding scope**

*1*f you're an experienced BASIC programmer, you can skip this chapter because it's too elementary for you. In fact, the next few chapters cover the fundamentals of VBA programming, which you perhaps already know.

However, if you're coming to BASIC (Visual Basic for Applications, the version of BASIC used in Office) from a different language, you'll want to at least read the parts that explain the variable types available, the various operators, and how BASIC handles *scope* (a variable's range, or duration, of influence).

Understanding Variables

I start from the beginning by explaining what variables do in computer programming. You create variables for the same reason that you might have a manila envelope on your desk with *VISA* written on it. Each month, when you get your new bill, you replace last month's bill with the latest bill. In other words, the envelope always contains your current Visa charge card balance.

The amount that you owe varies from month to month — hence the term *variable.* If someone asks about your current balance, you could just hand her the envelope. In other words, the envelope named VISA contains the current data about your credit card account. In a computer program, you can use variables the same way: the variable's name takes the place of the number that it contains. For example

```
MsgBox 214.15
```

displays the number 214.15. The same number would be displayed if you instead assigned that number to a variable (like `currentbill`) and then used the variable's name in the code rather than the literal number, like this:

```
currentbill = 214.15
MsgBox currentbill
```

This code also displays the number 214.15. After you create a variable in a running program, the computer's memory contains the variable's name along with its current contents (called the variable's *value*), which is the information that this variable holds. Later, the program might change the contents of the variable so a new value would be held by that variable. The value in a variable can *vary,* which is where it gets its name. A *constant* is similar, but as its name suggests, its value does not vary:

```
Const ReagansWife = "Nancy"
```

The distinction isn't really too significant, and constants are used much. In fact, if you were writing a program involving Ms. Spears, I'd strongly advise that you use a variable in that case:

```
BritneysHusband = "?"
```

Creating Variables

You can create a variable by assigning data to it, as in the earlier example:

```
currentbill = 214.15
```

This is an *implicit declaration* because you haven't specified a variable type: You let BASIC worry about the type of variable that you're creating. BASIC is smart enough to know that if you use quotation marks around your data, it's a text variable (a *string*), as in

```
MyName = "Richard"
```

Or, in the case of the Visa-bill example, you're assigning a fractional number, so BASIC knows that 214.15 should be a *floating-point* numeric variable.

BASIC is also smart enough to know how to perform *implicit conversions* in many situations — that is, it can change a variable's type from, say, numeric to string. An implicit conversion happened in the example earlier in this chapter. The MsgBox function displays string variables — not numeric variables. However, BASIC created a floating-point variable when you assigned it the fractional number 214.15:

```
currentbill = 214.15
```

Then, when you later use that variable with the MsgBox function, BASIC automatically translates it into a string variable:

```
MsgBox currentbill
```

Any time you use implicit declaration, BASIC simultaneously creates the variable's name (the label you want to give it, such as `currentbill`), assigns your data to that variable, and then assigns it an indeterminate type called the *variant* type, which is capable of changing into various kinds of data types as needed. The `Variant` type has been removed from VB.NET (because of the rounding problems and other kinds of errors it can introduce when the context in which it's used is ambiguous) and will likely disappear from Office programming as well in the future. The rounding error problem occurs when a variant changes to a less precise data type. For example, a *double precision floating point* data type can be quite precise because it permits such a small fractional portion — so many digits to the right of the decimal point, like this: 1.79769313486232. However, were that converted to a *single precision* data type, rounding would occur because the single only permits this many decimal places: 1.402823. If a high degree of accuracy were required — such as during laser surgery — rounding off decimal places could be catastrophic.

**Book II
Chapter 2**

Managing Data

Also, note that your program's users never see variables' names. You use those variable names when writing your program, so it's helpful to give your variables names that mean something to you. Most programmers give variables names that help them to understand the meaning of the contents of those variables. A variable named `X` is less helpful than one named `MyVisaBill` when you later read, test, or modify your program.

You can use any name you want when creating a variable except the name of a word that itself VBA uses, like `Print` or `Show` or `End`. VBA tells you if you make this error; it won't allow you to assign a value to one of these reserved words.

Explicit Variable Declaration and Data Types

Some languages don't permit implicit declaration or conversion. You can also force VBA to refuse to execute a program or macro if a variable isn't explicitly declared by typing **Option Explicit** at the top of your code window.

One reason for insisting on explicit declaration is that sometimes errors can be caused by BASIC's attempts to figure out what variable type you intend. Also, when variables are explicitly declared, BASIC can catch a particular type of programming error: namely, a typo where you incorrectly typed in the variable name (`curretbill` instead of `currentbill`, for example). Without `Option Explicit` turned on, your program would execute with no error messages when you used `curretbill` — and that could easily cause a mysterious and hard-to-track-down bug.

Never send a rocket to Tempe

Here's why NASA engineers must be explicit when declaring or converting variable types. A floating-point data type (which might hold a value such as 12.335) should not be permitted to automatically (that is, implicitly via BASIC's best guess) convert to an Integer data type because the conversion would strip off the .335 fractional portion of the number. Integers have no decimal point, and BASIC converts decimals to integers by truncating the fraction. Of course, stripping off that .335 is insignificant in many kinds of programming — for example, when calculating calories in a diet program. But when you're calculating a rocket's trajectory, every fraction must be accounted for. You might send the moon shot to Tempe, Arizona instead of its intended target.

What about the other way around? Is automatic conversion of an integer into a floating-point type permitted? Yes, because that type of conversion is safe; it merely increases the precision of the number.

With Option Explicit in force, it's not enough to simply assign a *datum* (some value) to a variable; you must formally declare the variable name and also declare its type as well:

```
Dim MyName As String
MyName = "Richard"
```

Also, implicit conversion isn't allowed in some languages. If you want to display a numeric variable in a text box or message box, you must formally and explicitly transform (also called *casting*, or *coercing*) the variable from a numeric to a text variable type. Here's an example. When converting one type into another type — such as changing a floating-point numeric type into a String type — you specifically do that transforming in your source code:

```
Sub Vars()

Dim currentbill As Single 'this is a floating point data type
currentbill = 214.15

Dim billString As String

billString = CStr(currentbill)

MsgBox billString

End Sub
```

In this example, two variables are explicitly declared, and their types are defined. Then the CStr (convert to string) function is used to transform the floating-point numeric type variable currentbill into a string so that it can be assigned to the string variable `billString`. Of the various ways to shorten this code, I wanted to show you the full monty so you could see the various steps. It can be shortened by doing the conversion directly before passing the data to the message box, like this:

```
Sub Vars()

Dim currentbill As Single
currentbill = 214.15

MsgBox CStr(currentbill)

End Sub
```

VBA lets you declare variables as one of the following data types: `Boolean`, `Byte`, `Integer`, `Long`, `Currency`, `Single` (a floating point data type with less precision — fewer digits to the right of the decimal point — than the `Double` floating point type), `Double`, `Date`, `String` (for variable-length strings), `String * length` (for fixed-length strings), `Object`, or `Variant`. The details and specifications for each of these types are described in Table 2-5, later in this chapter.

Whether you turn on the `Option Explicit` feature is your decision. If you're working for NASA, calculating orbital velocities, you'd better turn it on and force yourself to be explicit. You don't want a moon shot heading off-course. If you're just writing a little geography quiz program for Junior, however, I wouldn't worry too much about explicit declaration.

Using Operators and Expressions

Variables can interact with each other. Here's one example:

```
Donkeys = 15
Monkeys = 3
TotalAnimals = Donkeys + Monkeys
```

In other words, you can use the variable names as if they were the same as the contents of the variables. If you write `Monkeys = 3`, you assign the value 3 to the word `Monkeys`. You can thereafter use `Monkeys` just as you would use the number 3:

```
TotalAnimals = Donkeys + Monkeys
```

The preceding line is the same as the following:

```
TotalAnimals = Donkeys + 3
```

When you combine variables on the same programming line and make them interact, you're using an *expression*. Here's how it works: If someone tells you that she has a coupon for $1 off a $15 Mozart CD, you immediately think *$14*. In the same way, VBA reduces the several items linked into an expression into its simplest form.

 A *numeric expression* means anything that represents or results in a single number. Strictly speaking, the numeric expression *evaluates* into a single number (or true or false, which is another way of saying 1 or 0, the binary numbers).

When an intelligent entity hears an expression, the entity collapses that expression into its simplest form. In plain English, if you type **15 – 1** into one of your programs, Visual Basic reduces that group of symbols — that *expression* — to a single number: 14. Visual Basic simply evaluates what you've written and uses it in the program as the essence of what you are trying to say.

We humans always reduce things, too. Sometimes we call it *intuition;* sometimes we call it *putting two and two together*. But we routinely reduce complicated expressions or ideas to their simpler forms, their essence.

5 * 3 is a numeric expression, and as far as BASIC is concerned, 5 * 3 is just another way of expressing 15 (a single number). 5 * 3 collapses into 15 inside the program and is essentially that single number.

You can combine many kinds of numeric entities into expressions. Any combination of any of the following entities is acceptable in a numeric expression:

+ A numeric variable.

+ A numeric variable in an array.

+ A function that returns a number.

+ A literal number. (12 is a literal number, as opposed to a variable.)

    ```
    Print Sqr(12) 'literal number
    Print Sqr(N) 'Variable
    ```

+ A numeric constant, like `Const Pi = 3.14159265358979`.

+ Any combination of literal and variable numbers.

    ```
    Print X + 14
    ```

Any combination of the preceding examples that can evaluate to a single numeric value is an expression. An expression is made up of two or more of the preceding items connected by one or more operators. For example, the plus symbol in 2 + 2 is an operator. Altogether, there are 23 different operators. (I get to operators shortly in the following section.)

Testing True or False

An expression can be evaluated by Visual Basic as either 0 (False) or not 0 (True). See how this works:

```
BobsAge = 33
BettysAge = 27
If BobsAge > BettysAge Then Print "He's Older"
```

BobsAge > BettysAge is an expression making the assertion that *BobsAge is greater than BettysAge*. The greater-than (>) symbol is one of several relational operators. Visual Basic looks at the variables *BobsAge* and *BettysAge* and at the relational operator (see Table 2-1) that combines them into the expression. VB then determines whether the expression is True. The If...Then structure bases its actions on the truth or falsity of the expression.

Table 2-1	Relational Comparison Operators
Operator	*Means This*
<	Less than
<=	Less than or equal to
>	Greater than
>=	Greater than or equal to
<>	Not equal
=	Equal
Is	Do two object variables refer to the same object?
Like	Pattern matching* (see upcoming example)

*The Like pattern-matching operator works like this:

```
Sub LikeTest()
    X = "Farina"
    If X Like "F*a" Then MsgBox "Yes, like!"
End Sub
```

The patterns are case-sensitive, so "f*a" in the above Like example would fail: that is, would not be true and the message box would not display. Here are the Like patterns that you can use:

✦ ?: Any single character. ("BETTYboohoo" Like "B?T*")

✦ *: Zero or more characters.

✦ #: Any single digit (0–9). ("a2a" Like "a#a")

✦ [charlist]: Any single character in charlist. ("F" Like "[A-Z]")

✦ [!charlist]: Any single character not in charlist. ("F" Like "[!A-Z]") (This returns False.)

Note: You can use the relational operators with text as well. When used with literal text (or text variables), the operators refer to the *alphabetization* qualities of the text, with *Andy* being "less than" *Anne*.

The relational operators make comparisons, and the result of that comparison is always True or False.

Using arithmetic operators

Just like relational operators make comparisons based on such criteria as *less than* and *greater than,* the arithmetic operators (as shown in Table 2-2) describe mathematical relationships, such as multiplication.

Table 2-2	Arithmetic Operators
Operator	*Means This*
^	Exponentiation (the number multiplied by itself: 5 ^ 2 is 25, and 5 ^ 3 is 125).
–	Negation (negative numbers, such as –25).
*	Multiplication.
/	Division.
\	Integer division (division with no remainder, no fraction, no floating-point decimal point: 8 \ 6 is 1. Integer division is easier, and the computer performs it faster than regular division).
Mod	Modulo arithmetic.
+	Addition.
–	Subtraction.
&	String concatenation.

Dividing the Mod way

The modulo (Mod) operator gives you any remainder after a division but not the results of the division itself. This operation is useful when you want to know whether some number divides evenly into another number. That way, you could do things at intervals. If you wanted to print the page number in bold on every fifth page, for example, you could enter the following:

```
If PageNumber Mod 5 = 0 Then
    FontBold = True
Else
    FontBold = 0
End If
```

If this program were to check each page number in turn, the results of the expression at the beginning would look something like this:

15 Mod 5 results in 0.

16 Mod 5 results in 1.

17 Mod 5 results in 2.

20 Mod 5 results in 0 again.

Combining Variant variables

Variant variables can be combined in a way that is similar to how traditional text variables are concatenated:

```
A = "This":B = "That":MsgBox (A & B)
```

results in ThisThat.

When adding numbers, use the + operator. When adding (concatenating) text, use the & operator:

```
MsgBox (A & B)
```

When you use *variants* (recall that unless you specify otherwise, VBA defaults to the Variant data type):

```
x = 5:a = "This"
MsgBox (x & a)
```

results in 5This.

Variants are in an indeterminate state, like Schrödinger's Cat, until they are used. For example, if you add two `Integer` variable types, you get an overflow error if the result is larger than 32767, which is the biggest number that a variable of `Integer` type can hold:

```
Dim x As Integer, y As Integer
x = 32760
y = 22
x = x + y
MsgBox x
```

results in `Overflow Error`.

The `TypeName` command can tell you what subtype a variant currently is. Notice in the following code how the variant variable x changes from an `Integer` type into a `Long` type to accommodate the addition that results in a number greater than an integer can hold:

```
Sub Vars()

x = 32760
MsgBox TypeName(x)
y = 22
x = x + y
MsgBox x
MsgBox (TypeName(x))

End Sub
```

results in `Integer, 32782, Long`.

Using logical operators

Logical operators (as shown in Table 2-3) are rather specialized and not too often used in most programming. They compare two entities, resulting in `True` or `False`. For example, you can use the logical operator `And` to see whether two conditions are true, like this:

```
X = 12: Y = 22
If X > 0 And Y > 0 Then MsgBox "true"
```

This evaluates to `True`, and the message is displayed because both expressions — X is greater than zero *and* Y is greater than 0 — are true.

Table 2-3	Logical Operators
Operator	*Means This*
Not	Logical negation
And	And
Or	Inclusive Or
XOR	Either but not both
Eqv	Equivalent
Imp	Implication — first item False or second item True

In practice, you'll likely need to use only Not, And, XOR, and Or from among the logical operators. These four operators work pretty much the way they do in English:

```
If 5 + 2 = 4 Or 6 + 6 = 12 Then MsgBox "One of them is true."
```

Understanding XOR

For years, a number of respected journals published articles on computer encryption that suggested using the binary operation XOR. XOR remains widely used in computer-based encryption because XOR has the pleasant feature that it toggles things. XOR a character once, and it is changed into another character; XOR this new character, and it is restored back to the original.

XOR does this to bits:

0 XOR 0 = 0

0 XOR 1 = 1

1 XOR 0 = 1

1 XOR 1 = 0

In computers, the letters of the alphabet are already in the ASCII code (or the double-byte Unicode). Each letter has a numeric equivalent; in ASCII code, capital A is 65, B is 66, and so on. That's already one level of substitution. Now, when you XOR capital A with something, you get another number. But XOR it with what? The thing that you use to make substitutions unique is a *key*. This obviously helps "mess up" the original because using a different key will produce different patterns in the resulting encrypted document.

For example, if you XOR the characters *RM* against the key it, you get the symbols ;9.

If you then XOR the encrypted text (;9), you restore the original text: RM.

In effect, XOR is a black box that you can feed an original into and get a garbled result. Then feed that garbled result into XOR a second time, and you get back the original text. Sounds like a perfect way to encrypt and then decrypt a message, right?

You can go both ways with this same little box. For this reason, XOR was widely used as the basis for computer encryption. It has fallen out of favor, however, because this type of encryption is too easily cracked.

Because one of these expressions is `True`, the message box will be displayed. Remember that with the `Or` operator, only one or the other needs to be `True`.

```
If 5 + 2 = 4 And 6 + 6 = 12 Then MsgBox "Both of them are
    true."
```

As before, only one expression is true. This makes the `And` operator evaluate to `False`, so nothing is displayed. Both expressions (the first and the second) must be `True` for the message box to be displayed.

Use the `XOR` operator to change an individual bit within a number without affecting the other bits. `XOR` has been used for some crude, easily solved encryption schemes. There was a time when people actually thought `XOR` was a useful computer encryption tool.

Operator precedence

When you use more than one operator in an expression, you have to be aware that operators follow an *order of precedence*. In other words, some operators are executed before others, without regard to their physical position in a line of code. In simple terms, you sometimes need to specify which operator should be evaluated first in an expression.

For instance, multiplication might need to be carried out before addition. To illustrate the importance of operator precedence, try this example:

```
MsgBox (10 + 5 * 3)
```

Does this mean to first add 10 + 5 (getting 15) and then multiply that by 3 for a final result of 45? (Thank you for playing, Contestant Number 1.) Or does it mean to multiply 5 * 3 (getting 15) and then add 10 for a final result of 25? (Contestant Number 2 wins the vacation to Hawaii.) You see the ambiguity here. Expressions are not necessarily evaluated by the computer from left to right. Left-to-right evaluation in this example results in 45, which is incorrect.

To make sure that you get the results you intend when using more than one operator, the simplest approach is to just use parentheses to enclose those items you want evaluated first. For example, if you intend to add 10 and 5 and then multiply that result by 3, write the expression like this:

```
MsgBox (10 + 5) * 3
```

By enclosing the addition operation in parentheses, you tell VBA that you want the enclosed items to be considered a single value and to be evaluated before anything else happens.

In complicated expressions, you can even nest parentheses to make clear which items are to be calculated in which order, like this:

```
MsgBox 3 * ((9 + 1) + 5)
```

This expression adds 9 and 1 (getting 10), which is then added to 5 (getting 15), which is multiplied by 3 (getting, finally, 45). If you work with numbers a great deal, you might want to memorize the following table. However, most people just use parentheses and forget about this precedence order.

Table 2-4 shows the order in which VB will evaluate an expression, from first evaluated to last:

Table 2-4	Arithmetic Operators in Order of Precedence
Operator	**Means This**
^	Exponents. (6 ^ 2 is 36. The number is multiplied by itself *x* number of times.)
−	Negation (negative numbers like −33).
* /	Multiplication and division.
\	Integer division (division with no remainder, no fraction, no floating-point decimal point. 8 \ 6 is 1).
Mod	Modulo arithmetic (any remainder after division; 23 Mod 12 is 11. See the sidebar, "Dividing the Mod way").
+/−	Addition/subtraction.

Expressions combined into larger expressions

Expressions themselves are acceptable elements of expressions. In other words, you can put expressions together, building a larger entity that itself is an expression, like this:

```
Sub Vars()

Z = "Tom"
R = Right(Z, 2) 'Pick off "om," the two characters on the right side
L = "om"
N = 3
M = 4
o = 5
P = 6
If N + M + o + P = 18 And Z = "Tom" Or R = L Then MsgBox "Yes."

End Sub
```

This expression, complicated as it is with various operators and interior expressions, evaluates in the end to `True`, so the message box is displayed. Also notice that no matter how complex an expression becomes, *it always ends up evaluating in only two possible ways: true or false.*

Expressions with literals, constants, and variables

You can include literals as well as variables in an expression. In the following, `Z` is a variable, but `"Tom"` is a literal in the preceding example. `M` is a variable, and `4` is a literal. You can mix and match. You could also create the preceding example with some literal numbers mixed, as well as a constant or two, in

```
const Nance = "Morphing"
```

```
If 3 + M + 5 + P = 18 And Z$ = "Tom" And Nance = "Morphing"
    Then MsgBox "Yes."
```

Expressions and functions

Expressions can include functions, in addition to all the other elements described earlier that are legally included in expressions. In this example, the `Val` function tests the number at the start of the variable `A`. Finding `True`, the string variable `A` doesn't match 55.

```
A = "44 Rue Madeline"
```

```
If Val(A) <> 55 Then MsgBox "The text variable doesn't start
    with the digits 55."
```

Variables versus Constants

Although a variable's name remains the same while a program runs, the contents of the variable can vary, which is how a variable differs from a constant. Constants are not changed while a program runs; they are a known quantity, like the number of donuts in a dozen or months in a year:

```
Const MONTHSINYEAR = 12
```

Variables, um, vary:

```
MyVisaBillAtThisPoint = 1200.44
```

but a month later . . .

```
MyVisaBillAtThisPoint = 1530.78
```

In practice, a few programmers love constants, but most others avoid them. If you read some people's programs, you can see they are making their programs more readable — more English-like — by including several constants:

```
BackColor = vbBlue
```

The preceding line is preferred by many people over the following line:

```
BackColor = RGB(170, 170, 170)
```

VBA includes many constants built into the language. With built-in constants, you can just use them in your programming. You don't have to declare them; they're just there. To see what constants are built in, press F2 to get the Object Browser and select All Libraries in the top drop-down list. Then in the Classes list, look for words that end in *constant,* such as `ColorConstants` or `KeyCodeConstants`, as shown in Figure 2-1.

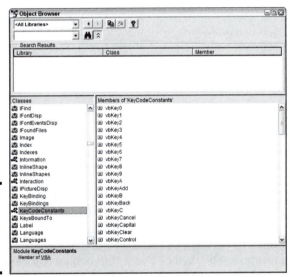

Figure 2-1:
Look up constants in the Object Browser.

Arrays — Cluster Variables

Arrays, unlike constants, are universally regarded as extremely useful. *Arrays* are variables that have been gathered together into a structure, so you can manipulate the data by using loops.

An array is a group of variables that all have the same variable name and are distinguished only by an index number. This way, you can refer to each item in the array by referring to its index number, thereby manipulating the items serially and mathematically.

This approach might look like a small savings of effort, but imagine that your program will probably have to use a set of variables in many situations. And eventually, you'll have to save them to disk. If you had to refer to each item by name, you couldn't go quickly through the group, like this, to add sales tax to each item:

```
For i = 1 To 12
ArrayName(i) = ArrayName(i) * 1.06
Next I
```

If you don't understand how loops work, like the `For...Next` loop here, they're explained in Book II, Chapter 3.

Variable Types

The terms *variable types* and *data types* are interchangeable. However, I'm now pulling back and looking at a larger, more abstract set of variable categories. All numeric variables can be thought of as one category and strings (text) as a separate category. Finally, objects form a third major type. Just remember that within the numeric and object types, there are many subcategories, but the text type has only one version: the string.

`Text` and `Numeric` are the two basic kinds of variables; they're defined as follows:

✦ **Text variables (often called *string variables*):** Can be used in captions, text boxes, and so on. Text variables are made up of the symbols — the characters in text. They can't be divided or used to calculate the amount of linoleum that you would need to redo your kitchen floor. Text is for communication, not calculation. Text is merely a group of graphic symbols; for example, the word *Europe* can't be divided by the word *spaceship*.

✦ **Numeric variables:** Are used to calculate things; they are numbers rather than symbols. The digits 1 and 2 stamped on top of a carton of eggs are *text*, but the actual number of eggs in that carton is *numeric*.

How do you change a text variable into a numeric variable and vice versa? The `Str` and `Val` commands mediate between the two kinds of numbers. `Str` translates a true number into digits (text characters) that can be displayed. `Val` does the opposite; it turns a text digit like 5 into a real number that you could multiply. However, VBA doesn't require that you use `Str` or `Val` much because VBA uses implicit type conversion automatically. Just remember that those commands will cure the problem if you ever get a `Type Mismatch` error message.

Although only one kind of text variable is available, you can pick from several types of numeric variables because there are several ways of expressing numbers in a computer. The term *variable type* is also sometimes expressed as *data types*.

Object variables

A new, third major variable type has been introduced to VBA. You can use variables to point to objects, including forms and controls (which are objects). (*Point to* is a common usage among programmers, meaning technically that the variable contains the memory address where the value of a variable resides.) This provides you with efficient ways to access, manage, and create copies of forms and controls and also to get your feet wet programming with some object-oriented programming (OOP) features, such as classes. Several metaphysical-sounding commands support object variables in VBA: Is, Set, New, Null, Empty, Nothing, and Me. They mostly disappear from BASIC when you move to Visual Basic .NET, so I won't waste your time exploring them in this book. You're unlikely to use them in your VBA, either. And Help is always only an F1 keypress away if you think you might want to look at them.

As a reminder of how object variables are used, here's an example from some code in Book II, Chapter 1:

```
Sub TestClass()

Dim o As Class1  'create object variable
Set o = New Class1 'assign object variable

o.TheMessage = "Hi, Bobbi!"
o.OurClass

End Sub
```

The value of numeric types

Computers calculate in different ways with different numeric variable types. They can do arithmetic faster with integers than with floating-point types because integers have no decimal point and thus no bothersome fractions manipulate.

Why? The simplest explanation is found in the fact that elementary school teachers have to spend much more time teaching division than teaching multiplication. These operations — addition, subtraction, multiplication, and division — are not symmetrical. Multiplication is pretty easy to get after you understand the idea of addition. (Anyone who has written a list for Santa or made a stack of cookies understands addition. Subtraction, too, is clear enough — especially when your older brother steals some cookies from the stack.)

But division is in a class by itself. Division can cause something to go below unity, below one, into the problematic world of fractions. Suddenly, two simple digits like 3 and 1 can expand into a list of digits bigger than the universe, like .3333333333333333, the infinitely long answer to dividing 1 by 3. And then there are those remainders — you know, those unsettling things left over after the arithmetic is supposedly finished.

Computers have exactly the same problems working with division; there's more to consider and more to manipulate. Just like us, the computer calculates more slowly when using floating point variables. If you want to speed up your programs, allow the computer to use integers instead. If you don't need the precision fractions offer — and most of the time you don't — use an Integer.

In Table 2-5 is a list of the numeric variable types that you can use in VBA, along with their symbols, the range of numbers they can hold, and the amount of space each requires in the computer to store a number of that type:

Table 2-5		Variable Types	
Name	*Symbol*	*Range*	*Storage Required*
Boolean	None	True or False	2 bytes
Byte	None	0 to 255	1 byte
Integer	%	−32,768 to 32,767	2 bytes
Long Integer (or Long)	&	−2,147,483,648 to 2,147,483,647	4 bytes
Single (single-precision floating point)	!	−3.402823E38 to −1.401298E-45 (negative numbers); and 1.401298E-45 to 3.402823E38 (positive numbers)	4 bytes
Double (double-precision floating point)	#	1.79769313486232E308 to −4.94065645841247E-324 (negative numbers); and 4.94065645841247E-324 to 1.79769313486232E308 (positive numbers)	8 bytes
Currency (scaled integer)	@	−922,337,203,685,477.5808 to 922,337,203,685,477.5807	8 bytes
Decimal	None	+/−79,228,162,514,264,337,593,543,950,335 if no decimal point; +/−7.9228162514264337593543950335 with 28 places to the right of the decimal. The decimal type is removed in VB.NET.	14 bytes

Name	Symbol	Range	Storage Required
Date	None	January 1, 100 to December 31, 9999	8 bytes
Object	None	Any Object	4 bytes
Text (string) (a string of variable length)	$	1 to roughly 2 billion	The length plus 10 bytes
Text ("string") (a string of fixed-length)	$	1 to roughly 2 billion (roughly 65,400 for Windows 3.1)	Length of string; the length of the text
Variant (when holding a number)	None	Any number	16 bytes; can be as large as a Double
Variant (when holding text)	None	1 to roughly 2 billion (roughly 65,400 for Windows 3.1)	The length of the text plus 22 bytes
User-defined Variable (use the Type command)	None	The size of the defined contents (You, the programmer, establish the range.)	Whatever is required by the contents

Some programmers type **DefInt A–Z** at the very top (in the general declarations section above any Subs) of each form and module. This forces all undeclared variables to default to the integer rather than variant type. This used to offer a more significant gain in program execution speed than it does now, but there is still some improvement. The A–Z means every variable name starting with any letter between A and Z: in other words, all variables.

Scope: The Range of Influence

So far the variables in the examples in this chapter have been located inside procedures (between Sub and End Sub). When you declare a variable inside a procedure, the variable works only within that procedure. While the program executes the procedure or event, the variable comes to life and does its thing but then dies and disappears as soon as the End Sub line is executed. Variables that live only within a single procedure are *local* variables.

Local variables have two qualities that you should understand:

✦ **Limited scope:** No programming outside their own procedure can interact with them, either to read their value or to change their value. Their scope is limited to their own procedure. (I discuss the concept of scope at greater length in the next section.)

✦ **Disappearing value:** When VBA finishes executing the procedure in which they reside, the local variable's value (whatever data it holds) evaporates. If that procedure is executed a second time, whatever value the local variable once contained is simply no longer there.

Preserving the values of local variables

In some programming situations, you want a local variable's value to be preserved. In those cases, use the `Static` command, like this:

```
Sub Minx()
    Static x
End Sub
```

In this example, the variable x retains its value until the program is shut down. Another way of putting it is this: When you use the `Static` command to declare a local variable, the value of that variable is preserved for the lifetime of your application. If you don't use `Static`, a local variable exists only for the lifetime of the procedure within which it sits.

What do you think would happen if you click somewhere in the `RunThis` macro (to put the blinking insertion cursor there) and then press F5 to execute it?

```
Sub RunThis()
First
x = x + 3
MsgBox x
End Sub

Sub First()
x = 12
x = x + 5
MsgBox x
End Sub
```

Here's what happens when you execute `RunThis`. The first command that the computer encounters is `First`, which refers to the macro of the same name. By using the command `First`, the `First` macro is executed, which first defines the value of x as 12, and then 12 + 5 or 17. A message box then pops up displaying 17, which is the value of the variable x.

Then the line x = x + 3 executes, and a message box displays 3. The variable x inside the `RunThis` macro is not the same variable as the x inside the `First` macro.

But what if you want both of these procedures to be able to access and manipulate the *same* variable? To do this, move your insertion cursor to the very top of the code window — above any procedures. When you do this (press the up arrow until you move the cursor to the top, or click your mouse at the top), you'll notice that the two list boxes at the top of the code window now read (General) and (Declarations), as you can see in Figure 2-2.

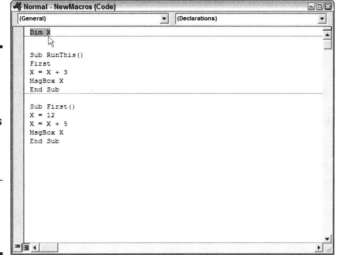

Figure 2-2:
Declare a
variable in
the General
Declarations
zone if
you want
it usable
anywhere —
in all the
procedures
— in this
module.

Having created a module-wide variable by declaring it outside any particular procedure (using `Dim X` to declare the variable X), try executing the `RunThis` procedure again. Now, the variable x is the same variable in both procedures, so the second message box displays 20 this time.

When a variable has module-wide scope like this x, it's available to all the procedures in that module. It's not available, however, to the procedures in any other modules or forms in the project. Instead of `Dim`, you can use the declaration `Private`. `Private` has that same effect as `Dim` but is a bit more descriptive because it makes it clear that the variable is *private* to its own module rather than *public* to all modules in the project. Also, `Dim` is more frequently used within procedures.

What if you want to make a variable available to all the procedures in all your modules and forms? (In other words, you want to create a variable with project-wide scope.) To do this, declare the variable with the `Public` command rather than `Dim`. What's more, you have to put the declaration into a module, like the one named `NewMacros` that I use for the programming examples in this chapter.

A module is similar to a form, but it doesn't have a user interface. Forms display buttons, text boxes, or other user-interaction objects. Forms are covered in Book II, Chapter 4.

Modules are never made visible to the user. Modules also contain no events. A module is just a code window — a location where you put your programming and also put public declarations that then become project-wide in scope). A public `Sub` or `Function` in a module is available to the entire program, too.

Form-wide, module-wide, and project-wide variables are preserved for the lifetime of your application. They never lose their value, as does a local variable declared with the `Dim` command.

It's considered good programming practice to try to avoid using `Public` variables when possible. Variables with that much scope can make your programming harder to debug. Looking at the status of variables is one of the primary ways to find out where a problem is located in a program. If you use a local variable, a problem with that variable will be confined to its procedure. That really narrows your search for a bug. You have more code to search if there's a bug involving a form-wide variable, but at least this kind of variable limits the problem to a single form rather than the entire program.

You might have noticed that procedures themselves also have scope. All procedures are default to public scope, except for event procedures that default to private. (You find them within forms, which I discuss in Book II, Chapter 4.) To make your procedures private to their module, insert the `Private` command:

```
Private Sub RunThis()
```

Scope Blowout

Classic BASIC, of which VBA is an example, limits itself to the four primary scoping declarations discussed in this chapter: `Dim`, `Private`, `Public`, and `Static`. (There's also a `ReDim`, but it's arcane.)

However, when you get into OOP languages — such as Visual Basic .NET — scoping becomes more complex. It can be *much* more complex. Quite a bit of time and effort is spent on scoping rules and techniques in OOP. Among the OOP scoping commands are `Protected`, `Friend`, and `Shared`. You even find *combination scoping,* which is using two scope declarations at the same time, such as `Protected Friend`, `ReadOnly Public`, and `WriteOnly Friend`. So far there's no `Prison Pen-pal Friend` declaration, but give it time.

The fundamental purpose of OOP is to promote encapsulation, which is a security measure that attempts to hide data and code in an effort to reduce confusion and bugs. For more on this, see Book II, Chapter 1.

You can ignore this OOP explosion of scoping behaviors and commands as long as you limit your programming to VBA. OOP is often overkill for individual programmers or small projects anyway. However, throughout this book, VB.NET is covered along with VBA, so you find out what `Friend` (and lots of other terms) means when used to declare scope.

Chapter 3: Looping and Branching

In This Chapter

✔ **Handing repetition**

✔ **Making decisions with** `If...Then`

✔ **Branching with** `Select...Case`

This chapter is for people who are new to programming. However, if you're new just to Visual Basic (VB), you might want to skim through it to get a feel for how VB handles looping and branching, which are two of the most important techniques in programming.

Looping means repeating a task until a condition is met; *branching* means choosing between carrying out a set of different tasks, based on a condition.

Going 'Round and 'Round in Loops

Often a job requires repetition until a result is achieved: Polish your boots until they shine, or add spoonfuls of sugar one at a time until the lemonade tastes good. This kind of repetitive behavior is handled with *looping* in a computer program.

Repetition is often needed in computer programs, and the most common loop structure is `For...Next`.

Using a For...Next loop

Between the `For` and the `Next` are *program lines,* which are instructions that get carried out repeatedly. The number of times that the computer executes the loop is defined by the two numbers listed right after the `For`:

```
Sub Iterate()

For I = 1 To 4
    A = A + I
Next I

MsgBox A
End Sub
```

In this example, the loop's counter variable is named I. (There's a tradition to use the name I in For...Next loops.) But the important thing to understand is that the counter variable is incremented (raised by 1) each time the program gets to the Next command.

The Next command does three things.

✦ Adds 1 to the variable I.

✦ Checks whether I has reached the limit set in the For statement (4 in this example) and makes sure the limit has not been exceeded.

✦ Then Next *loops* — that is, it sends the program back up — to the For statement to repeat the code one more time. The lines of programming code within the loop are executed each time the loop cycles.

The answer displayed by the message box in the previous example is 10. Try single-stepping through the execution of this loop (press F8 repeatedly), pausing your mouse cursor over the counter variable I and also over the variable A each time you go through the loop. You'll see that the first time through I is 1. (Look at For I = 1 To 4; the counter starts with 1.) The variable A is empty, but as soon as its line of code is executed, it contains the value of I plus whatever was in A. The second time through the loop, A first has a 1 in it, but the value of I is 2, so A then contains 3. The third time through the loop, 3 is added to 3, resulting in 6. Finally, the last time through the loop, I has a value of 4, which when added to 6, becomes 10. The program then exits the loop and displays the MsgBox.

Using the Step command with For...Next

Step is an optional command that works with For...Next. Step can be attached at the end of the For line to allow you to skip numbers — in other words, to "step" past them. When the Step command is used with For...Next, Step alters the way the loop counts.

By default, a loop counts by 1:

```
Sub Iterate()

Dim a As String


For i = 1 To 12
    a = a & i & " "
Next i

MsgBox a
End Sub
```

And results in 1 2 3 4 5 6 7 8 9 10 11 12.

However, when you use a `Step` command, you change how a `For...Next` loop counts. For example, use `Step 2` to count every other number:

```
Sub Iterate()

Dim a As String


For i = 1 To 12 Step 2
    a = a & i & " "
Next i

MsgBox a
End Sub
```

And results in 1 3 5 7 9 11.

If the mood strikes you, you can even "step" every 73rd number (`Step 73`), count backward (`For I = 10 to 1 Step -1`), or count by fractions (`Step .25`).

Nesting For...Next loops

`For...Next` loops can be nested, one inside the other. At first, this sort of structure seems confusing (and it often remains confusing): The inner loop interacts with the exterior loop in ways that are instantly clear to only the mathematically gifted, although a couple of beers also helps.

Essentially, the inner loop does its thing the number of times specified by its own counter variable, multiplied by the counter variable of the outer loop. Got it? It's like the moon. It's revolves around the Earth, but both are simultaneously revolving around the sun. So the moon's path resembles a corkscrew. To make matters worse, the entire solar system is revolving around the galaxy, but let's not get into that.

When working with nested loops, simply keep substituting counter numbers (and maybe moving code from one loop to the other) until things work the way you want. One meaning of *hacking* to a programmer is similar to what carving is to a sculptor: messing around until the desired result emerges. In this example, I want to display two sets of numbers: 1 2 3 and 1 2 3. After a frosty, cool one, I finally figured how to do it. The outer loop (`I`) should loop twice, and the inner loop (`J`) should loop three times. And the value of `J` should be used each time to display the numbers that I want. Here's the code:

```
Sub Nested()

Dim a As String
cr = vbCrLf ' move down one line

For I = 1 To 2
    For J = 1 To 3
        a = a & " " & J & cr
    Next J
Next I

MsgBox a
End Sub
```

Any numeric expression can be used with `For...Next`. However, the range that you're counting must be possible. For example, the following is not possible:

```
For i = -10 To -20 Step 2
    MsgBox "loop"; i
Next
```

This loop does nothing. It can't. You're asking it to count downward, but your `Step` command is positive. As any intelligent entity would when confronted with a senseless request, Visual Basic does nothing with these instructions. It ignores you. You have to make the `Step` negative with `-2` before something will happen.

Early exits from loops

If you want to exit the loop before the counter finishes, use the `Exit For` command. The `Exit For` command is rarely used, but here's an example of when you'd want to use it. Suppose you're filling an array that should only hold 500, and you don't want to overflow it. You avoid this by making a provision for an early exit from the loop if necessary. If the `Exit For` is carried out, execution moves to the line of code following the `Next` command.

```
If n > 500 Then Exit For
```

You can use `Exit Do` (for `Do` loops), `Exit Function`, `Exit Property`, and `Exit Sub` commands as well.

Working with Do...Loops

Sometimes you might prefer the `Do...While` loop structure to `For...Next`; in fact, some programmers favor it over `For...Next` because it can be a bit more flexible. `Do...Loop` structures can be handy in special looping situations. Read on.

Choosing Do While over For...Next loops

In its most common use, `Do...While` employs a comparison operator at the start of the loop to test something (is it = or =>, and so on). If the comparison succeeds, the statements in the loop are executed at least once. However, the first time the comparison fails, the loop is skipped, and execution continues on the line following the `Loop` command. The `Loop` command signals the end of the `Do While` structure, just as the `Next` command signals the end of the `For...Next` loop structure.

```
Sub Iterate()

Dim a As String
cr = vbCrLf ' move down one line

Do While y < 11
    y = y + 1
    a = a & y & cr
Loop

MsgBox a
End Sub
```

Book II
Chapter 3

Looping and Branching

Remember that you must do something in the code within the loop that changes the comparison value. Otherwise, you create an endless loop. Also note that if Y in the example above already holds a value of 11 or more when the program reaches this loop, the loop will never execute. The exit test will fail the very first time the loop is encountered, and none of the code within the loop will execute at all.

Using Do Until loops

A version of `Do While` is `Do Until`. It's just another way of expressing the same idea, but you might find it a little clearer. `Do While` loops as long as the comparison is `True`, but `Do Until` loops until the comparison is `False`:

```
Do Until y = 11
'Some behaviors
Loop
```

Using Loop While and Loop Until

If you want to put the loop exit test at the end of the loop structure, here are two additional ways to construct a `Do` loop:

```
Do
'Some behaviors
Loop While Y < 11
```

This works the same way as the earlier Do While example. The difference is that when you put the test at the end, the loop always executes at least once, no matter what value is in the variable Y when you enter the loop.

```
Do
'Some behaviors
Loop Until Y = 11
```

Which of these four structures should you use? Use Do While or Do Until if you don't want the loop to execute even once if the exit test fails at the start. As for the difference between the While and Until styles, it's often a matter of which one seems to you to be more readable, or which one works better with the exit test. Many times, it's merely a semantic distinction: the difference between *Do the dishes while any are still dirty* versus *Do the dishes until all are clean.*

Exploring While...Wend: A simple loop

Finally, at your disposal is the While...Wend structure, although it's little-used. It's simple but relatively inflexible:

```
While X < 7
'Some behaviors
Wend
```

As you can see, this looping technique is comparatively simple. While...Wend has no Exit command (like the Exit Do command). While...Wend is limited to an exit test at the start of the loop, and it does not permit you to use the alternative command Until.

For...Each: Looping in Object Collections

The job of moving through a collection of objects is made easy for programmers because the collection itself knows how many objects it contains. With collections, you can use the For Each structure.

For example, to see a list of the text fonts available on a given computer in VBA, you can create this macro:

```
Sub ShowFonts()

For Each F In FontNames
    Debug.Print F & ", "
Next F

End Sub
```

The results are displayed in the Immediate window.

To do the same thing VB.NET, you use the `System.Drawing.FontFamily` object, like this:

```
Dim F As System.Drawing.FontFamily

For Each F In System.Drawing.FontFamily.Families
    Console.WriteLine(F.Name)
Next
```

`For Each` is a quick and clean way to loop because you don't have to specify a literal number or some other exit test.

Creating a Very Useful File Search Utility

The macro you create in this next example is one of my favorites because it executes *so* much faster than the built-in Windows text search utility. If you write 800-page books as I sometimes do, you now and then find yourself near the end, writing Chapter 28, and thinking, "Didn't I mention *object collections* in one of the early chapters?"

Until I wrote the following macro, I had to rely on the search engine in Windows: the one you launch with Start➪Search, or by right-clicking in Windows Explorer and choosing Search from the context menu. Windows includes an indexing feature that works in the background during idle time, attempting to create lists to speed up the search process. Nonetheless, these Window searches are really quite slow if you're looking through dozens of DOC files for a particular word or phrase such as *object collections*.

Type in the following macro and then add it to a toolbar in Word. (Right-click the toolbar, click the Commands tab, click Macros in the left list of the Customize dialog box, locate the SearchText macro in the right list box and drag it onto the toolbar.) Or create a shortcut key combination for the macro. (Choose Tools➪Customize and click the Keyboard key.)

This example code also illustrates the `For Each` structure, so that's the excuse I'm using to include this high-speed search utility in this chapter.

The first time in a given session that you use this macro to search, it is about as slow as the Windows search utility. But thereafter, the documents being searched are cached in RAM, and the search is extremely fast. Try searching the same folder for two different phrases. You'll see that the search for the second phrase is lightning fast.

Press Alt+F11 to open the Word's VBA editor, and choose Tools⇨References. Ensure that the Microsoft Office 11.0 Object Library check box is marked. Then type Listing 2-1 into the Normal macros editor, where you put all the macros you want to make available to all Word documents.

Listing 2-1:   Search Macro

```
Sub SearchText()

'after the first search of a given path, this is faster than
    the built-in Windows search.
'and, unlike the Windows Explorer search, this one can be
    hard wired for a project's folder.

cr = vbCrLf
quot = Chr(34) 'quotes

Dim 1 As FileSearch
Set 1 = Application.FileSearch

s = InputBox("Please enter the search string...", "Enter the
    text you're looking for.")

With 1
  .NewSearch
  .LookIn = "C:\book OFFICE 2003"
  .SearchSubFolders = True
  .FileName = "*.doc"
  .MatchTextExactly = True

  .TextOrProperty = s

nFound = .Execute(msoSortByLastModified)

If nFound > 0 Then
        For Each F In .FoundFiles
           UserForm1.ListBox1.AddItem F
        Next
End If

End With

UserForm1.Caption = nFound & " hits for " & quot &
    1.TextOrProperty & quot & " found in" & 1.LookIn
UserForm1.Show

End Sub
```

In this macro, you first create a variable to move down one line (cr) and another to display quotation marks.

Then you define a `FileSearch` object variable and use `Set` to assign this application's `FileSearch` object to that variable. You ask the user for the text that should be searched for. You can also ask the user at this time to specify which folder or drive to search, but I prefer to hardwire it into the code with this line in the macro:

```
.LookIn = "C:\book OFFICE 2003"
```

For several months while working on a book, I generally search in the same folder, so it's quicker to just define that folder right in the code. This way I don't have to answer the `LookIn` question each time I use the search utility. It's easy enough to press Alt+F11 and type a new `.LookIn` filepath as need be.

Similarly, you can ask the user to enter the file specification (the `.FileName` property of the `FileSearch` object), but I like to hardwire `.doc` into the macro code.

Using the `With` structure so you don't have to keep repeating the object variable name 1, you then specify the various properties and use the `FileSearch` object's `Execute` method to iterate (loop) through each (`For Each`) item in the `.FoundFiles` collection built by the `Execute` method. These items are dumped into a `ListBox` on a UserForm.

This line does quite a bit of work:

```
If .Execute(msoSortByLastModified) > 0 Then
```

The `Execute` method returns the number of files found, so if it is zero, you don't use the `For Each` loop. Also, the `msoSortByLastModified` argument is one of several you can choose from to specify how the filenames are ordered in the collection of hits that the `Execute` method finds during its search. `msoSortByLastModified` orders them by (you guessed it) their date of modification. To get a list sorted alphabetically, use `msoSortByFileName`.

At the end of the macro, some statistics are displayed on the UserForm's title bar, and the UserForm is shown to the user so he can click one of the documents listed to view the document in Word.

The `.NewSearch` property is used because the other search properties are remembered between searches and reused during a given session. In other words, without specifying `.NewSearch`, filepaths, text to search for, and so on are retained and become the defaults. Also, the text you search for includes a search of the documents' properties (the name of the document's title, its author, and so on). I haven't found a way to leave out the document properties during a search and just look through the text. This `.TextOrProperty` seems the only option here.

Add the UserForm to this project now by choosing Insert⇨UserForm in the VBA editor. Drop a `ListBox` from the Toolbox onto the UserForm. Double-click the `ListBox` to get to its `Click` event and type in this code:

```
Private Sub ListBox1_Click()

n = ListBox1.Value

Documents.Open FileName:=n, ConfirmConversions:= _
        True, ReadOnly:=False, AddToRecentFiles:=False,
            PasswordDocument:="", _
        PasswordTemplate:="", Revert:=False,
            WritePasswordDocument:="", _
        WritePasswordTemplate:="", Format:=wdOpenFormatAuto,
            XMLTransform:=""

End

End Sub
```

When the user clicks a document name in this list box, Word's documents object's `Open` method is triggered, displaying the document so the user can read it.

You can include another property of the `FileSearch` object to allow users to specify a filter for the search based on the time the files were saved. If you don't include the `.LastModified` property in your code, it defaults to *any date* (`msoLastModifiedAnyTime`). However, you can select from these alternative time stamps: `msoLastModifiedLastMonth`, `msoLastModifiedLastWeek`, `msoLastModifiedThisMonth`, `msoLastModifiedThisWeek`, `msoLastModifiedToday`, and `msoLastModifiedYesterday`.

Making Decisions via Branching

Making decisions is central to any intelligent behavior. As a result, the `If...Then` structure is one of the most important features in any computer language — indeed, in any kind of language.

If...Then is the most common way that decisions are made. After the decision is made, actions are taken that respond to the decision. A program is said to *branch* at this point because the path it was following splits into more than one trail. The branch that the program chooses is decided here at the If...Then junction. For each of the branches, you write code appropriate to that path.

Many times a day, we do our own personal branching, using a similar structure: If you're hungry, you eat. If it's nice weather, you don't wear a jacket. If the car windows are fogged up, you wipe them off. This constant cycle of testing conditions and then making decisions based on those conditions is what makes our behavior intelligent and adaptive.

Understanding If...Then

This same kind of testing is what makes computer behavior intelligent, too. You put If...Then structures into a program so it reacts appropriately to various kinds of user input, as well as such additional events as incoming data from a disk file, the passage of time, or other conditions.

Here's a simple example of how If...Then is used:

```
Sub Branching()

Response = InputBox("How many calories did you take in today?")

If Response > 2200 Then
     m = "Keep that up and you'll have to buy new pants. Your bad self."
   Else
     m = "Good self-control on your part."
End If

MsgBox m

End Sub
```

The line of code starting with If tests whether something is True. If so, the code on the line or lines following the If are carried out. If the test fails (the test condition is false), your program skips the line(s) of code until it gets to an Else, ElseIf, or End If command. Then the program resumes execution. Put another way, the If test determines whether some lines of code will be executed.

Notice that if you're making a simple decision (either/or) with only two branches, you can use the Else command. In the above example, if the user's response is that he ate more than 2,200 calories, the first message is displayed. Or, if the opposite happened, the message following the Else command is displayed.

What if you want to branch into more than only two paths? Easy! You can use the ElseIf command:

```
If X = "Bob" Then
    MsgBox "Hello Bob"
ElseIf X = "Billy" Then
    MsgBox "Hello Billy"
ElseIf X = "Ashley" Then
    MsgBox "Hello Ashley"
End If
```

In a way, using ElseIf is like using several If...Thens in a row. But for situations in which you want to test multiple conditions, the better solution is to use the Select Case command, as you'll soon see.

As with loops, it's traditional to provide a visual cue by indenting all lines of code that will be carried out inside the If...Then structure. Also, there is a simple, one-line version of If...Then that you can use if your test is simple enough (True/False) and short enough that you can just put it all on a single line. In that case, you do not use an End If. (The If...Then structure is assumed to be completed by the end of the line of code.) The computer knows that this is a single-line If...Then because some additional code follows the Then command. In a multiline If...Then structure, the Then command is the last word on the line. Here's an example of the single-line structure:

```
Sub Branching()

Password = "sue"
Reply = InputBox("What is the password?")
If Reply <> Password Then MsgBox ("Access Denied"): End
MsgBox "Password verified as correct. Please continue."

End Sub
```

Notice the colon that appears at the end of the If...Then line in the preceding example code. It's used to combine separate programming statements (logical lines of code) on the same physical line. This is a rarely used technique, but you should be aware of it. It's handy for single-line If...Then code, as this example illustrates. You want to do two things should the password fail the test:

✦ Show a message box.

✦ End the program.

Normally, the `End` command would have to be on a line of its own in the code. When you use the colon, VBA reads the code that follows it as a separate logical line of code. Recall that you can use the space-underscore characters to break a single, long, logical line of code into two physical lines. (Logical here means *what VB acts on,* and physical means *what you see onscreen.*) Using a colon is the opposite of the space-underscore. A colon allows you to place two logical lines on the same physical line. (You can even cram more than two logical lines on one physical line: `X=X+1:A=B:N="Hi."`, for example.)

Remember that the condition you test with `If` is an expression, so it can involve variables, literals, constants, and any other valid combination of components that can make up an expression. For instance, you can use a function in an expression:

Book II
Chapter 3

Looping and
Branching

```
If InputBox("Enter your age, but it's optional") <> "" Then

        MsgBox "Thank you for responding"

End If
```

The `InputBox` function is executed, and its result is tested to see whether it does not equal ($<>$) an empty string (`""`), which would mean that the user failed to type anything into the `InputBox`.

A `Function`, like a `Sub`, is a procedure. However, a `Function` usually returns a value, and a `Sub` (usually) does not. In practice, over the years, the distinction between `Sub` (no return value) and `Function` (returns a value) has broken down, and now these procedures are fairly interchangeable. Generally, code that you execute with programming commands, such as `MsgBox` or `InputBox`, are called *functions* although they reside in the language's code library and you, yourself, do not write these functions. You merely *call* them (use them) in your programming.

Multiple choice: The Select Case command

`If...Then` is great for simple, common testing and branching. But if you're testing for more than two branches, `If...Then` becomes clumsy. Fortunately, here's the alternative decision-making structure in VBA that specializes in multiple-branching. `Select Case` should be used when there are several possible outcomes and several tests.

The main distinction between `If...Then` and `Select Case` goes something like this:

If CarStatus = burning, *Then* get out of the car.

But the `Select Case` structure tests many and various situations:

```
Select Case CarStatus
    Case Steaming
            Let radiator cool down.
    Case Wobbling
            Check tires.
    Case Skidding
            Steer into skid.
    Case Burning
            Leave the car.
End Select
```

`Select Case` works from a list of possible answers. Your program can respond to each of these answers differently. There can be one, or many, lines of code within each case:

```
Response = InputBox("What's your favorite color?")

Select Case LCase(Response)
Case "blue"
    MsgBox "We have three varieties of blue"
Case "red"
    MsgBox "We have six varieties of red"
Case "green"
    MsgBox "We have one variety of green"
Case Else
    MsgBox "We don't have " & Response & ", sorry."
End Select
```

This example illustrates that you can use any expression (variable, literal, function, compound expression, or other kind of expression) in the `Select Case` line. In this example, I use the `LCase` command to reduce whatever the user typed to all lowercase letters. Then VB goes down the list of cases and executes any lines in which the original expression on the first line matches one of the `Case` lines. Note that the final case is special: The optional `Case Else` command means that if there were no matches, execute the following code.

Using the Is command with Select Case

You can use the special `Is` command with each case to use comparison tests on each case:

```
X = InputBox("Your weight, please?")

Select Case X
Case Is < 200
        '(put one or more commands here)
    MsgBox "Good for you"
Case Is < 300
        '(put one or more commands here)
MsgBox "Not too bad."
End Select
```

In the above example, if the number is lower than 200, the first block of code lines executes; then execution jumps to the line of programming following `End Select`. If the number is lower than 300, the second block of code executes (any code between `Case Is < 300` and `End Select`). Note that as soon as one of the cases triggers a match, no further cases are even checked for a match. The `Case` structure is merely exited.

Using the To command with Case Select

If you want to check a range of values, use the `To` command. It can be a numeric range (`Case 4 To 12`) or an alphabetic range (based on the first letter of the string being tested):

```
Reply = LCase(InputBox("Type in your last name."))

Select Case Reply
Case "a" To "m"
    MsgBox "Please go to the left line."
Case "n" To "z"
    MsgBox "Please go to the right line."
End Select
```

You can also combine several items in a `Case`, separating them by commas:

```
Case "a" To "l", "gene", NameOfUser
```

This is an *or* type of test: that is, take action if

+ The answer begins with a letter between a and l.

  or

+ It's gene.

  or

+ It matches the value in the variable `NameOfUser`.

Chapter 4: Managing Files and UserForms

In This Chapter

✔ Understanding saving and loading

✔ Displaying a user interface

✔ Working with dialogs

✔ Using Windows controls

*T*his chapter continues the introduction to VBA, covering several topics of interest to anyone who doesn't know how to build a user interface. Specifically, here I cover UserForms, dialogs, and Windows controls. And because hard drive storage is also important, I start with a little background on loading and saving disk files.

Communicating with the Hard Drive

To preserve data, you need to load and save disk files. The syntax to do this differs between various Office applications, with Access, as always, being the odd man out.

Each Office application has its own type of file because the documents used within the applications have different internal structures representing their different purposes. Excel opens a workbook object (an XLS file), so it uses the `Open` method of the `Workbooks` object. Word opens a document, so it uses the `Open` method of the `Documents` object. And Access, of course, does things a little differently.

Loading files in Word and Excel

Here's how you open a file in Word, adding it to the collection of currently open documents:

```
Documents.Open "c:\test.doc"
```

Here's how to load a file in Excel:

```
Workbooks.Open "c:\test.xls"
```

You can also specify a slew of optional conditions when opening document or workbook files, such as the one that makes the file read-only, like this:

```
Documents.Open FileName:="C:\MyFiles\MyDoc.doc", ReadOnly:=True
```

Here's the full syntax for the Open command:

```
Workbooks.Open(FileName, ConfirmConversions, ReadOnly,
    AddToRecentFiles, PasswordDocument,
    PasswordTemplate, Revert, WritePasswordDocument,
    WritePasswordTemplate, UserFormat, Encoding,
    Visible, OpenConflictDocument, OpenAndRepair ,
    DocumentDirection, NoEncodingDialog)
```

If you want to open all recent files (those listed at the bottom of the File menu), use this code:

```
Sub OpenRecentFiles()
    Dim rFile As RecentFile
    For Each rFile In RecentFiles
        rFile.Open
    Next rFile
End Sub
```

Loading files in Access

Access, of course, does things differently. You import ordinary text files by using archaic Open commands that hearken back to the early days of BASIC. Here's an example that opens a file in sequential-input mode, and then reads and displays the contents. Follow these steps:

1. **Open a database in Access. If you don't have a file on your root C:\ directory named test.txt, create one in Notepad.**

2. **Choose Window⇨*the database name.***

   The main database window opens.

3. **Click Modules in the left pane of the main window, as shown in Figure 4-1.**

Figure 4-1:
To write a
VBA macro
(as opposed
to an
Access-
style
macro),
select
Modules.

4. Click the New button in the main database window (refer to Figure 4-1).

The Visual Basic editor opens, as shown in Figure 4-2.

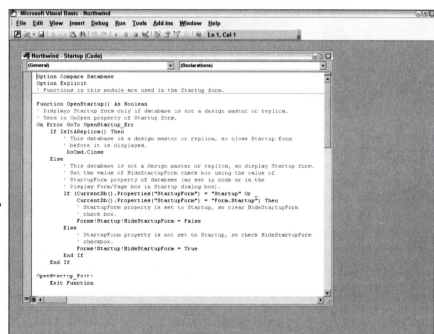

Figure 4-2:
The Visual
Basic editor,
ready for
you to write
your own
program-
ming.

5. **Type this macro into the editor:**

```
Sub opentext()

Open "c:\test.txt" For Input As #1

If LOF(1) > 0 Then
Do Until EOF(1)
Line Input #1, s
a = a & s
Loop
End If

' Close
Close #1

MsgBox a

End Sub
```

6. **Click somewhere in this macro so your blinking insertion cursor shows within the code.**

7. **Press F5 to execute the macro.**

The test.txt file is opened, and a message box displays its contents. You can use this technique to load data from some legacy databases.

You use the Open command for both loading and saving files in Access. This example opens the file in binary mode (which sometimes results in smaller file sizes) for writing operations only:

```
Open "c:\test.txt" For Binary Access Write As #1
```

Many variations on the Open command exist. See Access's VBA Help for a description of all the permutations.

Saving files

In most Office applications (Access excluded), you can simply use the Save method of the document, workbook, or other object to store the information on the hard drive. (See the preceding section for how to save a file in Access.)

For example, in Word, you can use this code to save the current document (the one you're looking at in the Word window) if it has been in any way modified since the last time it was saved:

```
Sub savedoc()

If ActiveDocument.Saved = False Then ActiveDocument.Save

End Sub
```

To save all opened documents, use the `Documents` collection's `Save` method, like this:

```
Sub saveAlldocs()

Documents.Save NoPrompt:=True

End Sub
```

Creating User Interfaces

In Visual Basic programming, the *UserForm* is a container that you use to arrange the visual elements of a user interface. When the program later executes, the UserForm appears to the user as a window, with whatever appropriate controls (buttons, text boxes, scrollbars, and so on) are necessary for the user to interact with the application.

The UserForm as a container

For a programmer, though, the UserForm is also a container for programming code that supports the behaviors of the controls and brings them to life. For example, if you put a button control on a UserForm and label that button `Click Me to see BBC!`, you can put underlying code for that button that responds when the user clicks the button by connecting to the Internet and showing the BBC news page.

Try an example; follow these steps to take the user to the BBC news page.

1. **Press Alt+F11 in Word.**

The VBA editor is displayed.

2. **Choose Insert⇨UserForm from the VBE menus.**

A new UserForm, along with a Toolbox containing controls, appears, as shown in Figure 4-3.

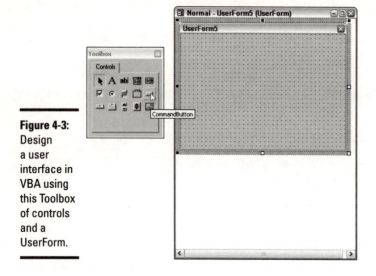

Figure 4-3:
Design
a user
interface in
VBA using
this Toolbox
of controls
and a
UserForm.

3. **Drag a** `CommandButton` **from the Toolbox (as shown in Figure 4-3) and drop it on the UserForm.**

   A new `CommandButton` appears on the UserForm.

4. **Click the button.**

   An insertion cursor appears, cluing you that you can edit the default caption.

5. **Type** Click Me to see BBC **as the new caption of the button.**

6. **Click outside the button on the UserForm.**

7. **Double-click the button.**

   A new code window opens, displaying the `Click` event of the button. Into this event (a `Sub` procedure, just like a macro), you can type whatever programming you want to execute when the user clicks this button.

8. **Type this code to open the user's browser and to display the BBC site:**

   ```
   Private Sub CommandButton1_Click()

   ActiveDocument.FollowHyperlink _
   Address:="http://news.bbc.co.uk", NewWindow:=True

   End Sub
   ```

9. **With the blinking insertion cursor inside this procedure, press F5 to test your user interface.**

   The UserForm appears as a window, just as the user would see it, as shown in Figure 4-4.

Figure 4-4:
Your pro-
gramming
UserForm
has been
transformed
into a
window.

Book II
Chapter 4

Managing Files and
UserForms

10. **Click the button.**

The BBC news page appears in your browser.

Displaying a UserForm from a macro

After you create a UserForm, you want to be able to display it to users. You can display UserForms from within macros by using the UserForm object's Show method. Follow these steps:

1. **In the VBA editor, choose View⇨Project Explorer.**

The VBA Project Explorer window pane opens.

2. **Click the + symbol next to the Modules node to expand it.**

The node opens, displaying all the modules in this document.

3. **Double-click the New Macros entry under Modules.**

The main macro editor window opens.

4. **Move down to the bottom of the macro window and type in this new macro:**

```
Sub savedoc()

UserForm1.

End Sub
```

As soon as you type the period following UserForm1, IntelliSense takes over and displays a list of all the members of a UserForm.

5. **Locate Show in the members list and click it to make your line of code read**

```
UserForm1.Show
```

6. **Press F5 to execute this macro.**

Your UserForm is displayed.

Using an object variable

A more formal approach to displaying and managing UserForms involves creating an object variable, which I name `MyForm` here, in a macro or application, like this:

```
Dim MyForm as New UserForm1
```

Thereafter, you can use the object variable to assign values to the form's properties and the properties of controls on the form. Here's a macro that manipulates a form and its contents:

```
Sub ShowForm()

Dim MyForm As New UserForm1
MyForm.TextBox1.Text = "Welcome"
MyForm.Caption = "Florida"
MyForm.Show

End Sub
```

You can also retrieve values from a form by using the object variable:

```
S = MyForm.TextBox1.Text
```

Hiding and destroying an object variable

When you're done with the form, use its `Hide` method to make it invisible:

```
MyForm.Hide
```

If you don't need it any more, destroy the object variable and its object:

```
Set MyForm = Nothing
```

Engaging the User with Dialogs

A set of standard Windows dialogs are available to you in several Office 2003 applications: printing, file access, color adjustments, and so on. Here is an example that displays the standard Open dialog box:

```
Sub ShowDia()
    Dialogs(wdDialogFileOpen).Show
End Sub
```

In addition to the standard Windows dialog boxes, dozens of application-specific dialogs are also available, such as Word's Date and Time dialog box (as shown in Figure 4-5), which you display with the following:

```
Dialogs(wdDialogInsertDateTime).Show
```

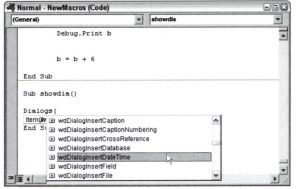

Figure 4-5:
You can manipulate dozens of built-in dialog boxes program-matically.

To see a list of all the dialog boxes available and their arguments, search the Excel or Word Help system for *Built-in Dialog Box Argument Lists.* (Outlook and PowerPoint don't offer this capability.) Or just type in **Dialogs(** (with a left parenthesis), as shown in Figure 4-5, and the VBA IntelliSense feature opens with a list of all the dialogs.

Access, of course, doesn't directly support a simple UserFormat for display-ing dialogs, although you can use this technique. However, to get it to work, you need to figure out which code library (Tools⊅References in the Access VBA code window) contains the standard Windows dialogs; then select its check box:

```
Sub ShowDia()

    Dim dlgOpen As FileDialog

Sct dlgOpen = Application.FileDialog( _
    FileDialogType:=msoFileDialogUpen)

With dlgOpen
    .AllowMultiSelect = True
    .Show
End With


End Sub
```

You can employ a variety of techniques with the dialog boxes. For instance, if you want to simply show a dialog box to the user but prevent the user from taking action, use the `Display` method. The Open button in this next dialog box will be disabled:

```
Sub ShowDia()
    Dialogs(wdDialogFileOpen).Display
 End Sub
```

A value is returned by the `Show` and `Display` methods, telling you whether the user clicked the Close, OK, or Cancel buttons:

```
Sub ShowDia()

    If Dialogs(wdDialogFileOpen).Show = -1 Then
        'user clicked OK
    End If


End Sub
```

A returned value of `0` means that the user clicked the Cancel button, and a returned value of `-2` means that the user clicked the Close button.

Understanding Controls

You can of course construct custom dialog boxes to display to the user. A simple approach is to use the `msgbox` and `inputbox` functions. More complex and satisfactory is to create a UserForm and interact with the user with it.

To see a control's properties, right-click the control on the UserForm and then choose Properties from the context menu. The Properties window opens, as shown in Figure 4-6.

To see how to employ the various controls in the UserForm Toolbox, follow these steps:

1. **Press Alt+F11 in Word.**

The VBA editor is displayed.

2. **Choose Insert⇨UserForm from the VBA editor menu.**

A new UserForm appears, along with a Toolbox that contains controls. A close-up of the Toolbox is shown in Figure 4-7.

Figure 4-6:
Adjust
properties in
this window.

Figure 4-7:
Here is your
set of
controls.

TIP

Excel's Toolbox has an additional control named RefEdit that displays the
address of a range of cells on one or more worksheets.

Figure 4-6 shows the default controls on the Toolbox, but you can add
dozens more to the Toolbox. Some controls might be installed on your computer from other Microsoft products. You can also get controls from third-
party sources, and there's even a set available from within Office that's not
considered as frequently used as the default set.

To see the list of controls that you can add to the Toolbox, right-click the Toolbox and choose Additional Controls. You'll see the list of controls, as shown in Figure 4-8. You can read more about these in Chapter 5, Book II.

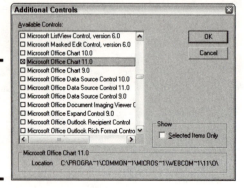

Figure 4-8:
A slew
of other
controls is
available to
add to your
Toolbox.

Read on to explore the purpose and behavior of each of the default controls.

The Label control

A Label is generally used to inform the user of the meaning of something visible on a window. For example, if you have a TextBox, you could describe its purpose to the user by positioning a Label that reads Please enter your address here just above the TextBox.

Here are some common uses for a Label:

+ Print information on a UserForm.

+ Add captions or other descriptive text to controls that have no Caption property of their own, such as ScrollBars.

+ Apprise the user of changing conditions while your program runs: that is, a file is being loaded, records are being sorted, and so on.

A Label normally has no border (the default) and appears to be printed on a UserForm. Labels are usually not changed while a program runs, although they can be. Often the Caption (the label's displayed text) and its other properties are adjusted while you design your program using the Properties window.

The most important element of a `Label` is its `Caption` property, which is where you put your descriptive text. Remember that the main purpose of a `Label` is to label something on your UserForm. `TextBox` controls are also designed to handle text, but they also accept input from the user and have much greater overhead.

A `Label` wraps its text at its right edge. (It breaks lines at a space character.) You can take advantage of this fact to add multiline notations on UserForms. First, create a `Label` that's a few lines high and then type some words separated by spaces into its `Caption` property. When you reach the edge of the `Label`, the words move to the next line. A `Label` is limited to 1,024 characters, and its `TextAlign`, `AutoSize`, and `WordWrap` properties determine how text is displayed within the label.

The TextBox control

The `TextBox` control and the `CommandButton` are probably the most frequently used of all the controls. The VB `TextBox` control is a simple (although surprisingly functional) word processor.

The `TextBox` control responds to all the usual editing keys: Delete, Insert, Backspace, PgUp, and PgDn. It can also automatically *word wrap:* that is, detect when the user has typed to the right side of the text box and then move the word down to the next line without breaking it in two.

You can add `ScrollBars` (via that property of the `TextBox`). By manipulating the `SelText` and related properties during runtime, you can create cut, copy, and paste features. By using the `KeyDown` event, you can capture characters while the user types them, thus adding special, additional features triggered by the Ctrl, Alt, or function keys.

A `TextBox` is like Notepad — elementary, but useful. For example, you can use text boxes for data entry or any situation where the user needs a convenient way to type something into your program. If you want to limit the number of characters the user is permitted to enter into a `TextBox`, use the `MaxLength` property. It can be set in the Properties window or while the program is running. When not 0 (the default), a `TextBox` will refuse to accept — will not print onscreen or add to the `Text` property — any more characters typed by the user. You can also use text boxes to display information, such as a disk file that the user will want to view or edit.

When using `TextBox`, you can't add a selective boldface or italics feature, however, or include varying typefaces or font sizes. These properties are set for the entire `TextBox`, so you can't mix and match them in the text inside the box.

**Book II
Chapter 4**

Managing Files and UserForms

However, a more advanced TextBox control is available — the RichText Box — and you might find it in the list of additional controls you can see by right-clicking the Toolbox. This control does permit formatting, such as italics, boldface, various type faces and type sizes, bulleted lists, and even color. You can import and export RTF files, thereby retaining the formatting. (Most word processors recognize the RTF codes.)

The TextBox MultiLine property is rather an annoyance, to the regret of millions of BASIC programmers (and a waste of man-centuries of time), ever since Visual Basic version 1 MultiLine has defaulted to False. The practical effect of this bizarre decision on the part of the designers is that you almost always have to change the property to True whenever you add a TextBox to a UserForm. That's because text boxes are almost always more functional with more than one line (and, consequently, with word-wrap activated).

If you add a horizontal ScrollBar with the scroll bar's property, all text will be on a single line. This single line can contain up to 255 characters. Any additional characters that the user attempts to type in or that your program attempts to add to the Text property will be ignored. It's therefore usually practical to use only a vertical ScrollBar, both horizontal and vertical bars, or none. A lone horizontal bar is restrictive.

There is no default limit (beyond the user's available memory) to the size of the text within a TextBox. A TextBox Text property (Text1.Text, for instance) behaves just like a text variable.

You can use the KeyDown event of a TextBox to intercept characters as they're typed in, which allows you to control user input — refusing to accept letters, for example, if the user is supposed to be entering a phone number.

You can also add shortcut commands with this technique, such as Ctrl+Q for Quit. To add a cut, copy, and paste feature, see the SelText property in the earlier section, "The TextBox control."

Windows uses the Tab key as a way of moving between the items — the controls — in a window. Pressing Tab cycles you through the various OptionButtons, CommandButtons, or whatever controls are on a UserForm (see "TabIndex" in Help). In a TextBox (unless it's the only control on the UserForm that can respond to tabbing), the user can't use the Tab key to move the cursor over as would be possible in most word processors (and typewriters). Pressing Ctrl+I, however, will tab in a TextBox.

The ComboBox control

ComboBoxes are similar to ListBoxes; however, a ListBox simply provides a list of options the user can choose from, whereas a ComboBox offers that list and also lets the user type in additional items.

Use ComboBoxes to offer the user choices but accept alternatives. For example, if your program dials the telephone and is an electronic substitute for a Rolodex, you can keep track of the six most-frequently dialed people.

When the program starts, it shows a ListBox with these people's names so the user can just click one and then press Enter to select the one that's highlighted. Pressing arrow keys moves the user up and down through the list. And — the main feature — there's a place for the user to simply type in a person who is not listed in the top six.

Your macro or program detects the user's selections, which trigger the text box's Click event. Your program also knows when the user starts typing: That act triggers the box's Change event.

Your program can add or remove items from a ComboBox:

```
ComboBox1.AddItem "New York"
```

Or to add an item, use this:

```
ComboBox1.AddItem N
```

Or to remove the fourth item from a ComboBox, use this:

```
ComboBox1.RemoveItem 3
```

The items in a List or ComboBox start with a zero-th item, so the fourth item is removed by requesting number 3.

Computer language designers still cling to the confusing habit of starting a count from zero (in some cases, not all).

The ListBox control

A ListBox is the same as a ComboBox except that the user can't type anything into a ListBox. He can click only one or more of the listed items, thereby selecting that item or set of items.

When using ListBoxes, remember these points:

✦ **Provide the user with a list of hardwired choices reflecting your judgment about appropriate options.**

For example, if you want the user to select between light, medium, and dark blue for the BackColor of a UserForm, put only those names in a ListBox. The user must follow your aesthetic rules because those are the only options that you offered.

✦ **Provide the user with the only possible choices.**

Only a limited number of font style settings are available, so your ListBox would contain only those options.

✦ **Make a ListBox more accommodating to the user.**

Add a TextBox or other controls to the UserForm as adjuncts to a ListBox, offering the user more flexible control than a lone ListBox would normally offer. Let the user, for instance, select from CheckBoxes or OptionButtons to AddItems to your ListBox.

ListBoxes can be made more efficient in some situations by adjusting their MultiSelect, ColumnCount, and TopIndex properties. MultiSelect permits the user to select more than a single item at a time; Columns displays more than a single vertical list of items; and TopIndex allows your program to scroll the list, independent of the user.

The Text property of a ListBox always contains the currently selected item (available as a text [string] variable). X = List1.Text would allow your program to examine and react to the selected item in the box. The Text property of a ComboBox, however, can contain something the user might have typed in — some text that's not part of the box proper.

The user can select an item from a ListBox by clicking it or by typing in its first letter. This triggers a Click event without using the mouse.

The CheckBox control

Check boxes allow the user to select from among several options, and more than one of these options can be simultaneously selected. The OptionButton is a similar, related control, but only one of them can be selected at a time.

The Value property of a CheckBox determines whether a given box is unchecked, checked, or grayed out (meaning that it can't be selected by the user at this particular time; it's inactive and unavailable as an option).

The user can trigger a CheckBox by clicking anywhere within the frame of a CheckBox (on the box image, on the caption, or even outside the caption if the frame is larger). The box that has the focus is indicated visually while the program runs by a dotted-line box around the caption. In other words, if a particular CheckBox (among all the controls on a window) has the focus, it will have a faint, gray line around it.

The OptionButton control

OptionButtons are similar to CheckBoxes, but OptionButtons allow the user to select one choice from a group of mutually exclusive choices. That is, selecting one button automatically deselects all the other buttons in the group. Only one OptionButton in a group can be selected at a given time.

This control is frequently referred to as a *radio button group* because it operates the way the buttons do on an old car radio (think Rambler or DeSoto, not Escort or Passat). Time-warp back (or ask your dad) about how you literally had to press a button to make the currently selected button pop out. In control terms, when you click a radio button, the currently selected button is deselected. In other words, only one radio button in a group can be selected at a time.

CheckBoxes are used in groups too, but any number of CheckBoxes can be selected (active) at a given time.

You could use a group of OptionButtons if you want to offer the user a choice of possible BackColors for a UserForm. Because there can be only one background color on a UserForm at a time, the choices are mutually exclusive. For example, if the button for Green were previously in effect and the user selects Magenta, Green should pop out and become inactive.

OptionButtons can be placed directly on a UserForm or grouped within a Frame control. If you want to create a group of OptionButtons that will cause each other to pop out when a new one is selected, they must all be on the same UserForm or within the same Frame. You can create more than one group of OptionButtons on a single UserForm by placing each group within a Frame, which acts as a container.

To place an OptionButton within a Frame, for example, first put a Frame control on a UserForm; then drag and drop the OptionButton icon from the VB Toolbox.

The group of OptionButtons that you place into a Frame all move together if you drag the Frame around. And, more importantly, the OptionButtons are now part of a team, and pressing one will automatically pop out any of the others.

The ToggleButton control

A `ToggleButton` is essentially a `CheckBox` in a fancy costume. It has two states, on and off, and the user can tell when it's on because it looks as if it's depressed into the UserForm. Like `OptionButtons`, `ToggleButtons` can be grouped inside `Frames`.

The Frame control

`Frames` have something in common with UserForms: They are dual-purpose entities that can assist you in organizing your program both visually and structurally. `Frames` subdivide a UserForm into logical zones (to visually clue the user about the relatedness of variously framed sets of controls).

A `Frame` can draw a visible line around a group of controls. This alerts the user that these controls, like a set of `OptionButtons`, are working together toward some purpose — such as selecting a graphic, or a record in a database. More importantly, a `Frame` can group controls drawn on top of it. This grouping has two effects.

One, while you are designing your program, you can drag the `Frame` around on the UserForm, and any other controls contained within the `Frame` will follow it as a unit. They have been contained within the `Frame`. This simplifies design and maintains the positional relationship between the grouped controls.

To group controls, you must first add the `Frame` to the UserForm. Then drag and drop the other controls from the Toolbox — or elsewhere on the UserForm — into the `Frame`.

VBA also allows you to surround a group of controls by dragging the mouse around them (or by clicking them while holding down the Shift key). Then they can be dragged in concert.

The second effect that frames have is that all `OptionButtons` contained within a particular `Frame` or `PictureBox` are considered a *unit*. If the user clicks one of these buttons, any other button in the unit that was selected will be deselected. For more on this, see the section, "The OptionButton control," earlier in this chapter.

A `Frame` sinks its Caption into the `Frame` border, to the left side. If this design style appeals to you, the `Frame` offers it.

**Book II
Chapter 4**

Managing Files and
UserForms

The CommandButton control

Just like the `Click` event is the most popular event in Visual Basic, so the `CommandButton` is perhaps the most frequently used control. It provides visually intuitive, direct access: The user sees the caption and simply clicks the command button to get something done. The animation offers good, strong feedback; there's a real sense that something has happened, unlike some other VBA selection methods.

Use `CommandButtons` any time the user needs to make something happen in the program. Accompany them with pictures (by setting their `Picture` property). Use `Label` controls to explain the button's purpose to the user.

The TabStrip and MultiPage controls

The `TabStrip` can be a useful control because it organizes information in a way similar to a card file of 3 x 5 cards, with divider tabs to indicate logical categories. In other words, it's similar to some of the dialog boxes and property windows displayed in various Windows applications.

Display large amounts of data

Use a `TabStrip` when you want to display a considerable amount of information to the user and need to organize that information into categories.

The `TabStrip` control offers the user a more visually intuitive and easier to use format than the traditional menu approach to changing an application's options or preferences.

`MultiPage` does basically what a `TabStrip` does except it's easier for the programmer to work with.

When an event fires in a `MultiPage` or `TabStrip` control, you see a different syntax than you find in other controls. An index is passed as an argument to the event, so that you (the programmer) can figure out which page or tab on the control was clicked (or otherwise triggered an event). For example

```
Private Sub TabStrip1_Click(ByVal Index As Long)

End Sub
```

Designing a MultiPage control

It's not difficult to design a `MultiPage`. Just drag it so that it fills the UserForm. (This looks best, and users expect to see a tab-style page as a single entity — not as a part of a larger window.) Then from the Toolbar, drag and drop whatever controls you want on page one. Click the Page2 tab and add controls to it. If you want additional pages, right-click the Page2 tab and choose New Page. You can also choose Move from this same right-click context menu to rearrange the pages.

The ScrollBar control

A ScrollBar is an analog control, like the volume knob on a stereo. The position of an analog control offers a visual analogy corresponding to, and illustrating, the status of the thing it adjusts.

Such controls can be turned all the way up or all the way down or can be moved gradually between the extremes. ScrollBars are, therefore, appropriate for allowing the user to adjust things that have a range of possible states, such as background color. This range of states should also be contiguous, like how the colors of a rainbow blend into each other across the spectrum.

And, of course, the classic use for ScrollBars is to help the user move data up and down in a window (or sideways).

You can reverse the direction of a ScrollBar. Normally, Max is at the far right of a horizontal bar and at the bottom of a vertical bar. However, if you set the Max property to a number lower than the Min property, the Max flips and becomes the far left of a horizontal bar and the top of a vertical bar.

A ScrollBars property of the TextBox control adds an internal scrollbar to that control.

The SpinButton control

This simple control increments and decrements numbers when the user clicks it. You can use it to manipulate the values displayed in other controls, such as changing the date displayed in a label. To get an idea how it works, add a SpinButton and a Label to a UserForm; then double-click the SpinButton to get to its Change event. Type this into the event, press F5, and click the SpinButton to observe the activity:

```
Private Sub SpinButton1_Change()

Label1.Caption = SpinButton1.Value

End Sub
```

Adjust the Min and Max properties to suit your needs.

The Image control

The Image control holds graphics, displaying BMP, GIF, JPG, ICO, and WMF graphics files. Graphics placed in an Image control can be freely resized. You can stretch or shrink the graphics to suit your needs by adjusting the PictureSizeMode property. Zooming, stretching, and clipping — to preserve the original resolution — are all available techniques.

Figure 4-9 illustrates the clipping mode in the image (top) and the stretch mode (bottom). Set the PictureSizeMode property to fmPictureSizeModeStretch if you want the entire graphic to display no matter how you resize the Image control that contains it.

Figure 4-9:
Clipping
mode
versus
stretch
mode.

UserForms can also display graphics, via their Picture property.

Chapter 5: Moving to the Internet

In This Chapter

✔ **Developing Web Pages**

✔ **Using Web controls**

✔ **Understanding database security levels**

*I*n this chapter, I show you how to use Office 2003 to build Web pages. You also discover how to manage Internet security features, use Web controls, and create a direct connection between a database and an Internet Web page by using the data-access page feature in Access.

Taking Office 2003 to the Web

Office 2003, like most other major applications, has provisions for the Internet, both in terms of input and output. The input "features" include hyperlinks embedded in documents that, when clicked, result in that annoying (to me, anyway) surprise when the Internet Explorer browser suddenly takes over a window, or a pane, within an application or utility. Press the wrong keys or click a hyperlink by accident, and suddenly Word or Windows Search utility transforms into a kind of faux browser. Even Windows Explorer also participates in this sudden and — I think unwelcome — transformation. When I want to surf the Internet, I prefer to do it in the full browser and not some partial browser that invades another program.

As for *output* — displaying your information in Web pages for the world to see — Office 2003 applications include some special controls, wizards, and other features to help you do just that. For example, the Microsoft Office Web Components are controls you can use to display charts, spreadsheets, and database contents on the Internet. And you'll likely be amazed at how the Access data-access page helps you easily and quickly create connections between databases and Web pages. That used to be quite a tough job.

Moving Office to the Web

Although the four Internet-related controls in the preceding steps are the most visible Internet-related elements in Office 2003, additional features in Office also contribute to the job of publishing on the Web. Many Office 2003 applications use the Web (or an intranet site) to assist in various kinds of collaboration and user communication.

One simple Web publishing feature is available in Word and Excel. Choose File➪Save as Web Page from Excel or Word, and an HTML version of your spreadsheet or document is stored. These versions can be directly displayed in Web pages. An HTML file is — for all practical purposes — simply a Web page. Loaded into a browser, it becomes a Web page.

If you open the .mht (a single-page version of HTML) file in a browser, it looks like Figure 5-1.

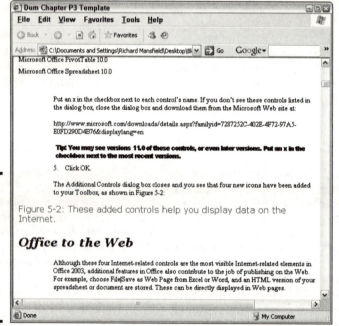

Figure 5-1: When you save a document as a Web page, it can easily be displayed in a browser.

You can also use the Save As Web Page dialog box to save your document as an ordinary HTML page or even as XML.

When you use the Save As Web Page feature, any elements in your document that must be translated for browser viewing are described. For instance, when I saved this Word page, I was told that

+ Decorative border styles will appear as single-line borders.

+ Pictures and objects with text wrapping will become left- or right-aligned.

However, these saved documents are not interactive. They're static, like snapshots. To permit the user to interact with your Office 2003 applications' data, you can use the special controls that you added to your toolbox earlier in this chapter.

Loading Additional Controls

When you add a UserForm to a VBA project in an Office application, a Toolbox also appears. This Toolbox contains a set of controls you can drag and drop onto the UserForm to build the user interface. However, this isn't the entire story; there are more controls you can employ for special purposes. To load additional controls to display Office applications' information on the Internet, follow these steps:

Book II
Chapter 5

Moving to the Internet

1. **In Excel, press Alt+F11.**

The VBA editor window opens.

2. **In the editor, choose Insert⇨UserForm.**

A new UserForm — and the Toolbox with its controls — appears. For more on UserForms, see Chapter 4, Book II.

3. **Right-click the Toolbox and choose Additional Controls from the context menu.**

The Additional Controls dialog box appears, as shown in Figure 5-2.

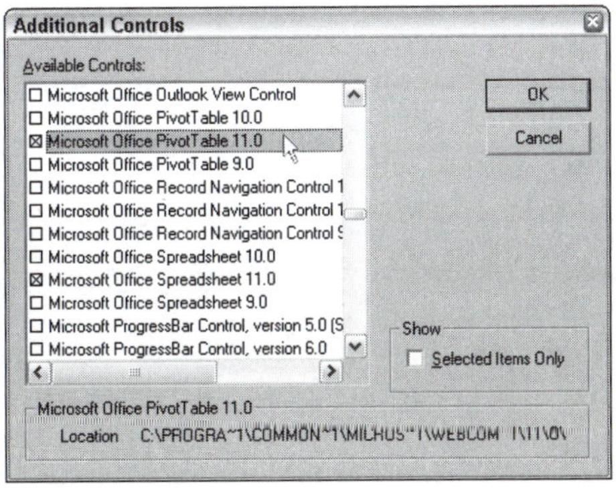

Figure 5-2:
Add new controls to the Toolbox with this dialog box.

4. **Scroll down until you find the following controls in the dialog box:**

- Microsoft Office Chart 11.0
- Microsoft Office Data Source Control 11.0

- Microsoft Office PivotTable 11.0
- Microsoft Office Spreadsheet 11.0

To see what these controls are used for, see the section, "Using the Web Controls," later in this chapter.

If you don't see these controls listed in the dialog box, close the dialog box and download them from the Microsoft Web site at

`www.microsoft.com/downloads/details.aspx?familyid=`
`7287252C-402E-4F72-97A5-E0FD290D4B76&displaylang=en`

You might see versions 10.0 of these controls or other versions. Mark the check box next to the most recent versions. Another name for Office 2003 is Office 11, so generally you'll look for Office 11 components when adding features.

5. **Click the check box next to each control name in Step 4.**

6. **Click OK.**

The Additional Controls dialog box closes, and you see that four new icons have been added to your Toolbox, as shown in Figure 5-3.

Figure 5-3: These added controls help you display data on the Internet.

The new control icons

Using the Web Controls

Here's a summary of the four Office 2003 Web Controls that I show you how to load earlier in this chapter:

✦ `ChartSpace`: The `ChartSpace` control lets you display graphs and charts from a worksheet or pivot table (Access and Excel) or a database table (Access). You can display more than one graph or chart at a time. (This control is a container, which is probably why it's called a *space*.)

+ `PivotTable`: The `PivotTable` control allows users to interact with a worksheet or database table. Options include filtering, outlining, and sorting. Pivot tables are reports that can be quickly switched to show various views on a set of data. You can find much more on pivot tables in Book IV, Chapter 4, "Data Diving with PivotTables."

+ `Spreadsheet`: The `Spreadsheet` control displays a basic version of a worksheet but does allow users to manipulate functions and recalculate.

+ `DataSource`: The `DataSource` control is not displayed to the user but does help the programmer create a connection between a data source and the Web page or controls on that page.

You can also drop these controls into spreadsheets or UserForms for Windows programming, rather than Internet purposes.

Publishing an Excel Spreadsheet

You can Web-publish a single Excel spreadsheet or pivot table but not an entire workbook. Obviously, publishing this kind of data might be especially useful as a way to share information with co-workers, even those on the road. To see how to display an interactive spreadsheet in a Web page, follow these steps:

1. **Run Excel and choose File⇨New.**

The New Workbook pane opens. (If it doesn't open, choose View⇨ Task Pane.)

2. **Click the <u>Templates on Office Online</u> link.**

3. **Choose an Excel template, such as the Buy vs. Lease Car Calculator template (listed under the <u>Finance and Accounting</u> link, then the Personal Finance link).**

4. **Click the Download button to bring it into your version of Excel.**

If you want to see how this entire sheet would look in a Web page, choose File⇨Web Page Preview.

5. **Drag your mouse to select the range of cells you want to publish, as shown in Figure 5-4.**

6. **Choose File⇨Save As Web Page.**

7. **Click the Selection radio button to publish only the range, as shown in Figure 5-5.**

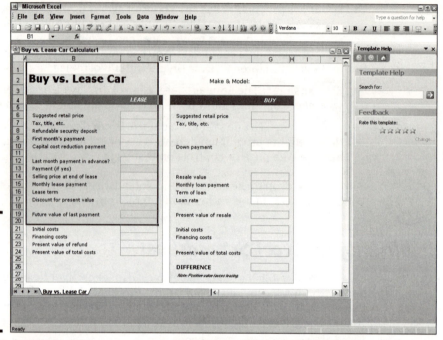

Figure 5-4: Select the range of cells you want to put in a Web page.

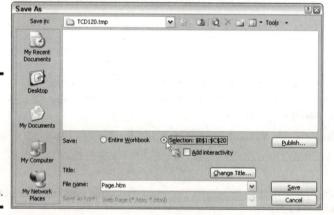

Figure 5-5: To publish only a selected range, click the Selection radio button.

8. **Click the Add Interactivity check box.**

   This determines that the spreadsheet isn't read-only when displayed in the Web page, permitting users to actually use the spreadsheet.

9. **Click the Publish button.**

   The Publish as Web Page dialog box opens, as shown in Figure 5-6.

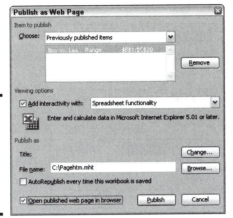

Figure 5-6:
Make any changes you wish to the published sheet here.

10. **Ensure that the Add *InteractivityActivity With* check box is checked.**

11. **Specify a filepath for your Web page.**

12. **Select the Open Published Web Page in Browser check box.**

13. **Click the Publish button.**

After some behind-the-scenes grinding away, the Web page file (.mht) is stored on your hard drive, and Internet Explorer opens with the spreadsheet range displayed, as shown in Figure 5-7. This spreadsheet range is a Web page, and it is dynamic. Users can type in data, formulae, and perform calculations.

Type some data into this Web page and then choose View➪Source in Internet Explorer to see the underlying HTML code that was generated to create your Web page. Here's one interesting part of the code, where the Excel spreadsheet object is defined:

```
<object
 id="Buy vs_26422_Spreadsheet"
 classid="CLSID:0002E559-0000-0000-C000-000000000046">
<param name=DisplayTitleBar value=false>
<param name=ViewableRange value="$A$1:$B$20">
<param name=Autofit value=true>
<param name=DataType value=XMLData>
```

In the preceding code block, note the classid. That's a unique number (or so you hope) that identifies the Microsoft Office Spreadsheet Web Component version 11. Version 10 has this similar but unique ID number:

0002E551-0000-0000-C000-000000000046

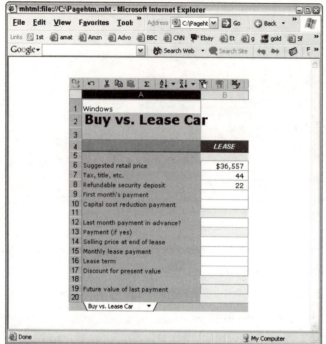

Figure 5-7:
Post a
functional
spreadsheet
range as a
Web page.

(See more about the version differences in the earlier section, "Loading Additional Controls.")

Securing a Spreadsheet: Protecting Cells

You might want to display some cells in a spreadsheet that are protected: namely, that the user is not permitted to modify. In the following example (using the Buy vs. Lease Car template), you want to freeze the Refundable Security Deposit cell at 0 (zero) and not allow users to make any changes to it.

To see how to publish a selectively disabled spreadsheet, follow these steps:

1. **In Excel, open the spreadsheet template from the preceding example.**

2. **Type 0 (zero) into one of the cells.**

   Your goal now is to disable this cell so that the user can't adjust it.

3. **Drag your mouse to select the cell (with the 0) that you want to disable. (It may appear selected after you complete Step 2, but it isn't. You must drag to see the context menu in Step 5.)**

4. **Right-click the selected cell.**

5. **Choose Format Cells from the context menu that appears.**

   The Format Cells dialog box opens, as shown in Figure 5-8.

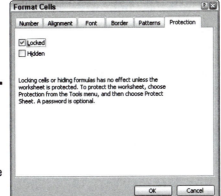

Figure 5-8:
Use this dialog box to protect (disable) a cell or range of cells.

6. **Click the Protection tab in the dialog box.**

7. **Click the Locked check box to add a check mark.**

8. **Click OK.**

   The dialog box closes.

9. **Choose Tools⇨Protection⇨Protect Sheet.**

   In the Protect Sheet dialog box that opens, you can choose various levels of protection.

10. **Leave the default settings as they are and click OK. These defaults allow the user to select, but not edit, the locked cell.**

    The dialog box closes.

    Don't choose the Password option in the Protect Sheet dialog box — if you do, the cells can't be used in a Web page.

11. **Select the range of cells you want to publish — perhaps a dozen cells surrounding the protected one — so you can test the protection feature.**

12. **Choose File⇨Save As Web Page.**

13. **Enable the Selection radio button to publish only the range.**

14. **Click the Add Interactivity check box.**

    Now all the cells in the spreadsheet (other than the protected one) can be modified by the user when displayed in the Web page.

15. **Click the Publish button.**

The Publish as Web Page dialog box opens.

16. **Ensure that the Add Interactivity With check box is checked.**

17. **Specify a filepath for your Web page.**

18. **Click the Open Published Web Page in Browser check box.**

19. **Click the Publish button.**

Now try to make changes to that 0 in the protected cell. Doesn't happen. Instead, a message box informs you that this cell is read-only, so your efforts to modify it are doomed, as shown in Figure 5-9.

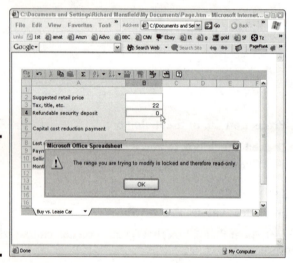

Figure 5-9: Not so fast, dude. This cell is read-only, so forget about changing it.

Publishing Access Data

Access doesn't work the way that Excel does; no File⇨Publish as Web page feature exists. Instead, you use the special data-access page, which is already an HTML document — and thus, already published, in a sense. You can permit users to interact with data — or indeed to use the Web controls (Chart, PivotTable, or Spreadsheet) — within a data-access page.

Although data-access pages are used to create Web pages, you can also employ them within the Access application itself in Windows. And, either within a browser or Access, a user can edit and add or delete records as well as sort and filter the data.

Data access pages can be created several ways:

✦ Convert an existing Web page or Access report (or table, form, or custom view).

✦ Start from scratch.

✦ Use a wizard in Access.

Whichever method you choose, you'll avoid the maddening tedium and downright waste of human time writing HTML by hand to accomplish the job of building an interactive, database-connected Web page. Programmers used to write this stuff by hand; fortunately, wizards and other automated features make a Web programmer's life far more pleasant these days.

Creating a data access page

To see how to create a data access page from an opened database, follow these steps:

1. **In Windows Explorer, open the Northwind sample database (Northwind.mdb) in Access.**

Northwind can be found at `C:\Program files\Microsoft Office\ Office11\Samples`. Choose Help|Sample Databases, then select Northwind Sample Database. If it's not there, go to Windows's Control Panel, choose Add/Remove Programs, then find and click Microsoft Office, click the Change button, and follow the instructions to install the Northwind sample database.

2. **Start creating a data-access page by choosing Pages (in the left pane of the database window, as shown in Figure 5-10).**

Figure 5-10:
Click the
Pages
object to
begin
building a
data access
page.

3. **Click the New button on the database window toolbar.**

   The New Data Access Page dialog box opens, as shown in Figure 5-11.

Figure 5-11:
Choose
here which
data access
page
approach
to take.

4. **Click the AutoPage: Columnar option.**

5. **In the drop-down list at the bottom of the dialog box, choose the** Employees **table as your data source (refer to Figure 5-11).**

6. **Click OK.**

   The dialog box closes, and your new data-access page appears, as shown in Figure 5-12.

Notice in Figure 5-12 that a set of database manipulation icons are available in a strip along the bottom. These include the usual first, previous, next, and last record navigation buttons, as well as new record, delete record, sorting and filtering buttons. The user has quite a bit of freedom to manipulate and view this table from the database.

Deploying a data-access page

To save the data-access page (so you can drop it into a Web site via FrontPage or other Web site-building tools), just click the data-access page's toolbar to select it. Choose File⇨Save, and you'll see a Save dialog box where you can specify where the .htm (HTML) file will be stored.

After the file is saved, you see a warning dialog box telling you that you've saved the file to an *absolute filepath* (a hard-wired address on your hard drive) as opposed to the more desirable network Universal Naming Convention (UNC) path. If you intend for others on your intranet to use this file, you should indeed correct the address. However, if you're deploying the file to a server for Internet Web site purposes, you undoubtedly know how and where to store the file — just store it in the same directory along with your other Web pages.

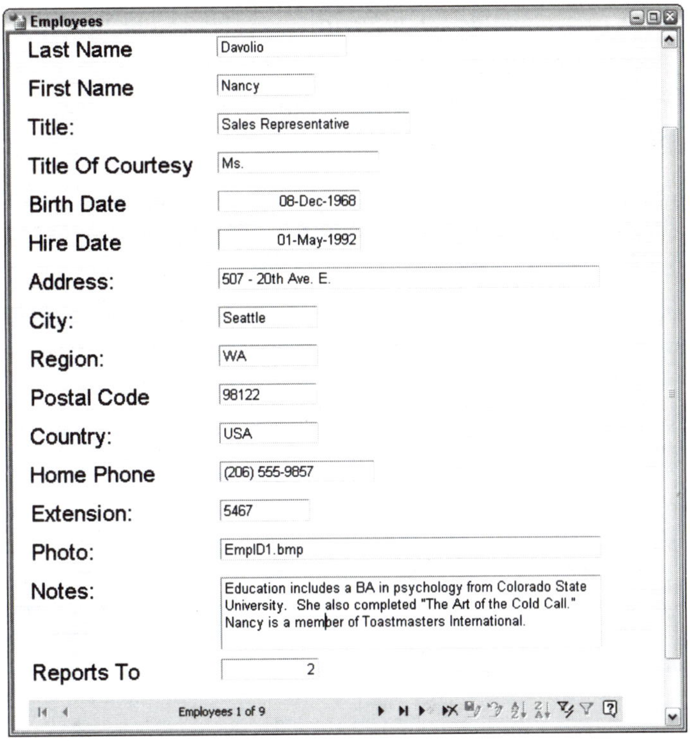

Figure 5-12:
A finished
data access
page,
showing the
first record
in the
Employees
table.

After the file is saved, it can be displayed in a browser, just like a Web page because it is in fact (hmmm) a Web page. In Windows Explorer, double-click the employees.htm file (or whatever name you saved the file). If you (or your machine's administrator) applied some permissions security measures to this location, you'll see a message like the one displayed in Figure 5-13.

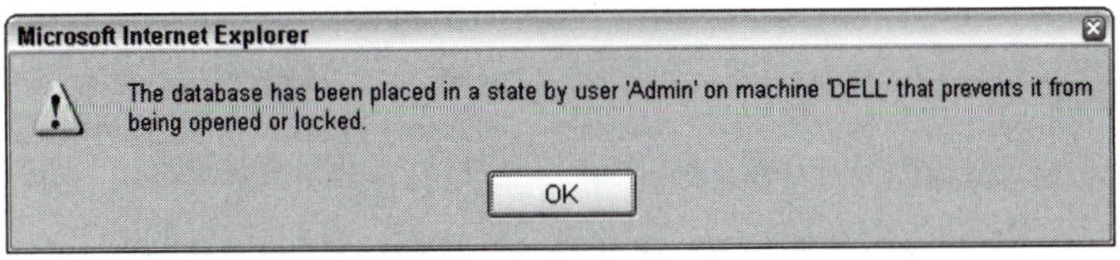

Figure 5-13:
Security
measures
can prevent
a database
from being
accessed
from a Web
browser.

However, precisely this same security warning can be displayed erroneously. The message should also state

> This file or database may currently be in use by another application or process.

If you haven't shut down Access and it's still displaying the data-access file, shut Access down now. Then try double-clicking the `employees.htm` file in Windows Explorer again.

This time you should see it appear in Internet Explorer, as shown in Figure 5-14. You've made a connection between your Access database and a Web browser; users can manipulate this database from the Internet.

Title:	Sales Representative
Title Of Courtesy	Ms.
Birth Date	08-Dec-1968
Hire Date	01-May-1992
Address:	507 - 20th Ave. E.
City:	Seattle
Region:	WA
Postal Code	98122
Country:	USA
Home Phone	(206) 555-9857
Extension:	5467
Photo:	EmpID1.bmp
Notes:	Education includes a BA in psychology from Colorado State University. She also completed "The Art of the Cold Call." Nancy is a member of Toastmasters
Reports To	2

Figure 5-14: Make a connection between your Access database and a Web browser.

Experiment a bit with the database records by trying some of the manipulation and maneuvering tools on the toolstrip at the bottom of the Web page.

Also, to give yourself a thrilling yet frightening treat, right-click the background of the Web browser and choose View Source from the context menu. You now see the enormous amount of HTML that's been created for you. This is why I said earlier that creating database-connected Web pages (indeed pretty much *any* kind of a Web page) used to be HTML hell. Imagine having to write this stuff by hand, as people used to do.

Also notice that buried in the HTML code is a `Data Access` control as well as the various parameters that it uses, including the Northwind sample database, the Jet database engine, and various security settings. Here is the portion of the HTML that defines the control:

```
<OBJECT id=MSODSC tabIndex=-1
classid=CLSID:0002E553-0000-0000-C000-000000000046>
<PARAM NAME="XMLData" VALUE="<xml xmlns:a=&quot;urn:schemas-
   microsoft-com:office:access&quot;>&#13;&#10;
   <a:DataSourceControl>&#13;&#10;  <a:OWCVersion>10.0.0.5605
   </a:OWCVersion>&#13;&#10;
   <a:ConnectionString>Provider=Microsoft.Jet.OLEDB.4.0;User
ID=Admin;Data Source=C:\Program Files\Microsoft
Office\OFFICE11\SAMPLES\Northwind.mdb;Mode=Share Deny
None;Extended Properties=&amp;quot;&amp;quot;;Persist
Security Info=False;Jet OLEDB:System
database=&amp;quot;&amp;quot;;Jet OLEDB:Registry
Path=&amp;quot;&amp;quot;;Jet OLEDB:Database
Password=&amp;quot;&amp;quot;;Jet OLEDB:Engine Type=0;Jet
OLEDB:Database Locking Mode=1;Jet OLEDB:Global Partial
Bulk Ops=2;Jet OLEDB:Global Bulk Transactions=1;Jet
OLEDB:New Database Password=&amp;quot;&amp;quot;;Jet
OLEDB:Create System Database=False;Jet OLEDB:Encrypt
Database=False;Jet OLEDB:Don't Copy Locale on
Compact=False;Jet OLEDB:Compact Without Replica
Repair=False;Jet
OLEDB:SFP=False</a:ConnectionString>&#13;&#10;
```

Security: Locks on Top of Locks

Always an interesting topic (to some of us anyway), security takes many forms in today's computers. Layers upon layers of technology exist these days, all trying to save us from intruders, probes, spies, and virii of various kinds. Security initiatives today have become rather overdone. Like doors you see in New York City apartments, there are locks upon locks, sliders, chains, multiple bolts . . . as if quantity were quality.

Of course, if you take a few, easy common-sense precautions, you have nothing much to fear. If you simply back up your documents frequently, refuse to open e-mail attachments or execute programs from unknown sources, and use a firewall when connected to the Internet, you're in little real danger from anything that the big, bad hackers and whackers can do to your machine.

Nonetheless, it's annoying to get spied on or have to reinstall your applications after a virus attack. Most careful people never experience a virus attack in their personal computers at home, but the danger in lost productivity in office situations is clear. And the more connectivity (the more people online at an office intranet for example), the more likely that someone in the office will be dumb enough to try to open an e-mail attachment named BIGFUN.EXE or something and infect the whole place.

With .NET, and the general thrust to make security a priority, security initiatives are flowing freely into every level of computation. This isn't merely a Microsoft phenomenon — almost everyone selling anything related to computing has security on the mind (and in the advertising). It's almost enough to make one bemused.

Securing databases

If you create a direct connection between a database and an Internet Web page by using the data-access page feature in Access, any visitor to this page can alter or delete records. Think about it. You've exposed your quivering hard drive to the depredations of the world's bad guys.

In the earlier section, "Securing a Spreadsheet: Protecting Cells," I show you how to post an Excel spreadsheet to the Internet and selectively specify some or all cells as read- only, thus preventing users from making any changes to it.

Likewise, you can protect databases in a variety of ways — everything from encrypting the data so users can't see what they shouldn't see to employing user-permissions (Tools⇨Security⇨User and Group Permissions) or passwords so that only authorized people get to look at the data — and perhaps only a subset of those people are given full permissions so they are able to actually modify the data.

An easy way to manage user-level security settings is to select the main database window and then choose Tools⇨Security⇨User-level Security Wizard.

If you assign a password to a database file, only people whom you tell the secret password are able to open it. After they're in, though, they're completely in and can do whatever they want (unless you've separately specified user-level security permissions), so passwords by themselves are sometimes an all-or-nothing approach. You can password-protect only .mdb database files (see the upcoming section, "Protecting your code," for the scoop on .mdb's cousin, .mbe.) Follow these steps:

1. **Choose File⇨Open in Access.**

The Open dialog box opens.

Here's a weird UI feature. The Open button on the lower right of this dialog box has a drop-down feature. A little arrow on it. This is the first time I've ever seen a drop-down *button* — but you never know. Somebody thought this unique approach was clever or something. Baffles me.

2. **Click an** .mdb **file in the Open dialog box to select it.**

3. **Click the down-arrow icon on the Open button, as shown in Figure 5-15.**

**Book II
Chapter 5**

**Moving
to the Internet**

Figure 5-15:
This odd
drop-down
button
offers
various
ways to
open a
database
file.

4. **Choose Open Exclusive in the drop-down button list.**

5. **Choose Tools⇨Security⇨Set Database Password.**

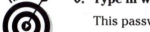

6. **Type in whatever password you want to use.**

This password is case-sensitive.

You can remove passwords by choosing Tools⇨Security⇨Unset Database Password.

Protecting data-access pages

In Book VIII, Chapter 7, I cover various Office 2003 security features in depth. For now, be aware that you can protect a data-access page by opening it in design view. (Choose View⇨Design View with the data-access page selected.) Right-click the section bar in the group that you want to make read-only. Then, from the context menu, choose GroupLevel Properties. The GroupLevel Properties dialog box appears, as shown in Figure 5-16.

GroupLevel : Employees		
All		
AllowAdditions	True	▼
AllowDeletions	True	
AllowEdits	True	
AlternateRowColor		
CaptionSection	False	
DataPageSize	1	
DefaultSort		
ExpandedByDefault	False	
GroupFilterControl		
GroupFilterField		
GroupFooter	False	
GroupHeader	True	
RecordNavigationSection	True	
RecordSelector	False	

Figure 5-16:
Protect
elements in
data access
pages in this
dialog box.

In the GroupLevel Properties dialog box, enable whatever kinds of protection you want to enforce: forbid additions, deletions, editing, or any combination of these permissions.

Protecting your code

Another aspect of security is protecting the programming that you do from others. Perhaps you've come up with an excellent solution that you want to hide from prying eyes. Or perhaps you just want to hide the code so others won't mess around with it and introduce bugs.

You can save an `.mdb` file in a different format (`.mde`; the *e* is for *encrypted*). Similarly, you can also transform `.adp` files into `.ade` files.

When saved as an `.mde` file, all your VBA modules are *compiled* (turned into machine language executables), and your readable source code (what you see when programming in the VBA editor) is removed. As a result, people can execute — but not read (or modify) — your VBA programming. This kind of security is pretty efficient. You don't have to subdivide your users into various levels of permissions, or manage passwords, and so on. You're just giving out the executable and not letting anyone into the source code that generates the executable. Users of `.mde` files can't use design view to import, export, or modify forms, reports, source code, or modules. Nor can they add, remove, or modify references to databases or code libraries. They can't even open the Object Browser. (Data access pages, tables, queries, and macros can, however, still be imported from, or exported to, databases that are not saved in the .mde format.)

Say you've written some VBA code in Access, and you don't want others viewing your macros or programs. Here's how to transform an unprotected Access database into an `.mde` database:

1. **Open your** `.mdb` **or** `.adp` **file and ensure that no one else on the network is currently viewing it.**

2. **Choose Tools➪Database Utilities➪Make MDE File.**

   If Access finds that you're trying to save an Access 2000 database in the `.mde` format, it informs you that the database must first be converted into an Access 2003 version. To do so, click the Main database window to select it, and then choose Tools➪Database Utilities➪Convert Database.

   The Save dialog box opens.

3. **Specify where you want the new database saved; then click Save.**

   The new `.mde` or `.ade` file is saved.

Your original `.mdb` or `.adp` file still remains on the hard drive. It's not deleted because you might want to modify it later, so you should keep your original in a secure place. Note that you can't revert an `.mde` or `.ade` database back into an `.mdb` or `.adp` version. Also be aware that you'll run into versioning problems if people have been modifying data in an `.mde` or `.ade` version, and then you want to make some changes to, say, a macro. You can't easily reconcile the versions.

**Book II
Chapter 5**

Moving
to the Internet

Chapter 6: Debugging

In This Chapter

✔ Handling typos

✔ Trapping errors within code

✔ Locating logic errors

✔ Using step-throughs, watches, and other debugging techniques

*B*ugs — errors in a computer program — are inevitable. You can be enormously painstaking, tidy, and thoughtful, but if your program is more than 50 lines long, errors are likely to occur. If it's longer than 100 lines, errors are virtually certain.

Macros are short enough that you might create five or six of them without a bug, but odds are that you won't. One reason, though, that short programs like macros are easier to write bug-free (aside from the obvious point that there's simply less code to err in) is that much of the job of debugging long programs is the work you must invest finding and fixing the very worst bugs (logic bugs). You'll spend a lot of time just figuring out *where* the little critters are. Locating bugs in large programs is usually much more difficult than actually fixing them. Most macros, though, are small enough that you already know where the bug is: It's right there in the few lines of code that you're staring at.

However, if you write programs in VB.NET (as I describe in several chapters in Book VIII), you'll have more code to look through. To debug longer programs, you want to avail yourself of several of the tools like *watches,* as I describe here, that help you track down exactly which line contains the bug.

Roll up your sleeves and see what tools the VBA and .NET editors offer for those who need to track bugs down and kill them dead. Because VBA programmers stand astride two different languages — classic Visual Basic represented by VBA, and the future of BASIC, VB.NET — this chapter covers the error-trapping techniques available in both languages. If you're not ready to transition to .NET just yet, simply ignore the comments applicable to that language.

Errors in computer programming fall into three primary categories:

✦ Typographical errors (includes syntax errors)

✦ Runtime errors

✦ Logic errors

I deal with each in turn, starting with typos, which are the easiest. Logic errors are the toughest.

Fortunately for us programmers, Visual Basic (VB) editors provide a powerful suite of tools to help you track down and eliminate bugs. Basic programmers have been the envy of the programming community for years. However, with the arrival of Visual Studio .NET, all supported languages (namely C and its derived daughter languages) now share the same editor (Integrated Design Environment; IDE) and, therefore, the other languages have finally caught up.

Typos in Commands and Variables

Typos are the easiest errors to locate and correct. For example, Visual Basic knows at once if you mistakenly type `Prjnt` instead of `Print`. If it doesn't recognize the word, it detects that kind of error and alerts you. When you give VB an impossible command like `Prjnt`, VB realizes that it can't do anything with that line of code because that word just isn't in the language's vocabulary.

VB also lets you know if you have a typo in a variable name. Typing an `Option Explicit` in the top of the code window forces you to explicitly declare all variables. This has the effect of preventing a particular kind of typo: If you misspell the name of a variable, an error message will warn you that the variable has not been declared. This alerts you that you've made a typo.

Command Name Errors as Typos

Perhaps you didn't mistype something but instead mistakenly thought that VB knew a command that it doesn't know. For example, type in the command `Pass the Salt`:

```
Sub Whaaa()

    Pass the Salt

End Sub
```

As soon as you press Enter after typing **Salt**, you have an error. VB expects to see a command at the start of that line, and `Pass` is not part of the list of commands that VB understands. To help you find your error, that line of code turns red (in the VB editor) or is underlined (in the .NET editor). (In .NET, VB also displays its best guess as to the nature of the problem in its Task List window, although the suggestions can be a bit vague.)

If you press F5 to run the `Pass the Salt` code, VB displays a message box informing you of compile or build errors. You can ask for Help in the VBA error message box, but it, too, is a bit vague, reporting in this case that the problem might be punctuation, a misnamed procedure, misspelling, and several other possibilities.

Understanding Syntax Errors

Related to typographical errors are syntax errors. Computer languages can be snippy little schoolmarms when it comes to correct punctuation. And languages don't tolerate it when you leave out required arguments or put them in the wrong order.

VB expects correct punctuation. This line — `UserForm1..BackColor = Blue` — will trigger a syntax error because there's no double-period punctuation in VB's Little Book of Correct Punctuation.

Another kind of error is when you don't provide the right type of information, or enough information, for VB to carry out a command:

```
CommandButton1.Top
```

The information in this statement is incomplete. You've given only the name of a control (`CommandButton1`) and one of its properties (`Top`), but you haven't provided the information that tells the `Top` method which location you want it to move to. That's as incomplete a statement as an English sentence like *Mary's Hair.*

A third variety of easily detected (and easily fixed) error is an inconsistency of some kind between parts of your program. For example, if you have a procedure that expects an argument, like the following:

```
Sub MultiBeep(numbeeps)
    For counter = 1 To numbeeps
        Beep
    Next counter
End Sub
```

and you try to call it but give no argument:

```
MultiBeep
```

VBA catches the error right away, displaying this message: `Argument Not Optional`. (.NET displays this somewhat more complete message: `No argument specified for non-optional parameter "numbeeps"`)

 If you have the AutoListMembers option selected in Tools⇨Options⇨Editor (or in .NET: Tools⇨Options⇨Text Editor⇨All Languages), VB displays the argument list for any procedure that you're trying to call. This happens as soon as you type the left parenthesis following the procedure's name. Of course, if you don't type any left parenthesis, this doesn't happen.

Handling Runtime Errors

Some errors occur only during runtime. Your code is valid code with no typos or syntax errors, but something unexpected happens when the program is running. This is often a problem related to contacting a peripheral, such as a hard drive. For example, if the user has no diskette in Drive A:, and your program executes this code:

```
Documents.Open "a:\test.doc" 'VBA
```

or the .NET version:

```
Open(5, "A:\Test.doc", OpenMode.Input) '.NET
```

VBA puts up an error message telling you that the file can't be found. VB.NET is somewhat more technical in its error message: `An unhandled exception of type 'System IO.IOException' occurred` and so on.

VBA's error message lets you choose between four buttons: Continue, End, Debug, and Help. .NET's buttons are Break, Continue, Ignore, and Help.

You need to prevent, or at least gracefully handle, runtime errors. It's no good having a smoothly running program that suddenly halts if the user has, say, forgotten to put a disk into Drive A: or failed to close the drive door.

How Runtime Errors Occur

Runtime errors include various kinds of unexpected situations that can come up when the program is running. While you're writing the program, there are a number of things you can't know in advance about the user's system. For example, how large is the disk drive? Is it already so full that when your program tries to save a file, there won't be enough room? Are you creating an array so large that it exceeds the computer's available memory? Is the printer turned off, but the user tries to print anyway?

Whenever your program is attempting to interact with an entity outside the program — the user's input, disk drives, Clipboard, RAM — you need to take precautions by using the `On Error` (VBA) or `Try...End Try` (.NET) structures. These structures enable your program to deal effectively with the unexpected while it runs.

Unfortunately, your program can't correct many runtime errors. For instance, you can only let the user know that his or her disk drive is nearly full. The user will have to remedy this kind of problem; you can't fix it with your code.

Using On Error or Try...End Try

If a runtime error can occur, you should use the `On Error` or `Try` commands to trap the error. If you don't use these error-trapping commands, Visual Basic will provide an error message to the user (which might be very confusing to the user), and VB might have to shut down your VB program as well. This scares the wits out of new users. They sometimes think they've broken the computer. Here's a comparison of the traditional (VBA) `On Error` error-trapping technique and the more advanced `Try` technique (.NET).

Using On Error (VBA)

.NET permits you to use the classic `On Error` technique: You don't have to revise this aspect of your older programs. However, for new programs that you write in VB.NET, you might want to consider the possibility that a superior error-trapping and handling approach exists. It's called *structured* error handling, which implies that your familiar, classic VBA error handling is . . . well . . . unstructured.

However, if you try to write some traditional VBA like `If Err Then`, you'll be informed that VB.NET doesn't permit the `ErrObject` to be treated as Boolean (`True`/`False`). But where there's a will, there's a way. You can test the `Err` object's number property. If you want to test the `Err` object within an `If...Then` structure, use this VB.NET code:

```
x = CInt(textbox1.Text)

If err.Number <> 0 Then

    textbox1.Text = "You must enter a number..."

End If
```

Consider first the classic VBA On Error syntax. Because there is no Drive Z:, the following input causes an error:

```
Sub Mungo()
    Open "Z:\MYFILE" For Output As #1
    Print #1, x
    Close #1
End Sub
```

When this macro runs, a Path Not Found message will appear. Many users will be baffled; some will undoubtedly go into a deep depression. Only experienced programmers or users will understand what Path Not Found means. However, if you modify the macro to insert an error handling structure, you can provide a more helpful message of your own and also make the program continue to run rather than shut down:

```
Sub SaveIt()

On Error Resume Next

Open "Z:\MYFILE" For Output As #1

If Err Then
MsgBox (Error(Err)) & ". There was a problem with the disk
    drive. Perhaps there is no Drive Z on your system?"
Close
Exit Sub
End If

Print #1, X
Close #1

End Sub
```

When this disk access fails, the user sees the helpful, custom error message shown in Figure 6-1 instead of VBA's cryptic, scary Path Not Found default message.

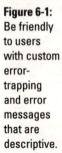

Figure 6-1:
Be friendly to users with custom error-trapping and error messages that are descriptive.

Notice in the above code that you put an `On Error Resume Next` command at the start of a procedure where you suspect that a runtime error might occur (such as contacting a peripheral like the disk drive). This command tells VB to not shut down the program if an error occurs. Rather, it should resume execution of the next line of code following the error.

You then place the line that starts handling the error (`If Err Then`) just following the possible error (`Open Z:`). This code is sometimes called an *error handler* or an *error trap*. The point is that you are saying this: If the `Err` variable contains some value other than 0, there is an error. Consequently, you must do something about that error in your code between the `If Err` and the `End If`, as I did in the preceding example. The `Error(Err)` command feeds the error code (`Err`) to the `Error` function — and you get back a text description of the error.

The VB.NET version: Structured trapping

If you're writing a .NET program, consider using the new `Try...Catch... Finally` structure rather than VBA's `On Error`:

```
Sub TryError()


    Try

Microsoft.VisualBasic.FileOpen(5, "A:\Test.Txt",
    OpenMode.Input)

        Catch er As Exception
            MessageBox.Show(er.ToString)
        Finally

        End Try



End Sub
```

Code between the `Try` and `End Try` commands is watched for errors. You can use the generic `Exception` (which will catch any error) or merely trap a specific exception such as the following:

```
Catch er As DivideByZeroException
```

The term *exception* is used in C-like languages (and now in VB.NET) to mean *error*. It sounds better, more PC, and certainly less embarrassing to tell the boss, "I have a couple of exceptions in my program" rather than "I have a couple of errors."

I use `er` in this example, but you can use any valid variable name for the error. Or you can leave that variable out entirely and just use `Catch`, like this:

```
Try
    Microsoft.VisualBasic.FileOpen(5, "A:\Test.Txt", OpenMode.Input)

Catch
    MessageBox.Show("problem")
Finally

End Try
```

When Catch executes

If an error occurs during execution of the source code in the `Try` section, the following `Catch` section is then executed. You must include at least one `Catch` section, but there can be many such sections if you need them to test and figure out which particular error occurred. A series of `Catch` sections is similar to the `Case` sections in `Select Case` structures. The `Catch` sections are tested in order, and only one `Catch` block (or none) is executed for any particular error.

You can use a `When` clause to further specify which kind of error you want to trap, like this:

```
Dim Y as Integer
Try

Y = Y / 0
Catch When y = 0
    MessageBox.Show("Y = 0")
End Try
```

Or you can specify a particular kind of exception, thereby narrowing the number of errors that will trigger this `Catch` section's execution:

```
Catch er As ArithmeticException
    MessageBox.Show("Math error.")
Catch When y = 0
    MessageBox.Show("Y = 0")

End Try
```

To see a list of the specific exceptions, use VB.NET's menu Debug⇨Windows⇨ Exceptions and then expand the Common Language Runtime exceptions. You might have to do a bit of hunting. For instance, the `FileNotFound` error is located two expansions down in the hierarchy: Common Language Runtime⇨ SystemException⇨IOException. So you have to expand all three nodes (click the + next to each) in order to finally find `FileNotFoundException`.

Also notice in the Exceptions window that you can cause the program to ignore any of the exceptions. (Select the Continue radio button in the Exceptions window.) This is the equivalent of `On Error Resume Next` in older versions of BASIC such as VBA or VB 6.

Here is a list of common errors that you can trap in VB.NET. The following errors are in the `System` namespace:

```
AppDomainUnloadedException, ApplicationException,
ArgumentException, ArgumentNullException,
ArgumentOutOfRangeException, ArithmeticException,
ArrayTypeMismatchException, BadImageFormatException,
Can'tUnloadAppDomainException, ContextMarshalException,
DivideByZeroException, DllNotFoundException,
DuplicateWaitObjectException, EntryPointNotFoundException,
Exception, ExecutionEngineException, FieldAccessException,
FormatException, IndexOutOfRangeException, InvalidCastException,
InvalidOperationException, InvalidProgramException,
MemberAccessException, MethodAccessException,
MissingFieldException, MissingMemberException,
MissingMethodException, MulticastNotSupportedException,
NotFiniteNumberException, NotImplementedException,
NotSupportedException, NullReferenceException,
OutOfMemoryException, OverflowException,
PlatformNotSupportedException, RankException,
ServicedComponentException, StackOverflowException,
SystemException, TypeInitializationException, TypeLoadException,
TypeUnloadedException, UnauthorizedAccessException,
UnhandledExceptionEventArgs, UnhandledExceptionEventHandler,
UriFormatException, WeakReferenceException.
```

The following errors are in the `SystemIO` category:

```
DirectoryNotFoundException, EndOfStreamException,
FileNotFoundException, InternalBufferOverflowException,
IOException, PathTooLongException.
```

You can list as many `Catch` phrases as you want and respond individually to them. You can respond by notifying the user as in the previous example or merely by quietly fixing the error in your source code following the `Catch`. You can also provide a brief error message with the following:

```
e.Message
```

Or, as in the previous example, use the following fully qualified error message:

```
e.ToString
```

Here's the full `Try...Catch...Finally` structure's syntax:

```
Try
    tryStatements

[Catch [exception [As type]] [When expression]
    catchStatements

[Exit Try]

Catch [exception [As type]] [When expression]
    catchStatements

[Exit Try]

. . .

Catch [exception [As type]] [When expression]
    catchStatements]

[Exit Try]

[Finally
    finallyStatements]

End Try
```

Recall that following the `Try` block, you list one or more `Catch` statements. A `Catch` statement can include a variable name and an `As` clause defining the type of exception or the general *all errors,* `As Exception` (er `As Exception`). For example, here's how to trap all exceptions:

```
Try
Microsoft.VisualBasic.FileOpen(5, "A:\Test.Txt", OpenMode.Input)

Catch e As Exception

    'Respond to any kind of error.

Finally

End Try
```

And here is how to respond to the specific `File Not Found` error:

```
Try

Microsoft.VisualBasic.FileOpen(5, "A:\Test.Txt", OpenMode.Input)

Catch FileNotFoundE As FileNotFoundException

    'Respond to this particular error here, perhaps a messagebox to alert the
    user.


Finally


End Try
```

An optional `Exit Try` statement causes program flow to leap out of the `Try` structure and to continue execution with whatever follows the `End Try` statement.

Using Finally

The `Finally` statement should contain any code that you want executed after error processing has been completed. Any code in the `Finally` statement is always executed, no matter what happens (unlike source code following the `End Try` line, which might or might not execute, depending on how things go within the `Try` structure). Therefore, the most common use for the `Finally` section is to free up resources that were acquired within the `Try` block. For example, if you were to acquire a Mutex lock within your `Try` block, you would want to release that lock when you were done with it, regardless of whether the `Try` block exited with a successful completion or an exception (error). It's typical to find this kind of code within the `Finally` block:

```
objMainKey.Close()
objFileRead.Close()
objFilename.Close()
```

Use this approach when you want to close, for instance, an object reference to a key in the Registry, or to close file references that were opened during the `Try` section (block) of code.

Mutex means *mutual exclusion object*. A Mutex object can help direct traffic when more than one thread attempts to access a file or other resource. When a thread makes a connection to the shared resource, it locks the Mutex. It's unlocked when the connection is no longer needed. Then other threads are free to make their connections in the same lock/unlock fashion.

Here's how source code that you put within the Finally section differs from source code you put following the End Try line.

If there *is* an error, here is the order in which code execution takes place:

1. Try section.

2. Catch section. (The Catch section that traps this error.)

3. Finally section.

If *no* error occurs, here is the execution order:

1. Try section

2. Finally section

3. Source code following the End Try line

Even if a Catch section has an Exit Sub command, the Finally section nevertheless will still be executed. Remember that Finally is *always* executed. However, the Exit Sub does get executed just after the Finally block.

Tracking Down Logic Errors

The third major category of programming bugs — logic errors — is usually the most difficult of all to find and fix.

Some can be so sinister, so well concealed, that you think you will be driven mad trying to find the source of the problem within your code. BASIC programming editors devote most of their debugging features and resources to assisting you in locating logic errors.

A logic error occurs even though you made no typos, followed all the rules of syntax, and otherwise satisfied Visual Basic so that your commands can be carried out. You and VB think everything is shipshape. However, when you run the program, things go wrong: Say, the entire screen turns black, or every time the user enters $10, your program changes it to $1,000.

BASIC's set of debugging tools help you track down the problem. The key to fixing logic errors is finding out *where* in your program the problem is located. Which line of code (or multiple lines interacting) causes the problem?

Some computer languages have an elaborate debugging apparatus, sometimes even including the use of two computer monitors: One shows the program as the user sees it; the other shows the lines of programming that match the running program. Using two computers is a good approach because when you're debugging logic errors, usually your main job is to figure out where the code is that's causing the problem.

It's not that you don't notice the symptoms: Every time the user enters a number, the results are way, way off. You know that somewhere your program is mangling the numbers — but until you X-ray the program, you often can't find out where the problem is located.

The watchful voyeur technique

Many logic errors are best tracked down by watching the contents of a variable (or variables). Something is going wrong somewhere, and you want to keep an eye on a variable to find out just where its value changes and goes bad.

Some of VB's best debugging tools help you keep an eye on the status of your variables. Type in a simple VBA macro, like this:

```
Sub Adder()

        Dim a As Double, b As Double

        a = 112

        b = a / 2

        b = b + 6

End Sub
```

Now press F8 once to take your first step into the macro. After you press F8 to take that first step, make the watch window visible: Choose Debug⇨ Add Watch (VBA) or Debug⇨Windows and select the Locals, Watch, and Immediate windows (.NET). Open the Immediate and Locals windows in VBA from the View menu.

Each time that you press F8 to execute the next line of code (called *single-stepping,* or *step into*), the program again goes into *break mode* (paused in its execution).

The .NET Watch and Locals windows share the same space, and you can switch between them by clicking the tabs on the bottom of their shared window.

In VBA's Add Watch dialog box, type **b** in the Expression field and then click OK to close the dialog box. This tells VBA to display the contents of variable b while the program is executing, while you're stepping through it, or while in break mode.

Press F8 several times to step through the code lines and keep an eye on the value in variable b, as shown in Figure 6-2.

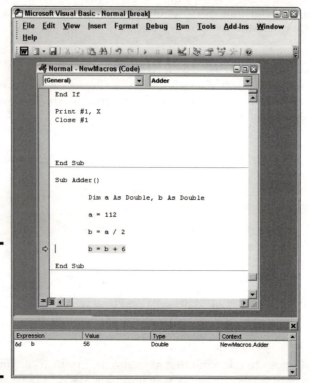

Figure 6-2:
The Watch window displays a variable's value while you're debugging.

In the .NET Locals window, you see the contents of all variables that have been declared within the currently executing procedure.

Also take a look at the Immediate window. In this window, you can directly query or modify variables, or expressions. To find out the value in variable b, for instance, just type the following into the Immediate window and then press Enter:

```
? b
```

The answer — whatever value b currently holds while you're in break mode — will be printed in the Immediate window. (The ? command is short-hand for the Print command.)

If you want to experiment and actually change the value in a variable during break mode, delete the number in the Value column in the .NET Locals or Watch windows, and then type in your new value. You can also launch and test procedures (events, Subs, or Functions) by typing their names and pressing Enter. VB.NET will execute the procedure and then halt again. This is a good way to feed variables to a suspect procedure and watch it (and it alone) absorb those variables to see if things are going awry within that procedure.

Book II
Chapter 6

Debugging

Using Debug.Write or Debug.Print

Some .NET programmers like to insert Debug.Print (or Console.Write in .NET) commands at different locations within their code. (I don't because I find that approach rather clumsy compared to setting watches or break-points. For one thing, with these printing/writing statements, you have to spell out the location and variable name yourself in the printed message.) This also has the effect of displaying the contents of the variable b in the Output window. But in this case, you're causing the values in the variables that you choose to show to be displayed via code within your program. Try inserting some Debug.Write (*MyVariableName*) lines here and there in a VB.NET program, and then run the program and watch the results appear in the Output window.

Actually, you can type any executable commands that can be expressed on a single line into the Immediate window to watch their effects. Notice that this is all done while the VB program is halted during a run. You can test condi-tions from within the living program while it's in break (pause) mode. You can get into break mode several ways:

✦ Insert a Stop command into your code.

✦ Set a breakpoint (which I discuss later in the section, "Setting Breakpoints") in the code.

✦ Single-step (press F8).

✦ Choose Break from the Run menu (or the toolbar).

✦ Press Ctrl+Break.

The Add Watch Technique

The Locals window in .NET is fine for local variables, but what about form-wide or project-wide variables? Although they show up in the VBA Watch window, they don't in the Locals window.

To watch one of these other kinds of variables in .NET, put your program in break mode, right-click the variable you're interested in, and choose Add Watch from the context menu. You can alternatively select and then drag a variable from the code window, dropping it into the Watch window. Also, while you're in break mode, you can simply pause your mouse pointer over a variable to see its contents in a small box.

When you add a watch, VB keeps an eye on whatever expression(s) you've asked it to watch. You can watch a single variable, an expression, a property, or a procedure call. The Watch window shows the current status of any watched expressions.

In VBA but not .NET, the Watch window permits some highly useful debugging techniques, like conditionally halting the program (throwing it into break mode so you can examine variable values, see where the break occurred, and examine surrounding conditions). You can break when a condition becomes true (such as the variable I holding a value, say, larger than 44 $I > 44$) and other tests. This ability to break conditionally is, in VB.NET, part of the break-point debugging feature, which I discuss in the next section.

Setting Breakpoints

Sometimes you have a strong suspicion about which line, macro, form, or module contains the error you're hunting for. Instead of single-stepping through the entire code, you want to press F5 to execute the program at normal speed but then stop when execution enters the dubious form or procedure. After halting the program in a suspect region, you can start pressing F8 to single-step through each line.

Breakpoints can be one of the most useful debugging aids. You can certainly press Ctrl+Break and stop a running program in its tracks. But what if it's moving too fast to stop just where you want to look and check on things? What if it's alphabetizing a large list, for example, and you can't see what's happening? What if you want to specify a condition ($n = 1445$, for example) that triggers a break?

You can specify one or more breakpoints in your program. While running, the program will stop at a breakpoint just as if you had pressed Ctrl+Break (or if you've made the breakpoint conditional — it will break when that condition occurs).

When the IDE enters break mode, the code window pops up, showing you where the break occurred so that you can see or change the code, or single-step, or look at the Watch window or other debug windows to see the values in variables.

You set a breakpoint by clicking the gray margin to the left of the line in the code window where you want the break. A red dot appears in the gray margin. The red dot alerts you that a line of code is a breakpoint. Execution will halt on this line (or perhaps not if the breakpoint is conditional), and VB enters break mode. Click the red dot a second time to turn it off.

Setting conditional breakpoints in VBA

Try creating a conditional breakpoint in VBA. For this example, you can use the code you created in the previous section. Say that you want to halt execution when the variable counter is greater than 1,000. Follow these steps to make this code break execution when this condition occurs:

1. **Click the gray margin to the left of the line that you want to break on (the** For **line, for example, as shown in Figure 6-3).**

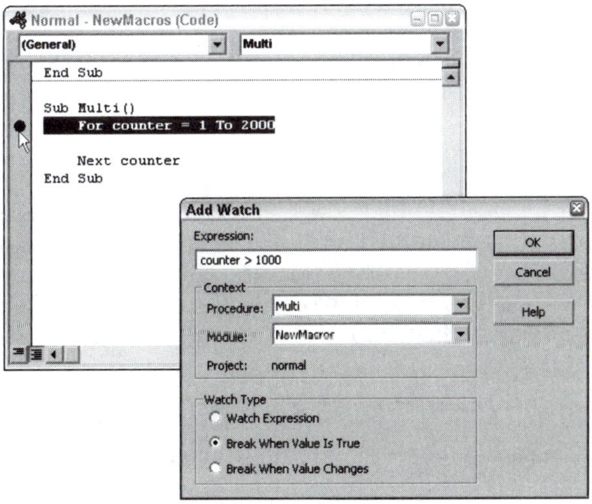

Figure 6-3:
The line is highlighted, and a dot appears in the margin — both signaling the location of a breakpoint.

A red dot appears where you clicked, and also the line of code is high-lighted where the breakpoint is set.

2. **Right-click the breakpoint line.**

3. **From the context menu that appears, choose Add Watch.**

The Add Watch dialog box opens.

4. **Type** counter > 1000 **into the Expression field.**

This is your condition that will trigger the break.

5. **Select the Break When Value Is True radio button.**

This means *break when the expression becomes true.*

6. **Click OK.**

The dialog box closes, and the breakpoint is now conditional on the value of the counter variable increasing above 1,000.

7. **Choose View➪Watch to open the Watch window and then press F5 to execute the procedure. Press F5 twice if necessary.**

The loop executes and then halts when the variable reaches 1001. The Value column in the Watch window turns from False to True.

Another use for breakpoints is when you suspect that the program is *not* running some lines of code. Sometimes a logic error is caused because you think that a subroutine, a function, or an event is getting executed, but the program never reaches that procedure. Whatever condition is supposed to activate that area of the program never occurs.

To find out whether (as you suspect) a particular event is never executing, set a breakpoint on the first line of code within that procedure. Then, when you run your program — and the breakpoint never halts execution — you have proven that this procedure is never called.

Sometimes you set several breakpoints in your code that you later want to delete because you've fixed the bug. If you've set a lot of breakpoints, the Clear All Breakpoints (Ctrl+Shift+F9) feature allows you to get rid of all of them at once without having to hunt them all down and toggle each one off individually by locating them and then clicking their red dot.

Setting conditional breakpoints in .NET

I use an example earlier in this chapter in which $10 grew to $1,000 for no good reason. If something like this happens to you, you'd obviously want to find out where that happened in your code. You could add breakpoints to stop the program when $10 grows larger than, say, $200 (that's your *condition*). Then, while the program is running and $10 is transformed into $1,000 — your logic error — VB halts the program and shows you exactly where this problem is located.

Type this code into the VB.NET editor:

```
Private Sub Button1_Click(ByVal sender As System.Object,
    ByVal e As System.EventArgs) Handles Button1.Click

        Static moneyvariable = 55
        moneyvariable = moneyvariable + 44


End Sub
```

To set a conditional breakpoint, go to the line in this procedure where `moneyvariable` is increased by 44. Click in the gray area to the left of that line of code. The red dot appears, and the line is changed to a red color as well. Right-click the red part of the line (*not* the red dot) and choose BreakPoint Properties from the content menu that pops out.

Click the Condition button in the BreakPoint Properties dialog box. In the BreakPoint Condition dialog box that appears, type your condition that will trigger the break: that is, `moneyvariable > 200`, when this variable goes above 200.

Press F5 and keep clicking Button1 five times. Then your variable will have exceeded the conditional value, and the editor will enter break mode. You can specify any kind of condition by using the Is True, Has Changed, or Hit Count options in the BreakPoint Properties dialog box.

Alternative Debugging Strategies

You likely noticed several other tools on the Debug menu. Although they're not as widely useful as breakpoints, single-stepping, or watches, when you need these lesser tools, you'll be glad that they're available. Here's a brief survey of the minor debuggers.

Step Over

`Step Over` is the same as single-stepping (pressing F8) except that if you're about to single-step into a procedure, `Step Over` ignores the procedure. No procedure calls will be carried out. All other commands will be executed. If you're single-stepping (pressing F8 repeatedly) and you come upon a procedure that you know isn't the location of the bug, press Shift+F10 on that line to step over the entire procedure, ignoring it entirely. This option gets you past areas in your program that you know are free of bugs and would take a lot of single-stepping to get through.

Keyboard shortcut: In VBA, press Shift+F8. In .NET, press Shift+10.

Step Out

You must be in break mode for the `Step Out` feature to work. It executes the remaining lines of the procedure that you're currently in, but it stops on the next line in the program (following the current procedure). Use this to quickly get past a procedure that you don't want to single-step through.

Keyboard shortcut: Press Ctrl+Shift+F8.

Run to Cursor

To use the `Run to Cursor` option, click somewhere in your code other than the line on which VB currently stopped. (You're moving the insertion cursor to a different line of code.) VB remembers both the original line and the new line where the insertion cursor now resides. Choose the `Run to Cursor` option, and the code between the original and new locations is executed quickly. This is a useful trick when you come upon, for example, a really large `For...Next` loop. You want to get past this loop quickly rather than waste all the time it would take to complete the loop by pressing F8 over and over. Just click a program line past the loop and then use the `Run to Cursor` feature. VB executes the loop at normal execution speed and then halts at the code following the loop. You can now resume stepping from there.

Keyboard shortcut: In VBA, press Ctrl+F8. In .NET, press Ctrl+10.

Set Next Statement

You must be in break mode to use this. With the `Set Next Statement` feature, you can move anywhere in the current procedure and restart execution from there. (It's the inverse of the `Run To Cursor` feature described above.) While the program is in break mode, go to the new location where you want to start execution from, and then click the new line of code where you want to resume execution. Now, pressing F8 will single-step from that new location forward in the program. This is how you skip over a line or lines of code. Say that you know that things are fine for several lines, but you suspect other lines further down. Move down by using `Set Next Statement` and start single-stepping again.

Keyboard shortcut: In VBA, press Ctrl+F9. In .NET, press Ctrl+Shift+10.

Show Next Statement

If you've been moving around in your program's code, looking in various events, you might have forgotten where in the program the next single-step will take place. Pressing F8 would show you quickly enough, but you might want to get back there without actually executing the next line. Show Next Statement moves you in the code window to the next line in the program that will be executed, but doesn't execute it. This way, you can look at the code before proceeding.

Keyboard shortcut: None.

Call Stack

The Call Stack feature is on the View menu in VBA, and the Debug⤵ Windows menu in .NET. Call Stack provides a list of still-active procedures if the running VB program went into break mode while within a procedure that had been called (invoked) by another procedure. Procedures can be *nested:* That is, one can call on the services of another, which, in turn, calls yet another. The Call Stack option shows you the name of the procedure that called the current procedure. And if that calling procedure was itself called by yet another procedure, Call Stack shows you the complete history of what is calling what.

Keyboard shortcut: None.

Book III

Maximizing Word

The 5th Wave   By Rich Tennant

"OK, TECHNICALLY THIS SHOULD WORK, JUDY, TYPE THE WORD, 'GOODYEAR' ALL CAPS, BOLDFACE, AT 700-POINT TYPE SIZE."

Contents at a Glance

Chapter 1: The Word Object Model

In This Chapter

- Beginning with the `Application` **object**
- Programming with `Document` **objects**
- Accessing enumerations
- Understanding ranges and selections
- Using bookmarks
- Handling events

The terms *object model* or *class hierarchy* refer to the system of categorization that is used to try to organize a set of classes into some meaningful arrangement. For example, the `Application` object is the largest object in Office applications. It contains many other objects, such as ranges, selections, toolbars, and so on.

In practical terms, the outermost (or largest container) object is often simply left out of coding; it's understood, so it's only optional. Lesser objects, such as a document, paragraph, or selection are contained within each other, like nested Russian eggs. These lesser objects must be named in your code (although `Document` is sometimes omitted).

In this chapter, you wrestle with the dodgy concepts of objects and object variables, and also see how some useful objects can be used to search and otherwise manipulate Word documents.

Understanding Objects

Objects are slippery things. Born of and nurtured by academic theoreticians, the idea of object-oriented programming (OOP) has spread throughout the computer world. Whether you consider this a good thing is beside the point; OOP is as pervasive among today's programmers as alchemy was in the Middle Ages. If you call yourself a programmer, you must deal with objects. You don't have to create them in your programming: Classes can be entirely left out in favor of simpler, shorter procedure-based programming techniques. VBA, VB 6, and all earlier versions of Visual Basic are only incidentally object-oriented.

However, if you wish to make use of the features built-into applications — and you certainly do — you must at least learn the fundamentals of OOP in order to employ the members of the classes (objects) that are *exposed* (you're allowed to use them) by Office 2003 applications. These members are properties and methods. *Properties* are generally qualities (similar to traditional variables); *methods* are just other names for what have always been called *procedures.* But you do need to learn the lingo and the syntax with which you instantiate an object and then access its members. You might never need to write your own classes when programming for Office 2003, but you'll certainly need to use the classes built into the Office suite of applications.

Objects are so widely used because professors mostly love the concept of OOP and have taught a generation of programmers to use them. In addition, when writing very large programs in groups (such as the people at Microsoft who collectively cobbled Excel together), OOP offers security/clerical benefits that traditional procedure-oriented programming does not.

However, objects do suffer from two undeniable weaknesses. The first is that they are not logical. How do you keep everything straight when everything is an object (as is true in the .NET languages)? In .NET, even an integer variable is an object. What good is the term *object?* What can it mean if it means everything? How much information do you convey if you describe everything with the word *thing?*

The second weakness is the fact that OOP nomenclature has little stability. The same object can be a collection, an object, and a property. For example, `Document` is an object in the Word object hierarchy, but it's simultaneously a collection of the current documents (`Documents`). The `Document` object has properties, yet it is also itself a property (of the `Application` object). This situation is more than simply amusing: It's as if biological classification had been designed by a bunch of drunk monks . . . as if a toad were classified as both land animal and fish. In a sense, this is vaguely accurate about toads — they are kind of intermediate — but how useful is a taxonomic system that can't effectively categorize any animal with any useful specificity?

Nonetheless, you're obligated to wrestle with the hierarchies and structures that OOP promotes, and programming in Office 2003 requires that you learn to work with objects and their members. You do want to be able to display dialogs, use the built-in search utility, and other features that are contained within the Office applications' class libraries.

As George Orwell said of communists, some are more equal than others. Some objects are more important than others. In Word, for instance, the `Application` object is the big one in hierarchical terms but is generally of little importance to programmers (unless you need to programmatically manipulate options, windows, views, and such).

The Application object is the object from which all other objects derive. However, you need not use it explicitly when programming the Document object in Word. (When contacting Word from outside applications, you do need to use an object variable referencing the Application object.)

In Word document programming, you can leave the Application object out of your code because derived objects such as the Document object are understood to be part of the application. Just as you don't have to say *America's California,* there's no other possibility.

Dissecting the Document

Much Word programming involves the Document object, the ActiveDocument object (the document with the focus — the one that you've been working with most recently) and the Documents collection (all currently open documents). You can be as granular as necessary because the Document object deconstructs into the components of a piece of writing: for example, a Paragraphs collection containing a Sentences collection containing a Words collection containing a Characters collection. Or so you would imagine. Read on.

You can retrieve the first paragraph in the first document by using this code:

```
Sub Gran()

    n = Documents(1).Paragraphs(1)
    MsgBox (n)

End Sub
```

This displays the first paragraph in the first document. However, you can't get the first word in that paragraph this way (as you logically would think):

```
n = Documents(1).Paragraphs(1).words(1)
```

Oops! (Get it, OOPs?) An error message appears: method or data member not found. With OOP, things aren't always what you might expect. The Words collection is a property of the Document object and not the Paragraphs object. Instead, use this, which searches in the ActiveDocument object of Document:

```
n = ActiveDocument.Words(5)
```

or

```
n = Documents(2).Words(5)
```

**Book III
Chapter 1**

**The Word
Object Model**

Note that the `Words` object is a property of various other objects, including the `Document`, `ActiveDocument`, and `Range` objects. Yet, to surprise us yet again, the `Characters` collection is a property of the `Words` collection and not the document:

```
n = Documents(2).Words(5).Characters(2)
```

So, you just never know. Patterns do exist, but they are unpredictable and vary from one application's object model to the next.

To keep your head from rolling off your shoulders when in OOP World, you must rely heavily on the *IntelliSense* (lists that pop out while you're writing code such as statement completion and AutoListMembers) in programming editors, Help, MSDN online, books that describe the object model, and perhaps to a lesser extent, the Object Browser.

Objects themselves aren't the problem. It's the inconsistencies and the randomness by which they are organized and manipulated in computer languages.

I can't think of an alternative to objects and the members that describe their capabilities and qualities. Indeed, what's best about working with objects is that you have the ability to manipulate essentially everything in an application. You can programmatically do pretty much anything a user can do with menus and toolbars and quite a bit that users can't do (such as directly redefining ordinary keys, like the accent grave key — as you'll see how to do at the end of Book III.) You'll also see why it's quite a useful adjustment to make to Word.

But the people — committees actually, as you might expect — who are designing the system are so terribly inconsistent. I'd use the word *blithe* to describe the general approach to classification.

So my advice is to approach objects deductively rather than inductively. Don't try to sit there like a philosopher and say, well, *logically,* the `Words` collection must be a property of the `Paragraph` object. Be deductive and try experimenting (and use Help features) until you get the answer in the real world. Logical assumptions don't get you too far with today's object taxonomies. The classification scheme is far from orderly, and the committees who design these schemes include some people who look exactly like Gyro Gearloose.

Object Variables

If you want to create or open a document, it's necessary in VBA to take the time to generate an object variable and then instantiate an object and assign it to that variable, like this:

```
Dim mydoc As Word.Document
Set mydoc = Documents.Add()
```

That creates a new document, giving it a default filename (Document1, for example). To specify your own filename (like, say, t.doc), use this:

```
Dim mydoc As Document

Documents.Add.SaveAs ("C:\t.doc")
Set mydoc = Documents("C:\t.doc")
```

The following statement opens an existing file:

```
Set mydoc = Documents.Open("C:\t.doc")
```

Editing text

You can do the usual things with document elements: add, delete, or modify (words, paragraphs, headers, or whatever).

To make these changes, use either the Range or Selection objects. You can have multiple Range objects but only one Selection object at any given time. Also, with a Selection, you must first *select* (highlight) before you can manipulate. A Range can merely be directly described in the code.

There is always a Selection object in a document's text. (If nothing is highlighted, the blinking insertion cursor — representing the insertion point — is the Selection object.)

Here's an example. In a Word document, type **this is selected**, and then drag your mouse across those three words to highlight (select) them. Now switch to the VBA editor and type this in:

```
Sub SelectionInfo()

s = "The selection contains  " & Selection.Characters.Count & " characters."

MsgBox s

Selection.InsertDateTime

End Sub
```

Press F5 to run the macro. You're told that there are 16 characters in the selected text, and then the InsertDateTime method replaces the selection with today's date.

**Book III
Chapter 1**

**The Word
Object Model**

Significant selection properties

As you might expect, various properties of the Selection object can tell you information about what's selected — or indeed, modify the selection. (The Range object shares many of these same properties.)

The End and Start properties

The End and Start properties tell you the character position, within the document's Characters collection, of the selection. For example, if your document starts like this:

One **two** three four five

And you select the word *two,* the Start property is 4, and the End property is 7. You can use these properties to *set* (change) the selection start and end points — moving the highlight.

The Font and ParagraphFormat properties

The Font and ParagraphFormat properties get or set objects describing the formatting. The Range object returns a range identical to the selection. You can go the other way with the ActiveDocument.Range.Select method. Notice that when you get a range from a selection, it's a property; but when you go the other way and get a selection from a range, it's a method. I tell you, there's no logic.

The StoryType property

An object called (who knows why?) Story represents the various kinds of text. You can use the StoryType property to get a built-in constant (also called an *enumeration*) telling what kind of Story is selected: ordinary document text = wdMainTextStory, wdCommentsStory is a comment, wdFootnotesStory for footnotes, and so on. The StoryLength property tells you how many characters long the story is (that contains your selection).

Enumerations do not directly report (in English) the answer you're after. Instead, you get a code — a number — and you have to look up the constant list to see what the number represents:

```
MsgBox Selection.StoryType
```

If this displays 1, what does it mean? Which of the constants is represented by 1? If you look up StoryType in Help, it doesn't give you the list of codes. Instead, you must search Help for constants, where you'll find the Word Enumerated Constants entry — and that includes a WdStoryType entry, shown in Figure 1-1.

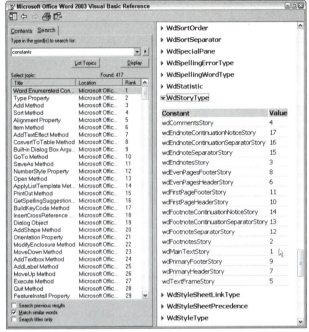

Figure 1-1:
Here's where you can find the many lists of enumerated constants in Word Help.

**Book III
Chapter 1**

**The Word
Object Model**

After you look up the constants, you discover that 1 means `MainText` story.

However, you can use the built-in constant names in expressions, like this:

```
If Selection.StoryType = wdFootnotesStory Then
```

The Style property

The `Style` property can get or set the style, which can either be one of the styles in the Styles drop-down list in the Formatting toolbar or one defined in the constant style's enumeration. But don't bother looking in the list of enumerations shown in Figure 1-1 for `wdStyles` or anything like that. You won't find it there. What do you imagine is the name they gave this enumeration? Boo! Surprise! It turns out to be `wdbuiltinStyles`! Who could have guessed?

There are 103 built-in styles, ranging from `wdStyleBlockQuotation` to `wdStyleTOC9`. If you want to change the style of a selection to, say, the third-level headline, use the following statement:

```
Selection.Style = wdStyleHeading3
```

Queerly, the numeric codes for all the style constants are negative! For example, `wdStyleBodyTextFirstIndent` is -78. Fortunately, when you query the style, you get back a string variable (not a code) telling you the name of the style:

```
n = Selection.Style
```

Please don't try to find patterns in these behaviors. Believe me, there aren't any useful rules here. Things can go any which way. Just, (I repeat), lean on Help and the various IntelliSense features, along with reference books.

The Text property

The `Text` property returns or sets the text:

```
s = Selection.Text
MsgBox s
```

The Words property

The `Words` property returns a collection of the words in the current selection. So, to make the third word in the selection boldface and 8 point (small), you can use this code:

```
Sub SelectionInfo()

With Selection.Words(3)
    .Font.Size = 8
    .Bold = True
End With

End Sub
```

In some versions of BASIC, you find the property `FontSize`, but in others, you find (as here) the `Size` property of the `Font` object. (The `Font` object is also a property of the `Selection` object, but that's another tale.)

Significant selection methods

When providing arguments to methods, you can use either the peculiar colon-equals (`:=`) punctuation or the traditional parentheses. Beware that the colon-equals approach has not survived in future versions of BASIC. The following two lines of code do the same thing:

```
Selection.Expand Unit:=wdParagraph
Selection.Expand (wdParagraph)
```

The following methods are of the `Selection` object, but many are also methods of the `Range` object. `Selection.copy` copies the selection to the Clipboard. The `Cut` and `Delete` methods are similar, but `Cut` puts a copy in the Clipboard (like pressing Shift+Del). `Paste` pastes.

Starting at 1 or 0?

Although nearly all other collections in VBA (`Paragraphs`, `Characters`, and so on) begin counting with the number 1, the `Range` object counts from 0 (zero). There's no reason for this discontinuity: Every list, group, array, or collection should begin counting with 1. That's the way our numeric system has worked for thousands of years, and there's no reason to start counting from zero in computer languages. We don't say, for example, "I've been to Greece five times, but the very zeroth time I went was the most fun." We quite reasonably say, "The *first* time I went. . . ." Why some computer language designers decided to count from 0 in some cases and from 1 in other cases remains one of those sad mysteries in the annals of human folly. And don't assume that you can ever know which of the two modes — start with 0 or start with 1 — applies in any particular case. Some collections, list box controls, arrays, and other groups in programming begin with 0 and some with 1. You just have to wrestle with this problem until sanity eventually gains the upper hand with computer language designers. Eventually, they'll realize how many man-centuries of debugging they've caused by authoring this confusion.

You can increase the size of the selection with the `EndOf` or `Expand` methods. The `InsertAfter` and `InsertBefore` methods insert a string where described. The `InsertBreak` method takes the following arguments, among others: `wdPageBreak` (default), `wdSectionBreak`, and `wdLineBreak`.

`InsertParagraph` replaces the selection, but `InsertParagraphAfter` and `InsertParagraphBefore` do not. `SetRange(Start, End)` specifies the starting and ending character positions. `Shrink` reduces the selection to the next smaller unit of text (following this pattern: entire document, section, paragraph, sentence, word, insertion point). For example, if you select a paragraph, only a sentence remains selected after using `Shrink`.

Creating ranges

You can create a range directly by specifying its starting position and length:

```
Sub Ranges()

Dim myrange As Word.Range
Set myrange = ActiveDocument.Range(0, 25)
myrange.Bold = True

End Sub
```

In this example, you ask VBA to create a range from the 0th to the 24th character.

Recall that you can create as many different ranges within a document as you need. Also, a whole slew of Word objects have a `Range` property that you can use to create a new range. The range that you get is the same unit of the object. (A `Paragraph` object returns, for example, a paragraph-long range.) Here are the objects with a range property: `Bookmark`, `Cell`, `Comment`, `Endnote`, `Footnote`, `FormField`, `Frame`, `HeaderFooter`, `Hyperlink`, `Index`, `InlineShape`, `List`, `Paragraph`, `Revision`, `Row`, `Section`, `Selection`, `Subdocument`, `Table`, `TableOfAuthorities`, `TableOfContents`, and `TableOfFigures`.

Here's an example that uses the `Range` property of the `Paragraph` object. Your goal here is to change the size and color of the first character in each paragraph in the active document. In addition, you change the character to the engraved style. You first define two object variables: one for the `Paragraph` object and one for the `Range` object. Then you specify the following for every paragraph (in turn) throughout this document's `Paragraphs` collection: If the paragraph has at least one sentence in it, create a range that spans merely the first character in the paragraph's range's `Characters` collection. Then, change that little range (that first character).

```
Sub Ranges()

Dim p As Word.Paragraph
Dim r As Word.Range

For Each p In ActiveDocument.Paragraphs
    If p.Range.Sentences.Count > 0 Then
        Set r = p.Range.Characters(1) 'point to first letter
        r.Font.Size = 12
        r.Font.Engrave = True
        r.Font.Color = wdColorBlue
    End If
Next p

End Sub
```

Bookmarking

Similar to the `Range` and `Selection` objects, the `Bookmark` object has a start and end position. It can also be as large as the entire document or merely the size of the insertion point (zero characters). Bookmarks, though, are kind of like ghost documents within the regular document. They can be used as place markers showing where addresses from a database — or perhaps boilerplate text — are to be inserted in a letter. Also, bookmarks can themselves contain text that, depending on conditions, is inserted into the main document.

Bookmarks are normally invisible but can be made visible by setting the View object's ShowBookmarks property to True (or by choosing Tools⇨Options⇨ View). Here's an example that inserts one of two messages at the end of a letter to a customer, depending on whether the customer's account is paid up. In a Word document, choose Insert⇨Bookmark and then name your new bookmark AreTheyPaidUp. Then switch to the VBA editor and type the macro in Listing 3-1.

Listing 3-1:   Bookmark Insertion Macro

```
Sub BookIt()


Dim Range1 As Word.Range
Set Range1 = ActiveDocument.Bookmarks("AreTheyPaidUp").Range

With Range1

If paidup = True Then
.InsertAfter vbCrLf & "Thank You for your business!" & vbCrLf
Else
.InsertAfter vbCrLf & "Where's the cash??!!" & vbCrLf
End If
.Select

End With

ActiveDocument.Bookmarks.Add "AreTheyPaidUp", Selection.Range


End Sub
```

When executed, this macro accepts a parameter named paidup (probably from a database) that describes whether the customer owes any money. A Range object is then created and set to point to the bookmark. Then you use the InsertAfter method to append your message to any text that might already exist in the bookmark. (In this case, there's none, but boilerplate text might well exist in a typical business or professional document.)

Surrounding the text with & vbCrLf, which is a constant representing pressing Enter, has the effect of making your text a separate paragraph. Finally, you use the Bookmarks collection's Add method to replace the existing bookmark with your new one. When you use the same name as an existing bookmark, the original bookmark's text (if any) is retained, but your new text is inserted. Unfortunately, bookmarks are deleted from a document if you use a range's Text property to replace the contents of the bookmark. Likewise, if you hadn't used the Select method to create a new selection, the bookmark in the above example would have been destroyed.

**Book III
Chapter 1**

**The Word
Object Model**

Search and Replace

Automating Word can sometimes require that you employ the `Find` and `Replacement` objects. This is another way to insert boilerplate text or to change a letter's contents based on information coming in from a database or other source. You could even display an `InputBox` to ask the letter writer to choose whether he wants to send the polite, neutral, or really exasperated version of the same letter. (The exasperated version searches for, and then deletes, all use of the phrases *thank you* and *please*.)

One quick way to program in VBA is to first record a macro and then see what VBA code was automatically created for you. You can modify that code as necessary, but at least you're not starting from scratch.

Follow these steps:

1. **In Word, open a document that you don't mind messing up.**

2. **Choose Tools⇨Macro⇨Record New Macro.**

   The Record New Macro dialog box opens.

3. **Click OK to close the dialog box.**

   The macro recording toolbar appears.

4. **Choose Edit⇨Replace.**

   The Find and Replace dialog box opens.

5. **In the Find What field, type** the; **in the Replace With field, type** xxxx.

6. **Click the Replace All button.**

   All instances of the word *the* are replaced with xxxx's.

7. **Close the dialog box.**

8. **Click the Stop button on the Macro toolbar.**

   The macro recording stops, and the toolbar disappears.

9. **Press Alt+F11.**

   You see the VBA editor.

10. **Locate your new macro. It should look like this:**

    ```
    Sub Macro8()
    '
    ' Macro8 Macro
    ' Macro recorded 12/19/2003 by Richard
    '
    ```

```
Selection.Find.ClearFormatting
Selection.Find.Replacement.ClearFormatting
With Selection.Find
     .Text = "the"
     .Replacement.Text = "xxxx"
     .Forward = True
     .Wrap = wdFindContinue
     .Format = False
     .MatchCase = False
     .MatchWholeWord = False
     .MatchWildcards = False
     .MatchSoundsLike = False
     .MatchAllWordForms = False
End With
Selection.Find.Execute Replace:=wdReplaceAll
End Sub
```

You can adjust any of the `Selection` or `Find` objects' properties to modify how your search and replace behaves.

The Find Object's Properties

The significant properties of both the `Find` and `Replacement` objects include `Font`, `ParagraphFormat`, `Style`, and `Text`. The important properties of the `Find` object (by itself) are `Forward`, `Found`, `MatchCase`, and `MatchWholeWord`.

The `Execute` method of the `Find` object has several optional arguments that are duplicates of some of the `Find` object's own properties. You can either specify these options as properties or arguments, as you wish. For example, the statement

```
myrange.Find.Execute Forward:=True
```

is equivalent to

```
With myrange.Find
     .Forward = True
     .Execute
End With
```

or

```
myrange.Find.Forward = True
```

The `ClearAllFormatting` method of the `Find` object eliminates any previously specified formatting rules. This way, you won't cause that frequently confusing result of finding no hits in a document that you know contains plenty of hits. Then, you notice that the italic or `Headline1 Style` formatting criteria are specified because your last search required them.

Trapping Events

Of the three members of any object model — properties, methods, and events — it's events that are generally less often discussed. Nonetheless, you frequently need to provide a programmatic response to something that happens to an object (such as the user clicking a button, or an incoming message arriving).

The document object offers six events: `New`, `Open`, `Close`, `Sync`, `XMLAfterInsert`, and `XMLBeforeDelete`. You can provide programming for these events in the `ThisDocument` object. Press Alt+F11 to open the VBA editor, and then right-click ThisDocument under the Normal node. Choose View Code from the context menu and select Document in the top-left, drop-down list box of the Code window. By default, the `Document_New` event is displayed, but you can select the document's other events by opening the drop-down list in the upper-right of the Code window.

For example, you put any code you want to execute when a new document is created inside the `New` event, like this:

```
Private Sub Document_New()

MsgBox "Welcome!"

End Sub
```

An alternative approach to using `ThisDocument` events is to trap events by giving your macros special names (such as `FileSave`). In this case, any time the user chooses File⇨Save from the Word File menu, your macro code is executed. Read about this technique in Book III, Chapter 5.

To respond to Word's `Application` or mail merge object's events, you must add a class module to your project to contain the event. Then create the event in the class module, like this:

```
Public WithEvents o As Word.Application

Private Sub o_Quit()

    MsgBox "bye"

End Sub
```

You can find out the syntax and any arguments required by the various events by searching for *application* in VBA Help, choosing Application Object, and then clicking the <u>Events</u> link at the top of the Help page. (The Quit event has no arguments.)

Before your event trapping works, you must also initialize the object. A good place to do that is in the ThisDocument Open event:

```
Dim X As New Class1 'this assumes your class module is named Class1

Private Sub Document_Open()

  Set X.o = Word.Application 'point object variable to app

End Sub
```

For an example of how to do this in Excel (Word works the same way), see the Book IV, Chapter 2.

**Book III
Chapter 1**

**The Word
Object Model**

Chapter 2: Power Editing

In This Chapter

✔ **Maximizing Word's editing features**

✔ **Viewing and maneuvering the smart way**

✔ **Introducing Smart Documents**

✔ **Understanding fields**

✔ **Importing data**

✔ **Using Mail Merge**

Many — perhaps most — Office workers don't take advantage of Word's many powerful editing features. Before exploring some VBA and programming techniques, this chapter first offers some useful (albeit underused) techniques that can improve productivity for nearly any kind of Office worker. You'll see how to do some power editing, maneuver efficiently, and use Smart Documents. Fields, data importing, and mail merge are also covered.

Selecting Text Quickly

Selecting text is a common job in Word, but few people realize the many shortcut ways to do this. For example, double-click any word to select it. To select an entire line, click the left margin. Double-click the left margin to select the entire paragraph. Drag in the left margin to select a group of lines. Triple-click the left margin to select the entire document (or press Ctrl+A). Quadruple click the left margin to send a Word document to the Space Station. (Let me know how this last one works out.)

To select a chunk of text of any size, do the same thing you do to select a contiguous group in a list box or a group of filenames in Windows Explorer. That is, click at the start of the text block and hold Shift while clicking the end of the block. Or click the start of the block, press F8, and then drag (or click the end point). To select all text formatted the same way, right-click the text and choose Select Text with Similar Formatting from the context menu.

Making Snappy Retorts . . . er, Repeats

Memorize the F4 key; it can be a real timesaver. If you have to do something repeatedly (such as formatting, typing in a phrase, or many other tasks), you don't have to repeat all the steps in the task. For example, maybe you want to change the style of all the headlines in a document, reducing them from the Heading1 style to Heading2. Instead of selecting each headline, dropping the style list in the Formatting toolbar, scrolling until you find Heading2, and then clicking it in the list — yipes — just take those steps for the first head-line in the document. Thereafter, merely click each headline and press F4. The style is correctly applied to each headline.

Going Backward with Undo

Always remember your Undo friend: Press Ctrl+Z to undo a mistake. If you delete some text and then wish you hadn't, the Undo feature restores the text. Sweet. Likewise, Undo is a lifesaver when you make foolish formatting mistakes. The downside: If you made your mistake several steps previously, of course, you could repeat Ctrl+Z until the problem is fixed, but this also undoes in-between things you probably don't want undone as well. Undo, unfortunately, undoes every action between the error up to and including your latest action.

To see a list of your actions — and I mean *everything you've done since you opened the document!* — locate the Undo icon on the Standard toolbar and then click the down arrow on the Undo icon. (Undo looks like a left-curved arrow.) Your most recent six behaviors are listed, but you can scroll down this list as far as necessary to find the problem. Then you click the error. Remember, though, that all previous actions will also be undone. It's up to you.

If the Undo button isn't visible, right-click the Standard toolbar and choose Customize from the context menu. In the Customize dialog box, click the Commands tab, click Edit, and drag the Undo icon and drop it on the Standard toolbar.

Note Undo's brother, the Redo feature (Ctrl+Y). Its toolbar button also includes a drop-down list with all the actions that you most recently undid. This is your lifesaver if you undo 143 actions and then regret having to repeat the 142 tasks that you correctly accomplished.

Mastering Quick Maneuvering

When editing a document, you sometimes want to see the forest, not the trees. You want to move around quickly, just locating a particular zone or type of style. Here are a couple of tips for how to view and search your document differently.

Viewing a document

Speed up your work by choosing different views in Office 2003. A change of view can help you see a document's outline, or maybe you want to see how two pages next to each other look. You can still rely on the stalwart Document Map, but you have some new choices, too.

Document Map

Use Document Map to collapse a document into a kind of outline format, based on the headings you've used in the document. One great thing about this view is that you still get to see the original document. This is handy when you want to make sure you have headings in a logical progression or when you want to jump to a certain heading in the document. Choose View➪Document Map to see this outline version, as shown in Figure 2-1. See a similar view in the upcoming "Thumbnail view" section.

Book III
Chapter 2

Power Editing

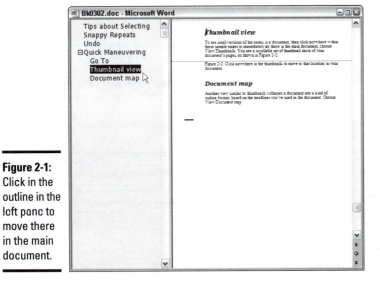

Figure 2-1:
Click in the outline in the left pane to move there in the main document.

Reading Layout view

New in Office 2003 is Reading Layout view. When you select this option from the View menu, you see two pages at a time, as if you had opened a book. This view makes it somewhat easier to scan larger amounts of text at a glance.

Thumbnail view

Also new in Office 2003 is a view of small versions of the pages in a document. When you choose View⇨Thumbnails, click anywhere within these sample pages to immediately go to that place in the main document. You see a scrollable set of thumbnail shots of your document's pages, as shown in Figure 2-2.

Searching within a document

Use these Office tools to help you quickly navigate a document, finding specific items such as page numbers, comments, bookmarks, and more.

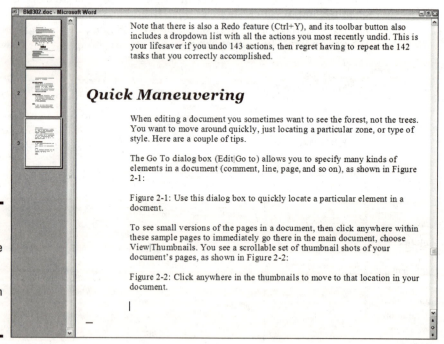

Figure 2-2: Click anywhere in the thumbnails to move to that location in your document.

Go To

Use the Go To tab of the Find and Replace dialog box (choose Edit⇨Go To) to search for many kinds of elements in a document (comment, line, page, and so on), as shown in Figure 2-3. Go To's cousin — Find — works much the same way but with a little more precision. Pressing Ctrl+F brings up the Find tab of the same dialog box, from which you can search for a word, word fragment, special characters or formatting, and so on.

Figure 2-3:
Use this dialog box to quickly locate a particular element in a document.

Bookmarks

Bookmarks are convenient for marking somewhere you want to return to, like the stopping point of the day's work. When you insert bookmarks throughout your document, you can use them to quickly locate and move to certain points in a document. To insert a bookmark, choose Insert⇨Bookmark to open the Bookmark dialog box, enter a name for the bookmark, and then click Add. To go to a bookmark, press Ctrl+G (which takes you to the Go To tab of the Find and Replace dialog box), click Bookmark (under Go To What), find the bookmark (under Enter Bookmark Name), and then click the Go To button. (Speed hint: Just double-click the bookmark's name in the dialog box.)

**Book III
Chapter 2**

Power Editing

Browsing with Select Browse Object

On the bottom of the horizontal scrollbar (in the lower right of your document), you'll see some symbols — icons that most people ignore. The central icon is a small ball, as illustrated in Figure 2-4.

Go Back

Press Shift+F5 to use Go Back to cycle among the most recently edited locations in a document. This feature is most handy when you reopen a document and want to find where you last worked. You can also make use of the

GoBack method of the `Application` object. To open the most recently edited document and then move the insertion cursor to the most recently edited location in that document, create this macro:

```
RecentFiles(1).Open
Application.GoBack
```

If you name this macro `autoexec`, this behavior automatically loads the most recent document, at the most recent edit, every time you start Word:

```
Sub autoexec()

RecentFiles(1).Open
Application.GoBack

End Sub
```

Any instructions you write in a macro named `autoexec` are automatically executed every time you run the Word application.

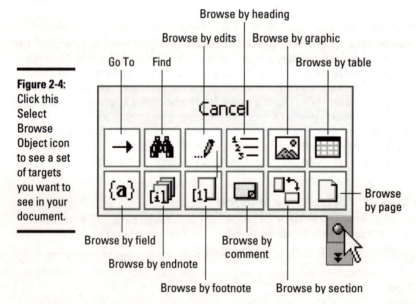

Figure 2-4:
Click this Select Browse Object icon to see a set of targets you want to see in your document.

Introducing Smart Documents

Although the new Smart Documents technology in Office 2003 (Word and Excel, specifically) certainly qualify to be included in a chapter about power editing, I cover this technology in depth in Book VII, Chapter 6. Still, a little preview here is useful.

To a user, on the surface, Smart Documents behave somewhat like wizards but without the step-by-step pages of instructions. Smart Documents are based on XML and offer you, the developer, a programmable solution to a variety of common Office tasks. You can semi-automate processes, like creating proposals, business plans, reports, and other kinds of documents that have predictable form and/or content. You can hand someone a Smart Document, and he can use the task pane (that you've built) to get help, lists of options, and other assistance in writing, editing, and publishing the document.

Smart Documents are built on XML, so you might suspect that there's an Internet connection here. Good guess, Office 2003 developer. Technically — and thankfully, someday all this will be kept under the hood — a Smart Document is built by using managed code that's Internet-connected with either a primary interop assembly or a COM interface. I only mention this because some readers like brief clouds of sophisticated-sounding nonsense. Unfortunately, at this time, Smart Documents are technically demanding because creating them is not yet smart (that is, not filled with useless buzzwords or pointless propeller-head verbiage). The main problem is that there's no wizard to guide you through the process of creating Smart Documents. One day soon there will be such a wizard, but not yet.

As you might suspect, the task pane is context-sensitive, so when a user maneuvers through a Smart Document, the commentary and other assistance offered by the pane changes. Exactly what kind of commentary appears in the task pane is up to you, the programmer. You can insert lists, calculation fields, all kinds of controls (such as list boxes), hyperlinks, and various other kinds of assistance.

Here are some ideas about what you could do with Smart Documents:

+ Facilitate import and export of data in a fashion similar to Mail Merge but with more flexibility (regarding the location, type, destination, and source of the data).

+ Take a single document and automate the process of transforming it into several versions, each appropriate for a different target (a database, a published report, an outline, and so on).

+ Programmatically build new Word documents more flexibly than previously, drawing on more diverse sources for the content.

+ Semi-automate various librarian functions (answering questions like, *Who has the latest version? Whose comments can be ignored?* and so on).

+ Increase document security and validation automation.

**Book III
Chapter 2**

Power Editing

Although creating Smart Documents is a mildly interesting new feature, it's far from ironed out. You have to manage quite a few details manually (ever try writing XML by hand?), and the opportunity for version conflicts (between different Smart Documents), deployment problems, and other new technology glitches is great. Smart Document creation cries out for a wizard, but there currently isn't one. As you can see in Book VII, Chapter 6, creating Smart Documents currently is not for the faint of heart.

Programming with Fields

Of the various ways to automate document creation and modification, fields are among the most venerable. The three types of fields are

✦ **Result fields:** These tell Word what text you want inserted.

✦ **Marker fields:** Rather simple, these resemble bookmarks, indicating a location in the document (so that Word can later return to this location and do something: for example, add a term to an index). Bookmarks, in fact, are themselves a field. A difference between fields and bookmarks is that you can delete fields in your text with the Delete or Backspace keys. However, to delete a bookmark, you must open the Bookmark dialog box (choose Insert⇨Bookmark), select the bookmark from a list, and click the Delete button.

✦ **Action fields:** These do something by themselves, such as launch a macro, but don't themselves add new text to the document. A hyperlink is considered an action field, for example.

In some ways, a field is similar to a variable in programming. Based on conditions or context, a field can be automatically changed without user or programmer intervention. For example, a field containing a date can change to always display the current date.

Fields can import data from files, from elsewhere in a document, or from data about the document (its word count, for example).

To see fields within a document, select the field (or the entire document if you wish), and then toggle field view by pressing Shift+F9. If you have a date field in your document, it will change from 1/30/2003 to {DATE \@ "M/d/yyyy" }. Fields are enclosed in braces.

Inserting fields

The simple way to insert a new field into a document is to choose Insert⇨ Field. Memorable, isn't it? The Field dialog box appears, as shown in Figure 2-5.

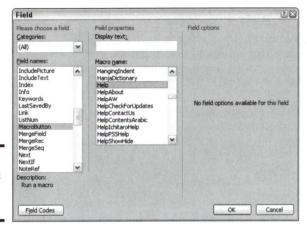

Figure 2-5:
Insert fields
from this
dialog box.

The Field dialog box includes a MacroButton option, as shown in Figure 2-5. And when you select that option, you can scroll through the macro name list and find all your macros, plus dozens of menu items (most everything available on a menu) such as HangingIndent and WindowNewWindow. Most of these menu items are named after the menu on which they reside. Thus, if the Word Count feature is on the Tools menu, the name of this item is ToolsWordCount.

Here are some helpful field tips:

✦ If you want Word to always update the fields before printing documents, choose Tools➪Options, click the Print tab, and then select Update Fields.

✦ If you prefer to type fields directly into your documents, type the field's name, select it, and press Ctrl+F9.

✦ To update all the fields in a selection, press F9.

✦ To prevent a field or fields from being updated, select the fields, and then press Ctrl+F11. To reverse this process — to permit the fields to be updated — choose Ctrl+Shift+F11.

✦ To move from one field to the next, press F11. To move in reverse, press Shift+F11.

✦ When you right-click a field, you can accomplish three things with this field from the context menu: update it, edit it, or toggle between results and the code.

Using the Fields collection

You can programmatically manage fields by using the `Fields` collection. In this example, the number of pages in the document is inserted:

```
Sub fieldwork()


Set myField = ActiveDocument.Fields.Add(Range:=Selection.Range, _
    Type:=wdFieldNumPages)

End Sub
```

To update all the fields in a selection:

```
Selection.Fields.Update
```

Using the Ref field

The `Ref` field is interesting. It allows you to both refer to a bookmark elsewhere in the document as well as insert that bookmark's text at the field location. To see how this works, select a block of text somewhere in your document and choose Insert⇨Bookmark. When the Bookmark dialog box opens, name this bookmark *ThisText.* Click somewhere else in the document where you want this text inserted, and then choose Insert⇨Field. The Field dialog box opens, as shown in Figure 2-6.

Select the `Ref` field in the Field dialog box, select name of your bookmark *(ThisText),* and click OK to close the dialog box. The bookmarked block of text is reproduced at the current location (of the field) in your document. Now go to the bookmark, make a change to the text, and move back to the field `Ref` copy. Click your mouse in the field, and poof! The entire block of text goes gray, indicating that it's a field. Press F9 to update the field. The change that you made to the bookmark text is now made in the updated field.

Advanced field tricks

If you feel that you'll use fields extensively in your documents, it's worth using Word Help to investigate various advanced tricks that you can do with fields. For example, you can customize your field's appearance in various ways, choose differently formatted numbers, create fields that calculate results from literals or variables (like a spreadsheet does), format date and time, and so on. You can even nest fields inside each other: This way, one field's changes or conditions can optionally update the nested field, or you can base the outcome of an IF field, for example, on the status of a nested field.

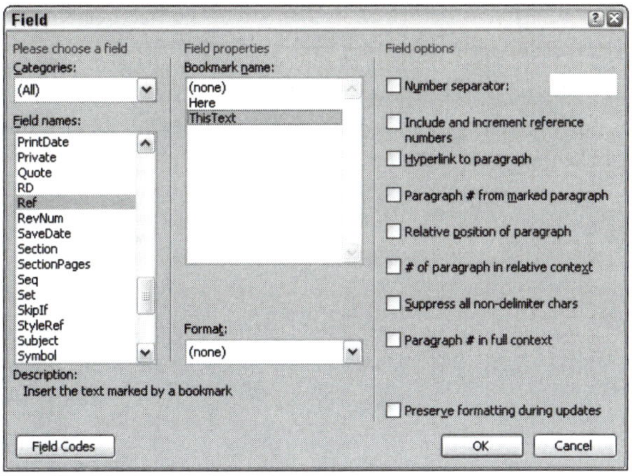

Figure 2-6:
Use the Ref
field to copy
updatable,
bookmarked
text.

Importing Data

You can bring data into a document automatically, using much the same style
of programming that works when programming .NET or older versions of
Visual Basic.

You can open the sample Access Northwind database and then insert a
comma-delimited (data separated by commas, such as *this, this, and this*)
list of all the customers' names into the current document. Sometimes individual data are *delimited* (separated) by commas or other special symbols.
To perform this task, follow these steps:

**Book III
Chapter 2**

Power Editing

1. **Press Alt+F11.**

   The Word VBA editor opens.

2. **Press F7.**

   The code window opens where you can write macros.

3. **You must first import a library of DAO (Data Access Objects) code, so
   choose Tools⇨References.**

   The References dialog box opens.

4. **Scroll down in the dialog box until you locate Microsoft 3.0 DAO Object
   Library, or versions 3.51 or 3.6.**

5. **Click the latest DAO library version to select it.**

6. **Click OK to close the dialog box.**

To open the Northwind database and bring in the customer name records, type this code into the VBA code window:

```
Sub datawork()

    Dim d As Document
    Set d = ActiveDocument

    Dim db As DAO.Database
    Dim r As Recordset


    Set db = OpenDatabase(Name:="C:\Program Files\Microsoft
        Office\Office11\Samples\Northwind.mdb")

    Set r = db.OpenRecordset(Name:="Customers")

    For i = 0 To r.RecordCount - 1
        d.Content.InsertAfter Text:=r.Fields(2).Value & ", "
        r.MoveNext
    Next i

    r.Close
    db.Close

End Sub
```

7. Click somewhere within the above macro; then press F5 to execute it.

You see a list of 91 names inserted into your current document, ending with the name Zbyszek Piestrzeniewicz, which is pronounced *Ziggy Stardust.*

If your version of `Northwind.mdb` isn't in the path used in this code, you'll get an error #3044 message (not a valid path). Use the Start⇨Search feature to locate `Northwind.mdb` on your hard drive. If it's nowhere to be found, rerun your Office 2003 setup CD and choose to install the sample databases.

In this example, you first create a document object and point it to the current active document; then you create database and recordset variables. (I talk more about recordsets and their sucessor, datasets, in Book V when I discuss Access.) The database variable is pointed to the sample database (which also opens the database), and the recordset is pointed to the `Customers` table in that database.

You can view the structure (tables, fields, views, stored procedures) of a database by opening the database in Access or by using the new and useful Server Explorer in the .NET IDE, as shown in Figure 2-7.

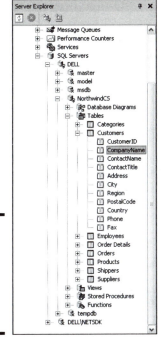

Figure 2-7:
Use this
Server
Explorer
to see
database
structures.

The fields within the Northwind `Customers` table include customer ID, contact, and other fields. But I'm interested in the `CompanyName` field (which happens to be field 2, as you can see in Figure 2-7). So the example code loops through the entire table by using the `MoveNext` method of the recordset object. Notice that you must start your loop with 0 and end it with `RecordCount-1` because recordset fields begin counting their lists with 0, and that throws everything off by 1, so you have to compensate in your code.

Each time through the loop, the `Content.InsertAfter` method is used to add text to the document. (This text is the `Value` property of the `Fields` collection.) A comma and a space are added to the text in the document. Finally, the two objects are destroyed with the `Close` method.

You can employ the various bookmarks, fields, paragraphs, and other collections and objects available in the Word object model to insert your data coming in from a database (or other source) wherever appropriate in your text. See Book III, Chapter 1 for additional information on the Word object model.

Mass Mailings with Mail Merge

Word's Mail Merge is a specialized combination of some of the techniques featured in this chapter: bringing data in from outside Word, and automating the process of inserting text into ranges, fields, or bookmarks. However, because merging names and addresses into a document for mass mailings is such a venerable and essential word processing task, a wizard exists to make the job fairly painless. The wizard sits in Word, but you can also get to it via Outlook. I show you both pathways.

Word's Mail Merge is a classic technique: From a data source, you insert unique information (such as addresses) into form letters. It's a cheap, easy way to customize anything from mass ad mailings to the Christmas letter that you send to all your friends.

You first create a form letter, specifying where you want custom content inserted *(merge fields)*. Then create a data source (a database table, a table in a Word document, a spreadsheet, or your Outlook Contact list.)

You use the Mail Merge Wizard to step you through the necessary tasks, and your form letter can actually take five different forms: a traditional form letter, e-mail, envelopes, labels, or directories (catalogs) — a single document containing all the merged data, including a repetition of any additional static text you want associated with the data.

To create a mail merge, follow these steps:

1. **Create a Word document, saving this document to your hard drive with the name** `MassMail.doc`.

   Fill your holiday letter full of news about little Billy and Betty, their many accomplishments, and an update on Uncle Bob and his dog Sam.

2. **Choose Tools⇨Letters and Mailings⇨Mail Merge.**

   The Mail Merge Wizard appears, as shown in Figure 2-8.

3. **Select Letters in the first step of the wizard, as shown in Figure 2-8.**

4. **Click the <u>Click Next to continue</u> link on the bottom of the task pane.**

5. **On the second step of the wizard, select Start from Existing Document.**

   A file browser opens in the task pane, asking you to identify the existing document.

6. **Select Use the Current Document.**

7. **Click Next.**

Figure 2-8:
Start here
to create a
mail merge.

**Book III
Chapter 2**

Power Editing

8. **Select Type a New List in the Select Recipients option button group.**

9. **Click the Create button.**

   The New Address List dialog box opens, as shown in Figure 2-9.

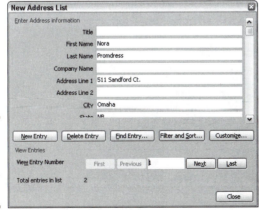

Figure 2-9:
Create a list
of targets
here for your
form letter.

10. **Click the Close button.**

The Mail Merge Recipients dialog box opens, as shown in Figure 2-10.

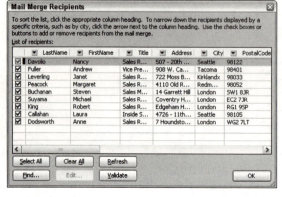

Figure 2-10:
Edit the
order or
other
properties
of your mail
merge data
list here.

11. **Click OK.**

The dialog box closes.

12. **Click Next.**

The task pane tells you to personalize the letter by adding address blocks, greetings, and so on.

13. **Click above the main body of the letter, where you want to write Dear *XXXXX*.**

14. **Click the <u>Greeting Line</u> link in the task pane.**

The Greeting Line dialog box opens, as shown in Figure 2-11.

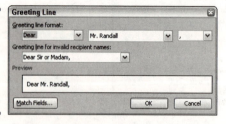

Figure 2-11:
Here's
where you
create a
greeting
merge field.

15. **When you're satisfied with the default greeting style, click OK.**

The dialog box closes.

16. **Click above the greeting line in your letter, in the location where you want the address field to appear.**

17. **Click the <u>Address Block</u> link in the task pane.**

The Insert Address Block dialog box opens, showing you the default style.

18. **Click OK.**

The dialog box closes. At this point, your document includes two merge fields, and looks something like this (although details of your Christmas mass mailing will undoubtedly differ slightly from those written by Karyn here):

```
<<AddressBlock>>
<<GreetingLine>>
Thank you for everything!!
Uncle Billy is getting better every week!! And little Billy still loves
    his bike!
Love,
Karyn ("Fluffy") Primstance-Mesuremaseur
```

19. **Click Next in the task pane.**

You see a preview of your form letter, with the merge fields filled in from the first record of data.

20. **Click Next in the task pane.**

The task pane tells you how to either print your mass mailing or edit the individual letters (making them even more deeply personal).

To start a mass mailing process from within Outlook (where perhaps you keep addresses of many of your Contacts), click the Contacts button in the left pane of the Outlook window and choose Tools⇨Mail Merge. When you finish making any selections in that dialog box that open and then click OK, Word opens with the merge document loaded. You then choose Tools⇨ Letters and Mailings⇨Mail Merge in Word, but you begin with the wizard's Step 3, as described in the earlier steps.

Chapter 3: Using XML in Word

In This Chapter

✔ Discovering WordML

✔ Using XML

✔ Using programmatic XML

✔ Selecting options

✔ Using the special Word XML editor

*I*n this chapter, you see how XML and Word now work together, synergisti-cally, to facilitate communication between any and all platforms, operating systems, data stores, applications, and whatever else might want to commu-nicate with Word. In a word, XML is today's *lingua franca.*

Lingua means *tongue. Franca* is a corrupted version of Italian that was once spoken on the Mediterranean coast. It was the language of the Franks blended into Italian. But the phrase *lingua franca* has come to stand for whatever means of communication can be used to make interaction possible between people who speak different languages.

Introducing Word XML

eXtensible Markup Language (XML) and associated technologies have become *de rigueur* in contemporary computing. Book VIII, Chapter 2 goes into the topic of XML in relation to all Office 2003 applications, but it's useful here to introduce the features of XML in Word specifically. Likewise, in the books on particular Office 2003 applications — Excel, Outlook, and Access most notably — you'll find explanations of how XML works in the context of each specific application.

Microsoft — although located in Seattle, home office of grunge — is no slacker. Do you imagine that Microsoft would sit idly by while others created versions of XML and not have a go at it, too? Actually, many flavors of XML float around in Microsoft operating systems and applications. And the one of interest here is *WordML,* which is the schema for Word 2003.

Making do with what you've got

Although XML files are bulky because they're wildly redundant, this just doesn't matter. Developers and programmers have undergone a paradigm shift in the past decade. In the early days (1985 and before), programmers had to be careful to conserve computer memory because it was expensive and quite limited. As a result, programming used every little corner of a RAM chip. This lead to such unhappy consequences as employing the number 0 as the first item in a list. (Arrays, lists, and collections sometimes still have a zeroth index, leading to lots of unnecessary programming bugs.) Y2K fears were also caused by programmers trying to conserve memory, storing dates using only two digits: *88* instead of *1988*.

Times change, and yet they don't. Hey, when paper was expensive, monks in the Middle Ages wrote on every scrap, sometimes writing on top of earlier manuscripts (which is how we lost some invaluable classics, like a treatise by Archimedes destroyed when a monk thought the parchment was more valuable than the genius's thoughts.) Of course, on the plus side, monks preserved quite a lot of classical knowledge, as well.

Excel (with its grids of orderly data) and Access (with its tables of organized data) seem ideally suited to XML. It's easy to see how an XML document's tidy structure can accommodate a database table or spreadsheet. But what about Word? Aren't Word documents fundamentally unstructured? Well, yes and no. Of course, there are sentences and paragraphs, but they're not really that predictable. Too, Word can include tables, numbered lists, and other comparatively more structured data. But don't worry; Microsoft has figured out a way to preserve Word's hidden structures (formatting, document statistics, and so on). That's WordML's job: to provide a schema to store a systematic XML version of a Word document, complete with all the necessary tag pairs that preserve all the underlying structures of a document.

You can save documents in XML (WordML) format in all versions of Word 2003, but the other XML features are found only in Office 2003 Professional (or the confusingly named *Enterprise Professional version*) and the standalone version of Word 2003.

XML — daughter of HTML and mother of countless child languages — differs from HTML in some fundamental ways. For one, XML is highly *extensible*. Anyone can invent any elements or attributes they want. XML also describes data (preserving the structure of the information it contains). HTML isn't designed to be customized by users, and it describes appearance, such as boldface or the location and size of a headline.

Although an XML file itself is highly *redundant* — often containing many repetitious tags and duplicated data — using XML in the workplace can paradoxically reduce another, more important redundancy.

Take this (intentionally long) example: A salesman writes down an order and faxes it to the office. There it's retyped into the home office computer, and another form is filled out by someone in the fulfillment department. Then some tags and mailing labels are typed in the warehouse, and the billing department retypes the details into an invoice while another worker retypes the order into the inventory management software — and on and on. Not only does all this repetition introduce obvious productivity losses, but it also greatly increases the opportunity for typographical errors. If the salesman had entered the order into his notebook and saved it as an XML file right from the start, software could take over the job of radiating the order into its various different forms in the various departments that handle the order.

Put another way, XML data is polymorphic and can easily be expressed, stored, and printed in a variety of formats — from invoices to mailing labels — without human intervention. This kind of system is a primary way that your local friendly SprawlMart differs from the corner mom-and-pop grocery.

Try an experiment. Create a blank Word document and type in **Hello, Snarky.** Saving this information in a simple TXT format takes up only 14 bytes, 1 for each character. Saving it as a WordML file requires 3,442 bytes, and saving it as a DOC file takes up 24,064 bytes. As you can see, storing all the extra information about formatting, author, styles, when it was last saved, line pitch, and whatnot requires quite a bit of space more than the simple characters themselves.

Although XML wallows in redundancy, the paradigm shift in computer programming is this: Computer memory is now so cheap that different programming styles are possible, such as XML's complete refusal to engage in any reduction of redundancy. When you can store a person's entire lifetime of e-mail messages on a CD that costs less than a penny, why not use redundant data storage methods if there's an advantage to be gained? And indeed there is: Computers don't make mistakes (although human data-entry or source code can make computers seem to err). The less that data is handled by humans (retyping it, for example), the safer that data is.

For more on XML, try *XML All-in-One Desk Reference For Dummies* by Richard Wagner and Richard Mansfield (Wiley).

XML in Word

XML, being extensible, invites people to create their own versions, so you've got different XML languages (*schemas,* or sets of rules and tags) for the baker, the butcher, and the candlestick maker. What's more, two different bakeries might each use their own proprietary XML. However, XML theorists were quite aware of the Tower of Babel problem. After all, XML was designed in part to solve the tremendous difficulties resulting from incompatible data storage schemes. So, most importantly, XML is stored as ordinary text — letters making words that people can actually read. If you can read and write your language, you can also read and write XML (not that you'll usually want to, but you can if you must).

Here are some of the things you can do with XML in Word:

✦ Mix XML into ordinary Word documents or save documents (convert them) in XML format.

✦ Validate Word XML files to ensure that the XML is *well-formed* (meaning that it makes sense, that all its tags appear in pairs, and that it otherwise follows the rules of XML documents).

✦ Import or export XML data when communicating with other XML-capable applications.

WordML is primarily a set of custom tags defining the elements of a Word document (and there are hundreds of potential elements). Before WordML, you couldn't make much sense of a DOC file if you loaded it into Notepad or otherwise tried to view it as text. *Note:* It's not text; it's a binary file. WordML, however, is a fully documented set of tags that you can actually read and (if you wish) manipulate programmatically.

For example, if you open a new document in Word (File➪New), you see a task pane open up with XML document as one of the options. Click the XML document link in the task pane. An XML Structure task pane opens. Type **hello**, select it, and then make it italic and underline it. Now choose File➪Save and click the Save button in the Save As dialog box. You can choose to optionally save only the data (no schema), or if you've attached a separate schema, Word saves that information along with the data.

You then use Windows Explorer to locate the file that you just saved. (Look for an .xml extension.) Right-click the filename, and choose Open with Notepad from the context menu. In the mass of information, you should be able to locate your *hello* twice in the document, but the one you want is down near the bottom:

```
<w:r><w:rPr><w:i/><w:u w:val="single"/></w:rPr><w:t>hello</w:t></w:r>
```

Note the `<w:i/>` tag (for italics) and the `<w:u w:val="single"/>` tag (u for underlining with the additional attribute, single underlining). Rumor has it that there are more than 3,000 different tags in WordML, which is more than I can explore here. Whenever possible, smart programmers let utilities and applications convert data and documents into HTML or XML. But do be aware that every Word feature is supported by an XML tag.

Here's the most basic XML document that Word can read — that Word can translate from XML into the native DOC format. (This is not the simplest form of XML file that Word can save, which is much more complex, as you can see in the preceding *hello* example.)

```
<?xml version='1.0'?>
<w:wordDocument xmlns:w='http://schemas.microsoft.com/
office/word/2003/wordml'>

<w:body>
    <w:p><w:r><w:t>Hello, World.</w:t></w:r></w:p>
</w:body>

</w:wordDocument>
```

If you type this into Notepad (or use Save As Plain Text from within Word) and then save this file with an .xml extension, you can use File⇨Open in Word to load it into Word. When you do this and you're asked whether you want to convert it from an XML file, click OK. You see the XML neatly formatted, as shown in Figure 3-1.

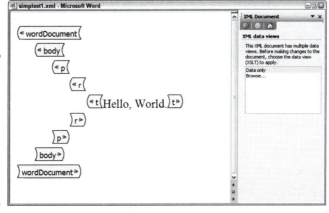

Figure 3-1:
The XML data view window, with the XML Document task pane at the ready.

All visible content in a Word document is contained within the <body> tag pair. The <p> is for paragraph, <r> for run (a *run* of text is a string of characters that all share the same formatting), and <t> is for text.

If you open a WordML file with a schema that you've attached *(referenced)* and Word cannot find the eXtensible Stylesheet Language Transformation (XSLT; schema file) in the Schema Library when opening this file, Word applies its default XSLT.

Deeper into WordML

You can, of course, automate the process of using XML by writing programming to manipulate it. One typical kind of XML programming involves translating traditional objects or data structures into XML and then back into their original formats (or indeed into other formats). You see here how that's done.

The Word XML Content Development Kit

Go to this address and download the Microsoft Word XML Content Development Kit (CDK) Beta 2. It assists you with your Word XML programming by providing sample code illustrating XML in Word 2003 and documentation about using XML in your own programming.

```
http://msdn.microsoft.com/library/default.asp?url=/downloads/list/office2k3.asp
```

After installing this software development kit (SDK), choose Start⇨All Programs⇨Microsoft Office 2003 Beta Documentation. Follow the pop-out menu items through Microsoft Word XML CDK, and click MSXML Reference. You'll see the Help window, as shown in Figure 3-2.

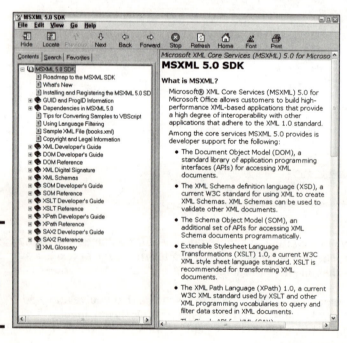

Figure 3-2: Locate information about using XML in Office 2003.

Programmatic XML

I talk more about manipulating XML data by using shocking-sounding techniques like SAX and DOM in my book *XML All-in-One Desk Reference For Dummies* (Wiley), but do note that communication is one of the advantages of using XML with Word and other applications. You can communicate between Office 2003 applications — and indeed with other entities such as .NET-created applications and utilities, or even between platforms — by using XML in your programming.

As an example, create a VBA program that builds a little XML file with two objects. (Pieces of data surrounded by schema tags can be called *objects,* but then, what can't?) First the program instantiates two objects; then it loads an XML string into each. (Read more about Word objects in Chapter 1 of this mini-book.)

Adding a reference

Open VBA in Word. In the Visual Basic editor, choose Tools⇨References. *References* attach outside code libraries to your projects; in this case, you want the XML library. Scroll in the References dialog box until you locate Microsoft XML, v 5.0 (or a later version). Select its check box to select it and then click OK to close the dialog box.

Book III
Chapter 3

Using XML in Word

Now type in this macro:

```
Sub XMLwerk()

    Dim d As New DOMDocument50
    Dim d1 As New DOMDocument50
    d.loadXML "<FirstName>Nitsy</FirstName>"
    d1.loadXML "<LastName>Aha</LastName>"

    Debug.Print d.XML, d1.XML

End Sub
```

When you press F5 to execute this macro, you'll see your XML objects printed in the Immediate window (View⇨Immediate Window). This is what you see:

```
<FirstName>Nitsy</FirstName>
<LastName>Aha</LastName>
```

You have programmatically created an XML document, added a couple of elements to it, and then printed the contents of both of those elements. In other words, you've manipulated an XML schema and its data programmatically.

Choosing XML Options in Word

When you're working with WordML, you might want to specify some behaviors regarding how XML will be validated, displayed, saved, and loaded. To do this, choose Tools⇨Templates and Add-Ins. When the dialog box opens, click the XML Schema tab and then click the XML Options button. The XML Options dialog box opens, as shown in Figure 3-3, with the following choices:

✦ **Save Data Only:** The Save Data Only option filters what data Word saves. Only data related to an attached schema will be saved; none of the other document information (such as author, date of origin, number of words, macros, and so on) is saved. This is a slimmer, less Word-specific version of saving the full XML data. If you don't choose this option (it's also available in the XML task pane), Word saves everything specified in the default WordML schema, including formatting, embedded graphics, and other such details.

✦ **Apply Custom Transform:** If you select Apply Custom Transform, Word runs the data through whatever XSLT transformation you request. Find more on transforms in Book VIII, Chapter 6.

✦ **Validate Document against Attached Schemas:** Selecting the Validate Document against Attached Schemas option causes Word to check the accuracy of the XML. In other words, it asks, *Does it conform to the schema?* Any errors are displayed in the XML Structure task pane.

✦ **Hide Schema Violations in This Document:** This option causes Word to eliminate the graphics (lines) in the document that alert you to any violations of the schema.

✦ **Ignore Mixed Content:** This option is used when you want to save DOT files (templates), and you expect users to enter data into your XML structures. Formatting that they enter along with their text causes no problems.

✦ **Allow Saving as XML Even if Not Valid:** This option permits XML to be saved even if it can't be validated via an attached schema. Use this to save your work even though you've not completely filled in the entire document (and it's thus invalid technically).

✦ **Hide Namespace Alias in XML Structure Task Pane:** This option causes Word to omit an attached schema's namespace alias (or even the entire namespace if no alias has been provided) after each element name. (*Namespace* is another clerical term used to specify a particular library of code. Read more about aliases in the following section.) Seeing the namespace repeated like this can be cumbersome, redundant, and unnecessary in the diagram displayed in the narrow task pane. You usually want a cleaner view — like the one in Figure 3-4 — especially if more than one schema is attached to your file.

✦ **Show Advanced XML Error Messages:** This option causes Word to display extra information about schema violations.

✦ **Show Placeholder Text for All Empty Elements:** This option takes effect if you've turned off the display of XML tags in the document (by deselecting the Show XML Tags in the Document option on the task pane). Word displays instead a placeholder when it finds an empty element.

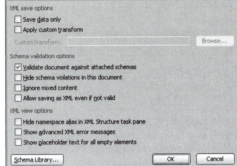

Figure 3-3:
Specify your
preferences
for XML
behaviors in
Word here.

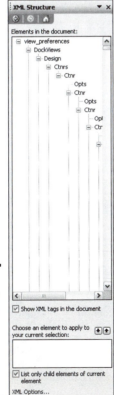

Figure 3-4:
Display only
the element
names
(as here)
without
namespace
clutter.

**Book III
Chapter 3**

Using XML in Word

Working with XML in Word's Special Editor

Try a couple of exercises to familiarize yourself with how XML documents can be manipulated by using the special XML editor window and its associated task pane. (See any of the task panes by choosing View➪Task Pane. Then click the small, inverted triangle symbol next to the X in the top-right corner to drop a list of available task panes.)

First, create a schema to use for practice. Type this simple schema (Listing 3-1) into Notepad (to avoid any extra formatting, and so on) and then save it as `PartyTime.xsd`.

Creating a practice schema

Remember that a *schema* is an XML structure into which data can be inserted. The particular schema in this example helps you plan a party by including fields for the names of all your friends as well as a Personality section describing their strengths and drawbacks as people.

Listing 3-1:   Practice XML Schema

```
<?xml version='1.0' ?>
<xs:schema id=' PartyTime'
    xmlns:xs='http://www.w3.org/2001/XMLSchema'
        >
    <xs:element name=' MyFriends' >
        <xs:complexType>
        <xs:choice maxOccurs=' unbounded' >

        <xs:element name=' NameAndComments' >
            <xs:complexType>
            <xs:sequence>
            <xs:element name=' Name'  minOccurs=' 1'  maxOccurs=' 1' >
                <xs:complexType>
                <xs:sequence>
                <xs:element name=' Firstname'  type=' xs:string'
                    minOccurs=' 1'   maxOccurs=' 1' />
                <xs:element name=' Lastname'  type=' xs:string'
                    minOccurs=' 1'  maxOccurs=' 1'  />
                </xs:sequence>
                </xs:complexType>
            </xs:element>

            <xs:element name=' Personality'  type=' xs:string'
                minOccurs=' 0'  maxOccurs=' 1'  />

            </xs:sequence>
            </xs:complexType>
        </xs:element>
        </xs:choice>
        </xs:complexType>
    </xs:element>
</xs:schema>
```

Now follow these steps to store your new schema:

1. **Choose File⇨New in Word and then choose XML Document from the task pane.**

2. **Click the <u>Templates and Add-Ins</u> link in the task pane.**

3. **Click the Add Schema button in the dialog box.**

4. **Browse your hard drive and choose** PartyTime.xsd.

5. **Type this in for the URL:** http://www.w3.org/2001/XMLSchema.

   You have to put one in, so just use this.

6. **Type** Party **for the alias.**

   It's nice to use aliases, or else you'll see the schema displayed with the entire cumbersome namespace. And sometimes you'll go hog-wild and use several schemas at once, each with its own cryptic namespace. Aliases make it easier to remember what each schema does.

7. **Close the dialog box.**

   Your new schema is displayed in the task pane as MyFriends{Party}. Party is the namespace alias.

You now have your empty shell into which you can pour data. This schema is also automatically added to the library of schemas maintained by Word (and it can be later used with other documents).

Using the XML Structure Task Pane

Word's XML Structure task pane offers several advantages to the busy XML document creator. With it you can

✦ See the entire structure of the attached schema(s), including child elements nestled within outer elements.

✦ See the structure displayed hierarchically.

✦ Edit the XML data by adding and removing elements.

✦ Show or hide tags within Document view.

✦ Get error messages if you abuse the schema's structure (removing an End tag, for example).

Building your XML document

Now build an actual XML document by adding some data. In the Element list at the bottom of the task pane, you see the top-level element (the outermost element, or the one within which all other elements are nested). It's MyFriends.

Book III
Chapter 3

Using XML in Word

Click it in the list to add to your document, and you see NamesAndComments, which is the second outermost pair of tags in this Russian dolls eggs-within-eggs structure of nested items.

You now see the outer element tag pair in your document, as shown in Figure 3-5.

Figure 3-5:
Your first
XML tag
pair ready
for editing in
Document
view.

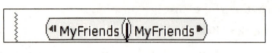

At this point, though, you've been a bad puppy and made a mess . . . temporarily. Notice the little question mark in the top of the task pane. Hover your mouse pointer over that ? to see Word telling you that you've violated one of the rules of your schema. That's right: This must contain other elements. In other words, just your outermost tag pair by itself does not a valid document make, according to your schema. And, should you be a really bad dog and try to save this as an XML file, you'll be told that you can't because it's in violation of the rules. You can save it as a DOC file but not as an XML file.

Word also alerts you to the violation with the vertical, saw-toothed purple line in Document view. Right-click that, and you get the same violation report at the top of the context menu. Anyway, you know what to do: Add more elements to correct the violation.

Notice in the lower box in the task pane that a new element (the second outermost) is now displayed: NameAndComments, which you should click. It's inserted where it should be between the outer MyFriends tags. Click Firstname in the task pane box. Notice that the box is now empty because no further nested tags are within the Name pair. However, there are two other pairs of tags: LastName and Personality. To see them in the box, press the right-arrow key. Now you see Firstname and Lastname. Click Lastname.

At this point, the two, innermost tag pairs become strange. They turn pink! And they also no longer display tag pairs but have been collapsed into a single pink icon, with ( ) closed parentheses. This is to save some space in the diagram. It's still the same old open-tag/close-tag pair in the underlying XML, but for your viewing pleasure, tags that can hold data automatically turn pink and collapse. You can force other (no-data) tags to collapse, too, if you wish. Click to the left of a tag and then press Tab. That tag-pair collapses, and any tags that it encloses (*child elements* as they're called) also collapse. Ctrl+Z reverses the collapse.

At this point, you might want to cursor around within the document and use the Enter key and others to format the diagram in the usual XML way, putting child elements on their own lines, indenting to show nesting, or whatever else rings your bell. The underlying XML is unaffected by these merely visual rearrangements.

To add the final data element, `Personality`, click between the `Name` and `NameAndComments` closing tags. You see `Name` and `Personality` listed in the task pane box. (You can add as many `Name` elements as you wish; that's why it's available.) However, just click the `Personality` element to add it to the diagram. `Personality` has no child elements. At this point, your document should look something like Figure 3-6.

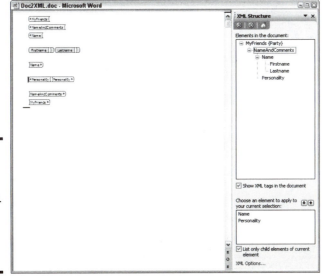

Figure 3-6:
Your complete `Party` XML document, displayed in two diagrams.

Book III
Chapter 3

Using XML in Word

Type in a first name, last name, and a brief description of the personality in the appropriate places between the parentheses and the tags. Then choose File⇨Save As and save the document as `Party.xml`. This time, Word doesn't object to your wish to save the file.

Extending the variety of uses to which a single XML data document can be put is not difficult in Word. You can manipulate the data or schema itself via SAX and DOM techniques, and you can convert XML into various formats via transforms. These and other topics are covered in various sections throughout this book, and specifically in Book VIII, Chapter 6.

Chapter 4: The Internet Connection

In This Chapter

- ✔ Creating Web pages in Word
- ✔ Understanding Web file types
- ✔ Changing Web options
- ✔ Using the Web Tools toolbar
- ✔ Using Web page controls
- ✔ Scripting Word Web pages
- ✔ Testing Web pages
- ✔ Understanding ASP

Can your Word documents be stored as Web pages and then viewed on the Internet? Indeed, they can. As you see in this chapter, you won't want to use Word as the front end for a big enterprise database-driven invoicing system. But for smaller jobs, such as displaying your pictures or blogging your feelings for all to see, Word does a serviceable job. And if you've already created documents that you want to display to the world, nothing could be easier than changing DOC files into Web pages.

Creating Web Pages in Word

Few areas of contemporary computing have been untouched by the impact of the Internet, which is currently estimated to comprise 92-million giga-bytes of data (and exploding). Office 2003 applications are no exception.

If you're creating a complex, huge Web site, use a dedicated Web page designer application. FrontPage, for example, includes helpful tools to make working with multifaceted sites easier than using Word. And if you want true power — including tools for creating dynamic, scalable Web pages — go for Visual Studio .NET.

However, if you're comfortable working in Word — you're familiar with its formatting features, tables, and so on — you can design perfectly fine Web pages in Word. Just do what you normally do to create and design a document, and what you see is what you will get on the Internet.

When you save a Word document as a Web page, you can then load that page into Internet Explorer and be pleased with what you see. Word does the tough job of translating the document into a Web page; all the HTML code is hidden from you. Yet, with the exception of a few items (headers, footers, and newspaper-style columns, which HTML doesn't support), the page should look pretty much as you designed it.

And if you need to build some interactivity built into your Web page, VBScript and JScript are available in Word as well. But don't be misled: Word-designed Web pages are largely for display and not serious interactivity. You can build nice advertisements, informative tutorials, and so on. But because Word is a document-processing system, it simply doesn't offer the tools necessary to build a database-driven, heavy-duty, or complex interactive Web site. For that, do consider using Visual Studio .NET instead.

Saving as a Web Page: The Three Kinds of Files

When you choose File⇨Save as Web Page, you're given a choice between three file types:

✦ **Ordinary, plain HTML:** Word calls this type *filtered* because all Word codes are stripped out and only HTML is left. Choose this if you plan to edit the page further in some other Web page editor that could trip on some of the proprietary Word formatting.

✦ **Web Page:** This includes both HTML and the codes that Word uses to construct the page's formatting in the Word editor. This choice creates a larger file, obviously, but it allows you to continue working on the page in Word.

✦ **Single File Web page** (Mime, MHTML with an `.mht` extension)**:** This format incorporates any necessary support pages (such as a graphics file) into a single file. If you don't choose this option, any support files are kept in a separate, dependency folder from the main HTML file.

Adjusting the Web Options Settings

You can make more specific adjustments for your Web pages in Word by choosing Tools⇨Options and then clicking the Web Options button of the General tab. Here, as shown in Figure 4-1, you can select specific target browsers, which is useful if you're creating pages for an office intranet and you know that your company is still using an old version of Internet Explorer or even Netscape.

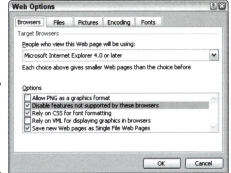

Figure 4-1:
Change Web options in this dialog box.

The Portable Network Graphics (PNG) and Vector Markup Language (VML) graphics formats are relatively new but do outperform the standard formats such as JPG. PNG is a beefed-up version of GIF, with support for 48-bit true-color or 16-bit grayscale and improved compression. VML uses equations to describe shape and fills, resulting in highly scalable drawings with very little bandwidth hit. (The drawings are described mathematically rather than transmitted as graphics files.) Of course, the results are essentially cartoonish, clip-art quality — not photographic.

Because cascading style sheets (CSSes) are pretty much universally understood now, you probably leave that option selected. Use the Files tab to refine how you want your Word Web pages saved, and the Pictures tab specifies the monitor resolution you want to target. Adjusting the pixels per inch (ppi) allows you to adjust the loading time of graphics-intensive Web pages (by, for example, speeding things up at the expense of some image quality by setting the ppi to 72). Leave this one alone for most applications. The Fonts tab allows you to specify different default fonts.

Building a Web Page in Word

You can take two approaches to creating a Web page in Word: Start with an ordinary Word document and then save it as a Web page, or begin with a blank Web page from Word's File➪New menu. I suggest that you take the second approach because Word knows from the beginning that you intend this document to end up on the Internet, so it offers you some additional help (some menu features specific to HTML, for example).

To create a new Web page, follow these steps:

1. **Choose File➪New.**

The New Document task pane pops out.

2. Click the <u>Web page</u> link in the task pane.

A new document opens, looking pretty normal (but don't be fooled). Take a look at the mouse pointer, for example. It's got some extra lines following it around the screen; it's a different icon than the usual I-beam shape, as shown in Figure 4-2.

Figure 4-2:
Your mouse cursor is followed by some extra lines when you're in the Web page design window.

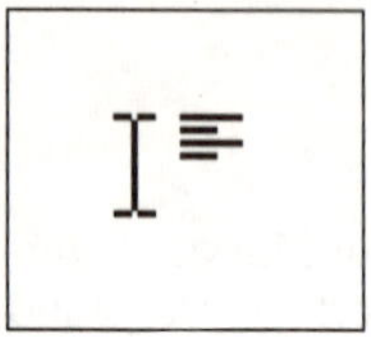

3. Create your Web page by typing in some text and maybe adding some pictures (choose Insert⇨Picture).

4. For a good scare, choose View⇨HTML Source.

The Microsoft Script Editor opens, holding your code. You can type in VBScript (or JScript) if you wish, using this editor. You also see the bloated HTML code that is necessary to display your few words and graphics in a Web page, as shown in Figure 4-3.

5. Close the Script Editor.

No point in spooking yourself by seeing what unfortunate Web programmers had to contend with a few years ago. You'll reopen this editor at the end of this chapter to fiddle around a bit with scripting, which isn't the same thing as writing HTML. Scripts are Visual Basic (or Java), somewhat pared down to remove file-access and other behaviors that could be used for bad purposes by hackers.

6. Choose File⇨Save As.

The Save As dialog box opens.

7. In the Save as Type list box on the bottom of the dialog box, choose Web Page.

The file is saved. If you inserted graphics, a subfolder is created to hold them.

Figure 4-3:
The Script
Editor,
displaying
the HTML
code.

8. In Windows Explorer, locate the HTM file that you just saved, and double-click its filename to open it.

Your browser (probably Internet Explorer) opens, and your Web page is displayed, as shown in Figure 4-4.

If you're creating a Web page, you'll probably enter a test-modify/code-retest cycle until you get things working as you want. It's simpler to view and test the Web page by using the File➪Web Page Preview feature than to save the file each time through the cycle and then activate it via Windows Explorer, as you did in Step 8 in the preceding example.

Figure 4-4:
A finished
Web page,
displayed in
a browser
as it would
be seen via
the Internet.

Using the Web Tools Toolbar

With the various buttons on the Web Tools toolbar, you can easily add a variety of useful controls, such as check boxes, option (radio) buttons, list boxes, text boxes, submit buttons, passwords — even movies and sound. Just click in your document where you want the control, and then click its icon on the toolbar.

Right-click any toolbar in Word and then mark the Web Tools check box in the drop-down list of toolbars. You see the Web Tools toolbar, as shown in Figure 4-5.

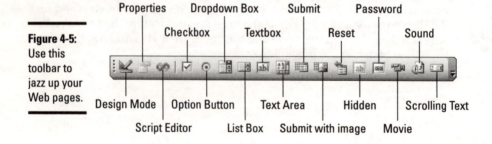

Figure 4-5:
Use this
toolbar to
jazz up your
Web pages.

You can also use this toolbar to add special effects, such as scrolling text (great, if you like annoying people) and background texture (okay if used in moderation).

Adding scrolling text

I ask that you avoid using scrolling text. (Shudder.) It's usually second only to animations and pop-ups as the most annoying features of vulgar Web sites. Used mostly for ads, scrolling text makes it hard to read the other elements on the Web page. But if you must (cough . . . if the boss insists), add it from the Scrolling Text dialog box, as shown in Figure 4-6.

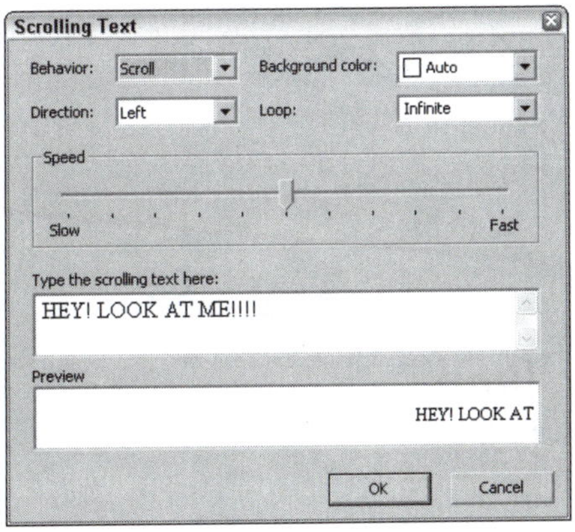

Figure 4-6: Add annoying scrolling or sliding text marquees to your Web pages. Sigh.

Open this dialog box by clicking the rightmost icon on the Web Tools toolbar.

Adding background texture

Background textures do add quality to your Web pages. From the Fill Effects dialog box (choose Format➪Background➪Fill Effects), you can add gradients, textures, or graphics to the background of your Web page. (Another option, patterns, I'd avoid. They're not only distracting; they're also cheesy.) A gradient adds interest to the Web page shown in Figure 4-7. Gradients, if not too extreme, add a nice metallic look. The one in Figure 4-7 goes from white to gray, but I recommend avoiding the default white-to-black gradient because it's too strong.

The textures available in this dialog box are also useful, but again, as with gradients, use a light touch and ensure that the background doesn't interfere with the foreground text and graphics, as it does in Figure 4-8.

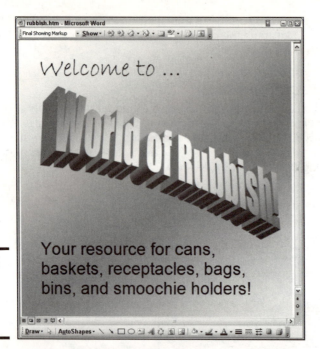

Figure 4-7:
Gradients
can add a
metallic
look.

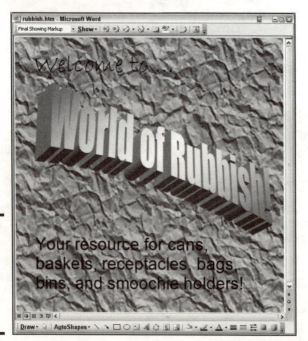

Figure 4-8:
A crumpled
paper
texture can
overpower
foreground
text.

Scripting in Word Web Pages

While viewing your Word Web page, press Alt+Shift+F11. There it is! A VBA-style editor, complete with a Toolbox for adding controls, debugging facilities, a properties window for adjusting controls' qualities, and a project window to show you the various documents and other files in the current project (which in this case is a Web site).

Although Word created the HTML that describes your Web page, strangely enough, you'll find lots of little, squiggly red underlines in the code. These are indications of various errors in the HTML code, but just ignore them. The editor's parser is evidently more uptight about HTML violations and illegal nesting than Internet Explorer is. And lucky for you, you don't have to worry about this stuff, anyway.

You can drag and drop controls from the Toolbox into the code, but do try to add them in the right places (not within attribute lists of other elements, not in the header, and so on). In fact, it's easier to add controls from the Web Tools toolbar. (See the earlier section, "Using the Web Tools Toolbar.") Remember that you're working in a design view (not this code view), and you can let Word worry about inserting the controls' code where it should be inserted. However, the Toolbox in the Scripting Editor does have a few controls not available on the Web Tools toolbar.

Scripting is inserted into an HTML page between `<SCRIPT>` tag pairs `</SCRIPT>`. Also, the script code is clumsily enclosed within the HTML tag pair for comment: `<!--`

`-->`

Normally in programming, a commented zone within code is ignored and not executed. In HTML, though, this merely prevents browsers that cannot execute script from instead displaying the source code to users (many of whom would be baffled by seeing it).

Scripting is similar to programming any other language, but note a few differences:

✦ **HTML pages are read from top to bottom by a browser, so you usually insert your script code in the** HEAD **section of a Web page.**

This way, it's decoded by the browser and is ready to respond to any action that later takes place in the lower BODY section of the page.

✦ **You can put your code within** Sub **or** Function **procedures, and that code executes only when the procedure is called (by other code in the page).**

Or, if you put code outside a procedure, that code is executed only one time — when the page first loads. So, you put your initialization code outside procedures in the HEAD section, which is the equivalent of using VB's Form_Load event.

To see how all this works, create a new Web Page (File⇨New⇨Web Page) and then press Alt+Shift+F11 to open the editor. In the HEAD section (just above the </head> tag), type this function:

```
<script language="VBScript">
<!--
Function SubmitIt()
n = Msgbox ("Thank you for your order!")
End Function

-->
</script>
</head>
```

You can name the function whatever you want. It's an event that will respond whenever a Submit button (a button-style control in HTML) is clicked by the user.

Whenever you want to insert script, you can get the template of the code by right-clicking the background of the code window and then choosing Insert Script from the context menu.

In the code view in the Editor, click in the BODY section of your HTML code and then double-click the Submit button on the Toolbox. This code is inserted for you:

```
<INPUT type="submit" value="Submit" ID=Submit1>
```

That's enough to display a Submit button in a browser, but you need to add an additional attribute to this element to make it trigger your function whenever the user clicks this button:

```
<INPUT type="submit" value="Submit" ID=Submit1 onclick="SubtmitIt()">
```

By adding an onclick attribute, you're telling the browser to execute the named procedure — SubmitIt in this case — whenever the user clicks the button. This is one way to interact with the user.

If you copy code from a word processor, the code will contain extra formatting codes when you paste it into a code editor such as the Script Editor or Visual Studio. It will look something like this:

```
<p class=Code>&lt;INPUT type=&quot;submit&quot;
    value=&quot;Submit&quot;ID=Submit1&gt; </p>
```

Understanding ASP

One of the best ways to interact with users — and to provide dynamic content in Web pages, such as database interactivity — is ASP and not ordinary scripting. *Active Server Pages* (ASPs) refers to a technology in which you can write scripting such as VBScript (or using ASP.NET, you can use the full VB.NET language) to respond to and interact with Web site visitors in a more efficient way than with ordinary scripting. The key is that security problems are solved because no script is ever sent to the user's browser. Instead, all *executables* (scripts or programming code) run on the server — only HTML is sent to the user.

When a Web page is loaded into a browser (when a user visits a Web site), the user's browser handles the typical HTML codes — for example, ⟨H1⟩, which causes the browser to display text as a large headline. (⟨H1⟩ means Heading #1, the biggest one.)

However, if a Web page contains ASP programming, something happens before the page is sent to the user. Any code in the page found between the special ASP percent symbol codes ⟨% and %⟩ is interpreted on the server where the Web site sits. The page is interpreted before that Web page is sent to the user's browser. The server translates the programming code into plain ordinary HTML, so there's no security issue — it flows directly into the user's browser.

What use is ASP in a real-world situation? Without ASP, Web pages can be mere exercises in publishing — not all that much more useful or advanced than the traditional advertisement. If you own a bookstore, you can print a flyer or take out an ad in a paper. You can do the same kind of thing with your Web site — list titles and display covers. Because users block scripts, your page is not interactive.

But by adding ASP to your Web pages, you enable users. They can, for example, tap into your databases directly (read-only, of course, unless you specify otherwise). With ASP, you could let a visitor to your bookstore's site see the latest discounts, see all the books you offer by searching your database, compare prices interactively, and even place orders. In other words, users can do dynamic things that used to require both a phone call to your office and a person in your office to provide assistance. Think of it this way: The ASP technology — to a great extent — lets users be their own customer service department.

When a user clicks a button or otherwise interacts with the page, a message is sent back to the server for a response. Executables execute on the server, and another HTML page is composed and sent back to the user. In this way, users can interact with your site without facing any danger of virus attacks. Thus, if you want to create Web pages that seriously, dynamically interact with users, abandon the features available in Word or other Office 2003 applications and start using Visual Studio .NET to build your Web site.

Book III
Chapter 4

The Internet Connection

To strip off all the unwanted codes, first paste the copied programming into Notepad. Then copy it from Notepad (select it and then press Ctrl+C) and paste it into the editor. It will then look like this, as it should:

```
<INPUT type="submit" value="Submit" ID=Submit1>
```

Testing your Web page

Now test your Web page. Go to the design view of your Web page (the Word document view) and click the Refresh button if necessary. You should see your Submit button. Choose File➪Web Page Preview. Click the Submit button in the browser, and you should see your message box. (If you don't see it, proofread your code to ensure that your `onclick` attribute includes the correctly spelled name of the function.)

In VBScript, you can avoid having to add an event trap to a Submit button. VBScript allows you to simply create a function with the ID of the object (`submit1` in this example) separated by an underline (_) from the name of the event you're handling (`onclick` in this example). So you could optionally omit the `onclick="SubmitIt()"` attribute and just name your function like this: `Function Submit1_OnClick()`. If you name the `Function` like that, it will be executed when the user clicks the Submit1 button.

Understanding scripting's drawbacks

Alas, scripting has been responsible for some virii — or blamed for it, anyway — so some people turn off scripting in their browsers. Then no script can execute. A more elegant and universally effective approach is available via Active Server Pages (ASP).

Chapter 5: Advanced Word Macros

In This Chapter

✓ Deciding what deserves to be automated

✓ Accessing other Office applications from within Word

✓ Modifying Word's built-in features

✓ Specialized formatting

✓ Advanced automation

✓ The best Word macros of all time

*W*ith VBA, you can use a macro to automate anything that you do repeatedly. Macros are a highly useful way to shift the burden of repetitive tasks from you to the machine. And don't forget that you can turn on the macro recorder and then follow the usual steps to accomplish your task (for the last time). When you're finished, just turn off the recorder, assign your macro to a shortcut key combination, and happily ever after just press a couple of keys to accomplish what you used to do slavishly by hand.

In this chapter, you see how to contact and manipulate other Office applications from within Word, access and modify the behavior of Word's built-in features such as FileSave, and are treated to what I consider the best Word macros available (at least for a writer).

Writing Macros 101

Perhaps the best way to master Office applications' macro programming is to record a macro and then look at the code that's automatically produced. (Choose Tools➪Macro➪Record New Macro.) In fact, if you ever get confused and need to see how a menu item or some other feature can be coded into VBA — the macro language — just record the behaviors, press Alt+F11 to open the macro code editor, and look at the code.

Additionally, macros can also do some things that are not available in normal Word. That is, they can do things that don't appear in any toolbar or menu. For example, you can contact other applications and send messages back and forth between Word and the outside application. To see how to send some data to an Excel worksheet, type the Sub in Listing 5-1 in the macro editor.

Listing 5-1:   Sending Interapplication Data via a Macro

```
Sub ContactExcel()

Dim ExcelSheet As Object
Set ExcelSheet = CreateObject("Excel.Sheet")

With ExcelSheet.Application
    .Cells(1, 1) = "Hello, Excel! This is Word speaking!."
    .ActiveWorkbook.SaveAs "c:\ExcelTest.xls"
    .Quit
End With
Set ExcelSheet = Nothing
End Sub
```

To execute the macro, press F5 while your blinking insertion cursor is inside this `Sub` in the code window. Although nothing seems to happen, use Windows Explorer to double-click the new file (`ExcelTest.xls`) on your C drive. When you do, the file loads in Excel, proving that Word started Excel running (`CreateObject`), sent your data to one of the cells in the current worksheet, saved the workbook that contained this worksheet, and then closed Excel — all with a few lines of code.

If you prefer to see Excel running, just the `.Visible = True` property in the above code.

```
With ExcelSheet.Application
    .Visible = True
    .Cells(1, 1) = "Hello, Excel! This is Word speaking!"
    .ActiveWorkbook.SaveAs "c:\ExcelTest.xls"
End With
```

If you want users to be able to see the names of your macros and execute them, create them as a `Sub` in the Macros dialog box (Tools⇨Macro⇨Macros). If you don't want a macro to appear in the dialog box, create it as a `Function`.

Interception: Modifying Built-In Word Features

Another great use for macros is their ability to intercept Word's built-in menu or toolbar features and make them behave differently. For example, to override the File⇨Save option through a macro — replacing the usual actions with your own preferences — just name the macro after the menu+item, such as `Sub FileSave()`. Now whenever someone chooses File⇨Save (or activates it otherwise, such as via a shortcut key combination), your macro — not the built-in Save action — will execute.

Here's a useful example. Perhaps you want to always save your documents in two different locations on your hard drive as a safety measure. After all, unless you're directly hit by a meteor, it isn't inevitable that two different locations on your hard drive will simultaneously fail. (Of course, they could, which is why you also back up your work to CDs or some other offline storage.) But saving your current document to two locations in your computer (or perhaps a separate, second disk drive) is a good precaution.

Suppose that whenever you choose File⇨Save, you want to save the document in the normal way, but you also want to save a copy of the document to a directory called `C:\archives`. First, record a macro that copies the File⇨Save As action. Listing 5-2 shows you the format for `SaveAs`, which is what you want when saving two copies because `SaveAs` is necessary if you're changing the filepath for the Save. Then press Alt+F11 to see your new macro in the editor.

Listing 5-2:   Double-Saving a Document

```
Sub doublesave()
'
' doublesave Macro
' Macro recorded 12/31/2003 by Richard
'
ActiveDocument.SaveAs FileName:= "bk0305 new.doc",
        FileFormat:=wdFormatDocument, _
    LockComments:=False, Password:="",
        AddToRecentFiles:=True, WritePassword _
    :="", ReadOnlyRecommended:=False,
        EmbedTrueTypeFonts:=False, _
    SaveNativePictureFormat:=False, SaveFormsData:=False,
        SaveAsAOCELetter:= _
    False

End Sub
```

Fair enough. But now you want to also save the backup copy as well. When you use `SaveAs`, the current directory is switched to the new target of the `SaveAs`. However, you don't want this to happen. You want to preserve the current directory. The way to do this is to first store the current directory:

```
Path = Selection.Document.FullName 'save current path
```

Then build a new filepath for the backup:

```
bakpath = "c:\archives\" & Selection.Document.Name 'create backup path
```

Now you can employ these paths to first `SaveAs` to the archive folder and then `SaveAs` to the original folder (which has the effect of restoring the original current directory). The complete macro is in Listing 5-3.

Book III Chapter 5

Advanced Word Macros

Listing 5-3: The Complete Double-Save Backup Macro

```
Sub FileSave()
'
' doublesave: archive and original, for backup

Path = Selection.Document.FullName 'save current path
bakpath = "c:\archives\" & Selection.Document.Name 'create
         backup path

    ActiveDocument.SaveAs FileName:=bakpath,
        FileFormat:=wdFormatDocument, _
        LockComments:=False, Password:="",
        AddToRecentFiles:=True, WritePassword _
        :="", ReadOnlyRecommended:=False,
        EmbedTrueTypeFonts:=False, _
        SaveNativePictureFormat:=False, SaveFormsData:=False,
        SaveAsAOCELetter:= _
        False

    ActiveDocument.SaveAs FileName:=Path,
        FileFormat:=wdFormatDocument, _
        LockComments:=False, Password:="",
        AddToRecentFiles:=True, WritePassword _
        :="", ReadOnlyRecommended:=False,
        EmbedTrueTypeFonts:=False, _
        SaveNativePictureFormat:=False, SaveFormsData:=False,
        SaveAsAOCELetter:= _
        False

    WordBasic.PrintStatusBar "This document, and a backup,
        were saved, honey."

End Sub
```

Finally, as a courtesy to myself, I display a subtle, yet heartwarming, message on the status bar.

If you get an error when running this macro, your security settings are likely to blame. The path specified might be read-only or something. As usual, when you're tripped up by security, consult your administrator. If you're the administrator, consult your own bad self.

Using Macros for Specialized Formatting

You should also consider employing macros to combine multistep jobs like specialized formatting. For example, one book publisher's editors do not like the phrase *do not*. They want you to replace it with *don't,* on the theory that this usage is more friendly, less academic, and less bossy. I suppose they're right. They go further: They want you to replace *cannot* with *can't, will not* with *won't,* and *for instance* with *for example.* So, the intelligent person records these various search and replace actions into a single macro. Then, each chapter can be instantly scanned and fixed in one single step by running the macro. In Listing 5-4, you can see what part of this macro looks like.

Listing 5-4:   Replacement Formatting in Word

```
Sub firstFormat()
'
' firstFormat Macro
' Macro recorded 12/2/2002 by   Richard Mansfield
'
    Selection.Find.ClearFormatting
    Selection.Find.Replacement.ClearFormatting
    With Selection.Find
        .Text = "cannot"
        .Replacement.Text = "can't"
        .Forward = True
        .Wrap = wdFindContinue
        .Format = False
        .MatchCase = False
        .MatchWholeWord = False
        .MatchWildcards = False
        .MatchSoundsLike = False
        .MatchAllWordForms = False
    End With
    Selection.Find.Execute Replace:=wdReplaceAll
    With Selection.Find
        .Text = "will not"
        .Replacement.Text = "won't"
        .Forward = True
        .Wrap = wdFindContinue
        .Format = False
        .MatchCase = False
        .MatchWholeWord = False
        .MatchWildcards = False
        .MatchSoundsLike = False
        .MatchAllWordForms = False
    End With
```

Macros should also be used when you want to combine formatting jobs that cannot be accomplished via a single Search and Replace dialog box. For example, you cannot simultaneously format both a paragraph and a font: These require two separate dialog boxes. However, you can accomplish this kind of thing with macros. Also, you're likely to find various jobs easier when you assign macros to keyboard shortcuts. Anyone who frequently writes or edits documents will understand.

For example, I frequently have to apply four headline styles while I'm writing a book. I could drop the list box of styles on the Standard toolbar and scroll through that list to find the appropriate headline style. I *could,* but I'd be nuts. It's far easier to create this macro (see the following steps):

```
Sub AltH()
    Selection.Style = ActiveDocument.Styles("Heading 1")
End Sub
```

Now assign this macro to the Alt+H key combination:

1. **Choose Tools➪Customize➪Keyboard.**

2. **In the Customize Keyboard dialog box, click Macros in the category list.**

3. **Find the appropriate macro in the list on the right and click it to select it (in this case, the macro named** `AltH`**).**

4. **Click in the Press New Shortcut Key text box and press whatever key combination you want.**

   I suggest Alt+H, for *headline.* Then I follow this same approach to redefine Alt+J (Headline Style 2) and Alt+K (Headline Style 3).

   If your new shortcut is already assigned to a different (perhaps Word default) shortcut, such as Ctrl+O (the Open standard), you see a message to that effect. You can usually override the default, but some presets are sacrosanct, like File➪Open (Ctrl+O). For more limitations on what keys you can (yea!) and can't (argg) reassign, see the later section, "Redefining ordinary keys." And for the scoop on how to override Word's overrides (woohoo!), see the later section, "Switching windows and deleting words."

5. **Click the Assign button.**

   The shortcut that you enter hops to the Current Key field.

6. **Click the Close button to exit the Customize Keyboard dialog box and then click the Close button of the Customize dialog box.**

Thereafter, any time I want a Level 1 (main) heading, I just press Alt+H anywhere on the line where the headline sits, and it's instantly formatted.

Naming shortcut keys

Follow these simple rules when assigning keyboard shortcuts.

✦ **Name the macro after the shortcut (**`AltH`, `AltJ`, `AltK`, `AltL`, **for example).**

   This way, you can always tell which keyboard shortcut triggers the macro.

   You can also look up this information by choosing Tools➪Customize➪ Keyboard and then clicking the name of the macro to see the macro's shortcut combination.

✦ **Name the macro after its purpose.**

Some people prefer to give their macros names that are descriptive of the macro's job: `LevelOneHeadlineStyle`, for example. This approach doesn't interest me because I find it quite easy to read the programming code in a macro to find out what it does. However, you could always add a descriptive comment to the code by preceding the line with a single quote character: `'`.

✦ **Group related macros together.**

For example, in my macros, `AltH`, `AltJ`, `AltK`, and `AltL` apply the four heading styles from largest to smallest, respectively.

✦ **When possible, use mnemonic first characters.**

For example, use `AltH` for *h*eadline style, `AltN` for *n*ormal style, and so on.

Storing macros

For the most part, you can store your macros in the `Normal.dot` (`NewMacros`) file, which is the template that's always loaded with any document you open, no matter what other templates might also be used. When you first record a macro, it's automatically stored in `Normal.dot` by default, as you can see in Figure 5-1.

**Book III
Chapter 5**

Advanced Word Macros

Figure 5-1:
Unless you specify otherwise, a newly recorded macro is stored in `Normal.dot`.

You can choose to store this macro only in the current document by selecting the Store Macro In drop-down list as shown in Figure 5-1. In that case, the macro is usable only when this document is the active one: that is, not in any other document. You can also store a macro in a template so that it works only in documents that use that template. Select this option from the Store Macro In drop-down list, too. Finally, you can store macros in add-ins, but I've never tried that.

Add-ins can, however, be useful in their own right, without using any macro code in them. In Book VIII, Chapter 1, you can read all about add-ins and see how to create them. One major advantage of creating an add-in is that you thereby bring VB.NET's powerful programming capabilities to your Office projects. Add-ins use compiled native code and also run in-process, thus avoiding the slight speed penalty exacted when either of these conditions are not met. Also, as the example in Book VIII, Chapter 1 illustrates, a single COM add-in can automatically load within multiple Office applications (either at application startup or on demand, depending on your specification).

Automating Macro Execution

To have Word automatically execute a macro at specified times, give the macro the following names:

- ✦ `AutoExec`: Runs each time you start Word
- ✦ `AutoNew`: Runs each time you create a new document
- ✦ `AutoClose`: Runs when you close a document
- ✦ `AutoExit`: Runs each time you shut down Word itself (not just a document)
- ✦ `AutoOpen`: Runs whenever you open a template (or any document based on a template) containing a macro with this name

To use one of these special macros, just name the macro using one of the words in the list above. For example, to display the word count each time you close a document, name your macro `AutoClose`, like this:

```
Sub AutoClose()

Dim dlg As Object: Set dlg = WordBasic.DialogRecord.Documentstatistics(False)
      WordBasic.Curvalues.Documentstatistics dlg

MsgBox "Words: " & dlg.Words

End Sub
```

The Best Word Macros of All Time

Well, perhaps I exaggerate, but the following macros are those that I've found most useful. I have been a busy beaver in the past two decades, using a word processor (on average) 5 hours a day for 20 years. I've used Word since it first became available, switching from Word Perfect (which was serviceable but less powerful and less well-thought-out).

We don't need no stinkin' f key

I had an extra computer keyboard in my study. (When you buy a new computer, you sometimes get a keyboard even if you don't want it.) A lady was visiting me and asked whether she could buy it because she needed a new one. I asked her: "Do you use the letter *f* very often? Could you work around it?" She replied: "Is it bad?" I told her, "The keyboard works just fine, but it doesn't print the letter *f*." She considered this for a moment and then said that yes, she needed the *f*. I told her that I was just joking and gave her the keyboard . . . but I don't think she ever really forgave me for my funny little prank.

My favorites list is, of course, skewed toward what's most useful for a writer because that's what I do. But I suspect some of these macros are universally worth using.

You can find other nifty macros earlier in this chapter, like `DoubleSave` (see Listing 5-2) and `FirstFormat` (see Listing 5-4). There are also some good macros sprinkled here and there throughout this book. If you have any personal favorite macros — for any Office 2003 application — I'd be interested in seeing them. Please send them to `richardm52@hotmail.com`.

Redefining ordinary keys

You can easily assign key combinations such as Alt+H to macros. See the earlier section, "Using Macros for Specialized Formatting." However, you aren't allowed to redefine ordinary character keys, such as *r* or *z*. And you sometimes want to do just that.

Frivolity aside, you really do need all the normal keyboard characters except for three: the accent grave (`; the one just under the Esc key) and [ ], the two square brackets. Only a few nationalities need an accent grave diacritical mark, and unless you're a typist for a mathematics professor, you don't much need brackets either. If you find you ever do need them (ahem, I just did to write this paragraph), you can always type them into Notepad and then copy and paste them into the Word document. A bit cumbersome, true, but rare. And by freeing up these keys, you can assign them to macros you use every time you use Word. They're the best because they're not even key combinations — you just press a single key, and the macro executes.

The next section illustrates how to assign macros to these keys.

Switching windows and deleting words

I often have two documents open at once — one containing notes and research, and the other in which I'm actually writing. I like to be able to switch quickly between them. I assign the accent grave key to this important job.

You can always use Word's Window menu to switch, but one of the most significant benefits of redefining keys is that you don't have to take your hands from the keyboard and reach for the mouse, or go through a series of shortcut key maneuvers to access the menu system. Here's the macro that switches to the next open document. If you want to use it, too, just type this into the macro editor, naming it `NextWindow`:

```
Sub NextWindow()
WordBasic.NextWindow
End Sub
```

If you want to ensure that the windows are always full-screen, add this line just above the `End Sub`:

```
Application.WindowState = wdWindowStateMaximize
```

I assign both bracket keys to a macro that deletes the word currently closest to the blinking insertion cursor. I use both because I so frequently have to quickly delete words, and using both bracket keys makes it almost impossible to press the wrong key. Repeatedly pressing this key sucks up whole strings of words quite rapidly, as if it were a vacuum. To me, it's an indispensable macro, and here it is:

```
Sub killword()

WordBasic.DeleteWord

End Sub
```

Now I don't need to select a word before deleting it, repeatedly press the Backspace or Delete key, or resort to any mouse/keypress interactions. I just press one of the bracket keys, and the word to the right of the insertion cursor vaporizes immediately.

Not out of the woods yet. Remember that you have to reassign keys: the accent grave key to point to the `NextWindow` macro, and the bracket keys to point to the `killword` macro.

This next `Sub` does the trick. Type this (Listing 5-5) into the macro editor.

Listing 5-5: Key Reassignment Macro

```
Sub Assignkey()
'219 is keycode for left bracket
'221 is keycode for right bracket
'96 is keycode for Circumflex (lowercase)

'run this macro to assign "killword" macro to the brackets
'just delete the assignment (in Tools@-->Customize@-->
           Keyboard) to 'restore the bracket keys

WordBasic.ToolsCustomizeKeyboard Category:=1,
           Name:="killword", KeyCode:=219, Add:=1
WordBasic.ToolsCustomizeKeyboard Category:=1,
           Name:="killword", KeyCode:=221, Add:=1
WordBasic.ToolsCustomizeKeyboard Category:=1,
           Name:="NextWindow", KeyCode:=96, Add:=1

'OR TO UNDO THIS CHANGE
'WordBasic.ToolsCustomizeKeyboard Category:=1,
           Name:="killword", KeyCode:=219, Remove:=1
'WordBasic.ToolsCustomizeKeyboard Category:=1,
           Name:="killword", KeyCode:=221, Remove:=1
End Sub
```

**Book III
Chapter 5**

**Advanced Word
Macros**

By going inside the engine room underneath Word and grabbing hold of the tube that routes keystrokes, you can assign a macro to a keycode (representing the tube through which the electricity flows when a particular key is pressed). By using the Add:=1 command, you tell Word to flip this switch and route this keystroke to your macro instead of simply printing the character onscreen. This is the same process that Word itself uses when you define a custom key combination, except here you're doing it on a low level — bypassing Word's refusal to permit some redefinitions in its Customize Keyboard dialog box.

If you are one of the few who rarely use the *f* key (see the sidebar, "We don't need no stinkin' f key") and wish to redirect it (or any other key) to a macro, you can find the codes by searching VBA Help for Character Set.

Assigning normal style

I assign Alt+N (for *normal*) to the normal style macro so that when I copy and paste text into my documents, I can quickly make it conform to the current document's primary body text format. Here's the macro:

```
Sub AltN()

    Selection.Style = ActiveDocument.Styles("Normal")

End Sub
```

Assigning an anti-table macro

The following macro is quite useful. It eliminates table formatting and leaves the text behind.

Text pasted into a document from a Web page is formatted often by Word as a table. You usually don't want this. For example, when I make a motel reservation at one of the better establishments (or any kind of establishment, for that matter, although I no longer stay in actual dives), I select the whole Web page containing all the reservation information. Then I copy and paste that into a Word document.

Alas, all kinds of havoc results: The various sections of the Web page are now separated by dozens of blank lines, boxes, frames, and what-not. I don't need all that mess, especially because what should print out as a one-page document requires five pieces of paper to accommodate all the pseudo tables. Just put your insertion cursor anywhere inside this fake tabled data and then run this macro. I keep it on my custom toolbar, triggered by a button I named Untable.

Sometimes these table formats are nested, so you might have to run the macro more than once to get rid of all the lines and stuff:

```
Sub Untable()

On Error Resume Next

    Selection.Rows.ConvertToText
            Separator:=wdSeparateByCommas, NestedTables:= _
        True
    Selection.MoveDown Unit:=wdLine, Count:=1

If Err Then MsgBox "No table was detected, dude."

End Sub
```

Toggling revisions

When working with another person on a document (an editor in my case), it's useful to turn on the revision marks feature so that the other person can quickly see the changes you made. This feature is particularly difficult to locate and select via the Word menu system or the Reviewing toolbar. (Microsoft calls this Track Changes instead of *revision marks,* so no wonder I have problems locating it, even when searching Help. You'd think it would be on the View, Edit, or Format menus, but it's on the Tools menu, instead.)

I add a macro — `RevTog` — to my custom toolbar that toggles revision marks on and off. Sometimes you make changes to a document that you don't want highlighted for others to see (either because they're cumbersome and unnecessary, or because they're deeply embarrassing). I find I need to toggle revision marks off and on rather frequently. Here's the macro:

```
Sub RevTog()

Dim DR As Object: Set DR = WordBasic.DialogRecord.ToolsRevisions(False)
WordBasic.Curvalues.ToolsRevisions DR

If DR.MarkRevisions = 0 Then
WordBasic.PrintStatusBar "Revision Marks ON."
WordBasic.ToolsRevisions MarkRevisions:=1
Else
WordBasic.PrintStatusBar "Revision Marks OFF."
WordBasic.ToolsRevisions MarkRevisions:=0

End If

End Sub
```

Add a macro to a toolbar by right-clicking the toolbar, choosing Customize from the context menu, and then clicking Macros in the left list box. From the right list box in this dialog box, drag the name of the macro to the toolbar and drop it. Right-click the new button to rename the button. By default, the entire path of the macro is included in the button's name, such as `Normal.NewMacros.Untable`. You don't want all that cluttering up your toolbars.

Accepting all changes

When you're looking at a document all messed up with revision marks — or should I say, Track Changes marks — you sometimes want to just get rid of them all and see the final, clean version. You can use Accept All Changes to do this, and it's another button on my custom toolbar:

```
Sub AcceptAll()
    WordBasic.AcceptAllChangesInDoc
End Sub
```

Using WordCount

I often need to know how many words I've written in a document. I don't want the entire document properties stats — paragraphs, characters, author's name, fishing tips, and everything else — just the word count. This macro does it:

```
Sub wordcount()

'update the statistics
    WordBasic.FileSummaryInfo Update:=1
```

```
      Dim dlg As Object: Set dlg =
            WordBasic.DialogRecord.Documentstatistics(False)
          WordBasic.Curvalues.Documentstatistics dlg

          WordBasic.PrintStatusBar "                         " +
            dlg.Words + " words in this document"
      End Sub
```

Book IV

Making the Most of Excel

"THE LCD DISPLAY WAS GOOD, PLASMA DISPLAYS WERE A LITTLE BETTER, BUT WE THINK THE LIQUID LAVA DISPLAY THAT JERRY'S DEVELOPED IS GONNA ROCK THE WEST COAST."

Contents at a Glance

Chapter 1: The Excel Object Model

In This Chapter

✔ Understanding the Excel object hierarchy

✔ Using worksheets and workbooks

✔ Working with cells

✔ Understanding Excel collection objects

✔ Accessing the `Application` object

✔ Using ranges

✔ Naming ranges

✔ Creating charts

This chapter begins the focus on Excel. You see how objects are organized in Excel and then work with the various members of important objects such as worksheets, workbooks, and cells. You also see how to manipulate ranges and charts.

Understanding the Excel Object Model

Excel's uses in an Office context include financial planning, modeling, and building charts. In some cases, it's even used as a kind of database (a repository of ordered information). But the trick that spreadsheets are famous for is recalculation: A cell can contain text, a numeric value, or a formula (such as the sum of all the values in a column). For example, if salesman Bob Racrette reports $2,000 worth of extra orders this month, you can change the value in the appropriate worksheet cell; if this cell is one of those governed by a SUM formula, the cell containing the total immediately changes to reflect Bob's success. Likewise, any Excel chart that gets its data from these changed cells will also be updated.

Like the Word object model (and most other application's models), Excel begins with the `Application` object at the top. (Read more about the Word object model in Book III, Chapter 1.) Within the `Application` object resides the `Workbook` object and a `Workbooks` collection.

The Application and Workbook objects have many members in common, but when you work with the Application object's members, you're usually accessing the current workbook (the one that has the focus). A workbook's members are specific to that particular workbook.

Within the workbook is the Worksheet object, referring to a particular worksheet. Note that the Workbook object has a Sheets collection containing a set of Worksheet or Chart objects.

Going further down is the Range object, and you'll use this one frequently. To read or write to any cells, rows, columns, or other elements within Excel, you usually first create a Range object. Compare this with Word, in which you work primarily with Range or Selection objects to manipulate text. In Excel, you define a Range object so that you can read, manage, or edit its contents.

The Excel Range object specifies a section of a worksheet, or it can also specify several sections at once. A *range* can be a single cell, a block of cells within a single worksheet, or even a set of blocks of cells in two or more worksheets.

There is an Excel Selection object, but I caution you against using it. Generally, use Range instead because the selection that the user creates will be lost if you activate a Selection in code: It is replaced by the selection that the code made. Also, the Range object is more flexible: You can have multiple ranges at a given time but only one selection. To see how to convert a Selection to a Range, see the upcoming section, "Transforming a selection into a range."

How to Use Excel VBA

To experiment with the Excel VBA example code, follow these steps:

1. **Start Excel.**

2. **Press Alt+F11.**

   You see the Visual Basic editor, which is probably empty — no place to write code yet.

3. **Choose View⇨Project Explorer.**

   You see a list of the worksheets and workbooks that are currently available in this instance of Excel.

4. **Double-click the default workbook's name, which is ThisWorkbook (unless you've changed it), as shown in Figure 1-1.**

Figure 1-1:
Double-click
a workbook
name to
make your
VBA macros
available to
the entire
workbook.

A code window opens where in which you can type in procedures, like
the Sub in the next section.

Adding a Workbook

When you start Excel, the Application object is automatically created. You
don't need to use the Application object in your VBA code because it's
understood. For example, you don't need to prepend Excel.Application
to code that closes the current workbook's Workbooks.Close. You can just
directly reference the Workbooks collection or any individual workbook or
other element without using the Application object.

The following code adds a new worksheet and then displays the names of all
the worksheets in the *current* (with focus) workbook:

```
Sub ShowSheets()

Set s = Sheets.Add(Type:=xlWorksheet)
For i = 1 To Sheets.Count
    s.Cells(1, i).Value = Sheets(i).Name
Next i

End Sub
```

With your blinking insertion cursor somewhere in this code, press F5 to execute the code. Press Alt+11 to return to the Excel workbook view. You'll see a
new worksheet added to your workbook, with the names of all the worksheets
listed in the first row. Note that the newly added sheet is not in the right order,
though. Suppose you want Sheet4 to appear after Sheet3. As with most anything in Excel, you can automate the task programmatically. In this case, add
the following bold line to this procedure that moves the new worksheet:

```
Sub ShowSheets()

Set s = Sheets.Add(Type:=xlWorksheet)

Worksheets(1).Move After:=Worksheets("Sheet3")

For i = 1 To Sheets.Count
    s.Cells(1, i).Value = Sheets(i).Name
Next i

End Sub
```

Notice that the worksheets here are referenced in two ways. The first reference specifies a worksheet by its index number in the `Worksheets` collection: `Worksheets(1).Move`.

The alternative way to reference a worksheet is illustrated by the second reference. In this case, you specify a worksheet by using its name: `After:=Worksheets("Sheet3")`. Note that this `After:=` specification works only if there is a worksheet named Sheet3.

Now when you execute the code, the sheets are in the order that you want them. As usual, you'll find a variety of approaches that you can take. For example, a `copy` method works the same way but adds a new sheet to the existing collection instead of merely moving one. If you prefer, you can replace the `after` argument with a `before` argument. Or, you can leave these out, and a new workbook is created with the moved or copied sheet. Finally, if you don't know how many sheets might be in the workbook — and you want the new sheet appended to the end of the collection — use `After:=(Sheets.Count)`.

Referring to Me

In Visual Basic .NET, you can specify an object itself with the `Me` command. For example, `Me.BackColor = Color.AliceBlue` turns the form (in which this code resides) a cunning, light blue. The object in which the code resides isn't necessarily the *active* object (the cell with the focus, with the black insertion frame, for example). Perhaps you have a macro that needs to reference an object in the same workbook where the macro resides. For example, you might want to display a `DialogSheet` from the workbook. You cannot always be sure that this workbook has the focus. The workbook might not be the currently active workbook. To ensure that a macro references its own workbook, use the `ThisWorkbook` property, like this:

```
ThisWorkbook.DialogSheets(2).Show
```

There is no equivalent `ThisWorkSheet` property.

Accessing the active cell

The smallest unit that you can manipulate is the cell. You can read or edit the currently active cell by using several equivalent code phrases (each of the following points to the same cell):

```
ActiveCell
ActiveWindow.ActiveCell
Application.ActiveCell
Application.ActiveWindow.ActiveCell
```

As usual, the `Application` object is optional in code unless you want to start a whole new instance of Excel running. Here's how to read the contents of the currently active (with focus) cell in Sheet2:

```
Sub accessCell()

Worksheets("Sheet2").Activate
MsgBox ActiveCell.Value

End Sub
```

Notice that something other than a worksheet might currently have the focus, so you use the `activate` method to set the focus on a particular worksheet — in this case, the one named Sheet2.

Creating a New Instance of Excel

The following code uses the `Application` object because no current `Application` object exists; for example, you're not running Excel but are instead executing this code from within Word. Or perhaps you want a second instance of Excel to run concurrently with the instance in which you execute this code. In other words, if you run the following VBA from within Excel itself, you spawn a new, second Excel instance:

```
Sub BringToLife()

On Error Resume Next

Dim e As Excel.Application
Set e = New Excel.Application
e.Visible = True

e.Workbooks.Add
e.Worksheets("Sheet1").Cells(4, 4).Value = 256

If Err Then MsgBox Error$

End Sub
```

Execute this, and you see a new Excel instance with a worksheet containing 256 in cell 4,4.

Note that when you instantiate Excel in this fashion (programmatically), no workbook or worksheets are automatically added to the instance. That is, you have an empty Excel instance, and thus your programming must explicitly create a workbook by using the Add method of the Application object's Workbooks collection. Also notice that you must specify whether a new instance of Excel created this way is visible. Similarly, if you programmatically create a new Workbook, it remains hidden until you set its Visible property to True.

As you might have noticed, when starting Excel yourself nonprogrammatically (from the Start menu for example), Excel does provide you with a default workbook, and it contains three worksheets. You can programmatically redefine the number of default worksheets by using the SheetsInNewWorkbook property of the Application object.

Using the Application Object

In Word is an Options object that you can use to manipulate various options (Tools➪Options). In Excel, however, you use the Application object to adjust options, like this:

```
Application.Calculation = xlCalculationManual
Application.CalculateBeforeSave = True
```

Recall that you can often leave out the Application object name when referencing other objects such as ActiveCell. However, when accessing application properties, you must use Application. For example, this code will fail to adjust the Calculation option:

```
Calculation = xlCalculationManual
```

Other options that are adjusted via the Application object can be found in this list of the Application object's 174 properties. Some of these are other objects (such as ActiveWindow), and others are options (CanPlaySound):

```
ActiveCell, ActiveChart, ActivePrinter, ActiveSheet, ActiveWindow,
ActiveWorkbook, AddIns, AlertBeforeOverwriting, AltStartupPath,
AnswerWizard, Application, ArbitraryXMLSupportAvailable,
AskToUpdateLinks, Assistant, AutoCorrect,
AutoFormatAsYouTypeReplaceHyperlinks, AutomationSecurity,
AutoPercentEntry, AutoRecover, Build, CalculateBeforeSave,
Calculation, CalculationInterruptKey, CalculationState,
CalculationVersion, Caller, CanPlaySounds, CanRecordSounds,
```

```
Caption, CellDragAndDrop, Cells, Charts, ClipboardFormats, Columns,
COMAddIns, CommandBars, CommandUnderlines, ConstrainNumeric,
ControlCharacters, CopyObjectsWithCells, Creator, Cursor,
CursorMovement, CustomListCount, CutCopyMode, DataEntryMode,
DDEAppReturnCode, DecimalSeparator, DefaultFilePath,
DefaultSaveFormat, DefaultSheetDirection, DefaultWebOptions,
Dialogs, DisplayAlerts, DisplayClipboardWindow,
DisplayCommentIndicator, DisplayDocumentActionTaskPane,
DisplayExcel4Menus, DisplayFormulaBar, DisplayFullScreen,
DisplayFunctionToolTips, DisplayInsertOptions,
DisplayNoteIndicator, DisplayPasteOptions, DisplayRecentFiles,
DisplayScrollBars, DisplayStatusBar, EditDirectlyInCell,
EnableAnimations, EnableAutoComplete, EnableCancelKey,
EnableEvents, EnableSound, ErrorCheckingOptions,
Excel4IntlMacroSheets, Excel4MacroSheets, ExtendList,
FeatureInstall, FileConverters, FileDialog, FileFind, FileSearch,
FindFormat, FixedDecimal, FixedDecimalPlaces,
GenerateGetPivotData, Height, Hinstance, Hwnd,
IgnoreRemoteRequests, Interactive, International, Iteration,
LanguageSettings, Left, LibraryPath, MailSession, MailSystem,
MapPaperSize, MathCoprocessorAvailable, MaxChange, MaxIterations,
MemoryFree, MouseAvailable, MoveAfterReturn,
MoveAfterReturnDirection, Name, Names, NetworkTemplatesPath,
NewWorkbook, ODBCErrors, ODBCTimeout, OLEDBErrors, OnWindow,
OperatingSystem, OrganizationName, Parent, Path, PathSeparator,
PivotTableSelection, PreviousSelections, ProductCode,
PromptForSummaryInfo, Range, Ready, RecentFiles, RecordRelative,
ReferenceStyle, RegisteredFunctions, ReplaceFormat, RollZoom,
Rows, RTD, ScreenUpdating, Selection, Sheets, SheetsInNewWorkbook,
ShowChartTipNames, ShowChartTipValues, ShowStartupDialog,
ShowToolTips, ShowWindowsInTaskbar, SmartTagRecognizers, Speech,
SpellingOptions, StandardFont, StandardFontSize, StartupPath,
StatusBar, TemplatesPath, ThisCell, ThisWorkbook,
ThousandsSeparator, Top, TransitionMenuKey,
TransitionMenuKeyAction, TransitionNavigKeys, UsableHeight,
UsableWidth, UsedObjects, UserControl, UserLibraryPath, UserName,
UseSystemSeparators, Value, VBE, Version, Visible, Watches, Width,
Windows, WindowsForPens, WindowState, Workbooks,
WorksheetFunction, Worksheets.
```

Working with Ranges

You can specify ranges either *absolutely* (specifying a particular cell or group of cells) or *relative to the active cell* (the one currently with the focus). Here's an absolute range, which is also being given a name:

```
Sub SetRange()

Names.Add Name:="Vac", RefersTo:="=sheet1!$A$3"

Range("Vac").Value = "This"

End Sub
```

When you put a dollar sign ($) in front of the row and column references, the range becomes absolute: No matter what cell is currently active (selected), this code puts the word `This` in cell A3. Also note that an exclamation point (!) is used to separate the name of the sheet from the cell reference.

However, if you remove the dollar signs, the range specification becomes relative to the active cell. If the active cell is A1, *only then* will $A$3 mean cell A3 in the above code. If instead the active cell is A2, like this, in what cell do you suppose the message will appear?

Here's an example that illustrates how to specify a relative reference:

```
Sub SetRange()

    Names.Add Name:="Vac1", RefersTo:="=Sheet1!" & "D3"

    Range("Vac1").Value = "This"

End Sub
```

You can also mix and match columns and rows (one can be absolute, the other relative). Here are the possible combinations:

✦ **$B$2:** Absolute column and absolute row

✦ **B$2:** Relative column and absolute row

✦ **$B2:** Absolute column and relative row

✦ **B2:** Relative column and relative row

The A1 style reference

One referencing system used in Excel is the *A1 style,* meaning that columns are labeled A–IV, and that the rows range from 1–65536. Mercifully, Excel doesn't start with row 0 (zero).

You can specify ranges and blocks of cells in the following fashion:

✦ The cell at column B and row 12 is B12.

✦ The range of cells from column A and rows 11–30 is A11:A30.

◆ The range of cells from row 16 and columns C–G is C16:G16.

◆ All cells in row 6 is 6:6.

◆ All cells in rows 2–4 is 2:4.

◆ All cells in column B is B:B.

◆ All cells in columns A–B is A:B.

◆ The range of cells in columns A–C and rows 9–20 is A9:C20.

A 3-D reference specifies cells across more than one sheet. For example, to get a total of all the values stored in cell R23 on sheets 4, 5, 6, and 7, you write it this way:

```
=SUM(Sheet4:Sheet7!R23)
```

The R1C1 style reference

The *R1C1 style reference* is an optional way of specifying cells that avoids using letters to represent columns: R1C1 uses numbers instead. This can be useful if you need to compute mathematically some row or column positions. (You can't do math on the letters A, B, and so on; you must use numbers.) In this system, *R* stands for *row,* and *C* stands for (you guessed it) *column.* It works like this:

◆ R is an absolute reference to the current row.

◆ R[-3]C is a relative reference to the cell three rows up in the same column.

◆ R[-1] is a relative reference to the entire row immediately above the active cell.

◆ R[4]C[2] is a relative reference to the cell four rows down and two columns to the right.

◆ R2C5 is an absolute reference to the cell in the second row in the fifth column.

Note that Excel itself often uses this style of reference when you record a macro. For example, if you click a cell and type in a value while recording, you get this mix of both the A1 style and the R1C1 style:

```
Range("F9").Select
ActiveCell.FormulaR1C1 = "22"
```

Using the Offset method

You can also reference a range relative to the current cell by using the `Offset` method. In this example, the word `Norma` appears six cells over and four down from the current cell:

**Book IV
Chapter 1**

The Excel Object Model

```
ActiveCell.Offset(4, 6).Value = "Norma"
ActiveCell.Offset(4, 6).Font.Underline = xlSingle
```

This notation might be a bit easier to visualize than the R1C1 style of relative addressing.

Using the Names collection

The `Names` collection of a workbook can contain as many named ranges as you wish, and you can thereafter refer to a named range by its name rather than its cell addresses, as you can see in the preceding example.

You can also assign temporary names, but if they're not added to the `Names` collection, they won't be saved when you shut down Excel:

```
Dim r As Range
Set r = Range("B3")
r.Name = "Total"
Range("Total").Value = 124
```

Accessing special ranges

In addition to the `ActiveCell` and `Range` objects, you can use other Excel VBA members to specify useful ranges in your code. For example, you might want to programmatically add some more rows or columns to a sheet but need to know where the outermost used cell is.

The SpecialCells method

The `SpecialCells` method of the `Range` object can come in handy. Suppose that you want to go to the end of used cells in a sheet (the cell in the farthest column, and down in the farthest-used row). This code does that:

```
Worksheets("Sheet2").Activate
ActiveSheet.Cells.SpecialCells(xlCellTypeLastCell).Activate
ActiveCell.Value = "Boo"
```

The format is

```
.SpecialCells(Type, Value)
```

The `Type` can be any of the following built-in constants:

- ✦ `xlCellTypeAllFormatConditions`
- ✦ `xlCellTypeAllValidation`
- ✦ `xlCellTypeBlanks`
- ✦ `xlCellTypeComments`
- ✦ `xlCellTypeConstants`

✦ `xlCellTypeFormulas`

✦ `xlCellTypeLastCell`

✦ `xlCellTypeSameFormatConditions`

✦ `xlCellTypeSameValidation`

✦ `xlCellTypeVisible`

Using `SpecialCells` is a way of filtering. It allows you to get only particular kinds of cells from a range. The `Value` argument is optional. You can use it to specify that you want only particular types of cells. `Value` is used only with two of the preceding constants: `xlCellTypeConstants` or `xlCellTypeFormulas`. You can use `Value` types either alone (such as `xlTextValues` by itself to get only text cells) or combine several `Value` constants to broaden the results. These are the `Value` constants that you can use: `xlErrors`, `xlLogical`, `xlNumbers`, or `xlTextValues`.

The UsedRange property

The `UsedRange` property of the `Worksheet` object returns the smallest rectangular region that can be drawn that includes all the used cells in the worksheet. For example, this could be useful if you want to color these cells to highlight them. This code applies a light gray pattern to the range of used cells in a sheet:

```
Worksheets("Sheet1").Activate
ActiveSheet.UsedRange.Interior.Pattern = xlPatternGray16
```

To find a list of the built-in constants, such as `xlPatternCrissCross`, `xlLogical`, and `xlBorderWeight`, search the VB editor's Help (while in the editor, press F1) and search for *Microsoft Excel Constants*.

The CurrentRegion property

The `CurrentRegion` property gives you the *current region* (all the cells that are in use: bounded by the white, unused cells). It works like a fill tool in a graphics program, searching from the current cell in all four directions until it finds blank rows and columns. Then it defines the region.

The blocks of data in Figure 1-2 are (as is often the case) framed by empty rows and columns. To specify a range for one of these blocks of data, you can use the `CurrentRegion` property, like this:

```
Sub dorange()

Worksheets("Sheet1").Activate
ActiveCell.CurrentRegion.Select

End Sub
```

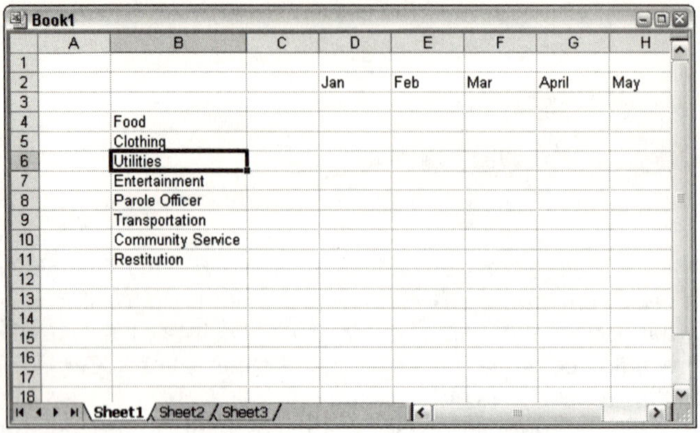

Figure 1-2:
A typical
spreadsheet
with empty
rows and
columns
surrounding
data.

After you execute this code, the block is selected, as you can see in Figure 1-3.

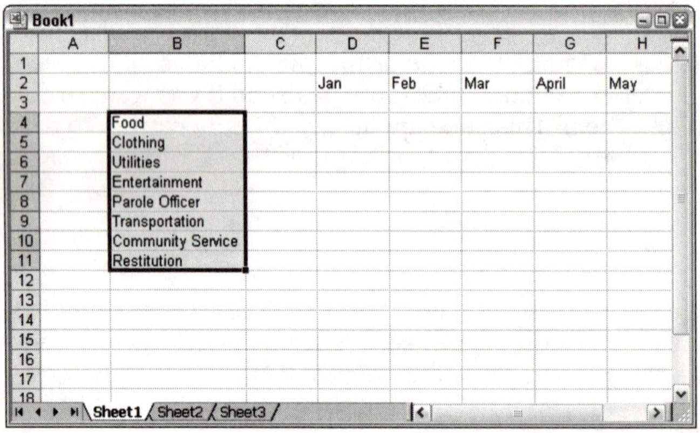

Figure 1-3:
Get a range
for a block
of data
with the
`Current`
`Region`
property.

If you want to access that range by using an object variable, this code does it:

```
Sub dorange()

Dim r As Range
Set r = ActiveCell.CurrentRegion
r.Interior.Pattern = xlPatternLightDown

End Sub
```

Transforming a selection into a range

Recall that generally you work with ranges in your programming. But now and then, you need to interact with users, who make selections. The following code shows you how to query the user about the current selection and then translate the `Selection` object into a `Range` object before you change its format in the code. This preserves the selection, which would be lost if you accessed it directly, programmatically:

```
Public Sub SelectionToRange()

Dim r As Range

Set r = ActiveWindow.RangeSelection
s = MsgBox("Do you want this range highlighted?", vbYesNo)
If s = vbYes Then
r.Interior.Pattern = xlPatternLightVertical
End If

End Sub
```

Here's code that returns the address of the current selection:

```
MsgBox ActiveWindow.RangeSelection.Address
```

Adding a formula

The following transforms the current selection into a range to specify that a SUM formula should be added to cell A1, displaying the total of the values in the user's selection:

```
Public Sub AddFormulaRange()

ActiveSheet.Cells(1, 1).Formula = "=Sum(" & _
        ActiveWindow.RangeSelection.Address & ")"

End Sub
```

Using the WorksheetFunction

Alternatively, you might need only to get the result programmatically. That is, you don't want it displayed on the sheet to the user. To do that, you can use the `WorksheetFunction` method, like this:

```
Public Sub ShowSum()

Set r = Worksheets("Sheet1").Range("G4:G6")
n = WorksheetFunction.Sum(r)
MsgBox n

End Sub
```

Creating a Chart

It's easy to create charts of data in Excel. Type these numbers into cells G4–G10 in Sheet 1: **45**, **66**, **33**, **33**, **44**, **55**, **66**. Then type in and execute this simple macro:

```
Public Sub ShowChart()

Dim ch As New Excel.Chart

Set ch = Charts.Add
ch.SetSourceData Source:=Worksheets("Sheet1").Range("g4:g10")
ch.ChartType = xl3DArea

ch.Activate

End Sub
```

You see the chart displayed in Figure 1-4.

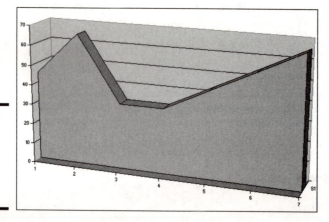

Figure 1-4: Adding charts to an Excel workbook is easy.

Dozens of varieties of charts are available in Excel. Search the VB editor Help (not Excel Help) for *Microsoft Excel Constants,* locate XLChartType, and click it to open the list, as shown in Figure 1-5.

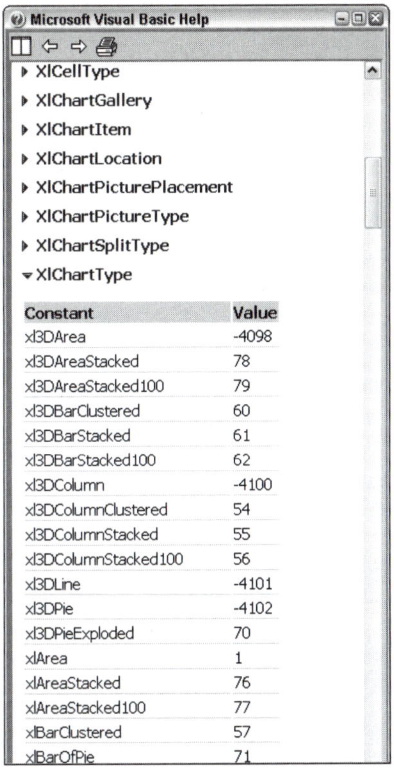

Figure 1-5:
Look here for all the chart types you can use in Excel.

Microsoft Visual Basic Help	

▸ XlCellType
▸ XlChartGallery
▸ XlChartItem
▸ XlChartLocation
▸ XlChartPicturePlacement
▸ XlChartPictureType
▸ XlChartSplitType
▾ XlChartType

Constant	Value
xl3DArea	-4098
xl3DAreaStacked	78
xl3DAreaStacked100	79
xl3DBarClustered	60
xl3DBarStacked	61
xl3DBarStacked100	62
xl3DColumn	-4100
xl3DColumnClustered	54
xl3DColumnStacked	55
xl3DColumnStacked100	56
xl3DLine	-4101
xl3DPie	-4102
xl3DPieExploded	70
xlArea	1
xlAreaStacked	76
xlAreaStacked100	77
xlBarClustered	57
xlBarOfPie	71

Chapter 2: Handling Excel Events

In This Chapter

✔ **Programming events in workbooks and worksheets**

✔ **Managing chart events**

✔ **Dealing with** `Application` **events**

✔ **Adding a class module**

*E*vents occur when programmers write code to respond to things that happen to an application. For example, when you write an application, you cannot know when (or even whether) the user will ever click one of your buttons. In an object's event procedures, you can write code to specify what happens when an event occurs: like when the program starts, when the user clicks a particular button, after a `PivotTable` report is updated, when the selection changes, and so on. All these (and many more actions) are *events*.

Generally speaking, events trigger (or *fire*) because the user does something to interact with your program. But events can also trigger when other objects interact with them. For example, the `SheetChange` event will fire whether the user changes a cell in that worksheet or whether some code in a macro (for instance) makes the change.

By default, the `Application` object's `EnableEvents` property is `True`, allowing events to trigger; however, if you want to prevent events from firing for some reason, you can turn it off like this:

```
Application.EnableEvents = False
```

In this chapter, you explore how to provide source code that executes when events trigger in workbooks, worksheets, charts, or other objects. Events are a way that a programmer responds to user interaction with their programs, although sometimes other code also interacts and triggers events. (Events are sometimes said to *fire* when triggered, just like a gun.)

Programming an Excel Event

To see a list of the events available in the `Workbook` object, follow these steps:

1. **Press Alt+F11 in Excel.**

The Visual Basic editor appears.

2. **Choose View➪Project Explorer in the VB editor.**

Project Explorer appears.

3. **Double-click This Workbook in Project Explorer.**

The editor window for this workbook is displayed.

4. **From the drop-down list in the upper left of the workbook's editor, choose Workbook.**

The `Workbook_Open` event (a `Sub` procedure, like a macro) appears with its basic structure typed in for you.

VBA chooses what it thinks is the most frequently used event to type in by default. For a `Button` object, for instance, it's obviously the `Click` event that you most likely want to use. If you wish, you can simply erase the default event procedure that VBA types in for you. Or you can just leave it empty, with no code in it. Nothing will happen when an empty event fires because there's no source code to execute.

5. **Open the drop-down list in the upper right.**

You see a list of all the events that can be programmed for a workbook, as shown in Figure 2-1.

Figure 2-1:
Find the events for the Workbook object here.

Now try writing code for a `Worksheet` object event.

1. In Project Explorer, double-click Sheet1 under the current VBA project.

Sheet1's code editor opens.

2. In the top-left list of the code window, choose Worksheet.

3. In the top-right list, choose the `BeforeDoubleClick` event.

4. Type in this code to display a running total of the number of times that the sheet has been double-clicked:

```
Private Sub Worksheet_BeforeDoubleClick(ByVal Target As
    Range, Cancel As Boolean)

    Static c As Integer
    c = c + 1

    Application.StatusBar = Caption & "Sheet 1 has been
    double-clicked " & c & " times."

End Sub
```

5. Try double-clicking Sheet1 to see the message in the lower-left corner of the Excel window.

Notice that a report appears in the status bar each time you double-click.

Also notice how event programming differs from ordinary programming: Ordinary procedures are executed when the program itself decides that they should be triggered. However, events execute when an outside agent (another program, an object, or the user) decides to trigger them. Think of it this way: An ordinary procedure in your day is when you, yourself, decide to make a sandwich. An event is when someone else asks you to make one.

Events in the Worksheet Object

As you can read in the preceding section, you can access the list of `Workbook` events by opening a workbook programming editor. Likewise, you can get to the events of a worksheet by opening its editor. To write code that triggers when a selection in a worksheet changes, for example, follow these steps:

1. Choose View⇨Project Explorer in the VBA editor.

Project Explorer appears.

2. Double-click Sheet1 in Project Explorer.

The editor window for the worksheet is displayed.

3. **From the drop-down list in the upper left of the worksheet's editor, choose Worksheet.**

   The `Worksheet_SelectionChange` event appears with its basic structure typed in for you.

4. **Open the drop-down list in the upper right.**

   You see a list of all the events that can be programmed for a worksheet.

To write a `Worksheet` object event, just type this into the `SelectionChange` event:

```
Private Sub Worksheet_SelectionChange(ByVal Target As Range)

MsgBox Target.Address

End Sub
```

Now each time you click a different cell in the worksheet, a message box displays its address.

Notice that some events include a parameter, such as `Target` here. You sometimes want to use this information. For example, if you plan to take some action on the newly selected range, you need that `Target` argument.

Writing Chart Events

To write event procedures for a chart, you must first add a chart to your workbook. Select some cells with some data in them: These cells provide the basis for the chart. Then press F11 to add a new chart to your workbook.

Now, go to the VBA editor and choose View⇨Project Explorer. Double-click Chart1 in Project Explorer to open its code editor window. Now you can open the drop-down list in the upper right to see (or choose) the various events available to the `Chart` object.

Writing Application Events

Application events are used for more generic behaviors than worksheet or workbook events.

Here are the events available to the `Application` object: `NewWorkbook`, `SheetActivate`, `SheetBeforeDoubleClick`, `SheetBeforeRightClick`, `SheetCalculate`, `SheetChange`, `SheetPivotTableUpdate`, `SheetDeactivate`, `SheetSelectionChange`, `WindowActivate`, `WindowDeactivate`, `WindowResize`, `WorkbookActivate`, `WorkbookAddinInstall`, `WorkbookAddinUninstall`, `WorkbookBeforeClose`, `WorkbookBeforePrint`, `WorkbookBeforeSave`, `WorkbookDeactivate`, `WorkbookNewSheet`, `WorkbookOpen`, `WorkbookPivotTableCloseConnection`, `WorkbookPivotTableOpenConnection`.

`SheetBeforeDoubleClick` and **Sheet**`BeforeRightClick` events can be useful if you want to respond via your code differently than the default responses built into Excel when these actions take place.

Defining an `Application` event requires some extra steps. Because there is no code window for the `Application` object, you have to add a class module to the VBA editor, defining a global application variable by using the `WithEvents` command. Suppose that you want to respond whenever the user adds a new worksheet to a workbook, but instead of using the `WorkBook_NewSheet` event, you decide to use the `Application` object's `WorkbookNewSheet` event. To respond in this way when the user chooses Insert⇨Worksheet, follow these steps:

1. **In the VBA editor's Project Explorer, right-click the project's name.**

   It's the one in boldface, not PERSONAL.XLS.

2. **Choose Insert⇨Class Module from the context menu that appears.**

   A new class module appears.

3. **In the General Declarations section of the class module (in other words, not inside any procedure), type this (as shown in Figure 2-2):**

   ```
   Public WithEvents objApp As Application
   ```

   As soon as you create this object variable, the list boxes at the top now contain additional information.

4. **Open the upper-left, drop-down list in the same code window (the class module window).**

   You see your new `objApp` listed there.

General Declarations

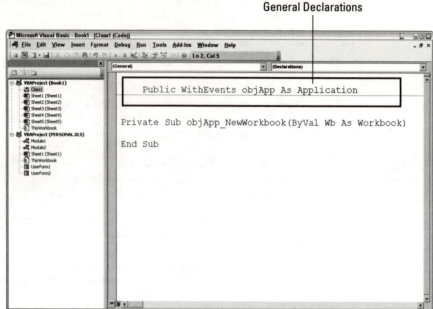

Figure 2-2:
The General
Declarations
section.

5. **Click it.**

6. **Open the upper-right, drop-down list.**

    You see all the `Application` objects available to you, as shown in
    Figure 2-3.

Figure 2-3:
The
Applica-
tion
object's
various
events are
listed in the
class
module.

7. **Type this into the** `NewWorkbook` **event:**

```
Private Sub objApp_NewWorkbook(ByVal Wb As Workbook)

MsgBox ("A new workbook has been created.")

End Sub
```

You're not done yet, though. You've still got to connect your declared object variable with the application in actual code. (The class module doesn't automatically run itself.)

Isn't object-oriented programming (OOP) fun when it forces you into these meaningless clerical contortions? You now have to put some activation code into one of the events that automatically triggers when Excel opens.

8. **In Project Explorer, double-click ThisWorkbook in the Project Explorer, and then type this into its General Declarations section:**

```
Dim X As New Class1
```

You've now created a reference (the variable `X`) to the class module, which you can use to access any of the members of this class (in other words, the procedures in this module, to avoid OOP-speak).

9. **Type this into this workbook's** `Workbook_Open` **event:**

```
Private Sub Workbook_Open()

Set X.objApp = Application
MsgBox "Application Object Active."

End Sub
```

10. **Save this project as** `TestAppObj.xls` **and then close Excel.**

11. **Now you can try out this twisted sister. Run Excel and open** `TestAppObj.xls`.

Because you inserted a macro that runs automatically (as opposed to writing new macros and testing them), a security warning message might appear (depending on your Excel macro security settings). If this happens, choose Tools➪Options, click the Security tab, and then click the Macro Security button. Change the setting to Medium so you can test your code. If you wish, restore your setting to High after testing.

Your message box appears, telling you that the `Application` object has been activated. From here on, any application events that you've coded will execute.

12. **Now test the application event by choosing File⇨New.**

A task pane appears.

13. **In the task pane, click Blank Workbook.**

A message box displays, informing you that a new workbook has been created.

Chapter 3: Advanced Worksheet Editing

In This Chapter

✔ **Importing data**

✔ **Importing XML**

✔ **Creating datasets programmatically**

✔ **Understanding the** Shape **object**

✔ **Augmenting Find and Replace**

Although this mini-book is about Excel, it's important to realize that of all the Office 2003 applications, Access is closest to Excel in many ways — not least in that both are frequently used to store tabular data. In this chapter, you go deeper into Excel programming, importing both traditional data structures, and XML-based data. Then you see how to build datasets, work with the Shape object, and improve on the built-in Find and Replace utility.

Importing Data into Excel

One easy way to programmatically import data into Excel is to first start recording a macro and then use the Data⇨Import External Data⇨Import Data feature. Then you can modify the code created by the macro recorder to import other data from other source. Here's the raw, unmodified code that you get when you record the importation of an Access database. In this case, I imported the Products table from the Northwind sample database:

```
Sub GetData()
' Macro recorded 4/9/2004 by Richard
'
    With ActiveSheet.QueryTables.Add(Connection:=Array( _

        "OLEDB;Provider=Microsoft.Jet.OLEDB.4.0;Password=""
        "";User ID=Admin;Data
        Source=C:\Northwind.mdb;Mode=Share Deny
        Write;Extended Propertie" _

        ";s=""""";Jet OLEDB:System database="""""";Jet
```

```
            OLEDB:Registry Path="""";Jet OLEDB:Database
            Password="""";Jet OLEDB:Engine Type=5;Jet
            OLEDB:Da" _
        , _
        "tabase Locking Mode=0;Jet OLEDB:Global Partial Bulk
            Ops=2;Jet OLEDB:Global Bulk Transactions=1;Jet
            OLEDB:New Database Password=""" _
        , _
        """";Jet OLEDB:Create System Database=False;Jet
            OLEDB:Encrypt Database=False;Jet OLEDB:Don't Copy
            Locale on Compact=False;Jet OLEDB" _
        , ":Compact Without Replica Repair=False;Jet
            OLEDB:SFP=False"), Destination:= _
        Range("A1"))
        .CommandType = xlCmdTable
        .CommandText = Array("Products")
        .Name = "Northwind Products"
        .FieldNames = True
        .RowNumbers = False
        .FillAdjacentFormulas = False
        .PreserveFormatting = True
        .RefreshOnFileOpen = False
        .BackgroundQuery = True
        .RefreshStyle = xlInsertDeleteCells
        .SavePassword = False
        .SaveData = True
        .AdjustColumnWidth = True
        .RefreshPeriod = 0
        .PreserveColumnInfo = True
        .SourceConnectionFile = _
        "C:\Documents and Settings\Richard Mansfield\My
            Documents\My Data Sources\Northwind Products.odc"
        .SourceDataFile = "C:\Northwind.mdb"
        .Refresh BackgroundQuery:=False
    End With
End Sub
```

In this recording, I imported a *connection* file (an ODC file) from the Northwind sample database. In the next section, I modify this recorded code to allow the user to both choose the data source and choose a table from a full MDB database file.

The Northwind sample database is supplied with Office 2003 to allow you to experiment using a realistic MDB (Jet/Access-style) database. Northwind. mdb should be found on your hard drive in C:\Program files\Microsoft Office\Office11\Samples. However, you might not have it installed or know where to look for it. Choose Help⇨Sample Databases in Access, and then select Northwind Sample Database. If it's not there, go to the Windows Control Panel, choose Add/Remove Programs, find and click Microsoft Office, click the Change button, and follow the instructions to install the Northwind sample database.

Importing an Access Database

The following macro asks the user to choose an Access database (MDB), displays a dialog box asking the user which of that database's tables to import, and then displays the results in an Excel worksheet.

Run Excel and press Alt+F11 to open the Visual Basic editor. Choose View⇨ Project Explorer and then double-click the ThisWorkbook entry in Project Explorer to open its programming window.

Type the macro in Listing 3-1 into the editor:

Listing 3-1:   Import an Access Database into a Worksheet Macro

```
Sub importdata()

On Error Resume Next

r = Application.Dialogs(xlDialogOpen).Show

With ActiveSheet.QueryTables.Add(Connection:=Array( _
        "OLEDB;Provider=Microsoft.Jet.OLEDB.4.0;Password="""";User ID=Admin;Data
            Source=C:\Documents and Settings\Richard Mansfield\My Documents\" _
        , _
        "Order Entry1.mdb;Mode=Share Deny Write;Extended Properties="""";Jet
            OLEDB:System database="""";Jet OLEDB:Registry Path="""";Jet
            OLEDB:" _
        , _
            "Database Password="""";Jet OLEDB:Engine Type=5;Jet
            OLEDB:Database Locking Mode=0;Jet OLEDB:Global Partial Bulk
            Ops=2;Jet OLEDB:Glo" _
        , _
        "bal Bulk Transactions=1;Jet OLEDB:New Database Password="""";Jet
            OLEDB:Create System Database=False;Jet OLEDB:Encrypt
            Database=Fal" _
        , _
        "se;Jet OLEDB:Don't Copy Locale on Compact=False;Jet OLEDB:Compact
            Without Replica Repair=False;Jet OLEDB:SFP=False" _
        ), Destination:=Range("A1"))
        .CommandType = xlCmdTable
    ' .CommandText = Array("Employees")
        .Name = "Order Entry1"
        .FieldNames = True
        .RowNumbers = False
        .FillAdjacentFormulas = False
        .PreserveFormatting = True
        .RefreshOnFileOpen = False
        .BackgroundQuery = True
        .RefreshStyle = xlInsertDeleteCells
        .SavePassword = False
        .SaveData = True
        .AdjustColumnWidth = True
        .RefreshPeriod = 0
        .PreserveColumnInfo = True
        .SourceDataFile = r
        .Refresh BackgroundQuery:=False
    End With
```

```
If Err Then MsgBox (Error)

End Sub
```

All the code from this book is available on the book's companion Web site. (Please see the Introduction for the specific URL.) You certainly don't want to type in lengthy code examples, so just copy and paste it from this Internet site.

The preceding code is quite similar to the code produced by recording a macro as when you use the Excel Data⇨Import External Data⇨Import Data feature. The modifications are these:

✦ Adding a couple of error trapping lines (`On Error` and `If Err`)

✦ Adding this line to allow the user to choose which database file to import:

```
r = Application.Dialogs(xlDialogOpen).Show
```

✦ Using the variable `r` to specify the `SourceConnectionFile` or `SourceDataFile` argument

```
.SourceDataFile = r
```

To test this data-import programming, click somewhere within the code that you just typed and press F5 to execute the code. When the Excel Open dialog box displays, use it to locate and open the Access `Northwind.mdb` sample database on your hard drive. Close the Open dialog box.

After you select the `Northwind.mdb` database from the Open dialog box, the Select Table dialog box opens, asking you to choose the table you want to see, as shown in Figure 3-1.

Figure 3-1: Choose the table you want to import from this dialog box.

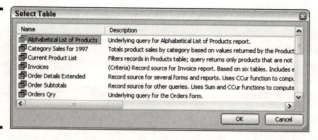

Double-click the table you want, and you see the data imported into Excel's current sheet, as shown in Figure 3-2.

Figure 3-2:
Behold!
Data
automati-
cally
dumped
into your
worksheet.

	A	B	C	D	E	F
1	Pro	ProductName	SupplierID	CategoryID	QuantityPerUnit	UnitPrice
2	1	Chai	1	1	10 boxes x 20 bags	18
3	2	Chang	1	1	24 - 12 oz bottles	19
4	3	Aniseed Syrup	1	2	12 - 550 ml bottles	10
5	4	Chef Anton's Cajun Seasoning	2	2	48 - 6 oz jars	22
6	6	Grandma's Boysenberry Spread	3	2	12 - 8 oz jars	25
7	7	Uncle Bob's Organic Dried Pears	3	7	12 - 1 lb pkgs.	30
8	8	Northwoods Cranberry Sauce	3	2	12 - 12 oz jars	40
9	10	Ikura	4	8	12 - 200 ml jars	31
10	11	Queso Cabrales	5	4	1 kg pkg.	21
11	12	Queso Manchego La Pastora	5	4	10 - 500 g pkgs.	38
12	13	Konbu	6	8	2 kg box	6
13	14	Tofu	6	7	40 - 100 g pkgs.	23.25
14	15	Genen Shouyu	6	2	24 - 250 ml bottles	15.5
15	16	Pavlova	7	3	32 - 500 g boxes	17.45
16	18	Carnarvon Tigers	7	8	16 kg pkg.	62.5
17	19	Teatime Chocolate Biscuits	8	3	10 boxes x 12 pieces	9.2
18	20	Sir Rodney's Marmalade	8	3	30 gift boxes	81
19	21	Sir Rodney's Scones	8	3	24 pkgs. x 4 pieces	10
20	22	Gustaf's Knäckebröd	9	5	24 - 500 g pkgs.	21
21	23	Tunnbröd	9	5	12 - 250 g pkgs.	9
22	25	NuNuCa Nuß-Nougat-Creme	11	3	20 - 450 g glasses	14
23	26	Gumbär Gummibärchen	11	3	100 - 250 g bags	31.23
24	27	Schoggi Schokolade	11	3	100 - 100 g pieces	43.9
25	30	Nord-Ost Matjeshering	13	8	10 - 200 g glasses	25.89
26	31	Gorgonzola Telino	14	4	12 - 100 g pkgs.	12.5
27	32	Mascarpone Fabioli	14	4	24 - 200 g pkgs.	32
28	33	Geitost	15	4	500 g	2.5
29	34	Sasquatch Ale	16	1	24 - 12 oz bottles	14
30	35	Steeleye Stout	16	1	24 - 12 oz bottles	18
31	36	Inlagd Sill	17	8	24 - 250 g jars	19
32	37	Gravad lax	17	8	12 - 500 g pkgs.	26
33	38	Côte de Blaye	18	1	12 - 75 cl bottles	263.5

Northwind

> If you want to import data from text files with low-level programmatic con-
> trol over *delimiters* (such as data separated by # characters or whatever),
> you can use the file input/output (I/O) commands available in VBA. For
> details, see Book II, Chapter 4.

Importing Data from an XML Dataset

Disconnected datasets (tables detached from their host database) represent a
valuable technology, providing a highly scalable solution when large numbers of users simultaneously need to access a database. They get in and out,
without needing to maintain an active connection to the database.

You can find out more about datasets in the following mini-book (Book V) on
Access, but here's an example of how you can import an XML dataset into
Excel. You'll import fields from the same `Products` table of the Northwind
database (see the preceding example in this chapter). Here, however, you
don't connect to the database directly; instead, you get your data from a
dataset.

To create an XML dataset by hand, follow these steps:

1. **Double-click the** `Northwind.mdb` **file.**

   The database is loaded into Access.

2. **In Access, double-click the** `Products` **table in the main database window.**

   The table opens.

3. **Choose File⇨Export.**

4. **In the Save as Type drop-down list of the Export dialog box, choose XML.**

5. **Click the Export All button.**

6. **Clear the Schema of the Data check box.**

   You want to let Excel format this data, not Access.

7. **Click OK.**

   The dialog box closes, and your XML dataset is saved.

8. **Close Access.**

9. **Run Excel.**

10. **Choose File⇨Open in Excel.**

11. **In the Open dialog box, locate on your hard drive the** `Products.xml` **dataset that you just created. Double-click it to open it.**

    The Open XML dialog box is displayed.

12. **Choose As an XML List.**

13. **Click OK.**

    You're notified that no schema exists for this data (no XSD or other associated formatting file). But you knew that.

14. **Click OK.**

    Your worksheet fills with the `Products` table.

Programmatically Creating a Dataset

To create a dataset from an Access-style database (MBD) programmatically, you can type in and then execute the following code (Listing 3-2) in Visual Basic .NET.

Listing 3-2: Creating a Dataset from an Access-style Database

```
Public s As String = "Provider=Microsoft.Jet.OLEDB.4.0;Data Source=" & _
      "C:\Program Files\Microsoft Office\Office11\Samples\Northwind.mdb;"



    Private Sub Form1_Load(ByVal sender As System.Object, ByVal e As
          System.EventArgs) Handles MyBase.Load

    Dim connect As New System.Data.OleDb.OleDbConnection(s)

    Try
        connect.Open()

        Dim SQ, fname As String, dset As New DataSet

        Dim adap As New System.Data.OleDb.OleDbDataAdapter

        SQ = "Select ProductName, CategoryID, QuantityPerUnit, UnitPrice from
         Products"

        adap.SelectCommand = New System.Data.OleDb.OleDbCommand(SQ, connect)

        adap.Fill(dset)

        fname = "C:\Products.xml"

        Dim fs As New System.IO.FileStream(fname, System.IO.FileMode.Create)

        Dim t As New System.Xml.XmlTextWriter(fs,
         System.Text.Encoding.Unicode)

        'this is a necessary first element for Excel to recognize the dataset
         as XML:
        t.WriteProcessingInstruction("xml", "version='1.0'")

        dset.WriteXml(t)
        t.Close()

        MsgBox("EXPORT SUCCEEDED")

    Catch ex As Exception
        MsgBox(ex.Message)
    End Try

    End Sub
```

Remember that all this book's code is available at this book's companion Web site. (Please see the Introduction for the specific URL.)

Press F5 to execute this and then follow Steps 9–14 in the preceding example to load your dataset into Excel.

In Listing 3-2, first the variable s is defined to hold the connection string to the database. This is done in the General Declarations section, in case you want to access this connection elsewhere in your project. In this code, though, you use it only in the `Form_Load` event. You first create a connection object named `connect`. Then within an error-trapping `Try` block, you open the connection to the database, create a string variable to hold an SQL `Query` string, and also declare a couple of variables to hold a filepath and a dataset. The dataset, being a particular kind of object (it has no special name, but it does behave differently than built-in objects like strings) requires that you use the `New` keyword when declaring it.

SQL (Structured Query Language) is the most widely used language for getting information from a database. You often don't want an entire chunk of data, such as a whole table, so you can write an SQL query, like this: *Show me all customers whose accounts are more than three months overdue.* This provides you with a useful subset of the data. SQL can also be used to modify a database, such as updating information.

A data adaptor object is created. Also, an SQL query is specified, asking that the dataset to be built from four fields in the `Products` table of the database. The specify query connection (a *command,* as it's called) is now made, and the dataset object is filled. Now the `New` .NET `FileStream` and `TextWriter` objects are used to save the XML data to a file on the hard drive.

Database management in the .NET world involves several objects that interact. Dividing the task of accessing data into these several objects is perhaps more of interest to the programmers at Microsoft who created this division than to the rest of us. But if you're curious, here are the four primary objects that are collectively known as the *data provider:*

✦ The data *connection* makes contact with a data store, such as a database.

✦ The data *adapter* makes a connection between a *dataset* and a data store.

✦ The data *command* allows you to specify how you want data retrieved or modified (similar to the idea that SQL can frame specific requests for subsets of data, or to modify the database).

✦ A data *reader* object provides a read-only, forward-only stream of data from a data store. (A reader executes very quickly.)

A *dataset* is a table, for example, that's been separated from its original database so you can work with it "offline," so to speak, without having to maintain an active connection to the original database.

Note that Access starts to buckle under the pressure of more than ten simultaneous connections; its performance seriously degrades. Disconnecting or "checking out" tables solves this problem. For more details about .NET database management, see my book *Visual Basic .NET Database Programming For Dummies* (Wiley).

OOP and the degeneration of languages

Object-oriented programming (OOP) theorists have offered convoluted explanations for the false "distinction" between objects that require New during instantiation and those that don't. But they (the explanations, not the professors) are too tedious to endure. Just note that some variable declarations in VB.NET require the New keyword, others don't, and there's no rule nor pattern that you can learn to differentiate them. It's the usual thing with OOP programming — you just have to try something. And if that doesn't work, insert a New command or some other fiddling until the compiler agrees with your grammar.

You've probably heard that the classic Chinese language cannot be typewritten because (being pictographic) the keyboard would have to be an acre wide and contain hundreds of thousands of keys. Chinese words aren't made up of 26 rearrangeable characters; instead, each word is a unique drawing, a little picture resembling the meaning (the word for *duck* looks like a duck).

Many of these words are quite lovely, and a language like this is easier to learn, but it certainly has drawbacks when you try to design a computer keyboard for it. Likewise, the many unique behaviors and interrelationships between objects and members in OOP languages increasingly baffle programmers. Even the people responsible for designing OOP languages themselves are often at a loss to explain the classifications systems, internal illogic, and absence of useful taxonomic rules. The Visual Basic language started off in 1990 with around 300 words. There are now hundreds of thousands of phrases — massive assemblies crammed with objects, each object's many members, and the many arguments and overloaded argument lists available to each member.

Computer programming is the second time in history (after Esperanto) that a human language was deliberately designed rather than simply evolving from grunts or accreting blindly over centuries of use. Programming offered a special opportunity to specify a logical grammar: a consistent set of rules. It's truly a shame that computer programming has now become the plaything of raging academics. To put the situation bluntly, confusion is triumphing over common sense. Our only hope is that sooner rather than later, the computer itself will design a programming language that is — like BASIC used to be — easy for humans to read and write.

Adding Shapes and Pictures

Now for a little recreation. Whether you've been naughty or nice, there's no use perma-sticking your nose to a grindstone. The following example shows you how to goose up your worksheets and presentations with some fun clip art. Also, graphics can have practical uses as well, such as drawing attention to important points.

You can use both the `AddShape` method of the `Shapes` collection and the `Insert` method of the `Picture` collection to liven up your work. The following code adds an explosion graphic, followed by a dropshadowed cloud drawing, and then a second explosion superimposed on the cloud.

The order in which you add these objects to a sheet defines the *z-axis format* — that is, which is superimposed on which.

```
Sub AutoShapes()

    'insert explosions
    ActiveSheet.Shapes.AddShape(msoShapeExplosion2, 425.25, 145.5, 86.25,
        101.25).Select


    'get a shape from the collection on the hard drive:
    ActiveSheet.Pictures.Insert("C:\Program Files\Microsoft
        Office\MEDIA\OFFICE11\AutoShap\BD18185_.wmf").Select

    'superimpose second explosion:
    ActiveSheet.Shapes.AddShape(msoShapeExplosion2, 465.75, 324.75, 72#,
        72#).Select


End Sub
```

Execute this `Sub`, and you see the graphics added to your worksheet, similar to the sheet shown in Figure 3-3.

6	18 - 500 g pkgs.	97
8	12 - 200 ml jars	31
4	1 kg pkg.	21
4	10 - 500 g pkgs.	38
8	2 kg box	6
7	40 - 100 g pkgs.	23.25
2	24 - 250 ml bottles	15.5
3	32 - 500 g boxes	17.45
6	20 - 1 kg tins	39
8	16 kg pkg.	62.5
3	10 boxes x 12 pieces	9.2
3	30 gift boxes	81
3	24 pkgs. x 4 pieces	10
5	24 - 500 g pkgs.	21
5	12 - 250 g pkgs.	9
1	12 - 355 ml cans	4.5
3	20 - 450 g glasses	14
3	100 - 250 g bags	31.23
3	100 - 100 g pieces	43.9
7	25 - 825 g cans	45.6
6	50 bags x 30 sausgs.	123.79
8	10 - 200 g glasses	25.89
4	12 - 100 g pkgs.	12.5

Figure 3-3: Surprise your co-workers with sudden, programmatically added graphics.

The `AddShape` method takes the following arguments:

```
AddShape(Type, Left, Top, Width, Height)
```

In the preceding code, note that the `AddShape` method specifies the absolute position in the sheet as well as absolute size of the graphic. However, when you insert a picture, its upper-left corner appears at the current selection point.

A collection of clip art `.wmf` (Windows Metafile) files can be found in the AutoShap folder in the path specified in the earlier code. Figure 3-4 shows some of the available drawings.

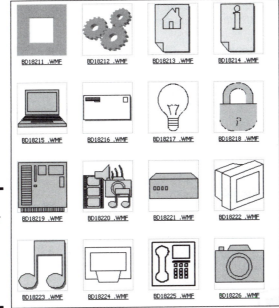

Figure 3-4: Tasteless or fun, adding clip art is your judgment call.

Augmenting Find and Replace

As in Word — or indeed many situations including programming itself — you sometimes need to locate a particular item or even mass-replace one item with another in Excel. It could be text, formulae, captions, values, or whatever else needs to be located or cleaned up.

Automating a find-and-replace isn't a difficult challenge; often you can record a macro that shows you the ropes by providing the necessary code. But do be aware of the limitations of recorded code. Sometimes it's too specific: It specifies the current selection, for instance, rather than using a relative programming command. Sometimes it's hard-wired rather than free-form. Other times it includes lots of extraneous code, such as line after line of default settings in Word.

In any case, you do want to be aware of your options for programmatic finding and replacing.

The Find method of the Range or WorkSheetFunction objects returns either nothing if no match is found or the single-cell range where the match was found. If you want to do a global find-and-replace, therefore, you must use a loop to iterate through the target cells.

Read more about loops in Book II, Chapter 3.

Understanding Find methods

The Range object offers Find, FindNext, and FindPrevious methods. Listing 3-3 illustrates how to use the Find and FindNext methods. It asks users what they want to search for, turns each *hit* (find) gray, and then displays how many hits occurred:

Listing 3-3:   Using Find and FindNext

```
Sub Count()

ActiveSheet.UsedRange.Style = "normal"

s = InputBox("Type in the search term.")

With ActiveSheet.UsedRange

    Set c = .Find(s, LookIn:=xlValues)

    If Not c Is Nothing Then
        firstAddress = c.Address
        Do
            counter = counter + 1
            ActiveSheet.Range(c.Address).Interior.Pattern = xlPatternGray16
            Set c = .FindNext(c)
        Loop While Not c Is Nothing And c.Address <> firstAddress
    End If

End With

If counter = 0 Then counter = "no"

MsgBox ("We found " & counter & " instances of " & s)

End Sub
```

Getting user input

You first *blank* (delete the contents of) any cells that have shading in the UsedRange (the entire group of used cells on the active sheet.) Next, you display an input box to get the user's target; it can be a number or text. Then you amend the ActiveSheet.UsedRange in a With block. You define c as the result of the search (via the Find method of the UsedRange object) — in other words, the first instance of the target that the user requested be searched for. If c is not nothing (meaning that something was found as a match for the requested target), you enter a Do loop, raising the counter variable each time through the loop and also turning the hit cell gray. You continue to loop as long as there's a hit (c has something in it) and the address of c isn't the same as the first hit. When finished looping, the results are displayed to the user.

The Find Format

Here is the argument list for the Find method:

```
Range.Find(What, [After], [LookIn], [LookAt], [SearchOrder],
    [SearchDirection], [MatchCase], [MatchByte],
    [SearchFormat])
```

✦ What: This is the target value you're looking for, such as *bottles* or *200*. It can be any type of data permitted in Excel. What is the only required argument; brackets mean optional arguments.

✦ After: This is the address of a single cell in the range where you want the search to begin. It's an offset; if omitted, your search begins in the top-left cell of your Range object's cells.

✦ LookIn: This can be one of three constants:

  • xlValues (the default)

  • xlFormula

  • xlComments

✦ LookAt: This can be one of two constants. (***Note:*** The entire value must be matched. For example, *Boy* will not be a match for *cowboy.*)

  • xlPart (the default)

  • xlWhole

✦ SearchOrder: This can be either xlByColumns or xlByRows.

✦ SearchDirection: This argument specifies the search direction. Choose from

- xlNext (the default)

- xlPrevious

✦ MatchCase: This is False by default. If True, the search is case-sensitive.

✦ MatchByte: If this is True, *Unicode* (characters represented by a two-byte code) matches only other Unicode characters. If False, Unicode characters can match ASCII code (single-byte) characters. This defaults to False, so just ignore it.

✦ SearchFormat: This argument is puzzling. If I were you, I wouldn't worry about it. It can be True or False and appears to interact with the FindFormat method, toggling it on or off. This code, for example, changes italicized cells to boldface but only because the Replace method's SearchFormat argument is True:

```
With Application.FindFormat
    .Clear
    .Font.Bold = True
End With

With Application.ReplaceFormat
    .Clear
    .Font.Italic = True
End With

Cells.Replace SearchFormat:=True, ReplaceFormat:=True
```

Some of the arguments for the Find method persist! In other words, the next time that you use the Find method in the same session, any values that you've previously assigned to LookIn, LookAt, SearchOrder, or MatchByte will be used again unless you change them in your new code. This strange persistence can certainly be expected to cause some confusing bugs.

The Replace method

A typical recorded version of Find and Replace looks like this:

```
Sub Macro1()

    Cells.Replace What:="10", Replacement:="4000", LookAt:=xlPart, _
        SearchOrder:=xlByRows, MatchCase:=False, SearchFormat:=False, _
        ReplaceFormat:=False

End Sub
```

Fortunately, Replace is a pretty straightforward method, and it doesn't require that you build a loop or anything as in the previous Find examples in this chapter. The arguments are also the same as those for Find except for Replacement (what you want to replace the targeted value with) and ReplaceFormat, which allows you to change the formatting of a cell, after this fashion:

```
With Application.ReplaceFormat.Font
        .Size = 12
        .Name = "Optima"
        .FontStyle = "Italic"
End With
```

Chapter 4: Data Diving with Pivot Tables

In This Chapter

- **Building pivot tables**
- **Using the PivotTable Wizard**
- **Revealing hidden data**
- **Creating pivot charts**
- **Modifying the data in pivot tables**
- **Updating pivot tables**

Pivot means to turn, yet remain in the same place, like a ballerina revolving *en pointe,* so you see her from all sides.

An Excel pivot table allows you to see data in new ways. Maybe you've heard about expensive, complex *data mining* technology: Sophisticated software explores a database and then presents users with ideas they never expected, predictions they never could have made themselves, and answers to questions they never thought to ask. (Check out *Excel Data Analysis For Dummies,* by Stephen L. Nelson, Wiley, for Excel data mining ins and outs.)

As you'll discover in this chapter, you can look at a set of data in several different ways and still miss something of importance. The first few figures in this chapter contain an interesting anomaly, but you're unlikely to spot it until I — with the help of a pivoting table — reveal it to you. Then you'll go back and say, "Why didn't I *see* that?" (Answer: You did see it, Bunky, but it was camouflaged by the data surrounding it. Only after some pivoting was it revealed to us all.)

This chapter also covers pivot charts and ways to modify or update the data in pivot tables.

What Is a PivotTable?

Data mining technology is becoming increasingly important in proportion to the increasing size and complexity of databases. No human has the ability to sort through millions of data and spot oddities, notable variants, and interesting trends.

Pivot tables aren't as advanced as data mining, but they're in the same ballpark. With them, you get to twist data around — to pivot it, as it were — to see it in new ways. I call it *data diving* because it's less extreme than mining although pivoting tables can (in their own way) yield valuable results in much the same way panning for gold by hand sometimes yields nuggets.

When you drag and drop fields to various locations within a pivot table, you're pivoting it. The pivot table re-sorts and recalculates the data, adjusting the subtotals and grand total(s) as necessary. You don't type in any formulae. You simply choose from a drop-down list in the PivotTable Field dialog box (double-click a field title button, the gray buttons, in the PivotTable) whether you want a COUNT, SUM, AVERAGE, MAX, MIN, PRODUCT, COUNT NUMS, STANDARD DEVIATION, or other options. If you need to perform calculations not available on this drop-down list, it's possible (see Excel's Help).

Here's an example of data too complex to be useful unless it's been pivoted or mined. Everyone entering the Super Bowl is watched by a video camera, and their face patterns are compared to stored photos. Tied to the photos is personal data, such as *young, male, pilot lessons, one-way tickets.* The visual and other patterns are automatically and rapidly transformed in various ways. This kind of analysis, although somewhat chilling for those of us who value liberty and privacy, might end up saving many lives.

Pivot tables are especially useful in a variety of situations:

+ Performing simple data-mining by hand, noticing significant facts otherwise hidden within the data.

+ Generating budgets and business plans, complete with easy ways to generate charts and reports.

+ Tracking expenses.

+ Discovering hidden patterns and relationships.

+ Improving inventory control.

+ Boosting productivity.

+ Spotting problems or trends early. (Which division wastes the most money on bad ads or sells the most widgets?)

+ Summarizing lengthy data in a compact format (see upcoming Figure 4-10).

+ Deciding what data to selectively hide.

+ Arranging data in ways that are easily charted (see Figure 4-10, which results in the chart shown in Figure 4-12).

Creating a Pivot Table

Like swimming, a pivot table is difficult to describe. The result is obvious in both cases, but the activity itself needs to be experienced, dear readers, so jump in here and experience it.

Start by creating a pivot table. Pivot it and twirl it around. Fool with it. Get a feel for it. To see how a pivot table works, follow these steps:

1. **Create a spreadsheet with four columns of fake data: Company, Year, Expense, and Amount.**

    You're pretending to be a wild greed engine, a mogul named Varla Vepp, who wants to examine the costs of three of her companies. She plans to decide which one to shut down during next year's New Year's celebration, just after many of her employees have maxed out their credit cards. Watch out for Varla's bad self; she's extremely scary when in high spirits.

2. **Fill in the data for 20 to 30 rows. Use three different company names, three different years, three expense categories (transportation, salaries, and utilities), and various different amounts of money, as shown in Figure 4-1.**

    Copying and pasting helps you quickly add this data.

	A	B	C	D	E	F
	COMPANY	YEAR	EXPENSE	AMOUNT		
2	MidState Sealant	2001	Transportation	24000		
3	Murrey's Fishfood	2002	Salaries	12500		
4	Murrey's Fishfood	2003	Salaries	45000		
5	MidState Sealant	2001	Transportation	17000		
6	MidState Sealant	2002	Utilties	4000		
7	Yo-Yo Clothing	2003	Transportation	33000		
8	Yo-Yo Clothing	2001	Transportation	5200		
9	MidState Sealant	2002	Salaries	17400		
10	Yo-Yo Clothing	2003	Utilties	23000		
11	Yo-Yo Clothing	2001	Transportation	4200		
12	MidState Sealant	2002	Utilties	4440		
13	Murrey's Fishfood	2003	Salaries	56800		
14	Yo-Yo Clothing	2001	Transportation	32000		
15	Murrey's Fishfood	2002	Transportation	42999		
16	MidState Sealant	2003	Utilties	25999		
17	Murrey's Fishfood	2001	Salaries	13000		
18	Yo-Yo Clothing	2002	Salaries	44400		
19	MidState Sealant	2003	Transportation	23880		

Figure 4-1: Create a sample set of data.

Book IV Chapter 4

Data Diving with Pivot Tables

3. **Click any cell in the data.**

4. **Choose Data⇨PivotTable and PivotChart Report.**

   The PivotTable and PivotChart Wizard opens.

5. **Leave the Microsoft Office Excel List or Database radio button selected as the data that you want to analyze.**

6. **Leave the PivotTable radio button selected.**

7. **Click Next.**

8. **In the second page of the wizard, specify A1:D300 as your range (in the Range text field).**

   You want to specify a range larger than the actual current data because you might add data in the future.

9. **Click Next.**

10. **In the final wizard page, select the New Worksheet radio button to set the location of your new pivot table.**

11. **Click Finish.**

    You now see a new worksheet containing a template for your pivot table, as shown in Figure 4-2.

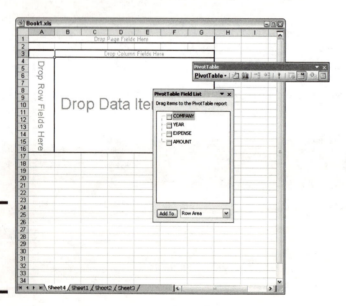

Figure 4-2:
Here's where you design the pivot table.

Now you're ready to build the actual pivot table. You begin by dragging and dropping items from the Pivot Table Field List dialog box, as shown in Figure 4-2. Follow these steps:

1. **Drag the AMOUNT header and drop it into the data field (Drop Data Items Here) in the template.**

   The template unhelpfully collapses. The template actually disappears at this point, and you're left looking at the usual Excel cells. (There's a solution to this, which I describe later in the tip in the section, "A sudden surprise." The upcoming Figure 4-11 illustrates the dialog box that solves the problem.)

   The item that you drop into the data field is the one that gets summarized by the pivot table.

2. **Click Company to select it in the PivotTable Field List dialog box.**

3. **Click the Add To button (with Row Area visible in the drop-down list) in the dialog box.**

   Your company field is added to the worksheet.

4. **Repeat Steps 2 and 3 to add the Year and Expense fields to the worksheet.**

   See the results in Figure 4-3.

Figure 4-3:
This Pivot Table is almost ready to pivot.

	A	B	C	D
1	Drop Page Fields Here			
2				
3	Count of AMOUNT			
4	COMPANY ▾	YEAR ▾	EXPENSE ▾	Total
5	Mid-State Sealant	2001	Transportation	2
6		2001 Total		2
7		2002	Salaries	1
8			Utilities	2
9		2002 Total		3
10		2003	Transportation	1
11			Utilities	1
12		2003 Total		2
13	Mid-State Sealant Total			7
14	Murrey's Fish Food	2001	Salaries	1
15		2001 Total		1
16		2002	Salaries	1
17			Transportation	1
18		2002 Total		2
19		2003	Salaries	2
20		2003 Total		2
21	Murrey's Fish Food Total			5
22	Yo-Yo Clothing	2001	Transportation	3
23		2001 Total		3
24		2002	Salaries	1
25		2002 Total		1
26		2003	Transportation	1
27			Utilities	1
28		2003 Total		2
29	Yo-Yo Clothing Total			6
30	(blank)	(blank)	(blank)	
31		(blank) Total		
32	(blank) Total			
33	Grand Total			18
34				

**Book IV
Chapter 4**

**Data Diving with
Pivot Tables**

5. **Close the PivotTable Field List dialog box.**

6. **Double-click Count of AMOUNT at the top of the data in this worksheet.**

   Refer to Figure 4-3.

   The PivotTable Field dialog box opens. (See Figure 4-4.)

Figure 4-4:
The Pivot-
Table Field
dialog box
offers you
a variety
of ways
to pivot
the data.

By default, Count of AMOUNT is displayed, which is rather odd. That's
not very useful information when you're looking at expenses or, indeed,
many other kinds of summaries. In this example, you want to see the
sum — the total cost — not simply a count of the number of expense
entries. (However, if you're summarizing non-numeric data, such as
company names, Count is the only possible choice — you can't perform
math on words.)

7. **Click Sum in the dialog box (in the Summarize By list) to choose
   Summarize by Sum.**

8. **Click OK.**

   The dialog box closes, and you see that the Total column has been recalculated to show various subtotals and totals. At this point, your worksheet should look like Figure 4-5.

Notice in Figure 4-5 that you're seeing expenses for each company, broken
down by yearly subtotals, company subtotals, and a final grand total. Now
drag the Expense button (in cell 4) and drop it on top of the Company
button. At this point, the pivoting takes place. Read on.

	A	B	C	D	E	F	G
	Book1.xls						
1							
2							
3	Sum of AMOUNT						
4	COMPANY ▼	YEAR ▼	EXPENSE ▼	Total			
5	MidState Sealant		2001 Transportation	41000			
6		2001 Total		41000			
7			2002 Salaries	17400			
8			Utilties	8440			
9		2002 Total		25840			
10			2003 Transportation	23880			
11			Utilties	25999			
12		2003 Total		49879			
13	MidState Sealant Total			116719			
14	Murrey's Fishfood		2001 Salaries	13000			
15		2001 Total		13000			
16			2002 Salaries	12500			
17			Transportation	42999			
18		2002 Total		55499			
19			2003 Salaries	101800			
20		2003 Total		101800			
21	Murrey's Fishfood Total			170299			
22	Yo-Yo Clothing		2001 Transportation	41400			
23		2001 Total		41400			
24			2002 Salaries	44400			
25		2002 Total		44400			
26			2003 Transportation	33000			
27			Utilties	23000			
28		2003 Total		56000			
29	Yo-Yo Clothing Total			141800			
30	(blank)	(blank)	(blank)				
31		(blank) Total					
32	(blank) Total						
33	Grand Total			428818			
34							

H ◄ ► H \ **Sheet4** / Sheet1 / Sheet2 / Sheet3 /

Figure 4-5:
Now you're seeing some interesting information.

The Table Pivots

Now the information is recalculated — the table *pivots* — and you see the subtotals for each category of expense, rather than by company subtotals. This is an interesting way to quickly reorient the view on the data, wouldn't you agree? You actually have a differently arranged, newly sorted, new table.

Try double-clicking the Expense button. You see the PivotTable Field dialog box from which you can select various options, such as hiding subtotals. Try clicking the Layout button in the dialog box to see the PivotTable Field Layout dialog box, as shown in Figure 4-6.

Figure 4-6:
Use this dialog box to change the format of a Pivot-Table to suit yourself.

Use the PivotTable Field Layout dialog box to change the way your pivot table looks to perhaps make the information clearer: Select Show Items in Outline Form, Display Subtotals at Top of Group, and Insert Blank Line after Each Item. Click OK twice to close both dialog boxes.

You now see a slightly different — and I think more readable — summary of the costs of each expense item, as shown in Figure 4-7.

Figure 4-7: You can adjust the layout to clarify what you're seeing.

	A	B	C	D	E	F	G
4	EXPENSE	COMPANY	YEAR	Total			
5	Salaries			189100			
6		MidState Sealant					
7			2002	17400			
8		MidState Sealant Total		17400			
9		Murrey's Fishfood					
10			2001	13000			
11			2002	12500			
12			2003	101800			
13		Murrey's Fishfood Total		127300			
14		Yo-Yo Clothing					
15			2002	44400			
16		Yo-Yo Clothing Total		44400			
17							
18	Transportation			182279			
19		MidState Sealant					
20			2001	41000			
21			2003	23880			
22		MidState Sealant Total		64880			
23		Murrey's Fishfood					
24			2002	42999			
25		Murrey's Fishfood Total		42999			
26		Yo-Yo Clothing					
27			2001	41400			
28			2003	33000			
29		Yo-Yo Clothing Total		74400			
30							
31	Utilties			57439			
32		MidState Sealant					
33			2002	8440			
34			2003	25999			
35		MidState Sealant Total		34439			
36		Yo-Yo Clothing					
37			2003	23000			

Just so we're all on the same page, for the next example, reverse your recent actions, again open the PivotTable Field dialog box, click the Layout button, and then deselect all three options: Show Items in Outline Form, Display Subtotals at Top of Group, and Insert Blank Line after Each Item.

Collapsing the pivot table

Try collapsing the entire report to see just the essentials. On the PivotTable toolbar, click the Hide Detail button (see Figure 4-8). If this toolbar isn't visible, right-click the Excel menu bar and mark the PivotTable check box. If the buttons on the PivotTable are disabled, click a cell within the worksheet's data to enable them.

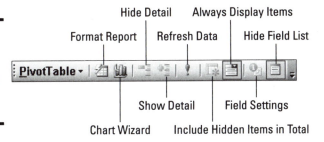

Figure 4-8:
The Pivot
Table
toolbar and
its various
buttons.

Now you see only the essentials. To see the fundamental difference between the two tables you've been looking at (broken down by expenses versus by company), drag the Expense button and drop it on the Company button. Now it's easy to see how different a table is when pivoted. This is still the same basic data (the grand total doesn't change), but when rearranged and recalculated, it tells you quite different things about your empire — and where the money goes — as shown in Figure 4-9.

Figure 4-9:
The table
organized by
expenses
(top) can be
pivoted to
reorganize
the data into
a table
organized by
companies
(bottom).

4	EXPENSE ▼	COMPANY ▼	YEAR ▼	Total
5	Salaries			189100
6	Transportation			182279
7	Utilties			57439
8	(blank)			
9	Grand Total			428818

4	COMPANY ▼	EXPENSE ▼	YEAR ▼	Total
5	MidState Sealant			116719
6	Murrey's Fishfood			170299
7	Yo-Yo Clothing			141800
8	(blank)			
9	Grand Total			428818

Now try pivoting again, working again with the wizard. Because in the earlier example, I originally asked the wizard to make a new worksheet when it created the first pivot table in this chapter, the original data still exists on Sheet1. That's what I use. Click Sheet1's tab on the bottom of the workbook (which should look like Figure 4-1, earlier in this chapter).

Click to select any cell in the table of data in Sheet1; then choose Data⇨ PivotTable and PivotChart Report to open the wizard. Drag Company to the Row field, Expense to the Column field, and Amount to the Data field. Double-click Amount and choose Sum. You've deliberately left out the year field, which simplifies your view of the table because there's less data to view and less to summarize.

Notice how different this view is from earlier pivots. The table has rotated again into a new view, as shown in Figure 4-10.

Figure 4-10:
This pivot
simplifies
seeing the
overall
picture by
eliminating
the time
factor (the
year-by-year
breakdown).

3	Sum of AMOUNT	EXPENSE ▾				
4	COMPANY ▾	Salaries	Transportation	Utilties	(blank)	Grand Total
5	MidState Sealant	17400	64880	34439		116719
6	Murrey's Fishfood	127300	42999			170299
7	Yo-Yo Clothing	44400	74400	23000		141800
8	(blank)					
9	Grand Total	189100	182279	57439		428818

Calendar data such as year, month, and so on can add needless complexity to a pivot table's data. You can either leave this field out of the pivot table entirely as I did in this example, or you can drop the Year (or other calendar field) into the Page section of the pivot table layout (see the upcoming Figure 4-11). Do this, and you can selectively view each unit of time — or all of them together — via a drop-down list. And if you're working with large amounts of data (such as comparing 200 companies), you can try the grouping continuous variables (see Excel Help).

A sudden surprise

One thing pops out in this new view of the data shown in Figure 4-10: Murrey's Fishfood never pays utilities! I wonder whom *they* know.

Take a look again at Figures 4-1 and 4-5. If you were looking particularly carefully at these tables of data, you might have noticed that Murrey's wasn't paying a utility bill. But many people would have missed this detail in the larger mass of data. That's precisely the value of pivoting data: You might see information that was previously hidden. By rotating the table in different ways, you can often get a deeper understanding of what the data means and how to perhaps make wiser decisions. I'm sure that Varla will want to know more about this Fishfood deal.

The sample table of data that I pivot in this chapter is actually rather small. Real tables can be quite a bit larger and, thus, quite a bit more likely to need pivoting to reveal their secrets.

You can rearrange the rows, columns, and data fields quickly in an existing pivot table (as opposed to using the original table's data as I did in the previous example). Right-click any cell in the pivot table, and then choose PivotTable Wizard from the context menu. Click the Layout button of the wizard. In the Layout dialog box that appears (as shown in Figure 4-11), you can freely rearrange the various field buttons by dragging and dropping them into the various zones in the diagram.

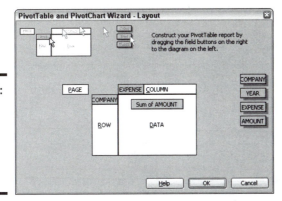

Figure 4-11:
Use the Layout dialog box to quickly pivot your tables.

Double-click any of the field buttons shown in Figure 4-11 to change that field's summary behavior from count to sum, or select from many other options. Between the wizards, context menus, dialog boxes, and drop-down lists, you have many ways to pivot, reformat, and manipulate pivot tables.

Try pivoting this table in various ways. Use the Layout dialog box (refer to Figure 4-11) to rearrange the field buttons and then close the dialog box to see your newly pivoted table. And don't forget these pointers:

✦ You don't have to include all the available fields in the pivot table.

✦ You can insert fields more than once.

✦ You can insert fields in more than one of the three layout locations (Data, Row, and Column).

Creating Instant Pivot Charts

Nothing could be simpler than seeing a chart of a pivot table — a *pivot chart*. Here is yet another view of your data, although this one is graphical. Pivot tables automatically generate subtotals for you, scaling the subtotals so that summary data can be easily displayed graphically.

Right-click any cell in the pivot table shown in Figure 4-10. Choose PivotChart from the context menu that appears. *Et voilà,* your data is charted. Here's another view where you might notice that the fishbait guy isn't paying his electric bill, as shown in Figure 4-12.

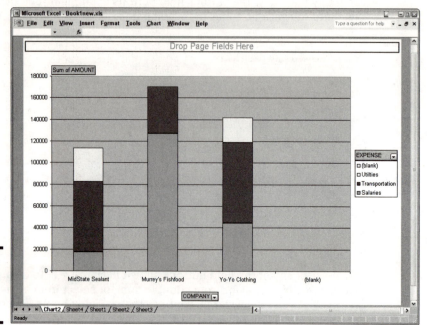

Figure 4-12:
Pivot charts
are just a
click away.

Modifying the Data in a PivotTable

You cannot directly edit the data in a pivot table. It's like a report — not a data source. But you can edit the source data and then choose Data⇨Refresh Data. The data that populates a pivot table need not be a loaded, active worksheet like the examples that I explore in this chapter. It can be a set of ranges, another pivot table, or various kinds of external data sources.

Refreshing pivot table data

If the data source is modified — for example, if you make changes to the values in the sheet shown in Figure 4-1 in this chapter — you can turn back to the pivot table and click the Refresh Data button on the PivotTable toolbar or choose the same option from Data menu. The pivot table is updated because it remembers the source of its data.

Pivot charts revert to their default formatting when refreshed. Pivot tables, however, stay formatted after being refreshed.

Automatically updating pivot table data

Perhaps you want to make the updating process automatic. Every time a pivot table's workbook is opened, any pivot tables in it are updated automatically. To do this, put your updating code in the workbook's special Open macro that executes automatically each time the workbook is opened. To do this, press Alt+F11 to open the Visual Basic editor (VBE) and choose View➪Project Explorer. In Project Explorer, double-click ThisWorkbook to open its macro window. Now type this:

```
Private Sub Workbook_Open()

For i = 1 To ActiveSheet.PivotTables.Count
    ActiveSheet.PivotTables(i).RefreshTable
Next

End Sub
```

Chapter 5: Business Analysis with Excel

In This Chapter

☑ Forecasting with Goal Seek

☑ Creating scenarios

☑ Using summary reports

☑ Exploring problems with Solver

*E*xcel includes a variety of tools that you can employ to assist your business with forecasting, planning, and general analysis. When it comes time to run your company stats through Excel, you might as well take advantage of some of these tools. In the preceding chapter of this mini-book, I cover in depth one of the most important data-analysis tools — the pivot table. In this chapter, you explore several additional tools useful for people whose job it is to combine computer expertise with business savvy.

Seeking Goals with Goal Seek

Excel's Goal Seek feature allows you to specify a particular goal value (such as profit = $12,000 monthly), and Excel will adjust the value in a second cell until the goal is achieved. Goal Seek has been called *what-if in reverse* because instead of adjusting the income cell to see the effect on the profit cell — the usual what-if behavior — you do the reverse: Specify what profit you want, and Excel adjusts income to achieve that goal. It's rather a simple tool, but it can be useful. And when you understand how it works, you'll have an easier time finding out how to use the more advanced tools such as scenarios and Solver, which I explore later in this chapter.

To see how the Goal Seek feature works, open a new worksheet and type in these three labels describing the cash flow of your cheese business: **Monthly Income**, **Monthly Expenses**, and **Profit**. Then type in these figures: **11000** for Monthly Income, and **4000** for Monthly Expenses.

The formula that you use to calculate Profit is B1 – B2. Click cell B4 to select it; in the formula (*fx*) line at the top, type =**B1 – B2**, as shown in Figure 5-1. As soon as you enter the formula, the result of the calculation, 7000, displays in the Profit cell, as shown in Figure 5-1.

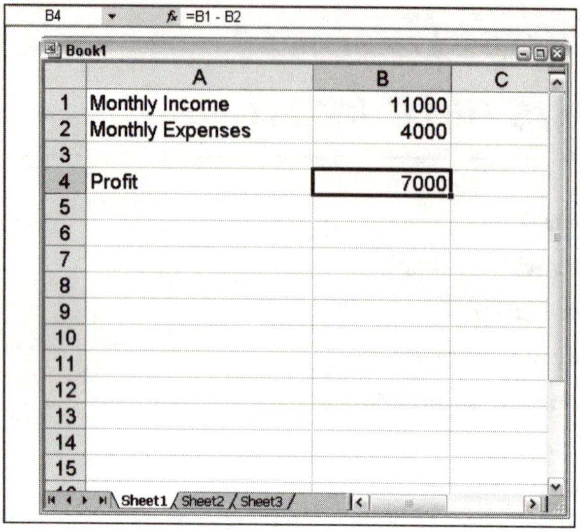

B4	▾	*fx* =B1 - B2		

Figure 5-1:
Here's some
simple
cheese
factory
cash-flow
analysis.

Book1

	A	B	C
1	Monthly Income	11000	
2	Monthly Expenses	4000	
3			
4	Profit	7000	
5			
6			
7			
8			
9			
10			
11			
12			
13			
14			
15			

Sheet1 / Sheet2 / Sheet3 /

Now to seek your goal. Click cell B4 to select it. Choose Tools⇨Goal Seek. The Goal Seek dialog box opens (as shown in Figure 5-2), and cell B4 is displayed as the cell that you want to change. For this example, you want to see how you can increase Profit, which is cell B4. You also need to enter the value that you want cell B4 to have (11000) as well as the cell that you want to adjust to reach this goal. Remember that when using Goal Seek, the goal cell itself must contain a formula, not merely data.

Figure 5-2:
Specify your
goal and
how you
want to
achieve it.

Goal Seek

Set cell: B4

To value: 11000

By changing cell: B1

OK   Cancel

To reach your goal in this example, you either have to increase your income (B1) or decrease your expenses (B2). Assume that you want to see what your monthly income must be to achieve the desired profit. Into the By Changing Cell field, enter **B1**. Click OK. You see the correct answer — 15000, in the Monthly Income cell — as displayed in Figure 5-3. The Goal Seek dialog box is replaced by the Goal Seek Status dialog box.

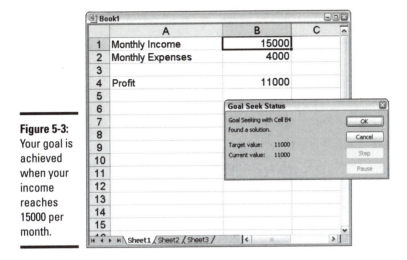

In the Goal Seek Status dialog box, click OK to leave the changed cell as is; then click Cancel to restore the original value.

To see how much you'd have to cut down on expenses to achieve your goal, follow the same steps as above, but instead type **B2** in the By Changing Cell field of the Goal Seek dialog box.

Using Scenarios

A step up from goal seeking, *scenarios* allow you to collapse what would require several worksheets into a single, easily viewed set of scenarios for a single worksheet. A scenario is a set of values that you offer to your formulae and that are displayable from within the Scenario Manager.

Try it by using the same sheet that I use in this chapter's earlier example for the cheese factory. Assume that you want to see the effect of various different expense levels on profits. One way to do this would be to create several sheets, each with a different value in the Monthly Expenses cell, but why do that when you can build a set of scenarios? Follow these steps:

1. **Use the cheese factory sheet shown in Figure 5-1.**

2. **Choose Tools⇨Scenarios.**

    The Scenario Manager dialog box opens.

3. **Click the Add button.**

    The Add Scenario dialog box opens.

4. **Type** Expenses @ 1000 **as the name for the scenario.**

5. **Click the Changing Cells field.**

The blinking cursor appears, indicating that a cell is selected.

6. **Click B2 in the worksheet, the Monthly Expenses cell.**

This is the cell you want to see adjusted to various values so you get to see the impact this item has on profits.

7. **Click OK.**

The Scenario Values dialog box opens.

8. **Type** 1000 **into the dialog box.**

9. **Click OK.**

The Scenario Values dialog box closes, and the Scenario Manager lists your new scenario.

10. **Repeat Steps 3–9 to add Expenses @ 2000 and Expenses @ 3000, respectively.**

You now have three scenarios from which to choose any time you open the Scenario Manager and click its Show button. At this point, your dialog box should look like the one in Figure 5-4.

Figure 5-4:
This dialog box now contains three defined scenarios.

11. **Click the Close button to close the Scenario Manager.**

If you want to see additional cells' values change in Step 6 in the preceding example, hold down Ctrl while clicking the additional cells to add them to the scenario.

Displaying Scenarios: Summary Reports

Can you display the results of several scenarios on a single worksheet? Sure. It's called a *summary report.* Follow these steps:

1. **Open the workbook from the preceding section's example.**

   It should contain the three scenarios that you built (Expenses @ 1000, Expenses @ 2000, and Expenses @ 3000).

2. **Choose Tools⇨Scenarios.**

   The Scenario Manager opens, as shown in Figure 5-4.

3. **Click the Summary button.**

   The Scenario Summary dialog box opens. Scenario Summary is selected by default.

4. **If B4 isn't selected, type that into the Result Cells field.**

   You want the results to be the Profit cell.

5. **Click OK.**

   The summary worksheet is displayed, as shown in Figure 5-5.

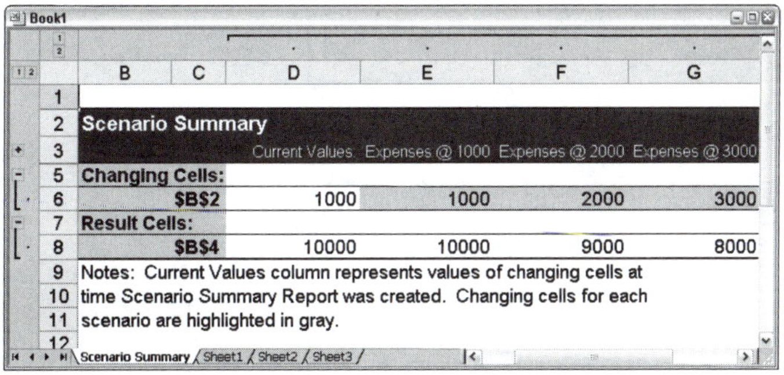

Figure 5-5:
Here's a summary report, created out of three scenarios.

Exploiting Solver

Solver, which was purchased by Microsoft and integrated into Excel, is similar to (but more advanced than) the Goal Seek feature. Goal Seek allows you to only directly specify a single cell as the variable (expenses, for example) to reach the goal that you specify (such as profit). Many real-world business problems, though, are more complex and involve multiple variables. With Solver, you can specify the goal (target cell) as well as constraints and multiple variables (changing cells).

For reasons known only to the privileged few, some features of Microsoft applications are not part of the menu system and must be added to the application. Solver is one of these mystery sisters that you have to invite explicitly to come down and join the party. Choose Tools➪Add-ins, mark the Solver check box, and then click OK. Excel shudders a little, and Solver becomes a member of the family: The Tools menu now displays Solver. (You might have to insert your Office 2003 CD.)

Solver works with a relatively complex worksheet. (Read more about this in *Excel Data Analysis For Dummies,* Stephen L. Nelson, Wiley.) Because of that, rather than creating a new worksheet to explore, take a look at the sample workbook of Solver examples that ships with Office 2003. Locate the file `SolvSamp.XLS` in this path: `C:\Program Files\Microsoft Office\ OFFICE11\SAMPLES`. If it's not there, find it on your Office 2003 CD. Load it into Excel by double-clicking its name. Click the Staff Scheduling tab at the bottom of the SolvSamp worksheet. It should look like Figure 5-6.

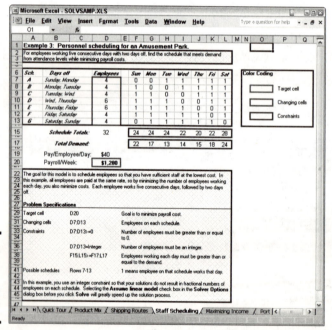

Figure 5-6: Use Solver to analyze complicated situations.

The problem to be solved by the Staff Scheduling Solver example is actually deceptive. It seems simple, but like the famous math puzzle involving the shortest route for a traveling salesman, it's actually rather complicated. This Solver model has three rules that must be followed *(constraints).* You can see these in the Problem Specifications area of the SolvSamp example in Figure 5-6:

1. The number of employees must be >= 0 (in other words, not negative).

2. The number of employees for each day must be a whole number and not a fraction.

3. The total number of employees must equal or exceed the number required to run the amusement park.

There's also a constraint not expressed in the sheet itself (but understood by the person filling in the sheet) that each employee must have two consecutive days off per week.

Check out the color-coded borders around the cells, showing which cells are constrained, which can be changed, and which is the target cell (the goal). By default, target cells are indicated by cyan (a rather bland color, similar to turquoise), changing cells indicated by green, and constraints by red.

The profit cell is the target, and you want to maximize profits by minimizing the number of employees on any given day while still remaining within the constraints.

Now solve the problem by asking Solver to take a look at it. Choose Tools⇨ Solver. The Solver Parameters dialog box opens, where you can specify Solver parameters and options. See Figure 5-7.

Figure 5-7:
Use this dialog box to adjust the behavior of the Solver.

The Guess button in this dialog box asks Solver to list all cells without formulae in them that are referred to by the formula in the target cell. These are likely to be, or at least contain, the cells that should be specified as the changing cells.

To avoid possibly slowing up your computer for hours, click the Options button. Notice that in this Solver Options dialog box, you can limit the amount of time that Solver will spend finding the solution. Some problems with many variables can take enormous computing power, so you might want to specify a limit.

Close this dialog box and then click the Solve button (in the Solver Parameters dialog box). This solution comes quickly, as shown in Figure 5-8.

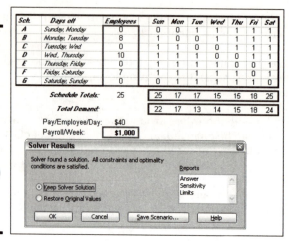

Figure 5-8: The first thing to notice here in the solution is that you've saved your company over $10,000 in annual payroll costs.

Sch.	Days off	Employees	Sun	Mon	Tue	Wed	Thu	Fri	Sat
A	Sunday, Monday	0	0	0	1	1	1	1	1
B	Monday, Tuesday	8	1	0	0	1	1	1	1
C	Tuesday, Wed	0	1	1	0	0	1	1	1
D	Wed., Thursday	10	1	1	1	0	0	1	1
E	Thursday, Friday	0	1	1	1	1	0	0	1
F	Friday, Saturday	7	1	1	1	1	1	0	1
G	Saturday, Sunday	0	0	1	1	1	1	1	0
	Schedule Totals:	25	25	17	17	15	15	18	25
	Total Demand:		22	17	13	14	15	18	24

Pay/Employee/Day: $40
Payroll/Week: $1,000

Solver Results

Solver found a solution. All constraints and optimality conditions are satisfied.

Reports
Answer
Sensitivity
Limits

⦿ Keep Solver Solution
○ Restore Original Values

[OK] [Cancel] [Save Scenario...] [Help]

Compare Figure 5-6 with Figure 5-8. The schedule itself didn't change (the 1s and 0s) remain fixed — they're not changing cells. But the changing cells (employees who have days off on any particular day), and consequently the schedule totals and profits, do change.

The various scenarios in this SolvSamp sample workbook make good templates for problems that many businesses must solve. Microsoft suggests that you see whether they might apply to problems you're facing. If so, adjust the data in the cells to reflect conditions that apply to your business, and then solve away to see various outcomes.

If you need to do advanced statistical analysis, choose Tools⇨Add-ins and then select Analysis ToolPak or Analysis ToolPak - VBA. You'll then have all the co-variance, exponential smoothing, random number generating, reverse transforms, and other fabulous (to statisticians anyway) tools at your fingertips. (You can find out more about this in *Excel 2003 Power Programming with VBA,* John Walkenbach, Wiley.)

Chapter 6: Ten Excellent Excel Macro Techniques

In This Chapter

↙ **Accessing other Office applications from within Excel**

↙ **Using UserForms to communicate with the user**

↙ **Adding macros to worksheet controls**

↙ **Automating formatting**

↙ **Trapping keypresses**

↙ **Selecting from a list box**

↙ **Sending workbooks via e-mail**

↙ **Differentiating between the** `Activate` **and** `Select` **methods**

*I*f you've read the earlier chapters in this book, you know what macros are and how to press Alt+F11 to open the macro editor in Word, Excel, and Access. In this chapter, you explore some useful macros that make working with Excel easier. Perhaps you haven't thought of some of these shortcuts or techniques.

If you want a macro to be available every time you run Excel (and from all worksheets), put it into `Personal.xls`. Do this by choosing Tools⇨Macro⇨ Record New Macro. In the Record Macro dialog box, open the Store Macro In drop-down list and choose Personal Workbook. This is similar to the `Normal.dot` template in Word that's always available to any Word document.

Accessing Other Office Applications

Contacting another application programmatically isn't difficult after you know the code. Obviously, being able to send data automatically between Office 2003 applications has uses. The different applications specialize in different jobs. For instance, if you want to run some scenarios, you might want to send data from Access to Excel because Excel excels in math. Word, of course, has the best facilities for creating reports and formatting documents. So sending information from Excel to Word is sometimes useful, too.

In this example, you send the Excel value in cell A1 to Word and then save the Word document. Follow these steps:

1. **Run Excel.**

2. **Type** Mrs. Murphy **into cell A1.**

3. **Press Alt+F11.**

   The Excel VB editor opens.

4. **Press Ctrl+R.**

   Project Explorer opens.

5. **Double-click ThisWorkbook and type in this procedure:**

   ```
   Sub SendToWord()

   s = Worksheets("Sheet1").Range("A1").Value

   Dim objWord As Object
   Set objWord = CreateObject("Word.Document")

   With objWord.Application
       .Selection.TypeText s & " is from Excel to you."
       .ActiveDocument.SaveAs "Word Test.doc"
   End With

   Set objWord = Nothing 'destroy the object

   End Sub
   ```

6. **Press F5 to execute this macro, and then you find that** Mrs. Murphy is from Excel to you **is typed into a new Word document.**

Understanding Scope

Notice the separate code windows for each of the three default worksheets, as well as one for ThisWorkbook. If you enter a macro (or module-level variable) into a worksheet VBA code module, its scope is limited to that worksheet unless you declare it Public (making it available to the entire project). If you create a standard or class module, using Public makes the procedure available not only to the entire project but also to any outside project that references the current project.

UserForms for User Interaction

You can simplify interacting with users by displaying a graphic form to accept and validate their input. In this example, I walk you through doing just that. Additionally, in this UserForm, you also want users to periodically change their password. For more on UserForms, see Book II, Chapter 4.

1. **Press Alt+F11 to open the Excel Visual Basic editor and then choose Insert⇨UserForm.**

An empty UserForm and a Toolbox appear, as shown in Figure 6-1.

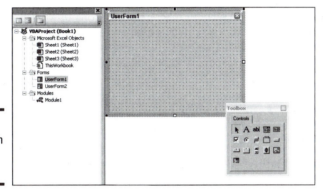

Figure 6-1:
Interact with users via this form.

Some people insist on calling this a UserForm *object,* but I just call it a UserForm in the interest of brevity and common sense. Because nearly everything is nowadays called an object — text boxes and even integers — it seems to add little to the communication to add the essentially meaningless term *object.* You might as well say, "Please fill the birdfeeder thing, using the scoop thing." Leaving out *thing* in this case doesn't decrease the information content one bit.

2. **Press F4.**

The Properties window opens, where you can modify the various properties of any controls that you place on the form or the form's properties themselves. I added a compelling (some would say *cunning*) gradient background to the UserForm by importing a graphic into its `Picture` property.

Sometimes the Toolbox disappears for no apparent reason. (There actually isn't any good reason why it should; it's just one of those funny little things.) If it disappears, click the background of the UserForm to make it reappear.

**Book IV
Chapter 6**

**Ten Excellent Excel
Macro Techniques**

3. **Click the UserForm to select it, click Caption in the Properties window, and then change the default** `Caption` **(title bar) property from UserForm1 to** `Type in your new password, please ....`

You want users to periodically change their password, so you automate the process by creating a macro under a UserForm that requests this information on a regular basis. You can use this technique to get any information from the user.

4. **Click the TextBox icon in the Toolbox to select it, and then drag your mouse in the UserForm to place the text box where you want it.**

5. **Add two command buttons to the UserForm and change their** `Caption` **properties to OK and Cancel, respectively.**

6. **(Optional) Add a graphic to the background of this form by clicking the form to select it. Then in the Properties window, click Picture and then click the ellipsis button (...) to browse your hard drive for a suitable background texture, like the cunning gradient I added.**

Drag your mouse around the text box and both control buttons to select all three. Then the Property window displays only those properties that they have in common. This is a quick way to increase the size of the font for these objects. (This is usually necessary, given that the default font size is 8 pt, which is pretty tiny.)

7. **Double-click the Font property in the Properties window and change the size from 8 to 11.**

8. **Press F5 to see your form.**

It should look something like the one in Figure 6-2, but perhaps without the gorgeous gradient graphic that I added using the `Picture` property.

Figure 6-2:
Users often respond better to custom dialog boxes.

9. **Close your UserForm to return to editor mode.**

10. **Complete the design of your form by clicking the text box and then double-clicking PasswordChar in the Properties window.**

11. **(Optional) Enter * if you wish to use asterisks as the characters that are displayed when a password is entered.**

I've never quite understood this feature. Is anyone really dumb enough to type in their password while some office snoop is standing behind them, watching them type it in? If the snoop is that close, he can just watch your fingers as your typing reveals which keys on the keyboard make up your password.

12. **Put the code into the buttons' events and double-click the OK button.**

Its `Click` event procedure opens, ready for you to insert code.

13. **Enter this:**

```
Private Sub CommandButton1_Click()

'write code here to send password to administrator

MsgBox ("Your password has been entered")
End

End Sub
```

14. **In the Cancel button's event, type this:**

```
Private Sub CommandButton2_Click()

End

End Sub
```

You can add lots of additional controls to the Toolbox by right-clicking it and then choosing Additional Controls.

Adding Macros to Worksheet Controls

In the preceding example, you display a UserForm with controls to the user. You can also add controls directly to worksheets if a UserForm seems overkill. If you need only one or two user-interaction controls, they can just be dropped right into a worksheet without cluttering it up.

Display a worksheet in Excel and then choose View➪Toolbars➪Control Toolbox. A set of controls similar to the ones in the VB editor Toolbox appears, as shown in Figure 6-3. (For more on controls, see Book II, Chapter 4.)

In the lower-left corner of the worksheet is Control Toolbox, a special icon (see Figure 6-3). Click it to add additional controls to the Toolbox.

Figure 6-3:
Use this
Toolbox to
add controls
directly
to Excel
worksheets.

Click the CommandButton icon in the Toolbox and then drag your mouse on
your worksheet where you want to display the command button. Right-click
the new button on the worksheet and then choose CommandButton Object⇨
Edit. Change the caption on the button to Click Me to Fill.

Click the worksheet to get out of editing mode. Then double-click the button
to get to its code window. Enter the code in Listing 6-1 into the button's
`Click` event. It will fill this worksheet with data when the user clicks the
`CommandButton` that you added to the worksheet:

Listing 6-1: Filling a Worksheet by Clicking a Button

```
Private Sub CommandButton1_Click()

    With ActiveSheet.QueryTables.Add(Connection:=Array( _
        "OLEDB;Provider=Microsoft.Jet.OLEDB.4.0;Password="""";User ID=Admin;Data
            Source=C:\Northwind.mdb;Mode=Share Deny Write;Extended Propertie" _
        , _
        "s="""";Jet OLEDB:System database="""";Jet OLEDB:Registry Path="""";Jet
            OLEDB:Database Password="""";Jet OLEDB:Engine Type=5;Jet
            OLEDB:Da" _
        , _
        "tabase Locking Mode=0;Jet OLEDB:Global Partial Bulk Ops=2;Jet
            OLEDB:Global Bulk Transactions=1;Jet OLEDB:New Database
            Password=""" _
        , _
        """;Jet OLEDB:Create System Database=False;Jet OLEDB:Encrypt
            Database=False;Jet OLEDB:Don't Copy Locale on Compact=False;Jet
            OLEDB" _
        , ":Compact Without Replica Repair=False;Jet OLEDB:SFP=False"),
            Destination:= _
        Range("A1"))
        .CommandType = xlCmdTable
        .CommandText = Array("Products")
        .Name = "Northwind Products"
```

```
.FieldNames = True
.RowNumbers = False
.FillAdjacentFormulas = False
.PreserveFormatting = True
.RefreshOnFileOpen = False
.BackgroundQuery = True
.RefreshStyle = xlInsertDeleteCells
.SavePassword = False
.SaveData = True
.AdjustColumnWidth = True
.RefreshPeriod = 0
.PreserveColumnInfo = True
.SourceConnectionFile = _
"C:\Documents and Settings\Richard Mansfield\My Documents\My Data
    Sources\Northwind Products.odc"
.SourceDataFile = "C:\Northwind.mdb"
.Refresh BackgroundQuery:=False

End With

End Sub
```

In Listing 6-1, replace the bold line with a path to a Northwind ODC file on your hard drive:

```
"C:\Documents and Settings\Richard Mansfield\
    My Documents\My Data Sources\Northwind Products.odc"
```

 The Northwind sample database is supplied with Office 2003 to allow you to experiment using a realistic MDB (Jet/Access-style) database. `Northwind.mdb` should be found on your hard drive in `C:\Program files\Microsoft Office\Office11\Samples`. However, you might not have it installed or know where to look for it. Choose Help➪Sample Databases in Access and then select Northwind Sample Database. If it's not there, go to the Windows Control Panel, choose Add/Remove Programs, find and click Microsoft Office, click the Change button, and follow the instructions to install the Northwind sample database.

Now return to the worksheet where your button resides. Click the Exit Design Mode button on the top of the Toolbox. The Toolbox disappears. Now click the button on the sheet, and your sheet should fill with data from the database.

Applying Formatting

If you have a favorite formatting scheme — a favorite way of presenting Excel data using certain fonts, colors, and so on — you can easily write it (or record it) into a macro and then assign it to a keyboard shortcut, toolbar, or menu.

Here's a macro that applies an AutoFormat to all the data in the current sheet instantly:

```
Sub FormatIt()

ActiveSheet.UsedRange.Select

Selection.AutoFormat Format:=xlRangeAutoFormatColor1,
        Number:=True, Font _
      :=True, Alignment:=True, Border:=True, Pattern:=True,
        Width:=True

End Sub
```

Format:=xlRangeAutoFormatColor1 gives you a black/cyan color scheme. Replace that with Format:=xlRangeAutoFormatColor2 for a brown/tan effect, or otherwise adjust the constants and parameters to get whatever formatting you prefer.

Adding Controls Programmatically

You can add controls to worksheets via programming. This example adds a command button to the active sheet and then adjusts its Caption property:

```
Sub AddButton()

ActiveSheet.OLEObjects.Add ClassType:="Forms.CommandButton.1", _
  Left:=120, Top:=100, Height:=20, Width:=100

ActiveSheet.CommandButton1.Object.Caption = "Click To Fill"


End Sub
```

If you want to add other controls, use this format to describe their class: Frame, Forms.Frame.1, Image, Forms.Image.1, Label, Forms.Label.1, ListBox, Forms.ListBox.1, and so on.

For more on controls, see Book II, Chapter 4.

Trapping Keypresses

In UserForms, you can use the KeyDown event to *trap* (react to with your own programming) user keyboard input. This event is available to any control that's sensitive to keypresses, such as check boxes, command buttons, forms, option buttons, and text boxes.

One use for this technique is to imitate the keyboard shortcuts in Excel that you can specify when you choose Tools⇨Macro⇨Record New Macro and then specify a shortcut key in the Record Macro dialog box. The same kind of keypress trapping is also available for your UserForms via the `KeyDown` event, and `KeyDown` is more flexible than the technique available in Excel itself.

In addition to creating custom keyboard shortcut "macros" within your UserForms, you can also use this technique to redefine the keyboard layout itself. For example, you could trap all Ctrl+C keypresses and then respond by clearing the text box (`TextBox.Text = ""`).

Another relatively uncommon use for trapping keypresses is to repeat some behavior based on how long the user holds down a key. For example, in order for a user to draw a line or border, you allow the user to hold down a key that repeats a character (like an underline) until the `KeyUp` event detects that the user has released the key.

To try this keypress capture technique, first add a `TextBox` control and then a UserForm. Then, from the drop-down lists at the top of the UserForm code window (double-click the `TextBox` control), locate and click the `KeyDown` event for the text box:

```
Private Sub TextBox1_KeyDown(ByVal KeyCode As
        MSForms.ReturnInteger, ByVal Shift As Integer)

End Sub
```

The `KeyDown` and `KeyUp` events provide you with two variables: `KeyCode` and `Shift`. `KeyCode` provides a unique number for every key on the keyboard — even distinguishing between the 3 on the numeric keypad and the 3 in the row above the alphabetic keys. In this way, you can have your program react to anything — the arrow keys, the Num Lock key, and so on.

The numeric codes can be located in the VBA Help. Search for *keycode constants*. You'll also notice a list of constant names (such as `VBKeyBack` and `VBKeyTab`). You should use these descriptive constants in place of the numeric codes if you wish — the constants are built into VBA.

For example, `VBKeyTab` is defined as 0x9 (this is an archaic numbering system known as *octal,* so you probably want to stick with the named constants), so you can then use the word `VBKeyTab` in place of 9 when you are testing for that `KeyDown`:

```
If KeyCode = VBKeyTab
```

or

```
If KeyCode = 9
```

The KeyCodes for uppercase and lowercase letters of the alphabet — *A* and *a,* for example — are the same. Also, the normal and shifted digits, such as 3 and #, are the same. To detect a shifted key, use the Shift parameter provided by the KeyDown events.

The KeyCodes

Table 6-1 shows the KeyCodes used by the KeyDown event.

Table 6-1	KeyCodes Used by the KeyDown Event	
Constant	*Code*	*Key*
vbKeyLButton	1	Left mouse button
vbKeyRButton	2	Right mouse button
vbKeyCancel	3	Cancel
vbKeyMButton	4	Middle mouse button
vbKeyBack	8	Backspace
vbKeyTab	9	Tab
vbKeyClear	12	5 on the keypad
vbKeyReturn	13	Enter (both keyboard and keypad)
vbKeyShift	16	Shift
vbKeyControl	17	Ctrl
vbKeyMenu	18	Menu
vbKeyPause	19	Pause
vbKeyCapital	20	Caps Lock
vbKeyEscape	27	Esc
vbKeySpace	32	Spacebar
vbKeyPageUp	33	Pg Up
vbKeyPageDown	34	Pg Dn
vbKeyEnd	35	End
vbKeyHome	36	Home
vbKeyLeft	37	Left arrow (←)
vbKeyUp	38	Up arrow (↑)
vbKeyRight	39	Right arrow (→)
vbKeyDown	40	Down arrow (↓)
vbKeySelect	41	Select
vbKeyPrint	42	PrintScreen
vbKeyExecute	43	Execute

Constant	Code	Key
vbKeySnapshot	44	Snapshot
vbKeyInsert	45	Insert
vbKeyDelete	46	Delete
vbKeyHelp	47	Help
vbKeyNumlock	144	Num Lock
vbKey0	48	0 and)
vbKey1	49	1 and !
vbKey2	50	2 and @
vbKey3	51	3 and #
vbKey4	52	4 and $
vbKey5	53	5 and %
vbKey6	54	6 and ^
vbKey7	55	7 and &
vbKey8	56	8 and * (not keypad *)
vbKey9	57	9 and (
vbKeyA	65	A
vbKeyB	66	B
vbKeyC	67	C
vbKeyD	68	D
vbKeyE	69	E
vbKeyF	70	F
vbKeyG	71	G
vbKeyH	72	H
vbKeyI	73	I
vbKeyJ	74	J
vbKeyK	75	K
vbKeyL	76	L
vbKeyM	77	M
vbKeyN	78	N
vbKeyO	79	O
vbKeyP	80	P
vbKeyQ	81	Q
vbKeyR	82	R
vbKeyS	83	S
vbKeyT	84	T

**Book IV
Chapter 6**

**Ten Excellent Excel
Macro Techniques**

(continued)

Table 6-1 *(continued)*

Constant	Code	Key
vbKeyU	85	U
vbKeyV	86	V
vbKeyW	87	W
vbKeyX	88	X
vbKeyY	89	Y
vbKeyZ	90	Z

The following codes in Table 6-2 for the ten digits occur when the Num Lock key is on.

Table 6-2   **KeyCodes When the Num Lock Key Is On**

Constant	Code	Key
vbKeyNumpad0	96	0
vbKeyNumpad1	97	1
vbKeyNumpad2	98	2
vbKeyNumpad3	99	3
vbKeyNumpad4	100	4
vbKeyNumpad5	101	5
vbKeyNumpad6	102	6
vbKeyNumpad7	103	7
vbKeyNumpad8	104	8
vbKeyNumpad9	105	9
vbKeyMultiply	106	Multiplication sign (*)
vbKeyAdd	107	Plus sign (+)
vbKeySeparator	108	Enter
vbKeySubtract	109	Minus sign (–)
vbKeyDecimal	110	Decimal point (.)
vbKeyDivide	111	Division sign (/)
vbKeyF1	112	F1
vbKeyF2	113	F2
vbKeyF3	114	F3
vbKeyF4	115	F4
vbKeyF5	116	F5

Constant	Code	Key
vbKeyF6	117	F6
vbKeyF7	118	F7
vbKeyF8	119	F8
vbKeyF9	120	F9
vbKeyF10	121	F10
vbKeyF11	122	F11
vbKeyF12	123	F12
vbKeyF13	124	F13
vbKeyF14	125	F14
vbKeyF15	126	F15
vbKeyF16	127	F16
vbKeyNumlock	144	Num Lock
none	145	Scroll Lock
	186	; and :
	187	= and + (same as keypad =)
	187	= (keypad)
	188	, and <
	189	- and _ (not keypad —)
	190	. and >
	191	/ and ? (not keypad /)
	192	` and ~
	219	[and {
	220	\ and ⇨
	221	] and }
	222	' and "

Detecting Shift, Alt, and Ctrl

The KeyDown event also lets you determine whether a key is being pressed at the same time as the Shift, Alt, or Ctrl key — in other words, a key combination. A typical macro might allow the user to press Ctrl+F, for example, as an alternative to accessing a menu or pressing a command button to start a text search within a text box.

The parameter name Shift that's passed to your programming by the KeyDown event tells you the status of the Shift, Alt, and Ctrl keys as follows:

```
Shift = 1
Shift + Ctrl = 3
Shift + Alt = 5
Shift + Ctrl + Alt = 7
Ctrl= 2
Ctrl+ Alt = 6
Alt = 4
```

So, to determine whether the user is pressing Alt+Shift+F3, use this programming, press F5 to display the UserForm, type some text into the TextBox, and then press Alt+Shift+F3 to see the trapping work:

```
Private Sub TextBox1_KeyDown(ByVal KeyCode As
          MSForms.ReturnInteger, ByVal Shift As Integer)

If Shift = 5 And KeyCode = 114 Then

MsgBox ("Trapped")

End If

End Sub
```

Selecting from a ListBox

If you frequently apply custom formatting styles to your worksheets — suppose you have four styles that you always seem to use — it's helpful to create a personal list box from which you can simply click any of the styles to apply. This same technique can be used whenever you find yourself frequently choosing between a set of behaviors.

In the VBA editor, choose Insert⇨UserForm, put a list box on the form, and then resize the form so it's only a bit larger than the list box. Double-click the ListBox to get to its Click event, and then enter this (Listing 6-2).

Listing 6-2: Choosing Custom Formats

```
Private Sub ListBox1_Click()

Select Case ListBox1.ListIndex

Case 0

    MsgBox ("Case 1")

Case 1

    ActiveSheet.UsedRange.Select
```

```
Selection.AutoFormat Format:=xlRangeAutoFormatColor2,
    Number:=True, Font _
    :=True, Alignment:=True, Border:=True, Pattern:=True,
    Width:=True

Case 2

    MsgBox ("Case 3")

Case 3

    MsgBox ("Case 4")

End Select

End Sub
```

Replace the message boxes with the formatting you want to apply.

The `Case` numbers in the preceding example are off by one; for example, the second case in the code is `Case 1`. This results from the fact that the first `ListIndex` number is 0 (zero), so you have a `Case 0`. Sure, it's daft, but you have to live with it. The first `Case` should of course be 1, but long ago some-one decided that programmers will continually create bugs and trip them-selves up when using indexes because, "Hey! Wouldn't it be weird to call the firstborn child *Boy Zero,* and the kid's third birthday *Birthday Number 2?*" Programming languages are unnecessarily difficult in this way. By now, so much legacy programming code exists that contains this wacky numbering system that it's probably impossible to rectify this moronic way of counting in computer programming. Bitter? Moi?

Put code to create the list in your UserForm's `Activate` event:

```
Private Sub UserForm_Activate()
    ListBox1.AddItem ("Red Border")
    ListBox1.AddItem ("Casual Style")
    ListBox1.AddItem ("Color #2")
    ListBox1.AddItem ("Formal Style")
End Sub
```

Now execute your UserForm by pressing F5 and click an item in the list to see it work. You can activate the UserForm in any of the usual ways: via a menu item, a toolbar, or a keyboard shortcut. You could alternatively add a `ListBox` control to your worksheet. If you want the UserForm to disappear after you've finished using it, add this line of code to the `ListBox Click` event:

```
Me.Hide
```

Sending a Workbook via E-mail

To send someone a whole workbook, type this code into a macro:

```
Sub sendit()
ThisWorkbook.SendMail "richrdm52@hotmail.com", "WorkBook for
    Rita"
End Sub
```

The format is

```
ThisWorkbook.SendMail "EmailAddress", "Subject Line in email"
```

To send the active workbook, replace *ThisWorkbook* with

```
ActiveWorkbook.SendMail
```

Differentiating Select from Activate

You might recall the difference between a selection and a range. (See Book IV, Chapter 1 for the full discussion if you don't.) But many people have difficulty understanding the difference between the `Activate` and `Select` *methods* — and indeed they appear similar. (Confusingly, you use the `Range` object's `Select` method to specify and create a *selection*.)

A range or selection can be, but isn't necessarily, a single cell. For example

```
Range("C6").Select
```

creates a selection comprising this single cell, but

```
Range("C6:D8").Select
```

creates a selection of six cells. Thus, a `selection6` can be, but isn't necessarily, a single cell. Specifying a selection that spans multiple cells, results, however, in a single cell in the upper-left corner of the selection being somewhat different from the others (in this case it's white, not shaded), as shown in Figure 6-4.

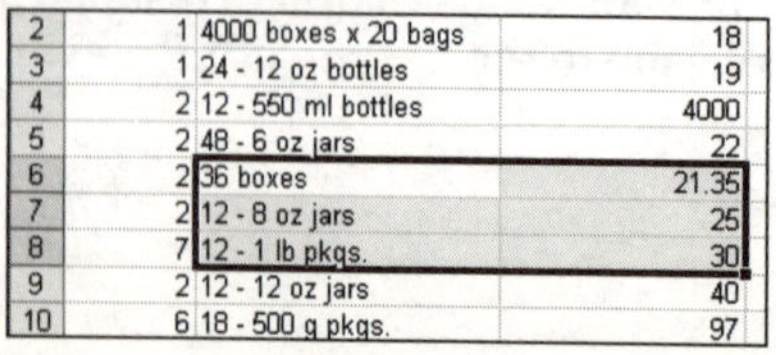

Figure 6-4:
The active cell is in the upper left of the selection.

2	1	4000 boxes x 20 bags	18
3	1	24 - 12 oz bottles	19
4	2	12 - 550 ml bottles	4000
5	2	48 - 6 oz jars	22
6	2	36 boxes	21.35
7	2	12 - 8 oz jars	25
8	7	12 - 1 lb pkgs.	30
9	2	12 - 12 oz jars	40
10	6	18 - 500 g pkgs.	97

Notice the active cell in the upper left. In Word, this is the *insertion point* — the location in the document where whatever the user types will appear. Cell C6 in Figure 6-4, is the active cell. ***Note:*** Only one cell can be the active cell at any given time.

If you want to move the location of the active cell from its default in the upper left of a newly created selection, you can do it with this code:

```
Range("C12:D14").Select
Range("D13").Activate
```

When this code is executed, it results in the selection and active cell shown in Figure 6-5.

Figure 6-5:
Programm-
atically
move the
active cell
by using the
`Activate`
method.

	B	C	D
1	CategoryID	QuantityPerUnit	UnitPrice
2	1	4000 boxes x 20 bags	18
3	1	24 - 12 oz bottles	19
4	2	12 - 550 ml bottles	4000
5	2	48 - 6 oz jars	22
6	2	36 boxes	21.35
7	2	12 - 8 oz jars	25
8	7	12 - 1 lb pkgs.	30
9	2	12 - 12 oz jars	40
10	6	18 - 500 g pkgs.	97
11	8	12 - 200 ml jars	31
12	4	1 kg pkg.	21
13	4	4000 - 500 g pkgs.	38
14	8	2 kg box	6
15	7	40 - 40000 g pkgs.	23.25
16	2	24 - 250 ml bottles	15.5

If you use the `Activate` method to move the active cell beyond the current selection, the selection itself becomes the same cell as the active cell. The previous selection is lost.

Unfortunately, the `Activate` method can be used to specify more than a single cell. You should avoid using it in this way, though, because it can cause mystery bugs. Take this example:

```
Range("B2:D4").Select
Range("C7:D13").Activate
```

After the first line with the `Select` command executes, its effects are ignored when the `Activate` method obliterates the selection and moves it down to C7:D13. Always use the `Select` method when creating a selection involving multiple cells.

**Book IV
Chapter 6**

**Ten Excellent Excel
Macro Techniques**

Book V

Advanced Access

The 5th Wave By Rich Tennant

"Your database is beyond repair, but before I tell you our backup recommendation, let me ask you a question. How many index cards do you think will fit on the walls of your computer room?"

Contents at a Glance

Chapter 1: Access Today

In This Chapter

✔ Discovering Access's strengths and weaknesses

✔ Using the new Access 2003 Developer Extensions

✔ Exploring the Package Wizard and Custom Startup Wizard

✔ Discovering the Property Scanner add-in

✔ Introducing Smart Tags

With Office 2003, Access has reached a new level of sophistication and efficiency. In this chapter, you see what Access does well and less well, and also discover some new tools that can make a developer's life easier.

Access has been improved in a variety of ways:

✦ The `ListBox` and `ComboBox` controls can now display four fields in ascending or descending order for reports and forms.

✦ You can adjust fonts in Query Design, and its Help system has been upgraded.

✦ Smart Tags can link fields.

✦ The Microsoft Data Engine (MSDE) — used for client-server and Internet program testing on a single machine — has been upgraded to a newer version, the SQL Server 2000 Desktop Engine.

✦ Improvements have been made to data access pages.

✦ Forms and reports have new methods, properties, and events.

✦ XML features have been either added or improved.

All in all, Microsoft continues to vigorously support Access with each new version of Office.

Understanding Access's Limitations

Access cannot do everything. There, I said it. Access, good for home or small office use, can also be used as a data store for large enterprise solutions (big companies that want to coordinate all their data and programming needs into a single, harmonious system). However, Access cannot be the database management tool for enterprise solutions because it's not scalable enough: It can effectively handle only ten simultaneous connections. A popular Web site — not to mention a large-scale, corporate intranet — simply grinds Access to a halt by the demands of the traffic that are brought to bear on Access.

Although you can use MDB files as databases, you cannot use Access as a database management system if your company wants to handle high traffic. And most companies at least hope to. (Don't they?)

For small business users, Access can build quick solutions via its many rapid application development (RAD) tools, such as wizards that walk you through various tasks. But if your business requires specialized coding — and many businesses do — you might find yourself spending quite a bit of time customizing via VBA or other programming tools such as VB.NET.

For large businesses, though, you quickly see performance degradation to unacceptable levels after you have more than 10 concurrent users or more than around 100,000 records. You can significantly reduce the network load that a heavily trafficked Access installation can cause by moving query processing to the back end (onto a server). When using this approach, Access itself merely acts as a front end (a user interface, essentially) for a client/server system; on the server, a more robust application such as Oracle or Microsoft's SQL Server handles the heavy duty processing. To the user, it appears that Access itself is managing the data, performing updates, sending back query results, and so on. In fact, another database management system (DBMS) is doing the heavy lifting. The net result of dividing the workload in this way is to take advantage of Access's RAD tools and many experienced Access programmers while simultaneously scaling up to handle heavy traffic.

If you plan to set up a large-scale client/server system with Access as the front end (and primary programming environment, via Access Data Project tools), you can benefit from the Access SQL Server 2000 Desktop Engine. It comes with Access and allows a developer to build the client/server application on a single machine — simulating a client/server installation on one computer. Then, after the system is built, it can be installed on SQL Server.

Adding Access 2003 Developer Extensions

If you're determined to go beyond Access's usual capabilities, you'll be interested in exploring a couple of new utilities in the Access 2003 Developer Extensions. You can give this suite of utilities, part of the Visual Studio Tools for the Microsoft Office System, a test run at this location: `http://msdn.microsoft.com/vstudio/tryit`.

Alas, there's a delicate interaction between Office 2003, Internet Information Server (IIS), Visual Studio, and other components used by developers. I use the term *delicate* because you have to install these various items in a specific order or suffer the consequences: That is, things won't work or won't work as expected.

In case you're interested in these utilities, here is a summary of the Access-specific tools in the Visual Studios Tools package. I cover the Package Wizard, the Custom Startup Wizard, and the Property Scanner.

The Package Wizard and the Custom Startup Wizard

The Package Wizard assists with deployment of Access systems, offering an easy way to build a setup installation utility, including automatic inclusion of dependencies such as the runtime files. Like the other utilities in this package, you get the source code for the Package Wizard so you can customize it to your heart's content. A related tool, the Custom Startup Wizard, allows you to easily create several different custom MDE files (MDB files stripped of your proprietary source code) — individualized MDE files for various customers.

The Property Scanner

This utility is like an industrial-strength search-and-replace. You can search an entire Access database solution *globally* (all the files) and replace a string semiautomatically via a list of links where the string appears. Anyone who's worked with a large distributed group of interrelated software projects (what Microsoft calls a *solution*) will understand how valuable a global search-and-replace tool could be.

Adding Smart Tags

Access can now link and export data from Windows SharePoint Services via *Smart Tags,* which are those small, context-sensitive icons that can be used in a variety of ways. (See Book VII, Chapter 5 for in-depth coverage of Smart Tags.) In Access 2003, you can add Smart Tags to any field in any query, table, form, report, or data access page in your databases. To see how to add a Smart Tag to a field, follow these steps:

1. **Open an Access database and select a table from the list of tables.**

2. **Choose View⇨Design View.**

3. **Click Smart Tags in the General tab of the property box (similar to the Properties window in other Microsoft applications), as shown in Figure 1-1.**

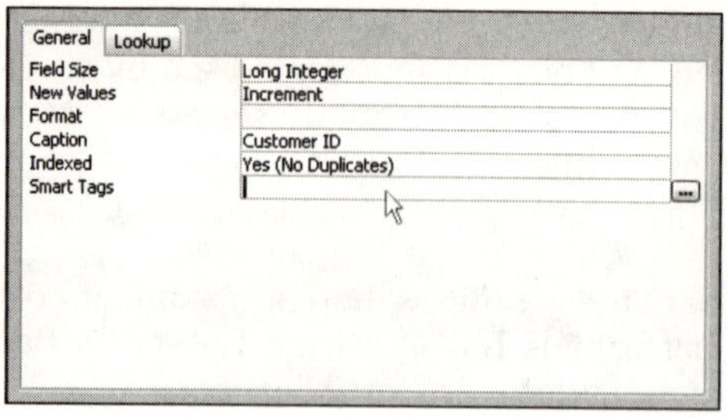

Figure 1-1:
This is the
Access
property
box.

4. **Click the ellipsis button in the Smart Tags field of the property box.**

   The Smart Tags dialog box opens, as shown in Figure 1-2.

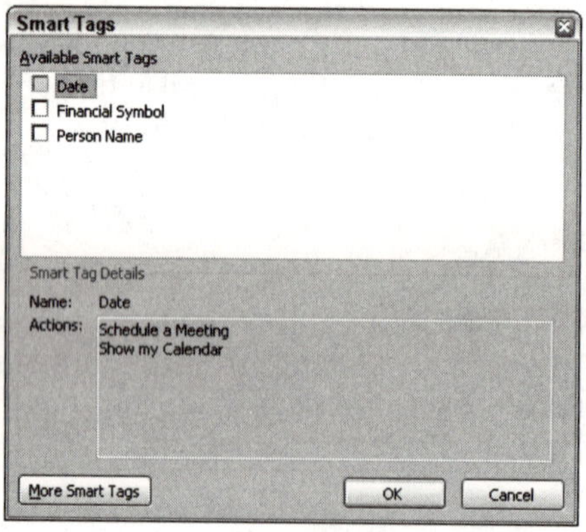

Figure 1-2:
Use this
dialog box
to add
Smart Tags
to your
Access
objects.

5. **(Optional) Click the More Smart Tags button to see third-party Smart Tags that you can purchase.**

   Your browser opens with a list of various tags. At the time of this writing, they included utilities allowing you to quickly create labels from Outlook Contact lists, build custom Smart Tags, and translate text into various languages.

6. **Select the Person Name check box in the list of available Smart Tags.**

   This tag style is selected. You now see a list of actions that this Smart Tag is capable of. For a person's name, the actions are Send Mail, Schedule a Meeting, Open Contact, and Add to Contacts. These are useful tasks that a user might well want to have available while working with your database table.

7. Click OK.

The dialog box closes, and a Person Name Smart Tag is now available in the field you assigned it to. In the property box, this specification is added to the Smart Tag property:

```
"urn:schemas-microsoft-com:office:smarttags#PersonName"
```

8. Choose View⇨Datasheet View.

Your table is displayed with small, dark-purple triangles added to each item in the field where Smart Tags are available. In addition, when you pause your mouse pointer on an item or select an item, an encircled *i* appears, symbolizing (perhaps) *information* — who knows? You can see this effect in Figure 1-3.

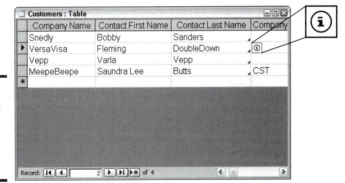

Figure 1-3:
Smart Tags always display a small *i* symbol.

9. Click the Smart Tag icon.

The available options for this Smart Tag open in a drop-down list for the user to select from, as shown in Figure 1-4.

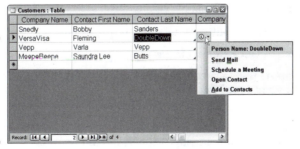

Figure 1-4:
The user can select Smart Tag options from this list.

Exploiting XML support

Of course, XML has invaded Access 2003 just as it has most other areas of contemporary computing. You can import or export XML *schemas* (structures) and data — in other words, both form and content. You can also use your own custom XSL transforms when bringing data in or out of Access, manipulating the XML prior to import or export.

Also, the old Access-specific schema that was obligatory in Access 2003 has been replaced by the newest XSD (schema) standard. This standard is now accepted as the preferred way to message data between data stores and data management systems.

It's generally quite simple to import or export XML-based data in Access 2003. You don't even need to use an XSD file to import data. If an XSD file is present, Access uses the structure defined within that file for importing the data. If no XSD file is present, Access 2003 deduces the incoming data's structure automatically and builds the structure for you.

Here's a simple example. Assume you have an old set of data in a comma-delimited list. It's just a long list of names separated by commas and carriage returns. You want to transform that list (stored in a Notepad TXT file) into a new XML file and also have Access generate an associated schema file (describing the structure of the XML file). You can import the original TXT file into Access as a table and then export the table as an XML/XSD file pair.

Importing text data

Here is how this works.

1. **Open Notepad and create a simple TXT file. Type this data into the file and save it as** c:\data.txt:

   ```
   Jones, Dottie
   Smith, Stan
   ```

2. **Open an Access database.**

   You cannot import unless a database is already open in Access.

3. **Choose File➪Get External Data➪Import.**

4. **In the Import dialog box, choose Text Files in the Files of Type list box and load your** data.txt **file.**

   The Import Text Wizard appears, as shown in Figure 1-5. Notice in Figure 1-5 that this wizard is smart enough to assume that commas delimit fields and that carriage returns delimit records.

5. **Click Next and leave the default Fields Are Separated by Commas radio button selected.**

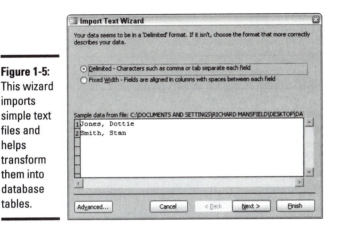

Figure 1-5:
This wizard
imports
simple text
files and
helps
transform
them into
database
tables.

6. **Click Next and leave the default New Table option selected.**

7. **Click Next and then click Advanced.**

8. **Rename the default Field1 to something more meaningful (use
   LastName) and rename Field2 to FirstName.**

9. **Click OK.**

10. **Click Next and choose No Primary Key (keep this simple).**

11. **Click Next and type** MyTable **in the Import to Table text box.**

12. **Deselect the check box that requests the wizard to analyze your table
    (again, keep this simple).**

13. **Click Finish.**

    A rather redundant message box appears, telling you that the importing
    has been accomplished.

14. **Click OK to close that message box.**

15. **Look in the main database window and double-click your new table
    named** data.

    You can see that a proper Access table has been created out of your
    original TXT file's data.

Exporting XML and XSD files

Take the data from the preceding section and transform it into XML and an
associated schema (XSD) file.

1. **Click Tables, and then click to select the table named** data **in the
   main database window.**

2. **Choose File⇨Export.**

3. **In the Export dialog box, choose XML in the Files of Type list box.**

4. **Click the Export button.**

5. **In the Export XML dialog box that appears, leave both the XML and XSD check boxes marked and then click OK.**

The job is done! You've taken a simple (perhaps a legacy) list of data, transformed it first into an Access database table, and then further transformed it into the newest XSD (schema) file and an associated XML file. These files can now be used to communicate with any other XML-aware database management system or other software that can understand XML.

The XSD file that you created specifies your table's structure and looks like this:

```
<?xml version="1.0" encoding="UTF-8"?>
<xsd:schema xmlns:xsd="http://www.w3.org/2001/XMLSchema"
            xmlns:od="urn:schemas-microsoft-com:officedata">
<xsd:element name="dataroot">
<xsd:complexType>
<xsd:sequence>
<xsd:element ref="Data" minOccurs="0" maxOccurs="unbounded"/>
</xsd:sequence>
<xsd:attribute name="generated" type="xsd:dateTime"/>
</xsd:complexType>
</xsd:element>
<xsd:element name="Data">
<xsd:annotation>
<xsd:appinfo/>
</xsd:annotation>
<xsd:complexType>
<xsd:sequence>
<xsd:element name="LastName" minOccurs="0" od:jetType="text"
            od:sqlSType="nvarchar">
<xsd:simpleType>
<xsd:restriction base="xsd:string">
<xsd:maxLength value="255"/>
</xsd:restriction>
</xsd:simpleType>
</xsd:element>
<xsd:element name="FirstName" minOccurs="0" od:jetType="text"
            od:sqlSType="nvarchar">
<xsd:simpleType>
<xsd:restriction base="xsd:string">
<xsd:maxLength value="255"/>
</xsd:restriction>
</xsd:simpleType>
</xsd:element>
</xsd:sequence>
```

```
</xsd:complexType>
</xsd:element>
</xsd:schema>
```

By default, if you double-click an XSD file and you have Visual Studio installed, the XML structure is loaded into a handy schema designer, as you can see in Figure 1-6.

Figure 1-6: Visual Studio includes powerful XML support, including this schema designer.

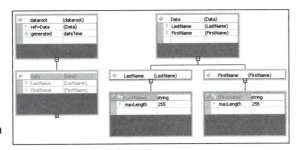

The actual XML data that you exported from your table looks like this:

```
<?xml version="1.0" encoding="UTF-8"?>
<dataroot xmlns:od="urn:schemas-microsoft-com:officedata"
          xmlns:xsi="http://www.w3.org/2001/XMLSchema-
          instance"
          xsi:noNamespaceSchemaLocation="Data.xsd"
          generated="2004-04-12T03:07:23">
<Data>
<LastName>Jones</LastName>
<FirstName>Dottie</FirstName>
</Data>
<Data>
<LastName>Smith</LastName>
<FirstName>Stan</FirstName>
</Data>
</dataroot>
```

Using the new desktop server

The venerable testing server — Microsoft Data Engine (MSDE) — has now been replaced with a new, improved version: SQL Server 2000 Desktop Engine. Added features include updatable views, linked servers, custom functions, additional properties supporting such Access capabilities as input masks and lookup fields, and copy and transfer database features.

MSDE isn't automatically removed when you install Office 2003, and you can continue to use it with Access. However, if you want to explore the newest features available in Access and also keep your prototyping system current, you likely want to replace MSDE with SQL Server 2000 Desktop Engine.

You can remove MSDE and then install the SQL Server 2000 Desktop Engine fresh (Microsoft suggests this), but you might want to instead choose the upgrade option if you've done considerable customization work on your existing system. Perhaps you've spent a lot of time customizing permissions or logon authentication for lots of users or you've worked hard to customize database roles for SQL Server. If so, you will likely want to choose the upgrade rather than clean install option when moving from MSDE to SQL Server 2000 Desktop Engine.

Using improved data access pages

Data access pages are Access's way of presenting its data in Web pages. Although they were introduced in Access 2000, they've only now come into their own in Access 2003. Data access pages are a way for you to efficiently build Internet or intranet pages that users can interact with easily. They're efficient for the programmer because the process of creating these pages is now assisted by a powerful and automated wizard and Page Designer. The resulting front end is highly scalable, and you can create Web pages that are highly sophisticated while letting Access do the dirty work of building the HTML.

Major improvements to data access pages include improved deployment, formatting, and updates to the Page Designer. Multiple Undo and Redo has been added, along with other features that bring data access pages from their relatively lame beginnings to what can now be fairly described as a full-featured form designer.

To see how easily scrollable tables can be dropped into a Web page, follow these steps:

1. **Load the Northwind sample database into Access.**

2. **Click the Pages icon in the main database window.**

   You see the first three options relate to data access pages — different approaches to the same goal:

   - Using design view

   - Using a wizard

   - Editing an existing Web page, as shown in Figure 1-7

3. **Double-click Create Data Access Page in Design View, as shown in Figure 1-7.**

   Depending on your version of the Northwind sample database, you might see a warning message. Just ignore it.

You now see the data access page, a Toolbox, and a list box containing the tables and queries in your database (ready to be simply dragged and dropped into the new Web page.)

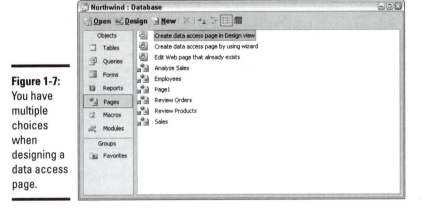

Figure 1-7:
You have multiple choices when designing a data access page.

4. **Click the title section of the data access page and rename it Northwind Orders, as shown in Figure 1-8.**

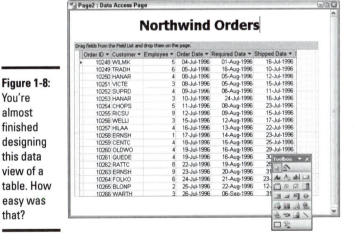

Figure 1-8:
You're almost finished designing this data view of a table. How easy was that?

5. **Drag the Orders table from the Field List dialog box and drop it into the Web page, stretching the table to make it a bit larger and dragging it wherever you want to position it in the page.**

Your new Web page now looks like the one in Figure 1-8.

6. **To complete the job, just save this Web page as an HTM file by choosing File⇨Save.**

   You see the Save as Data Access Page dialog box.

7. **Choose a location on the hard drive to save this file and click the Save button.**

   You might see a warning message describing how to deal with network addressing. Ignore it for now.

   When you double-click this HMT file that you just saved, it opens in Internet Explorer (as shown in Figure 1-9), and the user can freely browse.

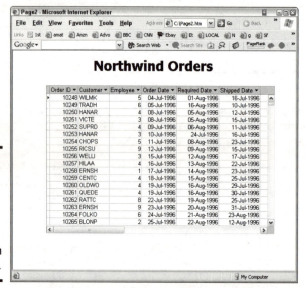

Figure 1-9: Here's the finished Web page, with a table of data that the user can freely scroll.

The user can also make modifications to the data displayed in this Web page, but to accept such modifications — that is, to permit updating of your database by users — you must handle such requests programmatically.

Using augmented forms and reports

Forms and reports both now include a `Move` method and a `Moveable` property with which you can change the position of forms or controls. New form events include `OnDirty` (is it being edited?) for controls and `OnUndo` for forms and controls. Reports now have the following properties previously only available to forms: `AutoCenter`, `AutoResize`, `BorderStyle`, `CloseButton`, `ControlBox`, `MinMaxButtons`, `Modal`, **and** `PopUp`.

Also note that the pivot table and pivot chart functionality in Excel was added to Access 2002. With these features, you can conduct sophisticated analysis on data in any query, form, table, ADP (Access Data Project) table, ADP view, ADP stored procedure, or ADP function. Pivot tables are described in depth in Book IV, Chapter 4.

Although introduced in Access 2000, ADP technology wasn't quite ready for prime time. However, now, most agree that ADP is quite a useful set of tools for creating client/server solutions. ADP files can contain the front-end objects (Access macros, data access pages, reports, forms, and so on) and then you connect to a back-end data store that holds the actual data (tables, views, procedures, and so on). After making this connection, you can use Access's efficient user interface to manage the tables and other objects stored on the back end. Build your client-server application on your personal machine using the SQL Server 2000 Desktop Engine described earlier in this chapter in the section, "Using the new desktop server." Then after building and testing is complete, port your finished client-server project to the SQL Server database.

Chapter 2: Programming Access

In This Chapter

✔ **Introducing Access objects**

✔ **Sorting out database technologies**

✔ **Using ODBC**

✔ **Abandoning VBA**

✔ **Abandoning DAO**

✔ **Understanding ActiveX Data Objects (ADO)**

✔ **Managing the concurrency problem**

✔ **Understanding RAD efficiencies**

*T*his chapter is for those who want to move their database programming forward, and, moving forward sometimes means leaving something familiar behind. In this case, your experience with DAO (Data Access Objects) technology — a well-loved, stable system — must be eventually abandoned in favor of ADO (ActiveX Data Objects). You also need to look past VBA to VB.NET. This chapter is something of a launching pad, then: sorting out the current Access object model but also looking forward to other, more advanced programming technology.

Access differs in many ways from other Office applications, both in its user interface and its programming technologies and tools. For one thing, Access programming relies relatively less than other applications on VBA. In Word, for example, you build solutions largely by using VBA to manipulate the objects built into Word. With Access, however, two additional technologies — and their object models and features — become significantly important in your programming. These technologies are SQL (for creating queries to extract subsets of data from a data store, or sometimes for modifying the data) and ADO (for database management, scalability, interoperability, and other efficiencies). Nonetheless, VBA can be the glue that ties the Jet engine's features, recordsets, SQL, and other elements together, so I cannot ignore the Access object model.

Introducing Access Objects

Like other Office 2003 applications, Access's highest object is the Application object, which embraces several essential secondary objects:

`Table`, `Query`, `Form`, `Report`, and `DataAccessPage`. In turn, these objects themselves contain sets of objects.

Because the `Application` object is generally understood, in many situations, it doesn't need to be explicitly named in code when working with other Access objects. Access also includes the usual collections: `Forms`, for example, is a collection containing all currently active forms.

Start Access, choose File⇨New, and then choose Blank Database from the task pane. Click the Create button to close the dialog box and accept the default name for the MDB file.

Press Alt+F11. Choose Insert⇨Module. A nearly empty module appears. Folks from MS (who enjoy enforcing rules on other people) have forced each new Access module to include a line of code at the top of the module that they think we should all use. They're wrong, but how fun! This line of code can introduce some bugs into your programming, but, well . . . so what?

`Option Compare Database` means that when strings are compared, they're not compared as you would expect on the binary level (case-sensitive, which is the normal Visual Basic default) nor on the text level (case-insensitive). Instead, the comparison is based on the *locale* (the language used by the culture) of the database itself.

Because few of us need this type of comparison — and because most programmers who do work in some cross-cultural, multidatabase environment surely know by now that they need to insert this line into their code — you can just erase it. This way, your string comparisons will work as they normally do in all other versions of BASIC — namely, case-insensitive and based on the cultural language of the computer system.

Now to ease into the world of ActiveX Data Objects (ADO), Data Access objects (DAO), Access objects, alphabet soup, and the lovely, busy world of object-oriented programming (OOP). Here's an example of OOP in Access:

```
Set db = CurrentDb
```

`CurrentDb` doesn't sound like the name of a typical method, but it is indeed a method of the Access `Application` object. It delivers an object variable *of the database type,* as techies like to say. In the code above, db is an object variable containing a reference to the currently open database in Access — the sample database Northwind, in the upcoming example.

Technically, this object variable contains a hidden reference to the Microsoft DAO Object Library, but I won't delve too deeply into useless OOP jargon. You can use it without knowing all the gory details about its taxonomy, which are usually only of interest to the people who classified all these things in the first place.

Adding a New Access Table

The structure of a database can be modified in many ways in your programming. Try this example. It opens the Northwind sample database, adds a new table to it (complete with four fields), and then closes it.

The Northwind sample database is supplied with Office 2003 to allow you to experiment using a realistic MDB (Jet/Access-style) database. `Northwind. mdb` should be found on your hard drive in `C:\Program files\Microsoft Office\Office11\Samples`. However, you might not have it installed or know where to look for it. Choose Help⇨Sample Databases in Access, and then select Northwind Sample Database. If it's not there, go to the Windows Control Panel, choose Add/Remove Programs, find and click Microsoft Office, click the Change button, and follow the instructions to install the Northwind sample database.

Before taking the drastic step of modifying the sample database, make a copy of `Northwind.mdb` so that you can restore it to its pristine state after you're through adding this table. Of course, you could also always get it off the Office 2003 CD.

Type the contents of Listing 2-1 into the Access VBA code window.

Listing 2-1: Adding a Table and Fields

```
Sub BuildTable()


    Dim dbNorthwind As Database
    Dim td As TableDef

    Set db = OpenDatabase("C:\Program files\Microsoft
    Office\Office11\Samples\Northwind.mdb")
    Set td = db.CreateTableDef("Arrests")

    With td
       ' Build the fields:
       .Fields.Append .CreateField("Alibi", dbMemo)
       .Fields.Append .CreateField("Name", dbText)
       .Fields.Append .CreateField("Alias", dbText)
       .Fields.Append .CreateField("PrisonerNumber", dbText)

       ' Append the new table to the database
       db.TableDefs.Append td
    End With

    db.Close

End Sub
```

Press F5 to execute this code. Now you've done it! Take a look at what happened to Northwind. Run Access, locate the Northwind sample database, and open it.

Look at the tables in Northwind and then double-click the new one: `Arrests`, created from the code in Listing 2-1. You see the fields that you created. By using this same technique, you can add, remove, or otherwise modify tables and their internal structures.

Understanding Microsoft Database Technologies

Before continuing with programming examples, draw back a bit to get a handle on Microsoft's various database-related initiatives.

Try to get a sense of the meaning of the many database programming terms and how they're related. Oh, yes: You must also always consider XML (the technology that, theoretically, will someday permit universal data access and messaging), the buried treasure toward which all the other roads — DAO, Open Database Connectivity (ODBC), and ADO — supposedly lead. XML packages are supposed to be *self-describing,* which means that they contain both an explanation of their structure as well as the data that fills that structure. For example, when `DataSets` are translated into XML, they are divided into two files: the *schema* (structure) and a separate file that holds the actual data.

Don't run for the exits just because the subject of contemporary database programming has some contradictions and is littered with acronyms. Understanding these variations and acronyms is important. They represent the yesterday, today, and tomorrow of database management . . . that is, if Microsoft has anything to say about it. And for the foreseeable future at least, Microsoft will have something to say about it.

The great Babel

You can store data in databases in thousands of ways. Most useful computer applications store data, but rarely do they store it the same way as other applications. They usually do it in peculiar, proprietary ways. For example, can you use Access to search the e-mail messages in your Microsoft Outlook Express Inbox database? Not directly.

One problem is the proliferation of structures. Some files are plain text delimited by commas; others are delimited in other ways. Some files are in proprietary binary formats; others are encrypted. And on it goes. To give you an idea of this problem, Outlook 2003 uses the following 36 file extensions: `.cfg`, `.chm`, `.csv`, `.dat`, `.dic`, `.dll`, `.ecf`, `.eco`, `.exe`, `.fav`, `.fdm`, `.htm`, `.html`, `.ics`, `.inf`, `.mdb`, `.msg`, `.nk2`, `.ocx`, `.oft`, `.oss`, `.ost`, `.pab`, `.pag`, `.pst`, `.rhc`, `.rtf`, `.srs`, `.stf`, `.txt`, `.vcf`, `.vcs`, `.vfb`, `.wab`, `.xls`, `.xnk`. Think about it.

You should (ahem, *should*) be able to search those files and extract useful data that can be stored and managed by Access — or indeed, any other database management system. True, you can search some of them; for example, MDB, TXT, XLS, and some other formats are readily accessible to Access. But all data files should be understandable, readable, and accessible unless they need to be encrypted for security reasons. (And even then, encryption isn't designed to destroy data but just to temporarily disguise it until it can safely be decrypted.)

More shoulds. You should be able to add a subset of your e-mail messages to your company's customer-service database if you want. You should be able to store or copy e-mail anywhere, but you can't. (Access saves data in files with an `.mbd` extension, Outlook Express stores e-mail in files with a `.dbx` extension, and the twain do not meet. Even Outlook Express itself has different database styles — a few years ago it stored your e-mail in MBX files!)

And how about plain TXT files produced by Notepad or other simple (but often useful) text editors? Why can't many database applications retrieve data from these kinds of files? Or from any and all kinds of files?

Data universality is hampered by various current trends, including the increasing importance of distributed computing and client/server computing. A primary trend today involves working harmoniously with applications and data that's spread across two or more machines. In other words, the Internet and intranets sometimes extract tables (sometimes as `DataSets`) from their database application or fracture an application into several parts running on several different computers and cause other divisions.

Increasingly, businesspeople are realizing that lots of important information remains unused or unintegrated because it's not in the proper format. Companies establish sites on the Internet and ask visitors for feedback on their products. More and more, that feedback comes in the form of e-mail. How many companies can make wide use of the information in that e-mail? Can they sort it, search it, and otherwise exploit it in an organized fashion? In other words, can they manage the data and store it for efficient integration into other data? Very few companies could do these things until ADO.NET technology arrived. And even fewer could make efficient use of HTML-based data such as the Web-based catalogs of their competitors. (Companies *do* like to check out competitors' catalogs, you know.)

Understanding Open Database Connectivity

Open Database Connectivity (ODBC) is a Microsoft database standard that is still widely used. ODBC takes on the burden of translating some proprietary database formats into formats that database applications can understand.

Simply put, ODBC sits on your machine or a user's computer (the client) and translates remote (server) relational databases into data packages that your client application can handle. On a fundamental level, your application can use Structured Query Language (SQL) to query or modify data held in a remote database without worrying about the details of the remote database's methods of storing that data (such as punctuation, organization, delimiting, and labeling).

One useful feature of ODBC is that you can specify ODBC connections. (Technically, they're *Data Source Names,* or *DSNs.*) You give these connections a name; then the next time you want to connect to that database, all the necessary information (password, log-on information, type of database, and so on) is already filled in, and you can just employ the DSN itself.

However, like many other acronyms you've gotten used to over the years, ODBC is now in the twilight of its useful life. Microsoft has announced its successors: OLE DB and, finally, ADO.NET. ODBC enables you to get relational data into a client computer. ADO.NET enables you to get any data source's data into a client computer — at least, that's the promise.

These days, a source of data is increasingly called a *data store* rather than a *database.* This new term is designed to help us broaden our sense of where useful data can be stored. It need not be in a proper database file; instead, you can now get data from simple TXT files, e-mail files, streams of data, and more. In what other job are new terms so rapidly invented and then killed off by newer jargon? Fashion? Advertising? Hair dressing?

ADO.NET can access data from many kinds of sources. Potential ADO.NET data stores cover the waterfront, including structured, semistructured, and unstructured data; relational and nonrelational data; and SQL-based and non-SQL data. Examples include desktop databases, flat files, mail stores, directory services, personal information managers (PIMs), multidimensional stores, and even those elusive OLAP cubes (don't ask).

Access and the Future of Database Management

Office 2003 developers might need to move beyond the programming capabilities built into the Office suite — namely VBA. VBA served for years as the best available programming technology for small businesses using Office. Now, though, with the demands of the Internet, larger intranets, security issues, and bandwidth conservation, creating robust solutions requires moving to VB.NET and Visual Studio (the editor and set of programming tools used by most serious developers).

With Access, you have a tested, effective system for small offices and home use. Access's many rapid application development (RAD) tools, such as its property pages, wizards, and other helpful utilities, are well known and quite functional on the small office/home level.

But as your view expands to Internet sales, distributed programming solutions, larger numbers of employees, and more complex Access programming, you need to expand your programming skills and move to .NET.

Access itself cannot support your needs with its efficient (although limited) built-in tools. You can still work with the actual Access database files (MDBs), and perhaps data entry can still be serviceable by using the Access facilities. Put another way, existing MDB files can sit on the back end, and you can employ Access to build a user interface on the front end. But other activities — such as multiple simultaneous Internet connections — can place too great a burden on Access's tools.

Access's performance degrades as you increase the scale of interaction (ramp up the number of users). In addition, Jet's (Access's engine) record-locking behaviors don't offer the necessary scalability for modern, enterprise-large applications. You can relieve this scalability pressure in some ways by using VBA to buffer user loads and manage security issues. But if you really want to prepare yourself, your co-workers, and your company for future needs, my advice is to move on from VBA to VB.NET.

You can download a 60-day trial version of Visual Studio .NET from this site:

```
http://msdn.microsoft.com/vstudio/productinfo/trial/default.
aspx
```

That said, take a look at the several technologies relating to database management.

The recent legacy: Data Access Objects (DAO)

Only a few years ago, the most popular database technology was Microsoft's Data Access Objects (DAO). Robust and well-tested, DAO was used by most database programmers until recently. They understood its object model (its syntax and how to program its methods and properties).

However, DAO had several weaknesses. It is best at single, desktop computer database management rather than distributed client/server, Internet, or intranet database management. In addition, DAO doesn't like old database formats — and lots of businesses have stuff stored in legacy formats.

Nor does DAO like new data formats all that much either, such as HTML, DHTML, e-mail, and plain text. DAO wants *relational data* — data organized into tables, fields, indices, and relations. You can't blame DAO for all this because it was never designed to do anything other than what it does (and does splendidly). Nevertheless, the time has come to phase out DAO and raise the curtain on the new stars of the database world. If your company is still using DAO, you're not preparing for the future.

What solution does Microsoft propose for addressing the shortcomings in DAO and other schemes? Universal data access through XML. This plan doesn't require that you massage data in any extreme ways. You don't have to pour e-mail files, a bunch of old DBF dBASE files, and Notepad TXT files through filters until they end up in a new, all-purpose file type.

Tools that support the XML strategy are designed to package data from its current format; provide self-describing, plain-text packages; and then send those packages freely (no firewall blockage) over an intranet or the Internet. When received, the XML data packages can be absorbed into whatever data store the receiving party uses. In theory, this approach will let you (the programmer) send or receive data without worrying about its native format. It doesn't matter whether the data comes from or goes into TXT, MDB, DBF, or DBX files. Microsoft supports XML, of course, and has built the .NET data storage and messaging systems on XML.

Now, you might be asking, "Isn't this universal access the same promise that we've been offered so many times before?" What about all the previous attempts to resolve the Babylon problem, such as the Symphony application suite offered in the mid-80s as the solution to the confusion of file types and data storage schemes? And Symphony's many successors?

Sure, for more than two decades, developers have been playing the universal data-access tune. XML is simply the latest attempt to offer everything to everyone in the Web-development crowd.

So, do I believe that XML is a step in the right direction? Yes. And to move toward XML and the .NET technology, you must begin to explore ADO.NET. If you work with databases, you should learn how to program ADO.NET. In all likelihood, it will become the technology of choice for database programming in the future.

Understanding ActiveX Data Objects

With ActiveX Data Objects (ADO), database programming became somewhat simpler to write, and new capabilities pointed the way to true distributed computing.

Consider just a couple of intriguing features of ADO: building recordsets from scratch (without any database connection) and disconnecting recordsets from the server. When disconnected, recordsets continue to work fine in your workstation (client) computer. Just like a worm chopped in half, each part behaves normally. And later, you can rejoin these recordsets to their original database or merge them into other databases. This can greatly improve the scalability of an application because lots of people need not maintain ongoing connections to the same database, thereby jamming the traffic on a server and taxing the abilities of aging applications like Access that were never designed to leap and twirl within the sudden-scaling world of the Internet.

Instead, users all work independently with disconnected recordsets sitting in their own personal machines. Recall that Access can effectively handle only ten simultaneous connections.

Also, when you know how to use ADO, you can use it with virtually any kind of data: HTML, e-mail, and plain text, as well as traditional relational data and even legacy data sources.

ADO offers all the features of its ancestors (DAO and RDO), but it requires some changes in programming techniques. For example, ADO is said to *flatten* the object model of DAO and RDO. Flattening means streamlining the model by reducing the number of objects but increasing the number of properties and methods of the objects that remain. Flattening also generally lessens the emphasis on the object hierarchy. Put simply, you can create objects without having to create other, higher objects. You can create a recordset without first having to create a `Connection` object for it, for example.

DataSets replace recordsets

Go deeper into the ADO.NET framework, and you discover various ways to manipulate and benefit from the new `DataSet` concept. You'll find many improvements, including ways to map aliases (make one-to-one substitutions) when, for example, you're using a `DataSet` from Greece and prefer to program using English words to name the various columns in the data store.

Note that with the move from ADO to ADO.NET, the ADO recordset has been replaced by the ADO.NET `DataSet`.

Some advantages of ADO.NET

The ADO.NET technology has been designed to provide you with as much flexibility as you might need — and database programming can require flexibility. Above all, remember that ADO.NET supports disconnected `DataSets`. The reason is that maintaining a continuously open connection between client and server is not only wasteful of system resources, it's often simply not possible in the world of Internet programming. So many people, so little power and memory in your server.

What's more, the typical database can handle only a few concurrent open connections. That pretty much eliminates old-style connected programming for any but the least popular Web sites. When you program for the Web, you must face the fact that 4 visitors to your site can suddenly swell to 400 — and many of these visitors might want to view your catalog or place an order at the same time. You hope, anyway.

Web programming is always essentially disconnected programming. For example, when a server sends an ASP.NET HTML page to a user's browser, it discards its copy of that page. It pays no more attention to the user's browser until another request arrives from the user. It's like the relationship between the president and hundreds of clamoring reporters.

ADO.NET and ASP.NET (its Internet-programming counterpart) are based on the premise that you'll often be programming for a disconnected architecture. You permit your application to connect to a database only while fetching data or saving changed data back to the database. Otherwise, you're not connected, and the database can therefore service some other request for data. If your application is designed to work on a single-user, standalone computer — therefore requiring a continual connection — use ADO instead of ADO.NET.

Microsoft sometimes now uses the term *column* to mean what used to be called a *field* in a database table. Likewise, MS now uses the term *row* for what used to be called a *record*. This seemingly endless shifting of terminology . . . well, it's the way things are. Keeps us all on our toes. IBM is using this terminology, too. I don't think it's going to catch on.

With ADO.NET, after data has been extracted from its data store, the resulting set of data (`DataSet`) is then translated into XML. If you need to store the `DataSet` as a file, it's stored in XML format. If you send the `DataSet` to another application, it is transmitted as an XML file. The translation to and from XML is handled for you automatically by ADO.NET.

In ADO, you were forced to use what is called *COM* when transmitting a disconnected recordset, but in ADO.NET, you use the simpler, cleaner XML stream. Among the benefits of XML is that no data-type conversions are required. With COM, ADO data types must be converted to COM data types, slowing things down.

Another advantage is that firewalls generally have no problem permitting the transmission of XML. (Ordinary HTML, from which XML is derived and which it resembles, is considered harmless by firewalls.) XML is seen as text — probably formatting or simple data — with no capability to spread viruses, inject worms, or otherwise threaten security. A COM transmission, on the other hand, makes a firewall slam shut because the transmission is fundamentally a binary — possibly an executable — form of information. Finally, the XML technology places no restrictions on the data types, unlike the limited set offered by the older COM technology.

Of course, there is no perfect technology. XML has its critics, too. The number-one defect is that platform independence — a frequently sought goal — has so far proved elusive. Already there are thousands of proprietary flavors of the supposedly universal XML data structure. Also, XML's claims that it is self-documenting are doubtful. Because artificial intelligence doesn't yet exist, the notion that a file could arrive at a server and explain itself to a receiving application — without any human intervention — seems more than a little far-fetched. There are other criticisms, too, including XML's famous verbosity.

Nonetheless, here are some reasons for you to consider switching from ADO to ADO.NET, particularly for distributed applications. Although ADO did introduce the concept of the disconnected recordset, ADO is nonetheless optimized for connected programming. ADO fundamentally assumes a continuous connection between the database and the application using it. ADO.NET, on the other hand, is optimized for the opposite: connect-on-demand programming.

Think of an ADO recordset as essentially a single table. If you want data from more than one database table, you have to use a `JOIN` query. The ADO.NET `DataSet` is a collection of one or more tables (`DataTable` objects). Therefore, data extracted from more than one table in a database is represented in the `DataSet` as more than one `DataTable` object. This is easier to visualize because there is essentially a one-to-one relationship between the structures in the database and the `DataTable` objects in the `DataSet`.

Working with the DataSet Object

Like objects everywhere, the `DataSet` class offers collections and properties. You need to understand the structure of the `DataSet` object to work with ADO.

Collections within collections

The `DataSet` has two primary collections: `Tables` and `Relations`. Lower in the hierarchy are several collections within the `DataTable` object: `rows`, `columns`, `keys`, `childrelations`, and `parentrelations`. The `DataRow` class includes a `RowState` property indicating whether and how the row (record) has been modified since its `DataTable` was first loaded from the database. The `RowState` property can be set to modified, new, deleted, and unchanged.

Substituting names (mapping)

When you first load the data from a database into a `DataSet`, the names of the tables and columns in the `DataSet` are the same as those used in the database or data store. If you prefer to use different names while working with the `DataSet`, just create your new names in the `DataSet` command and then map your names to the ones used in the original database. Both the `OleDbCommand` and `SqlCommand` use their `TableMappings` collections to map custom names to database names. When you return the data to the database, all will be well: Any edited data will flow into the correct columns and tables as named originally in their database.

Why would you want to map or rename tables and columns? Perhaps the database is written in a foreign language, and you find it easier to work with mapped aliases rather than foreign words. Or maybe you have an in-house naming scheme for your databases but are working with `DataSets` from some other organization. You want to maintain the custom naming scheme in your programming. So map.

What If Someone Else Modifies the Database in the Meantime?

While your `DataSet` is been disconnected from its database, someone might have also been working with some or all of that data in his or her separate `DataSet`. Maybe the person modified some of that same data and updated the database by restoring the contents of the `DataSet` to the database. What if the person edited a record that you also edited? Should you overwrite the other person's changes with your changes? Or vice versa?

Unfortunately, the ADO.NET `DataSet` commands cannot handle this problem automatically, but what technology can? The `DataSet` — like all other contemporary computing — is not artificially intelligent, after all. ADO.NET will not automatically lock a record in the database and then warn others that the record is being edited and that they must wait . . . and then solve the version problem that arises when multiple, duplicate `DataSets` compete for inclusion in the database update process.

It's up to you to write programming to solve a potential problem when new versions of a record conflict. If this is a possible problem for the database you're working with, you have to find a solution and write the source code for that solution yourself. What's more, if the database you're working with could have a problem with conflicting records, you have to find a solution and write the source code for that solution yourself.

The problem of two or more users in conflict during their attempts to flush back disconnected data into a database is the problem of *concurrency* or the *version problem*. When two or more users try to update a given record, should the changes made by the last person to update that record win?

Optimism versus pessimism

You can approach the concurrency problem in two fundamental ways: optimistic concurrency and pessimistic concurrency.

✦ **Optimistic concurrency:** This prevents outsiders from changing a record (row) only while another person is updating that record. The updating usually takes very little time, so the lockout is brief.

✦ **Pessimistic concurrency:** By contrast, this locks out others for a longer time. The lock starts when one user accesses a record (which that user might potentially edit or delete) and is in effect until the original user sends the record back to the database. (This is similar to the older style of database programming that maintained an open connection between an application and a database.)

Optimism

Optimistic concurrency locks a record only briefly, during the save to a hard drive. This prevents a nasty collision if two different records are simultaneously sent to the same record location in a database.

When a user attempts to update a record under optimistic concurrency, the updated data is compared with the existing record in the database. If there is any difference between them, the update is rejected. An exception is raised: An error message is generated. You (the programmer) must handle such errors in ADO.NET. You must write programming that responds to this type of error (using the `Try-Catch` error handling system in VB.NET) and decide what to do about the changed record. Do you accept it? Or do you have some criteria that can reconcile a data clash?

One version of optimistic concurrency is *last-in wins*. This version doesn't compare the updated record with the original record. It merely lets each new update replace the previous version of the record. The last-in wins approach is the most scalable approach that you can employ.

Pessimism

Pessimistic concurrency is useful if you need to freeze a record while making arrangements for a customer. For example, if an Amtrak agent is talking to someone about booking a sleeping car room on the train for a popular holiday, pessimistic locking will prevent two agents in two different stations from contending for the same room, thereby angering a customer. In that type of situation, you want to lock the record for that room until the first customer makes up his mind and either reserves that room or not.

The problem is that when you're using a `DataSet`, you can't use pessimistic concurrency. It's not practical in a disconnected architecture, and it's not scalable for the same reason that maintaining an open connection between an application and a `DataSet` isn't scalable.

Comparing versions with optimistic concurrency

When deciding which record gets saved, classic optimistic concurrency compares versions by checking their version number (or, in some cases, their time and date stamps) or by saving all the values (all the data in the `DataSet` is saved when the data is initially read).

If the version number approach is used, each record must have a version number (or datestamp) column. This special column is saved on the client computer when the record is first read. Then if that client has modified a record, the database is checked to see whether the stored version number matches the version number currently in the database. If they match, it proves that no other person has modified that record since it was "checked out" for use by the client. Therefore, it is safe to update the record with the client's edited version. You can use an SQL statement like the following to conduct this test:

```
UPDATE myTable SET Field1 = ChangedValue1, Field2 =
    ChangedValue2
WHERE ClientStoredStamp = OriginalStampInDatabase
```

If this SQL is attempted but the `ClientStoredStamp` doesn't equal the `OriginalStampInDatabase`, an error is returned, and you can write programming to make a decision about what to do. (You could store the client's editing and thereby replace the current record, extract the current record to compare it with the client's edited record, or save both versions and ask a human to make the decision.) It's also your responsibility to write the programming that updates the version or datetime column whenever a record is modified.

The other approach to managing optimistic concurrency is to save a copy of a record when it is first read. This means that your `DataSet` will have two copies of any record that is read: the one from the database and the one that the user modified. By using this approach, when the user attempts to update a record, the original version that came from the database is compared with whatever is now in that database. If they match, there's no problem. It proves that no one messed with the record while it's been "checked out" of your `DataSet`, so you can go ahead and save the updated version (containing the user's modifications) to the database without worrying about overwriting someone else's work.

Every `DataSet` command includes four parameter collections, one for each of the four commands: `Select`, `Update`, `Insert`, and `Delete`. Each parameter corresponds to a placeholder (? in an SQL statement) in the command text. The properties of a parameter specify both the column that the parameter is associated with and whether the parameter represents the edited version or the original version. These parameter collections make it possible for the `DataSet` command to generate dynamic SQL (or provide parameters to a stored procedure).

Getting Results in Seven Easy Steps

(Drum roll, please) I now conclude this chapter with a demonstration of some of the RAD features available to VB.NET. By progressing beyond VBA to manage database-related programming with .NET, you're not giving up wizards, add-ons, or other features that can assist you in quickly moving from need to solution.

This next example demonstrates how quickly you can connect to a server database (Northwind, to be precise) with VB.NET's RAD tools. No human hands will write any programming! Yet, in seven quick steps, you'll watch as a big Access table of data travels from its server database and is displayed in a client grid before your very eyes. You'll be slap speechless! Just seven quick steps!

I end this chapter by showing you how much VB.NET can do to help you with your Access database programming. In the following example, you see VB.NET make a connection, define a query, access the data, and preview the `DataSet` it created:

1. **After starting a new VB.NET Windows-style project, open Server Explorer in Visual Studio, as shown in Figure 2-1.**

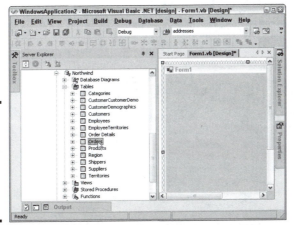

Figure 2-1:
Server Explorer is a very useful feature of Visual Studio .NET.

You can do lots of things with Server Explorer, including adding, editing, and deleting tables and columns. You can even create a new database!

2. **Drag a table (`Orders` for this example) and just drop it onto the VB.NET form, as shown in Figure 2-2.**

As soon as the `Orders` table is dropped onto the form, a `Connection` control and a `DataAdapter` control are automatically added to the project. They are placed in the tray below the form.

3. **To create a `DataSet` that contains the `Orders` table, right-click the SqlDataAdapter1 icon in the tray and then choose Generate Dataset from the context menu that appears, as shown in Figure 2-3.**

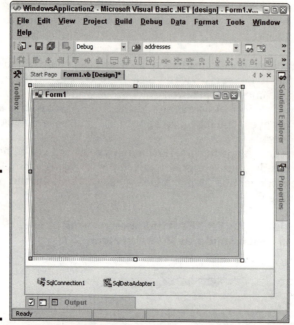

Figure 2-2:
Adding
tables from
an SQL
database is
as easy as
dragging
and
dropping.

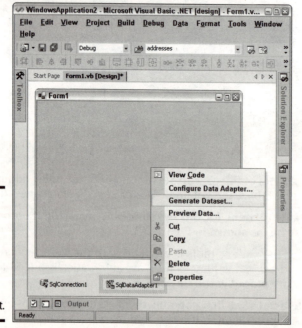

Figure 2-3:
A Data-
Adapter
can
generate
as many
DataSets
as you want.

The Generate Dataset dialog box appears.

4. **Your only job is to give this new** DataSet **a name.**

   Name it Maxie, as shown in Figure 2-4.

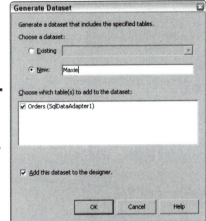

Figure 2-4:
Use this
dialog to
name a new
DataSet
(or modify
an existing
one).

5. **Click OK.**

   The new DataSet appears in the tray, as you can see in Figure 2-5. Your new DataSet was created courtesy of the DataAdapter control.

6. **Right-click the SqlDataAdapter1 icon again, but this time, choose Preview Data from its context menu.**

   The Data Adapter Preview utility opens.

7. **Click the Fill DataSet button.**

   All the data in the Orders table rolls into view, as you can see in Figure 2-6. That didn't take long, did it?

I believe that after you've used them a little, you'll come to consider the VB.NET DataSet your friend.

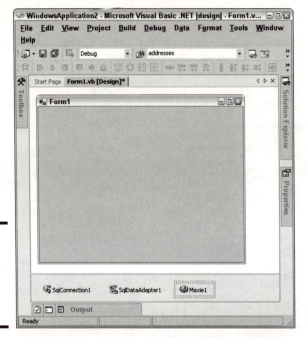

Figure 2-5:
There's
Maxie1
sitting
proudly in
the tray.

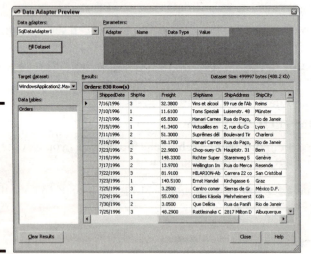

Figure 2-6:
The
`Orders`
table is
extracted
from the
server and
sent to the
`DataSet`.

Chapter 3: Manipulating Datasets

In This Chapter

✔ **Loading an Access database into .NET**

✔ **Filtering queries with** `Select`

✔ **Working with the** `DataView` **object**

✔ **Creating relations**

✔ **Communicating with a database**

✔ **Using the XML Designer**

✔ **Saving an XML dataset**

✔ **Loading XML into Access**

*A*fter tables get liberated from the usual restraints and proprietary restrictions within databases — after they're flying free as datasets — the sky's the limit. In this chapter, you see how to import a table or tables from an Access database into a VB.NET dataset, how to manipulate datasets every which way, and then how to send a dataset back into Access. The aging VBA language still built into Office applications comes nowhere close to VB.NET when free data management is concerned.

The techniques that I describe in this chapter, however, show you a way to retain your investment in Access. You can use it as a front end for user-interaction with a data store or even add Access databases to other back-end data. And of course, XML will often be the technology of choice when communicating between front ends, back ends, or any other ends.

Loading Access Tables into VB.NET Projects

Many offices use Access to both store data as well as to provide a way for users to view or update that data. However, Access isn't scalable enough by itself to manage data for large, enterprise systems. One approach to bringing Access into the world of distributed systems and Internet programming is to integrate Access databases and the Access user interface with .NET technologies. .NET is designed to be used with XML, to be Internet-ready, and to permit highly scalable solutions. For these reasons, you want to consider preparing for your company's future by finding out how to tie Access into .NET — how to send data stored in Access, for example, to a VB.NET project. To see how to import data from an Access (MDB) database into a VB.NET project, follow these steps:

1. **Start a new VB.NET Windows project.**

2. **Add a** `DataGrid` **control from the Toolbox (Windows Forms tab) to Form1.**

3. **Choose View⇨Server Explorer.**

Server Explorer appears, with a list of all your data connections. (Read more about Server Explorer in Book V, Chapter 1.)

4. **Right-click Data Connections in the Explorer.**

5. **Choose Add Connection from the context menu that opens.**

6. **In the Data Link Properties dialog box that opens, click the Provider tab.**

7. **Choose Microsoft Jet 4.0 OLE DB Provider.**

8. **Click Next.**

9. **Click the ellipsis button next to Select or Enter a Database Name.**

The Select Access Database dialog box opens.

10. **Locate the** `Northwind.mdb` **sample database on your hard drive.**

If it wasn't installed when you installed Office 2003, use Control Panel's Add/Remove Programs utility to install the samples from the Office CDs.

11. **Double-click Northwind.mdb.**

The Select Access Database dialog box closes.

12. **Click Test Connection.**

You should have no trouble passing this test.

13. **Click OK to close the Data Link Properties dialog box.**

Your new connection is displayed within Server Explorer, ready to be dropped into any form that you want to connect to this Access database.

14. **Drag and drop this new ACCESS connection onto Form1.**

15. **Click the Don't Include Password button.**

The Do You Want to Include the Password in the Connection String dialog box closes, and a new OleDbConnection1 icon appears in your tray.

16. **Close Server Explorer.**

17. **Double-click the OleDbDataAdapter icon in the Toolbox (Data tab) to add it to the form.**

The Data Adapter Configuration Wizard appears, ready for you to define which tables — and which fields — should be used to build your new disconnected dataset from the original Access database.

18. **Click Next.**

Your connection is automatically listed.

19. **Click Next again.**

SQL statements are selected (that, too, is what you want to use).

20. **Click Next and then click the Query Builder button.**

This opens the automated SQL Query utility, which is similar to Access's various query tools, such as the Simple Query Wizard or Expression Builder. You might find the .NET Query Builder easier to use, though, because there's no need to switch between design view and SQL view like there is in Access.

21. **Double-click Customers to add that table to the new dataset.**

22. **Click Close.**

Your Query Builder should now look like the one in Figure 3-1.

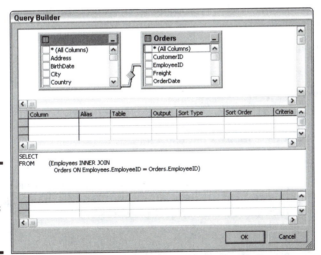

Figure 3-1:
Building
SQL queries
was never
this easy.

23. **Select the fields from this table that you want to include in the dataset. For the heck of it, select All Columns.**

Columns is the latest fad term for *fields*. Sure, it's been used by IBM and some others for years, but only recently has Microsoft been trying it on for size. Time will tell whether it sticks.

Notice that the SQL statement is automatically adjusted from this:

```
SELECT
FROM          Customers
```

To this:

```
SELECT      Customers.*
FROM        Customers
```

24. **Click OK to close the Query Builder.**

25. **Click Next and then click Finish.**

Generating a Dataset for an Imported Database

After you define a connection and specify the database contents that you want to import (in the preceding steps), you can generate a dataset for your VB project. In the preceding section, you can read how to specify a connection to the Access database, including an SQL statement that requests the Customers table from that database. Now that things are set up, you can do the actual work. You pull the data from the database and store it in a brand new dataset. The dataset is a detached table of data that can now be manipulated by the VB.NET application you're writing. It can be transmitted via XML, stored in other formats, filtered, or whatever your heart desires. Follow these steps:

1. **Right-click the OleDbDataAdapter1 icon in the tray.**

A context menu appears.

2. **Choose Generate Dataset.**

The Generate Dataset dialog box opens.

3. **Name your new dataset** dsCustomers.

4. **Click OK.**

The dialog box closes, and the new dataset's icon is added to the tray. Now you want to bind the DataGrid control to this dataset so that data will fill it when the VB.NET project executes.

5. **Click the DataGrid to select it.**

6. **Press F4 to display the Properties window.**

7. **Click the DataSource property in the Properties window.**

A down-arrow button appears.

8. **Click the button to drop the list down — it's like a list box.**

9. **Click dsCustomers1.Customers to select the dataset.**

The dataset is now bound to the grid control. Notice that the fields are displayed along the top of the grid control in the form.

The wizard's work is now over. You have to do a bit of programming (very little, calm down) to actually fill the dataset when your project executes. Double-click the form and type this into your Form_Load event:

```
Private Sub Form1_Load(ByVal sender As System.Object, ByVal e
    As System.EventArgs) Handles MyBase.Load

        OleDbDataAdapter1.Fill(DsCustomers1)

End Sub
```

Press F5 to see the results displayed in Figure 3-2.

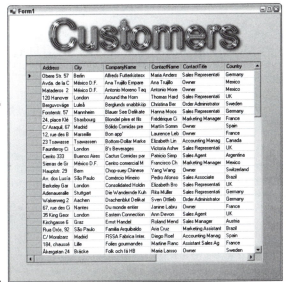

Figure 3-2:
There it is, your Access database moved into a VB.NET project, displayed and ready to be manipulated.

Case Study: Maintaining Alphabetical Order

So far, so good. Now for some manipulation — demonstrations illustrating the ways you can manage datasets — starting with figuring out how to alphabetize them.

Purists insist that relational data should not be maintained in alphabetical order. Well, those of us who design database solutions for actual living people here on planet Earth know that although data might not need to be *maintained* that way inside the database, it often has to be *displayed* in alphabetical order to users.

.NET `Arrays`, `ArrayLists`, `DataViews`, and `DataTables` are all objects that have a built-in sorting method. Oddly, `DataSet` object does not. You can, of course, specify that a particular column be indexed (and if it's a primary key column, its values are forced to be unique). However, although indexing a column makes searching more efficient, it does not maintain the rows in alphabetical order.

Precisely how indexing works varies among the different database types. Typically, databases include a primary key (also known as a *primary key index*). Some databases also feature a clustered index in which the rows are maintained in the same order as the index. In other words, when you add a new record, it is inserted into its alphabetical location within the set of existing rows rather than simply appended to the set. This kind of indexing is not available, however, to `DataSets`.

When you first create an SQL query to extract a `DataSet` from a database, you can specify that the result be ordered (alphabetized) in a particular way (ascending or, more rarely, descending). You can also specify that the `DataSet` be ordered by whatever column you want. Imagine a database table that works like a cookbook, filled with recipe titles in one field and recipe instructions in a second field. You could order this table alphabetically by recipe title column in a recipe database, for example.

This is all well and good, but what happens after the `DataSet` gets into the user's computer, and the user starts adding new rows of information? There's the problem. Each new row is not inserted alphabetically. If you permit the user to go to the next or previous row by clicking buttons to maneuver through the `DataSet`, or if you display the entire list of titles (for example, in a list box), some of the rows (at the bottom of the list box) will be out of alphabetical order. That's bad. You have to figure out a way around that problem. You want your `DataSet` to always be in alphabetical order, even when the user adds a new record or changes a title so that the recipe must now be listed elsewhere in the alphabetized list.

Providing an ordered list is such a common user-interface issue that it's surprising that the `DataSet` doesn't have a sort method.

Your first thought might be to just set a list box's `Sorted` property to `True`. That way, when you display all the titles, they are displayed in alphabetical order. True, but it doesn't solve the following two problems:

✦ When users add some recipes to the recipe database and then click the Next button to move up to the end of the rows, they go past recipes titled X, Y, and Z and find a mixture of S, R, A, Q, N, or whatever. (The added recipes are just sitting at the end, appended in no particular order.) The list box's `Sorted` property does not alphabetize items as they are browsed by the Next button.

✦ The order of the titles displayed in the list box gets out of sync with the recipes column. For example, if the user clicks the third title in the list box, it might or might not represent the third record in the `DataSet`. Why? Because perhaps the user has added a new row, and its title begins with `A`. That record shows up at the beginning (top) of the list box and bumps all lower titles down one in the list box (but not in the `DataSet` table). When users click in the list box, they expect to see the recipe for that title displayed in a text box. How do you, the programmer, figure out which row in the `DataSet` to display? You can't use the `SelectedIndex` property of the list box: It tells you which title the user clicked but not which row in the `DataSet` to display. The `SelectedIndex` number doesn't necessarily sync with the `DataSet` item number (`Tables(0).Rows(i).Item(1)`).

Of the several ways to deal with this, you could search the `DataSet` for the title that matches the one the user clicked and then display the recipe. As long as the title column contains unique entries (is a primary key), this works.

You can choose from two approaches to query and sort the records in a `DataSet`: the `Select` method and the `DataView` object. These two techniques are worth knowing about because sorting and searching are quite common database-related jobs. However, as you see, they don't solve the problem outlined in the preceding paragraphs. They do not permit you a way of sorting the `DataSet` itself.

I suspect that in the drive toward *scalability* (another word for one-size-fits-all), some features that are useful to small- or medium-size applications have been left out. Clearly, a huge database with 10,000 records isn't going to be interacted with by clicking Next and Previous buttons. Nor is it practical to display a huge list box with 10,000 titles. There are other, better ways to interact with monster databases. However, many of us work with smaller projects, such as a small office's inventory or personnel file. Creating utilities on this scale with a `DataSet` becomes problematic when you attempt to use a `DataSet` and find you can't sort it. However, probably the best solution is to simply search on your primary key field for a match to the string that the user clicked in the list box. This doesn't solve the Next and Previous button navigation method, though.

Filtering with Select

When you use the `Select` method of the `DataTable` object to get a list of data, the process is *filtering*. This is essentially the same process as querying, when you use SQL to extract a subset of the data in a database. In effect, you say something like, "Give me a list, ordered by age, of all the kids on the swim team who are still in the Minnows class." This process involves both searching and sorting simultaneously. Explaining SQL is beyond the scope of this book, but there are lots of other lovely books that just spend all their time on it. I recommend *SQL For Dummies,* 5th Edition by Allen G. Taylor (Wiley).

To experiment with the `Select` method, start a new VB.NET Windows-style project and add a `ListBox` to the form. In this example, I build a dataset from scratch rather than importing one from an Access database or some other outside source.

Type these `Imports` statements at the very top of the code window:

```
Imports System.Data
Imports System.Data.OleDb
Imports System.Data.SqlClient
Imports System.Data.SqlTypes
Imports System.Data.SqlDbType
```

You don't need them all, but what the heck. Why fiddle around? Just dump them in. Now type these declarations just above the `Private Sub Form_Load` line:

```
Dim ds As New DataSet(), dr As DataRow, dt As DataTable

' Used to create a new table, and an array of DataRow objects
Dim newRows() As DataRow
Dim newTable As DataTable
```

The `newRows` and `newTable` objects are used in later examples in this chapter.

In the `Form_Load` event, you define the schema of a `DataSet` and populate it with some rows of names. For simplicity, in this example, you use the same schema as in the example in the previous chapter. However, you let the computer generate a list of 30 rows that you can experiment with. Type the following code (Listing 3-1) into the `Form_Load` event:

Listing 3-1: Filling a Dataset

```
Private Sub Form1_Load(ByVal sender As System.Object, ByVal e
    As System.EventArgs) Handles MyBase.Load

        'define the dataset:
        dt = New DataTable("Recipes")
        dt.Columns.Add("title", GetType(String))
        dt.Columns.Add("desc", GetType(String))


        Dim colArray(1) As DataColumn
        colArray(0) = dt.Columns("title")
        dt.PrimaryKey = colArray
```

```
ds.Tables.Add(dt)

'create 30 random titles and descriptions, and add
  them to the DataSet:
makeupnames()

'display the random title and description columns in
  the listbox
Dim i As Integer, n As String
For i = 0 To dt.Rows.Count - 1
    n = ds.Tables(0).Rows(i).Item(0) & "..." &
    ds.Tables(0).Rows(i).Item(1)
    ListBox1.Items.Add(n)
Next i

End Sub
```

Just below the `End Sub` that ends the `Form_Load` event, add this next sub-routine, which makes up 30 fake, random titles and recipes and adds them to the `DataSet`. They are out of alphabetical order. (They're just random nonsense until you later alphabetize them by using the `Select` method.) Type in this `Sub` (Listing 3-2) below the `Form_Load` procedure's `End Sub`, just above the `End Class`:

Listing 3-2: Making Up Fake Names

```
Sub makeupnames()
        'create fake names
        Dim rndGenerator As New System.Random(1)
        Dim i, j, x As Integer
        Dim word As String

        For i = 1 To 30

            For j = 1 To 12
                x = rndGenerator.Next(97, 123) 'limit it to
        lowercase letters
                word += Chr(x) 'add a character (from the
        ASCII code value) to the word
            Next

            dr = dt.NewRow()
            dr!title = Microsoft.VisualBasic.Left
        (word.ToUpper, 6) 'make the titles uppercase to
        distinguish them
            dr!desc = Microsoft.VisualBasic.Right(word, 6)
            dt.Rows.Add(dr)
            word = ""
        Next

    End Sub
```

Notice that by seeding the random number generator with an integer in the first line of code — (1) in this example — you force it to provide the same list of random names each time the program runs. I chose this approach so that you can repeatedly test various aspects of these examples and tell at a glance how the records have been selected or ordered. Don't seed the generator if you want varying lists of random names. Now press F5 to see your DataSet titles column displayed. Notice that they are not in alphabetical order.

Alphabetizing with Select

In this next example, you alphabetize the list by creating a new array (of DataRow objects) and by specifying that the Select method should order them alphabetically (which is the default behavior of the Select method).

Add a button control to the form and change its Text property to Order by Select. Double-click the button and type this (Listing 3-3) into its Click event:

Listing 3-3: Alphabetizing

```
Private Sub Button1_Click(ByVal sender As System.Object,
    ByVal e As System.EventArgs) Handles Button1.Click

Dim i As Integer
        ListBox1.Items.Clear()

        ' Create a new table, and an array of DataRow objects
        Dim newRows() As DataRow
        Dim newTable As DataTable
        Dim n As String

        ' Get the DataTable of a DataSet.
        newTable = ds.Tables("Recipes")

        newRows = newTable.Select()


        ' Display the values in both columns of each DataRow.
        For i = 0 To newRows.GetUpperBound(0)
            n = newRows(i)("Title") & "..." &
          newRows(i)("Desc")
            ListBox1.Items.Add(n)
        Next i


End Sub
```

Press F5 and click the button. The titles are now alphabetized within the list box, as shown in Figure 3-3.

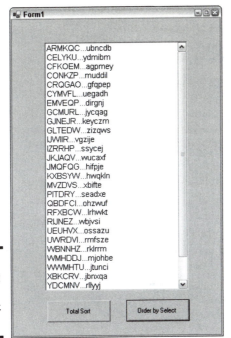

Figure 3-3:
A sorted list
created by
the Select
method.

Interestingly, in this array of DataRows (newRows), the Titles and Desc
columns remain synchronized. This is what you wanted to happen to your
DataSet, but you had to create a new array and use the Select method of
the DataTable to accomplish it. The DataSet doesn't have a Select
method nor any other way of sorting itself.

One is sorted, the other isn't

Even after creating this new array, notice that the DataSet itself isn't
alphabetized — just the new array. As you see in a moment, to alphabetize
the DataSet, you can try to replace the rows in the DataSet by deleting the
current DataSet's rows and then dumping this newRows array into the
DataSet. That sorts the DataSet, albeit in a rather roundabout way.

However, if you do try to replace the existing DataRows with the new array,
you run into all kinds of permissions problems: The primary key row already
exists and can't be duplicated, Row doesn't exist, and Column Title doesn't
allow nulls. Here is a way (Listing 3-4) to replace the rows in the DataSet
with the rows in the array without offending the security squad:

Listing 3-4: Replacing DataSet Rows

```
Private Sub Button2_Click(ByVal sender As System.Object,
    ByVal e As System.EventArgs) Handles Button2.Click
        Dim i As Integer
        Dim newRows() As DataRow
        Dim newTable As DataTable
        Dim n As String

        ListBox1.Items.Clear()

        newTable = ds.Tables(0).Copy()

        ds.Tables(0).Rows.Clear()

        newRows = newTable.Select()

        For i = 0 To newRows.GetUpperBound(0)
            ds.Tables(0).ImportRow(newRows(i))
        Next

        For i = 0 To dt.Rows.Count - 1
            n = ds.Tables(0).Rows(i).Item(0) & "..." &
          ds.Tables(0).Rows(i).Item(1)
            ListBox1.Items.Add(n)
        Next i
    End Sub
```

The overloaded Select method

When you use the `Select` method with no parameters (just empty parentheses), it automatically puts the result in alphabetical order by the primary key field. In this example, you specify that the Titles column is the primary key field. So you can simply use the no-parameter form to get the results you want:

```
newRows = newTable.Select()
```

However, three other forms of this method can be used, which means that it is overloaded. The arguments that you provide to this method determine how it behaves. You can specify a `Criterion`, which is an SQL-like string that defines how you want the rows to be filtered (queried). Here's an example that doesn't display any titles starting with A through E:

```
'find all rows matching the filter: (greater than F
  in the alphabet)
Dim Criterion = "Title > 'F'"
newRows = newTable.Select(Criterion)
```

This result is still sorted because the Title column is the primary key, but no rows beginning with letters lower than F in the alphabet are placed into the newRows array. The list of possible *expressions* (filters or criteria) is extensive and involves various special characters and punctuation rules. To see how to define a criterion to use with the Select method, open VB.NET's Help feature (choose Help⇨Index). Type **DataColumn.Expression** into the Look For text box, and then double-click the DataColumn.Expression property in the left pane of the Help window.

Yet another variation of the Select method permits sorting in descending order (backward from Z to A). The final Select method enables you to specify that only rows matching a particular DataViewRowState property are to be placed into the array. DataViewRowState includes Added, Modified, Deleted, Unchanged, and so on.

Which version is it?

To see the current version of the DataTable — as opposed to the original version that was loaded into the DataSet at the start — use code like this:

```
dv.RowStateFilter=DataViewRowState.Deleted
```

You can also test the status of individual rows in a DataTable by querying the RowState property. The following results are returned on these various rows when you run this code: Detached, Added, Unchanged, Modified, Deleted.

```
Dim dTable As New DataTable("dTable")
Dim dCol As New DataColumn("Title",
  Type.GetType("System.String"))
dTable.Columns.Add(dCol)
Dim dRow As DataRow

' Make a new DataRow.
dRow = dTable.NewRow()
Console.WriteLine(dRow.RowState.ToString())

dTable.Rows.Add(dRow)
Console.WriteLine(dRow.RowState.ToString())

dRow("Title") = "Moby Dick" 'edit the row
Console.WriteLine(dRow.RowState.ToString())

dTable.AcceptChanges() 'this makes the rowstate
  "unchanged"
Console.WriteLine(dRow.RowState.ToString())

dRow.Delete()
Console.WriteLine(dRow.RowState.ToString())
```

In VB.NET, `Console.WriteLine` is a common way of testing code when you want to print out and see some results. It prints to the Output window, which you can view by choosing View➪Other Windows➪Output, and then selecting the Debug variation in the drop-down list in the Output window.

When using the `Select` method, you can set the third parameter to specify which version of the rows you want to see, as in this pseudocode example. (*Pseudocode* uses descriptive names to illustrate the elements of source code, but the code isn't actually runnable.)

```
newRows = newTable.Select(filter expression, sort mode,
    DataViewRowState)
```

You have to replace the italicized parameters in the preceding sample line of code with actual VB.NET expressions or *enumerations* (various built-in constants). For example, before you could run this line, you must replace `DataViewRowState` with one of the enumerations shown when you type in the line of code. *Enumerations* are lists of constants. There are sets of constants built-into .NET, or you can create your own with the `Enum` statement.

If you are using a `DataView` object, set its `RowStateFilter` property to specify which version of the rows you want to see:

```
Dim drView As DataRowView
dv.RowFilter = "Title LIKE '*q*'"
dv.Sort = "Title"
dv.RowStateFilter = DataViewRowState.Deleted
```

Using the DataView Object

Datasets are disconnected from the database from which they drew their data. But what if you want to view the data in a dataset in a different way? For example, if you want to see only customers in Montana, should you go to the trouble of reconnecting to the original database and build a new dataset? That's not efficient. It's easier to use a *data view,* which provides you with a filtered and sorted view of the dataset's contents. A data view is not a copy of the data; it's just a different view of the dataset.

Using the `DataView` feature isn't too hard. You have to create a few objects and use `For Each` to iterate through them to display them. Add a button to the form used in the earlier example ("Filtering with Select") and change its `Text` property to `Display Dataview Q`. Then double-click that button and type this (Listing 3-5) into its `Click` event:

Listing 3-5: Building a Data View

```
Private Sub Button2_Click(ByVal sender As System.Object,
    ByVal e As System.EventArgs) Handles Button2.Click
        'Create a DataView and display it

        ' Get a reference to the Recipes table.
        Dim dtNew As DataTable = ds.Tables("Recipes")
        ' Create a dataview
        Dim dv As New DataView(dtNew)
        Dim drView As DataRowView
        ' Set the criterion filter and sort on title.
        ' This criterion says: list all records with a Q in
          the title field
        dv.RowFilter = "Title LIKE '*q*'"
        dv.Sort = "Title"

        'display the DataSet

        Dim i As Integer, s As String
        ListBox1.Items.Clear()
        Me.Text = "From DataView"

        For Each drView In dv
            s = drView(i)
            ListBox1.Items.Add(s)
        Next

    End Sub
```

Close Relations

One of the prime virtues of a `DataSet` is that it permits you to create relations, just like a real database. After all, the kind of database that's most popular these days — and that includes SQL Server and `DataSets` — is a relational database. So, just what are relations, and why are they so popular?

A *relation* is a connection between two tables that both share a common, *primary* key (a column in which each row contains unique data). The fact that they identify their rows uniquely, and both do it the same way, permits you to access data simultaneously from both rows but in sync. This can be useful when one table contains details not available in the other table. Recall that you sometimes use two tables to prevent redundancy.

Master-detail, parent-child

Data coming from multiple yet related tables is often referred to as *master-detail*. For example, a master table (the *parent*) could contain a list of publishers and their addresses, phone numbers, and other information.

However, because each publisher puts out many books, you don't want to have to repeat the publisher's address, phone number, and so on for each book. That's the redundancy that multiple tables solves. You simply put the main information about each publisher in one table, and you *link* (make a relation, or join) that table to a different detail (the *child*) table that lists all the books for each publisher. The child table doesn't contain the publisher's address, phone number, and so on; rather, it contains details about each book.

This master-detail relationship between tables is quite common. In a dentist's office, they put your name, phone number, and so on in one table; then they link it to a second table containing, for example, details about your payment history.

In the following sections, you first see how to create a relation between two tables programmatically, and then you see how to use wizards and the excellent, graphic *XML Designer,* which shows you a visual diagram of tables and any relations between them.

Programmatic relations

Start a new VB.NET Windows-style project. Double-click the form to get to the `Form1_Load` event in the code window. Type the following code above the `Private Sub Form1_Load` line:

```
Dim ds As New DataSet(), dr As DataRow, dt, dt1 As DataTable
```

Also add the usual `Imports` statements at the very top of the code window:

```
Imports System.Data
Imports System.Data.OleDb
Imports System.Data.SqlClient
Imports System.Data.SqlTypes
Imports System.Data.SqlDbType
```

You now want to create two tables, `dt` and `dt1`, and then define a relationship between them. Type this code (Listing 3-6) into the `Form1_Load` event. (In this example, the explanation of the various parts of the source code is provided by comments within the code itself.)

Listing 3-6: Generating Relations Programmatically

```
Private Sub Form1_Load(ByVal sender As System.Object, ByVal e
    As System.EventArgs) Handles MyBase.Load

        'define two new datasets:
        dt = New DataTable("Recipes")
        dt.Columns.Add("title", GetType(String))
        dt.Columns.Add("desc", GetType(String))
```

```
Dim colArray(1) As DataColumn 'make title primary key
   (unique)
colArray(0) = dt.Columns("title")
dt.PrimaryKey = colArray


dt1 = New DataTable("Calories")
dt1.Columns.Add("title", GetType(String))
dt1.Columns.Add("CalorieCount", GetType(Integer))

'make title primary key (unique) for this table, too.
colArray(0) = dt1.Columns("title")
dt1.PrimaryKey = colArray

'add both tables to the dataset
ds.Tables.Add(dt)
ds.Tables.Add(dt1)


'add three rows to the two tables:
dr = dt.NewRow()
dr!title = "First Title"
dr!desc = "Description of first title"
dt.Rows.Add(dr)

dr = dt.NewRow()
dr!title = "Second Title"
dr!desc = "Description of second title"
dt.Rows.Add(dr)

dr = dt.NewRow()
dr!title = "Third Title"
dr!desc = "Description of third title"
dt.Rows.Add(dr)

'second table:

dr = dt1.NewRow()
dr!title = "First Title"
dr!CalorieCount = 130
dt1.Rows.Add(dr)

dr = dt1.NewRow()
dr!title = "Second Title"
dr!CalorieCount = 220
dt1.Rows.Add(dr)

dr = dt1.NewRow()
dr!title = "Third Title"
dr!CalorieCount = 30
dt1.Rows.Add(dr)

'now create a relation between these two tables
```

```
'This next line of code creates a new relation object
  named
' "CalRel" and specifies that the first column
' (Recipes.Title) is the parent and the second column
' (Calories.Title) is the child (the parent/child
  relation is
' based on the order that you specify the two columns
  in the
' parameter list).

ds.Relations.Add("CalRel", ds.Tables("Recipes").
  Columns("Title"), _
                ds.Tables("Calories").Columns
  ("Title"))

' Now, loop through each row in the parent table's
  rows collection
' (it has three rows), and then loop through each row
  in the relation
' object (there is only one row), displaying the
  "count"
' (the parent table's row number), and both columns
  in the child.
' Note that you are not accessing dt1 directly (the
  child table)
' instead, you are accessing the relation object

Dim da As DataRow
Dim count As Integer

For Each dr In dt.Rows
    For Each da In dr.GetChildRows("CalRel")
        count += 1
        Console.WriteLine(count & "." & da("Title") &
  " " & da("CalorieCount"))
    Next
Next

    End Sub
```

Press F5 and look in the Output window for the results. You should see this:

```
1.First Title 130
2.Second Title 220
3.Third Title 30
```

Creating a Dataset with Relations

As you doubtless suspected, VB.NET offers you many interesting auto-coding features — wizards, designers, parsers, add-ins, and other helpers that let you drag-and-drop or answer a series of questions before they write source code for you. Sometimes you can get hundreds of lines of source code based on a three-minute little quiz from a wizard.

In the next example, you see how to connect to two different tables in the Northwind sample database and how to create a relation between the ID column that they have in common. You use both a wizard and a designer. You also see how to bind a `DataGrid` and a `ListBox` to the database connection. This example requires that you have SQL Server installed.

Relations via Wizards and Designers

You need to know how to summon wizards and designers to make your life as a programmer easier than you thought possible. To create a connection between a database and a `DataSet`, follow these steps:

1. **Start a new Windows-style VB.NET project.**

2. **On the form, place a `ListBox` and a `DataGrid` from the Windows Forms tab of the Toolbox.**

3. **Double-click the OleDbDataAdapter icon in the data tab of the Toolbox.**

   An OleDbDataAdapter is added to your form, and the Data Adapter Configuration Wizard opens. Recall that you can use either this OleDbDataAdapter (which is slower but more versatile because it connects to more databases) or the SqlDataAdapter used in most examples in this book. For variety, you use the OleDbDataAdapter in this example.

4. **Click Next.**

5. **Choose the Northwind database in the drop-down list.**

6. **Click Next.**

7. **Leave the Use SQL Statements radio button selected.**

8. **Click Next.**

9. **Click the Query Builder button.**

10. **Double-click Orders in the Add Table dialog box.**

    The Orders table is added to the Query Builder dialog box.

11. **Click Close to close the Add Table dialog box.**

12. **Click order_id and customer_id in the top pane.**

    This SQL query is constructed for you:

    ```
    SELECT     OrderID, CustomerID
    FROM       Orders
    ```

The order_id column is the one on which a relation will be created to link this table with another table in the Northwind database.

13. **Click OK and then click Finish. Choose not to add a password if the security patrol queries you.**

An OleDataAdapter1 and an OleDbConnection1 are added to your tray. You need only this one connection to the database, but to add a new table, you can add a second OleDataAdapter to your form. This new adapter also employs the existing OleDbConnection.

14. **Double-click the OleDbDataAdapter icon in the Toolbox.**

The Data Adapter Configuration Wizard dialog box opens again.

15. **Select the Northwind database and click Next.**

16. **Leave the Use SQL Statements radio button selected. Click Next.**

17. **Click the Query Builder button.**

18. **Double-click Order Details in the Add Table dialog box.**

The Order Details table is added to the Query Builder dialog box.

19. **Click Close to close the Add Table dialog box.**

20. **Click orderID, quantity, and unit price in the top pane to specify that you want to access the data from these fields (columns).**

This SQL query is constructed:

```
SELECT      OrderID, Quantity, UnitPrice
FROM        [Order Details]
```

Some databases refuse to permit spaces in table names. To avoid problems, you can enclose the name in brackets, as illustrated in the preceding SQL statement.

21. **Click OK and then click Finish. Click Yes to permit the primary keys to be added.**

22. **Now you need to build a `DataSet` that includes both of these tables.**

a. Right-click either of the OleDbDataAdapter icons in the tray beneath your form.

b. Choose Generate DataSet from the context menu.

c. Mark the check boxes next to both Order Details and Orders.

d. Name this **DataSet dsOrders** in the New text box on the dialog box.

e. Click OK.

You now see a new DataSet icon in your tray.

Using the XML Designer

At this point, you can open the XML Designer to create your relation. This illustrates the intimate relationship between tables, datasets, and XML versions of either. Follow these steps:

1. **Double-click the** `dsOrders.xsd` **file in Solution Explorer (VB.NET's equivalent of VBA's Project Explorer).**

The XML Designer opens, as shown in Figure 3-4. Notice the little key symbols next to the key fields in both tables. OrderID is a unique field, and you create your relation based on it.

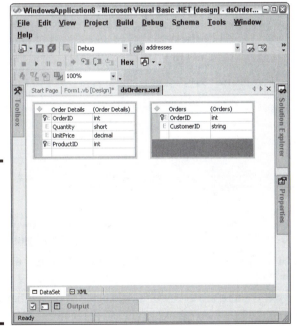

Figure 3-4:
This designer helps you graphically study and edit relations between tables.

If you don't see `dsOrders.xsd` file displayed in Solution Explorer, click the name of your project (which is in boldface in Solution Explorer) to highlight it, and then click the icon — it looks like three sheets of paper, one yellow — in the Solution Explorer title bar named Show All Files.

2. **Open the Toolbox.**

Notice that when the XML Designer is open, you see a number of XML schema icons that you can use to create a structure.

3. **The** Order Details **table is your child (details) table in this relationship, so drag a relation icon from the Toolbox and drop it on the** Order Details **table in the designer.**

The Edit Relation dialog box opens, as shown in Figure 3-5.

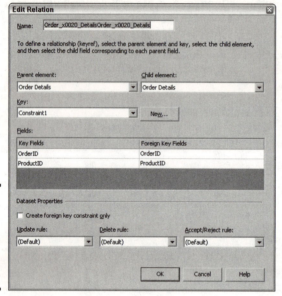

Figure 3-5: Use this dialog box to specify the details of a relation.

4. **In the Name field, the designer has provided a name for your relation:** Order_x0020_DetailsOrder_x0020_Details, **at this point.**

5. **Ensure that the parent element is** Orders **and the child element is** OrderDetails.

Now change the name to relOrders. You want to remember this name so that you can use it in a minute when you bind the ListBox and DataGrid to the relation.

Note the use of the term *element* here for what you normally call a *table*. *Element* is a term used in XML to refer to an item enclosed by <> </> symbols — tags — as in the following line:

```
<H1>This is a headline</H1>
```

The reason for using *element* here is that VB.NET has actually translated your DataSet (the tables, their schema, their relation, and eventually even their data) into XML. This way, they can be communicated over firewalls on the Internet. To see the XML source code that VB.NET has so thoughtfully generated for you, right-click either table in the designer and choose View XML Source.

6. **Ensure that Key Fields and Foreign Key Fields both read** `OrderID`.

7. **Click OK.**

   The Edit Relation dialog box closes, and you see something that looks like a necklace appear in the XML Designer, connecting the two tables graphically and symbolizing their relation, as shown in Figure 3-6.

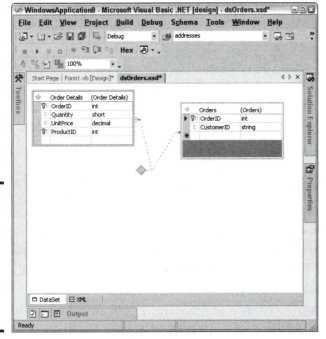

Figure 3-6:
This necklace symbolizes the relation established between these two tables.

8. **Right-click the dsOrders.xsd* tab at the top of the designer and choose Save dsOrders.xsd.**

9. **Click the Form1.vb[Design] tab at the top of the designer.**

   You see your form, almost ready to display this relation.

Binding the controls

You now need to bind the `ListBox` to the `Orders` master (parent) table and bind the `DataGrid` to the details (child) table, `Order Details`. To do that, follow these steps:

1. **Click the** `ListBox` **to select it.**

2. **Press F4.**

   The Properties window opens.

3. **Select the** `DataSource` **property and click the down-arrow icon next to that property.**

   You see a list of possible data sources.

4. **Click dsOrders1, your** `DataSet`.

5. **Select the** `DisplayMember` **property and click the down-arrow icon next to that property.**

   You see a list of columns (fields) within the table you chose as your data source.

6. **Choose ProductID, under the relOrders node.**

   A *node* is an entry with a – or + symbol next to it in a list, indicating that other items are listed underneath it and subordinate to it.

7. **Click the + to open this node and select UnitPrice.**

   The property should now read `relOrders.ProductID`.

8. **Click the** `DataGrid` **to select it.**

9. **Click the** `DataSource` **property in the Properties window and then click the down-arrow icon next to that property.**

   You see a list of possible data sources.

10. **Click dsOrders1.Orders.**

11. **Click the** `DataMember` **property in the Properties window and then click the down-arrow icon next to that property.**

12. **Click relOrders.**

    You see the relation, and the `DataGrid` control displays the four fields (the schema) of the child table in the DataSet.

At this point, your `DataGrid` is now able to point to all child rows in the child table whenever the user clicks on a product ID in the parent table (displayed in the list box). By selecting the relation object as the `DataMember` for the `DataGrid`, you make it possible to see the `Details` (child) fields.

Many people assume that with the `DataSet` created and the controls bound, you can just press F5 and see the data in the controls. Well, as you might remember from the first example in this chapter, you do have to write just a little source code to complete the process. Double-click the form to get to the code window and then type this into the Form_Load event:

```
Private Sub Form1_Load(ByVal sender As System.Object, ByVal e
     As System.EventArgs) Handles MyBase.Load
        DsOrders1.Clear()
        OleDbDataAdapter1.Fill(DsOrders1)
        OleDbDataAdapter2.Fill(DsOrders1)
End Sub
```

Using Clear

Using the Clear method isn't strictly necessary here because this is the first time that this DataSet is being used in this application. Nonetheless, it's a good habit to empty a DataSet of all its contents prior to filling it with new data. The Fill method of a DataAdapater object dumps the data from the database connection into the DataSet.

Saving an XML Dataset

As a final exercise, send this dataset via XML to Access. Change the Form_Load event code in the previous example to this:

```
Private Sub Form1_Load(ByVal sender As System.Object, ByVal e
        As System.EventArgs) Handles MyBase.Load
        DsOrders1.Clear()
        OleDbDataAdapter1.Fill(DsOrders1)
        OleDbDataAdapter2.Fill(DsOrders1)


        'SAVE
        Try

            DsOrders1.WriteXmlSchema("c:\test.xsd")
            DsOrders1.WriteXml("c:\test.xml")

        Catch ex As Exception
            MsgBox(ex.ToString)
        End Try

        Me.Text = "Saved..."

    End Sub
```

The new XML file Test and its associated schema file (XSD) are now available to Access.

Importing XML by hand

You can also use the manual import approach within Access:

1. **Choose File⇨Get External Data⇨Import.**

   The Import dialog box opens.

2. **Open the drop-down list next to Files of Type in the dialog box and select .XML (*.xml; *.xsd).**

3. **Locate the Test.xml file you created in the preceding section and double-click its name in the dialog box.**

The Import XML dialog box opens.

4. **Click the Options button in the Import XML dialog box.**

   The dialog box grows a bit larger. Notice that Structure and Data is selected by default. That's indeed what you want — both the schema (from the XSD file) and the data (from the XML file).

5. **Click OK.**

   You're informed that the importing has taken place, and you also notice that both tables — Orders and Order Details — have been added to your database.

6. **Click OK.**

   The message box and the dialog box both disappear.

7. **Double-click Order Details and Orders to see that indeed both tables from your original dataset have now been transferred to Access.**

Importing XML programmatically

If you prefer, you can import an XML file and its schema file by using the following VBA code in Access. Press Alt+F11 to get to the code window. Choose Insert⇨Module. Then type this code into the code window:

```
Sub GetXML()

Application.ImportXML _
    DataSource:="c:\test.xml", _
    ImportOptions:=acStructureAndData

End Sub
```

Chapter 4: Automating Access

In This Chapter

✔ **Using automation to connect to Access**

✔ **Working with** `SendKeys`

✔ **Automating the Access runtime**

✔ **Displaying a report**

*M*anaging Access from the outside is essential if you want to go beyond the built-in capabilities that VBA macros — much less old-style Access macros — offer.

For example, Access has limited Internet programming capabilities, relative to the splendid and efficient ASP.NET programming facilities built into .NET. Or, if you want to create a really rich front end for Access Windows projects, Access's VBA UserForm is not nearly as full of features — nor as well-tested — as the Windows Form in VB.NET. Beyond that, the security features, communication classes, and many other elements of the .NET framework are more advanced and far more plentiful than those built into Access (or any Office 2003 product, for that matter). Serious Office 2003 developers facing projects of any significance should become familiar with Visual Studio .NET programming. .NET is the future of Microsoft programming, and a programmer's future might well depend on his or her ability to make good use of it.

Automating How to Access a Form

Follow this example to see how to use automation to connect to Access. Here's the flow: Start Access, display a form from the Northwind sample database, move to the second record on the form, copy the data, and send the data back to the .NET application for further processing.

Before you can do all that, you have to get some DLLs in place — object collections, code libraries, communication tubes, and other such under-the-hood necessities. Go to this location and download the Office XP Primary Interop Assemblies (PIAs). (They're the same for Office 2003.)

```
http://msdn.microsoft.com/library/default.asp?url=/
downloads/list/office.asp
```

This set of *assemblies* (code libraries, in this case) isn't always absolutely necessary to control Office 2003 applications from within .NET. Other assemblies can do the trick. But the PIA is *primary* — it's the official set of libraries — so you can expect it to be supported and to cause the fewest side effects.

After you download the PIA, read the README.HTM file and follow its instructions to take a trip back in time to the command line. (That would be DOS, not much used for the past decade, except in cases like this.) Use the batch file to install the assemblies and update the Global Assembly Cache (GAC).

The README.HTM file doesn't mention this, but you probably need to restart Windows before Visual Studio .NET (which contains Visual Basic .NET) will work properly.

Read the section in the README.HTM file titled "Distributing solutions that rely on the Office XP PIAs" if you intend to deploy projects relying on the PIA to other computers. Creating a custom setup utility is likely the simplest solution to provide these other machines with the proper assemblies.

Now run VB.NET, choose File⇨New⇨Project, name the new project AutomateAccess (in the New Project dialog box), and then double-click the Windows Application icon. You must create a reference to your newly downloaded PIA, which is done indirectly by following these steps:

1. **To add a reference to the Access 11.0 object library, choose Project⇨Add Reference.**

2. **In the Add Reference dialog box that appears, click the COM tab.**

3. **Locate and double-click the Microsoft Access 11.0 Object Library.**

   It appears in the Selected Components pane.

4. **Click OK.**

   The Add Reference dialog box closes, and the reference (the assembly, actually) is added to your current project.

5. **Add a TextBox control to Form1; then double-click Form1 to get to the code window. At the very top of the code window, add this reference to Access's objects:**

   ```
   Imports Access
   ```

6. **Type Listing 4-1 into the Form_Load event.**

Listing 4-1: Moving Data from Access to .NET

```
Private Sub Form1_Load(ByVal sender As System.Object, _
     ByVal e As System.EventArgs) Handles MyBase.Load

   Dim s As String = "Customer Orders"
```

```
Dim oAccess As Access.Application ' "o" for object
Dim pathNorth As String = "C:\Program Files\Microsoft
  Office\Office11\Samples\Northwind.mdb"


' instantiate Access
oAccess = New Access.ApplicationClass
' show it
oAccess.Visible = True

' open Northwind
oAccess.OpenCurrentDatabase(filepath:=pathNorth)

'select the customer orders form
oAccess.DoCmd.SelectObject(ObjectName:=s, _
    InDatabaseWindow:=True,
  ObjectType:=Access.AcObjectType.acForm)

' display the form
oAccess.DoCmd.OpenForm(FormName:=s, _
            View:=Access.AcFormView.acNormal)

' send two Ctrl+Tabs to move to the second record
SendKeys.SendWait("^{TAB}")
SendKeys.SendWait("^{TAB}")

'select, then copy, the record
SendKeys.SendWait("^a") 'select all
SendKeys.SendWait("^c") 'copy


'get the copied data back to .NET from clipboard
Dim cl As IDataObject = Clipboard.GetDataObject()
If (cl.GetDataPresent(DataFormats.Text)) Then
    TextBox1.Text =
  cl.GetData(DataFormats.Text).ToString()
End If


' destroy the app object
oAccess = Nothing


    End Sub
```

The InDatabaseWindow argument of the SelectObject method selects the object in the database window, but it defaults to False, so you set it to True here to carry out the selection process. In effect, this argument sets the focus to the database window.

Press F5 to execute this code, and you see Access fire up and display the form. The data from the form is sent back to your VB.NET project and displayed in the text box.

This example illustrates a combination of techniques. Object instantiation is one technique. The Access application is instantiated by using today's fashionable object-oriented programming (OOP) approach:

```
New Access.ApplicationClass
```

A second technique is older — it used to be called *OLE Automation* — but it has its uses. You can use `AppActivate` or `Shell` commands to set the focus to another currently running application or start a new instance of an application, respectively. However, you then have to use `SendKeys` extensively to maneuver — macro-like — around the windows and other elements of the application. It's usually easier to first get an object variable (`oAccess` in Listing 4-1) referring to an instance of Access, and then use that and a form object variable to do the heavy lifting (that is, the main manipulations). `SendKeys` can then be used for other, smaller maneuvers. (For more on `SendKeys`, see the next section.)

Here's an example showing how `Shell` instantiates the Windows Character Map utility and then switches it to display the Times New Roman font:

```
Shell("CHARMAP.EXE", 1)
SendKeys.SendWait("Times New Roman")
```

Understanding SendKeys

`SendKeys` is worth spending a little time exploring because it can be helpful when you don't have the time to try to figure out all the ins and outs of a class library to know how to do a job that some simple keystrokes can accomplish.

When you import the `Access` namespace, as in Listing 4-1, you can then use the VBA commands available within the Access object model, including `SendKeys`. Alternatively, you can import a `VisualBasic` namespace (a reference to a code library, or class library, or object model — three ways of fundamentally saying the same thing) and get to use the Visual Basic 6 classic commands, of which `SendKeys` is one:

```
Imports Microsoft.VisualBasic
```

However you get to it — and whether you call it a function (as it was called traditionally) or a method (as it's now described) — `SendKeys` is nonetheless worth knowing about.

`SendKeys` allows your VB program to send keystrokes to another Windows program, just as if the user were typing those keys into the other program. In other words, `SendKeys` slips data — fake keystrokes — into the pipeline between the keyboard and a Windows program. `SendKeys` makes it seem that the user is typing something, and the program with the focus cannot tell that a user isn't simply typing away.

This technique allows applications to communicate with each other. (You cannot use `SendKeys` on the DOS command line.)

SendKeys and SendWait

The target program must be running and have the focus when `SendKeys` attempts to "type" something into it.

Normally, you'll want to use the `SendWait` method with `SendKeys` to cause your VB program to pause until the outside program has *digested* — processed — whatever keystrokes you have sent. Otherwise, keystrokes can get lost in the ether if focus is shifting or other events are interfering with a quick cascade of keystrokes. For example, here's how to send Ctrl+A:

```
SendKeys.SendWait("^a")
```

To directly send the following 12 text characters, use the following:

```
SendKeys.SendWait("MESSAGE SENT")
```

Or to repeat an individual key — in other words, to specify the number of repeats — put both items in braces. For example, to print seven *z*'s, use

```
({Z 7})
```

Sending nonprinting keys

You can also send the *nonprinting* keys: the keys that cause actions to take place rather than text to be printed, such as F1, Alt, Enter, PgDn, and so on. Many programs recognize and respond to special keys, like the Function keys and Alt+key combinations, for example. To "press" those keys by using `SendKeys`, you provide the name of the special nonprinting key and put it inside braces ({ }) using the following list. ***Note:*** The key names themselves are case-insensitive: It doesn't matter how you capitalize them. *Enter* is the same as *enter* or *ENTER*.

> `{Backspace}` **or** `{Bksp}` **or** `{Bs}`
>
> `{Break}`
>
> `{Capslock}`

```
{Clear}
```

{Delete} or {Del}

```
{Down}
```

```
{End}
```

{Enter} or ~

{Esc} or {Escape}

```
{Help}
```

```
{Home}
```

```
{Insert}
```

```
{Left}
```

```
{Numlock}
```

```
{Pgdn}
```

```
{Pgup}
```

{Prtsc} (for Print Screen)

```
{Right}
```

```
{Scrolllock}
```

```
{Tab}
```

```
{Up}
```

{F1} through {F16}

Or, you can simulate the Ctrl, Alt, or Shift keypresses in combination with other characters. For Shift, put the + (plus) symbol before the character you want shifted: +E, for example.

Many commercial programs save to disk by pressing the Alt+F, S — activating the File menu and selecting the Save option.

For Alt, put the % (percent) symbol before the character you want pressed simultaneously with Alt: %F S, for example.

For Ctrl, use the ^ (caret) symbol before the character you want pressed simultaneously with Ctrl: ^F, for example.

To hold down the Shift, Alt, or Ctrl key while several other keys are pressed, put the other keys in parentheses. For example, to send shifted ABC, use SendKeys "+(abc)".

Using "+abc" would shift only the A, resulting in Abc.

Because the braces characters are used in a special way, if you need to send one of them, enclose the brace itself in braces: {{}, for example.

Because the +, %, and ^ characters are used to indicate Shift, Alt, and Ctrl, respectively, enclose them in braces if you want to send one of them as a character or as printable text. For example, to print the percent symbol, use {%}.

If the program to which SendKeys is instructed to send keystrokes is not running or hasn't been given the focus (with the AppActivate command, for example), the keystrokes are sent back to your Visual Basic .NET program as if the keys were being typed into your program. This permits you to simulate keystrokes that the user might have typed while the VB program is running.

Automating the Runtime

The Developer Edition of Access allows you to deploy your Access 2003 applications to computers where no retail version of Access is installed. Instead, a *runtime* (code library) version of Access (named msaccess.exe) is installed on these machines. Your code will work, but the users themselves cannot write code nor customize your code unless they install their own copy of commercial — not runtime — Access, in which case they can go ahead and freely manipulate the objects and data that you gave them.

If you want to contact the runtime so you can automate this type of Access installation, you should start msaccess.exe and also load a database into it before attempting automation. You must revert to the command line style of programming to do this (DOS), and you must supply a database as an argument. Then use the GetObject command to get the Application object. You cannot use CreateObject or New to instantiate Access's runtime.

For valuable additional information about using the Package Wizard and deploying Access using the runtime, see the article, "Packaging Access 2003 Solutions" at this Web page on MSDN:

```
http://msdn.microsoft.com/library/default.asp?url=/library/
en-us/dnsmart03/html/sa03j8.asp
```

Displaying a Report

For a final example of automation, you see how to display an Access report. It's similar to displaying an Access form; see Listing 4-2:

Listing 4-2: Displaying an Access Report

```
Private Sub Form1_Load(ByVal sender As System.Object, ByVal e
    As System.EventArgs) Handles MyBase.Load


        Dim s As String = "Sales Totals by Amount"
        Dim oAccess As Access.Application ' "o" for object
        Dim pathNorth As String = "C:\Program Files\Microsoft
            Office\Office11\Samples\Northwind.mdb"

        ' instantiate Access
        oAccess = New Access.ApplicationClass
        ' show it
        oAccess.Visible = True

        ' open Northwind
        oAccess.OpenCurrentDatabase(filepath:=pathNorth)

        ' select the report
        oAccess.DoCmd.SelectObject(ObjectName:=s,
            InDatabaseWindow:=True, _
        ObjectType:=Access.AcObjectType.acReport)

        ' display the report
        oAccess.DoCmd.OpenReport(ReportName:=s, _
                View:=Access.AcView.acViewPreview)

        ' destroy app object
        oAccess = Nothing

    End Sub
```

Chapter 5: Troubleshooting in Access

In This Chapter

✔ Using the `Error` **event**

✔ **Understanding** `Option Explicit` **and** `Option Strict`

✔ **Adjusting macro security**

✔ **Using the new sandbox mode**

✔ **Backing up Access 2003**

✔ **Error-checking for forms and reports**

Error Management in Access

Access contains several built-in error-management (and avoidance!) features. A primary one is the `Error` event that's triggered in a form or report when something isn't right.

This `Error` event is not fired when any VBA errors occur in your programming code. For those errors, you must use the `On Error` trapping code, which I describe in detail in Book II, Chapter 6. The Access form and report `Error` event is fired when the Jet database engine or another outside source reports a problem. To see where this error trapping happens, follow these steps:

1. **Open the Northwind sample database.**

2. **Choose Help⇨Sample Databases and then select Northwind Sample Database.**

   If it's not there, go to Control Panel, choose Add/Remove Programs, find and click Microsoft Office, click the Change button, and follow the instructions to install the Northwind sample database.

3. **With the sample database open, press Alt+F11 to open the VB editor and then press Ctrl+R to see Project Explorer.**

4. **Open the Access class objects node in Project Explorer (click the +) and then double-click Form Employees to open its code window.**

Each object has its own private code window. Notice that the Programming Police have been busy in this code window. They've already turned off two options that they don't believe should be options:

```
Option Compare Database
Option Explicit
```

Hold everything. Why did the Programming Police turn off these options? Take a look at the next section for the answer, and then I'll resume this step list.

Understanding Option Explicit and Option Strict

`Option Compare Database` means that when strings are compared, the comparison is based on the *locale* (the language used by the culture) of the database itself. For more details on this dubious feature, see Book V, Chapter 1.

When `Option Explicit` is included in code, you cannot use implicit variables. You must declare every variable name formally (by using `Dim`, `Public`, or one of the other declaration/scoping/lifetime commands). In VBA and VB6, you are not required to explicitly declare variables. You can simply assign a value to a variable, which causes the variable to come into existence, like this:

```
MyVariablesName = 12
```

Also, you are permitted to forget about variable types and let VB decide for you which type was required at any given place in the code, based on the context. This is a *variant variable*. For example, if `MyVariablesName` contains numeric 12 yet you want to display this number in a text box, VB automatically transforms this numeric `Integer` data type into a text `String` type:

```
Text1 = MyVariablesName
```

This line causes `Text1` to display the digit characters 12. However, many programmers and professors of computer "science" (as they prefer to call it — some of them are quite certain that their style of programming should be *Zee Only Style of Programming!*) insist that all variables must be explicitly declared. It's not enough to simply assign some value to a variable; you should declare it and declare its type as well:

```
Dim MyVariablesName As Integer
MyVariablesName = 12
```

Not only that, if you want to transform (*cast*, or *coerce*) a variable of one type into another type — such as changing an `Integer` type into a `String` type — you must specifically do that transforming in your source code:

```
TextBox1.Text = CStr(MyVariablesName)
```

The `CStr` command is one of several commands that begin with `C` (`CInt`, `CByte`, and so on) that cast one variable type into another. In VB.NET, if you attempt to use a variable before explicitly declaring it, VB.NET informs you that you've made an error — that the variable name has not been declared. If you want to turn off this error message and use undeclared variables, type this line at the very top, on the first line, in your code window:

```
Option Explicit Off
```

However, you can avoid some kinds of bugs by explicitly declaring all your variables, and it doesn't take too much extra time to declare them.

Although VB.NET enforces `Option Explicit` by default, it does not enforce `Option Strict` by default. `Option Strict` governs whether an error message will be generated if you don't cast variables. You can use this line of code even though the text box displays a string and `MyVariablesName` was declared as an `Integer` variable type:

```
TextBox1.Text = MyVariablesName
```

This is perfectly legal in VB.NET. No error message will be displayed when you execute this code. However, some programmers insist that casting is important. If you are one of those, you can enforce casting by typing this line at the top of your code window:

```
Option Strict On
```

Now, try to execute the following line:

```
TextBox1.Text = MyVariablesName
```

The VB.NET compiler does not like that line and displays the following error message:

```
Option strict disallows implicit conversions from
System.Integer to System.String.
```

`Option Strict`, in spite of its charming name, does permit VB.NET to handle a few "safe" data type conversions itself. For instance, changing a 16-bit integer to a 32-bit integer cannot result in any loss of data, so it is permitted to take place automatically within VB.NET — there is no need for the programmer to explicitly do this conversion with special source code. The reverse, though (changing a 32-bit integer into a 16-bit version) is not permitted to take place automatically. You, the programmer, must use one of the data-conversion commands (see the "Searchable VBA/VB.NET Dictionary" in the online appendix. For more on this appendix, refer to this book's Introduction). Likewise, a floating-point data type (which might hold a value such as 12.335) is not permitted to automatically convert to an integer (which would strip off the .335 fractional portion of the number because integers have no decimal point). Is converting from an integer to a floating-point type permitted? Yes, because that is safe.

The point is that the Programming Police want `Option Explicit` to be embedded in every programming language — underneath, where you cannot choose to turn it off. They really don't want it to be an option at all. Like autocrats in any context, it's their way or the highway. Fortunately, some people enjoy the freedom of options, preferring to decide for themselves what's safe and what's an acceptable risk. That's why, in BASIC at least, these options still survive. But programming options — like any freedoms — are always under attack, and the newest version of BASIC (.NET) has now made explicit declaration the default.

Locating the Error event, part ll

After recovering from the shock of seeing someone else turning off some of your options by writing code for you in your code window, you can now locate the `Error` event. Let me restart my step list where I left off:

5. Open the list box in the top left of the code window.

6. In this list box, click Form.

7. In the other list box (top right of code window), locate and click Error.

You now see the event where you can insert programming to deal with Jet or other outside errors, as shown in Figure 5-1.

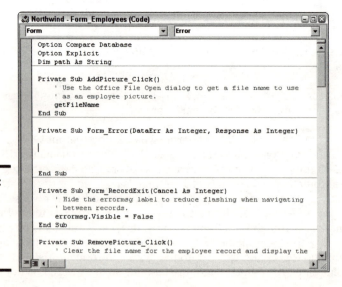

Figure 5-1: Add any database error handling here.

Recall that you cannot put VBA macro code error handling here. This event doesn't fire for those errors. Use `On Error` within your VBA code for that kind of problem.

Adding a custom error message

Most of the time, you employ the `Error` event shown in Figure 5-1 to keep your users calm. If they see the standard default Access error message, they might panic. You want to offer a gentler, kinder message — one that they can understand. Insert your custom error messages in this event, like in Listing 5-1:

Listing 5-1: Custom Error Message

```
Private Sub Form_Error(DataErr As Integer, Response As
        Integer)

 If DataErr = 2757 Then 'SQL Server error returned
        'don't display error message
        Response = acDataErrContinue

    Else 'deal with non-SQL Server errors here:

MsgBox "An error unrelated to SQL Server occurred. Please
        contact your IT professional."
    End If

End Sub
```

Unfortunately, SQL Server cannot return specific error codes to your `Form_Error` event. `DataErr 2757` includes all possible errors that could occur via SQL Server. Often, you want to handle errors in your programming rather than simply displaying an error message to your user and shutting down the application. To deal with SQL Server problems programmatically, you can add code like the following to get the error description returned from the SQL Server to a `Recordset` object. First create the object, like this:

```
Private WithEvents recSet As ADODB.Recordset

Private Sub Form_Open(Cancel As Integer)
    Set recSet = Me.Recordset
End Sub
```

Then use the `acDataErrContinue` command (illustrated in Listing 5-1) to cause an SQL Server error to be ignored by the `Error` event and handled instead within the `RecordChangeComplete` event, like Listing 5-2.

Listing 5-2: Dealing with SQL Server Errors

```
Private Sub recSet_RecordChangeComplete(ByVal adReason As
        ADODB.EventReasonEnum, ByVal cRecords As Long,
        ByVal pError As ADODB.Error, adStatus As
        ADODB.EventStatusEnum, ByVal pRecordset As
        ADODB.Recordset)

    If adStatus = adStatusErrorsOccurred Then

        s = pError.Description

        If InStr(s, "UPDATE statement conflicted with column
            check constraint") > 0 Then

            MsgBox ("You violated a check constraint.")

        ElseIf InStr(s, "Cannot insert the value NULL into
            column") > 0 Then

            MsgBox ("You cannot use a null value in this
            column.")

        Else
            MsgBox (s & " ... This error occurred in the SQL
            Server. Contact your administrator.")
        End If
    End If
End Sub
```

You can use `ElseIf` to trap as many error messages as you wish.

Sandbox Mode: Adjusting Macro Security

If you choose Medium or High macro security, you enter sandbox mode. This disables the usual problem commands (disk formatting and so on) of which virus writers are so fond. Authorization is used to see who can and cannot access these features. However, this mode protects you only from attacks originating in SQL statements or expressions in default values or control sources. VBA itself is not sandboxed.

Changing macro security levels should be easy, but it's not. In other Office applications, you can generally manage macro security easily. Just choose Tools⇨Macro⇨Security and adjust the settings. Alas, though Access Help says to do this, there's no Security option on the Macros menu at all. To get to the Security dialog box, you have to go through the following steps:

1. **Choose Tools⇨Customize.**

2. **In the Customize dialog box that opens, click the Commands tab.**

3. **Click the Rearrange Commands button.**

4. **In the Rearrange Commands dialog box that opens, select the Menu Bar option button.**

   From this drop-down list, choose Tools➪Macro.

5. **Click Add.**

6. **In the Add Command dialog box that opens, choose Tools from the Categories list.**

7. **Choose Security from the Commands list.**

   This list isn't in alphabetical order, but don't lose heart; Security is at the very bottom of the list.

8. **Click OK to close the dialog box.**

   The Security option appears in the Controls list for the Macros entry.

9. **Click both Close buttons.**

   The dialog boxes close, and the Security option — with sandboxing — is now available to you.

Backing Up for Safety

The single most important thing you can do to avoid virus and other data-loss problems is to frequently back up your work. Access 2003 has a new backup feature that you should become familiar with.

Choose Tools➪Database Utilities➪Back Up Database. The Save Backup As dialog box appears, like the one shown in Figure 5-2.

Figure 5-2:
Use this dialog box to save backups of your current database.

A new MBD file is specified, with a default filename incorporating the date in a strange year-first format, like this: `Northwind_2004-01-26.mdb`. I suppose the idea is that if you have huge numbers of otherwise identical backup filenames, it's most useful to sort them by year for display in Windows Explorer. The backup file is saved to the same path as the original MBD file.

Automatic Form and Report Error Checking

Access 2003 has an automatic form and report error-checking feature that does more than simply flag problems: It tries to offer ways to fix the problems.

Double-click the Products form in the Northwind sample database, choose Tools⇨Options, and click the Error Checking tab on the Options dialog box, as shown in Figure 5-3.

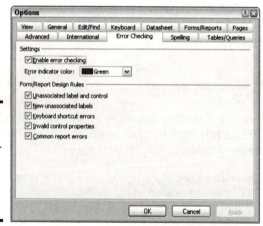

Figure 5-3:
Specify which error-checking features you want activated.

Error checking is turned on by default, as are all the design rules displayed in Figure 5-3. To see what happens if an error is on your form, click OK to close the Options dialog box. Then choose View⇨Design View so you can fiddle with the Products form.

Right-click the Product Name `TextBox` control on the form (*not* the label by the same name) and then choose Properties. The text box's properties dialog box appears, as shown in Figure 5-4. Click the Data tab and change the Control Source to a non-existent data source by typing in **x** (yup, one solitary x).

Close the dialog box and take a look at the form. A small, green triangle appears in the upper-left corner of the offending text box, and an exclamation point icon also appears, as shown in Figure 5-5.

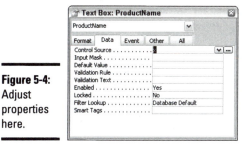

Figure 5-4:
Adjust properties here.

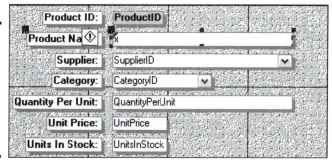

Figure 5-5:
The triangle and exclamation point icons signal an error in this form.

Click the exclamation point and notice that some very useful information is displayed, as shown in Figure 5-6.

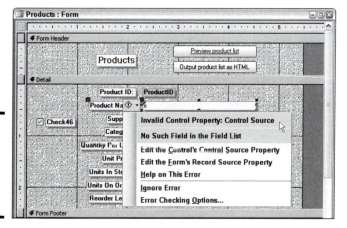

Figure 5-6:
Some error messages are quite useful, like these.

As Figure 5-6 illustrates, this error feature is quite helpful. You're not only told that the *control source* (the data field bound to this control) doesn't exist but also how to fix it: Edit the form's or the control's data source property. This is considerably more helpful than the usual computer language error message, although the new .NET languages do enjoy improved error messages and a continually improving Help system.

Specificity in error messages is a novel (and quite welcome) development. And information telling you exactly how to fix the problem is even more rare and more welcome. Too often, a single computer language error message is triggered by dozens of different causes. Also, error messages and Help entries are too often written by a raging propeller-head who knows the technical details brilliantly and cannot communicate his ideas to ordinary programmers to save his life. Here's an example of what I'm talking about, from an actual VB Help entry:

Changing the value of a field or property associated with any one instance does not affect the value of fields or properties of other instances of the class. On the other hand, when you change the value of a shared field and property associated with an instance of a class, you change the value associated with all instances of the class.

If you understand the previous paragraph, reach up and give the propeller on your beanie a spin for me.

Hint: The paragraph would be less confusing were the author, or editor, to make this change: ". . . a *shared* field or property . . ." Also, the words *associated* and *field* are used incorrectly here, but don't get me started. If The Powers That Be ever do manage to create comprehensible documentation, many of us computer book authors will be out of work. However, I take comfort in the fact that Japanese electronics manuals haven't improved much since the first transistor radios appeared in the 1950s, with their lively advice to *Replace the blue pull with the battery plastic, under the battery while shipped to you, before turning unit off. Or upward.*

Chapter 6: Access Macro Techniques

In This Chapter

✔ **Managing without a macro recorder**

✔ **Exploring the Object Browser**

✔ **Understanding** `DoCmd`

✔ **Using built-in functions**

✔ **Employing classic error trapping**

✔ **Adding keyboard shortcuts**

In this chapter, you see how macros work in Access. They're treated a bit differently from how other Office 2003 applications manage macros. You find out how to use the important `DoCmd` object, how to employ built-in functions, and how to trap errors. Access often goes its own way, using different dialog boxes and approaches than are found in other Office applications. Keyboard shortcuts are no exception; you see how they're created in Access.

Understanding the Languages of Access

Access's built-in programming languages (macro languages) have accreted over time, like barnacles on a ship. And unlike any other application known to man, Access currently includes three different built-in languages: BASIC, VBA, and VBScript, described as follows:

✦ **BASIC:** Access includes the ancient, limited, and essentially unsupported Access BASIC language, with its outdated — and relatively distinctive — point-and-click interface.

✦ **VBA:** VBA is actually a complete programming language, not merely a macro language. Although lacking inheritance and a few other object-oriented programming (OOP) features (that many programmers simply don't need or want anyway), VBA is a powerful, mature, and efficient language.

✦ **VBScript:** Finally, a subset of VBA's command set is found in the VBScript language, which is Microsoft's answer to JavaScript. VBScript is useful for Internet applications, where executables must be *lite* (not contain any commands that could do damage to a user's system) to pass through users' virus defenses. VBScript is a subset of VBA because it's missing certain potentially dangerous capabilities, such as hard drive access.

WordBasic

Truth be told, Word also had its aging WordBasic for a while, but remnants don't remain in Word 2003. Word 2003 automatically converts any WordBasic macros (which can be found embedded in Word 6 and Word 95 templates) to VBA. This happens if you create a new document based on one of these older templates, or simply open a template or attach it to a Word 2003 document. Macros in Word versions 97, 2000, or 2002 are already in VBA, not WordBasic, so no translation is necessary.

Creating Macros without a Recorder

Unlike Excel and Word, Access doesn't have a macro recorder, so you cannot use that helpful shortcut to generate sample programming that you can modify while creating your own macros.

Often, if you want to know the code to do a particular job (such as opening a file), the easiest way to get this code up and running is simply to record it, look at the code automatically generated, and adjust it as necessary. This approach can even be used with Access if you hit a brick wall. You could record something in Word, for example, and then see whether that code works in an Access macro. But this approach isn't that reliable because the Access object model has too many unique aspects.

One shortcut is to go back in time to the older Access macro creator and convert the result into VBA. To see how this works, follow these steps:

1. **Open the Northwind database in Access.**

2. **In the Objects list of the main database window, click Macros.**

3. **Click New on the window's icon bar.**

4. **In the Macro dialog box that opens, click the top line.**

5. **Open the list box from the top line.**

6. **Choose Quit from the list.**

Quit appears in the list of macro actions, along with a SaveAll option. You can click SaveAll to see another drop-down list of options. (Aargh. Why don't they just display the list instead of showing a drop-down arrow icon and making you click it? After all, if you clicked it, you want to see the list, right?)

7. **Choose Prompt as your option.**

8. **Close the Macro dialog box.**

A dialog box appears, asking whether you want to save changes.

9. **Click Yes.**

A Save As dialog box appears, allowing you to rename the macro.

10. **Rename it Quitting.**

11. **Click OK.**

The dialog box closes, and your macro is now officially a real macro. It appears in the list of macros in the main window.

12. **Click Quitting in the main database window.**

13. **Choose Tools⇨Macro⇨Convert Macro to Visual Basic.**

The Convert Macro: Quitting dialog box appears.

14. **Leave the default check boxes selected because you do want the error trapping and the comments so cunningly offered to you. (Who wouldn't?)**

15. **Click Convert.**

The Convert Macros to Visual Basic dialog box appears telling you that the conversion is finished.

16. **Click OK.**

This odd dialog box closes.

17. **Locate your new macro. Press Alt+11 to open the VBA editor and then press Ctrl+R to open Project Explorer.**

Its code window does not automatically open for you to view it.

18. **Under the Modules node in Project Explorer, double-click the Converted Macro-Quitting macro.**

The special module window devoted just to this particular macro opens, and you see Listing 6-1.

Listing 6-1: Converted Access Quitting Macro

```
'---------------------------------------------------------------
' Quitting
'
'---------------------------------------------------------------
Function Quitting()
On Error GoTo Quitting_Err

    DoCmd.Quit acPrompt


Quitting_Exit:
```

```
        Exit Function

Quitting_Err:
      MsgBox Error$
      Resume Quitting_Exit

End Function
```

Well, maybe you didn't need this commenting after all. It's not too useful, but the error trapping is good. And what's most useful is the translation that Access has — albeit, reluctantly, compared with the recording feature in other applications — now provided you. You know how to write code that quits with a prompt: DoCmd.Quit acPrompt.

I talk more about DoCmd and the error-trapping features shortly. However, I won't have anything to say about this line of code:

```
        Resume Quitting_Exit
```

I have no idea why this line of code exists. The End Function does the same thing without redirecting execution.

Using the Object Browser

To help you figure out the object model in Access, you can press Alt+F11 to get to the VBA code window; then press F2 to open the Object Browser, as shown in Figure 6-1.

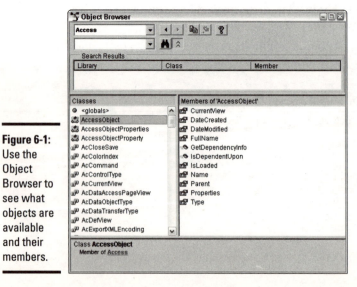

Figure 6-1:
Use the
Object
Browser to
see what
objects are
available
and their
members.

The object's members are symbolized by little icons next to their names. Properties are symbolized by a hand holding a VCR tape (collections add a small, cyan, floating ball to this icon), methods by a flying green eraser, enumerations by an equal sign, and events by a yellow lightning bolt.

Click a method in the Members pane, and you see the proper syntax for employing that method in the lowest pane of the browser. The method is called a *function* (the older name for *method*). For example, the `CompactRepair` method of the Access `Application` object looks like this:

```
Function CompactRepair(SourceFile As String, DestinationFile
    As String, [LogFile As Boolean = False]) As Boolean
```

This can be helpful, although the Access VBA editor includes IntelliSense features such as statement autocompletion and argument lists.

Using DoCmd

`DoCmd` is a class in the Access library. `DoCmd` contains many useful, commonly used methods such as `ShowToolbar`, `GoToPage`, `FindRecord`, `Maximize`, and so on. Indeed, by using the `DoCmd.RunCommand` method, you can trigger all the Access menu features programmatically, thus taking control over Access's behavior.

As you might expect, `DoCmd` has many methods. Press Alt+F11 to go to the Access VBA editor, and then press F2 to see the Object Browser. Click DoCmd in the Classes list in the Object Browser to see all the methods. The `RunCommand` method is especially full of variations and possibilities: It's your gateway to many Access behaviors. Although any custom menu and toolbar commands cannot be manipulated via `RunCommand`, all the built-in Access menus and toolbars are available. The menu and toolbar items are invoked by using a built-in constant starting with `ac`, such as `acCmdOptions`. For example, the following displays the Tools⇨Options dialog box:

```
Sub ShowOptions()

DoCmd.RunCommand acCmdOptions

End Sub
```

Notice that the argument for the `RunCommand`, `acCmdOptions` here, is oddly not enclosed in parentheses. Also, to see all the built-in constants (*enums,* as C programmers call them) that can be used with this method, choose Help in the VBA editor, choose Microsoft Visual Basic Reference in the Table of Contents, choose Enumerations, and then click the <u>Microsoft Access Constants</u> hyperlink. (Simply searching for *Microsoft Access Constants* won't do it — that would be too easy.) In the list of enums, click AcCommand, as shown in Figure 6-2, to see all the constants that you can employ with the `RunCommand` method.

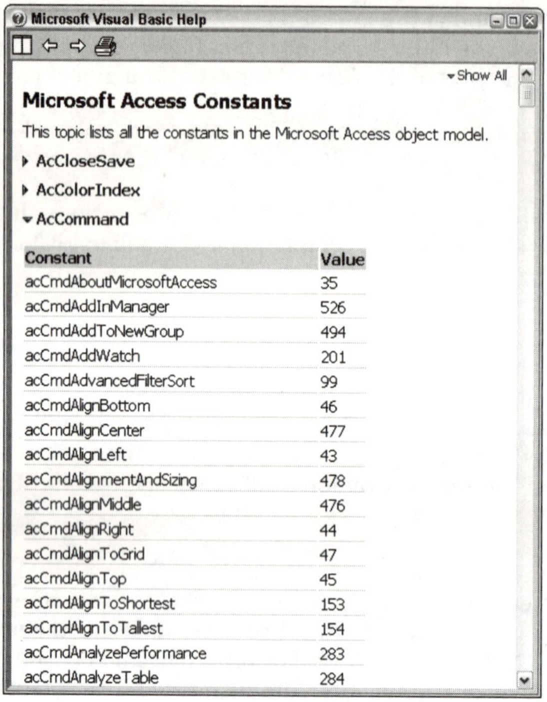

Figure 6-2:
Here are the
constants
that you can
use to
trigger
Access
menu items.

Microsoft Visual Basic Help
▼ Show All
Microsoft Access Constants
This topic lists all the constants in the Microsoft Access object model.
▸ AcCloseSave
▸ AcColorIndex
▾ AcCommand

Constant	Value
acCmdAboutMicrosoftAccess	35
acCmdAddInManager	526
acCmdAddToNewGroup	494
acCmdAddWatch	201
acCmdAdvancedFilterSort	99
acCmdAlignBottom	46
acCmdAlignCenter	477
acCmdAlignLeft	43
acCmdAlignmentAndSizing	478
acCmdAlignMiddle	476
acCmdAlignRight	44
acCmdAlignToGrid	47
acCmdAlignTop	45
acCmdAlignToShortest	153
acCmdAlignToTallest	154
acCmdAnalyzePerformance	283
acCmdAnalyzeTable	284

Seeing Built-in VBA Language Features

The Object Browser can provide you with a shortcut view — quicker than Help — of the commands that you can use to manage your macros. In the upper-left corner of the Object Browser, open the list and choose VBA. You see a list in the left pane showing all the various groups of functions, categorized by purpose such as FileSystem, Math, and so on. Click Strings, and you see all the classic Visual Basic functions. Click InStr, for example, and you can see the syntax, like this:

```
Function InStr([Start], [String1], [String2], [Compare As
    VbCompareMethod = vbBinaryCompare])
```

Using Classic Error Trapping

The On Error command helps you to avoid user panic. It also allows you to gracefully deal with the unexpected. In this example, what if the user has deleted a form that you expected to be left in the database?

```
Sub OpenForm()

DoCmd.OpenForm FormName:="Suppliers"

End Sub
```

This works fine in the Northwind database (opening the Suppliers form) unless that form doesn't exist or has been renamed. To deal with these possibilities, use this error structure:

```
Sub OpenForm()
On Error GoTo handler
Dim fn, s As String

 fn = "xx"

DoCmd.OpenForm FormName:=fn

Exit Sub
handler:

If Err = 2102 Then 'handle wrong form name:
s = InputBox("There is no form by the name of " & fn & ".
        Please enter the name of a form in this database.")

DoCmd.OpenForm FormName:=s

End If

End Sub
```

The *handler* is a labeled location to which execution is transferred if an error occurs. (Otherwise, the Exit Sub executes following a successful form opening.) If an error exists, the code following handler executes. Some (not all) error codes can be found by searching Help for Trappable Errors. Others can be discovered by inserting this line into your code and then deliberately triggering an error (such as supplying a bad filename or form name, as in the previous example):

```
MsgBox Err
```

Using Keyboard Shortcuts

The usual Microsoft keyboard redefinition feature accessible via the Keyboard button of the Customize dialog box (Tools⇨Customize) is available in Excel and Word, from which you can easily assign and reassign keyboard shortcuts. Access (sigh) lacks this feature. Instead, you have to assign keyboard shortcuts to macros somewhat less directly in Access. To assign a keyboard shortcut to a macro in Access, follow these steps:

1. **Open the Northwind database.**

2. **In the Objects list of the main database window, click Macros.**

3. **Click New on the window's icon bar.**

   The Macro dialog box opens, and a Macro Design toolbar appears.

4. **Click the Macro Names icon on the Macro Design toolbar, as shown in Figure 6-3.**

Figure 6-3:
Create
keyboard
shortcuts in
Access.

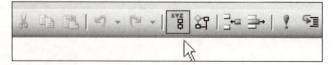

The Macro dialog box divides into three zones: Macro Name, Action, and Comment.

5. **In the Macro Name column, type the key combination that you want to use to execute your macro.**

   The syntax for key combinations involves braces:

Enter This	To Get This
^A	Ctrl+A
{F1}	F1
^{F1}	Ctrl+F1
+{F1}	Shift+F1
{INSERT}	Insert
{DEL}	Delete

6. **Click the Action column.**

7. **From the Action column list, choose RunMacro.**

   The Action Arguments changes to include a Macro Name field.

8. **Click the Macro Name field in the Action Arguments section of the dialog box.**

   Another drop-down list appears, containing all the macros in the current database.

9. **Click the name of the macro you want to assign this keyboard shortcut to.**

10. **Close the macro window. In the Save As dialog box that appears, name it AutoKeys.**

Book VI

Exploiting Outlook

The 5th Wave   By Rich Tennant

Contents at a Glance

Chapter 1: Outlook Power Tools

In This Chapter

✔ **Discovering the new reading pane**

✔ **Fixing a filter**

✔ **Blocking spam**

✔ **Using encryption**

✔ **Flagging e-mail**

✔ **Using special folders**

✔ **Seeing double Calendars**

*O*utlook 2003 is considerably changed from previous versions. This chapter covers the changes of most interest to developers, including the new reading pane, how to find "missing" e-mail, and the new spam-blocking feature. Also of interest are the double Calendars, how folders are employed, using flags to categorize e-mail, and how to manage encryption.

Using Outlook's New Reading Pane

Probably the first thing that you notice in Outlook 2003 is the reading pane on the right side. Many people find it easier to open their e-mail this way, although you can still use the older Mail view. To avoid opening multiple windows (one for each e-mail you double-click) or reduce the amount of scrolling, this pane might be the way for you to go. Figure 1-1 illustrates how efficient the reading pane can be.

Defaulting to Outlook

To make Outlook your default e-mail, Contacts, and Calendar application, choose Tools⇨ Options⇨Other. (See the Options dialog box here.) Under the General section, select the Make Outlook the Default Program blah blah check box, click OK, and you're good to go.

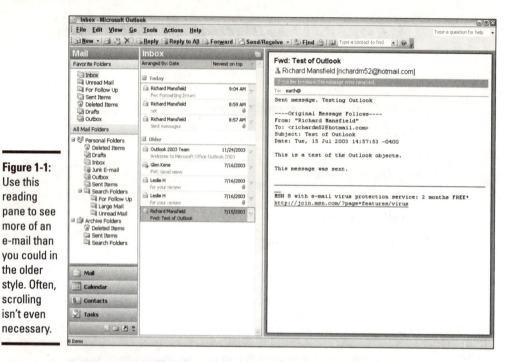

Figure 1-1:
Use this reading pane to see more of an e-mail than you could in the older style. Often, scrolling isn't even necessary.

Adjusting the Nasty Read Filter

Newcomers to Outlook 2003 are sometimes startled to find that as soon as they read an Inbox e-mail message, then do something else, or close Outlook, that particular message disappears! It cannot be found in Inbox or indeed in any of the mail folders. In fact, another frightening moment occurs when you realize that there are various categories of folders — personal, favorites, searches, archives — that aren't individual folders but rather *groups* of folders. And when you look in the three Deleted Items folders (yes, there are three of these, although they're different listings for the same folder) or look in the two For Follow Up folders, you won't find your e-mail anywhere. (This behavior is quite different from how Outlook Express works. It leaves all your Inbox e-mail alone unless you specifically delete it or move it.)

The problem is that a default filter is applied to the Inbox folder that automatically hides e-mail that you've read (or even just glanced at). You might find this a convenience, but if you don't (and I certainly don't), follow these steps to make Outlook straighten up and fly right: that is, unhide already read Inbox e-mail.

1. **Select the Inbox (in the Mail column).**

2. **Choose View⇨Arrange By⇨Custom.**

3. **In the Customize View dialog box, click the Filter button.**

4. **In the Filter dialog box, click the More Choices tab.**

At long last (sheesh), you see the culprit, displayed in Figure 1-2.

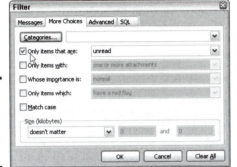

Figure 1-2:
Clear this
default filter
to see your
Inbox mail.

The check box next to Only Items That Are is selected by default, and
the filter is unread. This has the effect of showing you only those e-mails
that you've never seen before; all the other e-mails are not displayed.

5. **Clear this check box to restore all your e-mail in the Inbox.**

Why this is the default, and why you must maneuver through so many
twisted paths down into submenus and dialog boxes to finally rectify
this default behavior . . . well, it's beyond me.

Outlook 2003 is in many ways a marvel of efficiency and ergonomics. In this
case, though, it seems both wrong-headed and poorly designed.

Managing Multiple Accounts

If you're savvy about e-mail, you likely have a very private e-mail address
known only to a few friends and business associates, whom you ask to *please
never give out this e-mail address to anyone*. Then you create a public e-mail
address (the one you provide when you buy things online, enter contests, or
otherwise risk having the address published or sold, thereby attracting the
usual hailstorm of spam).

Online services such as Hotmail (www.hotmail.com) are useful for setting
up a public e-mail account. But then you have to look for your e-mail in two
locations: your private e-mail program (such as Outlook) and your public
address (your browser where you log on to Hotmail or another Web-based
e-mail service.) No more. Now you can add public accounts like Hotmail to
Outlook so you can see all your e-mail in one application. Outlook will automatically suck all your public account e-mail into a special Inbox.

To add a Hotmail e-mail account to Outlook, follow these steps:

1. **Choose Tools⇨E-mail Accounts.**

   The E-mail Accounts wizard opens.

2. **Select the Add a New E-mail Account radio button.**

3. **Click Next.**

   You see a list of server options.

4. **Click the HTTP option button.**

5. **Click Next.**

   You see the wizard's settings page.

6. **Type in your online name, your Hotmail e-mail address (which is also used as your User Name), and then type in your Hotmail password.**

7. **Click Next and then click Finish.**

   After a little background work, Outlook adds a new folder category named Hotmail to your All Mail Folders pane, as shown in Figure 1-3.

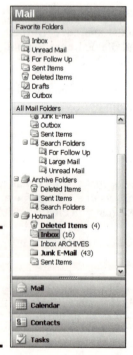

Figure 1-3:
Adding a
Hotmail
account to
Outlook is
easy and
convenient.

Strangely, the Deleted Items folder appears at the top of the Hotmail category (and other folders as well). I would prefer to have the Inbox located at the top. After all, Inbox is by far the most often used of the categories of mail, and the deleted mail folder is probably least used. And although you cannot drag these folders to reposition them (arrrg; perhaps in the next version of Outlook), you can rearrange the Favorite Folders.

To complete rerouting Hotmail to Outlook, follow the steps in Book VI, Chapter 4.

Blocking Spam and Virii

A relatively sophisticated spam-blocking system has replaced the old rules-based, anti-spam scheme that Outlook used to rely on (and that Outlook Express still does). Various telltale cues — you know, the ubiquitous You've Won! e-mail sent at 4 a.m. — are used to divide the good e-mail from the junk. However, these filters aren't perfect by a long shot, so you'll still get spam — and virus-writers are even more clever than spammers.

Outlook 2003 offers several layers of protection. You can modify the file types (executables like BAT, EXE, and so on) that are automatically blocked. You can also force HTML messages to display as text. The new Junk E-mail Filter can be modified by following these steps:

1. **Choose Tools⇨Options.**

2. **In the Options dialog box that opens, click the Junk E-mail button.**

   The Junk E-mail Options dialog box opens, as shown in Figure 1-4.

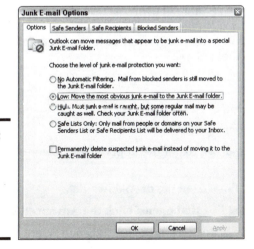

Figure 1-4:
Specify
here how
you want
Outlook
junk mail
handled.

By default, the level of blocking is set to Low, which probably makes sense for most people. It blocks obvious junk but does let some through. An alternative setting, High, seems rather pointless because it blocks so much that some authentic messages get blocked along with the junk. So, you have to read through the Junk E-mail folder to find which real messages got blocked by mistake. Given that this is what you have to do with no filtering selected, what's the point of even trying to redirect some e-mail? You have to check it, anyway.

Also, you can specify that particular senders should always be blocked from the settings available on the Blocked Senders tab (of the Junk E-mail Options dialog box; refer to Figure 1-4). However, this isn't much use unless you have a stalker sending you messages. Spammers constantly change their addresses, and virii writers often use your friends' address books to harvest your address, sending trouble your way by attaching a virus to e-mail that appears to come from this friend. You'll find more on Outlook security measures in Chapter 4 of this mini-book.

You can update the Junk E-mail Filter detector software as Microsoft continues to improve it. Go to this address:

```
http://www.microsoft.com/downloads/details.aspx?FamilyID=a
d3699f7-5cc3-4604-a768-32c4d044b630&displaylang=en
```

Using Encryption

Avoiding virii is only half of the e-mail security battle. The other half is protecting your privacy, including such things as confidential business details or even certain kinds of monkey business. Encryption provides protection against prying eyes, and digital signing authenticates that the person who appears to have sent the e-mail actually did. Signing can also ensure that a communication hasn't been tampered with.

To see the level of encryption currently in effect for your company's Office 2003 installation, follow these steps:

1. **Run Word.**

2. **Choose File⇨Save As.**

   The Save As dialog box opens.

3. **Click the Tools drop-down list in the upper-right corner of the Save As dialog box.**

4. **Choose Security Options from the drop-down list.**

5. **In the Security dialog box that opens, click the Advanced button.**

   The Encryption Type dialog box opens, as shown in Figure 1-5.

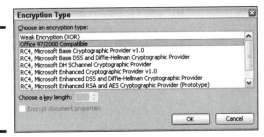

Figure 1-5:
Specify
more
advanced
encryption
from here.

As you can see in Figure 1-5, unless you've changed it, the default encryption scheme employed by your company is Office 97/2000 Compatible. Although not as laughably simple-minded as the XOR encryption system, the older Office version of encryption was not a massively complex problem to solve.

It took me about four hours to crack it and to write a utility that decodes any documents encrypted using the older versions of Word. I don't need to know the password; I just run my utility, and the document decrypts.

So, unless you absolutely require backward compatibility with earlier versions of Office applications, I suggest that you select one of the DSS (symmetrical encryption) options in the dialog box shown in Figure 1-5. DSS is quicker than RSA (public key), but RSA is stronger. Unless you have relatively small documents, you might find RSA too slow. And DSS is plenty powerful. These encryption systems are explored in depth in Book VIII, Chapter 8.

You can also specify various key (password) lengths. Most modern encryption schemes permit several key lengths: the longer the key, the greater the protection. Note, too, that the encryption schemes in the Encryption Type dialog box are listed roughly in order of security. DSS should be good enough for you; after all, it's good enough for banks.

Logged on at Administrator level access, you can modify your users' registries to beef up the security level for each machine. Employ a configuration maintenance file, a transform, an OPS file (Office profile settings), or distribute a Reg file (having used File⇨Export in Regedit).

To encrypt an individual e-mail message, follow these steps:

1. **While viewing the message, click the Options button on the toolbar.**

2. **In the Message Options dialog box that opens, click the Security Settings button.**

   The Securities Property dialog box opens.

3. **Select the Encrypt Message Contents and Attachments check box.**

4. **Click OK.**

If you don't already have a digital ID (used for both digital signatures and encryption), you'll have to choose Tools⇨Options, click the Security tab, and click the Get a Digital ID button. You'll be shown a Web site at Microsoft with some third-party companies offering digital signing. This same Options dialog box allows you to select the Encrypt Contents and Attachments for Outgoing Messages check box. This option automatically encrypts all messages that you send.

Flagging E-mail

The new Quick Flag feature allows you to rapidly categorize e-mail for later handling. With one click next to an e-mail message, a red flag replaces the pale gray flag, and the message is also automatically put into the For Follow Up folder. Click the red flag, and it turns into a check mark, meaning that the follow-up is finished and the message has been dealt with.

Right-click the flag, and a list of various additional flags appears, as shown in Figure 1-6.

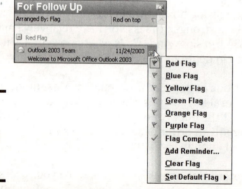

Figure 1-6: Easily tag your e-mail with these flags.

All these different colored flags have no built-in meaning (other than the red one and the check icon); Microsoft hasn't labeled them. You decide what a green or purple flag means. (I assume that purple represents royalty, so use it for messages you get from the queen.) Also, others who send e-mail to you can flag it; if their sense of its importance or category differs from yours, you can easily reflag the message.

Messages flagged by senders are displayed at the top of the Unflagged Group if you choose to arrange your messages by flag, as shown in Figure 1-7.

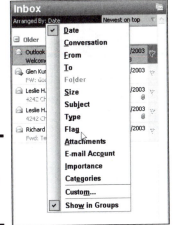

Figure 1-7:
Arrange
your e-mail
with these
options.

The Add Reminder option (refer to Figure 1-6) allows you to specify a date
and time to be reminded about this message.

Using Special Folders

Messages that don't belong in the built-in folders — Notes, Large Mail, and
For Follow Up — can be put into new folders that you create and name. For
example, right-click Personal Folders in the All Mail Folders list and then
choose New Folder. The Create New Folder dialog box appears, as shown in
Figure 1-8. Here, name the new folder, define what you want it to contain, and
give it a home; click OK.

Search folders are a special category of Personal Folders: For one thing, two
or more of these folders can contain the same message. Microsoft calls them
virtual folders, which should cue you that they're not quite as real as the
other, more traditional, folders. You can group and view messages in these
search folders without having to actually copy or move them there. The For
Follow Up, Unread Mail, and Large Mail folders are provided as the set of
default search folders, but you can add new ones.

Large Mail is where e-mail with big attachments or huge messages are displayed.

The trick involved with search folders is that messages are automatically
included in these folders based on specified criteria. For example, when you
click the red flag on a message, it is automatically then available in the For
Follow Up folder although it also remains in the Inbox or whatever other
folder you placed it.

Figure 1-8:
Create
custom
folders here.

To create a custom search folder, follow these steps:

1. **Right-click Search Folders in the navigation pane (the pane on the left in Figure 1-8).**

2. **From the context menu that opens, choose New Search Folder.**

3. **In the New Search Folder dialog box that opens, scroll down to Organizing Mail and then click Mail with Specific Words.**

4. **Near Show Messages That Contain These Words, click Choose.**

5. **Type** Richard **(or whatever other key term you want to use).**

6. **Click Add.**

7. **Click OK.**

   The new folder, named Containing Richard, appears under the Search Folders group. When you click this new folder, you see a list of all messages containing your keyword. Remember, this is a *virtual folder* — that is, a view of select e-mail — so the actual, real e-mails still reside within whatever folders they are really contained, such as Inbox.

In Step 3 of the preceding step list, if you choose Create a Custom Search Folder rather than Mail with Specific Words, click Choose, and then click Criteria, Advanced, and Field, you can go hog-wild in the Search Folder Criteria dialog box, specifying nearly any kind of criteria you can imagine, as shown in Figure 1-9.

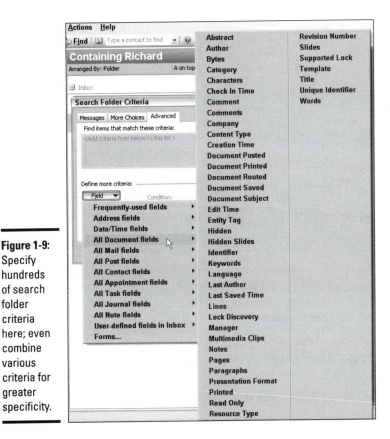

Figure 1-9: Specify hundreds of search folder criteria here; even combine various criteria for greater specificity.

Using Twin Calendars

Also new in Outlook 2003, you can now view two or more Calendars side-by-side, as shown in Figure 1-10. Comparing your schedule to a co-worker's calendar can be quite useful for setting up meetings and otherwise coordinating joint projects. Likewise, you might want to compare your personal and business calendars, or this year's calendar with last year's.

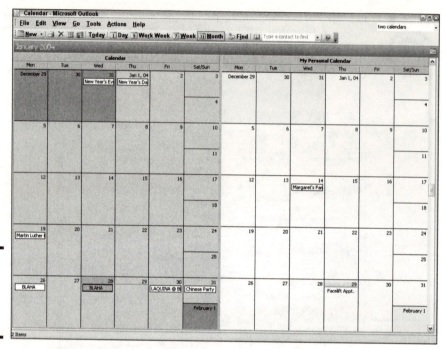

Figure 1-10:
Open more
than one
Calendar
at once.

To create a new Calendar, follow these steps:

1. **Choose Go⇨Folder List.**

The Folder List appears.

2. **Right-click the Calendar folder (*not* the colored, shaded Calendar bar button).**

3. **Choose New Folder from the context menu that appears.**

The Create New Folder dialog box appears.

4. **In the Name box, type whatever name you want to give to your new Calendar.**

5. **Click OK.**

The dialog box closes, and your new Calendar is added to your list of calendars.

Chapter 2: Programming Outlook

In This Chapter

✔ **Understanding the Outlook object model**

✔ **Discovering namespaces**

✔ **Using MAPI objects**

✔ **Using practical VBA**

✔ **Handling events**

*I*n this chapter, you see how to take control of Outlook, programming it to do your bidding. You see how the object model works and how to deal with the special Windows Messaging API (MAPI) objects. And, of course, you want to know how to trap events and respond to them programmatically. As always, I try to provide examples that are simultaneously illustrative and potentially useful in your efforts to improve Office efficiency and increase productivity.

Discovering the Outlook Object Model

The Outlook object model is similar to the other Office 2003 application's class hierarchies, but there are some differences. For one thing, in the other major Office applications, you can open multiple documents, workbooks, tables, and other objects. In Outlook, there's only one primary "document" — the current contents of your Calendar, Contacts, Inbox, and so on. In other words, there aren't alternative repositories of data that you can save from or load into Outlook the way you can open several documents in Word. For this reason, Outlook's library of objects contains no methods to save or load files and otherwise manipulate multiple primary documents.

Outlook also employs special objects named `explorer` and `inspector`. The former stands for each pane (zone onscreen) in which a folder's contents are displayed. The `inspector` is a pane in which a lone object is displayed. For example, the window displaying a list of all your Inbox folder's mail is an `explorer`. Double-click an e-mail listed in that `explorer`, and that individual e-mail is then displayed in an `inspector` pane or window. To see the Outlook object model, follow these steps:

1. **Press Alt+F11 to open the Outlook VBA editor.**

2. **Choose Insert➪Module in the VBA editor.**

   A new module window opens.

3. **Choose Help➪Microsoft Visual Basic Help.**

   The Help window opens.

4. **Click the book icon next to Microsoft Outlook Visual Basic Reference in the Help window.**

   A list of subcategories is displayed.

5. **Click Microsoft Outlook Object Model.**

   You see the diagram shown in Figure 2-1.

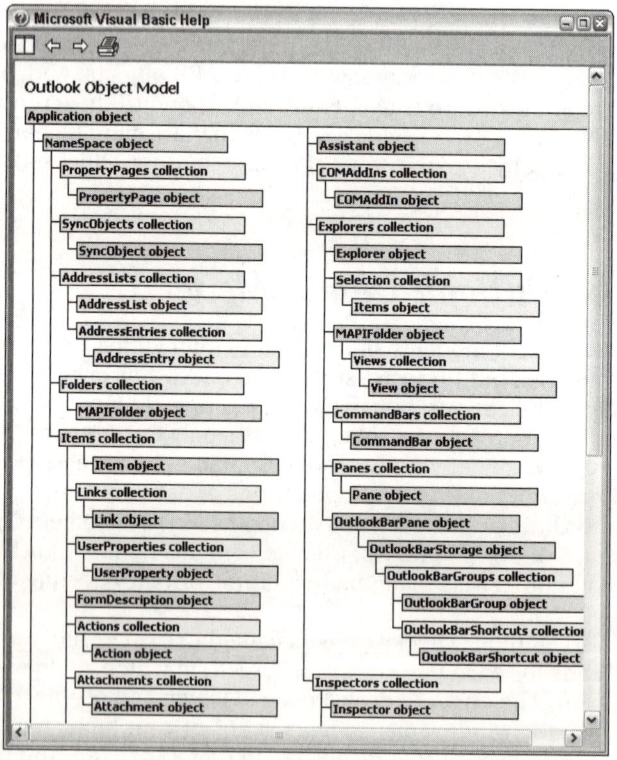

Figure 2-1: Here's the Outlook object model in all its splendor.

Using the Outlook Object Model

Try using the Outlook object model. Follow along to see how to automate sending an e-mail with an attachment from Outlook. Type Listing 2-1 into the module created in the preceding section:

Listing 2-1:   Automating Sending an Outlook E-Mail with an Attachment

```
Sub SendEmail()

'create the object variables
Dim o As Outlook.Application
Dim oMail As Outlook.MailItem

    'Instantiate the new objects:
        Set o = New Outlook.Application
        Set oMail = o.CreateItem(olMailItem)

    'Fill in fields and mail the message:
With oMail

.Importance = olImportanceHigh
.To = "richardm52@hotmail.com"
.Body = "Get this new message."
.Subject = "For YOU a new Message about our next Meeting!"
.Attachments.Add "c:\test.txt"
.Display
.Send

End With

'kill the objects
Set o = Nothing
Set oMail = Nothing

End Sub
```

This code creates a new e-mail message, specifies the target address, the message (Body in the object model), types in the subject line, sets the importance flag to High, attaches a file, and then displays and sends the e-mail.

Outlook's VBA has IntelliSense, so while you're typing lines of code, you'll usually see a list of options when you type a period (.) to signify a new element in a chain of objects or a left parenthesis to signify that you're beginning an argument list.

Regrettably, the usual classification problems and inconsistencies associated with object models plague Outlook VBA. Whereas you can access a Mail object via the Outlook Application object (as illustrated in the previous example), you cannot use the same technique to access a folder object. Instead, you must use a namespace object.

Namespaces are a relatively new category: They first appeared in BASIC with .NET. They're intended to prevent one of the less-charming aspects of object-oriented programming (OOP): name collision. In other words, you often program with more than a single code library at the same time — for example, a library of math functions and also a library of string functions. What happens, though, if both libraries include a function named Add? How is the compiler to know which of the two functions you intend to use? That's where namespaces come in.

Why namespaces?

Why are they using namespaces? It's a clerical thing, as is so often the case with OOP. Namespaces can help prevent name collisions, although not always. They're enigmas, really, but you have to deal with them just as maritime navigators must deal with sand bars. They're here and there, they're sometimes in the way, they shift around unpredictably from one Application Programmers Interface (API) to another — but can hang you up if you ignore them.

Import or qualify

In .NET, you can add Imports *namespaceName* statements at the top of the code window. Alternatively, you can qualify a function name each time it appears within the source code, like this: namespaceName. FunctionName. In effect, you're telling the compiler: "Use the function in *this* namespace — not the other one if there's one with the same name in some other namespace."

Confusingly, new terminology is constantly being introduced, often for no good reason. The latest term for code library (or Dynamic Link Library, DLL) is *assembly*. An assembly is a file containing a group of related functions, such as the Microsoft Office Web Components Function Library. Assemblies, when being added to a project, are called *references*. Now, one more point. Don't be upset, but I have to tell you that there can even be *multiple namespaces* within a single assembly — a single code library, a single DLL. So, you must think of namespaces as virtual libraries of functions because a namespace can refer to an entire physical library like a DLL, or it can refer merely to a subset of functions in a library containing several namespaces.

Sometimes, you might find that you need to actually add a library of code to a VB project. In other words, a function or functions that you want to use aren't part of the default set of libraries available to VBA or VB.NET. VBA and VB.NET both include a huge set of functions, so to write some programs, you don't need to import additional libraries. In other cases, though, you must specifically choose Project⇨Add Reference in VB.NET — or in VBA, choose Tools⇨References, as shown in Figure 2-2.

Figure 2-2:
These checked code libraries are available by default in Outlook's version of VBA. Just select new libraries to add them.

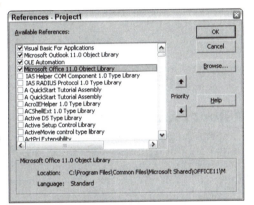

To see which code libraries are added by default in VB.NET, right-click the name of your project in Solution Explorer (it's the boldface line), choose Properties, and then select Imports in the Properties dialog box.

What happens, you might say, if you use the `Imports` command to specify two namespaces that have a pair of identically named objects? Now you *will* have a name collision — no doubt about it. `Imports` doesn't help you distinguish between these objects because you've used `Imports` for both namespaces. The classification system has a kink or two, as you can see.

You can also create your own namespaces when programming. For example, assume that you write code for a custom cursor class and put this class into a namespace called `NewCursors` within your library `MyObjects`. Then you reference it with the `Imports` command:

```
Imports MyObjects.NewCursors
```

And at the same time, you need to also reference the standard Windows objects namespace (which includes controls such as the `TextBox`, as well as other items such as default cursors):

```
Imports System.Windows.Forms
```

You don't need to actually use `Imports System.Windows.Forms`; it's already imported as one of the default libraries in VB.NET. I'm just showing you an example here.

Now you have two namespaces in your project, each containing a (different) `cursor` class. The only way you can distinguish them is to forget about the `Imports` trick and just use the long form (fully qualify the object) whenever you use the `Cursor` object. Here's how you specify that you intend to use the cursor in the `System.Windows.Forms` namespace:

```
Dim n As New System.Windows.Forms.Cursor("nac.ico")
```

Or, to use your personal custom cursor, fully qualify it like this:

```
Dim n As New MyObjects.NewCursors.Cursor("nac.ico")
```

Practical advice about namespaces

For VBA programmers: You can pretty much ignore namespaces because they're very rarely used in VBA. But do be aware of the concept of assemblies and namespaces because they're coming down the river toward you from the future. Eventually, .NET will replace the VBA languages built into Office applications, so it doesn't hurt to get used to these classification systems. True, they might be half-baked, not completely thought-through, and too often inconsistent and clumsy — but you just have to live with things like this as programming evolves through its current airy, academic phase into something more practical (I hope). After all, this isn't the first time that programming has suffered from the introduction of ill-conceived new ideas that upon later reflection had to be yanked from the languages because they caused so much trouble. Two examples of now-disgraced — although once-highly touted — concepts are dynamic link libraries (which resulted in the phrase *DLL Hell*) and the `Variant` variable type (which still exists in VBA but has been banished from VB.NET).

For .NET programmers: Don't worry about adding extra `Imports` statements that you actually use in your program: Namespaces neither increase the size of your executable (EXE) program nor slow execution. VB.NET is a huge language. It includes more than 60 .NET assemblies (code libraries), containing the hundreds of .NET namespaces. Each namespace contains many classes. In turn, these classes have multiple members (methods you can employ; properties you can read or change). Also, many of the methods are overloaded: They often permit you to provide a variety of arguments to make them behave in different ways. As you can see, hundreds of thousands of commands and variations of those commands are in this language.

What to do if you're a VB.NET programmer? You'll master the important tools fairly quickly — file input/output (I/O), printing, useful constants, interacting with the user, debugging, and so on. Most of these major programming techniques are different in .NET from their VBA counterparts but are not unrecognizably different. Also, you can use VB.NET Help's Search and Index features as well as the Object Browser when needed. To see the format, syntax, punctuation, and (sometimes) code examples of the many classes, try this approach. Run the Help Index and then type the following into the Look For field. (Cutting and pasting doesn't work; you must type this in.)

```
system.drawing.
```

You then see the massive number of classes listed in the left pane. Click any of these classes to see its members and other information about how to use it. Each page contains hyperlinks that take you to more specific information about particular members.

The more practice you get using VB.NET, the more you'll learn about which namespaces you need to import. The most common namespaces are automatically imported by VB.NET when you create a new project. These seven are imported by default: `Microsoft.VisualBasic` (a compatibility namespace, permitting you to use most VB6 and VBA constants and functions, such as `InStr` rather than the new .NET equivalent, `IndexOf`, `System`, `System.Collections`, `System.Data`, `System.Diagnostics`, `System.Drawing`, and `System.Windows.Forms`.

Using the MAPI Namespace

To manage folder objects in Outlook, you must refer to the Windows Messaging API (MAPI) namespace. This is the only namespace within the Outlook application object, but for some reason, when working with folders, you cannot simply use the `Application` object by itself as you do with most other Outlook objects. Perhaps more namespaces will be added later. (Search folders, though, are not included in the MAPI namespace, so you have to use different techniques with them.) MAPI itself puts you in touch with stored mail messages, among other things.

The following example illustrates how to use the `MAPI` object (yes, namespaces, like nearly everything else, are objects) to switch to the Tasks view in Outlook:

```
Sub SwitchToTasks()

    Dim o As Outlook.Application
    Dim n As Outlook.NameSpace
```

```
      Set o = CreateObject("Outlook.Application")
      Set n = o.GetNamespace("MAPI")

      Set o.ActiveExplorer.CurrentFolder =
    n.GetDefaultFolder(olFolderTasks)
End Sub
```

The first four lines of this code merely get you the *handle* (the address of) to the MAPI namespace inside the `Application` object. You can then employ the `GetDefaultFolder` method of the MAPI namespace to change the `CurrentFolder` property. The other possible arguments for the `GetDefault Folder` method are `olFolderCalendar`, `olFolderContacts`, `olFolder DeletedItems`, `olFolderDrafts`, `olFolderInbox`, `olFolderJournal`, `olFolderNotes`, `olFolderOutbox`, `olFolderSentMail`, `olFolderTasks`, `olPublicFoldersAllPublicFolders`, and `olFolderJunk`.

The `Explorer` object contains the contents of the currently viewed folder. In other words, when you look at your Inbox or view a list of Tasks, you're looking at an `Explorer`. There's also an `Inspector` object that displays more specific data, such as a single e-mail when you double-click in an Explorer view of your e-mail. These terms have no particular use nor pattern across different applications, so the only reason to pay any attention to them is that they're your passport to accessing this particular object model's behaviors and elements.

Using Practical VBA in Outlook

Suppose that a new wind of political change again sweeps the nation, and now you're supposed to refer to people as *Ms or Miss* rather than either single title. Whatever. But you, clever you, decide that you can automate this process. Instead of laboriously opening each name in your Contacts folder, and modifying some of them as required by the latest cultural shift, you whip up a little VBA code to do the job for you. Here's how.

You first want to change any name that begins with *Miss* to *Ms or Miss*. Use the code in Listing 2-2 to rifle through your contacts and make the changes:

Listing 2-2:   Search-and-Replace Example in Outlook

```
Sub MissToMs()

Dim n As Outlook.NameSpace
Set n = Application.GetNamespace("MAPI")
```

```
Dim f As Outlook.MAPIFolder
Set f = n.GetDefaultFolder(olFolderContacts)

Dim o As Object
Set o = f.Items.GetFirst

For Each o In f.Items

        If Left(o.FullName, 4) = "Miss" Then

            o.FullName = "Ms or " & o.FullName
            o.Save

        End If
Next

Set o = Nothing
Set f = Nothing
Set n = Nothing

End Sub
```

First, you do the usual drill of creating object variables and then instantiating objects for them to refer to. You end up with a generic object, a MAPI namespace, and a Contacts folder object. Your object uses the `GetFirst` method to point to the first item in the Contacts folder — the first Contact, in other words. Then you go through each item (each Contact) and see whether its `FullName` property begins with *Miss.* If so, you make the change by prepending *Ms or;* then you save the item back into the collection with the change. Then you go through the usual drill of destroying the objects you created. Setting things to `Nothing` causes some confusion. Some experts insist you always must do this to save memory, to free up resources, or to prevent problems. Others say that the garbage collection truck will be along in due time to automatically destroy unused objects. (It knows they're unused because they're only local in scope, having been instantiated within a procedure, and no other references to them exist.) So you can leave off the three lines ending in `Nothing` . . . and nothing is going to happen. That is, unless the other experts are correct in their warnings and memory or resources get all clogged up from pointers pointing to nothing. I've never noticed a problem.

The Contacts `Items` collection can contain distribution items as well as Contacts items. If this is the case, you might try to access properties that distribution items don't have. If this problem applies to you, add this test to the loop in the previous example to filter out the distribution items:

```
If o.MessageClass = "IPM.Contact" Then
```

Handling Events

You might want to insert some VBA code into one of Outlook's built-in events to customize Outlook's behavior. To see the available events for the `Application` object, choose View⇨Project Explorer, and then double-click ThisOutlookSession in the Project Explorer. Open the list box on the left top of the code window and choose Application. Then open the other list (right side), and you see all the events for the `Application`. Choose Quit (the event that fires when you close Outlook). In this event, type this code:

```
Private Sub Application_Quit()

MsgBox ("Tell Mary to go home.")

End Sub
```

Now close Outlook, and you see the reminder to tell workaholic Mary it's time to pack it in.

Open the Outlook VBA editor Help window. In the Table of Contents, choose Microsoft Outlook Visual Basic Reference; under that, click Events. You'll find a large number of events for various objects within Outlook. Unfortunately, creating code for most of these events is rather indirect and complex — you have to insert `WithEvents` commands, initialize the handler in the `Application_Startup` event, and such twists and turns. Fortunately, the Help system contains quite a generous number of code examples.

Advanced Searching

If simple searches aren't enough, Outlook also includes an object modestly named `AdvancedSearch`. Use this object to really take the bull by the horns. Interestingly, `AdvancedSearch` requires that you split your code into two procedures. You start the search in a procedure of your own. Then, when the search is finished, it triggers the `AdvancedSearchComplete` event where you write code to handle the results.

To see how it works, press Alt+F11 to open the Outlook VBA editor. Choose Insert⇨Module if no Module1 is listed in Project Explorer. Type this public variable at the very top of Module1:

```
Public r As results
```

Making a `Public` variable allows you to easily pass the `results` object between procedures. This object will contain the — you guessed it — results of the search, and you want to display in a text box the body of any e-mail message the user clicks in the list box.

Choose Insert⇨UserForm and put a small text box on the top left, a list box underneath it, a button on the top right, and a text box under the button. It should all look like Figure 2-3.

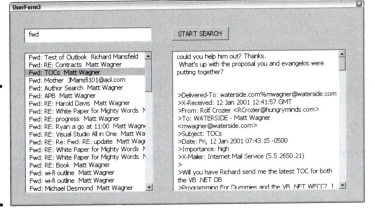

Figure 2-3: The results of the search appear in this UserForm.

Double-click the button on the UserForm and type this code into its `Click` event:

```
Private Sub CommandButton1_Click()

Dim s As Search

where = "'Inbox'"

n = "urn:schemas:mailheader:subject LIKE '%" & TextBox1.Text & "%'"

Set s = Application.AdvancedSearch(where, n, True)

End Sub
```

When the user clicks this button, the search is initiated in the Outlook Inbox (although you can change the `where` variable here to point to any target you want to search — perhaps put a group of radio buttons on the form, and let the user click the target).

Whatever the user has typed into the small text box will be the search term, and by surrounding it with % symbols, you're saying, *Include any additional text on either side*. In this way, searching for *bob* will also provide hits for *bobby, joe-bob,* and so on. This search looks through the subject headers of each e-mail — not the body text, although you can change that. (See AdvancedSearch in Outlook VBA Help for additional ways you can specify the search fields and the search term.) The final argument `True` in the preceding code means to search all subfolders.

In this same UserForm, double-click the list box so you can provide a way for the user to click an e-mail subject header and thereby cause that e-mail's text (the actual message) to be displayed in the text box to the right of the list box:

```
Private Sub ListBox1_Click()

Dim rr As results
Set rr = Module1.r


TextBox2.Text = rr(ListBox1.ListIndex + 1).Body


End Sub
```

Notice that you create an object variable rr to hold the results and point it to the public variable r that you previously declared in Module1.

Now all that's left to do is to write some programming in the AdvanceSearchComplete event. Double-click ThisOutlookSession in Project Explorer to open the module where Application events are located. Use the list boxes at the top of this module's code window to open the Application_AdvancedSearchComplete event and type this into it:

```
Private Sub Application_AdvancedSearchComplete(ByVal
          SearchObject As Search)

Set r = SearchObject.results

If r.Count = 0 Then
    UserForm3.ListBox1.AddItem ("NOTHING FOUND MATCHING " &
          UserForm3.TextBox1.Text)
  Else

  For i = 1 To r.Count

    UserForm3.ListBox1.AddItem (r(i).Subject & "  " &
          r(i).SenderName)

  Next i

End If

End Sub
```

Here you point Module1's public variable `r` to the results returned by the `SearchObject`. If the `count` property of this object is `0`, no hit was found, so you tell the user. Otherwise (`Else`), you display the `Subject` property for each hit that was found in the list box.

I suspect that you might prefer to use the above example code to construct your own custom search utilities for Outlook messages. Also note that you can conduct as many as 100 multiple simultaneous searches (for example, searching through several folders at the same time). To run multiple searches, just call the `AdvancedSearch` method in successive lines of source code.

Chapter 3: Managing Work and Life

In This Chapter

✔ Handling Contacts

✔ Sending Access data into Outlook

✔ Creating and displaying folders

✔ Modifying collections

✔ Searching Tasks

✔ Managing the Calendar

✔ Moving data from Outlook to Word

✔ Using the new Business Contact Manager

*I*n this chapter, I explore how to program several of Outlook's primary features: Contacts, Tasks, scheduling, and the Calendar. You begin by solving a common programming problem: how to transfer data from one application to another. Fortunately, the rich object model available in most Office 2003 applications makes the process of automating data transfer relatively painless. As usual, the only real pain is figuring out the necessary syntax. The objects are there; you just have to know how to reference them and punctuate correctly.

Do This First

For the example code in this chapter to work, you must first set the following references:

1. Press Alt+F11 to open the Outlook VBA editor.

2. Choose Tools➪References in the editor and ensure that you have selected the following three libraries:

   - Microsoft Office 11.0 Object Library

   - Microsoft Outlook 11.0 Object Library

   - Microsoft DAO 3.6 Object Library

Each of these libraries should have a check mark next to its name in the References dialog box.

3. Close the References dialog box.

Sending Access Data into Outlook

For this example, suppose that you have a table in Access containing a list of employees for a particular company — in this case, the Northwind sample database. You want to import this data into Outlook's Contacts folder.

If you execute this example code, you'll want to later delete the nine new Contacts that the example adds to your current list of Contacts. You don't want to clutter up your Contacts list with the fakes added during this example.

Choose Insert⇨Module in the Outlook VBA editor. A new module appears for you to type in the following subroutine (Listing 3-1):

Listing 3-1:   Importing Access Data into Your Outlook Contacts List

```
Sub ImportAccessData()

Dim DAOdb As DAO.Database
   Dim r As DAO.Recordset

   Set DAOdb = OpenDatabase _
      ("c:\Program Files\Microsoft Office\Office11\Samples\
         Northwind.mdb")
   Set r = DAOdb.OpenRecordset("Employees")

   'create outlook object variables
   Dim o As New Outlook.Application

   Dim c As Outlook.ContactItem
   Dim upr As Outlook.UserProperty

   With r
      .MoveFirst

      ' Loop through the Access records
      Do While Not .EOF

         ' Create a new Contact object
         Set c = o.CreateItem(olContactItem)

         ' Transfer data to existing Outlook contact
           categories:
         'If ![ACCESS FIELD NAME] <> "" Then
         OUTLOOK.FIELDNAME = ![ACCESS FIELD NAME]
```

```
        If ![LastName] <> "" Then c.FullName = ![LastName] &
            ![FirstName]
        If ![Title] <> "" Then c.JobTitle = ![Title]
        If ![BirthDate] <> "" Then c.Birthday = ![BirthDate]
        If ![HomePhone] <> "" Then c.HomeTelephoneNumber =
            ![HomePhone]
        If ![Notes] <> "" Then c.Body = "Personality defects
            or positives: " & ![Notes]

        ' Create an Outlook user property for any missing
            fields.
        Set upr = c.UserProperties.Add("Hire date at
            Northwind", olText)
        ' send the data from the appropriate Access field:
        If ![HireDate] <> "" Then upr = ![HireDate]

        ' Save then destroy the contact object
        c.Save
        c.Close olDiscard
        .MoveNext
    Loop
  End With
End Sub
```

**Book VI
Chapter 3**

**Managing Work
and Life**

Some Outlook fields are not named the same way that they are labeled in the Outlook Contact dialog box. For example, the Phone Numbers area in the Contact dialog box contains four possible entries, so PhoneNumber alone won't work. (One of these fields must be referred to as BusinessTelephoneNumber in programming code but is labeled Business in the dialog box.) To see the list of field names that you should use in your code, type **c.** in the code below this line of code:

```
Set c = o.CreateItem(olContactItem)
```

Typing **c.** (with the dot) opens the IntelliSense list with all the different field names for a contact object, as shown in Figure 3-1.

Figure 3-1:
To see the correct names for Outlook's Contact dialog box, display this IntelliSense list.

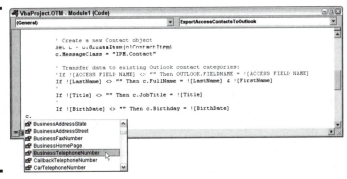

In this example, you declare DAO database and recordset objects, open the sample database, and then open the `Employees` table. Then you declare `outlook application`, `contact`, and `userproperty` objects. Next, a `With` block defines what you're going to do with r, which is the recordset containing the Access data from the Employees table. You move to the first record with the `.MoveFirst` method, and then begin a loop that iterates through the entire recordset via the `.MoveNext` method. The loop terminates when an `EOF` (end of file) is located.

You create a new `Contact` object each time through the loop and then stuff that object's fields with the data found in the various fields in the `Employee` table. The names of the fields don't always match. Indeed, in the first field (what Outlook calls `FullName`), you have to concatenate two fields from the Access table: `LastName` and `FirstName`. Likewise, Access's `Title` field becomes `JobTitle` in Outlook, and `Birthdate` becomes `Birthday`. So it goes.

Notice that what Access accurately calls `Notes`, Outlook (for some reason) calls `Body`. (Calendar notes are also in a field named `Body`.) Also, this line of code illustrates how you can add your own comments to incoming data. This line prepends your comment `"Personality defects or positives:"` to each incoming notes field value from Access:

```
If ![Notes] <> "" Then c.Body = "Personality defects
   or positives: " & ![Notes]
```

Why do this? Because field values (data) are raw data that, in some cases, you might want to prepend a description to (for the same reason that you might stamp *Personnel* on each resume sent to you). Prepending descriptions can help categorize and identify data.

Finally, for data that you want to transfer but which has no prebuilt field already defined in the Outlook Contact dialog box, you can define a user-defined field, displayed in the All Fields tab of the dialog box, as shown in Figure 3-2.

You create a user field by first using the `Add` method of the `UserProperties` object, defining the name of the new field:

```
' Create an Outlook user property for any missing
   fields.
Set upr = c.UserProperties.Add("Hire date at
   Northwind", olText)
```

Then you transfer the data from Access to your new field in the `Contact` object:

```
If ![HireDate] <> "" Then upr = ![HireDate]
```

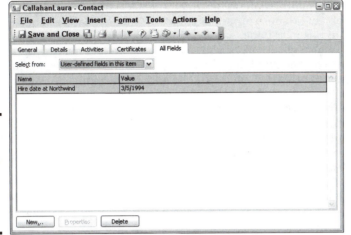

Figure 3-2:
Create your
own custom
fields from
this tab of
the Contact
dialog box.

Displaying a Folder Item

Sometimes you want to programmatically display a folder to the user. In this
next example, you see how that's done. In this case, you display the New
Contact form to the user. Type this procedure (Listing 3-2) into your code
window.

Listing 3-2:   Displaying a Folder for User Interaction

```
Sub ShowNewContact()

Dim o As New Outlook.Application
    Dim ns As Outlook.NameSpace
    Dim f As Outlook.MAPIFolder
    Dim c As Outlook.ContactItem

    Set ns = o.GetNamespace("MAPI")
    Set f = ns.GetDefaultFolder(olFolderContacts)


    Set c = f.Items.Add("IPM.Contact")
    c.Display

End Sub
```

This task requires that you create the usual Outlook objects, and then use
the GetDefaultFolder method of the Application object to access the
Contacts folder (via the enum in the method's argument). Then you use the
Add method to create a new Contact and display the dialog box for that
Contact.

TIP

For more information on the unfathomable, enigmatic world of namespaces and object-oriented programming (OOP) nomenclature schemes, see Chapter 2 of this mini-book. As an example, the Windows Messaging API (MAPI) namespace in Outlook is a strange requirement in many programming instances. You'll find that for much programming written in Outlook VBA, instantiating a MAPI namespace is required, although for other types of programming, it's not needed. Efforts on the part of this author to find any pattern or rule defining when this namespace must be included in your Outlook programming have failed. Undoubtedly, there's some arcane techie explanation, but I've never come across it. The only rule I know of is that you must instantiate a MAPI namespace whenever your program won't execute without it.

MAPI is the only namespace in Outlook, so including it is pointless: Having to declare it is rather like adding *Planet Earth* to every letter that you address. It's assumed because (as yet) there are no post offices in outer space . . . but never mind. Just follow the rules and, as Little Richard likes to say, "Shut up!"

You might think that MAPI would be needed for any programming that accesses the Outlook Mail folder's methods or sends e-mail via `Send` methods. Not so. You can leave MAPI out of your code when you use the `Send` method of the `AppointmentItem` object, as illustrated later in the section "Using Calendar Automation." So, do what's needed, don't try to figure out the taxonomy for heaven's sake, and just shut up!

Creating a New Contacts Folder

How about creating an entirely new folder? Declare the usual variables, instantiate the usual objects, and provide a name for the new folder (see Listing 3-3). It's now part of your Outlook, as shown in Figure 3-3.

Listing 3-3:   Creating a New Outlook Folder

```
Sub AddNewFolder()

Dim o As New Outlook.Application
Set o = CreateObject("Outlook.Application")

Dim ns As Outlook.NameSpace
Set ns = o.GetNamespace("MAPI")

Dim fo As Outlook.MAPIFolder
Set fo = ns.GetDefaultFolder(olFolderContacts)

Dim fn As Outlook.MAPIFolder
Set fn = fo.Folders.Add("NewContacts")

End Sub
```

Your new Contacts folder now appears in Outlook.

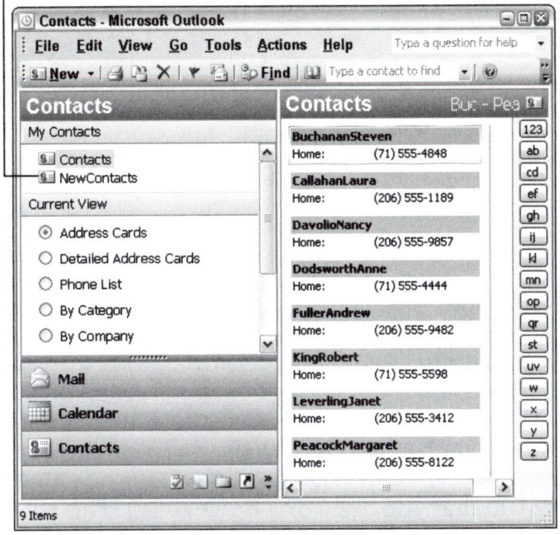

Figure 3-3:
Add new
folders
easily with
the
`Folders.`
`Add`
method.

Making Mass Modifications

Sometimes you need to loop through a set of data, gathering certain values and building the data into a list. In the following example, you use the `Items` collection — also very common in .NET programming — to access the data in a Contacts folder. Specifically, you want to build a list of names and birthdays of all the Contacts.

Type this procedure (Listing 3-4) into your Outlook VBA editor.

Listing 3-4: Building a List of Data

```
Sub Iterating()
    Dim o As Outlook.Application
    Set o = New Outlook.Application

    Dim ns As Outlook.NameSpace
    Set ns = o.GetNamespace("MAPI")

    Dim c As Outlook.Items
    Set c = ns.GetDefaultFolder(olFolderContacts).Items

    For Each i In c
```

```
If i.Birthday <> "" Then a = a & i.FullName & "," &
    i.Birthday & ","

    i.Close olDiscard
Next

    MsgBox a

    Set c = Nothing
    Set ns = Nothing
    Set o = Nothing
End Sub
```

Notice that in this code, you don't create an olContactItem object during each iteration through this loop, as you did in the ImportAccessData example earlier in this chapter (Listing 3-1) using Set c = o.CreateItem (olContactItem). Instead, you get an Items collection holding the items from the Contacts folder (in other words, all the individual contact records). Then you use a For Each loop, which doesn't care what variable you use (i in this example) to iterate through the collection, any more than a For Next loop cares whether you use i or j or whatever. This same technique can be used to write data to the fields instead of reading it as is done here. To write, simply use the syntax i.birthday =.

You inspect each record, reading the birthday field to see whether it has any data. If so, you add the name and birthday values to your list, delimiting them with commas. A list like this can be imported into other applications, such as Access.

Searching Tasks

You can search any of the Outlook collections by using a variation of the techniques described in previous examples, along with a Find method. This code (Listing 3-5) searches through a Tasks folder to see whether a Task is specified as high priority.

Listing 3-5: Searching the Tasks Folder

```
Sub searchTasks()

    Dim o As Outlook.Application
    Set o = CreateObject("Outlook.Application")

    Dim ns As Outlook.NameSpace
    Set ns = o.GetNamespace("MAPI")

    Dim ts As Outlook.MAPIFolder
    Set ts = ns.GetDefaultFolder(olFolderTasks)
```

```
Dim t As Outlook.TaskItem
Set t = ts.Items.Find("[Importance] = ""High""")

If t Is Nothing Then 'no high priority items
        MsgBox "No High Priorities"
        Exit Sub 'quit
Else
    MsgBox "The following high importance item was found:
        " & t.Subject
End If

End Sub
```

The Find method of the Items collection can be used to locate the first match. If you want to find more matches, use the FindNext method. This is an alternative way to search through a collection than techniques employing For Each or For Next.

Using Calendar Automation

In this chapter and the preceding one, I cover a variety of programming techniques involving Outlook Tasks, Mail, and Contacts. I don't want to ignore the important Calendar folder, though, and its scheduling capabilities. You can create new Calendar entries, send meeting notices, and, in fact, pretty much do anything you want with the Calendar features via VBA.

This example illustrates how to set up a meeting, require that some employees attend, and then send them e-mail notification of the compulsory meeting. Their Outlook calendars will be updated to include this meeting and its details. This example doesn't require that you instantiate the MAPI namespace, even though it sends messages. There's no accounting for OOP classification schemes, so there's often no predicting what objects are needed and what aren't in any given instance. Do you object to this kind of arbitrariness? Well, shut up!

Type this (Listing 3-6) into the VBA code window.

Listing 3-6:   Setting up an Outlook Meeting

```
Sub SetMeeting()

    Dim o As Outlook.Application
    Set o = CreateObject("Outlook.Application")

    Dim a As Outlook.AppointmentItem
    Set a = o.CreateItem(olAppointmentItem)
```

```
Dim required, required2 As Outlook.Recipient

'force these two to attend:
Set required = a.Recipients.Add("Janice Loez")
    required.Type = olRequired
Set required2 = a.Recipients.Add("Richard Mansfield")
    required.Type = olRequired

With a

.Subject = "Bob's Wife's Party"
.Body = "Everyone's invited to see their great new house and
            to provide presents."
.AllDayEvent = True
.MeetingStatus = olMeeting
.Start = #8/18/2004 8:30:00 AM#
.Duration = 600 'ten hours!
.Save
.Send

End With

Set o = Nothing
Set a = Nothing


End Sub
```

You want to send e-mail notices to two recipients in this code, so you define two recipient objects:

```
Dim required, required2 As Outlook.Recipient
```

Then you instantiate them and add them to your `Recipients` collection, specifying that their attendance is mandatory.

```
Set required = a.Recipients.Add("Janice Loez")
    required.Type = olRequired
Set required2 = a.Recipients.Add("Richard Mansfield")
    Required2.Type = olRequired
```

Then you enter a `With` block, where (no particular order is required) you define various properties of this new meeting:

```
With a

.Subject = "Bob's Wife's Party"
.Body = "Everyone's invited to see their great new house and
    to provide presents."
.MeetingStatus = olMeeting
```

```
.Start = #8/18/2004 8:30:00 AM#
.Duration = 600 'ten hours!
.Save
.Send

End With
```

Typing a period (.) anywhere within this block brings up an IntelliSense list of all the members of the AppointmentItem object.

In this example, you're only setting a few of the 68 total AppointmentItem object's properties. For one thing, the End property isn't necessary if you provide a Duration property. Outlook calculates the ending time for you, as illustrated in the End Time field displayed in Figure 3-4.

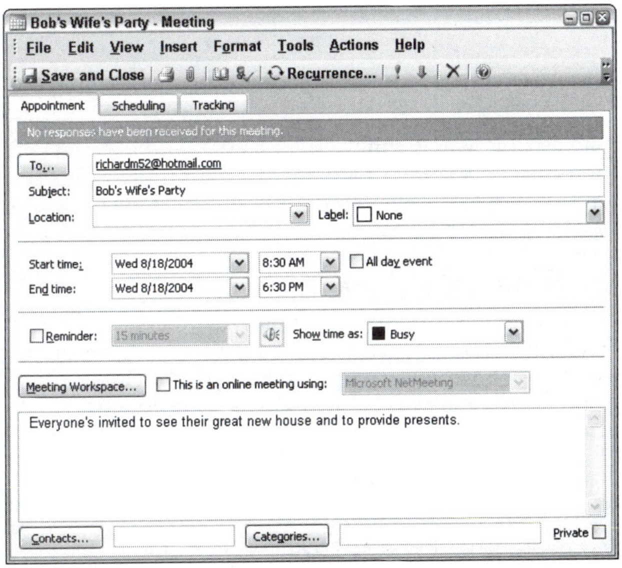

**Book VI
Chapter 3**

Managing Work
and Life

Figure 3-4:
The recipients of your meeting notice will find that this Appointment item has been automatically added to their Calendar.

Then, after the property fields have been filled in, you save this new item to your Calendar folder and send it to the previously instantiated Recipients objects. They will get e-mail notices, and their Calendars will automatically be updated.

Using non-Outlook e-mail programs

If the recipient gets e-mail in a program other than Outlook — such as in their browser via Hotmail while on the road — he simply finds an attachment to your message. If he opens this attachment in Notepad or some other text editor, he sees this:

```
BEGIN:VCALENDAR
PRODID:-//Microsoft Corporation//Outlook 11.0 MIMEDIR//EN
VERSION:2.0
METHOD:REQUEST
BEGIN:VEVENT
ATTENDEE;ROLE=REQ-PARTICIPANT;RSVP=TRUE:MAILTO:richardm52@hotmail.com
ATTENDEE;ROLE=REQ-PARTICIPANT;RSVP=TRUE:MAILTO:richardm52@hotmail.com
ORGANIZER:MAILTO:earth@triad.rr.com
DTSTART:20040818T133000Z
DTEND:20040818T233000Z
TRANSP:OPAQUE
SEQUENCE:0
UID:040000008200E00074C5B7101A82E00800000000703049E897E9C3010000000000000000000100
  0000034EF463C8AC0644D90F5284190214507
DTSTAMP:20040202T192154Z
DESCRIPTION:When: Wednesday\, August 18\, 2004 8:30 AM-6:30 PM (GMT-05:00)
  Eastern Time (US & Canada).\n\n*~*~*~*~*~*~*~*~*~*\n\nEveryone's invited
  to see their great new house and to provide presents.\n
SUMMARY:Bob's Wife's Party
PRIORITY:5
X-MICROSOFT-CDO-IMPORTANCE:1
CLASS:PUBLIC
END:VEVENT
END:VCALENDAR
```

Of course, some details will differ (such as `UID` and `DTSTAMP`), but this illustrates the interior structure of a Calendar appointment item as Microsoft transmits it between Outlook instances. You can think up a special code for the `Subject` property, such as this:

```
.Subject = "APPT: Bob's Wife's Party"
```

Then when one of your associates receives a message where the Subject line begins with `APPT:`, he knows to open it in Outlook. Opening this attachment in Outlook integrates the message into his appointments, as shown in Figure 3-5.

Figure 3-5:
Even people who don't get their mail directly in Outlook can import `Appointment-Item` attachments into Outlook, like this.

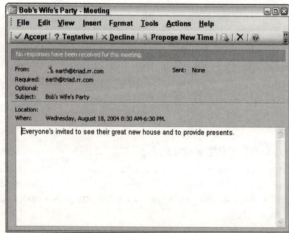

AppointmentItem members

The `AppointmentItem` **object offers quite a few properties and methods.**
Here are the 68 `AppointmentItem` **properties:** `Actions`, `AllDayEvent`,
`Application`, `Attachments`, `AutoResolvedWinner`, `BillingInformation`,
`Body`, `BusyStatus`, `Categories`, `Class`, `Companies`,
`ConferenceServerAllowExternal`, `ConferenceServerPassword`,
`Conflicts`, `ConversationIndex`, `ConversationTopic`, `CreationTime`,
`DownloadState`, `Duration`, `End`, `EntryID`, `FormDescription`,
`GetInspector`, `Importance`, `InternetCodepage`, `IsConflict`,
`IsOnlineMeeting`, `IsRecurring`, `ItemProperties`,
`LastModificationTime`, `Links`, `Location`, `MarkForDownload`,
`MeetingStatus`, `MeetingWorkspaceURL`, `MessageClass`, `Mileage`,
`NetMeetingAutoStart`, `NetMeetingDocPathName`,
`NetMeetingOrganizerAlias`, `NetMeetingServer`, `NetMeetingType`,
`NetShowURL`, `NoAging`, `OptionalAttendees`, `Organizer`,
`OutlookInternalVersion`, `OutlookVersion`, `Parent`, `Recipients`,
`RecurrenceState`, `ReminderMinutesBeforeStart`,
`ReminderOverrideDefault`, `ReminderPlaySound`, `ReminderSet`,
`ReminderSoundFile`, `ReplyTime`, `RequiredAttendees`, `Resources`,
`ResponseRequested`, `ResponseStatus`, `Saved`, `Sensitivity`, `Session`,
`Size`, `Start`, `Subject`, `UnRead`, **and** `UserProperties`.

Here are the 14 `AppointmentItem` **methods:** `ClearRecurrencePattern`,
`Close`, `Copy`, `Delete`, `Display`, `ForwardAsVcal`, `GetRecurrencePattern`,
`Move`, `PrintOut`, `Respond`, `Save`, `SaveAs`, `Send`, `ShowCategoriesDialog`.

Outside Outlook: Extracting Data from Outlook to Word

Because Office applications each specialize in different tasks, you often find
that you want to send data from one application to another. For example,
Word is clearly the best place to format documents, so if you have a list of
data in Outlook that you want to edit in a document, send the Outlook data
to Word. If this transfer of data is something you do often, automating the
process is quite a bit faster than copying and pasting individual data from
one application to another.

In this example, you write code that extracts a subset of `AppointmentItems`
from your Outlook Calendar and then sends the list to Word for distribution
to others or for printing as hard copy. It would be pretty slow and boring to
have to locate each item in this subset by hand, and then copy it to Word.

This code is designed to execute *from within Word.* So start Word up and put the code into Word's VBA editor. In Word, press Alt+F11 to open the VBA editor. Then (in the editor) choose Tools⇨References and select Microsoft Outlook 11.0 Object Library to add these functions to your project. Finally, type this macro (Listing 3-7) into the Word VBA editor.

Listing 3-7:   Sending Outlook Data to Word

```
Public Sub MonthsAppointments()

Dim o As Outlook.Application
Set o = New Outlook.Application

Dim ns As Outlook.Namespace
Set ns = o.GetNamespace("MAPI")

Dim m As Outlook.MAPIFolder
Set m = ns.GetDefaultFolder(olFolderCalendar)

Dim a As Outlook.AppointmentItem

' create a date one month from today:
mo = DateAdd("d", 30, Date)


Selection.TypeText "This Month's Appointments"
'move down two lines
Selection.TypeText vbCrLf
Selection.TypeText vbCrLf


For Each a In m.Items

d = a.Start

If d >= Date And d <= mo Then

    X = X + 1

        s = X & ".  " & a.Start & ":  " & a.Subject & vbCrLf

        s = s & "    Start: " & Format(a.Start, "Long Time") & vbCrLf

        s = s & "    End: " & Format(a.End, "Medium Time") & vbCrLf

        s = s & "    Location: " & a.Location

    Selection.TypeText s
    Selection.TypeText vbCrLf & vbCrLf

End If


Next

End Sub
```

When you press F5 to execute this, all the appointments in your Outlook Calendar for the next 30 days are listed in a Word document, starting wherever the blinking insertion cursor is currently located.

After the usual object instantiations, as described throughout this chapter, you create a date variable containing whatever date is 30 days from today:

```
mo = DateAdd("d", 30, Date)
```

Then you use the Word `Selection` object to type a title for the list and move down two lines with the `vbCrLf` enum (built-in constant). Then you move through the entire collection of appointments, checking whether any fall within the specified dates: `today to today +30`:

```
d = a.Start
If d >= Date And d <= mo Then
```

If so, data about the appointment is printed in the document, along with an incrementing number `X` at the start of each entry.

Using the New Business Contact Manager

A new add-in available for Outlook 2003 called Business Contact Manager (BCM) allows business people to record, track, and organize their professional activities from within Outlook (where their Contacts, schedules, Tasks, Calendar, and other utilities also reside). BCM becomes a new folder in Outlook. BCM is essentially a specialized database where you can enter and manage the following:

✦ **Leads:** Info about how to contact the potential human targets of your sales pitch (also know as *opportunities*)

✦ **Products:** What you want to sell to leads

✦ **Existing customers:** Former leads

✦ **Prospects:** Same as leads but perhaps closer to conversion into customers

✦ **Narratives:** Describing your various schemes and plots, and lessons learned from previously unsuccessful schemes and plots

Chapter 4: Expert E-Mail Administration

In This Chapter

✔ **Effective routing during vacation**

✔ **Managing multiple accounts**

✔ **Using Send/Receive Groups**

✔ **Blocking virii**

This chapter focuses on e-mail and the most significant, e-mail-related features that Outlook offers users, administrators, and others working with Office 2003. You see how to automate routing, handle multiple e-mail accounts from disparate sources, manage groups, and block virii.

Exploring Messaging Management

E-mail management and general messaging within Outlook 2003 is extremely flexible. Indeed, messaging throughout Office 2003 applications allows you to pretty much call the shots any way you want them.

For example, you can use Exchange to send a Word document to a folder in someone's Outlook application. In Word, choose File⇨Send To, and a context menu pops up with a nice choice of targets, as shown in Figure 4-1.

Choose Exchange Folder from the context menu (if Exchange Server is available to your office). You see a list of possible targets, including your own Outlook application, as shown in Figure 4-2.

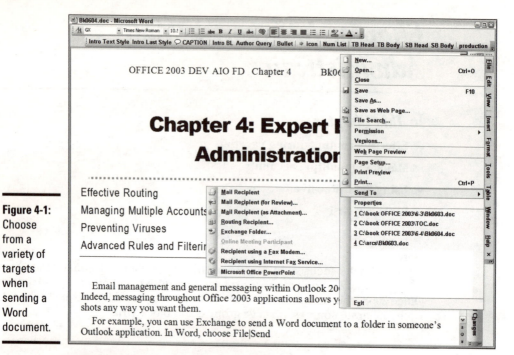

Figure 4-1:
Choose from a variety of targets when sending a Word document.

Figure 4-2:
Exchange Folder allows you to move a document into a folder of your choice.

Choose Mail Recipient (as Attachment) to employ the more conventional approach: ordinary e-mail. The familiar Outlook e-mail form appears, with your file attached, as shown in Figure 4-3.

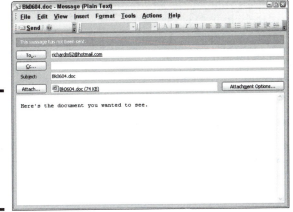

Figure 4-3:
Your docu-
ment is
automati-
cally
attached to
this e-mail.

 If you right-click a filename in Windows Explorer, you'll find a Send To context menu. It's not as full-featured as the Office 2003 applications' Send To
option, but you can choose Mail Recipient. If you do, an Outlook Mail dialog
box opens with the file attached to the message. Unfortunately, the message
is filled in for you, with the following sentence, which is sure to confuse the
recipient of this e-mail. Who thought this default message was a good idea?

```
Your files are attached and ready to send with this
message.
```

If you try to send a BMP file, you're offered the option of letting Outlook
"make all my pictures smaller." (The picture isn't actually made smaller, per
se, but its file size shrinks because it's compressed. This is an admission that
JPG graphics files are superior — less bloated — than BMP files.) If you
select this option, your BMP is converted to a JPG.

Routing: Out of Office Assistant

Using the routing feature requires an Exchange Server e-mail account. If
you're going to be gone for a while from your desk, you can use the Out of
Office Assistant to follow various rules about how to handle incoming e-mail.

E-mail can be automatically deleted (you know, those useless notes and gossip
from that pest, Anthony, in R&D), route other e-mail to particular folders,
respond with individualized replies, and so on.

You must leave Outlook running the whole time you're gone on vacation for this autoresponse technique to work.

To see how to automatically respond to incoming e-mail, follow these steps:

1. **Choose Tools⇨Options in Outlook 2003.**

2. **Click the Mail Format tab of the Options dialog box.**

3. **Deselect Use Microsoft Word 2003 to Edit E-mail Messages.**

This can be restored after you get back from vacation. This option cannot be used to autoreply because it must be turned off when you save a message as a template.

4. **Click OK.**

The dialog box closes.

5. **Click the Mail folder; then click New on the toolbar.**

A new e-mail message dialog box opens (see Figure 4-4), somewhat abbreviated because you have a more limited menu and toolbar features than you do in Word 2003.

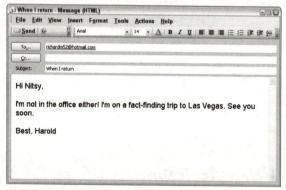

Figure 4-4:
This isn't the full-featured message box that borrows from Word 2003.

6. **Type the message you want automatically sent to your boss if she should e-mail you from her "study retreat" in Monte Carlo.**

7. **Choose File⇨Save As.**

8. **In the Save As dialog box that opens, name this file AutoNitsy.**

9. **Open the Save as Type drop-down list.**

You see a list of various kinds of file options.

10. **Choose Outlook Template.**

11. **Click Save.**

12. **Close the message dialog box and don't save a draft.**

13. **Choose Tools⇨Rules and Alerts.**

If the Rules and Alerts option isn't visible, you haven't closed the message dialog box. Repeat Step 11.

14. **In the Rules and Alerts dialog box that opens, click the <u>New Rule</u> link in the dialog box.**

The Rules Wizard opens. You've created and saved a message that can automatically be sent to the intended recipient, Nitsy, your boss, in this example.

In the following steps, you use the Rules Wizard to specify behaviors that result in an automatic response on Outlook's part.

1. **Select Start from a Blank Rule.**

2. **Select Check Messages When They Arrive.**

3. **Click Next.**

4. **Under Select Conditions, select the From People or Distribution List check box.**

Select Received in a Specific Date Span in this list if you want to reply with an out-of-office message to *all* incoming e-mail.

5. **In the Edit the Rule Description list, click the <u>people or distribution list</u> link.**

The Rule Address dialog box opens, as shown in Figure 4-5.

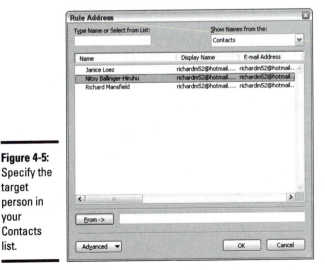

Figure 4-5: Specify the target person in your Contacts list.

6. Click the From button in the dialog box.

Your target person's e-mail is entered into the dialog box.

7. Click OK, and then click Next.

You see a new page in the wizard.

8. In the What Do You Want to Do with the Message list, choose Reply Using a Specific Template.

9. Click the <u>a specific template </u>link.

10. In the Look In list, choose User Templates in File System.

You should now see the template that you named AutoNitsy in Step 7 of the preceding step list.

11. Click AutoNitsy, click Open, and then click Next.

You see a list of exceptions, such as *(apply this rule) if sent only to me.* For example, you might want to respond at once — not automatically, but personally — if the boss sends you a personal e-mail.

12. Click Next.

13. Type AutoNitsy for the rule's name.

You gave the template underlying this rule this descriptive name, and it works just as well for the rule itself.

14. Click Finish and then click OK.

The dialog box closes, and your rule is in effect as long as someone doesn't turn off your computer or close Outlook. (You can, of course, turn off your monitor while you're in Vegas. What happens there, stays there.)

Using Multiple E-Mail Accounts

You can set up more than a single e-mail account, just as you can have a home, business, and PO box address for regular mail. With Outlook 2003, you can also redirect Web-based accounts, such as Hotmail, to Outlook.

An advantage of adding Internet-based accounts to Outlook is that your local machine has lots of storage for keeping Inbox and Sent Items e-mail. This can be important if you need to search your e-mail for addresses, discussions, and so on. Internet-based e-mail accounts are notorious for deleting e-mail that you don't want to discard. These accounts have limited storage, but when you dump your online folders into Outlook folders, you preserve these potentially important e-mail records.

Also, if you maintain several accounts within Outlook, you can use rules like those described in the preceding section to route incoming e-mail to the proper folder, set flags on it, adjusting priorities, sending automated replies, and so on. You often set up Send/Receive Groups for different connection settings. When using this technique, you can segregate e-mail accounts to prioritize your response, based on the different Groups.

Here's the difference between creating new folders and new Send/Receive Groups.

Folder: Create a folder if you're currently working on a project with several colleagues. You can set up this special folder just for communications about that project. This simplifies reading your e-mail because you would look in this account only when you were interested in working on that particular project.

Send/Receive Group: Create a separate Send/Receive Group for different kinds of e-mail connections. If you're a road warrior, you know that many hotels don't yet have broadband. To get around this limitation, you might want to set up a Send/Receive Group that initially downloads only message subjects rather than the entire body of the message. Slow Internet connections can make this technique a real timesaver. (Obviously, at home or the office where you've got a cable/modem connection, you wouldn't benefit from this approach.)

Using Exchange Server

Exchange Server has been around for about eight years in one guise or another. Although Exchange Server makes possible some of the more advanced features of Outlook, studies say that only about 50 percent of people using Outlook also employ Exchange Server. With Exchange Server, you get some offline features, allowing mail management while not connected to the Internet. These days, though, with always-on connections and high-speed, broadband throughput, the advantages of working offline are rapidly diminishing.

Also, when you maintain two folders — one on a server and one in a laptop or desktop — you face the old bugaboo of version control issues. That is, how can you reconcile two different versions of file collections? The process of reconciling files — either duplicated, edited responses, or two collections — cannot be successfully automated because no current programming language taps into the necessary artificial intelligence. Humans must step in and decide which collection, or file, is the current one. Simple rules that can be programmed, such as the *which comes last* rule based on deleted earlier versions, are not sufficient. Sometimes date/timestamps do not reveal which version should survive.

Some office situations, however, make server-based e-mail stores practical: for example, if you travel around the office and need to access e-mail from different computers, or if you're on the road. Also, some offices ask people to share accounts for one reason or another.

Working with Send/Receive Groups

To set up a Send/Receive Group, follow these steps:

1. **Start Outlook.**

2. **Choose Tools⇨Send/Receive⇨Send/Receive Settings⇨Define Send/ Receive Groups.**

   You see the Send/Receive Groups dialog box, as shown in Figure 4-6.

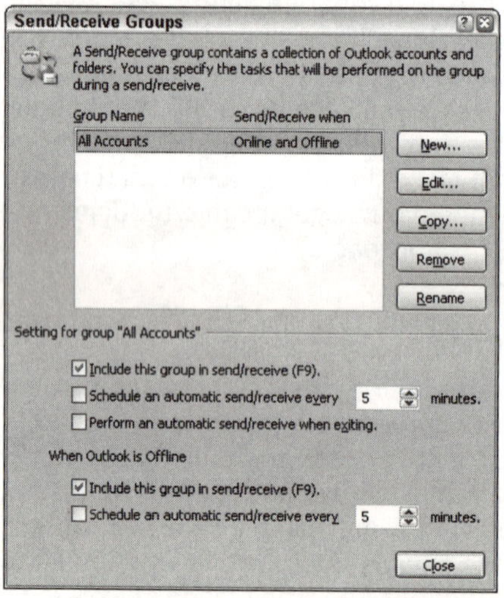

Figure 4-6:
Specify
new Send/
Receive
Groups
here.

You see that all your current accounts are in a single Send/Receive Group and any new account you might add will be automatically saved into this same Group.

3. **Click New.**

   A new Group can now be added.

4. **Type** Hotmail **or** Priority **or whatever other name describes this new group.**

5. **Click OK.**

   You see the Send/Receive Settings dialog box. You can specify qualities of your new Send/Receive Group in this dialog box. The left pane lists your e-mail accounts.

6. **To add an account, select Include the Selected Account in This Group.**

   You see the options for routing mail incoming from this account, as shown in Figure 4-7.

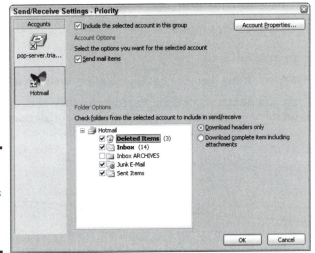

Figure 4-7:
This dialog box displays the options for your account.

7. **Click OK after specifying which folders you want included in this Group's Send/Receive.**

   The dialog box closes, and you're returned to main Send/Receive Groups dialog box where you can now see the new Group that's been added to your default Group.

8. **Click Close to complete the process.**

Avoiding Virii

The simplest and most effective advice on avoiding virii is to not open e-mail attachments and to maintain frequent backups. These two steps should prevent nearly all problems unless you have someone in your organization who deliberately introduces problems.

If you're an administrator, I suggest that you prevent most of your co-workers from opening attachments at all. Where transferring files is necessary, take steps to institute digital signatures, certificates, IDs, or whatever other secret code or authentication process makes sense for you. In a small office, where everyone inside can be trusted, your authentication process can be as simple as adding a line to the e-mail message, such as "This is from Betty. It's OK, as we agreed." Personalized or previously agreed-upon statements like this — or phone calls verifying the attachment — are unique to your organization and cannot easily be replicated by the bad guys.

Outlook automatically blocks executable attachments (`.exe`, `.scr`, `.bat`, and `.js`), but virii authors are becoming increasingly clever. Users simply cannot open these files at all.

To adjust Internet security settings, follow these steps:

1. **Choose Tools⇨Options.**

2. **In the Options dialog box that opens, click the Security tab.**

   You see available security options. Explore the Zone Settings and other buttons on this dialog box to see which levels of restriction should be enforced for your employees.

Chapter 5: Group Management in Outlook

In This Chapter

✔ Working with profiles

✔ Sharing schedules

✔ Planning meetings

*P*eople, of course, work together in groups in most businesses. Outlook can help you avoid stepping on each other's toes in various ways. In this chapter, you see how to establish profiles so that different users work with their own, custom virtual Outlook. You also explore the new shared Calendars feature — introduced in the first chapter of this mini-book — in greater depth. You see how to use the feature to make collaborative work more efficient by setting up a Web site to store calendar information. Another topic covered is Microsoft's Free/Busy Service, allowing you to automate the process of organizing meetings. The chapter concludes with various other utilities that assist with meetings, including reserving that slide projector.

Using Profiles

Profiles are yet another way to organize Outlook and its contents. Just as you might have various Windows profiles for each person who uses your home computer, you can also establish multiple Outlook profiles at work if more than one person uses a single machine. (You can also use a new profile to clean up a messy Outlook setup; read on.)

 With profiles, it's as if there were several different Outlooks, each with its own customizations for different purposes or for different people. When you turn on Windows and choose a Windows profile, the desktop and many other aspects of Windows can look different from different profiles on that same computer. Similarly, different Outlook profiles might have different default folders. For example, one profile might display the Mail folder first, and another the Calendar folder.

A profile includes toolbar settings, accounts, connection settings, AutoComplete files, views, navigation pane settings, security preferences, color and design choices, and others.

Creating a new profile can also be useful if you've really messed up your Outlook. Suppose you've created too many different folders, imported too many Contacts or Appointments, or otherwise have gotten confused. If you want to start over, create a new profile and make it the default folder (as shown in the upcoming Figure 5-3). You'll lose whatever data you've entered, but perhaps this is an easier path to follow than uninstalling/reinstalling if Outlook gets hopelessly mucked up. To create a new profile, follow these steps:

1. **Close Outlook.**

2. **In Windows XP, choose Start⇨Control Panel. In Windows 2000, Start⇨Settings⇨Control Panel.**

   The Control Panel opens.

3. **Double-click the Mail icon.**

4. **In the Mail Setup dialog box that opens, click the Show Profiles button.**

   You see the Mail dialog box.

5. **Click Add.**

   You see the New Profile dialog box.

6. **Type in a name for your new profile, perhaps** Private.

7. **Click OK.**

   The E-mail Accounts Wizard (sometimes oddly referred to as the *Custom Installation Wizard*) opens, as shown in Figure 5-1.

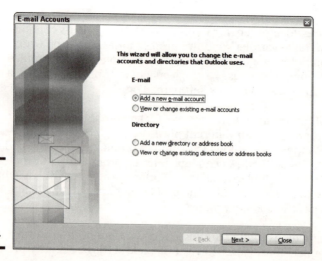

Figure 5-1:
Use this wizard to create a new profile.

8. **Following the successive wizard pages, create as many e-mail accounts as you wish for this new profile.**

9. **Click OK to close the wizard.**

   You see the Mail dialog box again, as shown in Figure 5-2, but now it includes your new profile.

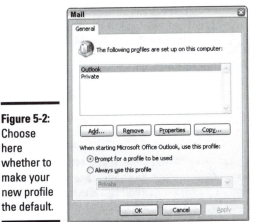

Figure 5-2:
Choose here whether to make your new profile the default.

10. **Decide which of your profiles should be the default when you open Outlook, or whether you want to see a dialog box each time and make a selection, as shown in Figure 5-3.**

Figure 5-3:
To select a profile, have this dialog box open whenever Outlook opens.

The option you choose, as well as any new profiles you've added, aren't available until you restart your computer.

Just as with your default Outlook profile, you can create multiple e-mail accounts. If you copy a profile, this resets its views and toolbar settings to their original default state yet retains any personalization done to e-mail accounts, connections, security settings, and folders. Bizarrely, there is some leakage between profiles. Most custom settings are correctly preserved for the different profiles, but some are not. For example, if you change the background color of the Calendar in one profile, all other profiles also reflect this new color.

If you get tired of always having to choose between profiles every time you start Outlook, it's not enough to click the Remove key in the Mail dialog box (as described in Step 4 of the preceding example). In fact, you need not remove a profile at all; just select the Always Use This Profile radio button in the Mail dialog box.

Sharing Calendars

You can use Exchange Server as a way of sharing schedules with your co-workers. This is fine if you're in an office that uses Exchange Server, but fewer than half of today's offices do. Also, if you have traveling salesmen, or other people who aren't always connected to your LAN, it's easiest to rely on Microsoft's Free/Busy Service. It's on the Web, so you can use it anywhere.

Why share Calendars? Meetings can be easily set up when you can see whether everyone is free at a particular time. Also, travel can be more easily planned, projects can be more efficiently organized, and so on. Collaborative work often requires that people take a look at each other's Calendar. In Office 2003, you can view two Outlook Calendars at the same time, but many times, you need to look at more than just two.

Setting up your own site

If you don't use Exchange Server, you can still employ any Internet site or intranet server that you control as a store for iCalendar information. (iCalendar is the format used to compare schedules.) Just publish your data and ask others to publish theirs — then everyone can see what times are free and what times are busy. Exactly why they're busy doesn't show up. To use an ordinary server, follow these steps:

1. **In Outlook choose Tools⇔Options.**

2. **In the Options dialog box that opens, select the Calendar Options button on the Preferences tab.**

   You see the Calendar Options dialog box.

3. **Click the Free/Busy Options button.**

    You see the Free/Busy Options dialog box.

4. **Select the Publish at My Location option.**

5. **Fill in your server's URL address, or LAN address, in the text box.**

Using Microsoft's Free/Busy Service

With the Free/Busy Service, you can share schedules with anyone who uses Microsoft Passport. This schedule sharing can be accomplished no matter where you might be located, thanks to the Internet. This is a good way to automatically remove scheduling conflicts when planning group activities, such as meetings. Everyone publishes his or her Calendar (free and busy times) and then Outlook's meeting request feature uses this Free/Busy Service to help you pick a good time for everyone to get together.

To use Microsoft's Free/Busy Service, everyone you want to schedule with must have a Microsoft Passport account. If you invite nonmembers to join in, they'll first be asked to get a Passport account. To use the Microsoft Free/Busy Service, follow these steps:

1. **Choose Tools⇨Options.**

2. **In the Options dialog box that opens, click the Calendar Options button on the Preferences tab.**

    You see the Calendar Options dialog box, as shown in Figure 5-4.

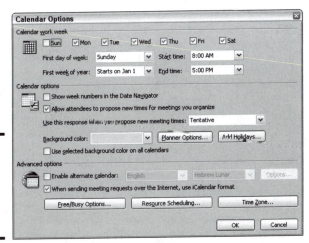

Figure 5-4:
This is your gateway to Internet-based scheduling.

3. **Click the Free/Busy Options button.**

   You see the Free/Busy Options dialog box.

4. **Select the Publish and Search Using Microsoft Office Internet Free/ Busy Service check box.**

5. **Click the Manage button.**

   Your browser opens displaying the Web site where this service is located.

If you already have a Passport account and are currently signed in, click the Sign Out button on the Web page (at the preceding URL), and then click the Sign In button. Things should work smoothly from there on.

After your Passport account has been reconciled with Outlook, you can permit Outlook to communicate automatically with the online service and display available meeting times when you or others request a meeting.

Planning Meetings

If you want to schedule a meeting, select the Calendar view and then choose Actions⇨New Meeting Request. You see the Plan a Meeting dialog box, as shown in Figure 5-5.

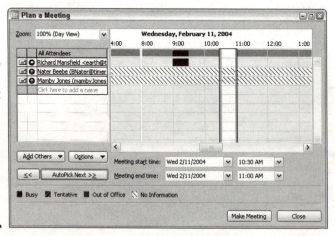

Figure 5-5: Specify start and end times, attendees, and other information for a new meeting here.

Note that you can visualize the start and end time of your meeting by the green (go) line symbolizing start and the red (stop) line for the end. These lines can be dragged with your mouse to adjust the meeting span.

You're essentially creating an e-mail in the dialog box shown in Figure 5-5, albeit a specialized one. ***Note:*** You can add graphics, files, or other attachments if you wish.

If you prefer, wait to add attendees until you click the Make Meeting button and go to the next dialog box where you can quickly add names by clicking the To button, as shown in the upcoming Figure 5-6. However, skipping this Planning dialog box doesn't allow you to check the free/busy status of your attendees (as I describe in the preceding section).

Notice in Figure 5-5 that a key to various colors appears in the lower left. People without *published* schedules (you don't have access to their free/busy information because they've refused to grant this permission, or they don't have an Exchange server or Free/Busy account) are indicated by slashed lines.

A solid block of color (under 9:00 in the Figure 5-5) shows that person is busy from 9:00 to 9:30.

If someone has slashed lines indicating that her schedule is unavailable to Outlook and she is on Exchange server, it's possible that somehow her Free/Busy data is corrupt. Try starting her Outlook by using the `/cleanfreebusy` command line switch. This will both clear up and regenerate her Free/Busy data.

Click the AutoPick Next button (refer to Figure 5-5) to have Outlook automatically find the next available time during work hours when all required attendees and resources are simultaneously available. You can refine how AutoPick Next works by clicking the Options button and then moving your mouse pointer down to AutoPick in the context menu.

If you click the Add Others button, you see a list from Exchange's global address list or from your Address Book or other source. Three buttons appear at the bottom of the Select Attendees and Resources dialog box. You can assign Required or Optional categories to each attendee or click the Resources button to specify resources. ***Note:*** Resources are things (not people), like PowerPoint projectors, models, videoconference setups, and so on. These resources must have previously been defined as *recipients* on the Exchange Server, but I must report that people *are* referred to as *resources* (and worse) by certain hard management types.

When you're satisfied with the details of the meeting, click the Make Meeting button. You then fill in an e-mail form that is automatically sent to anyone you specified as an attendee in the previous dialog box. Figure 5-6 illustrates how you prepare to send invitations to a meeting.

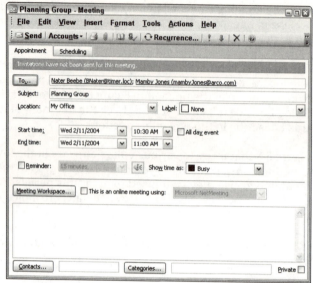

Figure 5-6:
Fill in the meeting title (Subject), location, and other details here.

If you want to further specify the nature of the meeting, click the Categories button or type in a message in the text box beneath the Meeting Workspace button. When you're finished, click the Send button on the toolbar, and e-mail is automatically sent to your attendee list, as well as notices and reminders (if any) entered into their Outlook Calendars.

Click the Scheduling tab shown in Figure 5-6 to get to the same free/busy view illustrated in Figure 5-5. You can check others' schedules either first (as described earlier) or after you've filled in the invitation e-mail, as shown in Figure 5-6.

Responding to invitations

After your invites have been sent out, the startled targets see a special e-mail in their Inbox, complete with several filled-in responses: Accept, Tentative, Decline, and Propose New Time. (Too bad *The Heck With You!* isn't on the list.) A user can click any of these responses to reply to the sender, as shown in Figure 5-7.

Tracking responses

Nothing is sadder than sending out birthday party invitations to your child's "friends" and then watching the clock tick-tock as the party start-time passes and nobody shows up. (It's no good telling the little person that popularity fades and surges throughout life: Sometimes you're nobody, and then a few years later, you might be elected prom queen!)

Figure 5-7:
Simplify your reply by clicking any of the links at the top of the meeting invitation e-mail.

To see how people are responding to your meeting invitations — and risk a possible personality collapse if nobody replies — right-click a meeting that you scheduled in your Calendar. Choose Open from the context menu. You see the same dialog box shown in Figure 5-6, but now it has a Tracking tab added to it. Click that tab, and you see the dialog box shown in Figure 5-8.

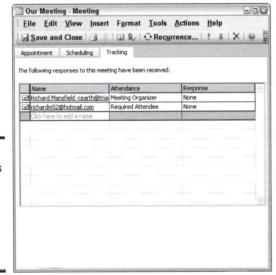

Figure 5-8:
Nobody has accepted your invitation. Could it be *unpopularity?!*

Setting up resource responses

Whoever manages company resources — meeting rooms, laser light shows, expensive catered hors d'oeuvres, company apartments, whatever — can work with administrators or developers to automate the process of allocating time at the apartment for visiting bigwigs or arranging a real nice spread for the next fancy meeting. (I suggest lobster-asparagus salad, a pile of giant shrimp mounded on crushed ice, rumaki, mushrooms stuffed with crab . . . things like that. Martha would know what to order.)

To make such arrangements do this, choose Tools⇨Options and then click the Calendar Options button. Click the Resource Scheduling button to open the dialog box shown in Figure 5-9.

Figure 5-9:
Automate
resource
allocation
here.

Select the check boxes shown in Figure 5-9 to specify the options you want. Then click OK to close the Resource Scheduling dialog box and begin the automatic process of coordinating and scheduling resources.

Chapter 6: Advanced Outlook Macros

In This Chapter

✔ Accessing other Office applications from within Outlook

✔ Trapping events

✔ Searching e-mail

✔ Paying attention to macro-ergonomics for the user

*T*o run the programming code in this chapter, you must first ensure that the necessary code libraries are referenced in the Outlook VBA editor. As grammars go, few world languages — either historical or contemporary — are as mangled and senseless as the mishmash grammar underlying computer languages.

Most features of computer languages have multiple names, often with no distinctions in meaning — not even subtle distinctions. For example, the term *function* has lately been less popular than the term *method,* although they mean the same thing.

Likewise, when you add a *reference* to a VBA project, you find many, many synonyms for what is probably best described simply as a *code library:* that is, a collection of code into a library that adds functionality (adds new functions, usually) to a programming language such as VBA. Synonyms for code library include

Assembly	Host object model
Control library	Proxylib
Control type library	Type library
Class library	Plug-in
Object library	Plug-in type library
Namespace	Services
Project model	Services library
Object model	Development environment

Core type library	Kernel
Extensibility	Helper (!? This one must have been named by a seven-year-old just before nap time.)
Runtime library	
Runtime execution library	DLL (for dynamic link library)
Runtime execution engine	

Some will argue that distinctions are here. Indeed, in some cases, adjectives such as *core, control,* or *plug-in* do shade the meaning a bit. But nearly all the terms in this list are mere synonyms without even a delicate distinction between them.

Some of the terms are simply bizarre. One popular usage, object library, just makes no sense. The distinction between classes and objects is that the latter exist only during *runtime,* during execution of a program. The proper term is *class library,* for the same reason that you don't confuse a cookbook with a cafeteria.

So, take a deep breath, kiddo, try to ignore the mess and confusion, and run Outlook. Press Alt+F11 to open the VBA editor, and then choose Tools⇨ References to open the References dialog box. Ensure that the check boxes next to following code libraries are marked:

✦ Visual Basic for Applications

✦ Microsoft Outlook 11.0 Object Library

✦ OLE Automation

✦ Microsoft Office 11.0 Object Library

Interacting with Other Office Applications

You can use the `CreateObject` command to instantiate an instance of an outside application and then send data to it. Here's an example that creates a Word document, sends an e-mail from the Outlook Inbox, and then prints it in the Word document.

Open Outlook and press Alt+F11 to get to the VBA editor. Type in this macro (Listing 6-1).

Listing 6-1: Sending Inbox E-mail to Word and Then Printing It

```
Sub SendEmailToWord()
    Dim o As Outlook.Application
    Set o = CreateObject("Outlook.Application")

    Dim ns As Outlook.NameSpace
    Set ns = o.GetNamespace("MAPI")

    Dim f As Outlook.MAPIFolder
    Set f = ns.GetDefaultFolder(olFolderInbox)

    On Error GoTo ErrorHandler

Title = f.Items(2)
Body = f.Items(2).Body

s = "Title: " & Title & vbCrLf & vbCrLf
s = s & "Body: " & Body & vbCrLf

'create word doc:
Dim oWord As Object
Set oWord = CreateObject("Word.Document")

With oWord.Application
    .Selection.TypeText s
End With

Exit Sub
ErrorHandler:

MsgBox Error

End Sub
```

You start off by creating the two always-necessary Outlook objects: Application and Namespace. You must have those objects before you can create any other objects, such as a folder. Then you create an Inbox folder object so you can get to its Items collection (the individual e-mails).

Now you're about to request actual data from this folder and send it off to Word, so you insert an instruction to VBA that if there's an error, jump execution down to the ErrorHandler: location in the code and execute a message box to display the string description of the error:

```
On Error GoTo ErrorHandler
```

Then you gather the actual data, using the folder.Items collection. When the folder is an e-mail type (such as olFolderInbox), the Item object is an individual e-mail. The e-mail's Subject line is the default data, so this gives you the subject:

```
Title = f.Items(2)
```

And the text of the e-mail is found in the Body property of the Item:

```
Body = f.Items(2).Body
```

You build a string s, separating the subject from the body with carriage returns by using the built-in constant vbCrLf.

```
s = "Title: " & Title & vbCrLf & vbCrLf
s = s & "Body: " & Body & vbCrLf
```

Finally, you instantiate a Word *instance* (the application opened and running under Windows) and then create a Document object (the ordinary Word document):

```
Dim oWord As Object
Set oWord = CreateObject("Word.Document")
```

Then use the TypeText method of the Selection object to enter your e-mail message into the Word document:

```
With oWord.Application
     .Selection.TypeText s
End With
```

After that, you exit the Sub. Without this exit, your execution would fall through to the error message section of the macro and display a message box.

```
Exit Sub
```

The final result is shown in Figure 6-1.

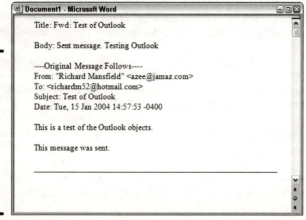

Figure 6-1:
This e-mail was plucked from Outlook's Inbox and printed in a Word document.

Trapping Events

You can go through a series of steps requiring initialization, special classes, event declarations, and so on to add event processing to an Outlook macro (see Book VI, Chapter 2), but if you want to trap events built into the Outlook `Application` object itself, the job is much easier. It's a trick, but it's extremely simple to do after you know how (rather like cooking rice).

Getting incoming mail

Suppose you want to display a message box each time mail is received in the Outlook Inbox. You could use this same technique to send automatic replies, process or route incoming mail, forward imported e-mail to your cellphone, or otherwise manage your mail as it arrives.

**Book VI
Chapter 6**

Press Alt+F11 to switch to the Outlook VBA editor. Press Ctrl+R to display the Project Editor. The `Application` object has its own special code window. To open it, click the + next to Microsoft Office Outlook Objects — a node that is inconveniently closed by default.

Advanced Outlook Macros

Open the Microsoft Office Outlook Objects node by clicking the + next to it. You then see ThisOutlookSession, the only entry in this node. Double-click ThisOutlookSession. A code window opens named ThisOutlookSession (Code), as shown in Figure 6-2.

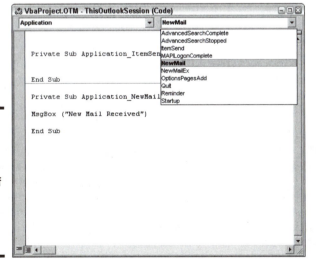

Figure 6-2:
Use this code window to trap a set of Outlook Application events.

From the top-left drop-down list, choose Application, as shown in Figure 6-2. Then open the top-right drop-down list. For this example, choose NewMail from the list of possible events you can trap.

A new subroutine is inserted into this code window: It's the event that *fires* (executes its code) whenever a new e-mail arrives:

```
Private Sub Application_NewMail()

MsgBox ("New Mail Received")

End Sub
```

Type in the message box, and then try sending yourself some e-mail to see that, indeed, the message is displayed whenever you get new e-mail.

And rice? Just dump a cup of it into a small saucepan, add 1¾ cups water, and bring to a boil. Immediately reduce to a simmer and let cook, covered, for 20 minutes. With the cover still on, remove from the heat, and let it sit for 20 more minutes. Perfect every time.

Intercepting outgoing mail

The ItemSend event, as shown in Figure 6-2, can also be a useful one. It allows you to tap into the pipeline through which outgoing mail flows before it actually hits the greater world of your LAN or the Internet itself. Type this into the ItemSend event, as I describe in the preceding section, send an e-mail, and see what happens:

```
Private Sub Application_ItemSend(ByVal Item As Object, Cancel
    As Boolean)

MsgBox (Item.Body)

End Sub
```

This event has several uses, most of them related to censorship. Maybe your husband is a golf fanatic and has dozens of expensive clubs, but both he and you know that clubs can be had for $2 at the Junior League Bargain Box. The trouble with hubby is that he realizes he has more than enough good equipment to service his rather meager skills on the green. Nonetheless, after a few liquid pick-me-ups, he sashays over to the computer and starts teasing himself with golf catalogs, golf club instant-shipping sites, and other irresistible fairway-fun enticements. Sooner or later, hubby is once again shopping under the influence. Perhaps you could put some code into the ItemSend event to quietly divert his e-mails to a folder for cooler heads to review in the morning.

Searching via Iteration

No built-in search feature can possibly provide the flexibility that you get when you program your own search. For example, what if you want to search your entire Sent Mail folder? (I never empty or archive mine; I just let them sit there for searches.) You could use Outlook's Tools⇨Find feature. Outlook's Find engine is unique among Office 2003 applications in two ways: It's on the Tools menu rather than the Edit menu, and it's more flexible and feature-rich than others. But what if you want to search for the two most recent e-mails?

Run an advanced search. Start by choosing Tools⇨Find⇨Advanced Find to bring up the dialog box shown in Figure 6-3.

**Book VI
Chapter 6**

**Advanced Outlook
Macros**

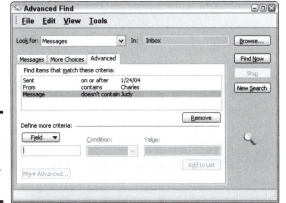

Figure 6-3:
The Outlook Find feature is extremely flexible.

You do have the limitation of not being able to specify OR searches, though, like finding any reference to *money* in messages from Fred or Suzy. Nor can you combine searches, like if you want to display all messages arriving only during the month of February for the past five years. And so on. Specialized searches can be important, particularly if the data store is quite large.

However, the following macro (Listing 6-2) allows you to specify whatever conditions you wish for the search. Here, the InStr function searches the body field (the message part) of each Sent Mail message for the word *reason*. You can use multiple InStr functions to specify the details of your search as well as the various fields you want to involve in the search. When finished, any e-mails that match the search criteria are printed in a Word document for you to read.

Listing 6-2: Outlook Search Macro

```
Sub FindIterate()

    Dim o As Outlook.Application
    Set o = CreateObject("Outlook.Application")

    Dim ns As Outlook.NameSpace
    Set ns = o.GetNamespace("MAPI")

    Dim f As Outlook.MAPIFolder
    Set f = ns.GetDefaultFolder(olFolderSentMail)

    On Error GoTo ErrorHandler


n = f.Items.Count

For i = 1 To n

If InStr(f.Items(i).Body, "reason") Then
x = x + 1

from = f.Items(i).SenderName
Title = f.Items(i).Subject
Body = f.Items(i).Body

s = s & x & "." & vbCrLf & " From: " & from & vbCrLf
s = s & " Title: " & Title & vbCrLf
s = s & "Body: " & Body & vbCrLf & "................." &
         vbCrLf & vbCrLf


End If

Next

If x = 0 Then MsgBox "No match found.": Exit Sub

'create word doc:
Dim oWord As Object
Set oWord = CreateObject("Word.Document")

With oWord.Application
    .Selection.TypeText s
End With

Exit Sub
ErrorHandler:

MsgBox Error

End Sub
```

This macro first uses the `Count` property to read the total number of messages in your Sent Mail folder (after having created the usual necessary objects via `Dim` and `Set`).

Then you use a `For Next` loop to search through the entire collection (`f.items`) of messages for a match to the word *reason*. You next look at each e-mail by using the `InStr` function; if there's a hit, you increment your hit counter (the variable `x`):

```
If InStr(f.Items(i).Body, "reason") Then
x = x + 1
```

If an e-mail matches, you pick off the From, Subject, and Message portions of the e-mail:

```
from = f.Items(i).SenderName
Title = f.Items(i).Subject
Body = f.Items(i).Body
```

And then you build a string `s` containing these items, separated by carriage returns.

A *carriage return* is an old term from typewriter days when you shoved the black paper roller — the *carriage* — back over to the left side each time you wanted to move down a line on the page. `Cr` stands for carriage return; `lf` stands for line feed (go down to the next line).

You continue through the loop, building the string with every new hit. Then when you've gone through the entire collection of messages, you send the completed string off to a new Word document.

Bringing Macros to the User

The preceding example cries out for a UserForm to interact with someone wanting to do a search. For one thing, you can provide the user with a text box in which to enter the search term(s). Putting Outlook macros that you use frequently on an Outlook toolbar is also useful.

Creating a UserForm

To create a UserForm so users can interact with your macros, first press Alt+F11 to switch to the VBA editor. There, choose Insert➪UserForm.

Drag two text boxes, two option buttons, and a button onto the UserForm. Press F4 to reveal the Properties window. Change the `Caption` property of the button to read `Click to Search`. Change the `Multiline` property of TextBox2 to `True` and its `ScrollBars` property to `Vertical`. Change the `Caption` properties of the option buttons, as shown in Figure 6-4.

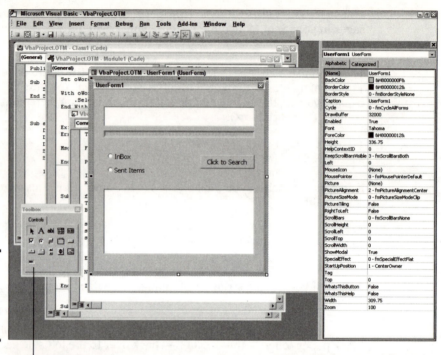

Figure 6-4:
Modify this
search form
any way you
want.

ProgressBar control

Because a large Inbox or Sent Items folder can take a while to search, you
want to add a progress bar for this kind of utility — something to show that
some progress is actually being made and that the program hasn't frozen.

By default, a progress bar control isn't on the Toolbox. To add a progress bar
to your Toolbox, follow these steps:

1. **Right-click the Toolbox.**

2. **From the context menu that appears, choose Additional Controls.**

3. **In the Additional Controls dialog box that appears, choose the
   Microsoft ProgressBar control by selecting its check box.**

4. **Close the dialog box.**

   The ProgressBar control is now available on the Toolbox.

Now add the progress bar control onto the UserForm.

1. **Drag the ProgressBar control onto the UserForm.**

   When users execute your search utility, they'll see how much time is left
   indicated by this progress bar, as shown in Figure 6-5.

TIP

Users expect to see movement in a progress bar like this, or at least a blinking light, to indicate activity if a job takes more than a few seconds.

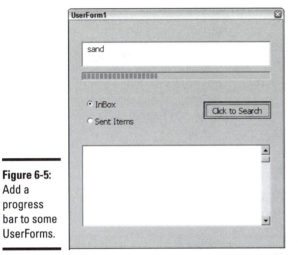

Figure 6-5:
Add a
progress
bar to some
UserForms.

2. **Double-click the command button to open its** `Click` **event in the code window. Type the code in Listing 6-3 into the** `Click` **event.**

3. **Press F5 to test the macro.**

   You should see results similar to Figure 6-6.

Figure 6-6:
The utility
works
flawlessly,
finding all
hits within a
folder.

Listing 6-3:   Searching with User Interaction

```
Private Sub CommandButton1_Click()

If TextBox1.Text = "" Then _
MsgBox ("You must type in a search term in the upper
           textbox."): Exit Sub

If OptionButton1.Value = False And OptionButton2.Value =
           False Then _
MsgBox ("Choose an OptionButton"): Exit Sub


    Dim o As Outlook.Application
    Set o = CreateObject("Outlook.Application")

    Dim ns As Outlook.NameSpace
    Set ns = o.GetNamespace("MAPI")

    Dim f As Outlook.MAPIFolder
    'figure out which folder:

    If OptionButton1.Value = True Then
        Set f = ns.GetDefaultFolder(olFolderInbox)
Else
        Set f = ns.GetDefaultFolder(olFolderSentMail)

    End If


    On Error GoTo ErrorHandler

n = f.Items.Count

ProgressBar1.Max = n

Target = TextBox1.Text

For i = 1 To n

ProgressBar1.Value = i

If InStr(f.Items(i).Body, Target) Then
x = x + 1

from = f.Items(i).SenderName
Title = f.Items(i).Subject
Body = f.Items(i).Body
```

```
s = s & x & "." & vbCrLf & " From: " & from & vbCrLf
s = s & " Title: " & Title & vbCrLf
s = s & "Body: " & Body & vbCrLf & "................" &
         vbCrLf & vbCrLf


End If

Next

If x = 0 Then TextBox2.Text = "No match found.": Exit Sub

TextBox2.Text = s


Exit Sub
ErrorHandler:

MsgBox Error

End Sub
```

This code begins by checking whether the user has chosen an
OptionButton and entered a search term.

The usual object instantiation follows, but the namespace object's Get
DefaultFolder method requires different arguments based on whether the
user chose the Inbox or the Sent Items, so you differentiate them this way:

```
If OptionButton1.Value = True Then
    Set f = ns.GetDefaultFolder(olFolderInbox)
Else
    Set f = ns.GetDefaultFolder(olFolderSentMail)

End If
```

You can add additional options such as searches of the Calendar, Notes,
Contacts, and so on, by using Select Case or a series of If...Then statements, like this:

```
If OptionButton3.Value = True Then
    Set f = ns.GetDefaultFolder(olFolderCalendar)
End If
```

However, if you go beyond an e-mail search, you need to modify the fields
(properties) of the Items collection by adjusting the properties specified in
these lines of code:

```
from = f.Items(i).SenderName
Title = f.Items(i).Subject
Body = f.Items(i).Body
```

You can execute a UserForm from the VBA editor for testing purposes by either clicking the UserForm to select it and then pressing F5, or by pressing F5 from within the code itself.

The progress bar must be given a `Max` property that reflects the total number of activities it is illustrating: in this case, the total number of e-mails being searched (the `Count` property of the `Items` collection): `ProgressBar1.Max = n`.

Then you get the user's search term: `Target = TextBox1.Text`. And within the loop, the progress bar is continually updated, employing the variable `i`, representing the current e-mail count as the loop increments:

```
For i = 1 To n
ProgressBar1.Value = I
```

Adding macros to your toolbar

You can execute macros from Outlook toolbars. To add a macro to a toolbar, follow these steps:

1. **If the target toolbar isn't visible, right-click an open toolbar. (If it is, skip to Step 3.)**

   You see a context menu.

2. **Click a new toolbar name if you want it visible.**

3. **Right-click the toolbar that you want to add a macro to.**

4. **From the context menu that appears, choose Customize.**

   The Customize dialog box appears.

5. **Click the Commands tab in the Customize dialog box.**

6. **Click Macros in the Categories list.**

7. **Drag the macro that you want and drop it onto the toolbar.**

Book VII

InterOffice: Working as a Team

The 5th Wave
By Rich Tennant

"IT'S A SOFTWARE PROGRAM THAT MORE FULLY RE-FLECTS AN ACTUAL OFFICE ENVIRONMENT. IT MULTI-TASKS WITH OTHER USERS, INTEGRATES SHARED DATA, AND THEN USES THAT INFORMATION TO NETWORK VICIOUS RUMORS THROUGH AN INTER-OFFICE LINK-UP."

Contents at a Glance

Chapter 1: Collaboration Features Overview

In This Chapter

✔ Using OneNote

✔ Using SharePoint for shared Contacts

✔ Exploiting document collaboration

✔ Tackling the versioning problem

✔ Setting up a Meeting Workspace

You'll find lots of ways to communicate between Office 2003 applications and between Office 2003 users. Sharing information can require that you resolve security issues, versioning problems (whose version of an edited document should be saved as the official, final one?), and other issues that arise when people try to avoid stepping on each other's toes.

Working in groups has its advantages. For one thing, many people think it's just fine to attend meetings on subjects they know nothing about. Also, when things go wrong, being in a group dilutes the blame.

This chapter is an overview, so several of the topics introduced here are covered in more depth in other chapters. For example, SharePoint is explored in detail in Book VII, Chapter 8, but presented briefly here.

Exploring OneNote

The first utility to consider when working with groups is *OneNote,* which is Microsoft's attempt to create an electronic equivalent of a legal pad. The idea is that laptops and notebooks flip up fence-like barriers at meetings — the portables' screens isolate participants from one another — so we should all migrate to the less intrusive writing pad, an electronic version of which is the Tablet PC. OneNote doesn't ship with any version of Office 2003. It's sold separately for a list price of $199.

In OneNote, you can type, insert pictures, write by hand, or even draw on the background or on top of pictures, which is useful for annotations and diagramming. (See Figure 1-1.) You can more easily (and portably) take written and oral notes (think meetings, classes, interviews, and lectures) or collect research. If you want something half-way between the power of Word documents and the simplicity of Notepad text files, OneNote might fill the bill for you. The side note feature alone is quite valuable because it automatically stores and saves short notes.

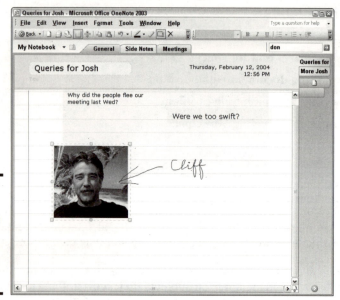

Figure 1-1:
Being able to draw and write in OneNote is a useful feature.

Handwriting in OneNote

OneNote can also be used on an ordinary computer, but its handwriting feature is awkward at best when using a mouse. A mouse is just not finely calibrated enough to reproduce pen-like strokes, so you end up with strange, five-year-old scrawling instead of your usual script.

Recording in OneNote

You can even record in your notes. In Figure 1-2, notice the audio recording icon. Just click it to hear its message.

Sending a OneNote document

To send a OneNote document, choose File⇨Email, and the document drops down to allow you to fill in the address and subject and also add any additional text you want, as shown in Figure 1-3.

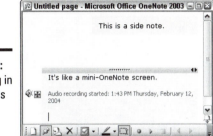

Figure 1-2:
Recording in
OneNote is
a useful
feature.

Figure 1-3:
Sending
OneNote
documents
via e-mail
is simple.

The recipient gets an interesting combination of embedded graphics and copyable text. One of the big drawbacks (to me at least) of PDF files (used with Adobe Acrobat Reader) is that the text is essentially a picture of text. That is, you cannot copy, cut, paste, or otherwise manipulate it. Perhaps there's a version of Acrobat that avoids this shortcoming, but OneNote does a good job of allowing text-editing while mixing in graphics or drawings of any kind.

When a OneNote message arrives in Outlook, it appears like the one in Figure 1-4.

Figure 1-4:
A recipient
of a
OneNote
message
can copy
and paste
its contents.

Side notes in OneNote

OneNote installs a tray icon, which is always near your clock. Click this icon for you to add a new *side note* (as shown in Figure 1-1), which is like an abbreviated version of the full OneNote utility. OneNote doesn't need to be open when you work with side notes; these are saved in a folder in OneNote, which is a nice touch of automatic organization.

The point of side notes is that they're fast and automatic: just as Notepad is often easier to use than Word when jotting down some brief text, so too is a side note easier than firing up the full OneNote application. In fact, side notes are easier than Notepad. To create a side note, you click its icon in the system tray, then when you're done writing your note, you just close its window, and it's automatically stored for you in the main OneNote application for later use.

Saving a side note

Saving a side note couldn't be any easier: You don't have to do anything. You open the side note, jot down whatever you want (or speak into your mike), and then just close the side note window. Even though you never saved the note, it's still there for you in OneNote's searchable Side Notes folder, as shown in Figure 1-5.

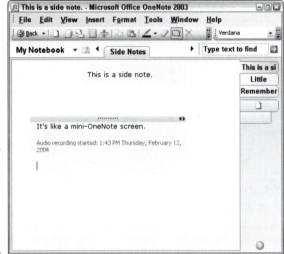

Figure 1-5:
Use the tabs here to identify stored side notes.

OneNote documents, as well as side notes, never require you to actually back up or save your notes. This is done automatically for you. Just close OneNote or side note windows, go about your business, and they're saved for you automatically.

More side note toys

Also, side notes go quite a bit beyond what you've done in the past with little text editors like Notepad. You can add importance flags, add new pages, choose from a set of different formatting pens and highlighters, add audio notes, and spell check. Side notes can also be made *modal* (always on top of other windows and applications) if you wish. The new Office 2003 Research pane is even available in these little note windows, as shown in Figure 1-6, where the squiggle line indicates a misspelled word.

The one feature that I wish were available is a way to link the notes to locations in Word documents and other Office 2003 applications.

Figure 1-6:
Little side notes can even be spell checked. A lot of functionality is packed into these little note takers.

Introducing SharePoint

SharePoint allows Office 2003 users to broadly communicate in various ways, depending on permissions levels and other factors. For in-depth coverage of SharePoint, see Book VII, Chapter 8, which is entirely devoted to that topic.

✦ Look at each other's Contact lists, events, and other Outlook items and folders.

✦ Manage files in shared documents folders and send copies of shared attachments to e-mail.

✦ Manage data located on the SharePoint Server with Excel.

✦ Create document workspaces and meeting workspaces, linked directly to Outlook meeting requests.

✦ Manage Web discussions while collaborating on presentations or other documents such as Excel worksheets.

✦ Share graphics libraries and other data stores.

In addition, various kinds of lists can be manipulated on the server, such as links, upcoming events (this list is built in), or pretty much any other kind of list.

Sharing Outlook Contacts

Here's one example of using SharePoint. You can share Contacts, among other items, when you're using an Exchange Server e-mail account. Click Contacts in the Outlook navigation pane (on the left side), and then click

Share My Contacts. Click Default in the Name box and select the permission level that you want to grant. Note that these permissions are similar to the schedule of various permissions granted by Windows administrators to others on the network.

Levels of permission

Here's a list of the levels of Outlook permissions and their features:

✦ **Owner:** Total control; can read, create, change or delete any items (like Appointments, e-mails, Tasks, and so on.) Can also do anything with folders, including adjusting permission levels for each folder, and can create subfolders.

✦ **Publishing Editor:** Same as owner but cannot manage permissions.

✦ **Editor:** Same as Publishing Editor but cannot create subfolders.

✦ **Publishing Author:** Can create and read items and files, create sub-folders, and can modify and delete items and files that this person creates.

✦ **Author:** Can create and read items and files; can modify and delete items and files that this person creates.

✦ **Contributor:** Can create items and files only.

✦ **Reviewer:** Can only read items and files.

✦ **Custom:** Folder's owner can specify permissions.

Shared Workspaces

Shared Workspaces allow a group working together on a project to maintain all their project-related files in a central repository on a Web server. In Word, choose Tools⇨Shared Workspace. A pane opens on the right side of your Word document, as shown in Figure 1-7.

By default, the pane lists any documents in the same library as the currently opened document. You can also create libraries of other shared items, such as graphics files.

After you create a shared workspace, you can then pester others sharing this space with hyperlinks, additional documents, and even task lists that contain to-do items for each other. It becomes a kind of group information manager.

Figure 1-7:
Use this
panel to
access
shared
documents
and
workspaces.

Conquering the version problem

Of course, sharing means (by definition) passing around the good with the bad. The bad, in the case of Shared Workspaces, could mean "Who knows which version of documents should be considered the best, final one?" And by *final,* I don't mean the most recent but instead the one that should ultimately be used (and all other versions discarded).

Document updating in SharePoint can be used with PowerPoint, Word, Visio, or Excel documents. When you open a copy of such a document for your own purposes, Office 2003 makes any updates to this document by others available for your perusal. Say that Sally deleted a paragraph that you want left in. This is your opportunity to compare your version with hers and make a final decision. Of course, others sharing this space with you and Sally will also have to incorporate this version with theirs. This versioning problem cannot be easily solved unless one person has the job of making the final review and the final decision. And documents within a Meeting Workspace are guaranteed to be the latest version, so that worry is eliminated.

Establishing a Meeting Workspace

Meeting Workspaces are another built-in feature available in SharePoint Services. Similar to the scheduling system in Outlook 2003, the SharePoint Meeting Workspace is a location where you can conveniently store lists of people scheduled to attend a meeting, notes, support data such as diagrams or reports, and other information relating to a meeting. This information is for the most part maintained and updated automatically for you after you create a Meeting Workspace subsite.

Perhaps this should be given a grander name than *meeting* because it's actually capable of more than managing single meetings. Indeed, this kind of store can hold information for an ongoing project — a series of meetings, not just a single meeting. Minutes from past meetings, as well as announcements of upcoming meetings, can all be shared and viewed by the collective participants. You can manage recurring meetings here and otherwise manipulate the data for your project or a set of related projects.

Meeting Workspaces also avoid the traditional flurry of e-mails, attachments, or paper documents that must be provided to someone who joins a project after a couple of meetings have already taken place. If you have a well-maintained Meeting Workspace — including details about the events that took place in each meeting after it's over — all you have to do is give the new project member access to the Meeting Workspace, and she can see all the information she needs to get up-to-speed.

This isn't a Messenger Chat or anything. You don't have to communicate and meet with the other attendees in realtime via the Meeting Workspace. Instead, it's merely a location to store relevant documents, agendas, lists, and so on. People in the meeting, however, might certainly want to be connected to the Workspace during the meeting to be able to view the documents.

To set up a Meeting Workspace, you must use Exchange Server and have access to a SharePoint Services or SharePoint Portal server site. The Workspace can grow out of an Outlook Calendar meeting request:

1. **Right-click the day in your Outlook Calendar when you want to have the meeting.**

   A context menu appears, as shown in Figure 1-8.

2. **Choose New Meeting Request.**

   The context menu closes, and the Meeting dialog box opens.

**Book VII
Chapter 1**

**Collaboration
Features Overview**

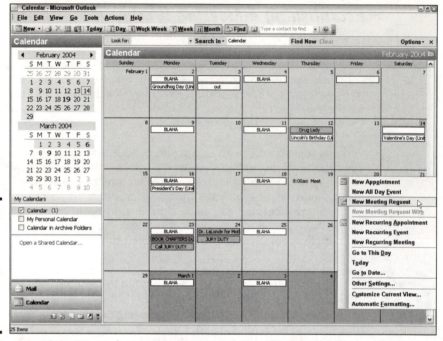

Figure 1-8:
Begin a
Meeting
Workspace
by request-
ing a
meeting in
Outlook.

3. Fill in the fields in the dialog box describing the details of the meeting and the recipients of the notice. Also look at the Scheduling tab to see whether this feature is available for the participants.

Outlook automatically modifies the Meeting Workspace data if you should later make any changes to the date, time, location, attendees, and so on. You make these modifications as you would for any ordinary meeting scheduled via the Outlook Calendar: by updating the information in the Request dialog box (double-click the meeting in the Calendar).

4. Click the Appointment tab in the dialog box.

5. Click the Meeting Workspace button.

A new right pane appears in the dialog box, as shown in Figure 1-9.

6. Click the Change Settings link.

7. Choose the Create a New Workspace option.

A new pane appears.

8. Choose the language, workspace template, or other options you want.

Your choices will reappear as default options when you set up future meetings with this pane.

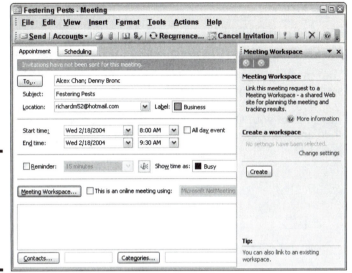

**Book VII
Chapter 1**

**Collaboration
Features Overview**

Figure 1-9:
Use this
Meeting
Workspace
pane to set
up a new
meeting.

9. **Click OK.**

You return to the first task pane.

10. **Click the Create button.**

Your new Meeting Workspace site's link is added to your meeting
request, and the subject, date, time, and location of your meeting
request are automatically added to the workspace site, as shown in
Figure 1-10.

Figure 1-10:
A new
Meeting
Workspace
has been
created,
and here's
its link.

11. **Click the link to see the workspace (named <u>Festering Pests</u> in the
example after the Subject specified when the meeting was initially set
up in Step 3).**

12. **Press Alt+Tab.**

You return to Outlook.

13. **Click the Send button in the Meeting dialog box (refer to Figure 1-9).**

Your meeting request and details about the Meeting Workspace are now sent to all the people listed in the To field.

Any meetings in your Outlook 2003 calendar that have a Meeting Workspace attached are easily identified by the little three-people-at-a-table icon shown in Figure 1-11.

Figure 1-11:
This icon next to a meeting in Outlook's calendar indicates that a Meeting Workspace is available for this meeting.

Chapter 2: Managing Shared Documents

In This Chapter

✔ Using the new Information Rights Management

✔ Setting permissions

✔ Changing Workspace options

✔ Protecting documents in Word

*W*hen collaborating on documents, it's too easy for co-workers to get in each other's way. Perhaps there's a wild writer trying to work with a very picky editor or vice versa. Or perhaps the accounting department wants an entirely different kind of document than the graphics department — one with fewer border decorations and a less-intense design.

In any case, group document-making, like group music, has to be orchestrated and controlled. First, participants all have to be together in rhythm, trying to harmonize if the end result is to be useful . . . not to mention appealing. Second, you need to manage the collaborators so that no one inadvertently (nor deliberately) damages the contributions of another. These goals are more likely to be achieved by using various features built into Office 2003, such as the new Information Rights Management technology, managing permissions and workspace options, and protecting documents in various ways. That's what this chapter is all about.

Restricting Documents with IRM

New in Office 2003 is *Information Rights Management* (IRM), which you can use to apply specifically restricted permission settings to documents, e-mail, and other files. You specify policies that govern who can copy, forward, print, or even *open* documents created in Word, Excel, Outlook, and PowerPoint.

Despite its strides, IRM isn't the panacea for all document protection, although it can prevent documents from being forwarded, copied, or printed. The PrintScreen key *is* disabled by IRM, but nothing prevents you from taking a digital picture using widely available screen capture utilities. Save the document as a graphic file and send it hither and yon.

IRM does have one rather slick trick up its sleeve, though. Like *Mission Impossible* tapes, you can give documents a *lifetime;* that is, set them to self-destruct at some point in the future. *Expire* is the polite term for this.

IRM's full feature set is available only in the Professional and Enterprise editions of Office 2003, with Windows Server 2003, and works only with documents created by Word, Excel, Outlook, or PowerPoint. However, users of the other Office 2003 editions (Standard, Small Business, and Student and Teacher) can, with your permission, edit or read IRM-protected files and e-mail.

Suppose you want to set permissions levels for a Word document — that is, access to the document with various specified degrees of control over the document. Begin by choosing File➪Permission. If you see the dialog box displayed in Figure 2-1, you need to install or update the new IRM feature. This requires that you have Windows Rights Management client (some software) installed on your system.

Figure 2-1:
If you see this, you have to install or update IRM on your system.

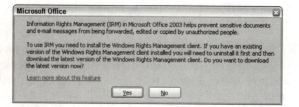

Viewing IRM-protected files

IRM protection might have its uses, but what about those folks who are not on your LAN and can't participate in the IRM system, such as a customer? And how do you take care of those folks who aren't using Office 2003?

Relax. You're covered. IRM-protected documents can be shared with outsiders even if they don't use Office 2003. A free IRM viewer (technically, the Rights Management Add-on for Internet Explorer) can be provided to outsiders, letting them view IRM-protected files. One small catch: The outsider must be granted explicit permission to view the file, though. This viewer can be downloaded from www.microsoft.com/windows/ie/downloads/addon.

When you install IRM on your machine — at least at the time of this writing — after some preliminaries, two apparently related entities (Activates Machine and the mysterious GIC, according to my firewall) access the Internet. After that, the installation completes. Then you move to Phase Two, authentication.

Phase Two: Authentication

After you install/update IRM, you have one more step before you can begin assigning permissions. You need some way to let IRM know — *authenticate* — the users who create or receive document with set permissions. You do this through the MS Information Rights Management server or your own rights management server.

MS offers a free trial service, but you must use .NET Passport. The Passport authenticates those people who are attempting to access restricted content.

Choose File⇨Permission⇨Restrict Permission As (after the IRM client is installed). The Service Sign-Up dialog box, as shown in Figure 2-2, appears. This is where you can opt for the free trial server authentication service from MS.

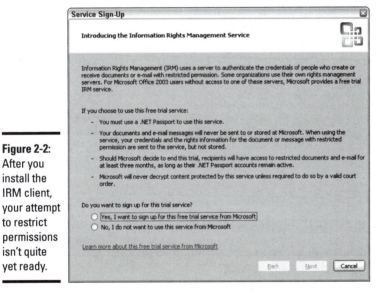

Figure 2-2: After you install the IRM client, your attempt to restrict permissions isn't quite yet ready.

If your company use custom rights management systems, you need not sign up for the Microsoft management service, which requires .NET Passport. The Passport authenticates people who are attempting to access restricted content.

Setting permissions in IRM

After you follow the steps in the preceding sections and are a full-power IRM user — that is, you have the IRM up and running and you've enabled an authentication server — you can set permissions. Lock and seal your documents by following these steps:

1. Choose File⇨Permission⇨Restrict Permission.

You see the Select User dialog box.

2. Choose the user account and click OK.

The dialog box closes, and the Permission dialog box opens, as shown in Figure 2-3.

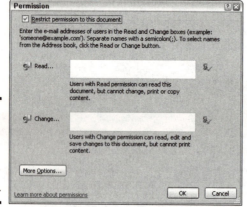

Figure 2-3:
Decide here who gets editing and read-only permissions.

3. Select the Restrict Permission to This Document check box.

4. Add the users to whom you're granting permission.

5. Click the More Options button.

You see a different Permission dialog box, as shown in Figure 2-4.

6. Select the various options you're interested in.

For example, specify when the document self-destructs.

7. Click OK to close the dialog box.

You now see your document with a special Shared Workspace pane on the right side, as illustrated in Figure 2-5.

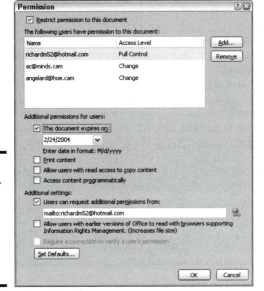

Figure 2-4:
Set permissions (and when this document goes up in flames) here.

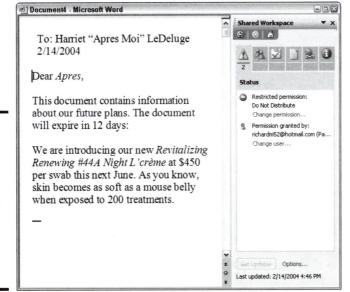

Figure 2-5:
These explosive details about the company's new unguent will self-destruct 2/24/04.

Using IRM in Outlook

IRM works in Excel and PowerPoint the same way it works in Word, as I describe earlier in this chapter. You have the same options and capabilities. In Outlook, however, things are a little different, given that this application focuses on messaging and scheduling. Here's one interesting feature: You can specify IRM behaviors and conditions for e-mail that you've already sent.

You can specify that e-mail cannot be printed, copied, or forwarded. This obviously is a limited protection. Recipients cannot use File⇨Print, Edit⇨ Copy, or the forward option, but they can certainly take a screenshot of the message. Interestingly, Microsoft's documentation for IRM doesn't say that it *prevents* copying. It only says this technology will *help prevent*.

To use IRM in Outlook, click the Mail folder, and then choose File⇨New⇨ Mail Message. In the Message dialog box, choose File⇨Permission⇨Restrict Permission As. Your e-mail is then given a header, as shown in Figure 2-6.

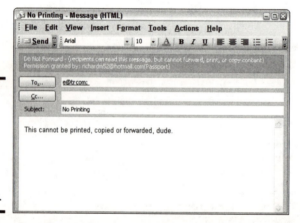

Figure 2-6: Notice the warning: Do Not Forward. Nor can you copy or print this.

When a protected e-mail is received, the Copy, Print, and Forward options are disabled. Further, any attachment to protected e-mail is given the same restrictions. And messages are encrypted during transmission so if someone intercepts them on the Internet or your intranet, the restrictions that you place on the contents cannot be adjusted by the outsider.

Changing Workspace Options

Shared Workspaces allow a group working together on a project to maintain all their project-related files in a central repository on a Web server. Shared documents are also *dynamic:* They can be changed and updated. Just as you can specify how frequently Outlook updates your e-mail by automatically sending and receiving, you can also specify how frequently you want shared documents updated.

You can also decide whether changes you've made to a document should be automatically the *final version* changes — that is, whether your version of this document should supersede anyone else's editing.

Click the Options link in the Shared Workspace pane. You see the various choices displayed in Figure 2-7.

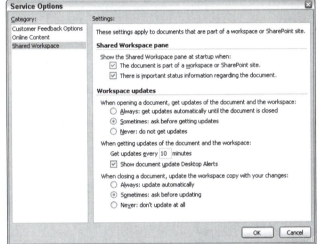

Figure 2-7: Adjust these options to specify how you want shared documents to behave.

Book VII Chapter 2

Managing Shared Documents

Using Word's Protect Document Feature

If you don't want to go to the trouble of using IRM, Word itself has a built-in protection scheme. Choose Tools⇨Protect Document, and you see the Protect Document pane, as shown in Figure 2-8.

Select the Limit Formatting to a Selection of Styles check box. Then click the Settings link, and you see the Formatting Restrictions dialog box, as shown in Figure 2-9. If a style in this list isn't selected, others cannot modify text written in that style.

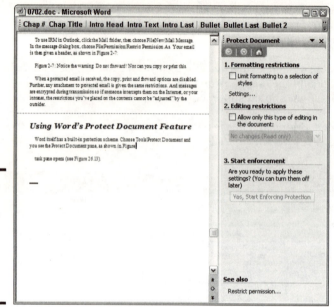

Figure 2-8:
Protect
documents
from
unwanted
changes
via these
settings.

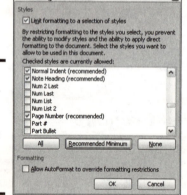

Figure 2-9:
The recom-
mended
minimum
restrictions
on styles
that others
can modify.

Now click Cancel to see the Protect Document task pane again; this time, try
the other options. Select the Allow Only This Type of Editing in the
Document check box. You see a couple of drop-down lists, illustrated in
Figure 2-10.

The final option is to drag your mouse to select areas within your document, and then specify who — on your list of groups; see the Groups list in
Figure 2-10 — is permitted to edit those selected zones. The editable zones
then turn a cunning, pale peach color, enclosed within gray brackets.

Figure 2-10:
Restrict
would-be
editors to
messing
around
with only
Tracked
Changes,
Comments,
Filling in
Forms, or
No Changes
(Read-only).

When you click the Yes, Start Enforcing Protection button, you see the dialog box shown in Figure 2-11.

Figure 2-11:
Either enter
a password
here or
choose
authenti-
cation to
control who
gets to
unlock the
protection.

Managing Versions in Word

Word 2003 includes a new way to keep track of various versions of a document: It maintains the versions in one file. This can assist considerably in preventing problems caused by a single document's various versions stored in files located here and there.

To create this kind of multiple-versions file, follow these steps:

1. **Choose File⇨Versions.**

You see the Versions dialog box.

2. **Click the Save Now button.**

The Save Version dialog box opens, as shown in Figure 2-12.

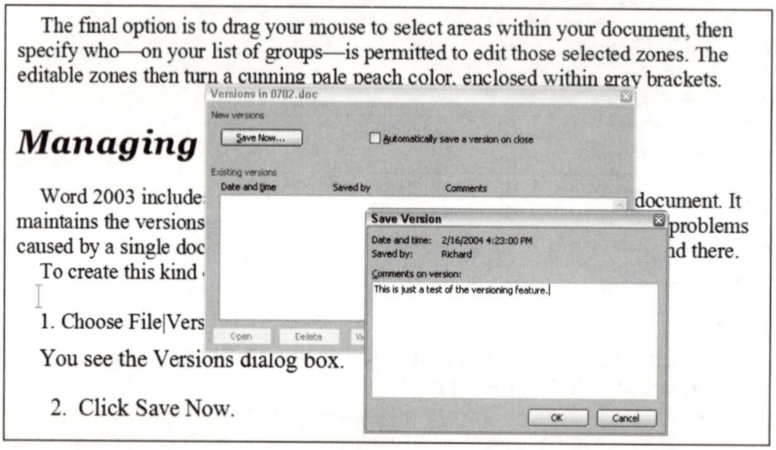

The final option is to drag your mouse to select areas within your document, then specify who—on your list of groups—is permitted to edit those selected zones. The editable zones then turn a cunning pale peach color, enclosed within gray brackets.

Figure 2-12:
Use these dialog boxes to store multiple versions of the same document in one file.

Managing

Word 2003 include~ document. It maintains the versions ~problems caused by a single doc~ ~d there.

To create this kind ~

1. Choose File|Vers~

You see the Versions dialog box.

2. Click Save Now.

Versions in 0702.doc

New versions
Save Now... ☐ Automatically save a version on close

Existing versions
Date and time   Saved by   Comments

Save Version
Date and time: 2/16/2004 4:23:00 PM
Saved by: Richard
Comments on version:
This is just a test of the versioning feature.

Open   Delete   Vi

OK   Cancel

---

3. **Type in any comments you want to include to identify this version, such as,** Marty really made some good suggestions on this one!

4. **Click OK.**

The new version is saved and date-stamped; both dialog boxes close.

5. **Choose File⇨Versions.**

You now see a list of all the previously saved versions, with descriptions, who saved them, and the date/time-stamp. They are shown in order of most recently saved version. You're free to delete any versions you no longer need and to choose to automatically save a new version each time you close Word. The file size increases by about 300 percent, from a typical 80K to 230K, but who cares? You can get 120MB hard drives these days for $60. The time it takes to save the file doesn't seem to increase much, if any.

Chapter 3: XML and Office

In This Chapter

- ✔ Displaying documents in a browser
- ✔ Building Web pages
- ✔ Adjusting properties
- ✔ Viewing code
- ✔ Writing scripts
- ✔ Scripting in Excel
- ✔ Debugging script
- ✔ Using forms

In this chapter, I explore ways to use Office 2003 applications to generate Web pages. You see both how to simply display passive data by merely saving documents as Web pages, and also how to interact with the user via scripting, using the built-in Script Editor. You also see how to employ forms and debug your projects.

Communicating via a Web Page

One way to communicate with customers, or between Office 2003 users, is to set up a Web page. Office 2003 provides various tools for this task, including displaying a Word document in HTML format in a Web page. There's even a special scripting editor built into Word 2003, Access, and Excel with which you can create programming and interactivity for your Web page. However, for the greatest power, scalability, design freedom, testing capabilities, and efficiency, I urge you to look into ASP.NET available in Visual Studio .NET. Displaying Office 2003 applications' documents and elements in a Web page is a quick and often functional solution. But if you need serious interactivity — such as allowing the user to interact with your online inventory, or place orders over the Internet — you need something more robust than the Web tools built into Office 2003 products.

Some readers at this point are saying under their breath: *Well!* If ASP.NET is a superior approach to Web programming, why spend the better part of this chapter covering scripting? Fair question. The answer is that scripting remains an important technology because it easily integrates into various XML technologies where full-featured languages do not, ASP.NET excepted. Also, scripting is a fairly mature technology, with its own efficiencies for use with small-to-medium programming tasks. For example, scripting is the programming technology built into Access's Data Access Pages, and also Microsoft's new InfoPath application, as you'll see in the next chapter of this mini-book.

To see how to build and program a Web page by using Word, follow these steps:

1. **Start a new Word document and build your Web page.**

2. **Type in two paragraphs of text.**

3. **Add a headline between the two paragraphs by choosing Format⇨ Styles and Formatting, and then choosing a headline style from the list displayed.**

4. **Add a diagram or photo (Insert⇨Diagram or Insert⇨Picture).**

Word does its best to generate usable HTML from whatever formatting and other elements you add to your Word document. HTML generally doesn't generate error messages itself when a page is displayed in a Web; it just ignores problems and displays the page as well as it can. You can use parsers and editors that will flag HTML errors, including the Script Editor built into Word or Excel (which I describe later in the section, "Scripting"). Also, the latest versions of Internet Explorer display a discreet icon in the lower-left corner when an error is detected.

You can save all support documents (such as a graphics file) in the same, single MHTML (Mime HTML) file. Older browsers don't support this convenient format, but who cares? Also, if you intend that your interactive features work in every possible browser (meaning some open source browsers as well as Netscape), you should use JavaScript rather than VBScript — but, again, who cares? I would never recommend that a programmer or developer struggle with the bizarre syntax in Java (derived from C) just to deal with the one or two percent of potential Web site visitors who still avoid using Internet Explorer. (It can handle either JavaScript or VBScript.) Netscape has become a mere ghost now, used by very few die-hards. Netscape never permitted VBScript to execute any code (some say because VB is a Microsoft product). Whatever.

TIP

Lots of cool features, such as dynamic HTML (DHTML; Web page animation), Active Server Pages (ASP; efficient user-interaction via active server pages technology, scrolling marquees, and many others) are supported in Internet Explorer. It's a mature, robust, and powerful Internet browser with no real competition. Whether this monoculture is good or bad, it remains a fact. Books that advise you to test other browsers (mainly meaning Netscape) should probably be updated. There's no reason to assume that any significant portion of your Web page audience will be using anything other than Internet Explorer.

Now take a look at your Word document as a Web page. Choose File➪Web Page Preview. It may take a minute or two for Word to get its act together and compose the HTML for the Web page, but be patient. Sooner or later, you'll see how the page looks in Internet Explorer, as shown in Figure 3-1.

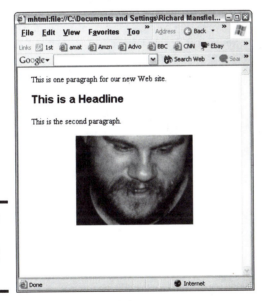

Figure 3-1:
Your new Web page, in preview mode.

Now save your Web page to your hard drive. (Preview mode doesn't require that the document be saved.) Choose File➪Save As Web Page. Then in the Save as Type box, choose Single File Web Page. Name it WebTest and click the Save button. The dialog box closes, and your MHT file (Mime HTML) is saved.

Adjusting Web page properties

The Web page title displayed on the title bar of the browser is determined by the title that you give your document. Choose File⇨Properties and then click the Summary tab in the Properties dialog box. Type in **Our Web Page** as the title. And, if you intend that your Web page be attractive to Google and other search engines, enter several appropriate keywords and some comments on this same page in the dialog box. Click OK to close the dialog box.

Seeing the code

In preparation for adding some scripting code of your own, take a look at Word's hard work. It translated your page into HTML, which is the verbose parent language of many others, such as XML. Sure, it's a huge amount of code to describe two paragraphs, a headline, and a picture, but so what? Memory is cheap, and broadband Internet is the future. Who cares about verbosity if it helps ensure clarity?

Choose Tools⇨Macro⇨Microsoft Script Editor. You now see the HTML code, and the scripting editor, as shown in Figure 3-2.

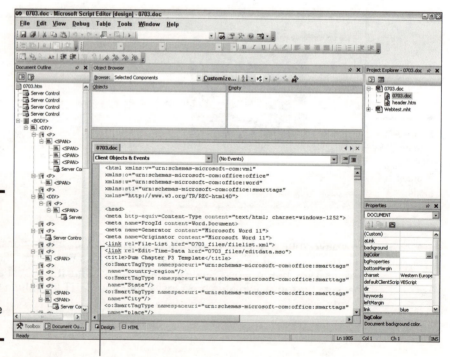

Figure 3-2: Here's the scripting editor, where you can make your Web pages come alive.

The saw-tooth underline indicates an error.

Notice that some of the HTML code has a saw-toothed, red underline, indicating that it violates some rule or other: That is, it's either an error or a potential error. For example, this line was generated by Word when it translated the example page into HTML, but Word's script parser is rejecting the work of Word's translator:

```
<body lang=EN-US style='tab-interval:.5in'>a
```

Note that both the `lang` and `style` attributes are underlined. If you pause your mouse cursor on either of them, you're informed by the parser that they are not attributes of the `body` element. Nonetheless, Word itself must have thought they were when it did the translation. (Perhaps the various workers in different sections of the Word programmer department should have a meeting.) In any case, you can ignore most HTML error messages. No harm done. Generally your page *gracefully degrades,* as the expression goes. (That is, it doesn't show all the formatting but does show the text and other essentials.) And don't forget that you can always preview your page (by choosing File➪Web Page Preview, as I describe earlier in this chapter) to look for any nasty surprises.

Notice that the title, keywords, and comments are also included in the code, and also that a zone of XML is embedded within the HTML:

```
<title>Our Web</title>
<!--[if gte mso 9]><xml>
 <o:DocumentProperties>
  <o:Author>Richard</o:Author>
  <o:Keywords>books, writing, developers</o:Keywords>
  <o:Description>We want this to be a successful
             site!</o:Description>
```

Book VII Chapter 3

XML and Office

The headline is enclosed in the largest headline style tags available in HTML, `<H1>`:

```
<h1>This is a Headline</h1>
```

Filling out the Web page

You can add additional features to your Web page before getting into coding a script language. Display the Web toolbar by right-clicking any other toolbar and choosing Web Tools. It has a number of controls that you can drag and drop into your Web page, as shown in Figure 3-3.

Figure 3-3:
This toolbar
includes
many useful
controls.

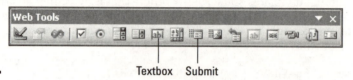

Textbox   Submit

Double-click the Textbox icon on the Web Tools toolbar. A text box appears
within a *form* (an HTML element). You can drag the text box to make it larger.
Also notice that you're put in design mode automatically when you add a
control.

Type **Please enter your name here... and click Submit when done** underneath the text box. Then double-click the Submit icon on the Web Tools toolbar. You can easily drag and drop controls to position them wherever on the
Web page you want them.

Now press Atl+Shift+F11 to see the Script Editor again. Notice in Listing 3-1
that that additional HTML has been added — two form elements and two
INPUT objects: a "TEXT" and "SUBMIT" type.

Listing 3-1:   Added HTML

```
<form>

<p class=MsoNormal><INPUT TYPE="TEXT" SIZE="63"></p>

</form>

<form method=Get enctype="application/x-www-form-urlencoded">

<p class=MsoNormal>Please enter<span style='mso-spacerun:yes'> </span>your
name here... <a name="OLE_LINK2"></a><a name="OLE_LINK1">
             <span style='mso-bookmark:
OLE_LINK2'>and click Submit when done:<span style='mso-spacerun:yes'>
             </span></span></a><INPUT TYPE="SUBMIT"></p>

<p class=MsoNormal><o:p> </o:p></p>

</form>
```

However, soon enough the Refresh button appears in the Script Editor,
and when you click it, additional information is added to this code
(see Listing 3-2), replacing the standard HTML objects (INPUT) with
custom Microsoft objects shown in boldface:

Listing 3-2: Custom Objects

```
<form>

<p class=MsoNormal><!--[if gte vml 1]>
            <v:shape id="_x0000_i1026" type="#_x0000_t75"
 style='width:249.75pt;height:56.25pt'>
 <v:imagedata src="Webtest_files/image003.wmz" o:title=""/>
</v:shape><![endif]--><![if !vml]><img width=333 height=75
src="Webtest_files/image004.gif" v:shapes="_x0000_i1026"><![endif]></p>

</form>

<form>

<p class=MsoNormal>Please <span class=GramE>enter<span
style='mso-spacerun:yes'> </span>your</span> name here...
            <a name="OLE_LINK2"></a><a
name="OLE_LINK1"><span style='mso-bookmark:OLE_LINK2'>and click Submit when
done:<span style='mso-spacerun:yes'> </span></span></a>
            <!--[if gte vml 1]><v:shape
 id="_x0000_i1027" type="#_x0000_t75" style='width:36.75pt;height:22.5pt'>
 <v:imagedata src="Webtest_files/image005.wmz" o:title=""/>
</v:shape><![endif]--><![if !vml]><img width=49 height=30
src="Webtest_files/image006.gif" v:shapes="_x0000_i1027"><![endif]></p>
```

This special code references graphics (GIF files) that are included in your MIME file (or if you've chosen to employ multiple dependency files, in separate files).

You're close to finishing designing this page. Note that ordinary Word effects (lines, diagrams, textures, and so on) can be added to a Web page document. Add a texture by choosing Format⇨Background⇨Fill Effects. Click the Texture tab and select one you like — just be sure you can still read the text on top of the texture. Click OK to close the dialog box.

Scripting

Scripting is programming, albeit with a somewhat abbreviated language. Scripting is designed to get past firewalls, browser security settings, and other security measures because it doesn't have potentially dangerous commands. Unfortunately, there *are* ways to make scripting dangerous, but Microsoft has come up with an ingenious solution: Do your code execution on the server, compose an ordinary HTML page after the computation has finished, and send that HTML back to the user's browser. HTML, like a television show, cannot introduce a virus into your house. It's the difference between seeing a picture of someone with a cold and sitting next to a contagious person who is hacking and wheezing.

ASP is the name Microsoft gave to this server-side code execution technique. It works quite well, allowing us programmers to enjoy the full VBA, VB.NET, or other languages rather than simply scripts. For serious, complex Web programming solutions (or what they now like to call *enterprise development*), you will find it much more efficient to work with the heavy-duty suite of tools available in the Visual Studio .NET suite.

But for now, see what you can do with the Script Editor: Simple Web solutions can be generated quickly and easily via scripting. First, in case there's some odd default, ensure that you're using VBScript and not JavaScript. Choose View⇨Property Pages to see the Property Pages dialog box, as shown in Figure 3-4.

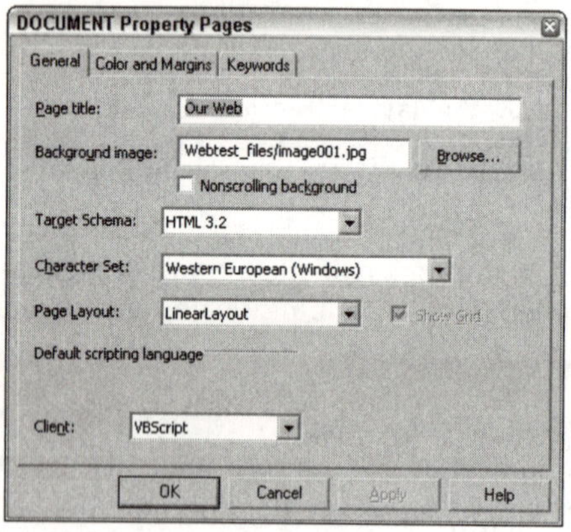

Figure 3-4:
Specify
the script
language
here.

Ensure that the Client list box displays VBScript. Then click OK to close the dialog box.

Typically, script is located just under the <HEAD> element's opening tag (the one without the backslash.) Locate <HEAD> in the code window of the Script Editor. It's near the top of the source code. Then click a blank line beneath the <HEAD> to put the blinking insertion cursor there.

Right-click at the insertion point and choose Insert Script Block⇨Client from the context menu. Why Client is a separate menu option is baffling, given that it's the only possibility. Nonetheless, you find this little bit of code is inserted for you. The <!-- means *start a comment,* and --> means *end a comment.* By writing your script within a comment, you can ensure that the HTML interpreter will ignore it and not try to figure out how to display it in the browser. A script engine, though, will pay attention to this code and try to execute whatever you write in the comment.

```
<script language=vbscript>
<!--


-->
</script>
```

Now type a simple command in the script area:

```
<script language=vbscript>
<!--
MsgBox("HI")
-->
</script>
```

Press F5. The page appears in a Web page, but first, a message box displays the word HI.

If you want to use an Access-style list of possible commands, press Ctrl+J. A list appears from which you can select commands. Properties and enums (such as built-in VB colors) are symbolized in this list by a hand holding a VCR tape. Functions (methods in OOP-speak) are symbolized by a flying purple eraser.

Try double-clicking the Abs function in this list of commands. (Formally, it's known as the *Object member list.*) The list disappears, and Abs appears in a lovely blue color in your code window.

Now press Ctrl+Shift+spacebar to see the *parameter* info (what arguments this function takes). You see Abs(number), so you realize that you must furnish a number. This somewhat limited IntelliSense help is available if you just need a brief reminder. Otherwise, there's a script Help engine available by pressing F1.

**Book VII
Chapter 3**

XML and Office

Commenting client-side programming

When HTML was first written, evidently nobody suspected that a computer might actually want to compute — to execute any real programming code. So HTML contains no provision for programming as such, just for displaying and primitive reactions like clicking a submit button.

That's why you write client-side programming inside a comment. It's one of those embarrassing little workarounds that testify just how much foresight goes into planning computer languages.

Scripting in Excel

Run Excel and then press Alt+Shift+F11 to get to the Script Editor. It's essentially the same as the Word Script Editor, but note one peculiar zone in the automatically generated, default script:

```
<script language="JavaScript">
<!----
function fnUpdateTabs()
  {
   if (parent.window.g_iIEVer>=4) {
    if (parent.document.readyState=="complete"
     && parent.frames['frTabs'].document.readyState==
                "complete")
    parent.fnSetActiveSheet(0);
   else
    window.setTimeout("fnUpdateTabs();",150);
  }
}

if (window.name!="frSheet")
 window.location.replace("../Book1.htm");
else
 fnUpdateTabs();
//-->
</script>
```

Right there in the middle of the script is a little bit of JavaScript! But don't be dismayed. Just because some (perhaps most) of Microsoft's own in-house programmers prefer to avoid using VBScript — the most popular scripting language in the world, and the one that Microsoft itself developed, promoted, and created — doesn't mean that *you* have to use Java.

You can mix and match script languages within a single script. For example, you can now extend this chapter's earlier example (written in Word's Script Editor) by creating one in Excel that accepts data from the user and returns it to the script for processing. This illustrates one way that you can have the user fill in a form, place an order, or otherwise communicate with your application online.

While in the Excel Script Editor, choose View⇨Toolbox. Then drag and drop a TextField (text box) icon into your script, somewhere within the <BODY></BODY> section of the HTML.

The HTML that's automatically created for you to represent these two controls looks like this:

```
<INPUT type="text" ID=Text1>
<INPUT type="submit" value="Submit" ID=Submit1>
```

Now on the line just under the `<HEAD>` tag, right-click; from the context menu, choose Insert Script Block⇨Client. If your default language isn't VBScript, choose View⇨Property Pages and change the Client field to VBScript. Then type into the script block the following lines of code (shown in boldface):

```
<script language=vbscript>
<!--

sub Submit1_Onclick

msgbox (text1.value)

end sub

-->
</script>
```

Press F5 to execute this code in the browser. You see your text box and submit button. Type something into the text box, and then click the submit button. You see a message box displaying the text that was typed in. Your script can in this fashion accept typed input from the user, and then process it by adding it to a database, sending e-mail, or whatever other response makes sense. Likewise, your script can respond to the `Value` property of other controls on the Script Editor Toolbox, such as the radio button or check box.

Now switch back to the Excel worksheet and notice that the controls you added to the script code — the text field and submit button — have also been added to the worksheet.

Here's what many think is the most reductive, simplest HTML document:

```
<HEAD>
<TITLE>New Page</TITLE>
</HEAD>
<BODY>
Message here
</BODY>
```

If you replace the current script in your Excel Script Editor with this and then press F5, you'll see that the browser's title bar displays `New Page` and the browser itself displays `Message here`.

The `HEAD` pair encloses the `TITLE` pair. Other commands can also appear within the `HEAD` pair, in particular scripts, but also meta-descriptions (references to support documents, comments, style specifications, and so on). In general, things not intended to be actually viewed by the user are often put into the `HEAD`.

The `TITLE` and `HEAD` pairs are not essential. You can leave them out of your source code with no harm done. Finally, the `BODY` pair encloses objects, controls, text, images, links, or other elements that you want to present to the user within the browser window. Not surprisingly, you can leave out the `BODY` pair if you want. In fact, contemporary browsers (namely Internet Explorer) are extremely forgiving when it comes to HTML.

The simplest page

Try this. Erase everything from your Script Editor and then type in only these words:

```
A Simple Page
```

Press F5, and you actually see this message in the browser. The Internet Explorer browser will display these words, even if you've included nothing else in your source code. No other computer programming language comes close to HTML's forgiveness. Try submitting A Simple Page to BASIC, C, or any other language. None of them will simply display the words; all will choke and throw out an error message.

The good news is that the user will rarely be baffled by an error message from an Internet browser and will almost never experience a browser freeze-up or crash as a result of your programming. HTML was designed this way. It was supposed to be robust, to avoid crashing the user's computer, or otherwise doing anything untoward. After all, when you go out into the Web, you're opening your computer and (in particular) your hard drive to the world. And as we all know, bad people are out there who would like nothing more than to have you visit an Internet site with this source code:

```
Format C:
```

Your hard drive would be reformatted, and they would jump up and down with glee.

Scripting errors

What happens if you write a script that seems innocent enough but still causes a problem? One of the classic errors in computer programming is the endless *loop*. By accident, you set up some condition that can never be fulfilled. After the VBScript interpreter gets to this loop, it can never get past it. In the following code, I'm saying to do this loop (to keep repeating the instructions between Do and Loop) as long as X is less than 3. And my instructions make sure that X always remains 2. All previous operating systems would *hang* on this (just freeze up), and the user would have to turn the computer off and then back on.

```
<HTML>

<script language=vbscript>
<!--


Do While X < 3
X = 2
Loop

-->
</script>

</HTML>
```

If you press F5, Internet Explorer quickly detects the endless loop and displays the message shown in Figure 3-5.

**Book VII
Chapter 3**

XML and Office

Figure 3-5:
Endless
loops don't
freeze
Internet
Explorer.

Internet Explorer refuses to be frozen by an endless loop. Naturally, people want an Internet browser to be robust and safe to use. As a result, a number of commands found in Visual Basic have been stripped from VBScript. There are no provisions for exploring or otherwise directly contacting the user's hard drive (with one exception, *cookies*). You can't adjust the user's clock although you can read their clock with the Time function:

```
CurrentTime = Time
```

There are no Link commands for dynamic data exchange, nor can you access the user's printer or Clipboard (or any other peripherals, for that matter) beyond the keyboard, mouse, and monitor. Of course, no access is permitted to the user's Windows API (low-level Windows functions).

In other words, the script is limited to working within — well within — the operating environment of the browser. No contact with the user's peripherals or operating system is permitted.

Debugging Script

Either errors in HTML source code are generally just ignored by browsers, or error messages are suppressed and made optional, as I discuss shortly. If you feed the following impossible HTML source code (there's no such command as OFF WHITE) to the Internet Explorer browser, the background inexplicably turns bright red:

```
<HTML>
<HEAD> <TITLE>HTML Bugs</TITLE>
</HEAD>

<BODY BGCOLOR = "OFF WHITE">
</BODY>
</HTML>
```

Bright red isn't quite what you intended, but at least the browser didn't freeze up or crash or otherwise do some damage and frighten the user. Actually, that red *is* a bit frightening.

Script errors, though, can be more serious. Typos and other kinds of bugs can interrupt your VBScript by displaying an error message to the user — a message that's unlikely to be understood by most users and that ensures they will avoid visiting your site again.

Logic errors (such as arithmetic miscalculation) won't generate an error message, but they can result in ridiculous information. For example, your document might announce to the user that the gas for a trip from Atlanta to Orlando costs $0.28. This kind of thing isn't reassuring to users, either.

The Script Editors in Office 2003 applications do have a subset of the usual suite of debugging tools, such as Step Into (F11, although it's usually F8 in all other versions of Visual Basic, demonstrating that C programmers wrote this editor). Take a quick look at the kinds of errors that crop up when writing computer programs, and what you can do about them in VBScript.

Microsoft Help online says that if you choose Tools⇨Options in the Script
Editor, click the Debugging node, click the JIT (Just in Time) button, and
then select the Enable Attach and the Enable JIT Debugging check boxes,
you'll see error messages when scripting (and HTML) has bad code. (On my
computer, they were selected by default. And oddly, the Enable Attach check
box cannot be disabled — nothing happens when you click it.) Although
Microsoft says that message boxes will display errors after these check
boxes are selected, on my computer, no message boxes were displayed
within the Script Editor. However, I noticed that Internet Explorer was displaying a little error icon in the lower-left corner, as shown in Figure 3-6.

Figure 3-6:
Double-click
this error
icon to
choose to
have error
messages
displayed.

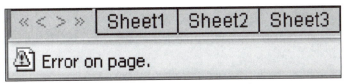

Evidently, Microsoft's recent browser versions suppress error messages
when script or other code generates problems. You, the developer, want to
see these messages, so double-click the error icon shown in Figure 3-6, and
you see the dialog box shown in Figure 3-7.

Figure 3-7:
Enable
seeing
debugging
error
messages
while
working
with script.

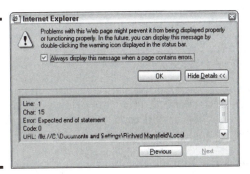

Typos

Typos are the easiest errors to deal with. If you have error messages turned on, the VBScript interpreter signals the browser to report them. For example, if you mistakenly type **MgsBox** instead of **MsgBox**, the interpreter doesn't recognize the command, and it flags the error with a message to you, the programmer, as shown in Figure 3-8. Here is the example code, complete with typo in boldface:

```
<HTML>
<HEAD>
<TITLE>Debugging</TITLE>
</HEAD>
<BODY BGCOLOR = "WHITE">
<SCRIPT LANGUAGE = "VBScript">
<!--
MgsBox "What gives?"
-->
</SCRIPT>
</BODY>
</HTML>
```

Note in Figure 3-8 that you're told that the error is located in line 9. Take a look at your source code in the Script Editor, count down from the top to line 9, look for the typo, and fix it. In this case, the error message is highly specific, mentioning the misspelled msgbox.

Given that error messages mention line numbers in your source code, you might want to turn them on in the editor. Choose Tools➪Options, click Text Editor, All Languages, and then select the Line Numbers check box. After doing that, your source code is numbered, like the code displayed in Figure 3-9.

Figure 3-9:
Display line
numbers to
make
tracking
errors
easier in
the Script
Editor.

**Book VII
Chapter 3**

XML and Office

Impossible commands

Also, another kind of typo — impossible commands — are easily noticed and reported: for example, `Erase the blackboard`. VBScript cannot digest this command, so it reports the problem. It does understand and recognize the command `Erase`, but it expects the `Erase` command to be followed by the name of an array because that's how `Erase` is supposed to work. Not finding the proper argument, the debugger reacts with an error message.

Unfortunately, error messages, even after over two decades of effort, remain generic and often confusing. For example, when reacting to `Erase the blackboard`, instead of offering `The function argument is wrong or something true`, the error message is `Expected end of statement`. Technically, this reference to punctuation isn't entirely wrong, but it does miss the main point: that `Erase` requires a specific kind of argument, namely an array. This information could be entered into a database and displayed to programmers. Too bad that with all the computing power we've got at our disposal, error messages are still as cryptic, brief, and often simply wrong as they were 20 years ago. When you do OOP programming, you're going to see `Object variable not set` and stuff like that hundreds of times.

Another generic and frequently seen message is `Type mismatch`. You get that if you provide the wrong argument, too, as in `X = Sqr("five")` (because you cannot square text).

A third variety of easily detected, easily fixed error is an inconsistency of some kind between parts of your script. Say you have a subroutine that expects three variables:

```
Sub Numbers (a, b, c)
End Sub
```

and you try to call it but provide only two numbers:

```
Numbers a, b
```

In this case, you get a really good error message: `Wrong number of arguments`.

Using MSXML Core Services

If you're interested in trying out sophisticated XML manipulation with Office applications and data but you're not ready to commit to the Visual Studio .NET XML tools, you might be interested in *XML Core Services* or, simply, MSXML. This is a powerful set of XML tools — including SAX and DOM facilities — that allows you to manage XML in many ways. MSXML can be used by all Office applications that have VBA built into them. You add MSXML as a reference in the VBA editor (choose Tools➪References). A description of how to add this reference and such interesting-sounding technologies that MSXML provides you with (such as SAX and DOM) can be found in Book III, Chapter 3.

Using Forms for Interaction

Although you can build Web pages with Word documents, forms are sometimes easier to manage because they have some built-in functionality that you don't need to code. Plus, many sample forms are in various Office 2003 applications that you can use as a starting point; simply edit them to make them specific to your needs.

Forms can contain zones that are frozen and cannot be edited by users (such as labels captioning fields like Name, Address, Phone). In other areas in forms, the user is expected to edit or fill in data, such as the text boxes next to the labels Name, Address, Phone. You can use macros, autocompletion (Tools➪AutoCorrect), and other features of the various Office 2003 applications to assist users.

Here is a summary of the best uses of forms in the various Office 2003 applications:

✦ **Access is your clear choice for database-related forms.** For example, if a user is interacting with a large database, Access has the tools and the strength to handle considerable amounts of data. Also, its comparative tools allow data to be manipulated and analyzed in a wide variety of ways. This suggests that Access is the choice when you want to generate various different kinds of reports in response to varying user needs. However, if you need What If analysis, recall that Excel offers specialized pivot table and pivot chart facilities.

✦ **Word is probably the first choice for forms that involve complicated layouts.** If you need to mix and match graphics, tables, lines, shading, backgrounds, links, and objects such as drop-down lists or option buttons, Word is optimized to generate documents with a complex design. By using VBA, input trapping (data validation), and other techniques, you can also guide the user through the process of filling in forms correctly and quickly.

✦ **InfoPath is best when you need to design forms resting on the XML technology.** InfoPath also includes some advanced controls only found elsewhere in the .NET environment, such as data repeaters. InfoPath has advanced features making it easier to add task panes, toolbars, forms for merging, and forms with alternative views the user can switch between while working with the form (such as the difference between design and HTML view in an editor). InfoPath is designed from the bottom up to work exclusively via XML for both messaging and data storage. It specializes in collecting data and generating reports but using the most advanced techniques. The following chapter (Book VII, Chapter 4) is all about InfoPath.

✦ **Outlook forms naturally focus on scheduling appointments, feedback (RSVP), and e-mail.**

✦ **Excel is a calculation engine with financial undertones.** So use its forms capability when your solution demands complex math, financial math, math analysis, math, math, and math.

✦ **FrontPage offers forms, but it specializes in building attractive Web pages.** You can design forms that display your database (such as online catalogs) or that gather information from users (such as order forms).

Office 2003 applications' built-in, form-generating features can be useful, but if you really want to see how dynamic and useful forms can be, take a look at InfoPath — the forms specialist — which I discuss in depth in the following chapter.

Chapter 4: Working with InfoPath

In This Chapter

✔ **Sharing information efficiently**

✔ **Designing with InfoPath**

✔ **Designing an InfoPath form**

✔ **Viewing the data hierarchy**

✔ **Generating InfoPath forms from XML and from databases**

✔ **Viewing sample scripts**

Available only for the Professional Enterprise edition of Office 2003, InfoPath deserves attention if you need to manage and report data in an XML-based environment. (Don't confuse the Professional Enterprise edition with the different Professional edition.) Users work with what appear to them to be simple forms, but unbeknownst to them, they're actually creating XML that programmers and developers can easily message or incorporate into pretty much any kind of a data store.

In this chapter, you see how to build InfoPath forms in various ways (from databases, from XML, directly designing from the ground up) and you also discover how InfoPath can improve Office efficiency by making it unnecessary for you to translate user-entered data into XML. When the user finishes filling in an InfoPath form, the data *is* in XML already.

Introducing InfoPath

InfoPath is a high-level, rapid development, Office-like interface that shields nonprogrammers from the murky depth of XML, data stores, schemas, and all the other mess down there.

InfoPath blends two primary technologies: form design and XML. You use InfoPath to build forms that users then fill in. But unlike classic forms, you can rigorously validate what they enter, and the data they provide is immediately cast into a schema. In other words, you don't have to take the user data and translate it later into XML — it becomes XML as they enter it. In fact, you can just save the data as an XML file right there and then. Or you can choose to stream the XML to a data store, to a Web Service, or e-mail it. Scripting capabilities are built into InfoPath, and you can of course send the XML that InfoPath generates to VBA or other languages for further processing.

InfoPath can work as a standalone application, or you can embed it into enterprise solutions: that is, large-scale, often-distributed, programming for business. If your company requires any significant access to back-end database information, you can let those who best know their own needs use InfoPath to craft their own custom forms. Even nonprogrammers should be able to create effective, personalized little programs to facilitate their data entry, access, or reports. Think of one of InfoPath's strengths as a customizable front end, easy enough for nonprogrammers to manipulate.

It's long been a goal to give tools to users with which they can manipulate data to suit their special circumstances. InfoPath, although not the final answer, is certainly a step in the right direction. And although users think they're simply filling out a form — albeit one with more flexibility and dynamism than usual — they're actually generating XML. (Rub your hands together and chuckle with me: "Little do they know.") Still, we developers understand how flexible and useful data in an XML format can be.

Understanding How InfoPath Is Divided

InfoPath is divided into two modes: form design and form completion. When InfoPath first opens, it's in design mode, ready for you to modify an existing form or create a new one.

InfoPath for the designer

InfoPath is tightly integrated with the other Office 2003 applications. You can, for example, begin designing a new form by pointing InfoPath to an Access database, and InfoPath will build a form template based on that database's structure (namely, its tables and fields). Other data store structures can also be used as starting points, including XML files, Web Services, Jet engine (Access MDB) databases and queries, XML schemas and SQL Server database views, some kinds of functions, tables, and stored procedures.

Although mature, powerful data entry and viewing tools are already available, InfoPath can be used as a user interface (UI) for databases. Because InfoPath is a technology specializing in XML contexts, it can provide considerable benefits as a UI for the creation and maintenance of XML-based data. For instance, although Web Services were originally employed in communications between servers, or between clients and servers, Web Services can be used in other ways. If users need a forms-based interface to XML documents, InfoPath is ideal.

Parts of an InfoPath form can be designed to display additional fields or data, depending on the context or events. In other words, like a helpful friend sitting next to the user, InfoPath can watch what the user does and *respond* in various beneficial ways. For instance, imagine an income tax preparation form. When users fill in a gross income higher than $50,000, you can display a section asking for additional information, informing them that they are a victim of the alternative minimum tax trick. This information becomes visible only when the InfoPath form detects a certain condition — in this case, the user's relatively high income. In this and other ways, InfoPath forms are intelligent, responsive, and dynamic.

When designing InfoPath forms, you'll notice the extensive error trapping and validation system available to you. Imagine a business travel reimbursement form with a field for dining expenses. If somebody enters an amount over her Las Vegas budget, you can inform her of that and refuse to accept any restaurant tabs greater than, say, $200 (unless it's that great Asian place in the MGM Grand, where you permit $400).

Rapid application development (RAD), first introduced to the world in 1990 via the Visual Basic Toolbox, is full of drag-and-drop controls. RAD revolutionized programming because you could add a fully functional text box or option button merely by dropping it into a prototype window (a *form*). Prior to that, you had to struggle with complex messaging and Application Programmers Interface (API) structures to do even the simplest GUI jobs. Even the C language eventually adopted RAD several years later.

Creating dynamic forms with InfoPath involves RAD technology, as you might expect. You employ the Layout toolbar to design the major zones of your page, and then fill those zones by using the Controls task pane, filled with check boxes, calendars, and so on that you can drag and drop. Just like in Visual Basic and its imitators, after a control is on a form, you can then further modify its behavior by changing its color, size, and other properties.

Specialized *container* controls are also available, helping you cue the user that various elements of the form are related because they're visually contained within a zone on the form. The InfoPath designer's equivalent of pressing F5 in Visual Basic (to execute your program so you can test it) is the Preview Form button found on the Standard InfoPath toolbar. Click it and you see your form the way a user sees it, allowing you to try filling in data, clicking buttons, displaying optional sections, and otherwise interacting with the fields and controls on the form. In other words, Preview mode allows you to give the form a trial run to see how it can be improved.

When describing form design, the term *field* is slightly different from the way that term is used in database programming. A *form field* is any area where the user can add information, but typically it's a text box — also called a *text field* — into which the user types a name, address, phone number, or whatever other piece of data is required. This form field, however, does typically map directly to a database field if the form's data is intended to be stored as a database record. Note that not all forms' data is saved to a database. Travel expense reports, for instance, can simply be thrown out as soon as the accounting department has combed through them for padding, errors, deliberate deception, falsification, and other freeloader attempts to gouge the company. Today we use the term *freeloader,* but our great grandparents had a more colorful phrase: *lounge lizard.*

Continuing with InfoPath's borrowing from Visual Basic's RAD system, you can bind databases directly to controls. Long available in Visual Basic, you can, for example, assign a particular text box to a particular field in a table. Also, when you design an InfoPath form, an associated XML schema is automatically created for you, representing the structure that you've designed visually. Fields and sections, along with their data types, are displayed as you move your mouse around your form.

Also, after a form has been filled in — and consequently its data and schema are in XML format — you can route the data in multiple simultaneous directions. One advantage of this flexibility is that a worker doesn't have to fill out multiple forms for the various departments involved in a single requisition. The data in the single InfoPath XML file can be absorbed into the various departments with their various data storage schemes and applications.

InfoPath for the user

Unlike simpler forms, InfoPath permits users to fill in data with various rich text features, such as using italics, shading, graphics, and other document capabilities typically missing from ordinary form-completion software, including tables, hyperlinks, and color schemes. You also have other capabilities at your disposal, such as spell checking, search and replace, and autocompletion.

Users can participate in the design of the forms, too, after the fact. If they need additional rows, they can add them to the form. Or if they want to add some notes explaining how they spent that extra $300 at that convention in Vegas, they can add this information. The forms are customizable.

After a form is filled in, the user can optionally interact with other Office 2003 applications: e-mail it, combine it with other forms' data, export the form's data to Excel for further analysis, and so on.

If you're an advanced developer, interested in additional sample forms (beyond those supplied by default with InfoPath), deployment information, programming tools, and sophisticated documentation, download the InfoPath software development kit (SDK) from

www.microsoft.com/downloads/details.aspx?FamilyId=351F0616 -93AA-4FE8-9238-D702F1BFBAB4&displaylang=en

This SDK is a way to really get under the InfoPath hood, integrating it with Office 2003 applications and other applications in large-scale solutions. (*Solutions* is the current name for computerized tasks of a certain size and complexity.)

When you're in design mode, the InfoPath title bar reads Design, and you also see lots of dashed lines around the various zone of your form. In design mode, you can press Alt+Shift+F11 to get to the Script Editor. As you'll see later in this chapter, default scripting underneath the sample forms is written in JavaScript by Microsoft's programmers. Of course, you want to use the more efficient VBScript because after the choice to use JavaScript has been made in a form, you cannot switch back to VBScript for your own programming in that form. These languages cannot be mixed within a given InfoPath form.

However, if you start designing a form from scratch, you get to decide which language should be used with that form. To set the default scripting language used in a new form, choose Tools⇨Form Options and then click the Advanced tab. For blank forms you build from the get-go, VBScript is the default language.

Even sample forms with no scripting — such as the Resume Builder sample — default to JavaScript, and you cannot change that default after you open the Script Editor. So, beware. After you open the Script Editor, the script language option is disabled in the Form Options dialog box. Other sample forms — such as Expense Report — contain prewritten JavaScript code and cannot be switched to VBScript no matter what you do. Even if you click the New Blank Form link on the Design a Form taskbar and then switch to the Script Editor, it becomes impossible to change the script language.

You'd expect to switch between design mode and preview ("fill-out-the-form") mode via the View menu or perhaps via a pair of tabs as in most other Microsoft applications and utilities. Not so with InfoPath. Somebody decided that this important switch belonged on the File menu. So, to switch, choose File⇨Design a Form or File⇨Fill Out a Form. (Or if the task pane is visible, use links there to switch modes as well.) How novel, but also how confusing.

Trying Out InfoPath

In this example, you want to design a form to gather information about employee disputes and flare-ups. You begin by adding tables to create the primary zones where the user provides data or gets information from you. Then you add controls. I also show you how to see the organization of your data.

Designing the main sections of a form

To get a feel for designing and using InfoPath forms, follow these steps. In my example here, I'm designing a form for documenting employee conflicts.

1. **Run InfoPath.**

   The Fill Out a Form task pane appears.

2. **Click the <u>Design a Form</u> link in the task pane.**

   The Design a Form task pane appears.

3. **Click the <u>New Blank Form</u> link.**

   The page changes from gray to white, hinting that you have an empty canvas on which to build your form. You also see the task pane come into its own. A set of tasks is listed in order: Layout, Controls, Data, Views, and Publish — the steps you take to get a form designed.

4. **Click the <u>Layout</u> link.**

   The Layout task pane appears, a shown in Figure 4-1.

Figure 4-1:
Use this task pane to design the main sections of a form (the broad outline).

TIP

5. **Drag a Table with Title from the task pane and drop it into the form.**

   If the task pane ever disappears — and it does sometimes — just choose View⇨Task Pane to bring it back.

6. **Type in the new title in the table, as shown in Figure 4-2:** Associate Conflict Resolution Form.

7. **Just below the title — where it reads Click to Add Form Content — type** General description of the dispute.

8. **Drag and drop a two-column table just below the previous table.**

9. **Where it reads Click to Add Form Content, type** Your Name:; **in the second section, type** Your Phone Extension:.

10. **Drag a one-column table and drop it beneath the existing two tables.**

11. **Where it reads Click to Add Form Content, type** Detailed description of this other person's problems....

That creates the basic form and its main zones, as shown in Figure 4-2.

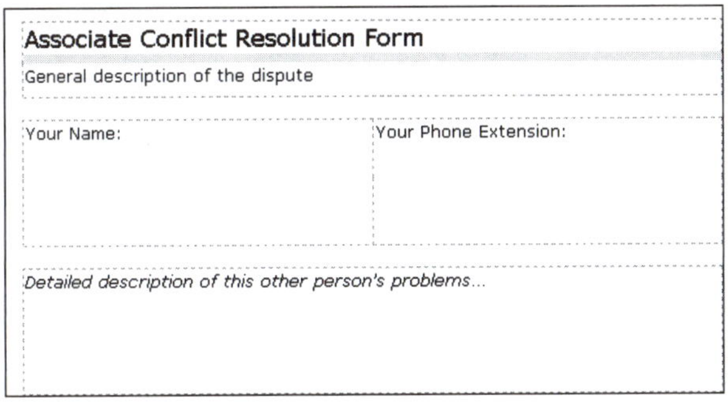

Figure 4-2:
Your first
step in
creating an
InfoPath
form is to
define the
primary
broad
zones.

Associate Conflict Resolution Form

General description of the dispute

Your Name: Your Phone Extension:

Detailed description of this other person's problems...

Adding controls

At this point, the form looks rather small, so add some controls to it to flesh it out with places where the user can provide data. Follow these steps to add controls:

1. **Click the <u>Controls</u> link in the task pane.**

   You see a Toolbox-like area in the task pane where you can drag and drop controls onto your form.

2. **Drag a text box from the task pane and drop it just next to the label you provided:** General description of the dispute.

   The text box appears on the line following your label, but it's too small.

3. **Click the text box.**

   Eight handles appear around the textbox, allowing you to resize it.

4. **To make the text box larger, drag down the handle in the middle of the lower line of the text box.**

   Your table size grows as necessary to accommodate your text box, as shown in Figure 4-3.

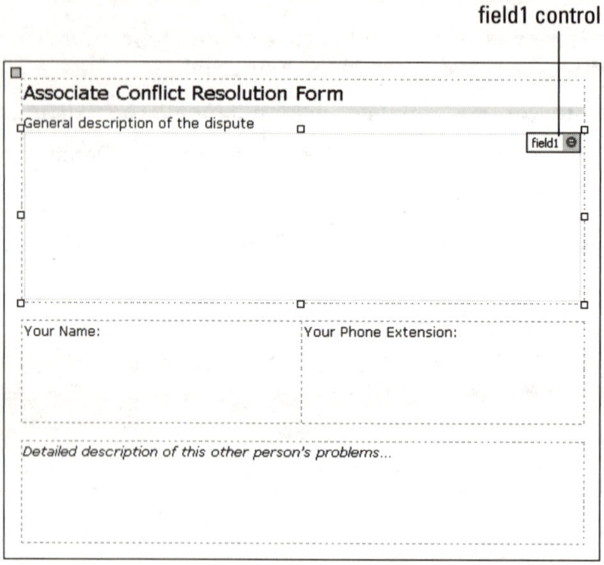

field1 control

Associate Conflict Resolution Form

General description of the dispute

field1

Your Name:

Your Phone Extension:

Detailed description of this other person's problems...

Figure 4-3:
Drag controls like this text box to resize them.

Notice that a control, when selected as shown in Figure 4-3, displays its element name (to use XML-speak) or its field name (to use database-speak). In other words, this is the tag that identifies whatever data the user types in. `field1` is the default given to the first control you place on an InfoPath form, but that's not descriptive enough. You want to help those on the back end who are absorbing this data into their systems by identifying in some descriptive way the data they're getting in this field (or element, as XML puts it).

5. **Right-click the text box.**

6. **From the context menu that appears, choose Text Box Properties.**

   The Properties dialog box appears, as shown in Figure 4-4.

   Instead of the traditional Properties window used in most Microsoft design environments, InfoPath uses this dialog box.

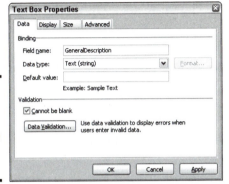

Figure 4-4:
Use this
dialog box
to adjust the
properties
of controls.

7. **Change Field1 to GeneralDescription.**

   Try to avoid using spaces in field names because that throws some data stores into a tizzy. If you use two words, push them together as here (GeneralDescription).

8. **The data type (string) is correct, but you want to insist that the user fill in this field, so mark the Cannot Be Blank check box.**

9. **Click the Display tab in the dialog box. In the Placeholder field, type** Please briefly describe the issues here....

   This provides a hint about what the user should do. The hint will appear in a subtle gray and will vanish as soon as the user starts to use the text box.

   If you want your text boxes to scroll, word-wrap, and display scrollbars (and you should if you've made them larger than a single line high), select the Wrap Text check box on the Display tab, and then adjust the Scrolling List Box options as desired.

10. **Click the Advanced tab to provide one additional cue for the user: In the Screen Tip field, type** Please briefly describe the issues of your conflict here....

    This appears as one of those yellow messages that display only when the user's mouse hovers over a control.

11. **Click OK.**

    The dialog box closes.

12. **Drag a text box and drop it under Your Name:.**

Book VII
Chapter 4

Working with
InfoPath

13. **Right-click the text box, choose TextBox Properties, and change the field name to** Name.

14. **Drag a text box and drop it under Your Phone Extension:.**

15. **Right-click the text box, choose TextBox Properties, and change the field name to** PhoneExt.

16. **Click the table outline at the bottom (the dashed line) and drag it up a bit because this table by default was a bit large.**

17. **Drag a text box and drop it under Detailed description of this other person's problems....**

18. **Right-click the text box, choose TextBox Properties, and change the field name to** DetailedDesc.

19. **You want to add one more table (zone) to this page, so click the <u>Layout</u> link in the task pane and drag a one-column table to the bottom of the form.**

20. **Where it reads Click to Add Form Content, type** Add optional additional complaints here.

21. **Into the new table you just added, add an Optional Section control.**

22. **Click the <u>Controls</u> link.**

23. **At the top of the optional section, type this:** Any further complaints about the company or its people?

24. **Drag a text box and drop it just below what you just typed.**

    Because this is a section (a *container control* similar to a `GroupBox`), InfoPath assumes that you might be putting several controls horizontally, so it might make this text box small. Drag the text box both wider and higher so it matches the width of the other large text boxes.

25. **Right-click the text box and change the field name to** OptionalComplaints.

    Try to avoid using spaces in field names.

26. **Click the Preview Form button on the toolbar.**

    You see your form as the user will see it, and you can type in data, click buttons, or otherwise interact with it to test it, as shown in Figure 4-5.

Notice in Figure 4-5 that the optional section's text box doesn't appear unless the user clicks the arrow icon to open it.

Figure 4-5:
Try adding
data and
otherwise
manipulating
the controls
on your form
to test it in
preview
mode.

Seeing the data hierarchy

If you want to see the organization of your data — what XML calls the
schema — click the <u>Data Source</u> link in the task bar. You see that *groups*
enclose fields. If you want to add additional fields to this schema that are not
visible to the user via controls, click the Add button. XML refers to these as
optional attribute fields.

If you add yet later delete a control to your form, it will still appear in the
Data Source list. This bug can confuse you later, so right-click the extraneous
phantom control's name in the Data Source list and choose Delete to remove
it from the schema.

Save your work to a disk file by choosing File⇨Save. The file is saved with an
.xsn extension, a proprietary InfoPath format — not XML. The form, when
filled in by a user, does store the schema and the resulting data that the user
entered as XML.

For example, try filling in the form created in this chapter's running example
(choose File⇨Fill Out a Form). Then choose File⇨Save and save it as
TestForm.xml. If you look at the resulting saved XML file in Notepad, you'll
see the schema. A filled-in form from the previous example generates this
XML schema. (The data, of course, depends on what you just typed in when
you filled in the form.)

```
<?xml version="1.0" encoding="UTF-8"?><?mso-infoPathSolution
          solutionVersion="1.0.0.2" productVersion=
          "11.0.5531" PIVersion="1.0.0.0" href="file:
          ///C:\book%20OFFICE%202003\7-4\
          ComplaintsPublished.xsn" ?>
<?mso-application progid="InfoPath.Document"?>

<my:myFields xmlns:my="http://schemas.microsoft.com/office/
          infopath/2003/myXSD/2004-02-21T19:57:12"
          xml:lang="en-us">

<my:GeneralDescription>Well, he tried to make faces at me
          during the Halloween
party!</my:GeneralDescription>
<my:Name>Marva Purisa</my:Name>
<my:PhoneExt>332</my:PhoneExt>
<my:DetailedDesc>Well, what can I say? I'm not used to
          getting faces made at me! Especially by people
          like this.</my:DetailedDesc>
<my:group2>
<my:OptionalComplaints>I don't like the donuts either!.
          </my:OptionalComplaints>
</my:group2>
</my:myFields>
```

Generating an InfoPath Form from XML

You can go the other way. Instead of generating XML from a form, you can
generate a form — a simple one that you can spruce up using InfoPath
tools — from an XML file. To see how this works, follow these steps:

1. **Open InfoPath.**

2. **Choose File⇨Design a Form.**

3. **Click the <u>New from Data Source</u> link in the taskbar.**

4. **Leave the default XML schema or XML data file option marked.**

5. **Click Next.**

6. **Click the Browse button to locate** `TestForm.xml`.

   This is the form you filled out and saved in the preceding section.

7. **Click Finish.**

   You're informed via a message box that your form will have a structure based on the chosen XML file. (The message confusingly calls this structure the *data source,* which makes little sense, but just ignore it.)

8. **When you're asked whether you want the actual data (called the** *values* **in this message) to be inserted into the form as well, click Yes.**

   The task pane automatically displays the data source, and you can drag and drop these fields onto the form to create a simple form, as shown in Figure 4-6.

Figure 4-6:
Drag the topmost node (MyFields in this example), and you can drop the entire schema into the form.

General Description: Well, he tried to ...
Name: Marva Purisa
Phone Ext: 332
Detailed Desc: Well, what can I...

Optional Complaints: I don't like the d...

⊕ Optional Section

Section

Note that you can drag individual fields. Or by dragging MyFields (the top, or parent, element, or node), you get the entire structure all at once as shown in Figure 4-6.

Generating a Form from a Database

You can also generate a form by importing a database and letting its structure shape the form. You have freedom to adjust and improve the visual design to assist the user by using optional sections for fields that aren't required to be filled in by the user.

To do it from a database, follow these steps:

1. **Choose File⇨Design a Form.**

   The Design a Form task bar appears.

2. **Click the <u>New from Data Source</u> link in the task bar.**

   The Data Source Setup Wizard appears.

3. **Select the Database option button in the wizard.**

4. **Click Next.**

5. **Click the Select Database button.**

6. **Locate the `Northwind.mdb` database file on your hard drive — or any other MDB file — and then double-click it.**

   The Select Table dialog box appears, as shown in Figure 4-7.

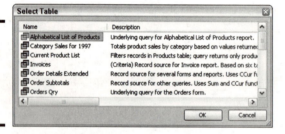

Figure 4-7: Choose the table or query from your data source.

7. **Double-click the Employees table (or some other table of your choice).**

   You see the structure (the data *fields* or *columns,* as they're called) of your chosen data source, as shown in Figure 4-8.

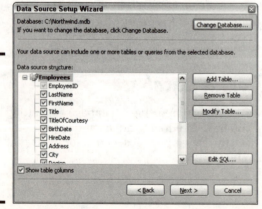

Figure 4-8: Here, choose the fields you want to include in your InfoPath form.

8. **Select or deselect any of the fields you wish in the wizard, as shown in Figure 4-8.**

9. **Click Next.**

You're shown the summary page of the wizard, as illustrated in Figure 4-9.

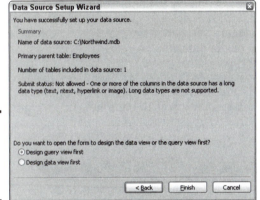

Figure 4-9: You can see any errors displayed here.

Book VII Chapter 4

Working with InfoPath

Text versus string

InfoPath cannot currently handle what is called a "long" data type (graphics, ntext, text, or hyperlink). Take a moment to catch up on some of the neologisms that have popped up here suddenly in this dialog box. Don't confuse the use of *text* here with *string*. These are specialized uses of the terms *text* derived from jargon used in *Transact-SQL*, which is a flavor of the SQL query language that adds programming capabilities for both Microsoft SQL Server 6.5/7.0 and Sybase version 11.5.

Ntext stands for *national text,* which should clue you that it involves *Unicode* — the replacement for the ASCII character code. Unicode's purpose is to embrace many of the languages on Earth, and their many peculiar characters: circumflexes, acute dieresis (ever suffered from *that?*), virgules, accents grave, acute, and aigu, Hungarian and French signes diacritique, umlauts, cedillas, macrons, ogoneks, ligatures, and the always popular Spanish tilde (that's the little ~ wormy looking character just beneath your Esc key).

ASCII used only the 256 code numbers available in a byte. Unicode is a two-byte code system used to accommodate all the other possible characters, including some of those Asian mega-character-sets. The `Ntext` data type can hold a string up to 1,073,741,823 characters, which means that it would use twice that many bytes.

Notice in Figure 4-9 that one or more of the fields (columns) in this table was not imported into InfoPath. (In this case, it was the graphics field, a photo of each employee.)

What the error message in Figure 4-9 refers to as the *text* data type has an upper limit of 2,147,483,647 characters. And of course *images* (graphics) data types can be huge, too. InfoPath doesn't deal with these gigantic data types, so it lets you know if you try to import them.

The wizard shown in Figure 4-9 also offers you two choices: whether to design the query first or the data view.

The query view (as in Figure 4-10) offers the user a way to search the database by filling in fields and then clicking the Run Query button. The data view is a form designed to allow users to enter new records into the data store.

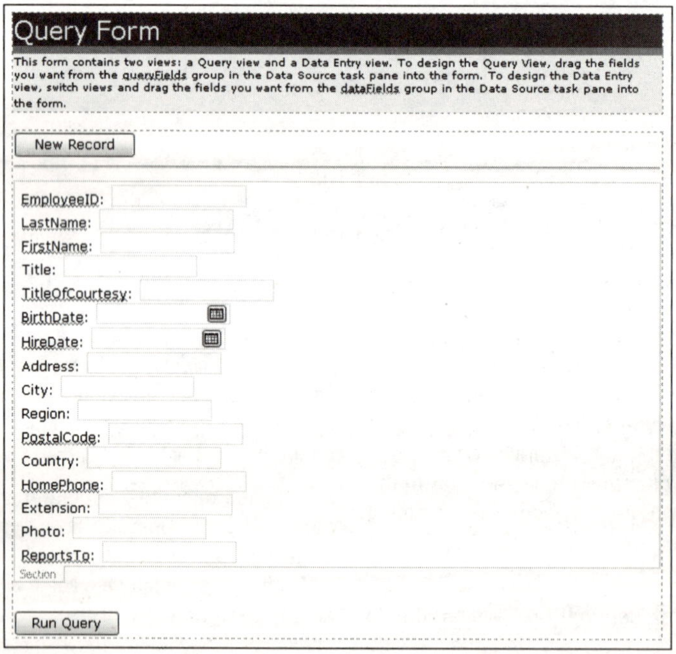

Figure 4-10: This is the query view of a Northwind database table.

If you chose the data view, the form is initially blank, but try dragging the `dataFields` entry in the taskbar and dropping it onto the form. You see a choice of Section with Controls or just Section. Choose the former, and you see the result shown in Figure 4-11. (In this example, there's only a single table, but there could be multiple tables.)

Figure 4-11:
This is the Section with Controls option when dragging a set of tables from the taskbar.

**Book VII
Chapter 4**

Working with
InfoPath

If you drag the table itself rather than entire `dataFields` set, you have three choices when you drop it: Repeating Table, Repeating Section with Controls, and Repeating Section. Choose the first option, and you see the result displayed in Figure 4-12.

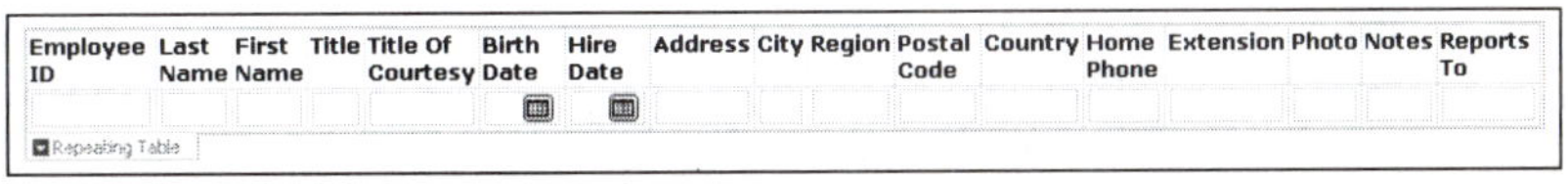

Figure 4-12:
This is the Repeating Table option.

The Repeating Section option looks like Figure 4-11, without the container section.

Jumping Java Babies

You might be tempted to look at the programming examples shipped with InfoPath. Resist, unless you're used to Java. The sample scripts, which demonstrate how to manipulate the behavior of buttons by event trapping, and other programming tricks, are (alas) written in Java. To see these samples, follow these steps:

1. **Choose File⇨Design a Form.**

   You're switched to design mode in InfoPath.

2. **Choose File⇨Open in Design Mode.**

   You see the Open in Design Mode dialog box.

3. **Browse until you locate the** `CD_Edit.xsn` **file — or one of the other four samples — in this path:**

   ```
   C:\Program Files\Microsoft Office\OFFICE11\SAMPLES\INFOPATH\
   ```

4. **Double-click the XSN file.**

   It opens in InfoPath, and you can examine it.

To see the documentation for these samples, follow these steps:

1. **Choose Help⇨Microsoft Office InfoPath Help.**

   The InfoPath Help task pane appears.

2. **Click Table of Contents in the task pane.**

   You see the TOC.

3. **Click InfoPath Developer's Reference.**

   Some additional topics appear in the task pane.

4. **Click Developer Sample Forms.**

   Of the four samples listed, choose the one you want to view.

When you look at the sample code, you'll know at once (thanks to all the semicolons) that you're dealing with a C-type language — in this case, JavaScript. It's not all that hard to translate Java into Visual Basic, but it's boring. Rather like rewriting a bad writer's work. You have to remove redundancies, rearrange illogically ordered syntax, and delete unnecessary punctuation. Not hard, just tedious.

Chapter 5: Adding Smart Tags

In This Chapter

✔ **Understanding Smart Tags**

✔ **Programming Smart Tags**

✔ **Creating and testing your own Smart Tags**

✔ **Feeding data to Web sites**

Smart Tags first appeared in Office XP, but they've been improved in Office 2003. Access and PowerPoint now offer them, along with Word, Outlook, Excel, and Internet Explorer. (Find more coverage on Smart Tags in Book V, Chapter 3.)

Smart Tags have a bit in common with OneNote's side note feature and other recent mini-applications. (Read about OneNote in Book VII, Chapter 1.) The idea is to provide quick access to a pared-down version of a full application.

Smart Tags are probably most like hyperlinks but with a twist. Smart Tags are dynamic, they can change (over time, based on the user's behaviors, based on other contexts). For example, in Word, Smart Tags parse your document as you write it and react by displaying themselves when they recognize a particular item, such as a date, a financial acronym, and so on. In Word, Excel, and PowerPoint, Smart Tags pop up based on phrases or individual words. In Access, Smart Tags attach to a field or form control.

In Office 2003, the developer doesn't have to tokenize the text so it can be detected by the *recognizer* (the parser that identifies terms as triggers for Smart Tags.) So a developer merely has to supply the recognizer with a list of trigger terms and the associated behaviors. It's similar to naming procedures and then writing code for those procedures to carry out. However, you can supply terms via a modified version of Perl (*regular* expressions, as they're called).

Before exploring the Smart Tags currently built into various Office 2003 applications or showing you how to create your own Smart Tags, first consider why you would actually want to bother programming Smart Tags in the first place.

Why Bother Programming Your Own Tags?

Smart Tags can provide the developer a way to add dynamic, updatable information to documents, presentations with PowerPoint, Excel spreadsheets, and other Office 2003 applications. Consider, for example, the need to instantly display the latest data about a company you're doing a presentation for. Just insert a Smart Tag in your presentation that can display a Web page that your research team keeps updated with the very latest data. You're on the road, but team members can update this page every day. It's a way of connecting a static document to up-to-the-minute data on a network or the Internet.

Or how about people working with reports? Insert a Smart Tag that sends their report to the next person who should review it or saves it to an Exchange folder or PowerPoint. Or your tags could merely offer optional assistance or information if the person filling out the form makes an error, such as leaving out an area code when filling in a phone number. Up pops a tag, asking the user to add the area code. Think of a spell checker that checks any kind of data.

Smart Tags are also a way for a developer to watch for key terms and then respond in pretty much any way that makes sense. In this way, each datum that a user enters into a document, spreadsheet, record, or form becomes an *event* — a trigger you can code for and respond to. Sound good? Read on.

Understanding Smart Tags

Smart Tags combine various concepts: hyperlinks, instant application access, Web Services, and third-party add-ons. You click a Smart Tag, and something happens: You get a weather report, e-mail a message, find reference material, and so on.

Try it in Access first. Follow these steps:

1. **Open the Northwind sample database.**

   Search your hard drive for `Northwind.mdb`.

2. **Click the Tables label in the left pane of the database window.**

3. **Click the Employees table to select it.**

4. **Press Alt+D.**

   You open the design view and see the fields of the Employees table.

5. **Click the LastName field to select it.**

6. **Look at the bottom of the properties under the General tab, as shown in Figure 5-1.**

Figure 5-1:
Smart Tags
are included
in the
properties
window.

General	Lookup	
Format		dd-mmm-yyyy
Input Mask		
Caption		Hire Date
Default Value		
Validation Rule		
Validation Text		
Required		No
Indexed		No
IME Mode		No Control
IME Sentence Mode		None
Smart Tags		

7. **Click the Smart Tags property in the properties window.**

   A button appears with an ellipsis.

8. **Click the button next to Smart Tags in the properties window.**

   The Smart Tags dialog box opens, as shown in Figure 5-2.

Figure 5-2:
Choose
whatever
Smart Tag
you want to
use in this
dialog box.

Smart Tags

Available Smart Tags
- [ ] Date
- [ ] Financial Symbol
- [✓] Person Name

Smart Tag Details

Name: Person Name
Actions: Send Mail
Schedule a Meeting
Open Contact
Add to Contacts

[More Smart Tags]   [OK]   [Cancel]

9. **Select the Person Name check box.**

   You see the various actions that a user can choose among: Send Mail, Schedule a Meeting, Open Contact, and Add to Contacts.

10. **Click OK.**

    The dialog box closes, and the Smart Tag definition is added to the properties window.

Working with a Smart Tag

To see how a user works with a Smart Tag, follow these steps.

1. **Choose View⇨Datasheet View.**

   The actual data from the Employees table appears.

2. **Click a person's name in the LastName field.**

   A small *i* icon appears, which is a Smart Tag icon, as shown in the top of Figure 5-3.

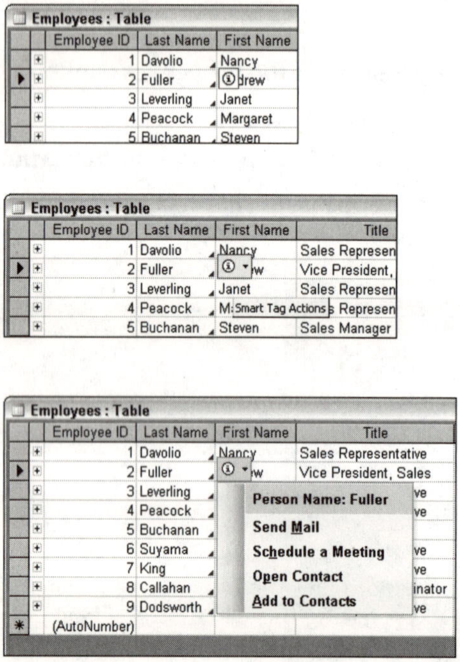

Figure 5-3: Smart Tags in action. The icon (top), the drop-down symbol (middle), and the task list (bottom).

3. **Move your mouse onto the Smart Tag icon.**

   It changes to a larger drop-down button, as shown in the middle of Figure 5-3.

4. **Click the Smart Tag icon.**

   A menu showing a choice of tasks appears, as shown in the bottom of Figure 5-3.

5. Select the Add to Contacts option in the drop-down list.

The Smart Tag in Access launches the Outlook dialog box, where you can add a new person to your Contacts list.

Only fields whose field names match in both Outlook's Contact database and Access's current database will be automatically filled in. Unfortunately, no standardized field naming convention exists (and XML certainly isn't helping this situation, allowing anyone, anywhere to define a unique custom schema). Thus, mapping is often necessary when programmers need to flow data from one table into another, and typing is often necessary when users need to flow data, as in this example from an Access table to an Outlook table.

Smart Tags in Word

Word recognizes various terms and phrases as Smart Tags, underlining them with purple dots, as shown in Figure 5-4.

Figure 5-4:
Word recognizes certain phrases as Smart Tags, underlining them like this.

123 Jones St.

You can ignore the Smart Tag or take action by hovering your mouse pointer over the Smart Tag and then clicking the drop-down button to see the list of options, as shown in Figure 5-5.

Figure 5-5:
An address in Word offers you these Smart Tag tasks.

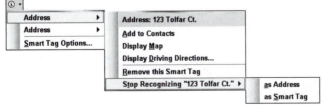

If you want to turn off Smart Tags in Word or manage them in other ways, choose Tools⇨AutoCorrect Options and then click the Smart Tags tab (this works in Excel as well), as shown in Figure 5-6.

Figure 5-6:
Edit Smart
Tags in this
dialog box
in Word.

Programming with Smart Tags

You cannot create Smart Tags by using the macro, VBA, or scripting languages built into Office applications, but you can manipulate existing Smart Tags programmatically. To actually create new Smart Tags, you need to use a Visual Studio .NET language.

Experimenting in Excel

Look at how to do some Smart Tag programming in Excel. Excel recognizes stock symbols, like MSFT, as you might expect. Type **MSFT** into an empty cell, and you see Excel's Smart Tag signal: a small triangle in the lower-right corner of the cell, as shown in Figure 5-7.

Figure 5-7:
Excel's
small
triangle
Smart Tag
symbol is
quite subtle.

Manipulating tags in VBA

This example activates a Smart Tag by typing a stock symbol for IBM. Then, selecting cell B1 has the effect of actually inserting the tag, making it possible to use. (The little Smart Tag symbol is now visible in cell A1, as if you'd pressed the Enter key.) Finally, you specify the #stockticker tag, its SmartTagActions, and use the Execute method.

To see how to manage Smart Tags with programming, follow this example:

1. **Start a new workbook in Excel.**

2. **Press Alt+F11 to open the VBA editor.**

3. **Choose View➪Project Explorer.**

4. **Double-click Module1 under Personal .XLS. Enter into this Module1 editor window the following code:**

```
Sub TagIBM()

    Range("A1").Select
    ActiveCell.FormulaR1C1 = "IBM"
    Range("B1").Select
    Range("A1").SmartTags("urn:schemas-microsoft-com:office:
        smarttags#stockticker") _
        .SmartTagActions("Insert refreshable stock price...").Execute

End Sub
```

5. **Press F5 to execute this code.**

You see today's report on IBM's stock price and other details about the stock inserted into your worksheet.

Creating Your Own Smart Tags

By simply creating an XML file containing the target words (terms) that should trigger a Smart Tag as well as the behaviors (actions) those words offer the user in the drop-down list, you can build your own Smart Tags. The example in Listing 5-1 handles stock symbols tags:

Listing 5-1:   Stock Symbol Smart Tags

```
<FL:smarttaglist xmlns:FL="urn:schemas-microsoft-com:smarttags:list">
    <FL:name>MSN MoneyCentral Financial Symbols</FL:name>
    <FL:lcid>1033,0</FL:lcid>
    <FL:description>A list of stock ticker symbols for recognition, as well as a
            set of actions that work with them.</FL:description>
    <FL:moreinfourl>http://office.microsoft.com</FL:moreinfourl>
```

**Book VII
Chapter 5**

Adding Smart Tags

```
<FL:updateable>true</FL:updateable>
<FL:autoupdate>true</FL:autoupdate>
<FL:lastcheckpoint>100</FL:lastcheckpoint>
<FL:lastupdate>5123942</FL:lastupdate>
<FL:updateurl>http://office.microsoft.com/smarttags/stockupdate.
        xml</FL:updateurl>
<FL:updatefrequency>20160</FL:updatefrequency>
<FL:smarttag type="urn:schemas-microsoft-com:office:smarttags#stockticker">
    <FL:caption>Financial Symbol</FL:caption>

<FL:terms>

<FL:termfile><FL:filename>stocks.dat</FL:filename>
</FL:termfile>

</FL:terms>


<FL:actions>
        <FL:action id="LatestQuoteData">
            <FL:caption>Stock quote on MSN MoneyCentral</FL:caption>
            <FL:url>http://moneycentral.msn.com/redir/moneycentralredirect.
        asp?pageid=SmartTag_1&amp;Target=/scripts/webquote.dll?ipage=
        qd%26Symbol={TEXT}</FL:url>
        </FL:action>
        <FL:action id="CompanyReportData">
            <FL:caption>Company report on MSN MoneyCentral</FL:caption>
            <FL:url>http://moneycentral.msn.com/redir/moneycentralredirect.
                asp?pageid=SmartTag_2&amp;Target=/investor/research/profile.
                asp?Symbol={TEXT}</FL:url>
        </FL:action>
        <FL:action id="RecentNews">
            <FL:caption>Recent news on MSN MoneyCentral</FL:caption>
            <FL:url>http://moneycentral.msn.com/redir/moneycentralredirect.
        asp?pageid=SmartTag_3&amp;Target=http://news.moneycentral.msn.
        com/ticker/rcnews.asp?Symbol={TEXT}</FL:url>
        </FL:action>
</FL:actions>

    </FL:smarttag>
</FL:smarttaglist>
```

You can likely find a file named STOCKS.XML in this path: C:\Program Files\Common Files\Microsoft Shared\Smart Tag\Lists. Depending on your version of Office, you might find additional XML files here, or this file might differ. But this path is the repository for XML files for Smart Tags lists.

Notice in this XML code that the <terms> section references a DAT file, which is in this same subdirectory. However, as you'll soon see, you can simply type a text list right in this <terms> element rather than provide a separate data file. You use the <termlist> rather than <termfile> tag pair.

The <termfile> DAT file is not written in XML or any of its offspring. It's a proprietary format, so unless you can track down the utility that creates it, you have to use a text list as illustrated in the next example.

The next section (*element*, if you insist) is <actions>, which includes a group of individual <action> elements, each with a caption, an ID, and a URL (address). The user selects one of these actions from the drop-down list displayed when the Smart Tag is activated. In this case, the actions are a series of what are (in effect) merely hyperlinks, not programming.

Creating your first Smart Tag

Following the pattern in the previous XML code example, you can build your own set of actions and your own list of trigger words. Try typing Listing 5-2 into Notepad:

Listing 5-2: Creating Triggers and Actions

```
<FL:smarttaglist xmlns:FL="urn:schemas-microsoft-com:smarttags:list">
<FL:name>Internet weather places for updates</FL:name>
<FL:lcid>1033</FL:lcid>
<FL:description>My list of various weather stations on the Internet
            </FL:description>
<FL:smarttag type="urn:schemas-microsoft-com:smarttags#msdnterms">
    <FL:caption>Weather Sites</FL:caption>
    <FL:terms>
        <FL:termlist>weather, storm, heat, temperature, forecast, weather
            outlook, travel</FL:termlist>
    </FL:terms>
    <FL:actions>
        <FL:action id="WeatherChannel">
         <FL:caption>The &amp;Weather Channel Web site</FL:caption>
         <FL:url>http://www.weather.com</FL:url>
        </FL:action>

        <FL:action id="CNNWeather">
          <FL:caption>&amp;CNN Weather Report</FL:caption>
            <FL:url>http://www.cnn.com/WEATHER</FL:url>
        </FL:action>

        <FL:action id="WeatherUnderground">
          <FL:caption>Weather &amp;Underground</FL:caption>
            <FL:url>http://www.wunderground.com</FL:url>
        </FL:action>
    </FL:actions>
</FL:smarttag>
</FL:smarttaglist>
```

**Book VII
Chapter 5**

Adding Smart Tags

Save this to the tag's list path: `C:\Program Files\Common Files\Microsoft Shared\Smart Tag\Lists.`

If you typed this in Word, copy it into Notepad to strip off the formatting codes. If you save it from Notepad, ensure that the extension is .xml, not .txt. Close Word and then reopen it. Opening an Office 2003 application causes any XML Smart Tag files to be scanned and their lists loaded so the application can work with the Smart Tags defined in the file.

Triggering your tag to test it

With Word freshly open, type **forecast** — one of the trigger Smart Tag terms you defined in Listing 5-2 — and then click the Smart Tag icon to drop down the list. You see the various actions (Internet sites in this case) that you defined in the XML file, as shown in Figure 5-8.

Figure 5-8:
Here's your new custom Smart Tag, working as you specified.

Click any of the actions to open Internet Explorer at that site.

 To provide shortcut keys in a Smart Tag's actions list, add the & code in the caption element's text, as illustrated in the code in Listings 5-1 and 5-2. When the user drops the actions list for the Smart Tag, the character immediately following & will be underlined, and the user can merely press that key rather than clicking the action in the list.

Feeding data to an Internet site

You can use the special {TEXT} code to feed specific data to a Web site or other target of a Smart Tag action. In this next example, you use {TEXT} code in a URL, and it gets replaced with the Smart Tag term. In other words, whenever the user types **27263** (my ZIP code), that triggers the Smart Tag, and the URL for the MSNBC weather Web page accepts a ZIP code variable. This URL has a czstr= attribute that wants a ZIP code, which is automatically supplied when the Smart Tag action is triggered.

```
<FL:url>http://www.msnbc.com/news/wea_front.asp?ta=y&amp;
      tab=BW&amp;tp=&amp;czstr={TEXT}</FL:url>
```

Type Listing 5-3 into Notepad, substituting your ZIP code for 27263 in the code below:

Listing 5-3:   Sending Data to the Internet

```
<FL:smarttaglist xmlns:FL="urn:schemas-microsoft-com:smarttags:list">
<FL:name>Local Weather</FL:name>
<FL:lcid>1033</FL:lcid>
<FL:description>My Local Weather</FL:description>
<FL:smarttag type="urn:schemas-microsoft-com:smarttags#msdnterms">
    <FL:caption>Local Weather</FL:caption>
    <FL:terms>
        <FL:termlist>27263</FL:termlist>
    </FL:terms>
    <FL:actions>
        <FL:action id="LocalWeather">

        <FL:caption>The &amp;Local Weather</FL:caption>


<FL:url>http://www.msnbc.com/news/wea_front.asp?ta=y&amp;tab=BW&amp;tp=&amp;
    czstr={TEXT}</FL:url>

        </FL:action>

    </FL:actions>
</FL:smarttag>
</FL:smarttaglist>
```

Save this XML file as `LocalWeather.xml`. Close Word, open it, and type your ZIP code into the document. Click the Smart Tag and choose Local Weather. You'll see your current weather report. The Smart Tag term — your ZIP code — replaced `{TEXT}` in the URL.

Chapter 6: Exploring Smart Documents

In This Chapter

✔ **Understanding Smart Documents**

✔ **Managing security issues**

✔ **Simplifying deployment**

✔ **Working with Smart Documents elements**

✔ **Using XML**

✔ **Attaching schemas**

✔ **Attaching the XML Expansion Pack**

✔ **Understanding the code**

✔ **Modifying a template**

*S*mart Tags — which you can read about in Book VII, Chapter 5 — are only part of the "smart" story. Microsoft's new Smart Document technology involves Smart Tags, but it also includes context-sensitive task panes. In fact, the term *Smart Document* generally refers to task pane behaviors, although Smart Tags are part of the concept, namely to provide users with various kinds of assistance by being aware of the user's current location in the document.

In this chapter, you see how to approach Smart Document technology the way a true developer/programmer should — not merely understanding how to use Smart Documents (users, after all, can do that) but instead rolling up your sleeves and controlling Smart Documents programmatically — managing security, deployment, and creating your own Smart Documents for users to, well, merely *use*.

First Things First: Downloading the SDK

Before exploring how to program Smart Documents, download the Smart Documents software development kit (SDK) from this URL:

```
www.microsoft.com/downloads/details.aspx?FamilyId=24A557F
7-EB06-4A2C-8F6C-2767B174126F&displaylang=en
```

When the setup wizard displays a screen with a Browse button and asks you to Choose Where to Install the Smart Document SDK, don't click the Browse button or follow the advice there. You *must* install the SDK to the default location suggested by this wizard, or some of the samples will not work: They're hard-wired to work here and here only.

With this download, you have samples, tools, and documentation that you can use to explore Smart Document creation.

Understanding Smart Documents

Like the wizards found in many of Microsoft's programming languages and some applications, a Smart Document is a new technology designed to assist users in completing a task. For example, you could create a Smart Document to assist a prospective employee in filling out your company's job application.

Both Word 2003 and Excel 2003 offer Smart Document capabilities. Smart Documents can

✦ Contain their own macros

✦ Access the features built into the host application

✦ Display controls and other objects to assist users

✦ Help manage version problems

For example, a Smart Document can define `range` objects in Word as read-only and can do so dynamically: Those ranges can be made read/write for certain users. How can Smart Document code know the current user? In Word's User Information dialog box (choose Tools⇨Options⇨ User Information) is a Name field. This translates into VBA code like this, which works in either Excel or Word:

```
MsgBox Application.UserName
```

Smart Documents can access this information, just like VBA can. Smart Documents can even use VBA. In fact, Smart Document programming sounds quite a lot like VBA, no? What's new and different about Smart Documents? What can you do with them that you cannot already do with VBA?

Microsoft's answer to this surprise question centers around the task pane feature, added to Office in the XP version. Improvements in the user interface (primarily the use of the task pane), deployment, and security distinguish Smart Documents technology from older VBA and ActiveX objects programming.

Smart Documents are sensitive to themselves: They can check whether they're the latest version. For example, when a user loads a Smart Document-based Suggestions form from their hard drive, this form can be programmed to quickly look on the network to see whether it's the most recent version — and if not, update itself. Sweet.

Smart Documents are also sensitive to the user's location within a document and can respond based on the context where it finds the user interacting. For example, if the user is asked to enter his birth date, the task pane can provide help by displaying the required format for entering dates if the user fails to employ that format. A specialized control can even be displayed to assist the user. But above all — Microsoft says — the functionality built into the Smart Documents technology makes life easier for us programmers. You can create solutions more easily than with previous technology and can also interact with data stores or other Office 2003 applications more easily.

Based on XML, Smart Documents employ an expanded version of the Smart Tag Application Program Interface (API). But whereas Smart Tags parse a document for terms that behaviors can be mapped to, Smart Documents instead employ XML schemas that are mapped to elements in the document.

Security measures

Because Smart Documents — like Smart Tags — are crawling with executables, security has to be tight. Before Smart Documents can be installed on a computer, they must be recognized by that machine's Registry as digitally signed by a trusted authority. Further, the user can be prompted (and can refuse) to permit a Smart Document to be installed. Users, though, are by far the greatest security weakness in any system of computer safeguards, so this last security measure doesn't provide much protection in most cases.

If you attempt to view the `SimpleSample.doc` Smart Document that's included with the Smart Document SDK, you see the security message displayed in Figure 6-1.

Figure 6-1:
Without the XML Expansion Pack, a Smart Document isn't so smart.

If you choose to download this Expansion Pack (which can mean simply registering it on your local machine because it's already downloaded), you see the following security warning that refuses your request, as shown in Figure 6-2. This message is displayed because your Registry blocks installation of potentially dangerous XML-based executables. Arrrg. See how to remedy this in the following section.

Figure 6-2:
Here's a
problem
with a
security
certificate.

Microsoft Office Word

The file could not be installed because there was a problem with the security certificate. The XML expansion pack may not work as expected. For more information, contact your administrator.

OK

Disabling security

The SDK samples are not digitally signed. To allow the Smart Document's SDK to work so you can explore and test this new technology, you have to run a little fixer at Start➪All Programs➪Microsoft Office 2003 Developer Resources➪Microsoft Office 2003 Smart Documents SDK➪Tools➪Disable XML Expansion Pack Manifest Security. Do this, and you're up and running. The SDK's Smart Document SDK Getting Started (same path as the Tools just listed) document, however, ominously warns:

> *IMPORTANT: You are strongly encouraged to disable XML expansion pack manifest security checking only within a testing environment. You should not disable security checking on users' machines.*

You've been warned.

Security is such a slippery slope . . . always a game of chess between the good guys and the bad guys. The odd thing about the signing safety measure for this XML Expansion Pack — if I understand it correctly — is that this SDK also includes an XML Expansion Pack Manifest Signing Utility. You can use this utility to digitally sign XML expansion packs and eXtensible Stylesheet Language Transformation (XSLT) files. And, also, presumably so can the bad guys. Some of them might even pose as you, a trusted source.

But what's truly intriguing is that you and I and everyone else can download the tool that disables the manifest security check in the Registry. You can even read the tool in Notepad because it's just a plain text Registry setting.

What is XSLT?

XSLT is one of the many variants or offspring of standard (ha!) XML. XSLT is designed to help XML by translating native XML into other formats, such as HTML that can be displayed in a Web page. XSLT is sometimes referred to as *XSL,* but according to the experts, XSL is a broader term that includes XSLT and also XPath and XSL (additional technologies used to help manage XML documents). Got it?

Deployment simplified

Using a technique introduced by .NET language solutions to avoid DLL Hell, Smart Documents gather their dependencies into a single XML manifest. (As you doubtless know, in the past code libraries such as DLLs were not well managed. Several applications would share a DLL, but when an updated version of that DLL was installed, it could easily cause some of the applications sharing it using it to fail. Sharing DLLs was an effort to conserve memory and disk space, but that's no longer a significant issue. Both memory and hard drives are now cheap, and therefore, capacious.

With Smart Document manifests, a user opens an Excel or Word template, and the manifest communicates the template's metadata and checks that the dependencies are current versions and are working. The programmer's job is to make the manifest file and save it with the Smart Document's dependency files on the server.

At the time of this book's writing, you could program Smart Documents by using Visual Basic 6.0, Visual Basic .NET, Visual C++, or Visual C#. Also, Smart Documents can be deployed to many locations, such as

◆ An intranet

◆ Web Services

◆ A corporate network

◆ The Internet

◆ SharePoint Portal Server 2003

◆ SharePoint Services

The Building Blocks of a Smart Document

Five interacting parts compose a Smart Document:

✦ **A Word document or Excel spreadsheet on which to build the Smart Document solution:** An XML file maps to sections of this document, providing a set of XML elements that are associated with components (controls, help messages, boilerplate text, and so on). These components are displayed in the task pane. Precisely what is displayed depends on where the user clicks (or moves the insertion cursor via the keyboard) in the document. The location of the insertion cursor triggers whatever XML element governs that section of the document.

✦ **An *XSD file* (an XML schema definition file) that expresses, in XML, the structure of a document:** Many business documents are already structured. They have a set of headlines, subheads, tables, and other formatting or organizing elements that define its structure. You, the programmer, merely then need to express the structure as an XML schema to prepare the document to become a Smart Document.

✦ **An action handler:** This is a code library containing the executable functions that carry out the actions the Smart Document is capable of.

✦ **The XML manifest file:** This provides any necessary server locations (for dependency files) and a list of those dependencies.

✦ **Dependency files:** This could be boilerplate text that the user can choose to insert, graphics, and so on that support the solution.

Programming Smart Documents

Smart Documents can be created in a variety of ways. For elementary Smart Documents, you need not create a DDL or a component, as illustrated in the following example. Or you can use COM components and Visual Basic 6 (unmanaged code) or .NET languages (managed code).

You first have to ensure that you're using the primary interoperative assemblies for Microsoft Office 2003 (usually found in the `C:\WindowsFolder\assembly` path). To see whether you've met this requirement, follow these steps:

1. **Open Control Panel.**

2. **Click the Add or Remove Programs icon.**

   The Add or Remove Programs dialog box opens.

3. **Click Microsoft Office 2003.**

4. **Click the Change button.**

   The Setup dialog box appears.

5. **Select the Add or Remove Features option button.**

6. **Click Next.**

   You see the custom setup page of the setup wizard.

7. **Select the Choose Advanced Customization of Applications check box.**

8. **Click Next.**

9. **Open the Microsoft Office Word entry in the list by clicking it.**

10. **Click .NET Programmability Support.**

11. **Choose Run from My Computer.**

12. **Repeat Steps 9–11 but this time for Excel.**

13. **Click the final item on the list, Office Tools.**

14. **Click Smart Tag .NET Programmability Support, Run from My Computer (under Office tools).**

15. **Click Update.**

    The installation process proceeds, complete with mystery Registry changes and other behind-the-scenes activity. Then, finally, the process is announced as being complete.

16. **Close the dialog box and then close Control Panel.**

Simple XML Smart Document programming

In this next example, you can use the sample document (`simplesample.doc`) from the Smart Document SDK download example earlier in this chapter ("First Things First: Downloading the SDK"). If you merely want to display links, help text, graphics, prebuilt controls (like buttons), and other simple items in the task pane, you can write an XML file that conforms to the Microsoft Office Smart Tag List (MOSTL) Schema, described at this MSDN site:

```
http://msdn.microsoft.com/library/default.asp?url=
/library/en-us/dnsmarttag/html/odc_stadvtools.asp
```

and elsewhere on the Microsoft site.

However, if you want to see how to view and explore the `SimpleSample.doc` example, I suggest that you use the following instructions to tour this sample. The instructions currently on the Microsoft site are difficult to

Book VII
Chapter 6

Exploring
Smart Documents

follow, to put it kindly. To be fair, creating a programmatic Smart Document is not child's play at this point in the technology's development. Significant security issues need to be worked around, and various support files are necessary for success.

The first step is to locate the `SmartSample.doc` in the default location where it was stored during the SDK download (from the earlier section, "First Things First: Downloading the SDK"). Open Windows Explorer and maneuver to this path:

```
C:\Program Files\Microsoft Office 2003 Developer
Resources\Microsoft Office 2003 Smart Document SDK\
```

If you did not install it to this location, *you must.* The sample won't work in other locations because it's hard-wired to look here for dependencies. If you try to execute it from elsewhere, you get this error message:

> *A file that's part of this solution could not be downloaded. The solution may not work properly. Contact your administrator for further information.*

This error message can also be triggered if a necessary dependency is missing from the files in this path or permissions aren't granted to load these files.

Via Windows Explorer, double-click `SmartSample.doc` in the following path:

```
C:\Program Files\Microsoft Office 2003 Developer
Resources\Microsoft Office 2003 Smart Document SDK\
Samples\SimpleSample\SourceFiles\SimpleSample.doc
```

You should see the unadorned document, as shown in Figure 6-3.

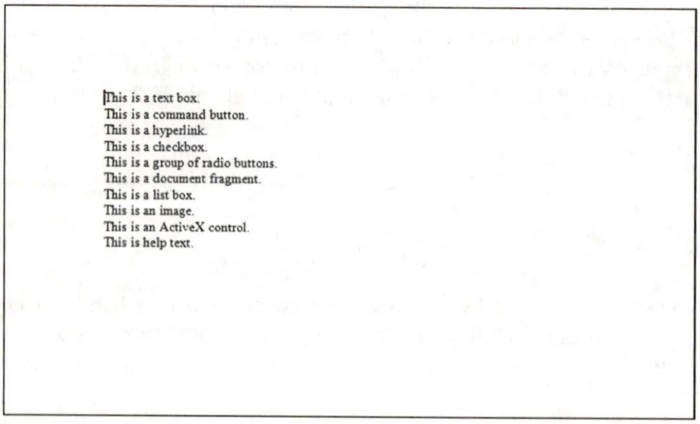

Figure 6-3:
Before the XML is added, this Smart Document-to-be looks like any other Word document.

This is a text box.
This is a command button.
This is a hyperlink.
This is a checkbox.
This is a group of radio buttons.
This is a document fragment.
This is a list box.
This is an image.
This is an ActiveX control.
This is help text.

Attaching a schema

The XML schema needs to be attached to the document, providing a map of its various zones. Follow these steps:

***1.* Choose Tools⇨Templates and Add-Ins.**

The Templates and Add-Ins dialog box opens.

***2.* Click the XML Schema tab.**

***3.* Click the Add Schema button.**

You can now add an XML schema to the Word Schema Library.

***4.* Browse this location to find the Source Files subdirectory:**

```
C:\Program Files\Microsoft Office 2003 Developer Resources\
    Microsoft Office 2003 Smart Document SDK\
    Samples\SimpleSample\SourceFiles\
```

***5.* Double-click the `SimpleSample.xsd` file (the schema).**

A dialog box opens asking you to provide an alias for this file.

If you see a security warning, you need to go to the same Source Files path in Step 4 and double-click the `DisableManifestSecurityCheck.reg` file. Answer Yes when asked whether you want to take this risk.

***6.* Type ssample as the alias.**

This alias (a *friendly name,* meaning *descriptive*) is displayed in the list of available XML schemas.

***7.* Click OK.**

You see the schema now added to your library, as shown in Figure 6-4.

Figure 6-4:
The schema is now attached to your Word document.

8. **Select the check box next to** `SimpleSample.xsd` **to ensure that it's attached to the** `SimpleSample.doc`.

9. **Click OK.**

The dialog box closes, and you see that a taskbar has been added to your document, as shown in Figure 6-5.

Figure 6-5: After you add a schema to a Word document, an XML Structure task bar appears.

You might see the dialog box shown in Figure 6-6 from time to time. It warns you that you've disabled Expansion Pack security (but you knew that, didn't you?). You either did it in Step 5 in the preceding example or earlier in the chapter. (The way to re-enable this security feature is to click Yes when you see the dialog box in Figure 6-6, but you don't want to do that now because you're exploring how to manage this technology.)

The `SimpleSample.xsd` file looks like Listing 6-1, describing the zones in your document (in this case, simple strings):

Figure 6-6:
Click No.
You want
the sample
Smart
Document
examples
to work.

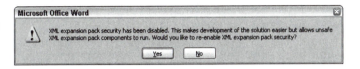

Listing 6-1: SimpleSample.xsd File

```
<xsd:schema xmlns:xsd="http://www.w3.org/2001/XMLSchema"
  xmlns="SimpleSample"
  targetNamespace="SimpleSample"
  elementFormDefault="qualified">

  <xsd:complexType name="exampleType">
    <xsd:all>
      <xsd:element name="textbox" type="xsd:string"/>
      <xsd:element name="commandbutton" type="xsd:string"/>
      <xsd:element name="help" type="xsd:string"/>
      <xsd:element name="radiobutton" type="xsd:string"/>
      <xsd:element name="checkbox" type="xsd:string"/>
      <xsd:element name="listbox" type="xsd:string"/>
      <xsd:element name="image" type="xsd:string"/>
      <xsd:element name="documentfragment" type="xsd:string"/>
      <xsd:element name="activex" type="xsd:string"/>
      <xsd:element name="hyperlink" type="xsd:string"/>
    </xsd:all>
  </xsd:complexType>

  <xsd:element name="example" type="exampleType"/>

</xsd:schema>
```

Book VII
Chapter 6

Exploring
Smart Documents

Attaching the XML Expansion Pack

You're not done yet. Now you have to add the Expansion Pack to this document to fully activate the Smart Document task pane features. Follow these steps:

1. **With the** `SimpleSample.doc` **visible, choose Tools⇨Templates and Add-Ins.**

   The Templates and Add-Ins dialog box opens.

2. **Click the XML Expansion Packs tab.**

3. **Click the Add button.**

   The Install XML Expansion Pack dialog box opens.

4. Browse to the same directory from which you opened
   `SimpleSample.doc`:

```
C:\Program Files\Microsoft Office 2003 Developer Resources\
      Microsoft Office 2003 Smart Document SDK\
      Samples\SimpleSample\SourceFiles\
```

5. Double-click `manifest.xml` to load it into your document.

If you see a security warning, you need to go to the same
`SourceFiles` path described in Step 4 and double-click the
`DisableManifestSecurityCheck.reg` file. Answer Yes when asked
whether you want to take this risk.

6. Click OK.

The dialog box closes.

You can now see the results of your trials and tribulations, as shown in
Figure 6-7.

Click any of the text zones (the areas enclosed by the XML tags from the
schema file). Try clicking This is a Checkbox in the left pane (see the selected
text in Figure 6-7), and you then see a couple of check boxes appear in the task
pane on the right, as you can see in Figure 6-7.

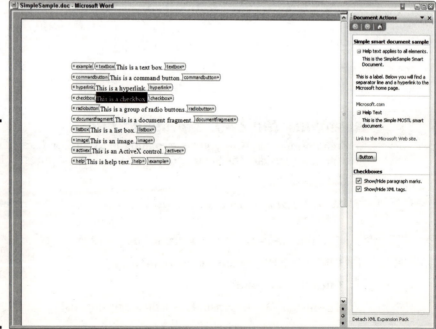

Figure 6-7:
Here's a
Smart
Document
in action,
showing the
results of
user clicks
by changing
what
appears in
the task
pane.

Select the Show/Hide XML Tags check box to conceal the tags in the document. The user would not normally see these XML tags but would rather simply see the text (as in Figure 6-3). However, with the schema and Expansion Pack added to this document — even with the tags not visible to the user — clicking any of these paragraphs changes what appears in the task pane. That's the heart of the user-interaction with a Smart Document. When users click somewhere in the document, help, controls, or other resources appear in the task pane, and users can then interact with these resources.

Try clicking the various other paragraphs in this document to see how the individual controls can be used in a Smart Document.

The manifest file looks like Listing 6-2.

Listing 6-2: Manifest File

```
<?xml version="1.0" encoding="UTF-8" standalone="no"?>
<manifest xmlns="http://schemas.microsoft.com/office/xmlexpansionpacks/2003">
   <version>1.1</version>
   <updateFrequency>20160</updateFrequency>
   <uri>SimpleSample</uri>
   <solution>
      <solutionID>{15960625-1612-46AB-877C-BBCB59503FCE}</solutionID>
      <type>smartDocument</type>
      <alias lcid="*">Simple Smart Document Sample</alias>
      <file>
         <type>solutionActionHandler</type>
         <version>1.0</version>
         <filePath>SimpleSample.dll</filePath>
         <CLSID>{14E38799-0AD2-4EA2-8EF6-B5754A9A7A90}</CLSID>
         <regsvr32/>
      </file>
   </solution>
   <solution>
      <solutionID>schema</solutionID>
      <type>schema</type>
      <alias lcid="*">Simple Smart Document Sample</alias>
      <file>
         <type>schema</type>
         <version>1.0</version>
         <filePath>SimpleSample.xsd</filePath>
      </file>
   </solution>
</manifest>
```

**Book VII
Chapter 6**

Exploring
Smart Documents

If you have problems

If you find yourself having difficulties with this example, try double-clicking a different `SimpleSample.doc` file in this path:

```
C:\Program Files\Microsoft Office 2003 Developer
Resources\Microsoft Office 2003 Smart Document SDK\
Samples\SimpleSampleVB6
```

It includes a DLL file, but if you attach the Expansion Pack and then follow the instructions in the earlier section, "Attaching a schema," you should be able to get this sample to work.

Understanding Smart Document source code

If you look at the `clsActions` file in the `SimpleSample.vbp` file found in the SDK directory:

```
C:\Program Files\Microsoft Office 2003 Developer
Resources\Microsoft Office 2003 Smart Document SDK\
Samples\SimpleSampleVB7
```

you'll discover how actual programming can be written to make a Smart Document respond to user movements (clicking or otherwise moving the insertion cursor in a document).

Source code inflation goes wild

Take a look at `SimpleSampleVB7.sln`, which is a *solution file* (the equivalent of the VB6 and earlier VBP Visual Basic project file). In fact, I urge you to use this example file as a starting place. Modify it and build on it to create your own solutions Why? Because when you attempt to interact with XML, your VB source code becomes XML-like — a bit more redundant, repetitive, and verbose than usual. Given the tremendous redundancy in this code, you'd have a difficult time imagining how to actually write the code from scratch. You would expect to use a single list to handle a set of ten controls — text boxes, check boxes, and so on. You would use this single list to provide object variables and property values all in one place. Or, you might use ten different property procedures to manage them. Instead, inflation goes wild in this code, and you find seven complete lists, each referencing an aspect of each of the ten controls in this project. In other words, you have 70 entries where 10 would have done the job in traditional (non-XML-inflected) programming.

Programming moves to the computer

You simply cannot write this kind of programming by hand, from scratch. Well, you could, just as some people spend a year building a model of the Eiffel Tower out of matchsticks. (It's called *torture art:* You're not impressed by the beauty of the result as much as by the persistence, struggle, and sheer determination required of the person who made it.)

When working with XML and its dreadful repetitiveness, the computer must increasingly take over the burden of generating source code. When you create a Smart Document of your own, it's virtually assured that you will not begin from scratch. Instead, you must use this class module as a template or some other prewritten code. Not only does XML have primitive debugging tools, its verbosity greatly increases the opportunity for error and the difficulty of reading and maintaining its code. To add insult to injury, it can be case-sensitive as well. In this case, it *is* case-sensitive.

Lists upon lists

For an example of verbosity and repetition, first refer to Figure 6-7. To set the properties of the check box captions, you must write this programming in your clsActions class module:

```
Case 501
    ControlCaptionFromID = _
    "Show/Hide paragraph marks."
Case 502
    ControlCaptionFromID = _
    "Show/Hide XML tags."
```

These lists are quite a bit longer than I'm displaying here. I'll generally just provide the first two items in each list rather than waste book space showing everything.

A complete list of controls specifies caption information for each control, like this:

```
Case 1
    SmartDocXmlTypeCaption = "Textbox"
Case 2
    SmartDocXmlTypeCaption = "Click"
```

Another list specifies how many controls of each type are being used in this Smart Document:

```
Select Case XMLTypeName
    Case cTEXTBOX
        ControlCount = 1
    Case cBUTTON
        ControlCount = 1
```

However, to define these check boxes as controls to be identified by the following case structure:

```
Select Case ControlID
```

you must include yet another list, another Public property, specifying the range of ID numbers used for each control type, like Listing 6-3.

Listing 6-3: Specifying ID Numbers

```
Public ReadOnly Property ControlID(ByVal XMLTypeName As String, ByVal
        ControlIndex As Integer) _
    As Integer Implements Microsoft.Office.Interop.SmartTag.
        ISmartDocument.ControlID
  Get
    Select Case XMLTypeName
      Case cTEXTBOX
        ControlID = ControlIndex
      Case cBUTTON
        ControlID = ControlIndex + 100
      Case cEXAMPLE
        ControlID = ControlIndex + 200
      Case cHELP
        ControlID = ControlIndex + 300
      Case cRADIO
        ControlID = ControlIndex + 400
      Case cCHECKBOX
        ControlID = ControlIndex + 500
      Case cLIST
        ControlID = ControlIndex + 600
      Case cIMAGE
        ControlID = ControlIndex + 700
      Case cDOCFRAG
        ControlID = ControlIndex + 800
      Case cACTIVEX
        ControlID = ControlIndex + 900
    End Select
  End Get
End Property
```

You must include a similar (and somewhat redundant) list of constant declarations:

```
Const cTEXTBOX As String = cNAMESPACE & "#textbox"
Const cBUTTON As String = cNAMESPACE & "#commandbutton"
```

And so on until you've specified one constant for each object you plan to use. Because this programming interacts with XML, the internal documentation — the comments in the source code — refers to these objects as *elements*.

Then you must create a constant representing the total number of elements. Don't confuse this with the total number of instantiated controls actually used but rather the total number of control objects. There are, for example, two check boxes actually used:

```
'Number of types (or element constants)
Const cTYPES As Integer = 10
```

No sooner do you find out that you must refer to controls or objects as *elements* (even though they've been called *controls* for decades) than you come upon yet another alien name for them: *types*. Found in the source code comments referencing the TextBox and other controls, *types* is a relatively meaningless term used by C programmers, even though this is purportedly a Visual Basic example. You'll find C and XML influences throughout the Visual Basic .NET Help system and code examples.

In another example of redundancy, after you define the cTYPES constant, you must also create a property representing this number of controls that you already defined:

```
Public ReadOnly Property SmartDocXmlTypeCount() As Integer Implements _
Microsoft.Office.Interop.SmartTag.ISmartDocument.SmartDocXmlTypeCount

      Get
           SmartDocXmlTypeCount = cTYPES
      End Get

   End Property
```

Likewise, each control constant must be listed in a property containing a series of SmartDocXmlTypeNames.

Stupidly, some XML code is case-sensitive, which is yet another source of bugs, but that some loony committee thought was a helpful feature. Visual Basic code is sensibly case-*in*sensitive, but when you're interacting with XML as you are when programming for Smart Documents, you must always remember to check that you've matched the capitalization as it's used in the XML schema. For example, Radiobutton does *not* match RadioButton. Also, because programming Smart Documents is distributed among .NET and XML source code, error messages won't be thrown simply because you've used one of those Option Explicit statements at the start of your .NET code designed to trap typos. (The source code comment refers to capitalization as a spelling issue.)

A global variable objApp is defined to represent Word itself, so you can access Word's features or a control:

```
   Private objApp As Microsoft.Office.Interop.Word.Application
```

In this code, this object is used only once to manage the calendar control:

```
   objApp.ActiveWindow.Selection.Range.Text = objCal.Value
```

This object variable is instantiated in what Visual Basic programmers would call the Form_Load event although here it's SmartDocInitialize. This is where necessary preliminary tasks are carried out:

```
   Public Sub SmartDocInitialize(ByVal ApplicationName As String, ByVal Document
           As Object, ByVal SolutionPath As String, ByVal SolutionRegKeyRoot As
           String) Implements Microsoft.Office.Interop.SmartTag.ISmartDocument.
           SmartDocInitialize
```

```
        Dim objDoc As Microsoft.Office.Interop.Word.Document
        objDoc = Document
        strPath = objDoc.Path & "\"
        objApp = objDoc.Application
    End Sub
```

As you can see by this procedure's arguments and `Implements` statement, object-oriented programming (OOP) can go quite wild with messaging between procedures and qualifications. In any case, this event triggers when the Smart Document process begins (when a Smart Document is loaded into Word, in this case). The primary task here is to instantiate the `objApp`, the object variable that refers to the executing Word application.

The `strPath` variable is used to reference dependency files, such as graphics, which (following the current fashion) are included in the same directory as all the other files used for the solution.

Also, the form itself needs a special definition, as does the calendar control:

```
Public ReadOnly Property ControlNameFromID(ByVal ControlID As Integer) As
        String _
    Implements Microsoft.Office.Interop.SmartTag.
        ISmartDocument.ControlNameFromID
  Get
    Select Case ControlID
        Case 901
            ControlNameFromID = "Calendar"
        Case Else
            ControlNameFromID = cNAMESPACE & ControlID
    End Select
  End Get
End Property
```

The calendar control needs this object variable, and it includes events that the user might trigger:

```
    Private WithEvents objCal As MSACAL.Calendar
```

Here's another lovely example of code inflation. This is just *the first line* of the code that builds a group of radio buttons (formerly known as option buttons):

```
Public Sub PopulateRadioGroup(ByVal ControlID As Integer, ByVal
        ApplicationName As String, ByVal LocaleID As Integer, ByVal Text
        As String, ByVal Xml As String, ByVal Target As Object, ByVal
        Props As Microsoft.Office.Interop.SmartTag.ISmartDocProperties,
        ByRef List As System.Array, ByRef Count As Integer, ByRef
        InitialSelected As Integer) Implements Microsoft.Office.
        Interop.SmartTag.ISmartDocument.PopulateRadioGroup
```

Notice that any code that calls this procedure must provide *ten* parameters to satisfy the argument list. Computer programming languages are moving into an *Alice in Wonderland* phase. Will they ever come back?

You'll also notice that HTML terminology is creeping into other programming as well. Instead of event procedures simply naming the control and the trigger action:

```
Sub Form1_Click
```

you get this:

```
Public Sub OnRadioGroupSelectChange
```

The addition of `On` to each event procedure name is typical of the unneeded repetitiveness characteristic of HTML, XML, and the many variants of these markup languages. You get the new `OnTextboxContentChange` event instead of the traditional and more sensible `TextBox_Change` event.

One other point of interest. In this next code, you handle controls or objects that are not handled in their own `OnClick` or other procedures. Put another way, some controls are handled differently than others. The primary events (`Click` in these cases) are gathered into a single procedure named `Invoke` (why not `OnInvoke`, one wonders). See Listing 6-4.

Listing 6-4:   Invoke Procedure

```
Public Sub InvokeControl(ByVal ControlID As Integer, ByVal ApplicationName As
            String, ByVal Target As Object, ByVal Text As String, ByVal Xml As
            String, ByVal LocaleID As Integer) Implements Microsoft.Office.
            Interop.SmartTag.ISmartDocument.InvokeControl
        Dim objXML As System.Xml.XmlDocument
        Dim objRange As Microsoft.Office.Interop.Word.Range
        Dim objNav As SHDocVw.InternetExplorer

        Select Case ControlID
            Case 101
                System.Windows.Forms.MessageBox.Show("This is an example of a
                    button.")
            Case 204
                objNav = New SHDocVw.InternetExplorer
                objNav.Navigate("http://www.microsoft.com")
                objNav.Visible = True
            Case 801
                objRange = Target
                objRange.XMLNodes(1).Text = "The quick red fox jumped over " & _
                    "the lazy brown dog."
            Case 802
                objRange = Target
                objXML = New Xml.XmlDocument
                objXML.Load(strPath & "gettysburgaddress.xml")
                objRange.XMLNodes(1).Range.InsertXML(objXML.InnerXml)
            Case Else
        End Select
    End Sub
```

As identified by their `ControlID`

- ✦ **101 is the test button on the task pane.**
- ✦ **204 is the label** `Microsoft.com.`
- ✦ **801 and 802 are** *document fragments* **(text that can be inserted into the document, or otherwise displayed).**

Click the button, and the response is a message box. Click the label (a hyperlink, actually) and the `Navigate` method of the Internet Explorer object takes you to the Microsoft site. Click a document fragment, and that fragment is placed at the location of the current range in the Word document.

Note that in `Case 801` in Listing 6-4, you can supply a literal fragment of text. Or, in `Case 802`, you can supply a reference to a file containing the text that gets dumped into an XML document before being, in turn, inserted into the Word document.

Modifying the Template

If you want to modify this Smart Document code, you're in for a bit of a struggle. Try to add a check box to those shown in Figure 6-7. There are many places where check boxes are referenced, and you have to find and modify some of these locations in the code to add a new check box.

First, locate this:

```
Public ReadOnly Property ControlCaptionFromID(ByVal ControlID
        As Integer, _
        ByVal ApplicationName As String, ByVal LocaleID
        As Integer, ByVal [Text] As String, _
        ByVal Xml As String, ByVal Target As Object) As
        String Implements Microsoft.Office. _
        Interop.SmartTag.ISmartDocument.
        ControlCaptionFromID
```

Then within this property, locate this reference to the number of check boxes:

```
Case cCHECKBOX
                ControlCount = 2
```

and change it to

```
                ControlCount = 3
```

Find this property:

```
Public ReadOnly Property ControlCaptionFromID(ByVal ControlID
          As Integer, _
          ByVal ApplicationName As String, ByVal LocaleID
          As Integer, ByVal [Text] As String, _
          ByVal Xml As String, ByVal Target As Object) As
          String Implements Microsoft.Office. _
          Interop.SmartTag.ISmartDocument. _
          ControlCaptionFromID
```

and then within the property, locate this code:

```
        Case 501
            ControlCaptionFromID = _
                "Show/Hide paragraph marks."
        Case 502
            ControlCaptionFromID = _
                "Show/Hide XML tags."
        Case 601
            ControlCaptionFromID = _
                "Select your favorite baseball team."
```

and, following the `Case 502` lines, add this:

```
        Case 503
            ControlCaptionFromID = _
                "Show User."
```

Find this property:

```
Public ReadOnly Property ControlTypeFromID(ByVal ControlID As
          Integer, _
          ByVal ApplicationName As String, ByVal LocaleID
          As Integer) As _
          Microsoft.Office.Interop.SmartTag.C_TYPE
          Implements Microsoft.Office.Interop.SmartTag. _
          ISmartDocument.ControlTypeFromID
```

and within it, change this line:

```
Case 501, 502
ControlTypeFromID = C_TYPE.C_TYPE_CHECKBOX
```

to

```
Case 501, 502, 503
ControlTypeFromID = C_TYPE.C_TYPE_CHECKBOX
```

Ignore this procedure because you want your new check box to default to unchecked:

```
Public Sub PopulateCheckbox(ByVal ControlID As Integer, ByVal
        ApplicationName As String, ByVal LocaleID As
        Integer, ByVal Text As String, ByVal Xml As
        String, ByVal Target As Object, ByVal Props As
        Microsoft.Office.Interop.SmartTag.
        ISmartDocProperties, ByRef Checked As Boolean)
        Implements Microsoft.Office.Interop.SmartTag.
        ISmartDocument.PopulateCheckbox
    Select Case ControlID
        Case 501, 502
            Checked = True
    End Select
End Sub
```

The key procedure you want to modify is this one. This is where the behaviors of the check boxes are coded (see Listing 6-5).

Listing 6-5:   Specifying Checkbox Behaviors

```
Public Sub OnCheckboxChange(ByVal ControlID As Integer, ByVal
        Target As Object, ByVal Checked As Boolean)
        Implements Microsoft.Office.Interop.SmartTag.
        ISmartDocument.OnCheckboxChange
    Dim objDoc As Microsoft.Office.Interop.Word.Document
    Dim objView As Microsoft.Office.Interop.Word.View

    objDoc = Target.Document
    objView = objDoc.ActiveWindow.View

    Select Case ControlID
        Case 501
            objView.ShowAll = Not objView.ShowAll
        Case 502
            objView.ShowXMLMarkup = Not
    objView.ShowXMLMarkup
        Case 503
            MsgBox(objView.Creator)
    End Select
End Sub
```

Add this code where shown in bold in Listing 6-5:

```
        Case 503
            MsgBox(objView.Creator)
```

Follow these steps:

1. **Choose Build⇨Rebuild Solution.**

2. **Double-click** `SimpleSample.doc` **in the** `SimpleSampleVB7` **subdirectory that you've been working with.**

3. **Attach the manifest and the schema files, if necessary, by choosing Tools⇨Templates and Add-Ins.**

4. **See whether you can see the new check box that you added to this example.**

   I can't. I do get the three controls on the task pane — the hyperlink to Microsoft.com, the text fragment, the button — but none of the other controls appear, including the check boxes.

Warnings in the Help file associated with this Smart Document SDK read like this:

After you make changes to the smart document code, delete the XML expansion pack, reboot the host application, and then re-add the XML expansion pack. Alternatively, change the version number for the smart document solution in the XML expansion pack manifest file every time the code is updated, and then delete and re-add the XML expansion pack.

However, following these instructions (and several variations of them) doesn't seem to help. Somewhere, deep in the Registry or elsewhere, some switch was thrown, and future attempts to see this Smart Document — even after removing the new 503 check box — fail. Please e-mail me at `richardm52@hotmail.com` if you figure out what's gone wrong. Perhaps we're in the famous *Version 1 Zone* and so must just be patient until this technology stabilizes.

Chapter 7: Using Project 2003

In This Chapter

✔ **Creating and editing projects**

✔ **Dealing with dependencies**

✔ **Understanding Gantt charts**

✔ **Adding Outlook features**

✔ **Handling the version problem**

Managing projects is a job that falls to many of us in our professional career, and Project 2003 assists you in the various phases of seeing a project through to its conclusion.

Project helps you deal with the complexities of any but the smallest projects. (You can send e-mails to make assignments and follow up for little jobs.) But if you have responsibility for a project of any size, you'll likely value Project's features — like Gantt charts, project templates, network diagrams, and task sheets — that can help you keep track of deadlines and otherwise organize things.

Taking a Look at Project 2003

As is often the case with its applications and utilities, Microsoft divides Project into different versions, adding additional features and/or scalability as the price goes up. Project Standard 2003 (list price $599) includes the essentials for planning and tracking a project. It is highly integrated with Office 2003 applications, although no version of Project is bundled with any version of Office 2003. The next version up, Project Professional 2003 ($999 list), can be integrated with Office Project Server 2003, providing special collaborative features, described by Microsoft as "Enterprise Project Management (EPM) capabilities such as up-to-date information on resource availability as well as skills and project status." For an in-depth comparison of the versions of Project, look here:

```
www.microsoft.com/office/project/howtobuy/choosing.mspx
```

Project 2003 demonstrates once again that Microsoft's various application development teams don't work under some sinister master plan — that is, sharing, plotting, and generally coordinating their efforts. As you perhaps know, Access goes its own way quite often, offering unique macro technologies; redefining keystrokes in its own, special way; omitting macro recording; and so on. Likewise, you get a surprise when you first fire up Project 2003. Notice anything odd in Figure 7-1?

The oddity in Figure 7-1 is that of all the Office 2003 applications, only Project puts the task pane on the left side. You can rectify that by grabbing the task pane by clicking and holding down the mouse button on the four vertical dots on the task pane title bar. Then drag the entire pane off to the right of the screen and drop it.

The Tasks pane (is it related to the *task pane?*) shown on the left in Figure 7-1, and in Figure 7-2, can be used like a browser: Click the links in it to see different views and options. Also note the useful pair of Back and Forward buttons to help you maneuver through the various levels of this pane.

However, the mouse buttons that can be used to move back or forward in a browser don't work here. Also, some features are strangely categorized. For example, to import data from Excel, you must click the <u>List tasks</u> link for some reason.

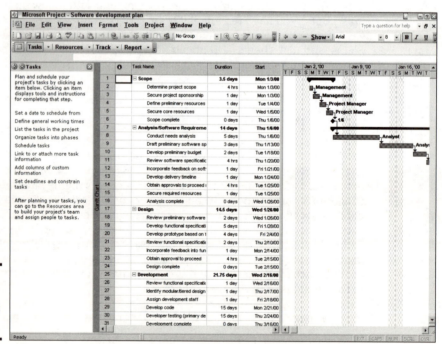

Figure 7-1:
The default
Project 2003
layout.

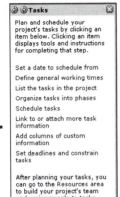

Figure 7-2:
Use the
Tasks pane
to plan your
project.

Creating a new project

Start to harness the power of Project by creating one — a project, that is. To help, Project offers a number of project management templates to choose from, including a software development plan, a project plan for a new business, a training rollout initiative, and many more.

Jump in and get a feel for it. Here I walk you through opening a software development plan template. After Project is up and running, do the following:

**Book VII
Chapter 7**

**Using
Project 2003**

1. **Click the <u>Create a new project</u> link in the task pane (or choose File⇨New if that link isn't visible).**

2. **Click the <u>Templates on Office online</u> link.**

The Microsoft Office Templates Home Page opens.

3. **Under Meetings and Projects in this home page, click Project Management. Or go directly to this page:**

```
http://office.microsoft.com/templates/category.aspx?CategoryID=CT06264042
    1033&CTT=4&Origin=ES790000301033
```

Notice the icons on the left side of each Project template. The ones with the green tablet are Project projects.

4. **Click the <u>Software development plan</u> link.**

5. **Click the Download Now button.**

This template is loaded into Project 2003 where you can view it and learn from it. But, whoops! First you notice that the task pane has flown back over to the left side again. (Oh well, this isn't technically the task pane.)

Exploring dependencies in Project

One major feature offered in Project is the relationships that you can specify between different tasks. This clearly goes beyond the simple task assignment features in Outlook.

Some tasks have inherent *dependencies:* That is, a certain task must be accomplished before a second one can begin. For example, if you need to submit a budget for your ambitious software development plan, you must first make a list of the necessary resources. In other words, the budget meeting should not take place until after the resources list task is completed. The budget *depends* on the completion of the resources list. You can relate tasks to each other in this fashion, specifying cause and effect. And if you try to rearrange tasks in a way that affects a defined dependency relationship, Project squawks and notifies you of the bearing that one task has on a subsequent (and dependent) task in the project.

A dependency can also develop when some action has ripple effects. Suppose a key employee runs off with her boyfriend to Alaska. You can quickly view the effect of her sudden departure on other tasks related to her jobs. Here's how to define a dependency:

1. **Click a row (a task) in a Gantt chart (described shortly).**

2. **Choose Task Information from the context menu.**

3. **In the Task Information dialog box, click the Predecessors tab.**

4. **Enter the ID of one or more previous tasks that must be completed before this task or have some other relationship to it (defined in the Type field in this dialog box).**

Arrows are drawn in the chart to illustrate dependencies, as you can see in the upcoming Figure 7-3.

Building a Project from Scratch

To launch a brand new project without following a template, choose File➪ New and then click the Blank project link in the Tasks pane. (You see the Tasks pane over on the left side with a list of steps that you should follow to structure and build your new project.)

Understanding a Gantt chart

Before seeing how to add functionality by integrating some of Outlook's capabilities into a Project job, take a look at *Gantt charts.* These charts are commonly used when planning because they allow you to visualize the timing involved in the various tasks that collectively result in a successful conclusion.

Projects should be broken down into tasks. Each task has its own row in a Gantt chart, with a running calendar of dates along the top of the chart, like a set of column titles. Because time is a major issue when manipulating projects, you'd expect the scheduling feature to govern much of what a project chart should be.

Take a look at the Gantt chart in Figure 7-3.

The time that you've allotted to each task is indicated by the bars on the right side of the chart, and the task names and categories appear on the left side. Major task name categories are indicated by bold text and lines that stretch across several tasks. However, individual tasks can also be parallel, or overlapping, in duration. It just so happens that many of the tasks in the template illustrated in Figures 7-1 and 7-3 are sequential (and also often dependencies as well, explaining their sequential nature).

Sequential (cause and effect) tasks are often found clustered at the beginning and end of a project, with more parallel or overlapping tasks occurring in the middle phase. This is the case with the template used earlier in this chapter (the Software Development Plan, as shown in Figures 7-1 and 7-3). However, if you scroll through that template's Gantt chart, you'll see quite a bit of parallel task behavior during the middle portion of the project.

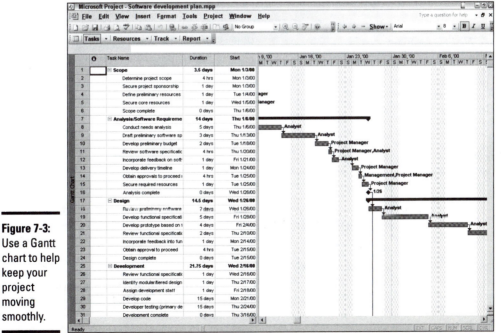

Figure 7-3:
Use a Gantt
chart to help
keep your
project
moving
smoothly.

As time passes, tasks are completed or in process, and the progress of the work on each task (its percentage of completion) is visually illustrated in the chart by a bar within the task's bar. For example, if you right-click a task and then choose Task Information from the context menu, you can specify the fraction of the task that's completed by adjusting the Percent Complete field, as shown in Figure 7-4.

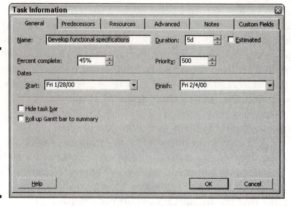

Figure 7-4: Track fractional completion of tasks by adjusting this Percent Complete field.

Set a task's completion to 45%, and it looks like the task shown in Figure 7-5.

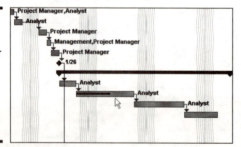

Figure 7-5: This bar-within-a-bar illustrates that one of these tasks is 45% complete.

When a task is 100% completed, a check mark appears in the Indicators field, just to the left of the Task Name field.

Seeing milestones

If you have events, or milestones — as opposed to tasks — that you want indicated on the chart, set their duration to 0 (zero), and they become milestones, visible as a diamond symbol. The Analysis Complete entry in the Task Name field of the Software Development Plan template is a milestone. It has no duration, but it does appear on the chart.

Some milestones do require a duration. For example, maybe the budget must be approved, and it will take your crack accounting department two days. To give a duration to a milestone, follow these steps:

1. **Right-click the milestone in the chart.**

2. **Choose Task Information from the context menu.**

3. **Click the Advanced tab of the Task Information dialog box.**

4. **In the Duration box, enter the task duration but select the Mark Task as Milestone check box.**

Adding Outlook functionality to a project

After you define your project and assigned tasks, you are ready to ride the horse. You, as project manager, must keep on top of things. One helpful way for a developer to assist in this process is to integrate the benefits of Outlook (the Contacts list, for example, and the ability to message and flag) into a Project job.

Take a look at how to merge some of Outlook's functionality into a Project project. (There's no way to get around this double word phrase, unless I use something vile like *undertaking*.) In this example, I show you how to create a reminder in Project that will, in turn, automatically create a task in Outlook. To add a set reminder feature to the default toolbar buttons in Project, follow these steps:

1. **With the Software Development Plan project loaded in Project (see the earlier section, "Creating a new project"), choose View➪Toolbars➪ Customize.**

The Customize dialog box opens.

2. **Click the Commands tab.**

3. **Click Tools in the Categories list box.**

4. **Click Set Reminder in the Commands list box.**

5. **Drag the Set Reminder button (looks like a bell) and drop it on the end of the Formatting toolbar, next to the blue ? (Help) button, as shown in Figure 7-6.**

Figure 7-6:
This bell is
the symbol
for the Set
Reminder
feature.

6. **Click Close.**

   The dialog box closes.

Now you can set reminders for any of the tasks in your Gantt chart.

1. **Ensure that the Gantt chart represents dates in the future.**

   What good is a reminder if the task is in the past?

2. **Go to the second row (Determine Project Scope) at the top of the Software Development Plan template and then click this row's Start field.**

   This field currently holds Mon 1/3/00.

3. **Click the down-arrow button to open a calendar.**

4. **At the bottom of the calendar, click the red circle next to Today.**

   This changes everything. Today's date is inserted into this field, the start date in row 1 also changes to today's date, and all the rest of the dates are also recalculated for the entire chart, based on the tasks' durations.

If you've changed any of the tasks' Percent Complete field, as described earlier in this chapter, you'll need to reset those to 0% complete before these tasks' start dates will be recalculated.

Add a reminder by following these steps:

1. **Click a task that you want to add a reminder to.**

   You can select a contiguous group of multiple tasks by dragging your mouse if you want to add them all at once. Each will become a separate task in Outlook.

2. **Click the bell button (the Set Reminder button; read about this earlier in this section and refer to Figure 7-6) on the Formatting toolbar.**

   The Set Reminder dialog box opens.

3. **Choose how much time prior to the onset of the task you want the reminder to pop up.**

   You can choose to set a reminder during a task instead of prior to the start of the task, if you wish.

4. **Click OK.**

   The dialog box closes.

Your reminder is now waiting to go off. When it does go off, you see a dialog box like the one in Figure 7-7.

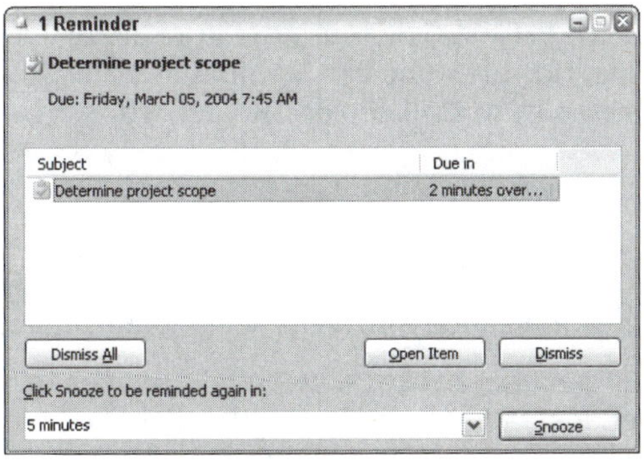

Figure 7-7:
Set reminders to tell you that a Project task should be attended to, pronto.

What does all this have to do with Outlook? By following the above steps in Project, this task is automatically added to the Tasks list in Outlook. Switch to Outlook and open the task window. You'll see your Project task in the Outlook list.

Managing the Version Problem

If you're working with a group, you always run into version problems. You know, you hand a copy of a document to everyone in a meeting and ask them all to edit it. And then when you get back this stack of documents, you have to go through them all and reconcile the various modifications made by each person.

Similarly, if you e-mail a document to several people working on a project, you'll get back several different versions of this document. You then have to go through that reconciliation process. It's not only tedious but also unnecessary. Here's a better way to get everyone's input without multiplying the documents: *routing*.

One way to avoid having multiple versions of a project document is to send a single copy of the document to only one recipient. When that person is finished marking it up with suggestions, he sends it in turn to one additional recipient, and so on down the chain. This is the equivalent of passing a single document around a conference table and asking each person to add comments or otherwise edit the document. When you get this document back, you can more easily merge the disparate editing into the final version. What's more, it saves team time as well because duplication effort is avoided. Say that you misspelled a word in the document. Why should various members of the team have to fix this error? After one of them fixes it on a routed document, none of the subsequent reviewers of the document need concern themselves with it.

Then again, you could use Project. The routing feature in Project sends the actual Project (MPP) file. However, you can add files of many different kinds — including Word documents — to your project file. Just choose Insert⇨Object.

To see how to route a Project file, follow these steps:

1. **Choose File⇨Send To⇨Routing Recipient.**

You see the Routing Slip dialog box (see the upcoming Figure 7-9).

Depending on your security settings, you might not see the routing dialog box just yet. Instead, you might see the dialog box displayed in Figure 7-8. If so, follow Step 2. If not, skip to Step 3.

Figure 7-8:
Security issues can be a terrible bore. Thanks, hackers, for burdening all the rest of us with your odious noise and stupid malice.

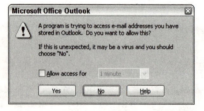

2. **Select the Allow Access For check box (to your Outlook Address) Book, enter a time setting, and close the security dialog box.**

   The Routing Slip dialog box appears, as shown in Figure 7-9.

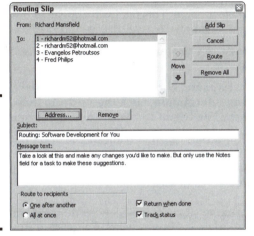

Figure 7-9: Use this dialog box to route your file through the team members.

3. **Click the Address button.**

   The Outlook Address Book opens.

4. **Double-click the names of each project member to whom you want to route the file.**

   Note that the order in which you add them is the routing order although you can change this order later in Step 6.

   Each name is added to the To list at the bottom of the dialog box.

   To delete any names that you've added, select them in the To list, and then press the Delete key.

5. **Click OK.**

   The Address Book dialog box closes.

6. **Double-click any of the names in your routine list, and then click one of the arrow buttons to adjust the routing order if you wish.**

7. **Leave the default settings marked as-is: One After Another, Return When Done, and Track Status.**

   - *One After Another*
   - *Return When Done:* Sends you a copy after the routing is finished.

- *Track Status:* Sends you e-mail each time the file moves from one group member to the next on the route. The message reads `Richard Mansfield routed the project Software Development to NancyDrew@hotmail.com` or something similar.

8. **Modify the Subject field if you wish.**

   It defaults to the project name. This field will appear as the message subject when your team members receive their e-mail.

9. **Type whatever message you want to include in the e-mail in the Message Text field.**

10. **To send the file on its route, click the Route button. To send it later but save the routing information, click the Add Slip button (and at sending time, choose File⇨Send to⇨Next Routing Recipient).**

    You see the security warning again. Go ahead and grant permission to use your Outlook Contacts list. You'll probably see a *second* security warning. Again, just put up with the unhappy necessity to protect your Address Book from harvester virii.

To modify an existing routing slip, choose File⇨Send To⇨Other Routing Recipient. The Routing Slip dialog box appears. To delete a slip, simply click the Remove All button in the dialog box.

When a recipient gets your e-mail, the following text will have been appended to any message you might have written in Step 9 in the preceding step list:

> *The project below has a routing slip. When you are done reviewing this project, choose Next Routing Recipient from the Send To menu in the Microsoft Office Project File menu to continue the routing.*

Why this says *below* is confusing. There's nothing below this text. The attachment and your custom message are above the text.

Chapter 8: Employing SharePoint

In This Chapter

- ✔ Choosing SharePoint over other collaboration technologies
- ✔ Specifying permissions
- ✔ Installing SharePoint
- ✔ Using the task pane
- ✔ Understanding SharePoint scalability
- ✔ Using SharePoint with Office 2003 Applications
- ✔ Discovering ASP.NET

*E*ven though it's been available for years under various different names, SharePoint only now seems to be getting off the ground. Perhaps it was an idea before its time. Microsoft hopes (one assumes) that with this latest version, now called SharePoint Services 2.0 for Windows Server 2003 (it's a free, optional component of this OS), it will catch on in a big way. I see no reason why it should fail. Like the .NET suite of languages, SharePoint is designed to be Web-based, and those who think they can continue to regard their local hard drives as the future of data storage (and indeed executables) are missing the boat.

SharePoint is a way for people to collaborate by efficiently sharing files and managing tasks and Web sites. SharePoint Services 2.0 is designed for workgroups, departments, and small- to medium-size businesses. A larger version, SharePoint Portal Server, is available for larger (enterprise) installations. Read on to discover when SharePoint should be chosen over competing collaboration technologies, how to handle permissions, ways to use the task pane and scale SharePoint, how to integrate SharePoint with other Office 2003 applications, and a bit about Microsoft's ASP.NET technology.

Deciding Why to Use SharePoint

Microsoft and others have already provided several ways for companies to accomplish many of SharePoint's jobs. What's the point of yet another collaboration technology, especially if your company is satisfied with its current solutions? After perhaps years of getting the kinks out of dealing with the version problem, security, and other file-share issues, why not stick with what you already have?

The simple answer is, I repeat, the Internet.

For one thing, consider that SharePoint offers an efficient way to permit users, via their browser, to access Office 2003 applications' features and data from anywhere, anytime. Office 2003 applications are designed to interact closely with SharePoint and vice versa. Setting up SharePoint Web sites and connecting them to Office 2003 elements is quite easy with SharePoint.

Unlike task management in Outlook or Project or older file-sharing systems, SharePoint is designed from the ground up as an Internet-based collaboration system for business. Of course, networks themselves are collaboration systems, and networks have been around in one form or another for decades. Tools already in place in most offices of any size permit people to share files, reconcile calendars to set up meetings (well, perhaps this tool is a paper calendar), send automated e-mail, and other features that SharePoint offers.

Indeed, throughout this book, you can find out how to accomplish many of these tasks by using Outlook's dual-calendar feature (Book VI, Chapter 1), Project's task management utilities (Book VII, Chapter 7), and other Office 2003 applications' built-in collaboration or Web-access features. What's more, if a needed feature isn't built in, programming sections in this book illustrate how you — the Office 2003 developer — can build your own solutions by using recorded macros, VBA, or .NET.

Seeing SharePoint features and integration

Nonetheless, SharePoint offers quite a tempting set of features, wizards, and other efficiencies, and it's well integrated with Office 2003 via the Shared Workspace task pane. This direct SharePoint access is available in Word, Excel, and PowerPoint.

To see the SharePoint task pane, follow these steps:

1. **Press Ctrl+F1.**

   This shortcut key combination is supposed to remind you of F1, the classic Help key.

   The default Getting Started task pane opens.

2. **Click the down-arrow symbol on the task pane's title bar (right next to the x).**

   You see a list of the available task panes, including Help, Search Results, Clip Art, Research, Clipboard, New Document, Shared Workspace, Document Updates, Protect Document, Styles and Formatting, Reveal Formatting, Mail Merge, and XML Structure. (Watch this space: More are to be added later.)

3. **Click Shared Workspace to see what's available if you're hooked up to SharePoint, as shown in Figure 8-1.**

In other words, you get direct access to SharePoint's site if you open a file residing on the SharePoint Services Web site. And with that direct access comes the ability to exploit various SharePoint features without leaving your Office 2003 application, including tasks, other documents, stored pictures (including thumbnails and slide shows), Web links, calendars, Contacts (or *resources,* as Project refers to your co-workers and acquaintances) links, communication with team members, issues lists (and many other kinds of lists), announcements, and even site management (if you have proper permission).

Lists have long been the neglected red-headed stepchild of most programming languages and database managers. However, SharePoint uses lists as its basic data structure, and these lists are quite similar to — and importable from or exportable to — Excel ranges and Access tables. Of course, Outlook data, such as the Address Book, is also stored as lists when used under SharePoint.

Book VII Chapter 8

Employing SharePoint

Figure 8-1: Many options are available when you open a SharePoint task pane.

Setting permissions in SharePoint

SharePoint users can selectively provide various levels of permission, including previewing the content of submissions, specifying that content should expire and when, direct site monitoring, site creation permission, and site membership control. Although you can delegate this kind of authority to your users, you can also retain special management privileges for yourself. Via Windows SharePoint Services, you can view data such as how long a SharePoint site has been inactive or even specify that sites that are unused for a certain period of time should be automatically deleted. You can see who created which sites. You can also impose quotas for sites, storage amounts, and users. You can also refuse users permission to add specific file types to sites.

Installing SharePoint

Getting SharePoint up and running is considerably easier than you might think. If you have other collaboration features installed — such as Exchange — you might find a bit more to deal with, but generally it's a smooth process, and the instructions are clear. It runs on IIS 6.0 in Windows Server 2003 and includes the Microsoft Data Desktop Engine as a database although you can connect to SQL Server.

The server where you install SharePoint must have at least 512MB of RAM, Windows Server 2003 (Standard, Enterprise, Datacenter, or Web Editions), and Web Application Server with ASP.NET, IIS 6.0 (including Common Files, Database, SMTP Service, and World Wide Web Service). Also required is SQL Server 2000 (Enterprise, MSDE 2000, and Network).

Using The SharePoint Task Pane

The SharePoint task pane offers a set of six icons across the top (refer to Figure 8-1). Click them to see the following information, from left to right.

✦ **Status** (the exclamation point icon inside a yellow triangle): This tells you details about the currently open document, such as its check-out status and version.

✦ **Members list** (two people): This indicates the online status of the people who are members of a group or meeting. You can interact with these people via instant messaging, add new members to the group, send mass e-mail to everyone in the group, and other options.

✦ **Tasks** (clipboard with a check mark): This shows the Project tasks list.

✦ **Document library** (dog-eared document): Here you can save files useful to the group or meeting.

 ✦ **Links** (the Earth with a chain on it; how disturbing): Here you add hyperlinks to whatever files or sites you feel are of value to the project.

 ✦ **Document information** (i-in-a-circle): This shows what was modified by whom, when last modified, and other *metadata* (data about data). What data appears in this store is customizable.

Exploiting Scalability in SharePoint

SharePoint used to be called SharePoint Team Services, riding on top of SharePoint Portal Server. The new 2003 version's official title is SharePoint Services for Windows Server 2003. A really large-scale version is also available: SharePoint Portal Server v2.0 sits on top of SharePoint Services and ramps up to the scale required to handle enormous companies' portal site needs. The Portal Server version adds enterprise-wide features — spanning the entire collection of individual SharePoint sites — including site navigation, site organization, searching and alerts features, and enterprise application integration. Ramp up to Portal Server if you need a high degree of customization or want to integrate multiple SharePoint sites into one large enterprise solution.

Portal Server (which costs extra) is installed on top of Windows Server 2003 and SharePoint Services. Well, perhaps *costs extra* is a bit too demure a term. For this huge enterprise version of SharePoint, I'm talking a starting price of $3,999 per server and $71 per user (volume pricing available). An external connector license (permitting unlimited user-access connections for non-employees) is $30,000 per server.

With Portal Server, you get BizTalk Server integration and Enterprise Resource Planning (ERP) integration with systems such as SAP and Siebel. You also get a more extensive library of Web Parts.

 SharePoint can use ASP.NET Web Parts (the latest name for *controls*) that execute server-side (like most ASP.NET code or objects) and then translate the results into HTML, which is sent to the user's browser. These Web Parts include news tickers, picture boxes to hold graphics, list controls, and so on.

The version of SharePoint that you might want for a small- or medium-size business is considerably more modest. In fact, it's free. SharePoint 2.0 (formerly Team Services) is an optional, free component of Windows Server 2003.

As you see, SharePoint is built for scalability. You can run Windows SharePoint Services on a single computer for small businesses or individual departments in larger businesses. Or you can set it up on a vast server farm handling 200,000 users and 40,000 sites or more. Load balancing for Web servers is supported, as is server clustering technology for all data, including documents, configuration, and list data.

Finding SharePoint Solutions

SharePoint can offer your business many solutions, including file sharing and collaboration, intranet capabilities, and Web page management. Here's an overview of SharePoint's capabilities.

File sharing and collaboration

With SharePoint, you can manage and share documents easily from anywhere (the Internet's famous *you're on from anywhere, 24/7* capability). Document libraries help you organize files in an organized way. Custom templates (or you can use Front Page), subfolders, security provisions (including role-based security), file versioning, and check-in/check-out features round out the file collaboration features. Collaboration features include online chats, document change e-mail alerts, and so on. The templates deserve particular mention. They're well-thought-out and effective, with a generous number of options and variations. You'll also find step-through wizards that make building various kinds of SharePoint-based Web sites quite easy.

Intranet capabilities

Each person who needs to use a SharePoint-based Web site can be given a custom login and individualized accounts, offering a secure way to publish your corporate data. Think of this as a secure intranet on the Web. Included are a bulletin board simulator, threaded discussions, and excellent wizards for such jobs as creating and managing surveys. Also, the current version of SharePoint is easier to use, so it might not be necessary for sophisticated IT support. Local users and team members should be able to manage their site in many situations. Backup, modification, and other maintenance tasks are now possible for users without sophisticated understanding of Web site management. Management is largely Web-based. Of course, creating solutions and systems with ASP.NET (described later in the section, "Introducing ASP.NET") isn't trivial, although that programming, too, has become more rapid and simple than it was only a few years ago with Active Server Pages (ASP).

Web page management

Like *FrontPage,* Microsoft's quick and easy Web page designer, SharePoint includes rapid page development features. You can use templates (or FrontPage) to get a site up and running quite quickly or to expand it. You can create your own custom templates for reuse. You can also create *subsites* (separate zones within the main site) to help segregate different projects and work groups. After the site is built (by using IIS Manager), maintenance is almost totally Web-based.

Using SharePoint with Office 2003 Applications

Given that SharePoint is designed to work well with Office 2003 applications, you shouldn't be surprised to see that task panes and other features can be used for collaborations with some efficiency. For example, you can link list data in a shared workspace to an Excel spreadsheet. (SharePoint has list-making and list-keeping features.) Word documents are a natural for starting docu-centric Document Workspaces. Here are some additional SharePoint features closely tied to other Office 2003 applications.

XML and InfoPath

You're probably wondering how InfoPath fits in (which I discuss at length in Book VII, Chapter 4.) Doesn't InfoPath include important tools for collaborative solutions? True enough, and you'll be happy to know that SharePoint takes InfoPath seriously. In fact, if you're looking to expand SharePoint features toward XML and back-end data stores, investigate the relationship between SharePoint and InfoPath.

You can store InfoPath forms in SharePoint form libraries. And, after forms have been filled out by users, Sharepoint's form library includes a location to store them as well.

Outlook and Document Workspaces

When you add an attachment to an Outlook 2003 message, an Attachment Options button appears on the Attachment field. Click this and you see the task pane shown in Figure 8-2.

**Book VII
Chapter 8**

**Employing
SharePoint**

Figure 8-2:
Select the
Shared
Attachments
radio button
here to
create a
Document
Workspace
in
SharePoint.

If you wish, a new Document Workspace can be created, and the attached file can be stored there. Everyone in the To and Cc fields are given access automatically to this new Document Workspace. You can also optionally create a new Meeting Workspace whenever you send out an Outlook meeting announcement.

The distinction between a Meeting Workspace and a Document Workspace is this: The former focuses the team on preparation for a meeting, and the latter involves collaboration centered around a document or set of documents.

OneNote

OneNote's file format is also recognized by SharePoint, enabling you to search side notes and OneNote files stored on a SharePoint site. In addition, you can save a shared OneNote notebook for all members of your team to use.

Access

For some reason (I have theories), Access is usually the odd-man-out of Office applications. It seems to stand alone in a variety of ways — different macro systems, fewer collaborative features, and so on.

However, SharePoint does pay attention to Access, even if a SharePoint task pane isn't available for it. You can import a SharePoint list into an Access 2003 table, or go the other way and export an Access table to a SharePoint list. Also, list grid views can be added to an Access table either as plain data or linked dynamically to the original SharePoint list. Thus, changes to the list are reflected in the Access table.

Dynamism — actively refreshing data to keep the information current in documents, task panes, Smart Tags, Web pages, and so on — is one of the most important contributions made by XML's integration into the Office 2003 application suite and orbiting technologies such as SharePoint and InfoPath. In many business situations, keeping data up-to-date is crucial. Some offices send copies of their database as e-mail attachments every day after work. Others have used aging, sometimes fragile, technologies such as OLE to cobble dynamic links to automate (at least to a degree) the job of maintaining current data. XML, though, promises to solve this problem once and for all. And XML is a fundamental feature of the documents, data, and applications in Office 2003. The back end can be attached to the front end more easily than ever before.

Introducing ASP.NET

Given that SharePoint rests on ASP.NET technology, if you want to customize SharePoint solutions, ASP.NET can be an important tool. You can also use ASP.NET to work with other Office 2003 customization and automation. For example, you can even create Web Services using .NET and then access them from VBA if you wish. Just install the Office 2003 Web Services Toolkit, available to download from Microsoft.com:

```
www.microsoft.com/downloads/details.aspx?FamilyID=fa36018a
-e1cf-48a3-9b35-169d819ecf18&DisplayLang=en
```

You can then integrate Web Services right from within the VBA editor (VBE) in Office 2003 applications. You use the Web Service References user interface to locate Web or just directly address a known Web Service's Web Services Definition Language (WSDL) file.

Adding dynamism to Web pages

ASP is designed to allow programmers to customize, automate, and connect Web sites to databases and other external systems, such as Office 2003 applications. In other words, although you can export a Word document to a Web site rather quickly (File➪Save as Web Page), it's inert. It's just a displayed document with perhaps some simple embedded controls. Or maybe you've designed a site by using the wizards in FrontPage or by translating other Office applications into HTML and publishing them. To create a truly dynamic Web page with custom behaviors, you often have to write some programming. Programming for Internet sites used to be a tedious and very difficult proposition. ASP was designed to help programmers speed up the job. ASP.NET replaces ASP and, in fact, realizes the ideal that ASP only strived for.

ASP.NET offers significant benefits to programmers and developers, so you should be aware of it. ASP has been used the world over since early 1997. However useful and widespread it became, ASP nonetheless had some really serious drawbacks, like requiring artists to insert their design code right in the same file used by programmers for their source code. ASP.NET avoids those drawbacks and offers a variety of valuable new rapid application development tools, including OOP support. ASP.NET is not merely the next version of ASP: ASP was thrown out, and ASP.NET was written from the ground up as a brand new, object-oriented language.

Aiding the programmer

In a white paper explaining the ASP.NET technology, Microsoft's Anthony Moore pointed out that ASP.NET and its Web Forms feature represent an important advance in programmer-friendly tools. He even compared these new tools with the vast improvement in traditional Windows programming efficiency that occurred when Visual Basic version 1 was introduced 14 years ago. Before VB came along, Windows applications were very difficult to build: time-consuming, complex, and disagreeable. The C language, with all its syntactic convolutions and needless complexity, was all that was available to Windows programmers until VB 1 made its welcome appearance.

Similarly, prior to ASP, programming Web sites was a pretty nasty business too. Now, though, ASP.NET, VB .NET, and improvements to the Visual Studio IDE (Integrated Design Environment) promise to bring VB-like efficiencies to what has previously been tedious and cumbersome CGI (common gateway interface) and ASP programming. Mr. Moore puts it this way:

As with creating Windows applications, creating a reliable and scalable Web application is extremely complicated. Our hope for ASP.NET is that it hides most of this complexity from you just as Visual Basic 1.0 did for Windows development. We also want to make the two experiences as similar to each other as possible so that you can "use the skills you already have."

ASP.NET is part of the suite of programming tools and languages bundled into Visual Studio .NET (which includes the database programming ADO.NET technology, Visual Basic .NET, and some other, less useful, languages like C). There's even a Java-esque language called C#, but it seems to me that they took the plain, understandable Visual Basic language, twisted its syntax around, added some unnecessary punctuation such as semicolons, and in general tried to make a C-like, yet relatively uncomplicated, new language. It's quite easy to translate between Visual Basic .NET and C#. So easy, in fact, that it can be automated. You can find a translator at `www.kamalpatel.net/ConvertCSharp2VB.aspx`.

Discovering the Purpose of ASP.NET

The core idea of Active Server Pages is that somebody (or many people at once) is surfing around the Internet (or a local intranet) and arrives at a page in your Web site. Instead of merely showing static, canned content on that page (simple, prewritten HTML), you can dynamically generate the page on your server right then and there, sending the resulting fresh HTML to the visitor.

This is how you can make your Web site attractive, up-to-date, varying, and interesting to the visitor. It's also how you provide dynamic content, such as allowing the user to see your latest catalog, place an order, communicate a suggestion and so on. In other words, *interaction*.

A given Web page might be used by thousands of people simultaneously. This possibility requires some adjustments in how you program, particularly in how you handle persistent global variables and connections to a database. (Access begins to groan under the strain when more than ten users are connected at once.)

ASP.NET addresses these and other Internet-related issues. It's not the same as writing a traditional Windows program wherein only one person at a time will be using your application, but ASP.NET makes it pretty easy.

Pure HTML merely describes how text and graphics should look — size, location, color, and things like that. You cannot do significant computing with HTML. For example, you cannot add 2+2. HTML merely specifies that a headline is relatively large, that the body text is colored blue, that one graphic is lower on the page than another graphic, and so on. HTML also includes a few, simple objects such as tables and list boxes. However, even its tables and list boxes are static and essentially lifeless display objects.

The *active* server premise permits you compute on your server. Then, as the result of the computation, you compose a page of HTML right then and there, sending it off to visitors' computers for viewing in their browser. This capability permits you to bring your Web pages alive.

ASP.NET uses a full language, such as VB.NET, to do its computing. You don't have to resort to crippled script languages — a subset of their parent language (Java or Visual Basic). With ASP, visitors don't need language features built into their computer: They get the results of your server-side computing translated into ordinary HTML and then sent to them.

ASP.NET, therefore, permits you to do lots of useful things on your server that you could never do with HTML. For example, you can access a database, insert prewritten components, revise your Web pages (include news about your company, today's date, and so on) so visitors don't get bored seeing the same content each time they visit, and many other valuable techniques. The visitor sees the most recent product announcements, today's date, and any other current information you want to provide. Your Web pages are responsive and timely.

Solved security

In addition, firewalls — designed to block access by hackers, whackers, viruses, worms, and other invaders — are built to permit HTML to pass unchallenged. Innocent, merely descriptive, and merely visual HTML can do no damage to your machine.

You can, however, insert scripting or executable objects (such as text boxes) into an HTML page and therefore let the visitor's computer do some computing. This is *client-side* scripting or execution. It's generally verboten, though.

Sure, client-side execution works fine if you're sure that all your visitors have the necessary language components installed on their machines, that their security settings permit scripting, and that they all use the same browser (and that browser supports scripting). So, if you're merely running a site intended for use in-house and everybody in your company uses Internet Explorer — and you're sure they all have the right components on their hard drives — go ahead and try some client-side computing. Intranets do sometimes permit scripting with certain security safeguards in place. However, there are many reasons to prefer server-side computing that sends mere HTML to clients. After all, you don't want executables — even scripts — running wild on your machine or network. That's an invitation to viruses, Trojan horses, and other bad things, isn't it?

If you see file and Web page extensions named ASPX, ASP.NET is being used. Here's an overview of the strengths and features you'll find when you begin using ASP.NET and Visual Basic .NET.

ASP.NET code is relatively easy to write, debug, and maintain. Also, with ASP.NET, you use the Visual Basic .NET language so you can leverage some of your existing programming knowledge, transferring your experience from the Windows OS platform to the browser intranet/Internet platform.

The Visual Studio .NET integrated design environment offers you all the support you've always enjoyed with mature, rapid application development (RAD) languages such as Visual Basic. In fact, for much functionality, you don't need to write any code at all: ASP.NET gives you a toolbox full of smart, rich, server-side components that you can just drop right into your ASP.NET projects (maintain state, validate, cache — you'll find that many programming problems are now handled for you by components); powerful debugging tools; WYSIWYG design and editing; and wizards to step you through tedious or complex tasks.

Segregated source files

In earlier versions of Internet programming, you had to mix your source code programming (such as VBScript) in with the HTML source code. These hybrid script/HTML files sometimes grew large and unwieldy. And two people often had to work with the same source code file. The person who is talented at designing the look of a Web site is often not the best person to write the programming that interacts with a database and vice versa.

ASP.NET solves this problem by separating programming source code and visual design (HTML) source code into two different files. Programming code is stored in a *code-behind file,* separate from the HTML file that the page designer works with.

Seeing the New Advantages of ASP.NET

The ASP.NET *runtime* (the library of functions that actually carry out the commands you write in the source code) has been built to take advantage of multiprocessor or clustered server structures. Also, the runtime ensures robust, continuous performance by keeping track of all running processes. If any process freezes or begins to leak, the runtime kills the process that is behaving badly and spawns a new process to take its place.

ASP.NET sits on top of the .NET runtime. .NET is designed from the ground up as an Internet-based platform (as opposed to a single-local-computer-based platform like Windows). Unlike previous versions of computer languages, all the languages that can be used with ASP.NET share the same runtime. (The .NET runtime is also called CLR, or *common language runtime.*) This means that you can write some code in VB, and someone else can write in Java or C# — and these pieces can be combined in the same ASP.NET project. .NET languages can also share each other's objects and libraries.

A shared IDE

A single IDE (programming editor) is now used by all the various .NET languages. A grand unification is going on here in the .NET programming model. Prior to .NET, you would choose your language based on what kind of work you were doing: ASP and script languages for Web page programming; VB for fast, efficient programming and RAD features-like forms; and the C-like languages when you wanted optimization and full object-oriented programming (OOP) inheritance. The programming you were working on — or, more likely, whatever language you were taught — forced you to choose a particular language. And your choice of language also determined which of the various APIs (runtime code libraries) you would be using. Now, with the single .NET API (Application Program Interface), all languages share the same IDE for designing your programs and also share the same API as well.

What's available to one language, then, is simultaneously available to all. No more learning various IDEs and various APIs if you need to switch between languages to accomplish your goals. All the new languages — ASP.NET, C#, VB.NET, and VC++.NET — sit on top of the same single .NET CLR.

Easier deployment

Deployment is simplified. You add an ASP.NET application to your server merely by copying the ASP.NET application's files to the server's hard drive. All the dependencies (files needed by your application, such as graphics) are stored together within the same folder and its subfolders.

No need to go through an elaborate setup and registration process. You can even upgrade an ASP.NET application on-the-fly while it's running without needing to reboot the server. (The Registry is not involved.)

In the past, if you had large, complex ASP n-tier apps that used components, the problems of registration, versioning and others (sometimes called *DLL Hell*) made life difficult for programmers and administrators alike. (The *n* in n-tier is math shorthand for *some number*. n-tier is also called *multi-layer* because sometimes the middle tier itself is subdivided.)

ASP.NET completely abolishes DLL locking, XML configuration files, and component registration. To deploy your ASP.NET Web app, just copy the main folder and its subfolders. Controls located in your application's BIN subfolder are simply available to your application: You don't need to worry about registering them or that they are locked: They're not locked, and they're not registered, but they work just fine. That's the new model. Do you have a newer, better version of a control that you've written and now improved? Just copy it into the folder on the server. It runs right away.

Book VIII

Power Techniques: Advanced Office Automation, VBA, and .NET

The 5th Wave By Rich Tennant

"It's a ten step word processing program. It comes with a spell-checker, grammar-checker, cliche-checker, whine-checker, passive/aggressive-checker, politically correct-checker, hissy-fit-checker, pretentious pontificating-checker, boring anecdote-checker and a Freudian reference-checker."

Contents at a Glance

Chapter 1: Advanced Office 2003 Programming

In This Chapter

✔ Surveying weaknesses in OOP

✔ Knowing when to use VBA and when to use VB.NET

✔ Discovering streaming

✔ Creating your own add-ins

Throughout this book, examples illustrate how to program Office 2003 — how to control both individual applications programmatically as well as control one application from another to develop larger scale Office solutions.

This chapter deepens your understanding of the interactions possible between Office 2003 applications as well as how to improve company productivity using tools like VBA and add-ins available to you as a developer/ programmer. I also demonstrate streaming as a way of contrasting VBA with VB.NET programming. The chapter concludes by showing you how to build your own add-ins, which is useful for simultaneously adding functionality to all Office applications and also an effective way to hook up VB.NET programming to Office 2003 solutions.

I start with a brief overview of class hierarchies.

Understanding Class Hierarchies

Consider these facts about the current programming classification system (also known as object-oriented programming, or OOP).

✦ **An object's properties or methods can return a second object,** called a *child* object. The first object is a *parent.* (OOP experts disagree what constitutes this parent-child relationship although they all agree that it exists. The disagreement is about which specific situations should be described as parent-child.)

✦ **The same object can have many parents and many children.**

✦ **A given action, such as changing a window's color, can be a property or a method.** In practice, these categories are imprecise. Lots of theory exists, but here in the real world of day-to-day programming with objects, it's anybody's guess which category will contain any given item. You essentially have to memorize the common members or for those you haven't memorized, guess — and if wrong, look it up in Help.

✦ **Properties can turn into objects,** depending on the context in which they're used. And vice versa.

✦ **The same object can be a child of its parent.** And vice versa. For example, in Excel 2003, the Range object is a child of the Worksheet object, but a Worksheet is also a child of the Range object.

Ready for a drink? Personally, I could use a stiff one right now.

Fighting Class Warfare

Don't break your brain trying to make too much sense out of object models. If you take them too literally, you'll be disappointed. For one thing, the term *object* has been inflated beyond belief.

In VBA, many elements of the language are considered objects. However, VBA's successor languages — VB.NET and the other .NET languages — move us closer to the truth about object-oriented programming. In .NET, everything — including the simple integer variable type — is now an object. And when everything falls into a category, that category becomes like water to fish: It's so omnipresent that it simply disappears from their consciousness.

The term *object* has little remaining meaning for a programmer. It has become as general and as meaningless as the term *thing.* How useful is it to say, "The thing is behind the other thing but not under the same thing, until later"?

Here's a programming example of what I'm saying. Consider this line of code:

```
CurrentWindow.Font.Size = 12
```

CurrentWindow is an object because it has properties (Font, for one). Font is a property of the CurrentWindow object. However, the Font property is simultaneously in this same line of code also an object itself, with a property named Size. Were you to refer to the collection of Window objects, CurrentWindow itself would become simultaneously an object and a property:

```
ScreenWindows.CurrentWindow.Font.Size = 12
```

A dual-monitor system would make the `ScreenWindows` collection a property/object of the `Monitors` collection, and so on and so on.

Move up or down an object hierarchy, and you find this Escher-like circularity. Indeed, consider this: The `Application` object sits at the top of most Office 2003 applications, and all other objects are child objects of the `Application` object. It's the parent object of most other objects.

However, to make life interesting, the `Application` object is also a property of nearly all other objects in Office 2003 applications. To put it bluntly, nearly every object in the object models of Office applications is a parent of the top object. Makes you wonder, doesn't it, just how useful this system of categorization is. It's as if biologists considered apes the ancestors of modern man, and modern man the ancestors of apes. Would this be a clear, useful classification system?

Properties are methods are properties

It gets worse. A primary distinction is made in object models between properties and methods. At least people claim to employ these categories. Alas, this is a distinction without a difference.

The division between the concepts of *property* and *method* is purely bogus. Most of the time, setting the color property of an object means changing a `Color` property. However, do you see that making a change in a color is an action? — which is the essential meaning of a *method*.

In practice, sometimes changing a color *is* classified as a method, yet sometimes it's a property. You find this kind of ambiguity throughout object models. That's why people are now spending more time struggling to get OOP syntax correct than they are debugging (unless they use inheritance, which can rapidly add bugs to code).

Tautology runs wild

OOP experts sometimes make statements like this, which are wonderfully revealing: A method can change a property or return the value of a property, but it's not itself a property. If I had a bell named *tautology*, I would be ringing it now, believe me! (And if you have a dictionary nearby, go look it up and learn a new word.)

Changing the color property *changes the color?*, just as executing a `ChangeColor` method changes the color. There is no distinction here between a `Color` property and a `ChangeColor` method. It's just a matter of whimsy, all too often, how things are categorized.

Deciding When to Use VB.NET

If you're familiar and comfortable with traditional Visual Basic (version 6 or earlier, or VBA), you might wonder why to bother with VB.NET. After all, VBA represents about ten years of perfecting a language that was pretty good to begin with.

The answer lies in the changes that are taking place for programmers. Increasingly, you must deal with distributed programming. A database manager might reside in Houston, with the inventory executable on a network in Toronto and customer fulfillment software in Boston. These distributed pieces *(tiers)* collectively represent a single, general program (or solution). They must work together smoothly (referred to as *interoperability,* although it used to be called *compatibility* or sometimes *platform independence*), must be stable *(robust)* and capable of handling a large volume of (or surges in) traffic *(scalable).* But distributed programs *(solutions)* are not a single, traditional Windows program residing on a single hard drive. A *solution* can contain several *programs* working together. The Internet drives this fracturing of resources and executable code.

VBA works well when you're working within or among Office 2003 applications. However, if you need a more powerful language, particularly for distributed or Internet-related programming, you'll want to move on up to VB.NET.

To illustrate a primary difference between VBA and VB.NET, consider code that saves and loads files. Traditionally, files resided on a local hard drive — right there in your machine. The worst confusion you had to deal with was specifying a path to a local area network hard drive. Today data still usually ends up in files, but it can also be elsewhere, coming in over the Internet, for example, in a stream.

Streaming is the metaphor that .NET language designers use for sending or receiving data. In the past, VB programmers used a somewhat more restrictive metaphor: saving and opening files. But in the brave new Internet world, data can be stored in more places than you can imagine — not just in files on your local hard drive. New times demand new thinking, so get ready for the data stream and all that it implies.

The Buzzwords

If you haven't been using any of these new terms — *tier, solution, interoperable, robust,* and *scalable* — you'd better start now. They help you sound oh so *au courant.* Oh yes, and *mission critical* means *essential to the task.* While I'm at it, let me also define a bit of additional computer jargon. (Why not?)

✦ **Solution:** A piece of software that handled a single job used to be called *application, program, project,* or *utility.* However, a new term, *solution,* is now used to mean a set of programs (and perhaps associated data stores and utilities) working together to achieve a common goal, such as sending invoices and tracking inventory for a business.

Traditionally, a single program did a single computing job. This is still true in some contexts (such as using a simple text processor like Notepad), but now several applications or utilities often work together to handle a common task — particularly for large or distributed tasks — so the term *solution* makes more sense, suggesting as it does that a set of programs is being used. A really large, complex solution is referred to as an *enterprise solution.*

✦ **Front end/back end:** *Front end* and *back end* refer to the distance between the user and a piece of software or a data store. *Front-end* is what used to be called the *user interface.* For example, it's the form the user sees onscreen and fills out, or the spreadsheet the user calculates with. The *back end* is the farthest part of the solution from the user, such as a data store or database management system residing on a server. The user never sees the back end, much less is permitted to directly access its data or use its features.

✦ **Tier:** *Tier* refers to the different pieces of a solution.

Understanding Streams

Streams are flows of data to or from your application. Streams now replace traditional VB communication techniques between applications and data. What mainly distinguishes the concept of streaming from traditional approaches is that a stream isn't limited to communication with disk files.

In the new world of distributed programming (typical of Web programming), data can be stored in more than one place. In addition to files, for example, collections of data can be in memory. In VB.NET, you can bind an array to a list box — treating the array, which resides in memory, as if it were a database file. The Internet might be another source of data streaming into your application. This, too, is a nontraditional source of data.

So, to take into account the various places where you might get or send data, the idea of streaming permits connections between all kinds of data sources (now known as *data stores,* to distinguish them from databases, which people traditionally associate with files). It's even possible to connect one data stream to another.

Understanding tiers and other new terms

Early on in network-based or Internet-based solutions were *two-tier* solutions (also known as *two-tier architecture* or *two-layer architectures*). This refers to splitting a job between a client and a server. Often the client holds the user interface and other executable code while the server simply acts as a storage location for data. However, the client can be relatively *dumb* (few or no executables), and the database management executables (or other programming) can reside and execute on the server.

A few years ago, *three-tier* architectures emerged, with the new tier (the middle-tier server or application server) mediating between the client (generally limited to user-interface tasks) and the server (the data store, or data management, components).

The middle-tier usually holds the *business logic* (or *rules*), such as managing the execution of utilities elsewhere in the solution (distributed processing, or *process monitoring*), queuing users (directing user traffic, *resourcing,* or *asynchronous queuing*), and other housekeeping and police work. Collectively, these tasks are sometimes called *centralized process logic.* (Are we having fun? Never mind.)

The primary goal of the middle tier is to permit increases in scale *(scalability).* Whereas a two-tier architecture might be able to handle 100 users, a three-tier system can ramp up to handle orders of more magnitude. Also, three-tier systems, if properly organized, can improve *maintainability* (making adjustments or solving bugs in a program), *flexibility* (this word means what it does in ordinary English; what a relief!), *reusability* (after you've written and tested a piece of programming, you can use it again in a different program), along with the improvement in scalability.

Can you have more than three tiers? Sure. There are *n-tier* solutions (*n* being math shorthand for *some number*), also called *multilayer.* Sometimes the middle tier itself is subdivided. There is a *light client* (as in *lightweight* or *trivial,* a favorite term of disparagement used by scientists and would-be scientists, such as some programmers) user interface display (markup) code, such as HTML. This layer ultimately simply shows up in a browser for some user to interact with. The other layer involves heavy-duty *(non-trivial)* programming (called *code-behind,* or *application servers*).

Consider this: Sometimes keeping data off hard drive files is desirable. For example, when you use .NET encryption classes, you can create a *cryptostream* in memory and feed it with a stream of data coming in over a secure line from Spain or wherever. The idea here is that you want to actually avoid storing this incoming data stream on your hard drive as a file. You don't want to encrypt from data in a file because even if erased, that original file could perhaps be reconstructed by disk analysis tools, and it contains the unencrypted data. So you keep everything as light, streams in RAM, evaporating as they move into your cryptostream. Then you can save the cryptostream to your hard drive because that stream is, by definition, encrypted and secure. In Book VIII, Chapter 8, I show you how to write a utility that encrypts text coming in from a stream rather than a file.

In sum, after you grasp the concept of streams and learn how to use them to send or receive data, you can then employ the same techniques no matter what data stores are involved. In theory, getting data from that remote computer in Spain should be no different from getting data off your own hard drive. I say *in theory* because as much as we might wish it were so, it's not possible to do everything the same way in all situations. For example, when you're working with a file on your local hard drive, you can ask the stream to tell you the length of that file — how much data is stored there. When working with a remote file coming in from Madrid, there is no `Length` property that you can query. The stream will stop when it's ready to stop. So you don't intercept the stream with a fixed loop like `For...Next`; you must use a `While` or `Until` loop instead.

You can still use the traditional VBA random access files techniques in VB.NET if you must. (In VB.NET, the syntax for these techniques is similar but not identical to traditional VBA.) But you're encouraged to make the transition to streams because of the greater flexibility they offer.

Also, programming is moving away from the random access file as a way of storing and accessing data. Instead, contemporary programming prefers databases and even XML files as data store constructs. It's all really pretty similar, when you get down to it — just labeled pieces of information organized one way or another. But fashions change, and right now, you really should start moving away from the classic, random access files and their record-number techniques. If nothing else, basing your data storage on databases or XML makes your information more compatible with other applications (at least for the next few years until a newer fashion in data storage takes the programming world by storm).

Streaming basics

Traditional Visual Basic file access assigns a file number to each opened file. The simplest traditional format is as follows:

```
Open filepath {For Mode}{options}As {#} filenumber {Len = recordlength}
```

For example:

```
Open "C:\Test.Txt" As 5
```

However, for reasons known only to those in charge of .NET, the actual syntax of the VB.NET version of the traditional VB isn't exactly the same as it used to be. `Open` becomes `FileOpen`, and the order of the arguments shifts around. So, you might as well just move on to streaming, no?

If you do want to stick with the older style file I/O, though, here's the VB.NET version:

```
FileOpen(5, "C:\Test.Txt", OpenMode.Random)
```

Streaming is quite a bit more flexible, but as usual, you pay a penalty for this flexibility. Streaming requires more programming because it offers more options for the same reason that the dashboard of a Lexus is more complicated than a VW.

To see a simple example of streaming, follow these steps:

1. **Using VB.NET in Visual Studio, chose File⇨New⇨Project.**

   You see the New Project dialog box.

2. **Double-click the Windows Application icon.**

   A new Windows-style application opens in the IDE.

3. **Double-click the TextBox icon in the Windows Forms tab of the Toolbox.**

   A TextBox is added to your Form1.

4. **Double-click a Button icon to add it also.**

5. **Click the TextBox in the IDE so that you can see its properties in the Properties window.**

   Press F4 if the Properties window isn't visible.

6. **Change the TextBox's Multiline property to True by double-clicking it in the Properties window. Also delete TextBox1 from the Text property in the Properties window.**

7. **Double-click the button.**

   The button's Click event is displayed in the code window.

8. **Type this in at the top of the code window (above Public Class Form1):**

   ```
   Imports System.IO
   ```

9. **To try the simplest example of VB.NET file streaming, type this into the button's Click event:**

   ```
   Private Sub Button1_Click(ByVal sender As
       System.Object, ByVal e As System.EventArgs) Handles
       Button1.Click

           Dim a As String = "This works fine."
           Dim b As String
   ```

```
Dim sw As New StreamWriter("c:\test.txt")
sw.WriteLine(a)
sw.Close()

Dim sr As New StreamReader("c:\test.txt")
b = sr.ReadLine
MsgBox(b)
sr.Close()

End Sub
```

10. **Press F5 to run this example.**

This code creates a new file (or replaces an existing one if you already have c:\test.txt on your hard drive). Then the code writes your test line of text and closes the StreamWriter. Next it opens that same file, reads the line of text, displays that text in a message box, and closes the file.

Here's a more flexible version of streaming. Replace the code in the button's Click event with Listing 8-1.

Listing 8-1:   More Flexible Streaming

```
Private Sub Button1_Click(ByVal sender As System.Object,
        ByVal e As System.EventArgs) Handles
        Button1.Click

Dim strFileName As String = "C:\test.txt"
        Dim objFilename As FileStream = New
                FileStream(strFileName, FileMode.Open,
                FileAccess.Read, FileShare.Read)

        Dim objFileRead As StreamReader = New
    StreamReader(objFilename)

        TextBox1.Text = ""

        While (objFileRead.Peek() > -1)
            TextBox1.Text += objFileRead.ReadLine()
            TextBox1.Text += ControlChars.CrLf
        End While

        objFileRead.Close()
        objFilename.Close()


    End Sub
```

Notice that you first create a `FileStream` object and then use it to create a new `StreamReader`. Later, within the `While...End While` loop, you use the `StreamReader` to control the duration of the loop (with the `Peek` method) as well as to read individual text lines, one by one, within the opened file (with the `ReadLine` method).

The `ControlChars.CrLf` command inserts a *line feed* (moves down one line in the `TextBox`) following each line that the `ReadLine` method retrieves from the file. However, if you don't need to examine the file's contents line by line, you can simply replace the entire `While...End While` structure with this simple line of code that brings in the entire file (including line feeds) in one big gulp:

```
TextBox1.Text += objFileRead.ReadToEnd()
```

Stream writing

Going in the other direction — dumping data into a stream — is similar to reading a stream as illustrated in the preceding section. Listing 8-2 shows how to write to a stream.

Listing 8-2: Writing to a Stream

```
Private Sub Button1_Click(ByVal sender As System.Object, ByVal e As
     System.EventArgs) Handles Button1.Click

    Dim strText As String = TextBox1.Text

    If (strText.Length < 1) Then
        MsgBox("Please type something into the TextBox so we can save it.")
        Exit Sub
    Else
        Dim strFileName As String = "C:\test.txt"
        Dim objOpenFile As FileStream = New FileStream(strFileName,
           FileMode.Append, FileAccess.Write, FileShare.Read)
        Dim objStreamWriter As StreamWriter = New StreamWriter(objOpenFile)

        objStreamWriter.WriteLine(strText)

        objStreamWriter.Close()
        objOpenFile.Close()
        TextBox1.Text = "Done. File saved."
    End If

    End Sub
```

This example actually appends to the existing `text.txt` file because you used `FileMode.Append`. Using `FileMode.Create` will either overwrite an existing file or create a new file if none exists.

Creating Add-Ins

Macros, wizards, templates, and toolbar customization are all features that allow you to personalize your Office 2003 applications. But if you want to be able to use features of the entire OS — to manipulate *anything* — you might want to try your hand at writing add-ins. You'll be delighted to know that Visual Basic .NET includes a wizard to make creating add-ins easier than it would otherwise be.

Add-ins can globally change the behavior or add functionality to several Office 2003 applications simultaneously and automatically. The following example illustrates how to do this. What's more, add-ins execute more quickly than the typical macro.

You might not think of a use for add-ins right now, but you should know that this technology exists to extend Office applications in powerful ways. When you write an add-in, you can tap the entire power of .NET. (I have written an encryption/decryption system that I'm planning to turn into an add-in, but describing it is beyond the scope of this book. You click a button on the Standard toolbar — or the Access Database toolbar — and instantly your current document will be encrypted and stored.) You'll also find commercial add-ins for sale.

The add-in that I describe in the following example adds itself automatically to the Office applications that it's designed to service. However, some add-ins must be attached to an application manually. To do that, follow these steps:

1. **Choose Tools⇨Templates and Add-Ins.**

   The Templates and Add-Ins dialog box opens.

2. **Click the Add button.**

   The Add Templates dialog box opens.

3. **Double-click whatever add-in you want.**

Programming your own add-in

Here's an example showing you how to create an Office 2003 add-in by using Visual Basic .NET. It adds a toolbar button named Time that when clicked, displays the current date and time.

To simultaneously add a toolbar button to Word, PowerPoint, Outlook, Excel, and Access — along with whatever behavior you want that button to trigger — follow these steps:

**Book VIII
Chapter 1**

**Advanced Office
2003 Programming**

1. **Run Visual Basic .NET in Visual Studio.**

2. **Choose File⇨New⇨Project.**

   You see the New Project dialog box.

3. **In the left pane of the New Project dialog box, click Other Projects to open this node.**

4. **In the left pane, under Other Projects, click Extensibility Projects.**

   Two templates appear in the right pane of the dialog box.

5. **Click the Shared Add-in template to select it.**

6. **In the Name field, type** comTIME.

   You can name your add-in whatever you want; this name will appear in the title bar of any message box that your add-in might display.

7. **Click OK.**

   The dialog box closes, and the Extensibility Wizard opens, as shown in Figure 1-1.

Figure 1-1:
Use the
Extensibility
Wizard to
simplify
building an
Office 2003
add-in.

8. **Click Next.**

9. **Select the Create an Add-in by Using Visual Basic option button.**

10. **Click Next.**

11. **Select Word, Outlook, Excel, and Access as your host applications, as shown in Figure 1-2.**

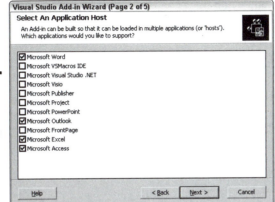

Figure 1-2:
Choose
here which
applications
you want
your add-in
to work
with.

12. **Click Next.**

13. **Type** TimeDisplay **as the name and** Shows current date and time **as the description of your Add-in.**

These are displayed to the user in the Templates and Add-ins dialog box in the Office applications, as described earlier in this section.

14. **Click Next.**

15. **Choose to have your add-in load when the host application loads and also to have the add-in available to all users of this machine.**

16. **Click Next.**

You see a summary of the choices you made while running this wizard.

17. **Click Finish.**

The wizard creates a public class, writing lots of code you'd never be able to think up for yourself. Included is this globally unique identifier (GUID):

```
<GuidAttribute("50861F26-00E5-4195-8F22-733EF51A7E82"),
    ProgIdAttribute("comTIME.Connect")> _
Public Class Connect
```

Listing 8-3 shows the code that you should enter into the various procedures of this class that the wizard built for you.

**Book VIII
Chapter 1**

**Advanced Office
2003 Programming**

Listing 8-3: Creating an Add-in

```
Imports Microsoft.Office.Core
imports Extensibility
imports System.Runtime.InteropServices


<GuidAttribute("79245F63-E547-43D3-BF16-1A22D780C972"),
        ProgIdAttribute("MyComAddin.Connect")> _
Public Class Connect

    Implements Extensibility.IDTExtensibility2



    Dim WithEvents OcButton As CommandBarButton

    Dim applicationObject As Object
    Dim addInInstance As Object


    Public Sub OnBeginShutdown(ByRef custom As System.Array)
            Implements Extensibility.
            IDTExtensibility2.OnBeginShutdown

        'get rid of the button
        On Error Resume Next

        OcButton.Delete()
        OcButton = Nothing


    End Sub

    Public Sub OnAddInsUpdate(ByRef custom As System.Array)
            Implements Extensibility.
            IDTExtensibility2.OnAddInsUpdate
    End Sub

    Public Sub OnStartupComplete(ByRef custom As
            System.Array) Implements Extensibility.
            IDTExtensibility2.OnStartupComplete

        Dim oToolbars As CommandBars
        Dim oStandardBar As CommandBar

        On Error Resume Next
```

```
' Add a button to the Standard toolbar
oToolbars = applicationObject.CommandBars

' Outlook must be handled differently.
' The CommandBars collection is a property of the
    ActiveExplorer object
' in Outlook. So see if the oToolbars object has been
    intantiated:
If oToolbars Is Nothing Then
    ' If it's nothing, then we're dealing with
    Outlook, so instantiate it now:
    oToolbars = applicationObject.ActiveExplorer.
    CommandBars
End If

'we're using the "Standard" toolbar, but you could
    use "Formatting" or whatever:
oStandardBar = oToolbars.Item("Standard")

' Another anomaly: Access calls the "Standard"
    toolbar the "Database" toolbar.
' so again, if instantiation has failed, we must
    instantiate this object differently:
If oStandardBar Is Nothing Then
    oStandardBar = oToolbars.Item("Database")
End If

' Try instantiating this particular button:
OcButton = oStandardBar.Controls.Item("Time")

'it's possible that there was a power loss or other
    disorderly exit from an application,
'in which case, the button was not deleted from a
    previous session
'the button is deleted in the OnBeginShutdown event
    in this class (above)

'but if it does not yet exist, then add the button:
If OcButton Is Nothing Then

    OcButton = oStandardBar.Controls.Add(1)
    With OcButton
        .Caption = "Time"
        .Style = MsoButtonStyle.msoButtonCaption

        ' The tag property is needed by some apps
(think of it as a variable name:
        .Tag = "Time"
```

**Book VIII
Chapter 1**

**Advanced Office
2003 Programming**

```
            ' The OnAction property deals with the
        possibility that the add-in isn't loaded
            ' but the user clicks the button. If this
        happens, the add-in will be
            ' loaded automatically, and the button's
        click event will be triggered
            ' the OcButton_Click event is located in this
        class (below).
            .OnAction = "!<MyCOMAddin.Connect>"
            .Visible = True
        End With
    End If


    ' kill these objects; they're no longer needed:
    oStandardBar = Nothing
    oToolbars = Nothing

End Sub

Public Sub OnDisconnection(ByVal RemoveMode As
        Extensibility.ext_DisconnectMode, ByRef custom As
        System.Array) Implements Extensibility.
        IDTExtensibility2.OnDisconnection

    On Error Resume Next

    ' kill the app object and trigger the shutdown event
        (if it's not automatically raised).
    If RemoveMode <> Extensibility.ext_DisconnectMode.
        ext_dm_HostShutdown Then _
        Call OnBeginShutdown(custom)

    applicationObject = Nothing

End Sub

Public Sub OnConnection(ByVal application As Object,
        ByVal connectMode As Extensibility.ext_
        ConnectMode, ByVal addInInst As Object, ByRef
        custom As System.Array) Implements Extensibility.
        IDTExtensibility2.OnConnection
    applicationObject = application
    addInInstance = addInInst

    ' If startup isn't in effect, call OnStartupComplete
        here.
    If (connectMode <> Extensibility.ext_ConnectMode.
        ext_cm_Startup) Then _
        Call OnStartupComplete(custom)
```

```
End Sub

Private Sub OcButton_Click(ByVal Ctrl As Microsoft.
        Office.Core.CommandBarButton, ByRef CancelDefault
        As Boolean) Handles OcButton.Click

    'display the time
    MsgBox(Now)


End Sub



End Class
```

After you add this code to the code that the wizard provided for you, test it. In the VB.NET editor, choose Build⇨Build ComTIME. Your new class will be registered. Start Word, Excel, Outlook, or Access. Look at the Standard toolbar. There it is: The Time button has been added. Click it. You see a message box displaying the date and time, as shown in Figure 1-3.

Figure 1-3:
Your add-in has been included in Excel, and when clicked, it does its job.

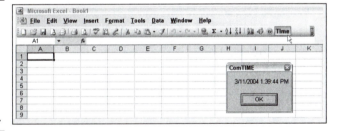

To remove this button or other add-ins from your applications, rebuild the previous code (choose Build⇨Build ComTIME, if that's the name of your add-in) after having added this exit line to the following event procedure:

```
Public Sub OnStartupComplete(ByRef custom As
        System.Array) Implements
        Extensibility.IDTExtensibility2.OnStartupComplete

Exit Sub
```

This will prevent the button from being added to the toolbars in the first place. Then you can right-click the Standard toolbar, choose Customize from the context menu, and drag the button off the toolbar. Or you can use

RegEdit to search the registry for ComTIME and get rid of references to it in the Add-Ins section for each application. Locate this registry entry for each host application. (Excel's is shown here.)

`HKEY_CURRENT_USER\Software\Microsoft\Office\`*Excel*`\Addins`

Adjusting add-in loading behavior

You can either delete the ComTIME entry under this add-in's Registry location or adjust the add-in's loading behavior according to the following `LoadBehavior` chart. Changing this value changes how the add-in works when one of its host applications starts running. You can combine these values; for example, a value of 3 means both *Is loaded* and *Load on application startup:*

Value	Name	Means This
0	Disconnect	Is not loaded
1	Connected	Is loaded
2	Bootload	Load on application startup
8	DemandLoad	Load only when requested by user
16	ConnectFirstTime	Load only once (on next startup)

The default value `0x00000003` means `Connected` and `Bootload`. Don't be put off by the bizarre numbering system. It's cute that some programmers always seem to think that confusion, noise, and oddity are preferable to clear, informative, ordinary notation.

Chapter 2: Exploring XML

In This Chapter

✔ Understanding XML

✔ Seeing how XML exploits extensibility

✔ Using XML and HTML

✔ Mastering the terminology

✔ Using namespaces

✔ Working with XSD

✔ Using XML data types

✔ Using schemas

✔ Using XML in Office 2003

✔ Programming manipulations

*T*his chapter begins with an overview of XML: its components, derivative languages, and uses. It concludes with examples illustrating how to manage and access XML features within Office 2003 applications programmatically via VBA code. I demonstrate a range of XML technologies, including namespaces, XSD, XML data types, and programming XML in Office 2003.

An XML Primer

The purpose of XML is to structure data, using an ordinary text file like those created in Notepad. In other words, no special codes, no executables, no tricky compression, no proprietary formats, no hidden constructs, and nothing behind the curtain. It's all out there, in plain text, without having to use a special program (such as the program that produced the data) to read it.

Even though it's a text file, XML isn't really read by anyone except a programmer, and even programmers try to avoid the tedium of translating into or out of XML. XML is stored as plain text because that makes it easier to debug. Also, it's easier to fix a bad XML file if you can edit it with simple, good old Notepad. And, alas, sometimes you do have to create filters that translate the raw XML into a format usable by a legacy application.

XML files are necessarily larger than a comparable amount of information when stored in binary format (particularly if you use a simpler, more compact way to delimit the data), but so what? A goal that drove early computer programmers was to conserve precious memory. That goal is no longer significant. Memory chips are cheap these days, and you can get a 120GB hard drive for under $100 on sale. If you're concerned about transmitting the XML (after all, data transmission is a major reason for XML's existence), many compression schemes are in use today that can effectively reduce the bandwidth requirements of a text file down to close to the load imposed by pure binary data.

Seeing XML Support in Office

The standard for sending messages in the computer world, XML — or its off-spring, such as Simple Object Access Protocol (SOAP) — is also being used in a variety of other ways to assist with data storage, interoperability, and so on. Office 2003 includes considerable support for XML, as does the .NET world.

XML implementation is limited in some editions of Office 2003 applications. For example, aside from being able to save documents in XML format, all other XML support in Word 2003 is available only in Office Professional Edition 2003 and standalone Microsoft Office Word 2003.

For example, a table in Access can quickly and easily be saved in XML. To see how, follow these steps:

1. **Run Access and load the** `Northwind.mdb` **sample database.**

2. **Click Tables in the main database window.**

   You see a list of the Northwind tables, as shown in Figure 2-1.

Figure 2-1: These tables are currently stored in Access's MBD format, but soon they'll be translated to XML.

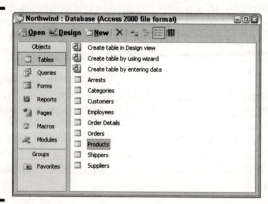

3. **Double-click Products in the main database window.**

   You see the Products table displayed.

4. **Choose File⇨Export.**

   The Export Table dialog box appears.

5. **In the Save as Type drop-down list, choose XML.**

6. **Click the Export All button.**

   You see the Export XML dialog box, as shown in Figure 2-2.

Figure 2-2:
Decide here
how many
XML files
you want
to save.

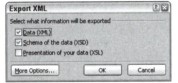

7. **Leave the default Data and Schema of the Data check boxes selected.**

   You want to save your table in two XML files.

   - *XSD file:* Describes the structure of the table (its fields and their data types)

   - *XML file:* Saves the actual data

   To preserve the formatting of a report or other formattable document, you could also choose to save a third file (XSL).

8. **Click the More Options button.**

   You see additional choices, as shown in Figure 2-3. Here you can specify which data is saved, how much of the schema to save, whether to include graphics (from the Presentation tab), and other options.

9. **Click OK.**

   The XSD and XML files are saved.

**Book VIII
Chapter 2**

Exploring XML

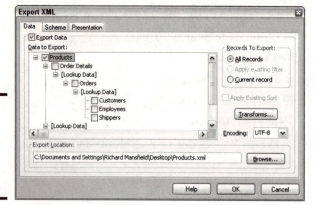

If you examine the schema file (the XSD file), you see the structure of your table described, using the element/attribute format typical of XML:

```
<xsd:element name="ProductID" minOccurs="1" od:jetType=
        "autonumber" od:sqlSType="int" od:autoUnique=
        "yes" od:nonNullable="yes" type="xsd:int"/>
<xsd:element name="ProductName" minOccurs="1" od:jetType=
        "text" od:sqlSType="nvarchar" od:nonNullable=
        "yes">
<xsd:simpleType>
<xsd:restriction base="xsd:string">
<xsd:maxLength value="40"/>
</xsd:restriction>
</xsd:simpleType>
</xsd:element>
```

The data file (the XML file) maps to the schema, with each record contained in a `<Products>` element:

```
<Products>
<ProductID>1</ProductID>
<ProductName>Chai</ProductName>
<SupplierID>1</SupplierID>
<CategoryID>1</CategoryID>
<QuantityPerUnit>10 boxes x 20 bags</QuantityPerUnit>
<UnitPrice>18</UnitPrice>
<UnitsInStock>39</UnitsInStock>
<UnitsOnOrder>0</UnitsOnOrder>
<ReorderLevel>10</ReorderLevel>
<Discontinued>0</Discontinued>
</Products>
```

The table has been rapidly transformed into XML. You can, of course, go in the other direction. However, Access (being Access) does things a bit strangely. Always the red-headed stepchild, instead of putting the Import option on the File menu next to the Export option, Access hides it away a bit. To import an empty table (XSD schema file) or a table filled with data (XSD plus associated XML files), choose File⇨Get External Data⇨Import.

In Book VII, Chapter 3, I explore various Office 2003 XML features that allow you to publish documents as Web pages. Most Office 2003 documents can be saved as HTML. However, when saved, Office-specific formatting can also be saved simultaneously. Not only can you export to a browser from an Office 2003 application, you can take the return trip and translate the HTML back into an Office document.

Word 2003 also permits a filtered style of document-to-Web page translation, resulting in simpler and more compact HTML files. This topic is examined in Book III, Chapter 4.

Exploiting Extensibility in XML

XML was designed to be *extensible* (you can add new descriptive categories to it), as unambiguous as possible, and (that long-sought-after yet elusive goal) platform-independent.

It's extensible because you can make up as many different descriptive names (element names and attribute names) as you wish. For example, if you're in charge of a summer camp, you can create a data structure in XML that contains elements (tags) like these: `Name`, `Age`, `SpecialMeals`, `PersonalityDrawbacks`, `Allergies`, `Hobbies`, `EmergencyPhoneNumber`, `PreviousExperience`, and so on. Within your summer camp and other places in your organization, you can easily establish rules about how to access these tags and how to manage the data contained between the tags. Even different organizations exchanging XML files across the Internet should be able to manage the tag structures without any great difficulties.

You can use XML to transmit and store a variety of kinds of information. Here are some of the different types of data that can be stored in an XML document:

✦ A structured record, such as a student's school records

✦ Regular text documents

✦ A `DataSet` (the result of a query against a data store)

✦ A control, such as a `UserControl`, an `ActiveX`, or a `Page` control

✦ A description of a user interface

✦ Other standardized graphics data

XML arrives at a client machine as a self-contained package. After it arrives at a client machine, the user can then manipulate, view, and otherwise interact with the XML package without requiring any round-trips to the server. This, of course, takes a load off the server.

Another efficiency of XML is *granular updating*. If some data has changed in an XML document, only the changed element (not the entire document) needs to be sent from server to client (or vice versa). Also, if new elements are added to an XML document, only those elements must be sent to the client browser. (ASP.NET, though, rebuilds an entire page of HTML each time it receives a request from a browser.)

Comparing XML and HTML

When you first see an XML file, you can be forgiven for thinking that it must be HTML. They share punctuation and structural features in common but no real underlying commonality. Both use < > symbols to bracket what both call *tags*. Quite often tags — elements — in XML are similar to arrays in Visual Basic, containing an entire set of variables. However, in a simple XML element (containing only one value), the element/value pair is similar to the VB variablename/value pair.

`<cookie>sugar</cookie>`

This XML code defines this particular value, `sugar`, as being a particular cookie. You might also have this element. (A start/end tag pair and the data within it are usually called an *element*.)

`<dancer>sugar</dancer>`

This other element, in the same file, defines a person and the name (sugar). Both HTML and XML use attributes name/value pairs written in the form `SomeName="MyValue"`, which also roughly corresponds to variablename/ variable value pairs in VB. However, XML is primarily a way of transmitting data from one place to another. The transmitting *agent* (the application that generates the XML) merely treats the tags and attribute names as *delimiters:* that is, as ways of naming and indicating the start and end of items of data. It is up to the receiving application to interpret the meaning of the tags although along with the XML file, a schema file is usually sent defining, via metadata in an XSD file (the structure of the XML data). Likewise, if formatting, graphics, or other presentation layout information exists for this data, an XSL file accompanies the other two.

Unlike HTML, in which the tag `<BR>` always means *line break* (move to the next line on the screen), in an XML file, `<BR>` could mean anything: *branch, broken cookies, Mrs. Simpson's bank statement,* or anything else. It's similar to the way you can assign a variable name such as `ArtView` to a particular graphic filename that might contain a picture of Toronto, your puppy, or indeed anything else (perhaps Art's opinions). It's up to your application how it interprets `ArtView` and what it does with the value represented by that word. Put another way, HTML is a simple computer language dedicated to describing the appearance of a document. (Its tags and attributes tell the computer how to arrange text, color, and so on.) Comparatively, XML is a way to structure and communicate data.

Attributes are not required, but an element can contain one or more of them, and they can be listed in any order. Attributes always use the = sign to separate the attribute's name from its value:

```
<BOSS BOXNUMBER="1">Jack Jackson</BOSS>
```

`BOSS` is an element, and `BOXNUMBER="1"` is an attribute of that element.

Each XML tag pair contains a datum. A *tag pair* is similar to a field (or column) in a database. However, there is no requirement for a one-to-one mapping between XML tag-pair content and the records in a database. Indeed, XML often packages information from various sources or even computed information (the way that a spreadsheet can combine two or more data into a third data that represents an arithmetic or other computation against the original data). Don't be concerned about *name collisions* — that different tags from different XML documents might share the same name. You'll see the solution to this potential problem later in this chapter in the section on namespaces.

Deciding Whether to Use an Element or Attribute

You might be wondering about the difference between an element and an attribute. In truth, you can store data in either one. Keep in mind, however, a few practical differences when designing an XML document or pouring a database table (or list) into it:

✦ **Elements can be contained within a structure similar to the** `Select Case` **structure.** In a schema, you can use a `<CHOICE>` tag to contain several elements in the source code, only one of which can be active in a given context.

✦ **The order in which attributes are listed in the source code is irrelevant.** However, you can specify in a schema that the order of elements does, in fact, matter.

✦ **Elements can be used more than one time in an XML schema.** Attributes cannot.

✦ **Elements can contain attributes.** Attributes cannot contain elements.

✦ **Attributes can limit their permitted contents to a small set of strings delimited by spaces.** Elements cannot do this. Limit an attribute's contents to these three strings, for example:

```
<AttributeType name="Temp" dt:values="cold warm hot" />
```

✦ **Attributes can have default contents.** However, the attribute must be left out of an element, like this:

```
<AttributeType name="Qualified" dt:type="boolean">
<attribute type="Qualified" default="0"/>
```

✦ **You cannot provide alternative attributes (for example, `"CheckedOut"` or `"Shelved"`).** You can do this with elements.

✦ **Your schema can specify that a particular attribute is either required or optional.** To make it required, use the following:

```
<AttributeType name="Rating" required="yes"/>
```

✦ **Elements encapsulate attributes, so different attributes in different elements in the same XML document can have the same name.** The beginning and ending tag pair of an element creates a scope for any attributes contained within the element. This is similar to how a procedure contains local variables in VB .NET. (You can reuse the same variable names with different local variables if they're in different procedures.)

Understanding XML Terminology

An XML element consists of a start tag, an end tag, and the data that the tags enclose. The enclosed data is sometimes called the element's *content*. One difference between XML and HTML is that HTML has a limited set of predefined tags whereas XML permits an unlimited number of tags (just as VBA permits an unlimited number of variable names). HTML tags describe how the content looks in a browser; XML tags describe the meaning of the content (`<DayOfThe Week>Monday</DayOfTheWeek>`). Just like coming up with descriptive variable names is the responsibility of the VB programmer, coming up with descriptive tag names is the responsibility of the XML programmer.

Nesting within XML

XML elements can be nested, like this:

```
<films>
  <film copyrightnumber="133117">
    <name>Annie Hall</name>
    <director>Woody Allen</director>
    <star>Diane Keeton</star>
  </film>
</films>
```

The preceding example, with its nested elements, begins with a unique first element (the *root note*). In this case, the films root node can contain many <film> elements; these element tags need not be unique.

Using data islands in XML

If you wish, you can insert XML data into an HTML page and then use VB to access that data. The ways to insert XML into HTML are *data islands.* To create a data island, use the HTML tag <XML> like this and put an XML document inside the tags:

```
<XML ID="Movies">
<films>
  <film copyrightnumber="133117">
    <name>Annie Hall</name>
    <director>Woody Allen</director>
    <star>Diane Keeton</star>
  </film>
</films>
</XML>
```

Or, if you prefer, you can provide a filename instead that contains the XML document, like this:

```
<XML ID="Movies" SRC="movies.xml"></XML>
```

Paying attention to XML strictness

Don't be misled: XML is far more strict in some ways than HTML. As you probably know, HTML ignores lots of kinds of broken rules. You can leave out the <HEAD> tag or sometimes write impossible attribute values or forget to use quotes around a value. Usually, when coming upon such an error, HTML simply ignores it and goes on to the next tag or attribute. HTML might punish you by not displaying something in the browser, but that's it. HTML will ignore various slip-ups on the programmer's part. In this respect, HTML is quite a bit looser and less demanding than (for example) VB or any other programming language.

XML, however, is very strict. Absolutely no missing quotes or missing tags are permitted. (XML is said to demand that your XML code must be *well-formed.*) If an application reading XML comes across such an error, that application is supposed to reject the entire XML file and stop in its tracks, raising an error. It's all or nothing. What's more, XML (unlike HTML or BASIC) is case-sensitive: `<cookie>` is a different tag than `<Cookie>`.

Fortunately, testing an XML document to see whether it is well-formed is relatively simple. XML has pretty simple punctuation rules; for example, each pair of tag names must be surrounded by `<>` `</>` symbols. Little, simple utilities called *parsers* can check through XML code to see whether it's well-formed in simple terms.

Validating a Word document

An XML file can also be validated against its own schema file. Word 2003 can validate XML if a schema is attached to a document. Any schema violations are shown in the XML Structure task pane. To activate this feature, choose Tools⇨Templates and Add-Ins. From the XML Schema tab, select the Validate Document Against Attached Schemas check box.

You can also watch the XML Structure task pane while working on an XML document to ensure its validity. Errors are flagged with icons next to each element.

Ensuring valid and well-formed XML

You can include a Document Type Definition (DTD) with an XML document. XML with a DTD (or XSD) is called *valid* XML. The DTD defines the rules that govern the structure and vocabulary of the tags in the document. If a programmer is writing an application that will receive and manipulate such an XML document, he can study the DTD to learn the rules that define the data structure. You could even write an XML parser utility to check XML documents to ensure that they conform to the DTD. DTDs are optional.

A well-formed XML document can be thought of as self-describing, particularly if the person who creates the tags and the structure does a good job. You will agree that this XML structure is pretty effectively self-describing:

```
<film copyrightnumber="133117">
    <name>Annie Hall</name>
    <director>Woody Allen</director>
    <star>Diane Keeton</star>
</film>
```

Seeing the Many Faces of XML

XML itself is merely a specification that describes what tags and attributes are and how they are to be used. However, several auxiliary technologies expand and assist XML. For instance, XML (like HTML) can use Cascading Style Sheets (CSSes) or the even more advanced styles technology XSL, which can reorder or add and delete tags and attributes. The XML Linking Language (XLink) provides a standardized method to include hyperlinks within an XML file.

The Document Object Model (DOM) is a way for programs to read and write to XML, adjusting the style, content, and structure of the XML file. DOM offers a standardized set of objects and also a standard framework that describes how the objects can be manipulated or combined. Therefore, the DOM can be considered an interface to the many proprietary Application Program Interfaces (APIs) and XML data structures, making it possible for a programmer to work with standard DOM interfaces rather than having to study proprietary APIs. For example, Ford and GM are likely to use different tags to represent the number of steering wheels in their inventory, and they are likely to use different applications and interfaces to manipulate those different tags. But with DOM, a programmer can count on a known, abstract interface that will work with either the Ford or GM APIs.

Also supporting XML are XML schemas, which assist programmers define their own, proprietary XML structures. Schemas, including one proposed by Microsoft, ultimately go beyond self-describing tags (understood by programmers) to self-describing data structures (understood by programs themselves, without the direct aid and translation of a programmer).

Using Namespaces in XML

XML *namespaces* help prevent collisions that can happen when attribute names or tags are identical if a document contains multiple markup vocabularies (more than one namespace). The namespace allows you to differentiate between different markup vocabularies. It works because each namespace is given a unique number. Commonly, a different URL is assigned to each namespace. By definition and design, URLs are unique: Only one possible number exists for each URL anywhere in the world of the Internet. Sometimes a Uniform Resource Number (URN) is used instead. In either case, the number is unique and prevents collisions of the names that you use in different vocabularies.

Using explicit declaration

Just like with variables in VBA, VB6, and earlier versions, you can either explicitly declare a namespace, or you can let it happen implicitly (more on this in the following section).

Explicit declarations keep things straight if your node contains elements from more than one namespace. You use a shorthand name for the namespace that you use as a prefix (like an alias) to specify which namespace an element belongs to.

```
<mo:film xmlns:mo="urn:FilmSociety.com:FilmData"
         xmlns:directors="urn:CinemaHistory.com:Directors">
  <mo:name>Annie Hall</mo:name>
  <directors:director>Woody Allen</directors:director>
</mo:film>
```

`xmlns` is the attribute used to declare a namespace and, at the same time, specify a prefix that represents the namespace. In the preceding example, I define a prefix (`mo`) that represents the namespace identified by the unique value of `"urn:FilmSociety.com:FilmData"`. I also declare a second namespace (`"urn:CinemaHistory.com:Directors"`) and assign `directors` as its prefix. Then I use the `mo` prefix to indicate that the `name` element belongs to the `"urn:FilmSociety.com:FilmData"` namespace. Next I use the `directors` prefix to specify that the `director` element belongs to the `"urn:CinemaHistory.com:Directors"` namespace. In this way, you can freely employ elements from different namespaces, not having to worry that you'll run into duplicate (and therefore ambiguous) element names. The prefixes prevent confusion if more than one element has the same name.

Using implicit declaration

With implicit declarations, all the elements inside its scope belong to the same namespace; thus, a prefix is not needed. You accomplish implicit declaration by simply leaving out the prefix when you declare the namespace, like this:

```
<film xmlns="urn:FilmSociety.com:FilmData">
  <name>Annie Hall</name>
  <star>Diane Keaton</star>
</film>
```

The Explosion of Schemes

As you probably can guess, the extensibility of XML is a double-edged sword. Allowing folks to create their own tag vocabulary and data structures could quickly result in thousands of unique, proprietary XML schemes.

In the early 80's, an intriguing language named Forth fascinated many programmers. It permitted a crude form of inheritance and polymorphism. You built a program by renaming the low-level language functions and redefining the language by adding functionality to the functions as you went along. The problem was that each application contained many unique statements that only the programmer could understand (if even he or she could figure it out after a few weeks passed).

Similarly, if every organization builds its own set of XML structures and tags, each organization generates a new language unique to itself. All these new languages will share the XML punctuation and syntax rules, but the actual vocabulary will be special to each implementation. How you navigate the structures, what the tags mean, the hierarchy, the relationships, and the diction . . . all this differs among the many thousands of versions of XML schema invented by each organization.

Microsoft and others have proposed sets of rules: *schemata.* One such initiative is Microsoft's *BizTalk,* a site that attempts to gather information about XML, XSL, and other data models used by all those thousands of organizations. See www.biztalk.org for further details.

Understanding XSD

Microsoft programming focuses on XSD (schema files) rather than DTD or other alternatives. (Read about DTD files in the earlier section, "Ensuring valid and well-formed XML.") Take a brief look at what you can do with XSD.

A *schema* is a structured framework (or diagram) that is meant to clarify and describe a set of related ideas. A blueprint, for example, is a schema that describes all the elements in what will be a house. If you are deeply into object-oriented programming (OOP) thinking, you might want to visualize a schema as a *class* and an XML document that uses that schema as an *object* — an instance of the class.

A schema is *metadata:* data about data. The metadata (or schema) for a database comprises the names and relationships between tables, fields, records, and properties of that database. Similarly, an XML document can be thought of as another kind of database. And an XML schema is a description of the structure of an XML document. If you own a grocery store, you can use XML to communicate your inventory needs to your suppliers as long as you both use the same XML schema.

VB.NET contains a tool, the XML Designer, which you can use to build and modify XML schemas and the resulting XML documents. This designer shows you both source code and diagrams of a schema.

Microsoft has selected XSD as its favored schema builder because it

✦ Permits you to group elements and attributes (to assist you in repeating the groups).

✦ Contains KEY and KEYREF statements, which allow you to create one-to-many relationships and uniqueness constraints.

✦ Supports inheritance, namespaces, and extensibility (not simple XML tag extensibility: rather, the extension of a schema itself).

✦ Employs XML to define the XSD schemas. (Thus, it has the benefits that XML offers over other data definition techniques.)

Here's an example of a typical XSD schema. Notice that there is no actual data content here (no proper names such as *Bobby* or numeric values such as a phone number). Instead, you have a list of elements, their data type, and a definition of their structural relationship within a sequence. This is quite like creating an array or type of declared variable names:

```
Dim FirstName as String
Dim LastName as String
Dim ZipCode as Integer
Dim Address as String
```

Here's the declaration of a complex data type using XSD:

```
<?xml version="1.0" encoding="utf-8"?>

<schema targetNamespace="http://CardCorp.com/XMLSchema1.xsd"
        xmlns="http://www.Nams.com/Ars/XMLSchema2">

<complexType name="customerType">
   <sequence>
      <element name="LastName" type="string"/>
      <element name="FirstName" type="string"/>
      <element name="StreetAddress" type="string"/>
      <element name="City" type="string"/>
      <element name="State" type="string"/>
      <element name="ZipCode" type="integer"/>
   </sequence>
</complexType>

</schema>
```

The line that begins with ?xml describes which version of XML this document uses. The following line, beginning with <schema, describes which XSD schema file is being used and also specifies the namespace.

Using XML data types

The type of an element or attribute can be either one of the standard types defined by the World Wide Web Consortium (W3C) or can be simple or complex types that you defined earlier in your schema.

Here in Table 2-1 is the full set of data types supported in XML.

Table 2-1	Data Types Supported in XML
Type	*Example*
bin.base64	MIME-style, base 64-encoded binary BLOB.
bin.hex	Hexadecimal digits representing octets.
Boolean	0 = false, and 1 = true.
Char	A string one character long.
Date	Date in a subset ISO 8601 format, without the time data. Example: 1945-12-26. (Note that this is different from normal American date expression, which uses the format month/day/year.)
DateTime	Date in a subset ISO 8601 format, with optional time and no optional zone. Fractional seconds can be as precise as nanoseconds. Example: 1998-05-04T17:22:01.
DateTime.tz	Date in a subset ISO 8601 format, with optional time and optional zone. Fractional seconds can be as precise as nanoseconds. Example: 1998-05-04T17:22:01-04:00.
fixed.14.4	Same as Number but no more than 14 digits to the left of the decimal point and no more than 4 to the right.
Float	Real number, with no limit on digits. It can potentially have a leading sign, fractional digits, and optionally an exponent. Punctuation as in U.S. English. Values range from 1.7976931348623157E+308 to 2.2250738585072014E–308.
Int	Number, with optional sign, no fractions, and no exponent.
Number	Number, with no limit on digits. It can potentially have a leading sign, fractional digits, and optionally an exponent. Punctuation as in U.S. English. Values have same range as most significant number, R8, 1.7976931348623157E+308 to 2.2250738585072014E–308.
Time	Time in a subset ISO 8601 format, with no date and no time zone. Example: 04:12:22.
time.tz	Time in a subset ISO 8601 format, with no date but optional time zone. Example: 04:12:22-04:00.
i1	Integer stored in one byte. Number, with optional sign, no fractions, and no exponent. Examples: 5, 110, –128.

(continued)

Book VIII
Chapter 2

Exploring XML

Table 2-1 *(continued)*

Type	Example
i2	Integer stored in one word. Number, with optional sign, no fractions, no exponent. Examples: 1, 323, –32768.
i4	Integer stored in four bytes. Number, with optional sign, no fractions, no exponent. Examples: 1, 323, –32768, 115295, –1000000000.
r4	Real number, with seven-digit precision; can potentially have a leading sign, fractional digits, and optionally an exponent. Punctuation as in U.S. English. Values range from 3.40282347E+38F to 1.17549435E–38F.
r8	Real number, with 15-digit precision; can potentially have a leading sign, fractional digits, and optionally an exponent. Punctuation as in U.S. English. Values range from 1.7976931348623157E+308 to 2.2250738585072014E–308.
ui1	Unsigned integer, stored in one byte. Number, unsigned, no fractions, no exponent. Example: 6, 255.
ui2	Unsigned integer, two bytes. Number, unsigned, no fractions, no exponent. Example: 6, 255, 65535.
ui4	Unsigned integer, four bytes. Number, unsigned, no fractions, no exponent. Example: 6, 999, 3000000000.
Uri	Universal Resource Identifier (URI). Example: urn:Myschemas-MyLocation-com:Teaoram.
Uuid	Hexadecimal digits representing octets, optional embedded hyphens that are ignored. Example: 246B7CC2–150E– 22C0– CD11– 3000D8987B29.

Some programmers prefer to use only the string type for XML files, and then in applications, convert the strings to other types as necessary.

If you want to use data types supported by Internet Explorer 5 and above, include the following datatypes namespace:

```
<schema name="YourSchema"
        xmlns="urn:schemas-microsoft-com:xml-data"
        xmlns:dt="urn:schemas-microsoft-com:datatypes">

 <!--  define your schema here  -->


</schema>
```

You are allowed to specify data types for attributes as well as elements; however, with attributes, there are fewer permitted types. The types permitted for use with attributes are string, id, idref, idrefs, nmtoken, nmtokens, entity, entities, enumeration, and notation. For example:

```
<AttributeType name="Overdue" dt:type="idref"/>
<attribute type="Overdue"/>
```

If an attribute has an `idref` data type, that attribute contains a unique identifying value in the document. (Think of the ID of a VB control that must be
unique in a given Web Form, or of the ID in an HTML document, which also
must be unique in that document.) However, note the two similar XML data
types in a schema: `id` and `idrefs`.

Attributes with the type `id` are references to the element that uses the same
`id`. `idrefs` is like `id`, but `idrefs` contains a list of `id`s separated by spaces:

```
<LateCharge creditcard="First Second Third">
```

Note that elements support the `id` attribute data type only in Internet
Explorer 5.01 and above:

```
<ElementType name="Factory">
   <datatype dt:type="id">
</ElementType>
```

Declaring simple XML data types

To declare simple (`Boolean`, `Float`, and such) data types for attributes in
your schema, just use the `<datatype>` element within an `<AttributeType>`
element, like this:

```
<AttributeType name ="MyAttributeType"/>
   <datatype dt:type="int"/>
</AttributeType>

<ElementType name="Points">
   <attribute type="MyAttributeType"/>
<ElementType>
```

Specifying Content in an XML Schema

You can use previously defined `ElementType`s to build a new, more complex
`ElementType`, like what you see in Listing 2-1.

Listing 2-1:   Building a More Complex ElementType

```
<schema xmlns="http://www.Nams.com/Ars/XMLSchema2">


<ElementType name="LastName"/>
<ElementType name="FirstName"/>
```

```
<ElementType name="StreetAddress"/>
<ElementType name="City"/>
<ElementType name="LastName"/>


<ElementType name="Voter" order="seq">
   <element type="FirstName" />
<element type="LastName" />
   <element type="StreetAddress" />
   <element type="City" />
</ElementType>

</schema>
```

In this example, I built the `Voter` element out of four previously defined elements. I also use `<seq>` to specify that the four elements must be in sequence.

XML that correctly follows the previous schema looks like this:

```
<Voter xmlns="Myschema:Voter-schema.xml">
<FirstName>Jon</FirstName>
<LastName>Popodoupolous</LastName>
<StreetAddress>922 W. Archer St.</StreetAddress>
<City>Bogotoa</StreetAddress>
</Voter>
```

Extending a Schema

Schemas can be freely *extended* (you can add new elements and attributes that go beyond what is defined in the schema) as long as you follow a few rules. This means that a schema's content model is by default *open,* although you can force it to be closed if you wish by using the `model="closed"` attribute.

If you want to extend an open-content model, you must remember that you can add new, undeclared elements only if they are in a new namespace. For example, here I add a new namespace with the prefix n:

```
<Voter xmlns= xmlns="Myschema:Voter-schema.
          xml" xmlns:n="urn:AnotherNamespace">
```

Now I can add an attribute from the n namespace, like this:

```
<FirstName>Jon</FirstName>
<LastName n:Alpha = "P">Popodoupolous</LastName>
```

or add a new element from the n namespace, like this:

```
<StreetAddress>922 W. Archer St.</StreetAddress>
<City>Bogotoa</StreetAddress>
<n:Country>Chile</n:Country>
</Voter>
```

You can't add (or delete) any content from the model that would violate the content model rules. In the original schema (Listing 2-1), I use the `order="seq"` attribute to require that the `FirstName`, `LastName`, `StreetAddress`, and `City` elements be sequential. You are allowed to add new attributes to these elements, but you are not allowed to violate the sequence of the elements. That is, you cannot remove one of the required four elements nor insert a new element above or within the sequence. The `<Voter>` element must begin with the four elements although you can add additional elements below those four elements. Also, if you want to add more `FirstName` elements to `<Voter>` (to accommodate people like many first names, like Prince Charles Albert James . . .), you can do it, but these new `FirstName` elements must be appended to the sequence. In other words, you must add new `FirstName` elements after the `<City>` element. Otherwise, you would violate the sequence as defined in the schema.

If for some reason you want to freeze a content model and not permit any extensibility, simply use the following attribute in the schema:

```
<ElementType name="Voter" order="seq" model="closed">
```

With this directive in place, any added or deleted elements — any changes to the original schema at all — will not validate. It doesn't matter if you add new namespaces. Closed means closed.

The `order` attribute can be used with the `seq` value in a schema to freeze a sequence of elements. You can also use the `one` value with the `order` attribute to require that only one, single *sub-element* (an element within another element) must be used (from a list of possible sub-elements). For example, you might want to specify that only one of the following elements can be used: `<ZipCode>` or `<CountryCode>` but not both. Here's how:

```
<ElementType name="Code" order="one">
    <element type="ZipCode" />
    <element type="CountryCode" />
</ElementType>
```

If you want to go in the other direction and throw all caution to the winds, use the `many` value with the `order` attribute. The `many` value says that there can be any number of sub-elements and that they can appear in any order as well.

Sometimes you might need to specify an order on some of the sub-elements but want to leave the rest of the sub-elements unaffected by the order rule. To do that, use the group element. For instance, isolate the ZipCode or CountryCode elements by forcing them to be either/or but not extending this rule to other sub-elements:

```
<ElementType name="Code">

<group order="one">
   <element type="ZipCode" />
   <element type="CountryCode" />
</group>

   <element type="PhoneNumber" />
   <element type="Age" />

</ElementType>
```

In this example, either ZipCode or CountryCode will be used but not both. However, both PhoneNumber and Age will be required.

The group element has two other possible attributes: minOccurs and maxOccurs. These attributes define how often a given sub-element can appear within a container element. You can specify maxOccurs by using an integer (maxOccurs="5" means that no more than five of this sub-element can appear) or an asterisk to indicate that there can be unlimited numbers of the sub-element:

```
<element type="Voter" maxOccurs="*" />
```

The default value for maxOccurs is 1; however, if the content="mixed", the default value for maxOccurs is "*".

MinOccurs defines the minimum number of times that a given sub-element can appear. MinOccurs defaults to 1, but if you set it to "0", the inclusion of that sub-element is then optional.

Using the Content Attribute

Elements can contain other elements (called sub-elements), and/or text, or simply be empty of content. You can use the values textOnly and eltOnly mixed and empty as values for the content attribute of an element. These values specify the permitted content for that element.

If you want to insist that an element contain text but can contain no other elements (nor be empty), use the `textOnly` value:

```
<ElementType name="FirstName" content="textOnly" />
```

If you use the `empty` value, no text or sub-elements are permitted. The `mixed` value permits you to use both text and sub-elements. Or, to specify that an element must contain sub-elements but no other content, use this variation. (`elt` is short for *element.*)

```
<ElementType name="Voter" content="eltOnly" />
```

If you define a data type for an element, `textOnly` becomes the default content specification.

If the `content` attribute is `eltOnly`, the order value defaults to `seq`. If the `content` attribute is `mixed`, the order value defaults to `many`.

Using Office XML Programming

Now that the tools are in place in Office 2003 applications, managing XML from within VBA is not difficult. Various classes added to the VBA object hierarchy permit you to accomplish pretty much anything with XML, including these tasks:

✦ Add, delete, cut, copy, move, and edit XML elements or attributes.

✦ Attach schemas to XML documents or the schema library.

✦ Save the document in either plain XML or with Word markup tags.

✦ React via code to events, including the user moving the insertion point, deleting elements, violating a schema, or adding a new schema.

✦ Apply custom eXtensible Stylesheet Language Transformation (XSLT) transforms.

✦ Add custom XML document validation error handling.

Try this example in Word:

1. **Open a new, blank document.**

2. **Press Alt+F11.**

The VBA Code window opens.

Book VIII Chapter 2

Exploring XML

3. **Press Ctrl+R.**

   Project Explorer opens.

4. **Click the name of the new, blank document.**

   Document names are in boldface.

5. **Choose Insert⇨Module from the VBA menu.**

   A new module appears.

6. **Create a sample XML and XSD file pair to work with in this example.**

   a. Run Access and load `Northwind.mdb` (the sample database that comes with Access).

   b. Click the Tables icon in the left pane of the main database window.

   c. Double-click the Employees table (in the right pane of the main database window) to open and view this table.

   d. Choose File⇨Export.

   e. In the Save as Type field of the Export table dialog box, choose .xml.

   f. Save it to `C:\`, your root directory.

   g. Click Export All.

   h. When the Export XML dialog box appears, click OK.

7. **Right-click the XSD file, choose Open with Notepad, and look in the XSD file for a** `targetNamespace`.

   If you're using the `Employees.xsd` created in Step 6, there is no `targetNamespace`. However, some XSD files will have one, and it looks something like this:

   ```
   targetNamespace="http://www.tempuri.org/dsOrders.xsd"
   ```

8. **Type the following into your new module.**

   Use whatever is your XSD file's `targetNamespace` for the `NamespaceURI` in the following code if there is a `targetNamespace`:

   ```
   Sub XM()

   ActiveDocument.XMLSchemaReferences.Add _
       NamespaceURI:="http://www.tempuri.org/dsOrders.
           xsd", _
       Alias:="Emps", _
       FileName:="C:\Employees.xsd", _
       InstallForAllUsers:=True
   End Sub
   ```

Otherwise (if there is no `targetNamespace`, as with the `Employees.xsd` sample file), you can just make up a `NamespaceURI`, like this:

```
Sub xm()

ActiveDocument.XMLSchemaReferences.Add _
    NamespaceURI:="Nspc", _
    Alias:="Emps", _
    FileName:="C:\Employees.xsd", _
    InstallForAllUsers:=True

End Sub
```

9. **Press F5 to execute this code.**

You've added a new XML schema to your document. You can see it by choosing Tools⇨Templates and Add-Ins and then clicking the XML Schema tab, as shown in Figure 2-4.

Figure 2-4:
You've program-matically added this schema to your Word document.

If you try to execute this code again — with the schema already attached — you'll get an error message (Error 6106, `Requested schema cannot be found.`) This error message is incorrect. The schema is obviously still there, but you are not allowed to try to import it if it's already active in the document.

Viewing and applying a schema

After the schema is attached to the document (from the preceding section), try viewing and applying the schema.

1. **Choose View⇨Task Pane.**

The XML Structure task pane should appear. If some other task pane shows up, click the down arrow in the task pane's title bar and choose XML Structure.

2. **At the very bottom of the XML Structure taskbar, clear the List Only Child Elements of Current Element check box to deselect it.**

You want to see the entire schema, as shown in Figure 2-5.

Figure 2-5: This task pane displays the schema you just added.

3. **Type the word** Betty **in your document and drag your mouse to select it.**

4. **Click the FirstName element (field) in the list of elements in the XML Structure task pane.**

Betty becomes surrounded with XML tags representing this field (element) name, as shown in Figure 2-6.

Figure 2-6:
This is how
XML data
can be
displayed
in a Word
document.

Dropping an entire XML file

Try another experiment. Using Windows Explorer, right-click the `Employees.`
`xml` file and choose Open With⇨Microsoft Office Word. When asked, agree to
view it as an XML document. You see the full set of tags. Now click the drop-
down arrow icon in the taskbar's title bar and choose XML Structure. You see
the full XML view, as shown in Figure 2-7. Templates like this can be passed
around for editing or filling in by co-workers. Then you're ready to export the
data back into Access, use it with a Web service or whatever.

Figure 2-7:
You can
drop an
entire
XML file.

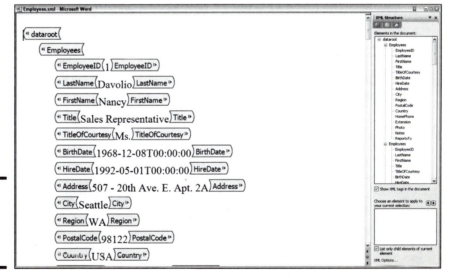

Programmatic XML Manipulations

You can, of course, manage an XML document entirely via code if you wish. Try some experiments to see how it's done.

Adding a node

With the `Employees.xml` file loaded in a Word document (as shown in Figure 2-7), press Alt+F11 to get to the code window.

Type this:

```
Sub xlAddElement()

 ActiveDocument.XMLNodes.Add _
     Name:="Employees", _
     Namespace:="Nspc"

End Sub
```

When you press F5 to execute this code, a new node is added to your document: in this case, an `Employees` tag pair. Note that this node can be only the `Employees` element and not any of the child elements. In this schema, `Employees` is the so-called *root element,* and that's what the `XMLNodes.Add` method works with.

If you get an error message, choose Tools⇨Templates and Add-Ins, click the XML Schema tab, and ensure that the `Emps` schema is selected (or whatever alias name you gave this schema in Step 8 of the earlier section, "Using Office XML Programming").

Adding child nodes and data

This code illustrates how to add a root node, its child elements, and the actual data. In database terms, you're adding an entire record with the example in Listing 2-2.

Listing 2-2: Adding a Node and Its Data

```
Sub xlAddChildren()

 Dim oActiveNode As Word.XMLNode

'Note that parentheses are necessary in this case:
Set oActiveNode = ActiveDocument.XMLNodes.Add _
    (Name:="Employees", _
    Namespace:="Nspc")
```

```
' Add child elements under the root node.

With oActiveNode.ChildNodes

    .Add(Name:="EmployeeID", _
        Namespace:=Nspc).Range.Text = "15"
    .Add(Name:="LastName", _
        Namespace:=Nspc).Range.Text = "De La Rouuage"
    .Add(Name:="FirstName", _
        Namespace:=Nspc).Range.Text = "Bonzit"
    .Add(Name:="Title", _
        Namespace:=Nspc).Range.Text = "Garage Associate"
    .Add(Name:="TitleOfCourtesy", _
        Namespace:=Nspc).Range.Text = "Dr. of Parking"
    .Add(Name:="BirthDate", _
        Namespace:=Nspc).Range.Text = "1952-02-19T00:00:00"
    .Add(Name:="HireDate", _
        Namespace:=Nspc).Range.Text = "1992-08-14T00:00:00"
    .Add(Name:="Notes", _
        Namespace:=Nspc).Range.Text = "Bonzit shows early signs of hyper-
            narco-compulsive personality disorder. There are the unsigned
            letters, the strange jokes about Venusians, the Betty Ford
            imitations."

End With
```

Notice that to save time, I didn't add every child element (database field) in this Employees record. I skipped address, postal code, phone, and other fields, but I did want to include the final element (the Notes field) because it's important to keep an eye on Bonzit.

This example illustrates how you can mix and match the child elements at will within a root element. You cannot invent new elements that are not already in the schema, though.

There are many more things you can do via VBA to Office 2003 applications' XML content and schemas. For additional information, search Office 2003 applications' Help systems and look online at MSDN for information on Office 2003 programming: http://msdn.microsoft.com.

Book VIII
Chapter 2

Exploring XML

Chapter 3: Employing Objects

In This Chapter

✔ Exposing the fundamentals of OOP

✔ Using objects in VBA

✔ Understanding .NET data types

✔ Exploring the differences between VBA and Visual Basic .NET

✔ Making declarations in VBA

✔ Using VBA events

✔ Working with collections

✔ Managing arrays of objects

*T*his chapter surveys the uses and syntax of objects in programming Office applications. Of course, VBA is covered, but you can also manage Office 2003 applications and solutions from above by creating VB.NET programs. Also, it's increasingly important for programmers to migrate from classic VB (as represented by VBA) to the future of BASIC, VB.NET. Therefore, this chapter also explores changes you need to make to your programming practices after you make the move from VBA to VB.NET.

Looking at OOP

First, briefly consider the implications of object-oriented programming (OOP) in general. Often, you should just ignore OOP classes when you write a program of moderate size by yourself. Just use traditional subroutines and functions to organize your code (classic procedure-based programming). Classes contribute nothing in this context.

However, you will have to work with the classes — and their members (methods and properties) — when you tap into Office applications' features.

It used to be that when you went beyond your own BASIC code, you used an Application Programming Interface (API). Now you use an object model (or several). So you do need to come to grips with object-oriented programming, if only to be able to exploit the features built into Office 2003 applications as well as other code libraries such as the extraordinarily powerful encryption features available in the .NET framework (set of code libraries).

And, of course, if you're creating a large program, a distributed program, or working with other programmers, OOP has several advantages to offer you over classic procedure-based programming. OOP is mainly a clerical utility, offering tools to keep programmers from stepping on each other's toes when they must write programs as a group.

Understanding Fundamental OOP

You face the practical job of migrating from essentially procedure-oriented traditional languages like VBA (and VB 6 and earlier) to object-oriented languages like VB.NET. You must migrate because the programming community is migrating and because VB.NET is worth learning — it's simply a much more powerful language than VBA, whether or not you're interested in using the (primarily clerical) benefits offered by OOP.

OOP theory claims that OOP offers three primary elements: encapsulation, inheritance, and polymorphism (although there's not much talk about polymorphism any more because it turned out to be essentially just an aspect of inheritance).

The main virtue of OOP is *encapsulation:* sealing off tested objects from outsiders. Inheritance is inherently dangerous and leads to many bugs. (Professors claim that inheritance is safe when done properly, but circus people say the same thing about walking a tightrope.)

Here's an example of encapsulation. A programmer hands you an object, telling you the public (meaning available to you) properties it exposes that you can read or write, and also the public methods you can invoke (along with the *parameters:* data that the methods need from you, and what, if any, data they pass back).

How is this different from traditional programming? Not much. Traditional programming uses variables, which are usually equivalent to properties. Traditional variables can be read or written to although properties can get so elaborate that in OOP, they can confusingly behave as if they were methods. Sometimes when you pass a value to a property, it checks (validates) if this value is acceptable. However, this same kind of validation can be built into functions just as easily.

Traditional functions and subroutines (collectively called *procedures*) are the equivalent of methods. Procedures tell you what parameters they want you to send them and what they pass back.

OOP differs from classic programming in that you could traditionally look at the source code written by another programmer. (Of course, languages, applications, and operating systems themselves contain libraries' built-in, or add-on, functions. These complied libraries are not readable by the programmer. So in this sense, encapsulation has always existed.)

With OOP, though, a particular clerical job is solved: You don't have to worry about one programmer editing the source code written by another programmer while they're working on a project together. Encapsulation ensures that people programming in groups can be sure that there's only one (presumably stable and tested) version of any given object. A programmer designs an object, tests it, and then seals it off (perhaps even compiling the object so it's as impossible to modify as a code library DLL). Other programmers are supposed to use the object's public properties and methods but not ask to view (and potentially modify) the object's source code. Another significant benefit offered by OOP derives from *instantiation:* You can quite easily reuse or manage code because you can simply instantiate as many objects as you want in any given context.

OOP projects can *sometimes* be more easily modified than traditional projects. And OOP objects are also often easier to reuse in a new project than trying to cut and paste the code that describes functions in traditional projects. If you write a class representing an individual book order for a bookstore program, you can instantiate this `BookOrder` object every time someone orders a book. Much of the functionality and most of the data needed to service a book order can be contained within each object. And, if you later write another program to manage books, you can probably reuse the `BookOrder` object relatively easily.

Employing Practical VBA Objects

VBA, like Visual Basic 6, permits the programmer to employ the most useful aspects of OOP. The main element that's missing is inheritance, but few VB programmers miss it, and few VB experts suggest using it even when it's available (as in VB.NET). Inheritance offers a way to modify the behavior of an object in spite of encapsulation. You inherit an existing object, but you specify different behaviors for that object. The problems this causes are famous among programmers. You modify an object whose internal structure (source code) is invisible to you; the side effects can be spectacularly unpleasant (and might not show up for years).

So you don't have to switch to .NET to experience OOP. You can work with it in VBA — a context with which you, as an Office developer, are likely quite familiar with.

Try some OOP in VBA. You often don't need to define an object variable (to reference an application's object, such as the Word `TaskPanes` object) because an object such as the `Application` object inherently exists whenever the program is running. Thus, the following VBA `Sub` displays the research task pane without requiring that you first *instantiate* (bring into existence) the `Application` object, the `taskpanes` collection of objects, or the specific research `taskpane` object. Just refer to them because they're already instantiated by Word itself. All you have to do is set this task pane's `Visible` property to `True`:

```
Sub ShowTask()

Application.TaskPanes(wdTaskPaneResearch).Visible = True

End Sub
```

However, if an object is not currently instantiated, you then need to instantiate it before you can access its properties or methods.

Object variables have a rather simple job: They act like shorthand references to their objects, just as a classic variable is a shorthand reference to the value it holds.

You can create object variables several ways in VBA. The best approach — and one that serves you well as you move from VBA to .NET — is to specify the object type. All you do is create an object variable that refers to an existing object, such as the `document` object in Word:

```
Dim oDoc As Word.Document
```

As for referencing objects that don't already exist, there are two VBA formats for this. First, you can declare the variable name and object type, and then `Set` that variable to a `New` instance of the object:

```
Dim o As Outlook.Application 'this is the type of variable
Set o = New Outlook.Application 'this is the actual object
```

A similar approach is called *implicit* object creation because when using this next approach, the object isn't instantiated until this variable is first used elsewhere in the code:

```
Dim MyWordApp As New Word.Application
```

People feel, however, that implicit declaration is slippery and undesirable because you, the programmer, are not certain where in your code the instantiation actually might take place.

Also, `New` works only as a way of creating top-level objects. (In Office 2003, this primarily means `Application` objects.) Objects below the top level in the hierarchy cannot be created with `New`. It's up to the top-level objects to provide a way to create their child objects, like when you use the `Add` method of the Excel `workbooks` collection to add a `workbook` child object:

```
Dim oEx As Excel.Application
Set oEx = New Excel.Application

oEx.Workbooks.Add
```

Distributed instantiation

You can also use `CreateObject` (to instantiate objects not currently in existence) or `GetObject` (to reference existing objects), in this fashion:

```
Dim oExSheet As Object
Set oExSheet = CreateObject("Excel.Sheet")
```

These functions are useful when the `New` command doesn't provide the necessary tools, particularly when you're attempting to instantiate an object *remotely* (on another machine, such as a server). Using the name of the server instantiates the object on the server:

```
Set oExSheet = CreateObject("Excel.Sheet","ServerName")
```

The server name is the machine-name part of a share name. For example, in this share name, `\\HomeBase\Public`, the server name is `HomeBase`.

It's traditional — at least among some programmers — to begin object variables' names with lowercase o to mean *Office,* as in `oDocument` or `oRange`.

You can alternatively use the following (generally less-desirable) ways to create an object variable. This variable can only hold objects, not other data types:

```
Dim oDoc as object
```

This variable is a `variant`, so it can hold objects or any other kind of data type, such as `string` or `integer`:

```
Dim oDoc as variant
```

This is the same as the `variant` because if you don't specify a data type, a declaration in VBA defaults to the `variant` type:

```
Dim oDoc
```

Early and late binding

`Dim VarName As Object` is an example of *late binding*. You're using the generic `Object` data type, not a specific object type. When you use a specific object type (as in `Dim oEx As Excel.Application`), `Excel.Application` is a particular object type. This is *early binding*. What's the diff?

Simply put: Use early binding whenever you can, and you almost always can. You almost always know what kind of object you're planning to deal with when declaring a variable, so specify it. (The generic `Object` data type can refer to any kind of object, so execution is slowed down while the reference is resolved.) Another benefit is that with early binding, VBA's *IntelliSense* feature kicks in (the lists of options displayed while you're programming, as shown in Figure 3-1). And IntelliSense makes programming with object models much easier.

Figure 3-1: IntelliSense lists are extremely helpful when wrestling with object models.

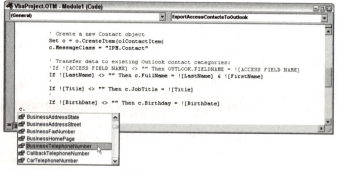

Understanding .NET Data Types

Before exploring objects further, consider some additional changes that you can look forward to in .NET concerning data types and variable declarations.

In .NET are some changes to the traditional VBA data types beyond the rejection of the `variant` type. A new `Char` type, which is an unsigned 16-bit type, is used to store Unicode characters. The `Decimal` type is a 96-bit signed integer scaled by a variable power of 10. The VBA `currency` type is now gone; use the `Decimal` type instead.

The VB.NET `Long` data type is now a 64-bit integer. The VB.NET `Short` type is a 16-bit integer. And in between them is the new VB.NET `Integer` type, which is a 32-bit value. If you are working with programming where these distinctions will matter, memorize these differences from the way that integers were handled in traditional VB programming.

Tables of both the VBA and VB.NET data types are included in this book's Cheat Sheet for easy reference.

Use the Integer type when possible because it executes the fastest of the comparable numeric types in VB.NET.

Table 3-1 lists all the VB.NET data types.

Table 3-1	VB.NET Data Types		
Traditional VB Type	*New .NET Type*	*Memory Size*	*Range*
Boolean	System.Boolean	4 bytes	True or False
Char	System.Char	2 bytes	0–65535 (unsigned)
Byte	System.Byte	1 byte	0–255 (unsigned)
Object	System.Object	4 bytes	Any type
Date	System.DateTime	8 bytes	01-Jan-0001 to 31-Dec-9999
Double	System.Double	8 bytes	+/–1.797E308
Decimal	System.Decimal	12 bytes	28 digits
Integer	System.Int16	2 bytes	–32,768 to 32,767
Integer	System.Int32	4 bytes	+/–2.147E9
Long	System.Int64	8 bytes	+/–9.223E18
Single	System.Single	4 bytes	+/–3.402E38
String	System.String	Character Count * 2 (plus 10 bytes)	2 billion characters

Declaring in VBA

The Dim command can either dimension an array or declare a variable (or a group of variables).

The default variable type is the variant, so if you wanted to use a different type, you have to explicitly declare it by using Dim or one of the other declaring commands such as Public. You can use Dim on a list of different variables on the same line:

```
Dim X As String, Y As Integer, Z
```

In the preceding code example, Z defaults to variant because you didn't specify a data type. Or you could use the DefType commands to change the default from variant to, say, Integer:

```
DefInt A-Z '(all variables become integer types unless
    otherwise declared).
```

The ReDim command could be used two ways: to resize arrays or to declare variables.

Discovering the Changes in VB.NET

As you can read here, .NET does things a bit differently.

Variants go away

The variant data type has been removed from Visual Basic; it's not permitted in .NET. For that reason (among others), you should probably abandon the habit of relying on variants even in your current VBA code. *Get used to it.*

Variants are disallowed in the .NET framework, although they were introduced only a few years ago with great fanfare as a helpful new technology. (With a variant, the language analyzes the context in which a variable is being used and then changes its data type automatically as necessary.)

As time passed, though, variants were found to introduce errors in some situations, particularly when rounding errors occurred if moving from a long numeric data type to a shorter one, thus chopping off some digits in the process. In many situations, this rounding wouldn't make any difference, but it can be a source of serious error in some kinds of programming (such as ballistics).

The variant type, efficient though it often was, had two additional fatal flaws from the VB.NET designers' perspective. In some cases, VBA had a hard time figuring out which type the variant should change to, so it had to guess. Sometimes it guessed wrong. Also, the other languages in the .NET universe do not use variants, and the .NET philosophy requires conformity between its various languages (at least on the fundamental issues, such as variable typing, if not case-sensitivity). Therefore, the variant variable is no longer part of the VB language; it has been banished in VB.NET.

DefType commands are gone

The DefType commands have been removed from the language. The now-removed DefType commands are DefBool, DefByte, DefCur, DefDate, DefDbl, DefDec, DefInt, DefLng, DefObj, DefSng, DefStr, and DefVar.

Mix types within a Dim list

You can mix types within a `Dim` list, but all variables are required to have an `As` clause defining their type (if you set `Option Strict On`). This next line of code is not permitted because of the `Z`:

```
Dim X As String, Y As Integer, Z
```

However, the following is allowed:

```
Dim X As String, Y As String, z As Integer
```

or

```
Dim X, Y As String
```

Note that in VBA, the `X` (because no `As` phrase defines it) would have been a `variant` type. In VB.NET, `X` is a `string` type. If you leave `Option Strict Off` and you don't attach an `As` clause, the variable will default to the `object` type:

```
Dim X
```

With `Option Strict On`, you must declare every variable and every array. You must use `Dim` (or use another declaring command such as `Private` or `Public`).

The default data type in .NET is the `object` rather than the VBA `variant`, but you must declare even this default type with `Option Strict`.

VB.NET has a streamlined way of declaring variables; it allows you to assign a value in the same statement that declares the variable:

```
Dim X As Integer = 12
```

Also, if you are using the latest version, VB.NET 2003, you can even declare a loop counter variable within the line that starts the loop, like this:

```
For i As Integer = 0 To 10
```

instead of the traditional style:

```
Dim i as Integer
For i = 0 To 10
```

You can no longer use ReDim in place of the Dim command

In .NET, you can no longer use ReDim in place of the Dim command. Arrays must be first declared using Dim (or similar); ReDim cannot create an array. You can use ReDim only to redimension (resize) an existing array originally declared with the Dim (or similar) command. (Look up the .NET ArrayList for a superior way to let VB.NET handle arrays that must dynamically change size. ArrayList also does other neat tricks.)

You can declare arrays in a similar way. Here's a two-dimensional array declaration:

```
Dim TwoArray(3, 4) As Integer
```

Use empty parentheses to declare a dynamic array:

```
Dim DynArray() As Integer
```

Declare the same variable name in more than one location

In .NET, you are allowed to declare the same variable name in more than one procedure. This can cause problems that are not flagged by any error messages. Here's an example: Assume that you originally declared n within the Form_Load event (so that it's local to that event only). However, you decide you need to make it Public so that other procedures can use its contents as well. Therefore, you type in a Public declaration at the top of the code window in the General Declarations section, outside of any event or procedure, but you forget to erase the local declaration. Unfortunately, you'll get hard-to-track-down bugs because the local declaration will remain in effect, and n will lose its contents outside the Form_Load event. Here's an example:

```
Public Class Form1
    Inherits System.Windows.Forms.Form
    Public n As Integer '(holds the number of files being
        renamed)

    Private Sub Form1_Load(ByVal sender As System.Object,
        ByVal e As System.EventArgs) Handles MyBase.Load

        Dim myfile As String
        Dim mydir As String
        Dim n, i As Integer
    . . .
End Sub
```

Strongly typed

VB.NET is strongly typed. Several changes to the language support this new approach. For one thing, the VBA `As Any` command has been deleted from the language. You can no longer declare a function `As Any` (meaning that it can return any kind of data type).

Declaring arrays in .NET

You declare an array in a way similar to how you declare a variable. To create an array that holds 11 values, ranging from `MyArray(0)` through `MyArray(10)`, type the following:

```
Dim MyArray(10)
```

You can simultaneously declare and initialize (provide values to) an array. You use the braces ({ }; punctuation marks that had never before been used in Visual Basic). Here's how to initialize a string array with two elements, `MyArray(0)` and `MyArray(1)`, which contain `Billy` and `Bob`:

```
Dim MyArray() As String = {"Billy", "Bob"}
MsgBox(MyArray(0) + MyArray(1))
```

Notice that you are not permitted to specify the size of an array when you initialize it with values, as illustrated in the previous example: `MyArray()`. This array has two elements: `(0)` and `(1)`.

Declaring with symbols

You can still use symbols when declaring some data types in VB.NET. For example, the following declares `N` as an `Integer` variable:

```
Dim N%
```

The following code is equivalent and also preferred:

```
Dim N as Integer
```

Changes to values and parameters

In VBA, you can use the following terms: `Empty`, `Null`, `Missing`, `IsNull`, `IsObject`, and `IsMissing`. They are deleted from VB.NET; they're gone with the variant.

In VBA, you can assign to the `variant` data type these special kinds of values: `Null` (not known), `Empty` (no value was ever assigned to this variable), and `Missing`. (The latter is used if this variable was not sent, for example, as part of a procedure's parameters.)

Null is sometimes used to identify fields in databases that are not available (or unknown), and the term Empty represents something that doesn't exist (as opposed to simply not being currently available). Some programmers use the IsMissing command to see whether an optional parameter had been passed to a procedure, like this:

```
Sub SomeSub(Optional SomeParam As variant)
   If IsMissing(SomeParam) Then
```

The VB.NET object data type does not use Missing, Empty, or Null. There is an IsDBNull function that you can use with databases instead of the now-missing IsNull command. Similarly, an IsReference command replaces the IsObject command.

An optional parameter can still be used with procedures, but you must declare that As *Type* and you must also supply a default value for them. You cannot write code within a procedure that will tell you whether a particular parameter has been passed. If you need to test whether an optional parameter has been passed, you can overload a procedure. *Overloading* is a new technique (to VB) wherein a function (or indeed a method or property) can be made to behave differently based on what is passed to it. Overloading is worth looking into because it allows your code to react in useful ways.

Bidding farewell to the Set command

When you migrate to VB.NET from VBA, you must remove all uses of the Set command. Just write the same line of code as before but without using VBA's Set.

In VBA, the Set command is used like this:

```
Set MyDataConn = Server.CreateObject("ADODB.Connection")
```

Also note that in VBA, when you change an object variable so that it references a different object, you use this syntax:

```
Set CurrentObjVar = DifferentObjVar
```

In VB.NET you leave out the Set command, like this:

```
CurrentObjVar = DifferentObjVar
```

If you omit Set in VBA, something entirely different occurrs. If the DifferentObjVar had no default property, an error is triggered. If it does have a default property, that default property is assigned to CurrentObjVar as its default property.

Not only does VB.NET omit the `Set` command, .NET (in general) doesn't allow default properties, anyway. For example, you can no longer use `X = Text1` as a way of assigning the text in a `TextBox` to the variable `X`. Instead, you must explicitly name any property, including what were previously default properties. In VB.NET, this works like so: `X = TextBox1.Text`.

However, just to make life interesting, some objects do have default properties that you can use in VB.NET. Specifically, objects that take arguments (the `dictionary` object, the `Item` property in a collection, parameterized properties, and so on) can be assumed to be defaults. Explicit reference to the property can, in these few cases, be omitted from your source code.

Parameterized properties (properties that take parameters) are still permitted to be defaults in VB.NET. For example, in VB.NET, most collections fall into this category. Here are some examples from the ActiveX Data Objects (ADO) data language:

```
Recordset object    (its default property is Fields)
Fields collection   (its default property is Item)
Field object        (its default property is Value)
```

For instance, this code illustrates two ways to reference the `Item` property of a recordset's field object:

```
Dim rs As Recordset
```

You can use the fully qualified code:

```
rs.Fields.Item(1).Value = "Hello"
```

Alternatively, you can omit the term `Item` because it is the default property of the `Fields` collection:

```
rs.Fields(1).Value = "Hello"
```

Using VBA Events

Objects are said to have three members: properties, methods, and events. *Events* are things that happen to objects — often things a user does to an object, such as the `Click` event of a UserForm. An event is quite like any other procedure. (It's sometimes called an *event procedure*.) It's a `Sub`, like this:

```
Private Sub UserForm_Click()

End Sub
```

And it's always empty of code unless you add some to respond to the event. You find events in the VBA editor by opening the drop-down list on the top left side of an editor window and then choosing an object. Then open the other, top-right list and choose one of that object's events, as shown in Figure 3-2.

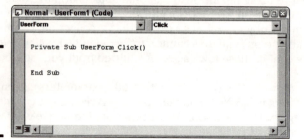

Figure 3-2: Events are found here, in the VBA editor.

A macro that you record or write in VBA is also a `Sub`, but the difference between an ordinary `Sub` and an event procedure is that the latter is automatically executed when something, such as a mouse click, happens to an object (such as a `UserForm`). Macros are not automatically executed, with the exception of a couple that can execute on application startup. Macros must normally be activated by assigning keystroke combinations, menu items, toolbar buttons, or other triggers to them.

Using VBA Collections

Collections are to OOP what arrays are to ordinary programming: items grouped together. In a database, you find a `tables` collection. And, in turn, each table has a collection of fields (describing the structure of the table) and a collection of records (holding the data). Thus, each `table` object contains a `records` collection.

Compared with traditional arrays, collections have more built-in functionality (although the VB.NET `ArrayList` is loaded with useful capabilities). Collections, for example, don't need to rely on the `For...Next` loop when you iterate through them. Instead, you normally use the `For...Each` statement, which knows how many items are in the collection, so you don't have to supply an upper limit as you do with `For...Next`.

Notice in this next code how many different parent objects must be declared and then instantiated before you can get to the calendar folder collection of appointment items:

```
Dim o As Outlook.Application
Set o = New Outlook.Application

Dim ns As Outlook.Namespace
Set ns = o.GetNamespace("MAPI")

Dim m As Outlook.MAPIFolder
Set m = ns.GetDefaultFolder(olFolderCalendar)

Dim a As Outlook.AppointmentItem

For Each a In m.Items
```

You're creating a new Outlook `Application` instance (this code runs within Word), so you have to declare an `object` variable and then instantiate the `Application` object. Next you have to do the same for a namespace object (this is peculiar to Outlook), followed by a folder object. Finally, you get to actually work with the appointment item objects. This mess isn't always necessary when working with objects. If, for example, you're working within an already executing (instantiated) application, such as Word, you need to instantiate a new Word object, or even many of its child objects (which already exist). The following example code illustrates this concept, formally know as *shortcut accessors*.

In a traditional `For...Next` loop, you use an ordinary variable — usually an integer — to count up through the loop. However, with `For...Each`, you must reference an object variable, and that variable must have been declared as being of the same type as the objects in the collection. In the preceding code, `a` is declared as an `Outlook.AppointmentItem`, which is the object collected within the calendar folder collection.

If an application is already running, you need not define all kinds of object variables just to be able to iterate through a collection. In the following example, you don't need to define all the object variables and their children (as in the preceding example) because this code is written in Word VBA and executes within a running instance of Word itself. Thus Word's `Documents` collection is directly available. All you need declare is a single object variable of the `document` type to use with the `For...Each` loop:

```
Sub DocInfo()
Dim oDocs As Word.Document

For Each oDoc In Documents

    If oDoc.Name = "0803.doc" Then

MsgBox ("Found")
```

```
End If

Next
```

Using the `Documents` collection without having to first instantiate all its parent objects can, as this example illustrates, be done. When you use short-cut accessors, you must be executing your VBA code inside the application itself. For instance, if you write VBA code for a macro designed to run within Excel, you can simply reference the `Workbooks` collection directly. (Or, as above, within Word you can directly access the `Documents` collection.)

However, if you're writing code executing within Word that's supposed to manipulate or access an Excel Workbook, you cannot simply directly access the `Workbooks` collection, much less a particular `Workbook` object held within that `Workbooks` collection. It works the same way with VB.NET code, which is by definition executing outside any Office applications you intend to access with the code. In those outside-access cases, you must drill down from the top-level object, through the hierarchy of objects, until you get to the specific document or workbook you're after. Here's an example of this drilling down through the hierarchy, starting with the top-level object — the `Application` object — and working downward:

```
Dim o As Outlook.Application
Set o = New Outlook.Application

Dim ns As Outlook.Namespace
Set ns = o.GetNamespace("MAPI")

Dim m As Outlook.MAPIFolder
Set m = ns.GetDefaultFolder(olFolderCalendar)
```

When you use *Active*Object names — as in *ActiveSheet* — you're referencing the object in a collection that currently has the focus. Word uses `ActiveDocument`, and some other programs use `ActiveWindow`. However, you might be unsure whether a particular object will have the focus when your code executes. In those cases, in Word, you can use the `ThisDocument` object; or, in Excel, use the `ThisWorkbook` object. These two ensure that your code references the document or workbook where the code itself executes.

Using Arrays of Objects

In VB.NET, you can create an array of objects. The trick is to first declare an array object variable and then instantiate each object in the array. Listing 3-1 illustrates how to create an array of seven objects:

Listing 3-1: Creating an Object Array

```
Dim arrRecipe(6) As recipe 'create the array object variable


Private Sub Form1_Load(ByVal sender As System.Object,
    ByVal e As System.EventArgs) Handles MyBase.Load

    Dim i As Integer

    'instantiate each member of the array:
        For i = 0 To 6
            arrRecipe(i) = New recipe()
        Next


' set the two properties of one of the array members
        arrRecipe(0).Title = "MyZeroth"
        arrRecipe(0).Description = "MyZeroth recipe goes like
            this"


    End Sub
End Class

Public Class recipe
    Private _Title As String
    Private _Description As String

    Public Property Title() As String
        Get
            Return _Title
        End Get
        Set(ByVal Value As String)
            _Title = Value
        End Set
    End Property

    Public Property Description() As String
        Get
            Return _Description
        End Get
        Set(ByVal Value As String)
            _Description = Value
        End Set
    End Property

End Class
```

Chapter 4: Advanced Internet VBA

In This Chapter

✓ **Understanding Web Services**

✓ **Using XML with Web Services**

✓ **Seeing Web Services in Office 2003**

✓ **Creating your first Web Service**

*V*BA takes classic Visual Basic to its limits: It's a powerful, flexible, and well-designed language. As Bach's music is to the Baroque period, VBA represents the summit and completion of traditional procedure-oriented programming. Yet even as VBA represents apotheosis of one kind of programming, it carries within itself the seeds of its successor: object-oriented programming, as represented by the .NET version of BASIC. And you must realize that VBA is in its twilight time. The sun is going down on our beloved VBA. So, if necessary, slap yourself. And prepare for the future.

In spite of everything, Microsoft continues to support VBA, even to the point of superimposing cutting-edge technologies onto it, such as Web Services. A *Web Service* is just an Internet-based program. It used to mean a small program (perhaps merely a single function that you *consumed* as a client), but now Web Services can be of any size. In this chapter, I describe how to exploit existing Web Services by connecting your Office 2003 VBA programming to them. I also show you how to create your own Web Services.

To be ready for examples later in this chapter, please slap yourself and download the Office 2003 Web Services Toolkit 2.01 from this location:

```
www.microsoft.com/downloads/details.aspx?FamilyID=fa36018
a-e1cf-48a3-9b35-169d819ecf18&DisplayLang=en
```

Looking at Web Services

A traditional VBA module contains procedures (like a Sub), and a VBA class module contains a class or several classes. However, neither of these types of modules has a user interface. (For a user interface, add a UserForm.) Remember that modules are just repositories containing a collection of procedures (like a small DLL) that do various jobs, such as a group of macros.

Suppose you write a series of Sub procedures that work together to translate one currency into another. You put those Subs together in a module to assist you organize your work. If you move that module to the Web, making it available to other programs to access over the Internet, it's no longer described as a *module* (or DLL, or set of VBA macros). Instead, it is now described as a *Web Service.*

Web Service is just the latest name for a function or set of functions that do a job for a program. You *call* (the term *de rigueur* is *consume*) the service. When you call a service, you also usually provide some data: the parameters that you *pass* to the service. Suppose you want to translate $125 into another currency, such as German marks. The programming in the procedure(s) of the Web Service figures out what $125 equals in marks and returns the answer to your application by sending back 249.697 deutsche marks. Your program makes use of this information. The only difference between this process and a traditional function is that the Web Service is on the Web.

As so often happens, the phrase *Web Service* has drifted from its original meaning. It is now used as a general term for any Internet-based programming, no matter how large. Originally, it referred to a small, self-contained function, such as a currency translator. Web Services then progressed to larger, more complex services such as local weather (you pass your ZIP code to the service, and it sends back a paragraph describing the current local conditions or perhaps even a map) or maybe a scrolling news ticker that you could insert into your own Web page. Lately, Web Service has been stretched to include huge, distributed *enterprise solutions* — in other words, the entire suite of programs and databases that work together to represent the computerization of a giant business.

Given that the phrase can now be used to describe anything from a single function to a huge enterprise solution, the phrase no longer indicates the scale of the programming involved. Web Service now merely means programming that you communicate with via the Internet.

One advantage of using Web Services is that they're dynamic: They remain up-to-date. Obviously, the ratio of $ to marks changes minute by minute. You can't define this ratio in your source code. Therefore, if you need current conversion data, your program can consume a $ to marks Web Service that always provides the current, accurate exchange rate (thanks to the Internet).

The main difference between a Web Service and functions in a module, DLL, namespace, or assembly is that a Web Service isn't located on your computer's hard drive. It's on the Internet; thus, it could be part of a distributed programming solution. And, because it is on the Web, it must communicate with the caller in a special way to avoid firewall rejection. That special way is XML.

Discovering Why Web Services Matter

Web Services could prove to be an important programming technology in the coming years. Simply put, Web Services are the latest effort to bridge the communication gap between applications, operating systems, and platforms. Sometimes called *platform independence* or lately, *interoperability,* this communication problem has proven surprisingly difficult to solve. However, unlike previous attempts that have all more or less failed, Web Services and XML might actually succeed.

Web Services are *stateless.* ASP.NET, for example, accepts a request from a client, and then usually fulfills that request by sending information back to the client and dropping the connection. End of story. The client might do all kinds of things on its end with the data it got from the Service, but the server is finished with the transaction: It treats every incoming request as a separate request (even if from the same client). The server sees all incoming messages as unique requests, distinct from any previous requests. (Traditional FTP servers maintained an interactive session with the client, and this session could be lengthy.)

Statelessness solves several server-side data storage, communication, and timing problems. Web Services communicate via ordinary text XML, which obviously simplifies searching, programming, and just plain understanding the messages.

Being stateless and text-based also makes Web Services fundamentally platform-independent. In theory — and usually in practice — Web Services freely communicate between Macs and PCs, between contemporary data formats and legacy structures, and between local processes and remote ones: in a nutshell, between your data store format and mine.

A Web Service, however, involves more than just sending a message from one computer, requesting that a remote computer perform a job (process some data).

Understanding distributed computing

Some very important implications arise when you divide data and processing between more than one machine. Think of it as the adjustment you must make when you get married. It's like figuring out how to manage your money jointly with your new spouse. A joint checking account forces you to behave differently than you did when you were single. It's more complicated. For example, you have to share data and synchronize your deposits and withdrawals to avoid bouncing checks. You might even have to figure out some security measures, such as ways to communicate about your finances without letting others in on your secrets. What was once merely a computation job within your single checkbook now also becomes a communication problem between two checkbooks.

Likewise, in traditional computing, a programmer wrote procedures knowing various facts about the environment in which the procedures operate: which operating system is used, the language in which other procedures are written, and the location and structure of any data used by the procedures. In other words, the programmer was working within a predictable, stable, and fundamentally *local* environment.

Distributed computing is not local: not self-contained on a single hard drive. Distributed programming does not offer the programmer that kind of predictability. For example, the data might reside in Des Moines, on a machine running Linux, but the procedure that processes that data might sit on a computer in London running Windows. Web Services simplify the exchange information between distributed computers.

Although Web Services themselves are designed to be platform-independent, we programmers of course use a particular platform — and usually a single language — during the process of creating the Web Service. Programmers and developers need to work within an environment that offers them a rich set of useful and familiar tools: debugging features, pop-up lists of methods, an effective help system, and so on.

Web Services make a special demand on the programmer. Exchanged information must be translated into XML and communicated via Simple Object Access Protocol (SOAP) calls, which are a subset of XML. (Don't be fooled by the hopeful, but often misleading, use of the word *simple* here.)

Discovering the tools for translation

Fortunately, Office 2003 applications and VBA itself provide some tools to assist you in translating documents and other data into HTML or XML, along with other tools you can use to consume Web Services. Also, as you might expect, Visual Studio .NET provides powerful tools for dealing with the verbosity and complexity of XML and SOAP. The majority of Web Services programmers will probably choose Microsoft's Visual Studio .NET and Visual Basic .NET as their programming environment. Although it isn't the only Web Services programming environment, it appears destined to be the dominant one. (This isn't the result of some Microsoft marketing trick; .NET is just plain well-done.) What's more, it features many useful tools, including the capability to automatically generate SOAP envelopes, thus lifting that significant burden from the programmer.

VS.NET includes other important tools. For example, ADO.NET brings database programming up to speed with its support for disconnected DataSets and the capability to automatically translate data into XML for transmission to a remote computer. And of course, ASP.NET does for Web programming what ADO.NET does for database programming. The security technologies built into the .NET framework are extremely powerful yet not difficult for you to use in your own programs, as you see in Book VIII, Chapter 8. In sum, VS.NET boasts a powerful set of tools to assist programmers and developers in consuming, creating, and maintaining Web Services.

Reviewing Web Services Highlights

Web Services are an important, still-emerging technology. You want to get your mind around what they are and what they do. The following list covers the main points to remember about Web Services:

✦ **They are free of physical (geographical) and computer language constraints.** Because Web Services are made available on the Internet (note the option of keeping some of them on your local hard drive), they can be accessed from anywhere: from within your local intranet, from Zambia, or from anywhere else.

✦ **They are essentially a set of functions (or a collection of functions, although this can be a large collection).** Therefore, they do not include a user interface that is sent to the consumer: no text boxes, buttons, and so on for people to interact with. Think of a Web Service as a utility that sits there and responds to requests coming in from the Internet (or an intranet). However, remember that a Web Service can be a huge enterprise solution.

✦ **They communicate with applications and with one another by using the XML-based technology SOAP.** This eliminates the difficulties that have traditionally hampered computer-to-computer communications. In the past, proprietary database structures, unique object models, and incompatible computer languages have made life very difficult for programmers trying to reach out and touch a computer beyond the one they are working on. All too often, even the various applications on the same computer's hard drive could not efficiently communicate.

✦ **They can't transmit viruses.** Because a Web Service merely sends text (XML) over the Internet (rather than an executable), a Web Service cannot transmit a virus. Remember that firewalls are designed to block executables but to permit text to pass right through, so firewalls do not block Web Service communications. It is possible to embed virii in text strings, but let's not get into that. So far, text at least doesn't self-start.

✦ **They are based on a universal standardized language: XML.** Because they are written in XML, any application that can deal with XML can access any Web Service.

✦ **They permit applications to consume (use) the functions that the Web Service exposes (makes available).** In this way, Web Services are just like traditional classes. However, unlike traditional classes, Web Services do not require that the consumer application employ the same object model as the Web Service. Both the Web Service and its consumers rely instead on XML as their shared protocol. Traditional objects are said to be tightly coupled to specific object models. Web Services are not.

✦ **They decrease inefficiencies.** Perhaps most important in the long run, Web Services can circumvent traditional inefficiencies within organizations. For example, a salesman in Santa Barbara should be able to pretty easily access the data and software at the home office in Des Moines, thanks to the relative simplicity and universality offered by the Web Services communication model. This, anyway, is the hope. We'll see how it plays out in practice.

Solving migration issues

Most programmers now face a daunting task: migrating from traditional Windows-based programming to Internet-based programming. For many programmers, this migration is as challenging as anything they will face in their entire career. Not only must they cope with a new platform — the Internet — but they must also learn to employ novel technologies to ensure the stability and security of their applications.

And, ideally — but perhaps too idealistically, and only time will tell — Web Services might permit many of today's nonprogrammers to join in the fun. Web Service programming can be quite high-level yet relatively easy to use, particularly for people using Visual Basic .NET. Smaller Web Services can be assembled as objects into modular applications that, hopefully, at least some business people will be able to fashion themselves rather than relying on overworked, understaffed, and chronically behind IT staffs. After all, who is in a better position to know what's needed, and thus to update a business or e-business utility, than the business people who use it daily?

Perhaps IT staff can generate sufficiently well-designed and clearly described Web Service objects so that the actual applications employing those objects can be put together by business people. Salespeople, department managers, analysts, and so on could then join in the effort to improve a company's efficiency. In the Internet Age, most businesses must try to be as agile as possible, and Web Services offer great agility to a company transitioning to e-business.

Solving interoperability issues

Whatever way things eventually turn out, many experts believe that Web Services might just be (at long last) the solution to interoperability, which is one of computing's most serious and persistent problems. And if Web Services *do* solve the backward compatibility, messaging security, and cross-platform communication difficulties (the Tower of Babel that has plagued programmers and developers for decades), you'll certainly want to be among the early adopters who start converting to this new technology relatively soon.

Remember, in the fast-moving information economy, only agile companies survive. Think of Polaroid, which until quite recently was among the bluest of the blue chip stocks. Nothing was ever supposed to happen to a powerhouse company like that. Then, of course, along came the digital camera. Not too many people shake it like a Polaroid picture any more.

Seeing How Web Services and XML Dance

Web Services are not written in XML; rather, the source code is most likely a .NET language. However, the Web Service's communication with its consumer is translated into XML. Here are the three basic steps:

1. **An XML message (an XML document) is built by the consumer, requesting the Web Service.**

   This is quite similar to calling a function. You send the name of the service that you want to invoke and (optionally) parameters (data) if required. This message is sent over the Internet (or possibly just an intranet).

2. **The Web Service receives the XML message, translates the XML message if necessary, and processes it.**

   For example, if `ChangeToMarks (123)` is sent to a currency converter function, the *conversion* — processing the request — is done on the server where the Web Service resides. What's received by the Web Service is the name of the Web Service as well as any parameters (such as `123` in this example, which denotes the dollar amount) required by the service.

3. **To send the resulting data back to the consumer, the Web Service creates its own XML document containing the response data.**

   This message is then sent back to the consumer. In some cases, this step is not necessary. The Web Service might be performing a job that doesn't require a response.

Seeing Web Services at Work in Office 2003

Although not as sophisticated or efficient as the Web Services features in Visual Studio, Office 2003 does endeavor to make the connection to this latest programming technology.

For example, Office 2003 expands XML support in its applications. Excel and Access 2003 improve their XML support, and it's been now added to Word 2003. Office 2003 is also now integrated (meaning more compatible) with Visual Studio .NET using the Visual Studio .NET Tools for Office.

Replacing VBA with VB.NET

Just as VBA replaced WordBasic and AccessBasic several years ago, it's clear that VB.NET will eventually replace VBA. Nonetheless, a large number of expert Office developers want to leverage their current expertise, pushing Office applications and VBA to the limit. That's perhaps why Microsoft is attempting with Office 2003 to build bridges between future technologies like Web Services and legacy technologies like VBA.

Adding a Web Service to VBA code

Time to become a consumer. Follow these steps to consume (call) a Web Service in VBA:

1. **Download and install the Office 2003 Web Services Toolkit 2.01 from this address:**

    www.microsoft.com/downloads/details.aspx?FamilyID=fa36018a-e1cf-
        48a3-9b35-169d819ecf18&DisplayLang=en

2. **Open Word and press Alt+F11.**

The VBA editor opens.

3. **In the VBA editor, choose Tools⇨Web Service References.**

The Microsoft Office 2003 Web Services Toolkit dialog box opens, as shown in Figure 4-1.

4. **Type c (just the letter c) or some other letter into the Business Name field.**

5. **Click the Search button.**

It takes a while, but the Web Services "Yellow Pages" listings at Microsoft are searched for all Web Services starting with the letter *c*.

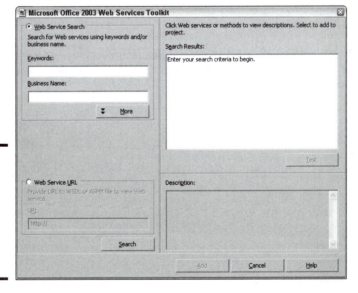

Figure 4-1:
Use this
dialog box
to add
a Web
Service to
your VBA
project.

**Book VIII
Chapter 4**

**Advanced
Internet VBA**

TIP

How do people let the world know of the existence of a Web Service? The "Yellow Pages" for Web Services is the UDDI (Universal Description, Discovery, and Integration) Business Registry (also known as *cloud services* or *UBR*). You can even set up your own registry in an intranet. It's just a searchable list of the names, addresses, and descriptions of Web Services.

6. When the list appears, click one of the services offered that sounds interesting to you.

You see a description of the service (although many don't offer this).

7. Click the Test button.

Internet Explorer opens with links to the service description (an XML-like file specifying with great redundancy the name, address, and parameters of the Web Service). You can examine this file if you wish or simply move on to Step 8.

8. Click the Web Service's name (a hyperlink).

You should now be able to test this service by entering parameters into a field and then invoking the Web Service to see the response. If you can't, go back to Step 6 and try a different service.

9. When you're finished testing a Web Service, you're ready to import it into your VBA module. Click Add.

Adding a Web Service to VBA is surprisingly easy because after you click Add, classes and code are added to your module.

After you add a Web Service, you're given instructions, error handling, class management, and example code demonstrating how to access the Web Service in your VBA projects, like this:

```
'This class was created by the Microsoft Office 2003 Web Services Toolkit.
'
'Created: 3/15/2004 05:01:18 PM
'
'Description:
'This class is a Visual Basic for Applications class representation of the Web
'service as defined by http://www.yorRM.com/Rea/Logon.wsdl.
'
'To Use:
'Dimension a variable as new clsws_Logon, and then write code to
'use the methods provided by the class.
'Example:
' Dim ExampleVar as New clsws_Logon
' debug.print ExampleVar.wsm_Logon("Sample Input")
'
'For more information, see Complex Types in Microsoft Office 2003
'Web Services Toolkit Help.
'
'Changes to the code in this class may result in incorrect behavior.
'
'*****************************************************************
```

You're not supposed to edit these new classes — just instantiate them and call them from other modules:

```
Dim ExampleVar as New clsws_Logon
debug.print ExampleVar.wsm_Logon("Sample Input")
```

For further information on consuming Web Services in your VBA Office 2003 applications, click the Help button shown in the dialog box in Figure 4-1. You can then examine the Office 2003 Web Services Toolkit Help file in your browser, as shown in Figure 4-2.

Figure 4-2: Find help here for using Web Services in Office 2003 VBA code.

Book VIII Chapter 4

Advanced Internet VBA

Creating Your First Web Service

In the preceding section, you can read how to consume (use) a Web Service. To *create* your own Web Services, you need to use Visual Studio .NET. In this section, you write and test Web Services of your own. Start by creating a Web Service template; just follow these steps:

1. **Choose File▷New▷Project in VB.NET.**

The New Project dialog box appears.

2. **Double-click the ASP.NET Web Service icon.**

A new project is created.

If the new project can't be created, you'll get a message to that effect. You need to ensure that you've installed IIS — Internet Information Services — and the necessary dependencies that support ASP.NET. Look at MSDN on the Web for instructions at

```
http://msdn.microsoft.com/library/default.asp?url=/
     library/en-us/iissdk/iis/newsystemarchitecture.asp
```

You first see a design window, and you can add controls to this window. But remember that a Web Service doesn't display any user interface, so it would be rather eccentric of you to add a button that no one will ever see. However, you might want to use some nonvisible controls, such as data connection controls.

3. **Click the <u>Click here to switch to code view</u> link in the center of the design window.**

You now see the code template. When VB.NET first creates a Web Service template for you, it provides this source code in the code window (Listing 4-1).

Listing 4-1:   Web Service Source Code

```
Imports System.Web.Services

<WebService(Namespace := "http://tempuri.org/")> _
Public Class Service1
    Inherits System.Web.Services.WebService

" Web Services Designer Generated Code "

    ' WEB SERVICE EXAMPLE
    ' The HelloWorld() example service returns the string Hello World.
    ' To build, uncomment the following lines then save and build the
    project.
    ' To test this web service, ensure that the .asmx file is the start
    page
    ' and press F5.
    '
    '<WebMethod()> Public Function HelloWorld() As String
    '      HelloWorld = "Hello World"
    ' End Function

End Class
```

To see how you write a Web Service and then test it, try creating a new Web Service that provides the current time and date. To write your own Web Service, follow these steps:

1. **Replace the** WEB SERVICE EXAMPLE **in Listing 4-1 (all those commented lines that begin with the ' character) with your own code.**

Delete the commented lines in the template and then type the following source code, shown in boldface:

```
Imports System.Web.Services

Imports System

<WebService(Namespace := "http://tempuri.org/")> _
Public Class Service1

     Inherits System.Web.Services.WebService

" Web Services Designer Generated Code "

<WebMethod()> Public Function WhatTimeIsIt() As String

        Dim s As String

        s = Now.ToString

        Return s

     End Function

   End Class
```

The `<WebService(Namespace:="http://tempuri.org/")>` element specifies that this is a special kind of class: a Web Service. Notice the `< >` symbols, which traditionally enclose an element in HTML. This `WebService` element can be omitted because ASP.NET understands that you are writing a Web Service: Its file extension is `.asmx`, which makes that clear. However, the element has its uses. It can include various attributes, including the namespace and also a `Description` attribute, like this:

```
<WebService(Description:="Provides the current date and
    time", Namespace:="http://tempuri.org/")> Public
    Class Service1
```

Also, you use the `<WebMethod()>` element to make it clear that the function is part of a Web Service. (You can include a `Description` attribute in this element, too.) *Note:* The `<WebMethod()>` element is not optional: You must include it because it's the only way that a remote client can see and access your function (method) from the outside.

This mingling of HTML-style source code (elements and attributes) with VB.NET code might seem a bit awkward at first, but you get used to it. Aside from those elements, the source code in this function is typical, familiar VB.NET.

2. **Press F5 to test this Web Service.**

You should see your browser fire up and display the information shown in Figure 4-3. (You can ignore the information about `tempuri` — temporary URI — and changing the default namespace for now. That's information you must deal with when deploying a real Web Service on the Internet.)

Figure 4-3:
If you include a Descrip-tion attribute, it is displayed at the top of this page.

The name of your Web Service is displayed as a hyperlink, as shown in Figure 4-3. In this example, it's named <u>WhatTimeIsIt</u>. (*Note:* If you provide a `Description` attribute for your `WebMethod`, it is displayed just below the link.)

3. **Click the Web Service name link.**

An Invoke button appears, as shown in Figure 4-4.

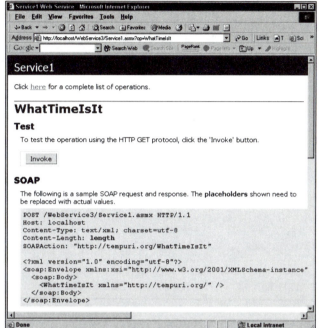

Figure 4-4:
Click the
Invoke
button to
run your
Web
Service.

4. **Click the Invoke button to imitate a request to your Web Service —
as if someone had sent the request over the Internet.**

Your service responds; see the result shown in Figure 4-5. Your Web
Service sent back the date and time as a string in XML format to the
remote client.

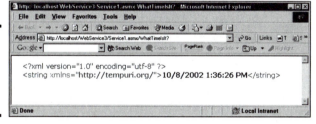

Figure 4-5:
This is
the Web
Service test
result.

Chapter 5: Working with .NET

In This Chapter

✔ **Discovering .NET**

✔ **Using software services**

✔ **Understanding Internet initiatives**

✔ **Using .NET database technologies**

✔ **Programming VB.NET**

*I*n the late 1990's, various Microsoft products began sporting the name *active:* Active Desktop, Active Directory, ActiveX, and so on. More recently, Microsoft began favoring a different term, namely the suffix *.NET,* as in Visual Studio .NET, Visual Basic .NET, ASP.NET, ADO.NET, and so on.

Time marches on. .NET enjoyed vogue status for approximately five years, but this term, too, is gently fading away. Microsoft server products aren't called .NET any more. And instead of referring to the upcoming version of Visual Studio as *.NET,* it's officially called *Visual Studio 2005.* Nonetheless, .NET is still used to describe the underlying technology, such as the collection of code libraries (the .NET framework). We might as well continue to use the term while acknowledging that it's in the twilight of its life.

Nevertheless, .NET gives you quite a variety of new skills for your programmer's bag of tricks. This chapter introduces you to the .NET tools and techniques that you might want to learn. This chapter is all about .NET for the BASIC programmer. You see how to employ software services, deal with issues involved in Internet programming, employ the powerful .NET database technologies, and, in general, continue on the path to .NET guru status.

Understanding .NET

The central concept around which all the .NET-based products circle is a technology designed for (you guessed it) programming that's Internet-centric.

.NET, like Microsoft's older COM technology, is not a single entity. Rather, it's a collection of tools and rich (feature-full) components, a programming and development environment, a runtime, a library of classes, a set of languages, and a group of robust built-in security features. .NET is also a highly effective way of programming for the Internet with strong database features. In .NET, you find the commitment to support XML-based, object-oriented, easily deployed, scalable, and reliable multiplatform computing.

Oh, yes, .NET is also an excellent system to use for traditional Windows programming, too.

That's quite an ambitious little solar system of new objects and technologies, all in orbit around the central idea of .NET.

.NET represents a major shift for developers and programmers. Driven by an effort to make programming more coherent and secure, and by the nature and requirements of Internet computing, it's being called the next wave in computing. Some argue that this shift from Windows-based to Internet-based computing is as profound as the shift from the text-based, colorless DOS world to the rich graphics of Windows. Perhaps. What isn't arguable is that .NET requires us programmers and developers to learn many new techniques, habits, and attitudes. Well, maybe we can keep some of the old attitudes. If you were snarky then, you're going to be snarky now, most likely.

Seeing the need for .NET

Think back to the late 70's when computing was mostly confined to IBM mainframes. These large centralized computers fed information to *dumb* terminals, which had very little computational power of their own: They were simply display devices with a dumb keyboard. Their entire reason for existence was to act as an interface between a human and the mainframe. Both memory and processing were contained on the central mainframe.

At the start of the 80's, processing and memory split off into millions of personal computers. And for the past 20 years, discrete, self-contained machines have dominated computing.

Perhaps we're now coming full circle back to where we started . . . but with a twist. In the next few years, some input/output units could become as small (and as dumb) as a cellphone. Your data might reside somewhere on the Internet, perhaps in a massive, centralized server farm or even distributed among many servers.

And that data might also be processed by services on the Internet that you subscribe to rather than applications that you purchase in a shrink-wrapped package. This computing model avoids the need for a dedicated personal computer, with its hard drive for storage, and lots of RAM and processing power located right there at your desk. Instead, you can access your virtual personal computer anywhere, anytime, using anything from a PDA to a huge wallscreen TV. Once again, I/O terminals might become dumb, connecting to remote data storage and processing.

If these predicted changes do occur (and some of them already appear to be underway), programmers will be required to make quite a few adjustments to their ways of working. .NET attempts to ease this transition while simultaneously anticipating the platform demanded by Internet-centric computing. For one thing, traditional method-driven (or procedure-driven) programming styles might have to shift to a more message-driven model.

Of course, you aren't forced to abandon your familiar programming techniques. You can use the Visual Studio .NET editor as well as VB.NET tools and techniques to produce traditional Windows programs just as you always have. In fact, you can produce better programs faster after you learn .NET techniques and discover how to tap into the huge .NET set of built-in classes (the Framework).

.NET includes many familiar VB elements but sometimes gives them new names. Errors, for example, are now called *exceptions,* which sounds so much nicer. "Yes, boss, I'm going to work on some of my exceptions today." (Oh, yes, I forgot. You can't use the word *boss* anymore. We're all *associates* now, aren't we? Some of us are just more *associated* than others.)

Seeing the benefits of VB.NET

VB.NET brings with it many new ideas and capabilities — such as overloading and inheritance — which were never part of traditional (VB 6 and earlier) Visual Basic.

For decades, people have been trying to design languages and operating systems that are platform-independent. In other words, in theory, a language or system should be able to run on all kinds of different machines, of all sizes, made by different manufacturers, with different operating systems. Internet programming is similar: A program should adapt itself to both a large-screen TV as well as a PDA. So far, this has been an elusive goal.

But with all the new and varying sizes of computer display devices (television/ Internet boxes, hand-helds, car computers, cellphones, and videogame/ Internet devices) as well as all the new platforms (the Internet itself is a platform, in a sense), platform-independence is becoming more than merely an aspiration. It's becoming a necessity.

.NET must be able to run in a variety of environments. One primary thrust of .NET is that it has to be compatible with many possible devices as well as various programming languages, data stores, and even different processes running at different speeds from different hard drives located different places around in the world. The programmer's world is no longer a predictable, coherent place.

The Internet is, of course, driving these changes, and the changes run deep. There must be new programming styles, new user interfaces, and new ways of communicating between applications and objects. By definition, the Internet is a vast collection of loosely connected objects. Another way of saying this is that the Web is *highly distributed.* The Internet stores bits and pieces here and there, and each new page you visit can contain a different collection of information coming from different servers, working in different computer languages.

And of course, large-scale applications must be able to ramp up from zero to perhaps thousands of simultaneous users: That is, they must be *scalable.*

Using .NET to Facilitate Software Services

Another feature of this Internet-centric trend is that software might increasingly be sold as a *service.* You won't buy a CD/manual package in the store; instead, you'll sign up for a subscription to an application, and the application will be automatically upgraded as bugs are fixed and new features are added. This marketing model resembles cable TV subscriptions, from which you choose among various packages of channels, and the service is delivered to you continuously.

Imagine that your data, applications (services), and any other computing items are stored in a secure location (or spread among several locations) on the Internet rather than on your local hard drive as they are now. This Internet-storage approach has several advantages.

✦ **You can access your data from any Internet device,** no matter where you are or what kind of localized storage the device has.

✦ **You also lessen the version problem,** no longer having to use the old Windows "briefcase" utility to attempt to synchronize your files between your home, office, and portable machines.

Wireless Internet access is an important element in this next phase of personal computing.

Another facet of services is that small, self-contained libraries or components can reside on the Internet (or intranets) and easily be accessed thanks to the light, flexible communications protocol SOAP (Simple Object Access Protocol), built upon XML and usable throughout the .NET technology.

Using .NET for Internet initiatives

How about .NET capabilities for Internet programming? Are you kidding? With ASP.NET technology, the entire VB.NET language is at your disposal (not just some limited scripting language, as in the past) when you want to create Web pages and sites. .NET is Internet-centric, to be sure, but you can also write dedicated Windows-style programs quite effectively with .NET. Using a technique called *code-behind,* you can program with VB.NET in one editor window while a separate window contains HTML (the traditional Web programming language). The code-behind technique is also used as a way of bringing VB.NET to Office programming, as you can see later in Book VIII, Chapter 6.

Using .NET and databases

Don't overlook the new .NET database management capabilities. ADO.NET works well with XML and also takes detached recordsets (now called *DataSets*) to a new level of detachment. This feature is particularly useful when you're using ASP.NET Web Services to transmit and receive data. ADO.NET has been designed to accept data in many formats and from a variety of sources. It's object-oriented, of course, and also works well with relational data.

The main reason to move to ADO.NET is to make database management highly scalable. Briefly, ADO .NET neatly solves problems related to large local area networks and the Internet. For most of the history of personal computing, your database application could establish a connection to a database and keep that connection open until the user was finished reading or modifying the data.

This approach works okay if only a few people (perhaps ten or so) need a connection with the database at the same time. However, hundreds (or possibly thousands) of people on the Internet can't simultaneously look through your catalog of Irish flannel sweaters. They simply can't all be connected at once! This problem is *scalability.*

For example, can your application handle 5 clients and then grow gracefully to deal with 5,000 in the days before Christmas? Or like Microsoft's Access database system (and others), will it grind to a halt and smolder as soon as more than 10 connections are open?

In ADO.NET, you use *disconnected DataSets,* which are copies of data from a database. Here's what happens: A brief connection to the server's database is made while a DataSet is checked out. Then the connection is broken. The DataSet is sent to the requesting client application. The client can keep the DataSet as long as necessary and manipulate the data as much as permitted. When the client is finished and if the client wants to update the database, a new (and brief) connection is established with the server database. The DataSet is submitted to the server, which decides whether to merge the changes into the database. When using this library model (check out/check back in), your database system becomes quite scalable. The server database is uncoupled from any sustained connections to clients. Do you see how similar this approach is to Web Services statelessness described in Book VIII, Chapter 4?

Finding .NET Programming Help

Time to examine the actual programming. True, .NET programming is unforgiving, but so are earlier versions of Visual Basic (or indeed, any other computer language).

Yet in many ways, a computer is the least flexible thing you'll ever try to communicate with. Put a comma — just one little innocent comma! — in the wrong place, and the computer language completely misunderstands what you're asking it to do. Misspell a word, even only slightly, and the compiler doesn't understand it at all. There's no getting around it: At this stage of their development, computer languages are extremely literal critters. Communicating with them means doing it their way or not at all.

However, in spite of this literal-mindedness, VB helps you out in many ways when you're programming. First, some of VB's *commands* — the words in VB's language — are familiar English words like *stop, end, text,* and *timer.* Second, you can sometimes combine VB commands into statements that are quite similar to English sentences: for example, `If Dollars = 12 Then PayBill()`.

To be sure, punctuation, word order, and other elements must be exact, but Visual Basic hates to let you fail. While you're learning to program, you can turn on various kinds of training wheels that are built into VB.NET. For example, if you make a punctuation error or misspell a command, VB.NET (even more frequently than VBA) makes suggestions.

Unforgiving gestures

Of course, human languages are sometimes unforgiving, too, as any American who hitchhikes in Europe quickly discovers. If you move your thumb up and down, a passing driver might slam on his brakes but only so he can jump out and pound you to a pulp. That thumb gesture means something very nasty in some other parts of the world, politely expressed as *sit on this.*

Computers may indeed be highly literal, but they make up for it by offering you tireless and watchful assistance. For example, if you mistype a VB command, VB itself immediately shows you the error and suggests how to fix it. And if you're still not exactly sure what a particular command does — or how to use it — descriptions of each command (and often source code examples) are only a keypress away (F1, to be specific). Just click a command in your programming code to select it and then press F1. With VB, you're rarely left hanging and twisting in the wind.

Too, IntelliSense features such as Auto Syntax Check and Auto Quick Info are always available. If you don't remember the various capabilities (members) of a given object, IntelliSense lists them for you and also shows you their parameters and the syntax. Even experienced programmers are unlikely to turn off IntelliSense features. And although you're still getting used to the idea of telling a machine what you want it to do (also known as *programming*), these various kinds of helpers are invaluable.

Chapter 6: Using Visual Studio Tools for Office 2003

In This Chapter

✔ **Understanding installation issues**

✔ **Dealing with setup problems**

✔ **Communicating between .NET and Office**

✔ **Does this tool have a use?**

✔ **Considering alternatives**

✔ **Creating your first VSTO project**

*W*ith Visual Studio Tools for Office (VSTO) installed, you get some help building a bridge between traditional Office programming with VBA as well as the future of Office programming, VB.NET. VSTO also supports the quasi-Java, hybrid language C#.

Just as using ASP.NET's code-behind feature allows you to employ all the tools and power of the VB.NET language in your Internet programming, so, too, are these advantages yours when you use VB.NET as code-behind your Office 2003 programming.

However, note these two warnings before you run out and spend $200–$450 for a version of VSTO:

✦ You can do pretty much the same things that VSTO does with other technologies — technologies that you probably already own, might already understand how to use, and that are likely more stable (at this point in VSTO's life cycle). These technologies are explored in various other chapters in this book, but they're explicitly listed in the upcoming section, "The five ways to program Office." You might want to choose to avoid VSTO until it's a bit more, um, *finished.* Or maybe VSTO will work better for you than it did for me.

✦ Continuing with this "more stable" concept, I simply cannot get the version of VSTO that I have to work at the time of this writing. So the example in this chapter goes fine up to a certain, crucial point, and then stops with my confession that I cannot go any further. The crucial point? When I press F5 to actually see the program that I built execute. It's supposed to send some data from the VB.NET VSTO template code to Excel. Excel does open up, ready, indeed fairly quivering, to receive this data.

But, alas, a security warning appears. This warning tells me that *current .NET security policy does not permit this project to run from this folder. . . .* Well, ho-hum. Never mind that this is a development computer, with .NET security set at its lowest possible level (no security at all), and that for years I've written and tested all kinds of other .NET projects on this machine, with no such security troubles. Don't hate me for suspecting that it's VSTO, not me or my machine, that is likely the source of this little problem here.

So, you've been warned. This chapter must remain theoretical. Unlike all the other chapters in this book, I cannot present you with working examples. I can only lead you to the final step, where what should happen — data moving from .NET to Excel — simply does not. Thanks, virii authors, under whatever rocks you hide, for making all our lives more difficult by making all these convoluted, multilayered, deliberately confounding security measures necessary.

Some programmers on the VSTO public newsgroup have not had the problems I faced. Some on the newsgroup report problems; others have gotten the system up and running okay. Maybe you'll be one of the lucky ones. The newsgroup is `microsoft.public.vsnet.vstools.office`.

Following Correct Setup

You must follow a particular order when installing the technologies that work together with VSTO. First, Visual Studio .NET 2003 must be installed, then Office 2003, and finally VSTO. You can obtain VSTO via an MSDN subscription or purchase it from software sources such as Amazon. It's around $200 for the upgrade version (if you currently own versions of VB, some Office development products, Visual InterDev, Visual Studio, and lots of other products). VSTO costs $450 for the non-upgrade version.

If you're interested in VSTO, visit the Microsoft site titled "How to Buy: Visual Studio Tools for the Microsoft Office System."

If You Have Problems

Before going any further, you might have difficulties when first installing VSTO. I certainly did. Dealing with temperamental software isn't uncommon when the software is brand-new. There are many glittering, interacting side effects, and several things have to be *just so* for things to work correctly. This technology, of course, will stabilize over time.

The first problem popped up when I chose File⇨New⇨Project, selected Microsoft Office System Projects in the left pane to open that node, and then under that, selected Visual Basic Projects. I double-clicked Word Document in the right pane.

The wizard opened. I left the defaults (Create New Document) but changed the location of the document to a temp file on drive C:. I clicked Finish, and the wizard wrote the code.

However, at the top of the code window, an error was flagged (with the saw-tooth underline) on this line of the code:

```
Imports Office = Microsoft.Office.Core
```

This reference is supposed to be automatically added to any new VSTO project that you start in VB.NET, but it wasn't. The solution is to choose Project⇨Add Reference, click the COM tab, locate Microsoft Office 11.0 Object Library in the list of code libraries, double-click it, and then click OK to close the dialog box. The reference is then added to the project and also now appears in the Solution Explorer list of References.

However, if your problem is deeper than this (because you cannot find Microsoft Office 11.0 Object Library in the COM libraries list), you now need to reinstall the PIAs (Primary Interop Assemblies; don't ask) for Office 11. To do that, follow these steps:

1. **Open Control Panel and close all other applications.**
2. **Double-click the Add Remove Programs icon.**

    The Add Remove Programs dialog box opens.
3. **Click Microsoft Office Professional Edition 2003 to select it.**
4. **Click the Change button.**
5. **Select Add or Remove Features.**
6. **Click Next.**
7. **Select the Choose Advanced Customization of Applications check box.**
8. **Click Next.**

**Book VIII
Chapter 6**

Using Visual Studio Tools for Office 2003

9. **Ensure that the .NET Programmability Support node is assigned to Run from My Computer from the following nodes:**

   - Microsoft Office Excel.

   - Microsoft Office Word.

   - Office Tools. (This node is called Microsoft Forms 2.0 .NET Programmability Support here.)

   - Microsoft Graph (under Office Tools).

10. **Click Update.**

    Your PIAs should be added (or repaired). Now you can rerun VB.NET and add the Microsoft Office 11.0 Object Library as described earlier in this chapter.

Communicating between .NET and Office Applications

Given that you can instantiate Office applications from .NET programs without resorting to VSTO, why bother with it? For example, this next VB.NET code example (Listing 6-1) instantiates Word, types something, saves the document, and then closes the instance. First, choose Project⇨Add Reference and then click the COM tab. Add the Microsoft Word 11.0 Object Library to your project by double-clicking it in the list box and then clicking OK to close the Add Reference dialog box.

At the top of the code window, type this:

```
Imports Microsoft.Office.Interop
```

Then type Listing 6-1 into the `Form_Load` event.

Listing 6-1:   Instantiating Word via Plain .NET

```
Private Sub Form1_Load(ByVal sender As System.Object, ByVal e
        As System.EventArgs) Handles MyBase.Load


    Dim WordApp As Word.Application
    Dim WordDoc As Word.Document
    WordApp = CType(CreateObject("word.Application"),
        Word.Application)
    WordDoc = CType(WordApp.Documents.Add, Word.Document)

    Dim s As String = "See, this text has been added
        to our new document. Now we'll save it as
        C:\test.doc."
```

```
Dim sln As Word.Selection
sln = WordApp.Selection
sln.TypeText(s)

WordDoc.SaveAs("c:\test.doc")

WordDoc = Nothing
WordApp = Nothing


End Sub
```

Why use VSTO?

Aside from the fact that I cannot yet get VSTO to actually work, the more I worked with it, the more I wondered why VSTO actually exists. Why use it at all? What benefits does it offer that you cannot get from other, more tested and traditional technologies?

If you attach the `Microsoft.Office.Interop` assembly to a .NET project, you can quite easily instantiate and manipulate Office applications' objects from within .NET. This has the advantage of allowing you to create Office solutions that work with Access, Outlook, and all the other apps, while VSTO is limited to Word and Excel.

There must be something gained by VSTO or it likely wouldn't have been invented, would it?

Various white papers and other documents describing VSTO mention all the benefits of .NET. Well, I agree that .NET certainly brings lots of goodies to the programmer's toolkit. .NET offers many advantages over older technologies. But you can easily add .NET to your Office solutions without resorting to VSTO. All .NET benefits are also available to a programmer when you create a front end in .NET and just instantiate Office apps. Likewise, those .NET benefits are available as well if you build COM add-ins. (See the section on programming your own add-in in Book VIII, Chapter 1.)

White papers also mention such benefits as in-process execution, event handling, and managed code. But none of these features is exclusive to VSTO; you can get them using other approaches (described later).

These white papers (and some mauve papers, too) also put forward the idea that VSTO is *document-centric*. (Users can click an XLS file in Windows Explorer, for instance, Excel starts running, and that workbook is loaded.) The user opens a document (or a creates a new document based on a template), and your code is loaded along with that document.

But again, it's not at all difficult to achieve this behavior without using VSTO. Just put a VBA `AutoExec` macro into a DOC (or other) file. This macro automatically executes your VB.NET application (via the VBA `Shell` function) when the document is loaded. Docu-centricity, right?

What, I ask, finally, what does VSTO offer that cannot otherwise be achieved using existing technologies? The answer seems to boil down to *nothing*. E-mail me at `richardm52@hotmail.com` if you know of some advantage that VSTO confers.

When you use VBA code, the code does stay in the document. So, if you need to update that code or fix a bug, you have lots of copies to replace all over the office. That, along with various other drawbacks and weaknesses of the VBA language (such as XML deficiencies) are solved when you add .NET to your Office programming tools.

When you use VSTO, you can take the more convenient .NET approach and store your assembly (code libraries) at a public network location. This way, all user's documents — no matter how many of these exist or where they're located — use this single assembly. This simplifies security somewhat and considerably simplifies maintenance. To change something in the assembly, just delete the existing version and replace it with the new version. (Of course, this seems simpler to describe than it turns out to be in practice. You must confront the multitudes of .NET security settings for your clients, install .NET itself, deal with PIAs, and other issues.)

But using VSTO is simply not the only way to add .NET capabilities to Office programming. And unless I — and others — are missing something, VSTO brings nothing to the table that you cannot find by using alternative, more stable and tested, approaches. VSTO is merely one way among several to manage Office 2003 applications programmatically. You might want to consider the advantages of employing alternative technologies rather than VSTO. To be fair, perhaps VSTO is more stable and effective now than it was when I worked with it while writing this book. Products do improve. You might want to research VSTO a bit more to see whether it fits in with your plans or needs.

The five ways to program Office

Here is a list of the ways you can program Office; there are five primary approaches:

✦ **Use classic VBA and instantiate other Office applications as necessary if you want to create a solution larger than a single application.**

VBA code executes and (except for Outlook) is stored within the application where the code resides. A Word DOC file, therefore, can contain a VBA application. Such code executes in process. VBA code is p-code, not compiled native code, so there is some degradation of performance, if slight. However, because the code executes in-process, you gain a compensating speed boost when interacting with Office object members.

✦ **Use Visual Basic 6 or some other COM-aware language.**

✦ **Create a front end in VB.NET that manipulates instantiated Office objects, as illustrated by Listing 6-1.**

You get all the benefits of .NET. You can choose to use .NET forms as your user interface, or you can even make this approach Office-document-centric. To do that, the user can click a DOC file that includes a VBA macro named AutoExec that automatically executes your VB.NET application (via the VBA Shell function).

✦ **Create an add-in, as illustrated in Book VIII, Chapter 1 in the section about programming your own add-in.**

Add-ins use compiled native code and also run in-process, thus avoiding the slight speed penalty exacted when either of these conditions are not met. As the example in Book VIII, Chapter 1 illustrates, a single COM add-in can automatically load within multiple Office applications (either at application startup or on demand, depending on your specification). COM add-in code created in .NET is managed code.

✦ **Use VSTO.**

VSTO offers a way to employ managed code that runs in-process and can respond directly to Office application events, but these behaviors are simply not unique to VSTO.

Of course, add-ins run in-process, and you can handle events with add-ins or other VB.NET front-end applications. For example, to respond to a document close event from within VB.NET code, you can modify Listing 6-1 (the example code earlier in this chapter) by adding an event handler:

```
Dim WithEvents WordApp As Word.Application
Dim WithEvents WordDoc As New Word.Document


Private Sub Form1_Load(ByVal sender As System.Object,
        ByVal e As System.EventArgs) Handles MyBase.Load
```

```
        WordApp = CType(CreateObject("word.Application"),
            Word.Application)
        WordDoc = CType(WordApp.Documents.Add, Word.Document)
        WordApp.Visible = True

        Dim s As String = "See, this text has been added
            to our new document. Now we'll save it as
            C:\test.doc."

        Dim sln As Word.Selection
        sln = WordApp.Selection
        sln.TypeText(s)

    End Sub
    Private Sub EventHandler() Handles WordDoc.Close
        MsgBox("EventHandler caught event.")    ' Handle the
            event.
    End Sub
```

Understanding VSTO

VSTO is limited at the present time to creating Word (DOC or DOT) or Excel projects, although it's likely that the technology will be extended to other Office 2003 applications, particularly Access and Outlook.

The .NET IDE (Integrated Design Environment) is a very powerful suite of tools for the programmer — far more capable and sophisticated than the VBA editor in Office 2003 applications. Given a choice, any serious Office 2003 developer — or indeed pretty much any programmer doing most kinds of Windows or .NET programming — likely prefers the Visual Studio programming environment.

Microsoft marches on. The term *IDE* is being replaced with *MDE* in some products. What do you suppose the *M* stands for?

Here's a little list (not in order of importance) of many of the things that I like about .NET, and why I left my familiar, beloved VBA and Visual Basic 6 for it:

✦ **Immense power:** The .NET framework is huge and really quite wonderful. You cannot exhaust it. The framework contains effective, specialized, generally powerful classes that can accomplish whatever you might need to do. (Database, Internet, security, and nearly all other kinds of programming are supported here with advanced tools and versatile classes.)

✦ **A brand-new language:** VB.NET language is not merely a revision of VBA or VB 6. Instead, it was rewritten from the ground up to be a brand-new, fully object-oriented programming (OOP) language. And if you aren't all that much of a fan of OOP, VB.NET allows you to easily ignore those extra features.

✦ **Server Explorer:** The .NET IDE also includes Server Explorer (choose View⇨Server Explorer), which is handy for adding database connections, creating schemas in the XML designer, accessing your intranet, adding, editing, and deleting tables and columns. You can even create a database with it.

✦ **Backward compatibility:** In .NET, you can use classic VBA and VB6 functions if you prefer, mixing them in with .NET code as you will. You can also add classic VB Windows forms to Office solutions. These forms are superior to the UserForms available via VBA.

✦ **The best programming editor tools:** Just one example (of many) is the VB.NET debugging facilities, which are among the most thoughtfully organized and robust available.

✦ **XML:** Extensive XML and namespace support.

✦ **ADO.NET:** An advanced, highly scalable, database management technology.

✦ **ASP.NET:** Ditto for highly scalable Internet programming.

VB.NET — like the other VS.NET languages — runs under the supervision of the common language runtime (CLR), thereby earning Microsoft's new phrase *managed code.* Such code is *validated* (checked to see that it doesn't violate memory restrictions and other illegal behaviors). It also offers code-based security features unavailable to unmanaged (that is, non-.NET languages) code. However, compared with older languages — particularly the VBA built into Office applications — .NET requires that you deal with a bit of a learning curve with the programming, deployment (this is actually quite a bit easier), and security settings. Also, although communication between .NET and Office objects is generally quite smooth, there are a few data type discrepancies that must be dealt with, although rarely.

Creating Your First Visual Studio Tools for Office Project

To see how to work with VSTO, first install VSTO on your computer and then follow these steps:

1. **Choose File⇨New⇨Project in Visual Studio.**

   You see the New Project dialog box.

2. **In the Project Types pane on the left side of the dialog box, open the Microsoft Office System Projects node, as shown in Figure 6-1.**

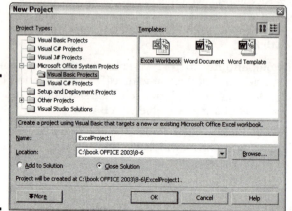

Figure 6-1: Here you see the new project types that VSTO adds to Visual Studio.

3. **Click the Visual Basic Projects entry, as shown in Figure 6-1.**

   You see the three possible project templates: Excel Workbook, Word Document, and Word Template.

4. **Double-click the Excel Workbook icon in the dialog box.**

   The dialog box closes, and the VSTO Wizard opens. You can build your new project by using either an existing document or a new one.

5. **Select the Create New Document radio button.**

6. **Click Finish.**

   The wizard builds a template for you. Actually, it's an Excel Workbook, with some code in it. The template includes `Open` and `BeforeClose` events.

7. **Click the + next to Generated Initialization Code in the code window.**

   You see the code in Listing 6-2, along with some warnings not to tamper with some of the code.

Listing 6-2: **Look but Don't Touch!**

```
Region "Generated initialization code"

    ' Default constructor.
    Public Sub New()
    End Sub

    ' Required procedure. Do not modify.
    Public Sub _Startup(ByVal application As Object, ByVal
            workbook As Object)
        ThisApplication = CType(application,
            Excel.Application)
        ThisWorkbook = CType(workbook, Excel.Workbook)


    End Sub

    ' Required procedure. Do not modify.
    Public Sub _Shutdown()
        ThisApplication = Nothing
        ThisWorkbook = Nothing
    End Sub

    ' Returns the control with the specified name on
            ThisWorkbook's active worksheet.
    Overloads Function FindControl(ByVal name As String) As
Object
        Return FindControl(name, CType(ThisWorkbook.
            ActiveSheet, Excel.Worksheet))
    End Function

    ' Returns the control with the specified name on the
            specified worksheet.
    Overloads Function FindControl(ByVal name As String,
            ByVal sheet As Excel.Worksheet) As Object
        Dim theObject As Excel.OLEObject
        Try
            theObject = CType(sheet.OLEObjects(name),
            Excel.OLEObject)
            Return theObject.Object
        Catch Ex As Exception
            ' Returns Nothing if the control is not found.
        End Try
        Return Nothing
    End Function
#End Region
```

Visual Studio added this interesting feature to Visual Basic: code that is displayed to you but that you are not supposed to modify. That's a bit like leaving a bone near a dog and saying, "STAY" to the poor creature, but there you have it: ' Required procedure. Do not modify. (Look at this, honey . . . but don't touch it. Microsoft programmers can be such *teases!*)

Actually, you should make up your own mind. Some areas of "hidden" regions *can* be usefully modified. (Psst: You *do* sometimes want to modify parts of the forbidden source code zones, no matter what the police say.)

For example, if you want to make something happen when an object (such as this Public Class OfficeCodeBehind) is instantiated, you can insert your code into the *constructor* (the procedure that executes when an object is constructed):

```
' Default constructor.
Public Sub New()
End Sub
```

When to touch the untouchable

Even though you'll find the ominous *do not modify* warnings here and there in the template's code, you sometimes must make changes. For example, this line of code would have to be edited were you to change the name of the class. This class is instantiated when a user opens the workbook you're working on, and its name is OfficeCodeBehind:

```
<Assembly: System.ComponentModel.DescriptionAttribute
           ("OfficeStartupClass, Version=1.0, Class=
           ExcelProject1.OfficeCodeBehind")>
```

Adding your code

Now you want to try adding a bit of code to find out how to work with a code-behind project like this one. Into the workbook's Open event, type this:

```
' Called when the workbook is opened.
    Private Sub ThisWorkbook_Open() Handles ThisWorkbook.Open

        Dim r As Excel.Range = ThisApplication.Range("A1")
        r.Value = 12

    End Sub
```

Press F5. If all security systems permit it and if the code-behind system is stabilized, you should see Excel start running and the value 12 placed into the worksheet.

In my computer, security settings *somewhere* (perhaps VSTO mucked up .NET) refuse to permit the code to execute behind the worksheet. So, although Excel does start, it refuses to engage. The VB.NET project is not permitted to execute from this folder.

The .NET code-access security system is complex. As this book goes to press, the version of VSTO that I have has no security configuration options in its wizard. They are evidently supposed to be accessible on the second page of the Microsoft Office Project Wizard, as shown in Figure 6-2.

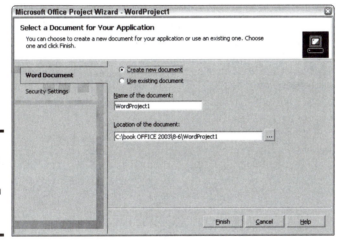

Figure 6-2:
No security options are available on this wizard page.

Figure 6-2 appears just before you click the Finish button (described in Step 6 in the step list in the earlier section, "Creating Your First Visual Studio Tools for Office Project"). It seems that you should be able to obviate security, as shown in Figure 6-2. But the version of the wizard that I had while working on this book had those capabilities disabled.

If you have a similar experience, you might be tempted to try adjusting the .NET security settings. However, I suggest that if your other .NET programming executes just fine — as mine has for years — the .NET settings are likely as they should be. You must wait for a version of VSTO that deals more effectively with security issues for us programmers who, obviously, need to be able to test our own programming on our own machines.

Or, as I did, you could ask questions on the VSTO newsgroup mentioned earlier in this chapter. Or you could retire and move to Florida with Amber or Mysti, David or Joe, your preferred other.

Adjusting .NET security (don't do this)

If you want to look into your computer's .NET configuration, here's how:

For Windows 2000 Professional, go to the Administrative Tools group in Control Panel and run the Microsoft .NET Framework Configuration. For Windows 2000 Server or Windows .NET Server, choose Start⇨Programs⇨ Administrative Tools⇨Microsoft .NET Framework Configuration. In XP Professional, from Control Panel, double-click the Administrative Tools icon and then double-click the Microsoft .NET Framework Wizards (or Configuration).

But it's really not .NET that's causing this problem: It's VSTO. So I advise you to just use the other .NET-Office 2003 bridges described in this chapter until VSTO gets its act together. And even then, what does VSTO really bring to the table that other approaches don't? E-mail me if you know the answer: richardm52@hotmail.com.

Chapter 7: Office 2003 Security

In This Chapter

✔ Understanding Office 2003 security

✔ Using Information Rights Management (IRM)

✔ Going beyond IRM

✔ Virus protection

✔ Using file- and folder-based security

✔ Managing encryption

✔ Removing comments

✔ Preventing tracing

✔ Setting macro security

✔ Signing and hashing code

You've seen those New York apartment doors covered with multiple deadbolts, chains, and rods. Is there a funnier or sadder topic in computing today than security? All the storm and fury, all the king's men, all the billions of dollars thrown at the problem — and it's no closer to being solved than it ever was or ever will be.

News flash: This problem cannot be solved. Technology cannot eliminate viciousness or foolishness without destroying human nature in the process. Has bank robbery been stopped? Mail fraud? Con games or pipe bombs? As long as there are people, some will be mean and childish, and others will be foolish enough to be vulnerable to the mean ones.

What *can* be done is to improve computer security so that malicious and foolish people have less impact than they currently do. For example, Office 2003 now includes an Anti-Virus API (Application Programmers Interface) that, among other things, allows commercial antivirus software to examine a document for virii after a user opens it but before any VBA code is permitted to execute. That's in addition to examining executables when first downloaded, always watching what's running in RAM, looking at e-mail, and so on.

The same phenomenon — layer upon layer of security measures like a door covered with locks — describes current computer security measures, yet virii routinely blossom around the world, rapidly infecting millions of machines within a few days.

Getting to the Heart of the Problem: People

The primary security problem is people: to be more specific, people who are nitwits. You can spend $20,000 to install professional hardware firewall, antivirus utilities, spyware detection, worm blockers, and all the rest, but when one silly person on your network opens an infected e-mail and executes the attachment, you've got trouble.

Think of it this way: Install a solid steel door in your apartment and add 35 deadbolts. But how much good does all this do if you're brainless enough to open the door to a stranger who says, "Hey! I'm trying to get $25 million out of Nigeria. Will you help if I give you some of the millions?" Knock, knock. "Want to see a *shocking* picture of Misti or Amber?" "Well, heck yeah!" Candygram. Land Shark.

Hope springs eternal

In spite of the fact that there's no way this side of heaven to ever be entirely secure, people do keep trying. Some of it is understandably psychological: Installing that steel door probably makes you feel more secure, and that is worth something. At least they can't set fire to it.

Note the implicit paradox here: You're reading information about security technologies in Office 2003 and Windows. But some information should remain secret, no? And there's lots more info out there on the Internet.

Someone has to implement, maintain, and enforce security measures. Administrators, IT professionals, developers . . . all of us need to know how to manage these security technologies (I couldn't get VSTO to work in the preceding chapter of this mini-book because of security issues.) But face it: Some technically astute people work for the dark side and have access to the same information that we do.

Security in today's computing systems often suffers from the weakest-link problem. For example, everyone in an organization must protect their password effectively for the LAN to remain entirely secure. Everyone must be sophisticated enough to understand the danger if they answer a phone call like this: "Hi, Jimmy in IT here. We're conducting a routine password test. Please type in your password now. Done? OK. That's working fine. Good. Now read it back to me off your screen, just for verification. Thanks! Bye." Whammo! That bad guy is *in*.

Some protection helps

However, layered security can offer some protection against such tricks. For example, even if an employee gives out a password, that employee might belong to a restricted group: that is, someone without unlimited permissions. So the damage (to file erasure or privacy attack) remains limited to the extent of that person's file-access permission level. In most security situations, multiple security strata do offer this kind of buffering against a total breach of your intranet.

Also, today's best systems tend to require extreme verification. All the layers of a security system must grant permission to the caller (human or computer) trying to access a hard drive, registry, or the security features themselves.

Understanding Office 2003 Security Initiatives

If you and your co-workers already know how to intelligently encrypt your documents, how to use a firewall effectively, not to open e-mail attachments or otherwise expose your machines to executables, and to frequently back up your work, you can probably skip this chapter. Encryption and backing up are the primary defenses against attacks of any kind. Other defenses — such as antivirus software — are less useful. Nonetheless, Office 2003 comes with lots of security features that, in many cases, can limit the damage if you don't carefully follow the two golden rules: encrypt and back up your work.

The security features in Office 2003 and .NET are considerable. You owe it to yourself to familiarize yourself with them and to find a balance between sufficiently strong security and the inconvenience that too much security causes.

Why consider .NET security along with Office 2003? Just as .NET will eventually replace VBA for Office programming, .NET security features will replace VBA security features. What California is to the rest of America, .NET is to the rest of Microsoft products: the wave of the future. However, covering .NET security is beyond the scope of this book.

Office 2003 continues the endless process of adding new security features, albeit a claim made by everyone, everywhere, about everything. You must come to grips with the new security features, though, if only to understand what they can and cannot do to protect us.

Using IRM

Consider Information Rights Management (IRM), which works with Word, Excel, and PowerPoint but not Access. You can specify that a document cannot be sent as an attachment to e-mail, has a limited lifetime, and cannot be copied. (The PrintScreen key is disabled.) But someone can still take a picture of the screen with a camera. Also, third-party screen capture utilities can sometimes be used to capture a graphic version of the document.

IRM can restrict individual users from

✦ Copying a document or portions of it

✦ Printing a document

✦ Using VBA to access a document programmatically

✦ Accessing a document following a specified expiration date

IRM won't work unless your system can verify users' identities via Microsoft's Passport authentication or Windows Server 2003 with the necessary Client Access Licenses.

Permissions can be tailored to each user with potential access to a document. To see the Permission dialog box, choose Tools➪Protect Document. At the bottom of the Protect Document taskbar, click the Restrict Permission link. The Permission dialog box appears, as shown in Figure 7-1.

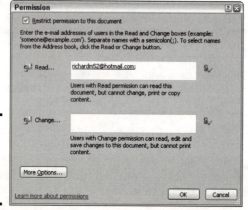

Figure 7-1: Manage IRM permissions here.

To refine the permissions, click the More Options button to see the expanded version, as shown in Figure 7-2.

Notice the Set Defaults button in Figure 7-2. Click this to make the current permission settings the default for any Excel workbook, PowerPoint presentation, or Word documents that you create in the future (that is, if you choose to add IRM protection to them). The settings in the dialog box shown in Figure 7-1 also apply to the default.

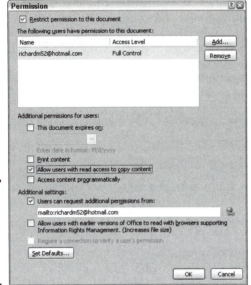

Figure 7-2:
Refine user
permissions
in the
expanded
dialog box.

Someone using a pre-2003 version of Office cannot read a document protected by IRM. However, there's an add-in for Internet Explorer that such a user can employ to read IRM-protected documents if you grant this permission. To do that, select the Allow Users with Earlier Versions of Office to Read with Browsers Supporting Information Rights Management check box as shown in Figure 7-2. Book VII, Chapter 2 includes additional information on IRM.

Hiding files

Another way to protect data is to hide files on your hard drive from other users. For Windows 2000 and later

1. **Right-click a filename in Windows Explorer.**

2. **Choose Properties from the context menu.**

3. **Select the Hidden check box.**

Two things can now happen: Either the file's listing in Explorer disappears, or the file's icon merely gets pale. If the latter happens, you've previously changed the default Windows Explorer setting to Show Hidden Files and Folders. (In Explorer, choose Tools⇒Folder Options, click the View tab, and find the Hidden Files and Folders section under Advanced settings.)

**Book VIII
Chapter 7**

Office 2003 Security

If you do hide a file this way, you can restore it to view by following the steps just mentioned, and selecting the Show Hidden Files and Folders check box at least temporarily: that is, long enough to right-click the hidden file and deselect its Hidden check box in its Properties dialog box.

NTFS file systems also permit you to specify behaviors and permission levels for entire folders. To do so, follow these steps:

1. **In Windows Explorer, right-click a folder and choose Properties.**

2. **Click the General tab.**

   You can select hidden or read-only properties on this tab.

3. **Click the Advanced button to choose to encrypt the contents of this folder.**

4. **Click the Sharing tab to adjust local or network sharing settings.**

 If other users share your computer, they won't be able to see your hidden files or folders as long as their Windows Explorer Tools⇨Folder options still has the default setting: Do Not Show Hidden Files and Folders.

Going beyond IRM

In addition to IRM, Office 2003 adds several new security features and improves existing features. For example, Access has a peculiar security warning when you load an MDB database: `This file may not be safe if it contains code that was intended to harm your computer. Do you want to open this file or cancel the operation?` Similar warnings appear in Outlook and other Office 2003 applications, depending on the security settings that the user or administrator have specified.

Beyond this, at your disposal are other security measures involving macros, warnings about loading ActiveX objects, trusted sources, password protection, certificates, and encryption. For example, administrators can go ahead and disable VBA although that can have a serious impact on employee productivity. Also, some Office 2003 add-ins, downloads, and programming of various kinds will not run.

Macros and other programming are like cars: inherently dangerous precisely because they're powerful. Rather than entirely eliminating such dangers, the best course is usually to establish rules about who can use the technology and how they can use it. You never entirely eliminate the dangers, but you reduce them to tolerable levels.

If you feel you must turn off VBA, you can change the option for VBA to Not Available or Not Available, Hidden, Locked. This can be done in three places:

✦ The Set Feature Installation States page of the Custom Maintenance Wizard

✦ The Setup.exe Advance Customization page

✦ The Custom Installation Wizard

If you choose the Run from My Computer option for Access, VBA is required for Access to execute in this fashion.

The alternative to turning macros off entirely and eliminating VBA from your Office 2003 environment is to goose up the security options settings. Choosing a High or Medium macro security prompts your users when unsigned macros are about to run, giving them the option to refuse to permit the macro execution. (This likely has little impact on George Nitwit, so it's no real protection against wanton foolishness.)

For details on managing macro settings in Office 2003 applications, see the section on adjusting macro settings in Book I, Chapter 2.

If you set macro security to Very High, no macros can execute unless they're stored in a trusted location on the user's hard drive.

If you're in charge of managing Office 2003 security, you should know that most Office security settings are specified either via policies or when using the Custom Installation Wizard. The improved Custom Maintenance Wizard permits you to adjust security settings after Office 2003 has already been installed. Nearly all the features that you can specify during setup can also be adjusted later with the Custom Maintenance Wizard.

Setting Up Virus Protection

Various improvements have been made in Office 2003 applications to guard against virus attack. Some of them rely on the user (!?), such as warnings/ questions that a database might contain executables and whether you want to load it, anyway. Others involve changes to the object model and application behaviors. For instance, the Outlook Address Book defaults to allowing only user-specified programmatic access to it, with an additional time limit on that access. If you write a program that wants to see your Address Book, you'll see a dialog box pop up asking whether you permit access to this information — and if so, for how long. This is to guard against currently notorious Address Book harvester viruses.

SharePoint and InfoPath offer some security features, discussed in this book in chapters on those technologies. Read about SharePoint in Book VII, Chapter 9 and InfoPath in Book VII, Chapter 4.

Because Office 2003 macro languages are fully capable of doing damage (file deletion, for example), you do have to be aware that a virus in VBA code is just like a macro. Typically, an infection via VBA results when the user opens a document. That triggers a macro, which starts to replicate itself, going into `Normal.dot` and other files. As with e-mail attachments, don't open documents from strangers.

Office 2003 applications default to automatic Internet connections (to provide automatic online Help features, descriptions of new templates and features, and so on). This connection can, of course, be unwise for some kinds of employees or if your company works on top-secret projects. To change this default, deselect this option by following these steps:

1. **Choose Tools➪Options.**

You see the Options dialog box.

2. **Click the General tab.**

3. **Click the Service Options button.**

You see the Service Options dialog box.

4. **Click the Online Content link in the left pane.**

You see the default settings, as shown in Figure 7-3.

Figure 7-3:
Prevent
automatic
Internet
connections
here.

5. **Clear the Show Content and Links from Microsoft Office Online check box.**

6. **Click OK.**

   The dialog box closes.

The Security Properties Dialog Box

Individual security settings for Office 2003 applications can be adjusted via the Security tab of the Options dialog box (choose Tools➪Options). (Access, as usual, differs from the other Office 2003 applications. There, you choose Tools➪Security.)

The Security tab of the Options dialog box is shown in Figure 7-4.

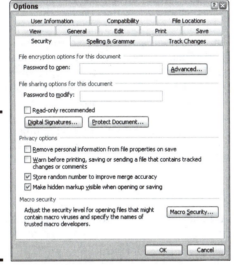

Figure 7-4:
Adjust various security settings of Office 2003 apps here (except Access).

Encryption options

As you see in Figure 7-4, you can *encrypt* the document: mangling it so that others cannot read it. A variety of encryption schemes exists, including the powerful RSA system. Precisely which encryption systems are listed for you depend on which ones are installed on your machine.

RSA

RSA (named after its inventors, Professors Rivest, Shamir, and Adleman) is quite an unusual system. Until RSA was invented, encryption depended on a secret key that you and your recipient used to decrypt the cyphertext message. RSA makes a key public information, yet RSA is the strongest encryption available today (unless the government is keeping something from us). For details on how you can add RSA to your own programming, see Book VIII, Chapter 8.

In any case, avoid the Office 97/2000 Compatible encryption scheme, even though it's the default in the dialog box. That system is rather lame; it took me only a few hours one day to crack it and write a little utility that automatically decrypts any document so encrypted (without even having to use brute force or password guessing). And, obviously, you should avoid the first system listed: the self-describing Weak Encryption (XOR). Interestingly, XOR was used for years until someone pointed out that zeros in the *plaintext* (the unencrypted document) provided a wide-open door into the cyphertext (the encrypted document). Choose a version of RSA or another of the strong encryption systems. If asked, choose the largest possible key length. (Specify the encryption and the key length by choosing Tools⇨Options and then click the Advanced button of the Security tab.)

In the Security dialog box, you can also manage digital signing to verify yourself as a trusted source. (For details on digital signatures, see the section on dealing with macro security issues in Book I, Chapter 2.)

File saving considerations

If you encrypt a document, be aware that versions of it in plaintext might still exist on your hard drive — you know, backups, recovered versions, and those odd temp files (like this: ~WRL2772.tmp) that Word creates but that sometimes remain undeleted. Even if you (or Word) delete them, the data in these documents might still exist magnetically on the hard drive, if no longer in the file allocation directory. In other words, you might not see them listed any longer in Windows Explorer, but they can often be recovered and viewed with special utilities.

As long as those plaintext copies of your document reside in one form or another on the hard drive, your data is not secure. The solution is to encrypt the document *before* you do any work on it or save it. This ensures that the encrypted version will be the only one extant. (For example, if you intend to keep a document secure, start the new document and then immediately encrypt it without actually typing anything into it yet. Then after it's encrypted, no other earlier/unencrypted version will remain behind on your hard drive.)

Choices on the Save tab (in Word, Excel, and PowerPoint, choose Tools⇨ Options) can also have security consequences. Most of today's speedy machines don't require the Fast Saves option because files save quickly enough as is. The Fast Saves feature simply appends changes to a document rather than integrating them. In some cases, however, opening a Fast Saved document with programs like Notepad or other text viewers can reveal text that was deleted. You might not want people seeing this deleted text.

Similarly, deleted text can remain in documents saved if you select the Always Create Backup Copy option. (Neither option is on by default.) If you select the second option, a backup copy of each document (a WBK file) is stored with the original. However, this backup is the previous version: namely, the one that might include text you deleted from the current version.

If you provide a password when encrypting a document, public key encryption is not used. The password is used as a *secret key;* that is, both you and the recipient must know this password to decrypt the document.

Nobody can decrypt a strongly encrypted file. That is the idea, after all (isn't it?). For one thing, the password isn't stored in the file. The password might exist only in your mind after you've typed it in when first encrypting the file. Will you remember it? Passwords can also cause a different problem: What if Patti suddenly leaves the company, perhaps because of a fatal yoga mishap? If she's the only one who knows her password, all her encrypted files are useless. It's the administrator's job to keep copies of employee passwords in a secure place.

Pas en France (Not in France)

However, France, like Access, does things its own way. In this context, France has outlawed 128-bit keys. If you're sending a document to Claudette, she'll likely have her Regional and Language Options in Control Panel set to French. She won't be able to open 128-bit key encrypted documents. Let's not pretend to understand how a government thinks it can outlaw a technology that's available worldwide with the click of a mouse. America, too, outlawed public key encryption until recently. *Je m'amuse.*

I suggest creating a secure, encrypted data store for this purpose, as I describe in Book VIII, Chapter 8. I use this utility several times a week. It's a very practical place to store such things as logon/password pairs, financial information, and sensitive data of any kind. You can create this utility following the simple instructions in Book VIII, Chapter 8, or you can get someone who knows VBA to do it for you. If I were in charge of a group of employees, I'd give each of them a copy of this utility. It's that helpful. Everyone has data they'd like to keep secret, and it has features that make it faster and easier to use than other encryption-based data stores.

Anyone who knows the password (or finds a file open on someone's machine) can remove the password from a document. The encrypted document must first be opened — requiring that someone know the password — before the password can be deleted. To remove a password, follow these steps:

1. **With the file open, Choose File⇨Save As.**

   The Save As dialog box opens.

2. **Click the drop-down arrow labeled Tools (in the upper-right of the dialog box, near its title bar).**

3. **Choose Click Security Options from the drop-down list.**

   The Security dialog box opens.

4. **Delete the asterisks in the Password to Open box.**

5. **Click OK.**

   The dialog box closes.

6. **Click Save.**

   The now-unprotected file is saved.

Using strong encryption

Strong encryption systems are available in Office 2003 for Word, Access, and Excel. Outlook uses Secure Multipurpose Internet Mail Extensions (S/MIME) security extensions with which you can both digitally sign and encrypt your e-mail and any attachments.

You can automate password protection with a macro, but if you do, be sure to display a dialog box asking the user to type in the password. *Don't write the password in the source code.* Including the password in an encrypted document used to be fairly common practice, but it's almost as foolish as leaving your front door key in the lock for any passing stranger to gain entrance.

Editing permission settings

Click the Protect Document button to prevent others from applying various kinds of formatting or editing, as shown in Figure 7-5.

Figure 7-5:
Use this taskbar to specify limits to the formatting or editing of this document.

You can also use the task pane shown in Figure 7-5 to assign different levels of editing permission to different users.

Don't confuse document protection with encryption. A protected document cannot be edited via the application, but parts of it can certainly be viewed with disk view utilities or even (in some cases) document readers as simple as Notepad.

Removing embarrassing comments

The primary value of the privacy options group of settings on the Security dialog box is to prevent you from letting others see the editing process as well any perhaps unkind comments you made about the document or a co-worker. By default, the Make Hidden Markup Visible When Opening or Saving option is selected. This helps to prevent you from adding revisions or comments that remain with the document when you, say, submit it to the boss with a comment like, *"As you know, Big Mike has no idea how to punctuate, so after he reviews this, be sure to check it one more time."*

In Word, Excel, and PowerPoint, you can remove sensitive metadata when saving a document. (Choose Tools⇨Options, click the Security tab, and then select the Remove Personal Information from File Properties on Save check box.)

Preventing tracing

The Store Random Number to Improve Merge Accuracy option is peculiar. It's on by default, and it does evidently serve a purpose when merging or comparing documents, but it has a perhaps sinister side effect. It's like an invisible digital signature or hidden watermark that can uniquely identify you as the document's author. If you have a reason to remain anonymous when creating documents — that is, you don't want them traced to you — deselect this option.

You can fire up the Office 2003 Resource Kit, available from `www.microsoft.com/office/ork/2003/default.htm`.

You can employ the Resource Kit's System Policy Editor to make sure this random number option is in effect for all your users. You can also use this approach to mass-enforce the Make Hidden Markup Visible option discussed in the preceding section. However, the Remove Personal Information from This File on Save option is individual for every document and thus cannot be mass-enforced.

Macro security

Click the Macro Security button to adjust the settings that govern whether macros are permitted to execute or whether warning dialog boxes are displayed. I discuss these options are discussed in detail in Book I, Chapter 2. Clicking this button also allows you to specify *trusted sources* — organizations or people who have digitally signed their macros or other VBA code, and whom you've specified can be trusted. Digital signatures are designed to verify that code originated from the signer and has not been subsequently modified. You can add your own digital signature to a document by clicking the Digital Signatures button on the Security tab of the Options dialog box. Digital signatures are now considered legally binding in the U.S. and Europe.

Signing your VBA code

To add a signature to VBA code, choose Start➪All Programs➪Microsoft Office➪Microsoft Office Tools➪Digital Certificate for VBA Projects. You see the dialog box shown in Figure 7-6. Beware, though, because this self-signing is rather limited. It only works only on the machine where it was created, it could be a forgery, and it's limited to personal use only.

Figure 7-6: A limited kind of digital signature can be added to your VBA code.

Signatures and hashing

Office 2003 employs powerful, public key technology to sign data blocks (such as Word documents, workbooks, and other blocks of data or files). This process provides *validation:* that the document comes from whomever it says it does (as long as you know the author; clearly, the bad guys can sign documents, too). Also, the private key generated by RSA public key encryption is used to encrypt a hash of the data. (.NET allows you to programmatically hash, along with many other powerful security features that you can add to your solutions. Hashing is explained in Book VIII, Chapter 8.) The encrypted hash value is then generated by the recipient of the data block and compared with the hash value transmitted along with the data. It they match, you can be virtually certain that this data block has not been altered (and thus can be trusted).

Like any security measure, digital signatures don't provide complete protection from the people on the dark side. Troubled individuals who write viruses could themselves get a digital certificate, just as good people can. They might not have the best certificate or even have it for very long, but a spree is a spree. Also, innocent folks might accidentally send you a signed yet poisoned document as a result of adding a valid certificate to what they did not realize was a toxic file.

Avoiding Data Loss

If you have really interesting secrets to protect, Office 2003 encryption features, if intelligently used, can guard your privacy quite adequately. By *intelligently used,* I mean the following:

✦ Use a strong encryption like RSA.

✦ Guard the password.

✦ Encrypt the document before adding any data to it so you don't leave any plaintext copies around on your hard drive.

The other great threat to security in computers is attacks on data. This kind of assault isn't an attempt to expose your secrets. It just wants to do damage: delete files, slow down your system, launch smash-and-grab raids, turn your machine into a zombie, and so on. The list of variations on childish malice is lengthy and growing. Probably the worst kind of attack destroys your work. You've spent days building a spreadsheet or writing a great proposal, and then, whack! It's deleted along with useful historical information like your Address Book and Inbox.

The solution is to back up your data often. With blank CDs costing five-for-a-penny or cheaper at your local computer megamart store and CD-R/W drives at $19, you have no excuse for avoiding what takes only minutes and costs nearly nothing. Also, ensure that any auto-backup features are turned on and set to high-frequency (such as every 30 minutes), so even a power outage won't cost you more than a half hour of work.

If you're working on an Office 2003 document and the application freezes, don't resort to manually shutting down (Ctrl+Alt+Del) the not-responding application. Instead, choose Start⇨All Programs⇨Microsoft Office⇨ Microsoft Office Tools⇨Microsoft Office Application Recovery. This utility attempts a graceful shutdown that tries to preserve the data.

Chapter 8: No More Paranoia: Programmatic Encryption

In This Chapter

✔ **Understanding encryption**

✔ **Reviewing the two main encryption techniques**

✔ **Building your own encryption solutions**

✔ **Working with public key encryption**

✔ **Exploring high-speed DES encryption**

✔ **Discovering encryption in .NET**

To me, encryption is one of the most interesting aspects of computing. There's something intriguing about the contest of intellects on either side — the bad people cooking up new attacks versus the good people thinking up new defenses. And the computer brings an entirely new dimension to this ancient spy-versus-spy game.

For example, computers can try millions of passwords in less than an hour. Known as a *brute force attack,* this technique (not possible before computerization), is countered by brute force encryption systems, as you'll see in this chapter. When you finish this chapter, you'll be able to employ today's strongest encryption systems in your own programming.

By contrast, I don't find virii all that interesting. They're usually just the computer version of some teenagers' infantile need to spray-paint public places. Sad, childish people trying to get attention because they're pretty much ignored in real life. Well, maybe they're ignored for a reason. But encryption is quite another level of intellectual achievement. Oddly, though, although the importance of computer security is universally recognized, very few books even mention .NET security classes, much less provide code examples. This book does. This chapter gives you the tools you need to protect your sensitive information.

The vast .NET security classes are far too extensive to cover in a single chapter, so I concentrate here on demonstrating how to use two of the most important (and, I think, most interesting) features: encryption and decryption. But trust me: You can do this.

Securing Your Private Information

Knowing how to create encryption utilities can be valuable in both your professional and personal computing. In this chapter, you build your own utility that swiftly secures data. This utility will likely prove quite, quite useful to you. I use it all the time.

You can use the utility to securely hide your logon/password combinations, your private financial data, and so on. The fact that you write it yourself (and thus have the source code) means that you can personalize it to suit yourself. At the end of this chapter, I suggest various customizations that you might find useful.

You see how to add encryption features to other, larger Office 2003 programming solutions as well.

In this chapter, you see how to include in your programs both *RSA,* the strongest possible encryption, and *Triple Data Encryption Standard* (TripleDES), a system strong enough for nearly any purpose. (The banks use it.) You also see how to encrypt files of any kind as well as how to employ the elegant .NET cryptostream and memorystream classes to conceal all traces of your secrets. By using these streams, your sensitive information is never stored in a file on a hard drive where even if you "delete" it, it usually remains behind for easy retrieval by commonly available, disk-read utilities.

With the information in this chapter, you can equal the skills of encryption gurus and ensure that Office 2003 data, or your personal data, is entirely secure because it's entirely disguised.

As politicians say: Those are my principles, and if you don't like them, I have others.

Comparing the Two Encryption Tactics

First, a bit of background. Experts divide secret messaging into two broad categories.

✦ **Steaganography:** This is the attempt to hide that a secret message is being sent. Invisible ink; microdots; shaving a runner's head, tattooing a message there, and letting the hair grow out; burst radio transmissions posing as static — all these approaches involve pretending that nothing sly is going on. Recently, terrorists have been accused of using the Internet to communicate by concealing messages in graphics files (A picture of a rose can contain hidden information, if you know where to look.)

✦ **Cryptography:** More common and generally more secure, cryptography doesn't try to hide the fact that a message is being sent. Instead, the message is mangled *(encrypted),* thus transforming the original (called the *plaintext*) so that it can't be read. After being encrypted, the message is called *cyphertext.*

Encryption can solve several computer security problems. For example, when you send something over the Internet, it can easily be intercepted. Encrypting the message, however, can make it impossible for the interceptor (*intruder* is the usual term for this person) to understand. Thus, an effectively encrypted message is useless to any intruder.

Cryptography can also protect information that isn't transmitted, such as information that merely sits on your hard drive but you don't want others to see. Perhaps it's your diary, a list of all your ID/password combinations, your opinions about sensitive subjects, investment details, or whatever. In this chapter, I walk you though building a utility program that you can use to save a file to your hard drive that nobody but you can decipher.

Understanding Office Encryption

Useful, quality encryption is now available in some Office applications. Only a few years ago, exporting the most powerful encryption technologies to foreign countries — or even discussing them with any specificity — was illegal. Fortunately, that law has been revoked. Lawmakers were finally made to understand that widely discussed ideas such as public key encryption cannot be made illegal.

You can encrypt Excel, PowerPoint, and Word documents. Outlook e-mail offers a form of encryption. Access has an encoding feature that compacts the database, but this isn't really encryption. In any case, the default encryption schemes in Office 2003 are not the strongest. I recommend maximizing the *key length* (how long the password is). For sensitive data, you'll even want to specify a superior encryption system. With your administrator's permission level, you can change these Registry entries:

✦ `HKCU\Software\Microsoft\Office\11.0\Common\Security`

✦ `HKCU\Software\Policies\Microsoft\Office\11.0\Common\`
   `Security`

✦ **Value name:** `DefaultEncryption`

✦ **Value type:** `MultiString`

✦ **Value data:** `"<Encryption Provider>","<Encryption Algorithm>","<Encryption Key Length>"`

For example:

```
DefaultEncryption="Microsoft Enhanced Cryptographic
        Provider v1.0","RC4","128"
```

Write Your Own Encryption Utility

For complete freedom and the strongest possible encryption, you'll want to write your own VB.NET code and thereby utilize the extremely powerful .NET encryption tools. This chapter also shows you how to employ these encryption functions in Office 2003 programs or other programs you might write.

When you build your own encryption utility, you can encrypt whatever kinds of information you want: documents (of course) but also graphics, database files, or whatever you wish. And you can automate or customize the process to suit yourself.

First, take a look at how to create an RSA encryption utility. It illustrates how to use the strongest possible encryption available today in your own programming (unless the government has made some unannounced breakthroughs in quantum encryption).

RSA (named after its inventors, Professors Rivest, Shamir, and Adleman) is quite an unusual system. Until RSA was invented, encryption depended on a secret key that you and your recipient used to decrypt the cyphertext message. This key (think of it as a password) had to be kept secret or an intruder — someone getting hold of the cyphertext — would be able to decrypt the message.

RSA, however, works differently. It employs two keys: a public key that anyone can see, and a private key that each recipient keeps secret. To receive an encrypted message, you generate a public key and a related private key mathematically. Then you give the public key to the person who is sending you a secret message. In fact, you can give the public key to everyone in the office. Public keys are even sometimes provided in the same way that a company provides a list of phone extensions.

The sender uses the public key to encrypt the message. When he sends you the encrypted message, you mathematically combine the public and private keys, which are used together to decrypt the message. Key generation is done via functions in the .NET security code library. It's simple. Trust me.

In fact, the entire process of using public key encryption is pretty straightforward after you see how to use the brief source code. It's easy to plug this technology into your own programs. However, note this drawback to RSA: It's quite slow if you need to send messages longer than, say, a paragraph. And a paragraph can even take a minute or two to encrypt on today's typical desktop computers.

The example code I provide shortly in Listing 8-1 is limited to encrypting 58 characters (the limit in the .NET Framework RSA implementation). However, you can obviously feed a longer message into a loop and repeatedly, and very slowly, encrypt multiple 58-character packets. But what use is this? In fact, RSA is not usually employed to send the actual messages. Instead, it's excellent for sending passwords (keys) for use by another encryption system called Data Encryption Standard (DES; explored at the end of this chapter). It's a division of labor. Each technology gets to do what it does best. Fast, secure DES sends the long messages; lumbering, ultra-powerful RSA sends the key to unlock those messages. This approach works great. The government and banks use this dual technology approach. Why shouldn't you?

DES is very fast and actually quite secure although not as secure as RSA. DES is a classic encryption scheme in which the sender and recipient share a secret key. Sharing a secret key between two people has always been a real problem — often the main problem — with ensuring encryption security. Simply put, how do you send the key from one person to another without some intruder finding it? And, in fact, how would you even know if an intruder intercepted it and were reading all your private stuff?

The answer used by many corporations, banks, governments, and others today is to use RSA to encrypt the key, transmit the encrypted key, and then decrypt it on the recipient's end. With the key now safely in both the sender's and recipient's possession, the speedy DES system can be used to encrypt and exchange messages of any length.

Using RSA

You don't need to understand the inner workings of RSA to use it any more than you need to be a mechanic to drive a car. So don't bother your pretty head trying to fathom asymmetric encryption, prime number theory, and all the rest. Just copy the following code and plug it into your own programming.

RSA is called *asymmetric* because it doesn't use the same secret key for the encryption that is used for the decryption. DES does use the same key on both ends of the process, so it's referred to as *symmetric* encryption.

Start a new VB.NET Windows-style project in Visual Studio.NET by choosing File⇨New⇨Project and then double-clicking the Windows application icon.

Put three text boxes (set their `MultiLine` property to `True`) and two buttons on `Form1`, so it looks like Figure 8-1.

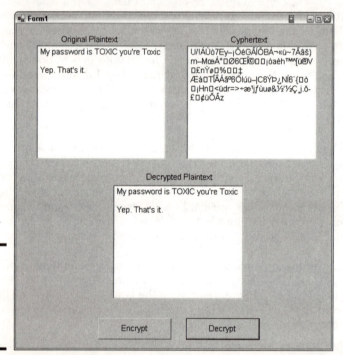

Figure 8-1: RSA encrypts and then decrypts a secret key.

Type this at the very top of the VB.NET Code window:

```
Imports System.Security.Cryptography
Imports System.Text
```

These namespaces provide access to the cryptography and text code libraries needed in this utility. Then, just above `Private Sub Form1_Load`, type these global variables:

```
Dim bArrayPlainText As Byte()
Dim bArrayCypherText As Byte()

Dim xPublicKey As String
Dim xBothKeys As String
```

Both the cyphertext and plaintext are manipulated in byte arrays, so you create those. The public key and the public/private key pair are held in simple string variables.

Now type this into the `Form_Load` event:

```
Private Sub Form1_Load(ByVal sender As System.Object,
        ByVal e As System.EventArgs) Handles MyBase.Load

    Dim rsa As New RSACryptoServiceProvider

    xBothKeys = rsa.ToXmlString(True)
    xPublicKey = rsa.ToXmlString(False)

End Sub
```

When this utility first executes, you use the `RSACryptoServiceProvider` object to generate a public/private pair (when the `ToXmlString` method's argument is set to `True`). And, when set to `False`, this same method provides only the public key, which you can send. When I executed this code, here's the public key I got:

```
<RSAKeyValue><Modulus>mkKN+zBCrrNrhJ+EY+7j78Nwr9/
    CHSOJripMIALHmoScu2k8juGlLa+uQSXP3gBqW5ATp9/
    YI3mST5Foo9Rmq9e6UyEnEpkRvTyLLNnzk3rpW34nYG89zgQZBR9v5XSRR
    xKPbONvoOVOdkagIV/MhsLD8p4uBCLlkjRHGqz/
    ov8=</Modulus><Exponent>AQAB</Exponent>
    </RSAKeyValue>
```

Your key will differ because they're generated randomly. The default key is 1,024 bits long, but you can specify any size key from 384 up to a whopping 16,384 bits. Also, note that each character in this key can represent any number between 0–255, not merely the digits 0–9. The number expressed in this key is larger than it appears when expressed in characters.

Finally, type in the following encryption and decryption procedures, as shown here in Listing 8-1.

Listing 8-1:   Exchanging a Key with RSA

```
Private Sub encrypt()

        TextBox2.Clear()

        Dim rsa As New RSACryptoServiceProvider

        rsa.FromXmlString(xPublicKey)

        Dim sPlainText As String = TextBox1.Text

        If sPlainText.Length > 58 Then MsgBox("You must use fewer than 59
                characters") : Exit Sub

        bArrayPlainText = (New UnicodeEncoding).GetBytes(sPlainText)

        bArrayCypherText = rsa.Encrypt(bArrayPlainText, False)


        For i As Integer = 0 To bArrayCypherText.Length - 1
            TextBox2.Text &= Chr(bArrayCypherText(i))
        Next i


End Sub



Private Sub decrypt()

        Dim rsa As New RSACryptoServiceProvider

        rsa.FromXmlString(xBothKeys)

        Dim sDecryptedPlainText As Byte() = rsa.Decrypt(bArrayCypherText, False)

        For i As Integer = 0 To (sDecryptedPlainText.Length - 1)
            TextBox3.Text &= Chr(sDecryptedPlainText(i))
        Next i

End Sub


Private Sub Button1_Click(ByVal sender As System.Object, ByVal e As
            System.EventArgs) Handles Button1.Click
     encrypt()
End Sub

Private Sub Button2_Click(ByVal sender As System.Object, ByVal e As
            System.EventArgs) Handles Button2.Click
     decrypt()
End Sub
End Class
```

In the `Encrypt` procedure, you get the public key:

```
rsa.FromXmlString(xPublicKey)
```

Then you get the message from the first text box, transforming the message into a byte array in preparation for feeding it to the `Encrypt` method of the `CryptoServiceProvider`. Finally, you loop through the cyphertext byte array to display the mangled message in the second text box. Notice that not only are you limited by the `CryptoServiceProvider` limit of transforming only 58 characters in one chunk, but also that no matter what size the plain-text message you feed in, the encrypted result is always expanded into a 128-byte cyphertext block.

The decryption procedure must use the same key pair that was originally generated in the `Form_Load` event. This is accomplished by using the `FromXmlString` method and providing the original XML key (`xBothKeys`) as an argument. Then you dump the cyphertext into a byte array and feed it to the `Decrypt` method. The resulting restored plaintext is displayed in the third `text box`. If you get strange results in the third text box, add Step 2 to the loop, like this:

```
For i As Integer = 0 To (sDecryptedPlainText.Length - 1) Step 2
    TextBox3.Text &= Chr(sDecryptedPlainText(i))
Next i
```

Powering Up DES Encryption

DES — and variants of it — is the strong encryption system of choice for most contemporary secure communications.

I enjoy programming in Visual Basic and have enjoyed it for over a decade. However, if I were limited to creating one application for myself — if I could write only a single program in my life — it would probably be the one that I show you how to build in this chapter. It's interesting to build, interesting to modify, and quite useful. I wrote it several years ago, and I still use it every few days. Of all the programs you might write for yourself, it's likely that an encryption program to safeguard your information benefits more than most from your intimate knowledge of how it works, how it can be made secure in your environment, how you can modify it, and from your hands-on customization.

Think first about your security needs. Do you want a secure repository to save all your logon/password pairs? Do you have secrets that you need to save in a particular way, for only a certain length of time? Do you want a quick way to cut and paste your credit card numbers? Do you want a secure place to store order numbers and e-mail receipts when you buy something online or make a reservation? A place to describe and record your finances? To keep a secret diary? Whatever your security needs are, they are highly specific to you. Thus, being able to satisfy those needs by designing and maintaining your own personal security zone can be invaluable.

The DES encryption technology was created by IBM in the early 70's. Back then, IBM was one of the few games in town, and the government requested that the brilliant IBM R&D people come up with a way of protecting bank money transfers, government communications, and other sensitive information. In 1972, the National Bureau of Standards asked for a reliable, fast, inexpensive, standardized, and very robust United States encryption system. They got what they wanted.

It was clear that computer communications would become increasingly essential in the modern world, and those communications had to be secured in some way. After all, the only difference between $1,000 and $1,000,000 in your savings account is three tiny, changeable magnetic patterns.

Formally introduced in 1976, DES to this day is routinely used for the great majority of business and government encryption. With the DES technology built into .NET, you, too, can protect your secrets as well as the big guys.

Making it public

Strangely, the DES algorithm was made public! In the past, the primary reason that people couldn't crack an encryption scheme was precisely because they didn't know how the scheme worked. For example, you might cook up a scheme to encrypt a message by spelling all the words backward. And while you're at it, you also substitute *x* for *e.* Having invented this system, you certainly don't tell people that these are the steps you're taking to mess up the messages. You don't let people know the algorithm.

However, the process used by the DES technique was published. Made public. For one thing, those in charge wanted software written to automate the encryption process (and possibly for other more mysterious reasons). The inventors of DES said that knowledge of how a DES message was encrypted wouldn't provide an intruder with a way of decrypting it.

How IBM's DES system works isn't really that tough to understand if you've done any bit-level programming. It's just that DES performs many, many transformations (such as rotation) of the key against the plaintext. So even though you can grasp the machinery that makes it work, you nevertheless cannot use that knowledge to break the code.

Each individual DES transformation is simple. A typical rotation left of a 4-bit unit, for example, changes 0101 into 1010, or 1001 into 0011. However, DES does so many transformations, each one impacting the next one, that a cumulative distortion occurs: a sum-greater-than-the-parts effect. It's as if you started a rumor that was passed along through a million people. You certainly wouldn't recognize your original message when they finished with it.

Can it be cracked?

A dispute among cryptologists concerns whether the government (or amateur groups) has actually cracked DES and can read DES encrypted messages. (Some even claim that there was always a secret, so-called trap door built into the DES system right from the start to permit government agencies access any time they wished. Like most conspiracy theories, this seems doubtful.)

However, if the government has cracked DES in the past 30 years, we wouldn't likely be told, would we? Some experts claim that the fifteenth cycle, of the 16 cycles used by DES, has been successfully penetrated. Now and then, an amateur group claims to have cracked DES completely. A 1999 attack on a DES message, during a contest, is said to have found a solution in a little more than 22 hours by testing 245 billion keys per second. This claim seems to me believable.

In fact, it does appear likely that the rudimentary 56-bit version of DES is no longer secure from supercomputer (or massive parallel processing) brute force key searches. Therefore, if your diary contains information so exciting that you think someone is going to rent 24 hours on a supercomputer to crack your secret file, you should consider moving up to TripleDES, which uses three times as many key bits (but runs three times slower, unfortunately). In this chapter, I show you how to use ordinary 56-bit DES and also 192-bit TripleDES. If you do decide to opt for TripleDES, be warned that you have to come up with a 24-character password instead of the easier-to-remember 8-character DES password. And don't try to get clever, dude: Simply repeating an 8-character password three times compromises the benefits of TripleDES.

If you do want to use TripleDES, simply change this DES declare statement in the code examples that use DES in this chapter:

```
Dim des As New DESCryptoServiceProvider()
```

and replace it with the following TripleDES declaration:

```
Dim TripleDes As New TripleDESCryptoServiceProvider()
```

Also, you must adjust the source code to expand the key (and the initialization vector) three times larger than the DES key and vector pair. (You expand from DES's 8-byte to TripleDES's 24-byte.)

**Book VIII
Chapter 8**

No More Paranoia: Programmatic Encryption

Choosing a good password

DES encryption — whatever size you use — requires a password. It's the password that DES uses to uniquely encrypt, and later decrypt, your file. You must be able to remember the password, or you'll never be able to decrypt the file.

The password should include digits (1–9) as well as alphabetic characters. What's more, you should choose the most random password that you will be able to remember. No matter how much encryption power you use, if people can guess your password, they're in! Your entire message rolls out for them to read.

Or if you write down the password and tape it to your desk drawer, well, you don't deserve to work with encryption. Some people actually choose the term *password* as their password. And if you walk through any large office, you're likely to see that some 15-watt bulb has this sticky note attached to his monitor: My Password *1422S*.

Your dog's name is not a good password . . . likewise for your address, your birthday, or your favorite food. All these would probably be tried by an even moderately motivated, semi-talented intruder. Don't write the password down. *Memorize it.*

Although computers make it possible to run millions of transformations on a message to encrypt it, computers are value-neutral. A computer doesn't know whether it's running an encryption program written by you (the innocent good person, trying to protect his personal information) or running an intruder's (the bad person trying to get into your bank account) key-testing hacking program that goes through entire dictionaries of possible passwords in a flash.

Encrypting in VB.NET

Time to get down to specifics. Here's a class, named `crypt`, that you can use to encrypt or decrypt a file on your hard drive. Before it encrypts (or decrypts) a file, you must provide this class with four pieces of information:

+ **What file you want encrypted:** Set its `filetoopen` property.

+ **The filename you want to give the new, encrypted version:** Set its `filetosave` property.

+ **Your password:** Set its `password` property.

✦ **Whether you want to encrypt or decrypt:** Set its `whichway` argument. You do this by setting a parameter when you create the `crypt` object. You might have noticed that when you create certain objects, you can provide them with parameters, just like you do when using a function. When you write a class, you can add this feature by using a parameterized constructor. It's just a `Sub New`, and that `New` tells VB.NET that you intend to receive a parameter when the object is *instantiated* (created) during runtime.

The `crypt` class requires three `Imports`, so start a new VB.NET Windows-style project and type the following at the very top of your Code window:

```
Imports System.IO
Imports System.Text
Imports System.Security.Cryptography
```

Now, move your cursor to the very bottom of the code window, below the final line of code that reads `End Class`, and type in the following new class (Listing 8-2).

Listing 8-2:   Practical Encrypting with DES

```
Public Class crypt 'user must provide "whichway" (encrypt or decrypt) filetoopen,
            filetosave and key.

    Sub New(ByVal WhichWay As String) ' parameterized constructor
        '  store their choice: encrypt or decrypt
        Way = WhichWay
    End Sub

    Private Way As String 'encrypt or decrypt
    Private pfname As String 'filename of incoming file
    Private efname As String 'filename of outgoing file
    Private pword As String ' the password the user enters


    Public WriteOnly Property password() As String
        Set(ByVal Value As String)
            pword = Value
        End Set
    End Property

    Public WriteOnly Property filetoopen() As String
        Set(ByVal Value As String)
            pfname = Value
        End Set
    End Property

    Public WriteOnly Property filetosave() As String
        Set(ByVal Value As String)
            efname = Value
        End Set
    End Property
```

```vbnet
Function cryptIt()

    If efname = "" Or pfname = "" Or pword = "" Then

        MsgBox("You must set the password, filetoopen, and filetosave
            properties of this encrypt object before using the CryptIt
            method.")
        Return ("error")

    End If

    'create the key from the password:

    Dim the_key(7) As Byte
    Dim doKey As New make_key(pword)

    the_key = doKey.MakeKey


    'random bytes for the initialization vector (see description in text)
    Dim Vector() As Byte = {&H22, &HD1, &H11, &HA8, &H82, &H62, &HDA, &H36}
    Dim buffer(4096) As Byte
    Dim tb As Long = 8 'Keeps track of number of bytes written
    Dim packageSize As Integer 'Byte block size


    'Create the streams.
    Dim fileIn As New FileStream(pfname, FileMode.Open, FileAccess.Read)
    Dim fileOut As New FileStream(efname, FileMode.OpenOrCreate,
            FileAccess.Write)
    fileOut.SetLength(0)

    Dim tf As Long = fileIn.Length 'find out file size.

    Try
        'create the cryptography object
        Dim DES As New DESCryptoServiceProvider()

        'flow the streams

        If Way = "encrypt" Then

            Dim cryptStream As New CryptoStream(fileOut,
            DES.CreateEncryptor(the_key, Vector), CryptoStreamMode.Write)

            While tb < tf
                packageSize = fileIn.Read(buffer, 0, 4096)
                cryptStream.Write(buffer, 0, packageSize)
                tb = Convert.ToInt32(tb + packageSize / DES.BlockSize *
            DES.BlockSize)
            End While

            cryptStream.Close()
            fileIn.Close()
            fileOut.Close()

        Else 'decrypt

            Dim decryptStream As New CryptoStream(fileOut,
            DES.CreateDecryptor(the_key, Vector), CryptoStreamMode.Write)
```

```
        While tb < tf
            packageSize = fileIn.Read(buffer, 0, 4096)
            decryptStream.Write(buffer, 0, packageSize)
            tb = Convert.ToInt32(tb + packageSize / DES.BlockSize *
        DES.BlockSize)
        End While

            decryptStream.Close()
            fileIn.Close()
            fileOut.Close()
        End If

    Catch e As Exception
        MsgBox(e.Message & "Perhaps you're using a bad password?")
    End Try

    End Function


End Class
```

At this point, you can't press F5 to see any results yet. You have to add some more elements to this project to be able to try this encryption class. Notice the squiggly line in your Code window under make_key. That class has not been coded yet.

After the various properties are created at the top of this code, you come to Function cryptIt(), which is the method in this class that does the actual work. First, cryptIt checks whether the user has set the necessary properties. If so, a *key* (a series of eight numbers) is created out of the user's password. The .NET DES encryption routine wants a byte array with 8 bytes in it, so you first create the byte array, and then you instantiate a doKey object (created by the MakeKey class). MakeKey transforms the user's password into a random series of numbers (and I explain how this class does its job soon in this section):

```
        Dim the_key(7) As Byte
        Dim doKey As New make_key(pword)
        the_key = doKey.MakeKey
```

Next, in the cryptIt class, several necessary housekeeping variables are created. The initialization vector is required by the .NET DES encryption routine. It's rather interesting, but you can skip the sidebar describing it if you're uninterested; you can easily use the encryption code without understanding the vector.

Streaming the encryption

After the initialization vector is defined in the cryptIt source code, a pair of filestreams are defined. They carry the data in from the plaintext file and out to the cyphertext file during the encryption process. (This class can also decrypt, so if that's what's going on, these same streams instead carry cyphertext in and send plaintext out.)

Finally, the actual encryption takes place, starting with the creation of a `DESCryptoServiceProvider()` object. After that object is instantiated, the code determines whether the user wants to encrypt or decrypt. The only difference between the two processes is that you use two different cryptostreams: one `CreateEncryptor` and the other `CreateDecryptor`. I put those declarations within the `If...End if` structure. Then, as long as `tb < tf` (the bytes written are less than the total bytes in the source file), the streams flow. The encryption process reads in a chunk from the `FileIn` stream; then it's encrypted and streamed out to `FileOut` (via the `cryptoStream`). Finally, the number of bytes written is updated into the variable `tb`.

When the process is complete, all three streams are closed. Interestingly, if someone provides the wrong password for decrypting a file, the DES `Crypto` class knows that it is the wrong password. Many decryption schemes simply spew out nonsense text when given the wrong password. (They simply go ahead and generate the nonsense that results from grinding a bad password against cyphertext.)

The .NET DES scheme, however, throws a `Bad Data` error message. This means that the correct password is somehow contained within the encrypted file (either somehow disguised, or in the form of a hash or checksum, described shortly). In any case, if an exception is thrown, you can display a message to users asking whether they supplied the wrong password and asking them to try again, as I did in this example.

Generating a password

To actually use the `CryptIt` class, you must also include a class to generate the key out of the user's password, so type in the following class (Listing 8-3) at the very bottom of your Code window, below all the other existing lines of code.

Listing 8-3: Creating a Key

```
Public Class make_key

    Sub New(ByVal TheirPassword As String) ' parameterized
            constructor
    '   store the password
    kpassword = TheirPassword
    End Sub

    Private kpassword As String 'the password string
```

```vb.net
    Public ReadOnly HashedKey(7) As Byte

    Function MakeKey()
        ' Declare a byte array that will hold the key
        Dim arrByte(7) As Byte

        Dim AscEncod As New ASCIIEncoding()
        Dim i As Integer = 0
        AscEncod.GetBytes(kpassword, i, kpassword.Length,
            arrByte, i)

        'Generage a hash value from the password
        Dim hashSha As New SHA1CryptoServiceProvider()
        Dim arrHash() As Byte = hashSha.ComputeHash(arrByte)

        'store the hash into the key array
        For i = 0 To 7
            HashedKey(i) = arrHash(i)
        Next i

        Return HashedKey

    End Function


    Function Create() 'method to transform password string
            into a key

        '   Save the current value of the LastFile property to
            the registry.
        Dim arrByte(7) As Byte

        'change the password string into a byte array:
        Dim AscEncod As New ASCIIEncoding()
        Dim i As Integer = 0
        AscEncod.GetBytes(kpassword, i, kpassword.Length,
            arrByte, i)

        'Get the hash value of the password byte array:
        Dim hash As New SHA1CryptoServiceProvider()
        Dim arrHash(7) As Byte
        hash.ComputeHash(arrByte)

        'return the key:

        Return arrHash

    End Function

End Class
```

This `Make_Key` class begins with a parameterized constructor (the `Sub New`), which requires that when clients using the class instantiate the class, they must provide a password as a parameter, like this:

```
Dim doKey As New make_key(pword)
```

Then the `MakeKey` method creates an 8-byte array, and the password is separated by the `ASCIIEncoding` class into individual bytes (each character's ASCII code value) and stored into the array. After that, the `SHA1CryptoServiceProvider` class generates a hash out of the array.

The user's password `strKey` is passed to this procedure; then the password is separated into individual ASCII values held in a byte array. This byte array is fed to the `ComputeHash` method of the `SHA1CryptoServiceProvider` class, which returns the hash value. I put the hash into my `TheKey` array, for later use in the encryption (or decryption) procedures.

Understanding what does a key does

A key is used in encryption to provide a way of distorting the plaintext. Here's a simple example. Assume that you think up an encryption scheme. Your idea is to stick the password's characters between each letter of the plaintext, like this:

+ **Key:** `Mike`

+ **Plaintext:** `Ring of fire`

+ **Encryption:** RMiinkge Moifk efMiirkee

As you can see here, the key is repeated as often as necessary throughout the plaintext. For illustration purposes, I used alphabetic characters here. However, with the arrival of the computer, modern encryption generally involves mathematical transformations rather than the simple character substitutions or transpositions characteristic of classic encryption schemes.

Computers are so good at math, compared with us, and so much faster at it as well. So, before being used mathematically in a modern encryption scheme like DES, the text password is transformed (hashed, for example) into a numeric value (the key) that can then be employed in the mathematical encryption. Remember, DES wants an 8-byte numeric array, not a password. That's the job of the `make_key` class in this chapter.

Finishing the Program

To complete the DES encryption application that's been developed in this chapter, you should add two buttons and two text boxes to the form. Ensure that `TextBox2` is fairly small and drag it down near the bottom of the form; `TextBox2` is where the user enters the password, so it only needs to be a single-line `TextBox`. Set the `TextBox1 MultiLine` property to `True` and stretch it to make it fairly large so that users can enter as much text as they wish, as shown in Figure 8-2.

Figure 8-2:
Arrange your DES crypto program's user interface like this.

It's nice to show the user some mangled text from the resulting encryption. Mangled text excites users. They think, "Wow! That's pretty messed up. Who could figure that out?" It excites *me,* to be honest. I've got to sit here quietly now and wait until I've stabilized.

This chapter's example program, therefore, displays some of the encrypted text after users click the Encrypt button. They type something into the text box, type in a password, click the Encrypt button, and *voilà!,* the transformed result appears in the text box, as illustrated in Figure 8-2.

Displaying mangled text

Here's a function you should type into the Form1 class to display the encrypted result. This same function also does a second job; it displays the decrypted plaintext if the user clicks the Decrypt button instead. Don't worry about it; you'll see what I mean when you run it. Move down through Public Class Form1 in your Code window until your blinking insertion cursor is just above the line End Class. (Be sure you're still in the Form1 class, not in the Crypt class or some other class beneath the Form1 class.) Now type in this function (Listing 8-4) just above the line End Class:

Listing 8-4: Show the Encrypted Text

```
Function showcrypt(ByVal fname As String) 'displays a file in
    the textbox

        Dim fs As FileStream = New FileStream(fname,
            FileMode.Open)

        Dim r As New StreamReader(fs)

        Dim x As Integer = fs.Length
        Dim i As Integer

        ' Read in all the data from the file:

        TextBox1.Text = r.ReadToEnd

        r.Close()
        fs.Close()

        'kill the temp file
        Dim fa As New FileInfo("c:\temp")
        fa.Delete()

    End Function
```

The CryptIt class creates a temporary file on the hard drive (named C:\temp) to hold the intermediary results of encryption or decryption. This file must be destroyed, however, or it would hold the plaintext after encryption had been performed on it. That would be bad: People could read all your secrets if they could locate the temp file. So at the end of this ShowCrypt function, the temp file is deleted.

Of course, even using a temp file isn't a good idea. For stronger security, you should use a cryptostream (illustrated in the example code in Listing 8-11 at the end of this chapter).

All that remains to be done to complete this application is to respond when the user clicks the two buttons. Type in the following code (Listing 8-5) for the button that encrypts.

Listing 8-5: Encryption

```
Private Sub Button1_Click(ByVal sender As System.Object,
        ByVal e As System.EventArgs) Handles
        Button1.Click
      'encrypt the contents of the TextBox

      Dim sfd As New SaveFileDialog()
      sfd.ShowDialog()

      Dim objCrypt As New crypt("encrypt")
      objCrypt.filetoopen = "c:\temp"
      objCrypt.filetosave = sfd.FileName
      If Len(TextBox2.Text) <> 8 Then MsgBox("Your password
        must be eight characters long") : Exit Sub
      objCrypt.password = TextBox2.Text.ToUpper

      'save textbox1 to c:\temp

      Dim strText As String = TextBox1.Text

      If (strText.Length < 1) Then
          MsgBox("Please type something into the TextBox so
          we can encrypt it.")
          Exit Sub
      Else
          Dim strFileName As String = "C:\temp"
          Dim objOpenFile As FileStream = New FileStream
          (strFileName, FileMode.Create, FileAccess.Write,
          FileShare.None)
          Dim objStreamWriter As StreamWriter = New
          StreamWriter(objOpenFile)
          objStreamWriter.WriteLine(strText)
          objStreamWriter.Close()
          objOpenFile.Close()
      End If


      Dim n As StringBuilder
      n = objCrypt.cryptIt()
      showcrypt(sfd.FileName)


      'delete the password
      TextBox2.Text = ""


End Sub
```

This button's `Click` event first displays a Save dialog box and asks the user to specify where on the hard drive to store the encrypted file and what name to give it. Then it streams the contents of the large `TextBox1` to a temporary file in preparation for encrypting the text. Finally, the `cryptIt` method is invoked. After the encryption is finished, the `showcrypt` function displays the results (mangled text like this: `10!@09jd ()#JF&`).

Finish the application by typing in the following code (Listing 8-6) for `Button2`, which decrypts.

Listing 8-6:   Decrypting

```
Private Sub Button2_Click(ByVal sender As System.Object,
        ByVal e As System.EventArgs) Handles
        Button2.Click
'decrypt a saved file

Dim ofd As New OpenFileDialog()
ofd.ShowDialog()

Dim objDecrypt As New crypt("decrypt")
objDecrypt.filetoopen = ofd.FileName
objDecrypt.filetosave = "c:\temp"
objDecrypt.password = TextBox2.Text
Dim n As StringBuilder
n = objDecrypt.cryptIt()
showcrypt("c:\temp")


'delete the password
TextBox2.Text = ""


End Sub
```

Trying the program

Okay, time to try it out.

1. **Press F5 and type an 8-character password into the lower text box.**

In the future, you can use any password you want, but while experimenting in this chapter, use the password MYSTERY2. Later in this chapter, you will see why this is important.

2. **Copy and paste a few paragraphs of text into TextBox1, the upper text box.**

3. **Click the Encrypt button.**

You see the Save As dialog box.

4. **Use the drop-down list at the top of the dialog box to move to your C: drive, and then type secrets as the filename for your encrypted file.**

   Again, for a technique explained later in this chapter, please use `C:\secrets` as the filename.

5. **Click the Save button.**

   The dialog box closes, and the upper text box's text is replaced with encrypted text.

Now try going the other way.

1. **Type in the password you used to encrypt the file and click the Decrypt button.**

   The Open dialog box appears.

2. **Double-click the filename you used when encrypting.**

   There you are: Your plaintext is restored.

Some Suggested Improvements to the Crypt Program

If you've followed this chapter to this point, you can use the project you've created as-is. It will calm the paranoiac in you by efficiently hiding your secrets. However, here are some exciting and sinister improvements I want to suggest to conclude this chapter. Read on, friend.

Fifty years ago, still struggling with their categories, crack psychologists combined the term *paranoia* with *maniac* and came up with the delightful word *paranoiac*. With today's political correctness, cracked (I mean *crack*) shrinks have been forced to rename many kinds of mental disturbances in an effort to soften the insult by using words such as *borderline*. This suggests that with a little help, the person can come over the line to join us happy, smiling normal people, over here where we all gather on this side of the line. Tennis, anyone?

Whatever you call it, surely nothing is wrong with being moderately paranoiac about your personal information. After all, some of your secrets, if known, could be used against you in various ways.

In this chapter, you constructed encryption/decryption and key-making classes, which make use of the sophisticated security classes built into .NET. Now I want to suggest some additions and customizations that can make your crypt utility even more useful to you as a way of protecting your private information.

For one thing, if only you are going to use it and you're going to create only one file that holds all your private data, why not simplify things and hard-wire the filename? (Put it into the source code rather than displaying Open or Save dialog boxes to have the user type it in.) That way, when you run the program, you only have to type in the password, and the file is automatically opened, decrypted, and displayed. Then, when you've finished editing the information and want to store it encrypted, you simply click a button, and it's all done for you automatically.

Remember that all the source code for these additions, as well as all the code for this book, is available for quick downloading from this book's companion Web site. (Refer to the Introduction for the URL.)

Here's an example of code you can type into the Form_Load event to automatically open, decrypt, and display plaintext:

```
Private Sub Form1_Load(ByVal sender As System.Object, ByVal e
            As System.EventArgs) Handles MyBase.Load
    'load and decrypt the encrypted file

        Dim objDecrypt As New crypt("decrypt")

        objDecrypt.filetoopen = "c:\secrets"
        objDecrypt.filetosave = "c:\tem"
        objDecrypt.password = passwordFromForm2
        Dim n As StringBuilder
        n = objDecrypt.cryptIt()

        showcrypt("c:\tem")

        'kill the temp file
        Dim fa As New FileInfo("c:\tem")
        fa.Delete()

End Sub
```

Note that the filetoopen is simply hardwired here (shown in boldface). Also note that the password comes from another Form, Form2. The variable passwordFromForm2 is currently underlined with a squiggly line because it hasn't yet been declared. This leads us to another clever trick that you might want to try, which adds one more layer of protection.

Choose Project⇨Add Windows Form. You now have to change the startup object from Form1 (the default) to Form2. That way, the code in Form2 is the first code executed when your project starts running. To make this change, follow these steps:

1. Choose View⇨Solution Explorer.

Solution Explorer displays.

2. Right-click the name of your project.

It's the only line in boldface in Solution Explorer.

3. Click Properties in the context menu that appears.

Your project's Property Pages dialog box opens.

4. Open the drop-down list under Startup Object by clicking its down-arrow button.

You see the forms and module listed here as potential startup objects.

5. Click Form2 in the drop-down list.

`Form2` is now displayed as the new startup object.

6. Click OK.

The dialog box closes.

When people run your program, just show them at first an empty `Form2`. Put no buttons on `Form2` — nothing to interact with. I like to set its `FormBorderStyle` property to `None`, its `BackGroundImage` property to some ominous-looking graphic file, and its `Opacity` property to 75%, just to make it look scary to someone who stumbles upon this utility. It just sits there, ghostly, teasing the paranoiac qualities in the intruder. You could even add a loop and a timer to slowly decrease its opacity, making it evaporate like smoke in front of their eyes. That can be *spooky,* and I say that in a helpful, caring way. Boo! (Let them worry what other tricks you might have up your sleeve.)

However, `Form2` is doing something behind the scenes: It's waiting to accept any keystrokes users might type. Whatever you type becomes the key used to decrypt your secret file. (It's passed to `Form1`.) Intruders will probably never be able to figure this out, but if they do, they still don't know the key. You know the key, though, so when you run the program and the spooky `Form2` shows up, you just type in your 8-character password and `Form2` disappears, `Form1` appears, and the decrypted file is displayed. All in a flash, but highly secure.

Making it happen

Use Project⇨Add Windows Form to add `Form2` to your project and Project⇨ Add Module to add `Module1`.

When this project runs, `Form2` is not supposed to do anything until the user types the number **2** above the keyboard, thereby making `Form2` disappear and `Form1` appear. (You can, of course, change this trigger character to suit yourself.)

In `Module1`, type the following variable. Putting it in a `Module` permits both `Form2` and `Form1` to access the variable. This technique is a way to communicate information between forms:

```
Module Module1
    'this variable can now be seen in both Form1 and Form2

    Public passwordFromForm2 As String

End Module
```

Now, switch to the Code window for `Form2` and type Listing 8-7 into the `Form_KeyDown` event. (To create the `KeyDown` event, open the drop-down list on the top right of the Code window and click KeyDown.)

Listing 8-7:   Inter-Form Communication

```
Public Class Form2
    Inherits System.Windows.Forms.Form

Windows Form Designer generated code

    Dim presses As String

Private Sub Form2_KeyDown(ByVal sender As Object, ByVal e As
            System.Windows.Forms.KeyEventArgs) Handles
            MyBase.KeyDown

    presses += e.KeyCode.ToString

        If e.KeyCode = Keys.D2 Then 'pressing the number 2
            triggers the end of the key input
            'form one is displayed and the user's key input
            is then sent as the password
            'to decrypt. If the wrong password was entered,
            the program will shut down in
            'form1@mdno text will be decrypted or displayed.

            'this will be in all uppercase
            passwordFromForm2 = presses.Substring(0, 7) & "2"


            Me.Hide()
```

```
        Dim n As New Form1
        n.Show()

    End If

  End Sub
End Class
```

Notice that just above the line `Private Sub Form2_KeyDown`, you must add the following line to declare the variable `presses`:

`Dim presses As String`

For this key-detection feature to work, you must switch to design view and set the `Form2 KeyPreview` property to `True` in the Properties window.

Notice that the variable `presses` here continues to accumulate all the characters that the user types in until the user types the digit **2**. Then all characters in `presses` (except the first eight) are discarded, and the `passwordFromForm2` is filled with those first eight characters. Interestingly, the numbers are identified in the `e.keycode` with a `D` in addition to the digit. If you press 3, `e.keycode` contains D3.

Here's what happens if your password is `treatww2` and you type that in. As soon as you press the 2 key, the `presses.Substring(0, 8)` contains `treatwwD` because the variable `presses` contains `treatwwD2`, but only eight of its characters are retained when you use the `Substring` method to strip off any extras.

Anyway, `Form2` hides, `Form1` is displayed, and `Form1`'s `Load` event triggers, bringing in the entire decrypted text for you to view.

Also in `Form1`, you can change the process of encryption by hardwiring your filename and avoiding having to interact with a `SaveFileDialog`. Remember, too, that the password is already available for the encryption process in the variable `passwordFromForm2`.

**Book VIII
Chapter 8**

No More Paranoia: Programmatic Encryption

Going beyond paranoiac to psychoiac

Here's another feature I find useful. Sometimes I get distracted while computing. I make some changes to the decrypted data in the `TextBox`, but I forget to shut down the `Crypt` program. Or I switch to Internet Explorer for a little browsing or leave the computer to get something to drink. I've done this while the crypt program is running, leaving my entire private life gaping open there in the text box for anyone to read.

To prevent this problem, I like to add two timer controls that shut down the Crypt program automatically if there have been no keypresses for one minute. Also, the following code adds a useful search feature so that you can quickly locate passwords and so on in your text box.

First, remove the main, large text box (not the password text box) and add a RichTextBox from the Toolbox in its place. The document in a RichTextBox automatically scrolls to display a match if one is found when you're searching. Also, set the Form1 KeyPreview property to True. Then type the following variable declarations at the top of the Code window:

```
Dim freezer As Boolean

    'these next variables are used by the Searchit routine
    Dim searchstring As String, pos As Integer
    Dim pressedonce As Boolean
    Dim Search, Where    ' Declare variables as objects
        (default).

        Dim isdirty As Boolean 'has the user changed the
        textbox at all?

Private Sub Form1_Load(ByVal sender As Object, ByVal e As
        System.EventArgs) Handles MyBase.Load
    'load and decrypt the encrypted file
```

Search (press Ctrl+H) all references in your code to TextBox1 and replace them with RichTextBox1. Now add two Timer controls to Form1 and type in this code (Listing 8-8).

Listing 8-8:   Timers

```
'These timers prevent you from forgetting to shut down
    'this application. If no keypresses are made for 1 minute,
    'the program is shut down:

    Private Sub Timer1_Tick(ByVal sender As System.Object, ByVal e As
            System.EventArgs) Handles Timer1.Tick
        'Timer1's Interval should be set to 6000 (six seconds)
        ' and it's enabled to true (in the Properties window).

        Static Counter As Integer

        If freezer = True Then
            Counter = 0
            Me.Text = "      Frozen      "
            Exit Sub
        End If

        Counter = Counter + 1
        If Counter = 9 Then End 'Shutdown!

    End Sub
```

```
Private Sub Timer2_Tick(ByVal sender As System.Object, ByVal e As
        System.EventArgs) Handles Timer2.Tick

    'Timer2's Interval should be set to 60000 (one minute)
    ' and it's enabled to false (in the Properties window).


    '1 minute has elapsed so turn freezer off
    freezer = False
    Timer2.Enabled = False

End Sub
```

The Form's `KeyDown` event detects keypresses (affecting the `freezer` variable used by the timers) and also detects whether the user presses F3 or Crtl+F, either of which triggers a search of the `RichTextBox` contents (Listing 8-9).

Listing 8-9:   Searching

```
Private Sub Form1_KeyDown(ByVal sender As Object, ByVal e As
        System.Windows.Forms.KeyEventArgs) Handles
        MyBase.KeyDown
        'For this to work, the Form's KEYPREVIEW PROPERTY
            MUST BE SET TO TRUE! (default=false)

        'This procedure searches through the TextBox
        'when the user presses F3 or Crlt+F...

        freezer = True 'a keypress, so stop the Timer
            countdown
        Timer2.Enabled = True 'watch to see if 1 minute
            passes
        'after last keypress and if so, turn freezer false


        If e.KeyCode = 114 Then ' pressed f3 to search

            searchit()

            Exit Sub

        End If

        If e.KeyCode = Keys.F And e.Control = True Then
            'pressed CTRL+F to search

            searchit()

            Exit Sub

        End If

    End Sub
```

Listing 8-10 shows the procedure that searches the RichTextBox.

Listing 8-10: Searching a RichTextBox

```
Private Sub searchit()


        Dim x As String, n As String
        x = LCase(RichTextBox1.Text)
        If pos = 0 Then pos = 1

        If pressedonce = True Then GoTo cont

        If searchstring <> "" Then n = searchstring

        Search = InputBox("Please enter your search text", , n)
        If Search = "" Then pressedonce = False : Exit Sub 'they clicked the
                cancel button on the Search Input box
        pressedonce = True
        Search = LCase(Search)
        searchstring = Search

cont:

        Where = InStr(pos, x, Search) ' Find string in text.
        Dim ra = x.Length

        If Where Then    ' If found,
            RichTextBox1.SelectionStart = Where - 1 ' set selection start and
            RichTextBox1.SelectionLength = Len(Search)  ' set selection length.
            pos = Where + Len(Search)
        Else
            MsgBox("Search text not found.")  ' Notify user.
            pressedonce = False
            pos = 0
            Search = Nothing
            Where = Nothing
        End If

    End Sub
```

Finally, here's another optional improvement. I sometimes make changes to the RichTextBox but forget to press the button to actually encrypt and save those changes to the disk file. Instead, I go ahead and click the x in the top right of the form or press Alt+F4 to shut down the program.

Saving changes

Here's a way to alert the user that editing hasn't been saved when the program is about to shut down. You test the isdirty variable (which is set if any changes are made to the RichTextBox), and you also check the freezer variable:

```
Private Sub Form1_Closing(ByVal sender As Object, ByVal e As
        System.ComponentModel.CancelEventArgs) Handles
        MyBase.Closing

    If isdirty and freezer = True Then

        Dim r As Integer
        r = MsgBox("You have made changes in the TextBox.
        Do you really want to quit without encrypting
        those changes? Click Yes to END the program,
        click NO to return to the program.",
        MsgBoxStyle.YesNo, "Do you really want to quit?")

If r = 6 Then End
'OR
e.Cancel = True 'cancel the closing

        End If

End Sub
```

Recall that if `freezer` is `False`, there has been one minute of activity. In that case, you don't want to halt the shutdown. (You don't want the message box holding up shutdown.)

Be very careful if you use the preceding technique. Message boxes can be dangerous in a secret program like this one. If you were to shut down this program and walk away from your computer, it's possible that you wouldn't notice the message box. A message box will prevent the program from shutting down, allowing others to view your secrets if they come upon the computer while you're away. Rather than using a message box, a safer approach would be to add a form to the project and simply display it for 20 seconds or so (put a `Timer` control on it to keep track), informing users that they can click a button on that form to encrypt if they wish to. Then after 20 seconds elapses, `End` the program if the user has not clicked the button.

I wanted to show you in this example utility how to encrypt files that are already on your hard drive, including any Office 2003 files, or indeed files of any type. But you should consider revising the utility *to never store plaintext in a file anywhere.* To do that, you can use some of the code in the DES utility described in this chapter but remove the part that encrypts a disk file or stores a temporary file.

Instead, encrypt the text you've typed into a text box and save only the resulting cyphertext to a disk file. When you want to modify your cyphertext file, load it, decipher it, display and modify it in the text box, encrypt it again, and save only the encrypted result to the hard drive. The plaintext need never be stored on the hard drive. To accomplish that, you can use cryptostreams and memorystreams. I think those are lovely names, even if they do derive from the C language. Here's how they work.

Using Streams to Avoid Storing Plaintext on Disk

To conclude the code examples in this chapter, here's how you can avoid storing your plaintext in a disk file. Instead, you will encrypt it in memory. Data manipulated in RAM memory is as evanescent as smoke drifting through the air. No record of the plaintext can be found by intruders because here only the cyphertext is stored on the hard drive. The plaintext existed only within RAM and in the pixels on your monitor (or maybe in a temporary disc cache, but that's volatile). When the program shut down, the plaintext evaporated.

Start a new VB.NET Windows-style project. Type these `Imports` statements at the top of the Code window:

```
Imports System.Security.Cryptography
Imports System.Text
Imports System.IO
```

Then type in the rest of the code (Listing 8-11).

Listing 8-11: Avoiding Disk Files

```
Private Sub Form1_Load(ByVal sender As System.Object,
        ByVal e As System.EventArgs) Handles MyBase.Load
    encrypt()
    decrypt()

End Sub

Public Sub encrypt()

    Dim des As New DESCryptoServiceProvider

    Dim bArrayIVector() As Byte = {2, 4, 46, 141, 8, 5,
        99, 2}
    Dim bArrayKey() As Byte = {12, 13, 44, 22, 21, 44,
        22, 128}

    'Create a file stream to hold the cyphertext:
    Dim fs As New FileStream("c:\CypherText.txt",
        FileMode.Create, FileAccess.Write)
```

```
    Dim bArrayMessage As Byte() = (New UnicodeEncoding).
        GetBytes("This could be from TextBox1. But for
        this example it's just a literal string, OK?")

    des.IV = bArrayIVector
    des.Key = bArrayKey


    Dim desencrypt As ICryptoTransform =
        des.CreateEncryptor()

    Dim cryptostream As New CryptoStream(fs, desencrypt,
        CryptoStreamMode.Write)

    'Save the cyphertext
    cryptostream.Write(bArrayMessage, 0,
        bArrayMessage.Length)
    cryptostream.Close()

End Sub


Public Sub decrypt()

    Dim des As New DESCryptoServiceProvider

    Dim bArrayIVector() As Byte = {2, 4, 46, 141, 8, 5,
        99, 2}
    Dim bArrayKey() As Byte = {12, 13, 44, 22, 21, 44,
        22, 128}

    des.IV = bArrayIVector
    des.Key = bArrayKey

    Dim fs As New FileStream("c:\CypherText.txt",
        FileMode.Open, FileAccess.Read)

    Dim desdecrypt As ICryptoTransform =
        des.CreateDecryptor()
    Dim cryptostreamDecrypt As New CryptoStream(fs,
        desdecrypt, CryptoStreamMode.Read)

    MsgBox(New StreamReader(cryptostreamDecrypt, New
        UnicodeEncoding).ReadToEnd())

End Sub
```

Press F5 to see the wonders of cryptostreams and .NET security libraries. With the example code in this chapter, you can do pretty much whatever you need to do to guard the privacy of your corporate data, whether in Office 2003 or outside it.

Index

A

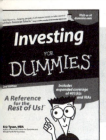
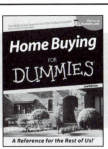
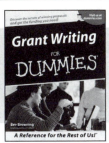

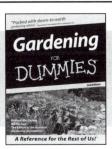

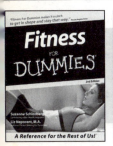
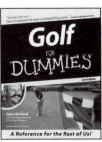
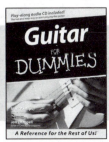

FOR DUMMIES®

A world of resources to help you grow

TRAVEL

Italy
0-7645-5453-0

Hawaii
0-7645-5438-7

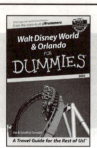

Walt Disney World & Orlando
0-7645-5444-1

Also available:

America's National Parks For Dummies
(0-7645-6204-5)

Caribbean For Dummies
(0-7645-5445-X)

Cruise Vacations For Dummies 2003
(0-7645-5459-X)

Europe For Dummies
(0-7645-5456-5)

Ireland For Dummies
(0-7645-6199-5)

France For Dummies
(0-7645-6292-4)

Las Vegas For Dummies
(0-7645-5448-4)

London For Dummies
(0-7645-5416-6)

Mexico's Beach Resorts For Dummies
(0-7645-6262-2)

Paris For Dummies
(0-7645-5494-8)

RV Vacations For Dummies
(0-7645-5443-3)

EDUCATION & TEST PREPARATION

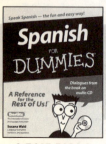

Spanish
0-7645-5194-9

Algebra
0-7645-5325-9

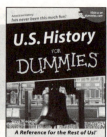

U.S. History
0-7645-5249-X

Also available:

The ACT For Dummies
(0-7645-5210-4)

Chemistry For Dummies
(0-7645-5430-1)

English Grammar For Dummies
(0-7645-5322-4)

French For Dummies
(0-7645-5193-0)

GMAT For Dummies
(0-7645-5251-1)

Inglés Para Dummies
(0-7645-5427-1)

Italian For Dummies
(0-7645-5196-5)

Research Papers For Dummies
(0-7645-5426-3)

SAT I For Dummies
(0-7645-5472-7)

U.S. History For Dummies
(0-7645-5249-X)

World History For Dummies
(0-7645-5242-2)

HEALTH, SELF-HELP & SPIRITUALITY

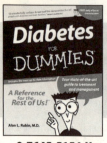

Diabetes
0-7645-5154-X

Sex
0-7645-5302-X

Parenting
0-7645-5418-2

Also available:

The Bible For Dummies
(0-7645-5296-1)

Controlling Cholesterol For Dummies
(0-7645-5440-9)

Dating For Dummies
(0-7645-5072-1)

Dieting For Dummies
(0-7645-5126-4)

High Blood Pressure For Dummies
(0-7645-5424-7)

Judaism For Dummies
(0-7645-5299-6)

Menopause For Dummies
(0-7645-5458-1)

Nutrition For Dummies
(0-7645-5180-9)

Potty Training For Dummies
(0-7645-5417-4)

Pregnancy For Dummies
(0-7645-5074-8)

Rekindling Romance For Dummies
(0-7645-5303-8)

Religion For Dummies
(0-7645-5264-3)

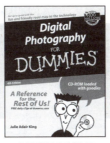

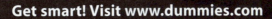

FOR DUMMIES®

Helping you expand your horizons and realize your potential

GRAPHICS & WEB SITE DEVELOPMENT

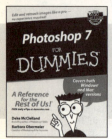

0-7645-1651-5

0-7645-1643-4

0-7645-0895-4

Also available:

Adobe Acrobat 5 PDF
For Dummies
(0-7645-1652-3)

ASP.NET For Dummies
(0-7645-0866-0)

ColdFusion MX For Dummies
(0-7645-1672-8)

Dreamweaver MX For
Dummies
(0-7645-1630-2)

FrontPage 2002 For Dummies
(0-7645-0821-0)

HTML 4 For Dummies
(0-7645-0723-0)

Illustrator 10 For Dummies
(0-7645-3636-2)

PowerPoint 2002 For
Dummies
(0-7645-0817-2)

Web Design For Dummies
(0-7645-0823-7)

PROGRAMMING & DATABASES

0-7645-0746-X

0-7645-1626-4

0-7645-1657-4

Also available:

Access 2002 For Dummies
(0-7645-0818-0)

Beginning Programming
For Dummies
(0-7645-0835-0)

Crystal Reports 9 For
Dummies
(0-7645-1641-8)

Java & XML For Dummies
(0-7645-1658-2)

Java 2 For Dummies
(0-7645-0765-6)

JavaScript For Dummies
(0-7645-0633-1)

Oracle9i For Dummies
(0-7645-0880-6)

Perl For Dummies
(0-7645-0776-1)

PHP and MySQL For
Dummies
(0-7645-1650-7)

SQL For Dummies
(0-7645-0737-0)

Visual Basic .NET For
Dummies
(0-7645-0867-9)

LINUX, NETWORKING & CERTIFICATION

0-7645-1545-4

0-7645-1760-0

0-7645-0772-9

Also available:

A+ Certification For Dummies
(0-7645-0812-1)

CCNP All-in-One Certification
For Dummies
(0-7645-1648-5)

Cisco Networking For
Dummies
(0-7645-1668-X)

CISSP For Dummies
(0-7645-1670-1)

CIW Foundations For
Dummies
(0-7645-1635-3)

Firewalls For Dummies
(0-7645-0884-9)

Home Networking For
Dummies
(0-7645-0857-1)

Red Hat Linux All-in-One
Desk Reference For Dummies
(0-7645-2442-9)

UNIX For Dummies
(0-7645-0419-3)

Available wherever books are sold.
Go to www.dummies.com or call 1-877-762-2974 to order direct

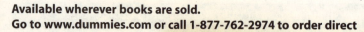